Fundan
International Business

THIRD EDITION

Fundamentals of International Business

THIRD EDITION

Michael R. Czinkota
Georgetown University

Ilkka A. Ronkainen
Georgetown University

Michael H. Moffett
Thunderbird School of Global Management

Bronxville, New York
http://www.wessex21c.com

Fundamentals of International Business

Michael R. Czinkota, Ilkka A. Ronkainen, Michael Moffett

Editor
Susan R. Petty

Copyeditor
Sheryl Nelson, OffCenter Concept House

Book / Cover Design / Production
Anna Botelho, Anna B Type & Graphics

Indexer
Wilbur Nelson, OffCenter Concept House

For more information contact Wessex Inc., One Oval Court, Bronxville, NY 10708
Or you can visit our Internet site at **http://www.wessex21c.com**

Library of Congress Cataloging-in-Publication Data

ISBN 978-0-9907405-3-7 (hardcover)
978-0-9897013-4-1 (softcover color interior)
978-0-9907405-2-0 (softcover black & white interior)

Cataloging information is on file with the Library of Congress.

About Wessex

Wessex publishes college- and graduate-level textbooks at significantly reduced prices compared to traditional publishers. Wessex textbooks are also available as PDF e-books. For information on *Fundamentals of International Business*, see **http://www.axcesscapon.com**. For information on *Managing Marketing in the 21st Century*, *Capon's Marketing Framework*, *The Virgin Marketer*, and *Sales Management*, see also **http://www.axcesscapon.com**.

Wessex also publishes trade books like *Managing Global Accounts*, *Strategic Account Strategy*, *Case Studies in Managing Key, Strategic, and Global Customers*, and *Transformative Selling*.

About the typeface

This book was set in 10 point ITC Berkeley Oldstyle from Bitstream. ITC Berkeley Oldstyle was created by Frederic W. Goudy of Bloomington, Illinois. Frederic W. Goudy was a prolific American book and type designer active 1896–1946, and whose consciously archaic style is readily recognizable.

To my personal fundamentals: Ilona and Margaret—MRC

To my family: Sanna, Sirkka, Susan, Alex, and Alpo—IAR

To Caitlin Kelly and Sean Michael—MHM

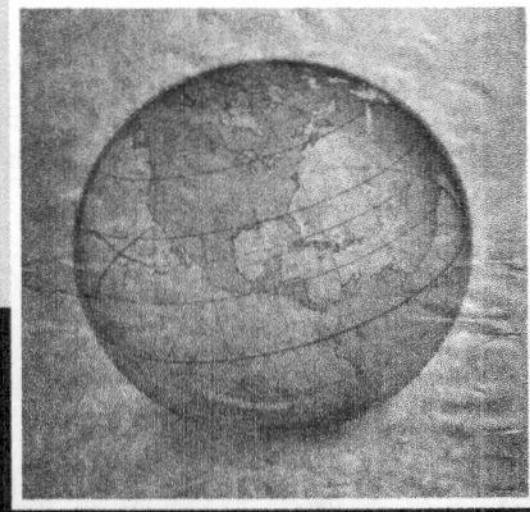

PREFACE

Fundamentals of International Business is an introductory international business text for use at the undergraduate level. Its comprehensive coverage of the subject also makes it appropriate for compressed teaching in MBA programs.

The book's content is streamlined along the core international issues when compared to the array of international business texts now available and sufficiently rigorous and demanding to satisfy the professional integrity of the instructor.

The ever-growing cultural diversity of students attending U.S. colleges and universities has influenced the development of this text. These students bring a wide range of learning experiences and a richness of cultural backgrounds to the classroom. We are sensitive to these conditions and to the educational opportunities presented to instructors by such diversity, which is reflected in our approach to the field and to learning.

Coverage

Here is what makes this book special:

Individuals, business, and government are mutually interdependent. Therefore, we work hard to highlight the interrelationships and linkages among these three pillars of international business. In the chapters, questions, and vignettes, the reader will discern this nexus of personal needs, policy requirements, and business activities.

Because globalization is regarded from more than one point of view, both the instructor and the student are provided with the insights and the materials to obtain an overview of the different perspectives and gain the ability to integrate the learned insights with their own personal views. We do so by providing not only the different arguments, but also by the facts and logic that allow for a scrutiny of these arguments.

As a result of our work with companies, we know that international business is the realm of small and medium-sized firms as well as large, multinational corporations. This text presents a balanced coverage of the subject matter, analyzing decision-making in the context of their corporate conditions. We have incorporated cutting-edge primary source research to provide students with invaluable insights into the worldview of contemporary real-life practitioners. Also addressed are important topics that are only marginally discussed in other international business texts, such as supply-chain management (logistics), countertrade, north–south economic integration, and the development of global management talent.

Conscience

We place major emphasis on international business in the context of the environment, sustainability, and responsibility. Both in the text itself as well as in the different vignettes of the chapters, we stimulate thinking about the way we affect the world and how the world affects us. We raise the concept of the Honorable Merchant introduced by the Hanse in

Europe during the 1500s and reintroduced by us in major conferences and discussions because we see this concept as crucial to the further development of international business. We also present the growing adherence to "curative marketing," which postulates that firms and governments identify conditions in which they have caused local problems and find ways to make good on those mistakes.

The roles of culture, policies, and politics, both domestic and international, are given in-depth exploration as well. The dimensions of ethics, social responsibility, diversity, and demographics are addressed through examples and vignettes. We appreciate the role, present and future, of corporate transparency, veracity, and vision. For example, the effects of grass-roots consumer pressure and sweatshops are explored, highlighting the need for acceptable working conditions and internationally enforced standards, as well as the rise of a new type of socially conscious, organized consumer base. We also offer an entirely new chapter titled "The Firm and Society," which allows the reader to delve in depth into issues such as social and personal responsibility, areas where expectations are growing rapidly.

Commitment

Our work in international business has also taught us that commitment and trust are key to global success. We are firmly committed to our work and personally stand fully behind it. If you have questions or concerns about this book, feedback of praise or complaint, please contact us at any time. Here is our contact information:

Prof. Michael R. Czinkota czinkotm@georgetown.edu
Prof. Ilkka A. Ronkainen ronkaii@georgetown.edu
Prof. Michael H. Moffett michael.moffett@thunderbird.edu

Organization

The global orientation of this book is reinforced by drawing on worldwide examples, trends, and data, rather than relying only on U.S.-based information. The reality and pragmatism of our content is ensured by always addressing the issue of "What does all this mean for employees and firms in terms of implementing international business activities?"

Fundamentals of International Business contains fifteen streamlined chapters, which translates into approximately one chapter per week for the traditional fifteen-week semester. Organized into six parts of two to four chapters each, the text flows logically from introductory material to the global environment to marketing and financial considerations in the global marketplace.

Part One provides an overview of the key issues facing international business today and explains how these topics will be dealt with in the text.

Part Two focuses on the similarities and differences between cultures, and how global politics both influences and is influenced by cultural factors.

Part Three shifts to the theoretical foundations surrounding global trade and investments, explaining the environment in which these occur.

Part Four explores the international monetary system, including the discussion of global financial management.

Part Five introduces the new discussion of the firm and society and is devoted to global operations and investigating strategic management issues.

Part Six describes the future of global business and the future opportunities for students of the field.

Distinguishing Pedagogical Features

A number of unique features in this text make substantial contributions to the learning process. These features deliver hands-on ease of learning that captures student interest, facilitate understanding of content, and lead to practical knowledge retention.

1 LEARNING OUTCOME

- **Integrated Learning System:** This text uses the integrated learning system to structure the text and the teaching supplements around learning outcomes. The numbered outcomes are identified in the chapter introduction, and each is precisely addressed in the summary section at the end of the chapter. Numbered icons within the chapter margins mark where each learning outcome is covered within the text.

The integrated learning system also makes lecture and test preparation easier. All of the text's major supplements are organized around the learning objectives, helping students and instructors focus on the key points of each chapter.

Opening Vignette: An opening vignette sets the stage for the chapter and includes one or two questions for students to consider and debate as they read the chapter.

- **World View:** This box offers concrete examples of the issues confronting global business decision makers in the classroom.

- **Quick Take:** A "Quick Take" vignette is a real-world example to provide context for concepts presented in the text.

Culture Clues

- **Culture Clues:** Interspersed throughout the text are "Culture Clues" that provide practical tips and insights to different cultures.

- **Fast Facts:** Throughout the text, these facts are presented in a question-and-answer format. They focus mainly on geography-oriented topics and are meant to provide immediate feedback to the student about their knowledge of the text material at hand.

GLOBALIZATION
Awareness, understanding, and response to global developments and linkages

- **Marginal Glossary:** An extensive marginal glossary makes it easier for students to define and understand key terms. An end-of-the-book glossary contains all key terms and definitions in a convenient alphabetical form.
- **Chapter Summary, Review Questions, and Critical Skill Builders:** Each chapter closes with a summary of key points that students should retain, organized by learning outcome. The review questions and critical skill builder questions are complementary learning tools that will enable students to check their understanding of key issues, to think beyond basic concepts, and to determine areas that require further study. All these tools help students discriminate between main and supporting points and provide mechanisms for self-teaching.
- **On the Web:** Each chapter contains two to three Internet exercises to involve students in the high-tech world of cyberspace. Students are asked to explore the Web for research into topics related to each chapter. This hands-on experience helps to develop Internet, research, and business skills.
- **Brief Format:** This text focuses on the essentials to provide a practical and inexpensive alternative to the standard texts on the market.

- **Up-to-Date Research:** Extra effort has been made to provide extensive current research information. The endnote resources enable the instructor and the student to incorporate additional information where it is useful and desirable.
- **In-Depth Tables and Figures:** Many of the tables and figures have been specifically designed and developed to enhance student understanding of the text material.
- **Critical Presentation and Explanation:** The complexity of topics and theories in international business is presented with pros and cons. The goal is to allow students an in-depth exploration of the struggles among various theories, policies, strategies, and structures.

Acknowledgments

We are grateful to many reviewers for their imaginative comments and criticisms and for showing us how to get it even more right:

Larry Colfer
Drexel University

Dharma DeSilva
Wichita State University

Robert Edwards
County College of Morris

Philip Kearney
Niagara Community College

Gary Knight
Willamette University

Steve Kober
Pierce College

Anthony Koh
University of Toledo

Behnam Nakhai
Millersville University

Scott Norwood
San Jose State University

Brian Peach
University of West Florida

Harold Purdue
Urbana University

Pollis Robertson
Kellogg Community College

Cory Simek
Webster University

Charles Skuba
Georgetown University

Nini Yang
San Francisco State University

A key role was played by Susan Ronkainen and Charles Skuba, editorial contributor, who provided insight and editorial talent galore. He was essential to this project and enabled us to reach a new level of excellence through his very substantial support. As both authors and colleagues, we are all the better for working with Susan and Charlie.

Valuable research assistance was provided by Kimberly Boeckmann and Ireene Leoncio. We appreciate all of your work!

Foremost, we are grateful to our families, who have had to tolerate late-night computer noises, weekend library absences, and curtailed vacations. The support and love of Ilona Vigh-Czinkota and Margaret Victoria Czinkota, Susan, Sanna, and Alex Ronkainen, Megan Murphy, Caitlin Kelly, and Sean Michael Moffett gave us the energy, stamina, and inspiration to write this book.

Michael R. Czinkota
Ilkka A. Ronkainen
Michael H. Moffett
July 2014

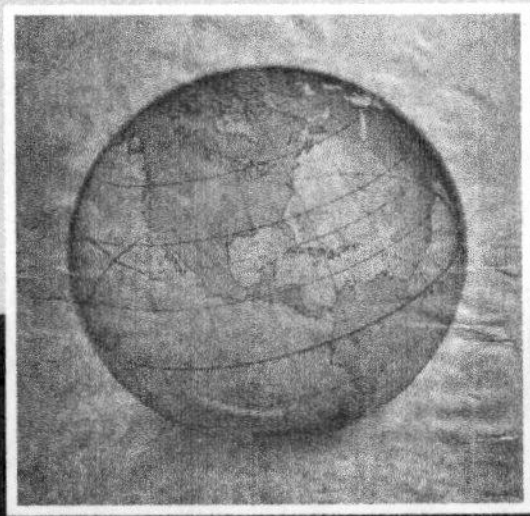

ABOUT THE AUTHORS

Michael R. Czinkota is on the faculty of marketing and international business of the Graduate School and the Robert Emmett McDonough School of Business at Georgetown University. He is the chair emeritus of International Marketing at the University of Birmingham in the United Kingdom and has held professorial appointments at universities in Asia, Australia, Europe, and the Americas.

Dr. Czinkota served in the U.S. government as Deputy Assistant Secretary of Commerce. He also served as head of the U.S. Delegation to the OECD Industry Committee in Paris and as senior trade advisor for Export Controls.

Dr. Czinkota's background includes eight years of private sector business experience as a partner in a fur trading company and in an advertising agency. His research has been supported by the National Science Foundation, the National Commission of Jobs and Small Business, the Organization of American States, and the U.S. government.

Dr. Czinkota has testified twelve times before Congress and is a sought-after speaker for businesses. He was listed as one of the three most published contributors to international business research in the world by the *Journal of International Business Studies*. His key books (of 42) are *International Marketing* (10th edition), with I. Ronkainen, and *International Business*, (8th edition) with I. Ronkainen and M. Moffett.

Dr. Czinkota serves on the Global Advisory Board of the American Marketing Association. For his work in international business and trade policy, he was named a Distinguished Fellow of the Academy of Marketing Science, a Fellow of the Chartered Institute of Marketing in the United Kingdom, and was honored with the Lifetime Achievement Award of the American Marketing Association. He has been awarded honorary degrees from the Universidad Pontificia Madre y Maestra in the Dominican Republic and the Universidad del Pacifico in Lima, Peru. In the fall of 2012, the Universidad Ricardo Palma of Lima, Peru, named its new International Business and Marketing School after Czinkota.

Dr. Czinkota serves on several corporate boards and has worked with corporations such as AT&T, IBM, GE, Nestlé, and US WEST. He serves as advisor to the National Economic Council, the General Accountability Office, United Nations, and the World Trade Organization's Executive Forum on National Export Strategies.

Dr. Czinkota was born and raised in Germany and educated in Austria, Scotland, Spain, and the United States. He studied law and business administration at the University of Erlangen-Nürnberg and was awarded a two-year Fulbright Scholarship. He holds an MBA in international business and a Ph.D. in logistics from The Ohio State University.

Ilkka A. Ronkainen is a member of the faculty of marketing and international business at the McDonough School of Business at Georgetown University. He also serves as a docent of international marketing at the Aalto University (Helsinki School of Economics).

Dr. Ronkainen has published extensively in both academic journals and the trade press. He is co-author of *International Marketing* (10th edition) and *International Business* (8th edition). His trade books include *The International Marketing Imperative* and *Mastering Global Markets*. He serves on the editorial review boards of *Journal of Business Research*, *International Marketing Review*, and *Multinational Business Review*.

He has received the undergraduate teaching and research award twice, as well as recognition from the International Executive MBA program at Georgetown as the Outstanding Professor of the Year. He is the founder and director of the McDonough School of Business's summer program in Hong Kong.

Dr. Ronkainen holds a doctorate and a master's degree from the University of South Carolina as well as a master's of science (economics) degree from the Helsinki School of Economics. He has served as a consultant to a wide range of U.S. and international institutions. He has worked with entities such as IBM, the Rand Organization, and the Organization of American States. He maintains close relations with a number of Finnish companies and their internationalization and educational efforts.

Michael H. Moffett is Continental Grain Professor in Finance at the Thunderbird School of Global Management. He was formerly an associate professor of finance at Oregon State University. He has also held teaching or research appointments at the University of Michigan, Ann Arbor; the Brookings Institution, Washington, D.C.; the University of Hawaii at Manoa; the Aarhus School of Business (Denmark); the Helsinki School of Economics and Business Administration (Finland); the International Centre for Public Enterprises (Yugoslavia); and the University of Colorado, Boulder.

Professor Moffett received a B.A. (economics) from the University of Texas at Austin (1977), an M.S. (resource economics) from Colorado State University (1979), an M.A. (economics) from the University of Colorado, Boulder (1983), and his Ph.D. (economics) from the University of Colorado, Boulder (1985).

He has authored, coauthored, or contributed to a number of books, articles, and other publications. He has coauthored two books with Art Stonehill and David Eiteman, *Multinational Business Finance* and *Fundamentals of Multinational Finance*. His articles have appeared in the *Journal of Financial and Quantitative Analysis, Journal of Applied Corporate Finance, Journal of International Money and Finance, Journal of International Financial Management and Accounting, Contemporary Policy Issues, Brookings Discussion Papers in International Economics*, and others. He has contributed to a number of collected works including the *Handbook of Modern Finance*, the *International Accounting and Finance Handbook*, and the *Encyclopedia of International Business*. He is also coauthor of books on multinational business with Michael Czinkota and Ilkka Ronkainen, *International Business*, 8th edition, and *The Global Oil and Gas Industry: Strategy, Finance, and Management*, with Andrew Inkpen.

Moffett has served as an executive education consultant to numerous global companies and organizations, including ADP, BP, ExxonMobil, Fluor Corporation, Solar Turbines/Caterpillar, IBM, Kimberly-Clarke, Kelloggs, Mattel, Statoil, the East Asiatic Company, ONGC of India, Brasil Telecom, Hypertherm, Vitro de Mexico, Woodward Governor, Briggs & Stratton, SK of Korea, Juniper Networks, State Farm, Phelps Dodge, RasGas of Qatar, Texaco, Legrand, Teleflex, Engelhard, EDS, General Motors, Dow Chemical, Pfizer, and Ranbaxy of India.

BRIEF CONTENTS

Preface

About the Authors

PART 1 GLOBALIZATION 1

Chapter 1 Globalization 2

PART 2 GLOBALIZATION DRIVERS 18

Chapter 2 Cultural Environment 19

Chapter 3 Global Trade Environment 44

Chapter 4 Politics and Laws 70

Chapter 5 Economic Integration and Emerging Markets 96

PART 3 GLOBAL TRADE AND INVESTMENT 127

Chapter 6 Trade and Investment Theory 128

Chapter 7 The International Movement of Trade and Capital (The Balance of Payments) 151

PART 4 GLOBAL FINANCE 173

Chapter 8 Global Finance 174

Chapter 9 Global Financial Management 194

PART 5 GLOBAL OPERATIONS 216

Chapter 10 Exporting and Global Expansion 217

Chapter 11 Global Marketing and Social Networks 247

Chapter 12 The Global Supply Chain 275

Chapter 13 Managing Globally 297

Chapter 14 The Firm and Society 328

PART 6 THE FUTURE 351

Chapter 15 The Future 352

Glossary

Name Index

Subject Index

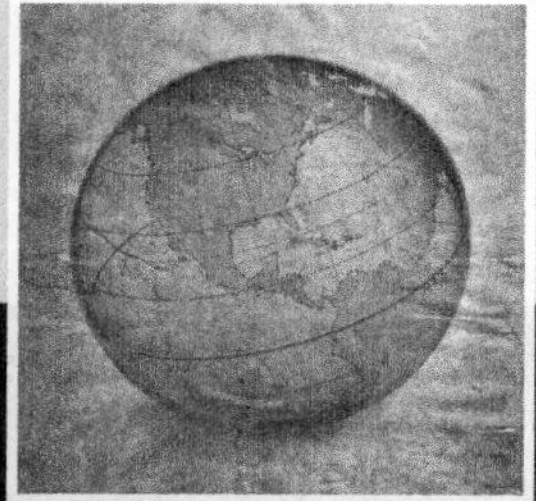

CONTENTS

PART 1 GLOBALIZATION 1

Chapter 1 Globalization 2

It's Not Just Money Anymore: Conditions of Rising Prices? **2**

Welcome to the World of Global Business 3

What Is Global Business? 4

Global Links Today 4

U.S. International Trade Position 9

Global Business Imperative 10

International Business in a New Era of Risk and Uncertainty 11

The International Reaction 12

Structure of the Book 13

Summary **15**

PART 2 GLOBALIZATION DRIVERS 18

Chapter 2 Cultural Environment 19

Not Just Cream Filling **19**

What Is Culture? 20

Elements of Culture 22

Language 22

Nonverbal Language 25

Infrastructure 26

Education 28

Social Institutions 28

Religion 30

Values and Attitudes 33

Manners and Customs 33

Aesthetics 34

Understanding Cultural Differences 35

Gaining Cultural Knowledge 37

Developing Cultural Competence 38

Formal Training Programs 38

Culture Shock 39

Summary **41**

Chapter 3 Global Trade Environment 44

Yes, Virginia, The Ham Is Chinese **44**

What Are Trade and Investment Policies? 45

Influence of Domestic Policy 45

Influence of Foreign Policy 46

Conflicting Policies 46

Post-War Global Trade Regulation 48
The World Trade Organization 49
Changes in the Global Policy Environment 49
Reduction of Domestic Policy Influences 50
Weakening International Institutions 53
Conflict Between Industrialized and Developing Nations 55
Policy Responses to Changing Conditions 56
Import Restrictions 56
Investment Policies 59
Host-Country Perspective on Investment Policies 60
Positive Effects 60
Negative Effects 61
Home-Country Perspective on Investment Policies 64
Restrictions on Investment 66
Investment Promotion 66
***Summary* 67**

Chapter 4 Politics and Laws 70
***Finding Safe Harbor in Data Privacy* 70**
Home-Country Perspective 71
Embargoes and Sanctions 73
Export Controls 74
Regulating International Business Behavior 75
Host-Country Perspective 80
Political Action and Risk 80
Economic Risk 84
Managing Risk 86
Legal Differences and Restraints 88
Influencing Politics and Laws 89
International Relations and Laws 90
International Politics 90
International Law 91
***Summary* 92**

Chapter 5 Economic Integration and Emerging Markets 96
***Worldwide Free Trade* 96**
Levels of Economic Integration 97
The Free Trade Area 98
The Customs Union 98
The Common Market 98
The Economic Union 99
Costs and Benefits of Economic Integration 99
Trade Creation and Trade Diversion 99
Reduced Import Prices 100
Increased Competition and Economies of Scale 100
Higher Factor Productivity 101
Regionalism Versus Nationalism 101
Regional Groupings 102
European Union 102
North American Economic Integration 106
Integration in Latin America 109
Integration in Asia 110
Africa 112
The Middle East 112
Cartels and Commodity Price Agreements 113

Emerging Markets *114*
Adjust Entry Strategy 117
Manage Affordability 117
Invest in Distribution 118
Supplier Base and Logistics 118
Build Brands 119
Labor Markets 119

Developing Markets *119*
Research 120
Creating Buying Power 120
Tailoring Local Solutions 120
Improving Access 120
Shaping Aspirations 121

Economic Integration and the Global Manager *121*
Effects of Change 121
Strategic Planning 121
Reorganization 122
Lobbying 122

Summary ***123***

PART 3 GLOBAL TRADE AND INVESTMENT 127

Chapter 6 Trade and Investment Theory 128

Millennium Development Goals: The Role of International Trade ***128***

Why Countries Trade *129*

The Age of Mercantilism *130*

Absolute Advantage and the Division of Labor *132*
Comparative Advantage 132
A Numerical Example of Classical Trade 133
National Production Possibilities 134
The Gains from International Trade 135
Applying Classical Trade Theory 136

Factor Proportions Trade Theory *136*
Factor Intensity in Production 136
Factor Endowments, Factor Prices, and Comparative Advantage 137
The Leontief Paradox 138
Linder's Overlapping Product Ranges Theory 138

Product Cycle Theory *139*
Stages of The Product Cycle 139
Trade Implications of The Product Cycle 140

The New Trade Theory *142*
Economies of Scale and Imperfect Competition 142
The Competitive Advantage of Nations 143

Theory of International Investment *144*
The Theory of Foreign Direct Investment 144
Firms As Seekers 145
Firms As Exploiters of Imperfections 145
Strategic Implications of Foreign Direct Investment 146

Summary ***147***

Chapter 7 The International Movement of Trade and Capital (The Balance of Payments) 151

International Payments and the Migration of People ***151***

International Transactions and the Balance of Payments *152*
Basics of BOP Accounting 153
Identifying International Economic Transactions 153
BOP as a Flow Statement 153
BOP Accounting: Double-Entry Bookkeeping 154
Bop Current Account *154*
Goods Trade 155
The BOP Capital and Financial Account *157*
Direct Investment 158
Portfolio Investment 160
Current and Financial Account Balance Relationships 160
Net Errors and Omissions 161
Official Reserves Account 161
The BOP in Total *162*
The Balance of Payments and Economic Crises 162
Capital Mobility *165*
Current Account Versus Financial Account Capital Flows 165
Historical Patterns of Capital Mobility 166
Capital Controls 167
Globalization of Capital Flows 169
Summary ***170***

PART 4 GLOBAL FINANCE 173

Chapter 8 Global Finance 174
Venezuela Fights a Currency War Against...Itself ***174***
The Purpose of Exchange Rates *175*
What Is a Currency Worth? 175
The Law of One Price 176
The Market for Currencies *177*
Exchange-Rate Quotations and Terminology 177
Cross Rates 179
Foreign Currency Market Structure 179
Evolution of The Global Monetary System *181*
The Gold Standard 181
Interwar Years, 1919–1939 181
The Bretton Woods Agreement, 1944–1971 182
Times of Crisis, 1971–1973 182
Floating Exchange Rates, 1973–Present 183
The International Money Markets *184*
Eurocurrency Markets 184
Eurocurrency Interest Rates 184
Linking Eurocurrency Interest Rates and Exchange Rates 185
International Capital Markets *187*
Defining International Financing 187
International Banking *189*
International Security Markets *189*
The International Bond Market 189
International Equity Markets *190*
Gaining Access to Global Financial Markets 191
Summary *191*

Chapter 9 Global Financial Management 194

***Korres Natural Products of Greece* 194**

Corporate Stakeholders and Governance 195

Corporate Stakeholders 196

Corporate Responsibility and Sustainability 197

Global Financial Goals 199

Operational Goals 200

International Corporate Investment 201

International Capital Budgeting 201

Capital Budget Components and Decision Criteria 201

Evaluating a Proposed Project in Singapore 202

Risks in International Investments 203

Capital Structure: International Dimensions 204

The Capital Structure of Foreign Subsidiaries 204

International Working Capital 204

Operating and Financing Cash Flows 204

Cash Flow Management 205

Foreign Exchange Exposure 206

Managing Transaction Exposure 206

Managing Economic Exposure 207

Managing Translation Exposure 207

International Accounting 208

Worldwide Accounting Standards 208

Principal Accounting Differences across Countries 209

International Taxation 209

Tax Jurisdictions 210

Tax Types 211

Financing Import/Export Operations 212

Trade Financing Using a Letter of Credit 212

***Summary* 213**

PART 5 GLOBAL OPERATIONS 216

Chapter 10 Exporting and Global Expansion 217

***Apples Go International* 217**

Globalization Drivers 218

A Comprehensive View of International Expansion 219

Why Go Global? 220

Strategic Planning for Global Expansion 221

Management Commitment 222

Internal Organizational Factors 223

Market and Competition Analysis 223

Competitive Strategy Formulation 223

International Business Research 224

Why Conduct Research? 224

Pre-Entry Research 224

Market Expansion Research 225

Conducting Secondary Research 226

Government Sources 226

International Organizations 226

Electronic Information Services 227

Interpreting Secondary Data 227

Conducting Primary Research 228

Determining Research Techniques 228

Interviews 228

Focus Groups 228

Observation 229

Survey Research 229
Experimentation 231
Ongoing Research 231
Target Country Selection 232
Target Market Segmentation 232
Global Program Development 233

Global Market Entry Strategies 234
Exporting and Importing 234
International Licensing 237
International Franchising 238

Global Market Development Strategies 238
Strategic Alliances 238
Informal Alliances 240
Contractual Agreements 240
Management Contracts 240
Equity Participation 240
Joint Ventures 241
Consortia 241
Elements of Successful Alliances 242
Full Ownership 242

***Summary* 244**

Chapter 11 Global Marketing and Social Networks 247

***How Hollywood Conquered the World* 247**

Standardization Versus Adaptation for Global Markets 248

Product Strategies 249
Product Characteristics 251
Company Considerations 253
Global Brand Strategy Decisions 253
Product Counterfeiting 254

Pricing Strategies 255
Export Pricing 255
Individual Market Pricing 256
Pricing Coordination 257
Transfer Pricing 257

Distribution Strategies 258
Channel Design 258
Managing the Channel Relationship 259
E-Commerce as a Distribution Channel 260

Promotional Strategies 261
Advertising 261
Personal Selling 265
Sales Promotion 265
Public Relations 266
Sponsorship Marketing 267

Social Network and Media 267
Opportunities and Challenges 268

***Summary* 271**

Chapter 12 The Global Supply Chain 275

***Tracking the International Shipment* 275**

Global Logistics 276
Supply-Chain Management 277
New Key Dimensions of Global Logistics 278

Global Transportation Issues 278
Transportation Infrastructure 278
Availability of Modes 280

Ocean Shipping 280
Air Shipping 281
Selecting a Mode of Transport 281
Export Documentation 285
Terms of Shipment and Sale 285

Global Inventory Issues 288
Order Cycle Time 288
Inventory as a Strategic Tool 289

Global Packaging Issues 290

Global Storage Issues 292
Storage Facilities 292
Special Trade Zones 293

Summary 294

Chapter 13 Managing Globally 297

Strength in Structure 297

Organizational Structure 298
Little or No Formal Organization 299
The International Division 300
The Global Organization 301
Evolution of Organizational Structures 304

Implementation 306
Locus of Decision-Making 306
Factors Affecting Structure and Decision-Making 306
Global Networks 307
Promoting Global Internal Cooperation 308
Role of Country Organizations in Decision-Making 311

Controls 311
Types of Controls 312
Bureaucratic and Formalized Control 312
Cultural Control 313

Managing Global Managers 314
Early Stages of Globalization 314
Advanced Stages of Globalization 314
Selecting Managers for Overseas Assignments 315
Compensating Global Managers 316
Non-Salary-Related Allowances 317

Managing the Global Workforce 320
Labor Participation in Management 320
The Role of Labor Unions 321
Human Resource Policies 323

Summary 324

Chapter 14 The Firm and Society 328

Bank Bonuses and Aristotelian Finance 328

The Power and Responsibility of International Business 329

Recognizing Challenges and Dilemmas 330

The Increased Role of Government 331
Diminished Trust 333

The Leadership Challenge 336
Aligning Strategy, Products and Societal Interests 337

Corporate Social Responsibility 337
What Is the Responsibility of Business? 337
Defining Corporate Social Responsibility 338

Strategic Focus *341*
CSR Reporting 341
Sustainability *342*
A Sustainable Future? *343*
Sustainable Practices *345*
Growing Importance to Consumers and Governments *345*
Summary ***347***

PART 6 THE FUTURE **351**

Chapter 15 The Future 352
No More Global Currency ***352***
The Global Business Environment *353*
The Political Environment 353
Planned Versus Market Economies 353
The North-South Relationship 354
Emerging Markets 355
The Effects of Population Shifts 355
Financial Environment *356*
A Changing Growth Perspective 359
Technological Environment *359*
The Internet 359
Data and Information 361
Global Trade Relations and Government Policy *363*
Government Policy 363
Environment, Conservation, and Sustainability 364
Terrorism 366
The Future of Global Business Management *368*
Reputation Management 370
Reforming the Global Corporation 370
Global Product Policy 371
Global Pricing 371
Distribution Strategies 372
Global Communications 372
Careers in Global Business *373*
Further Training 373
Employment Experience 373
Self-Employment 375
Summary ***375***

Glossary
Name Index
Subject Index

PART 1

GLOBALIZATION

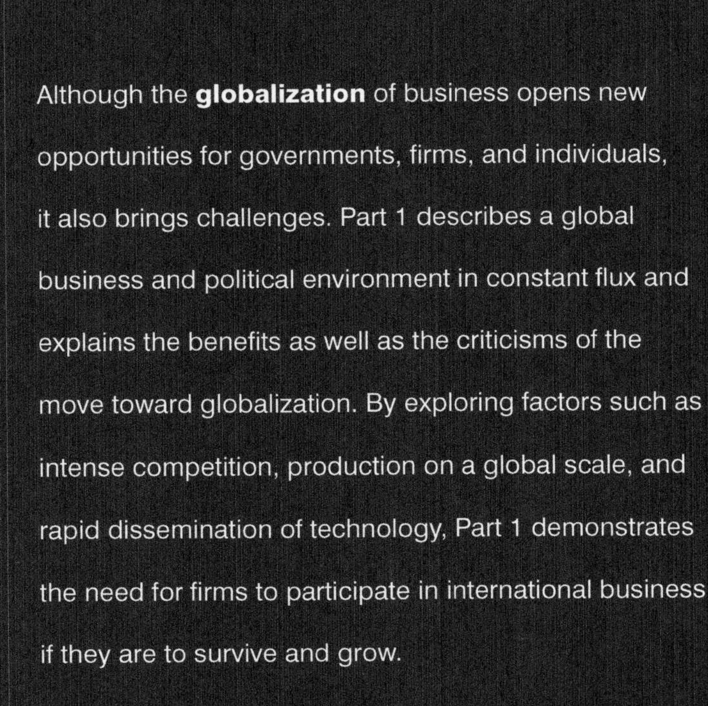

Although the **globalization** of business opens new opportunities for governments, firms, and individuals, it also brings challenges. Part 1 describes a global business and political environment in constant flux and explains the benefits as well as the criticisms of the move toward globalization. By exploring factors such as intense competition, production on a global scale, and rapid dissemination of technology, Part 1 demonstrates the need for firms to participate in international business if they are to survive and grow.

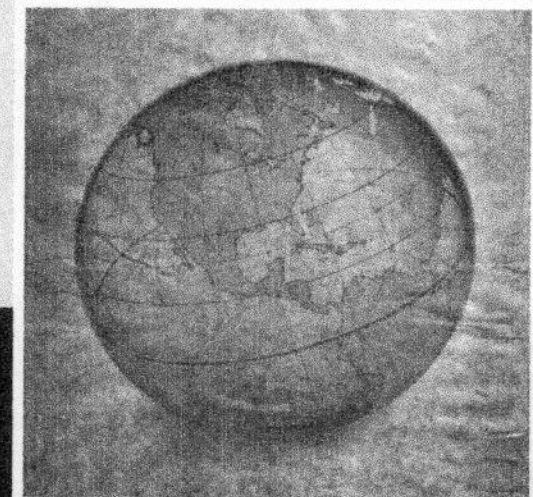

CHAPTER 1

GLOBALIZATION

It's Not Just Money Anymore

The sole purpose of international business used to be the maximization of profit, but today's executives have new questions to answer: Who pays the environmental and social costs of bringing a product to the global marketplace? When loggers take more timber than nature replaces or fishermen deplete a fishery, it is society that foots the bill. The prices resulting from clear-cutting and overfishing do not take into account the societal costs of losing a forest or the catch of fish for future generations. Who protects farmers whose sales and incomes are at the mercy of big customers, such as Walmart or Tesco?

Increasingly, product labeling and branding are proving an effective means of bringing the environmental and social costs of a product's production into the marketplace. Product labels inform consumers about a product's environmental background and often include the processes and production methods used. The Forest Stewardship Council's "FSC" label, the Marine Stewardship Council's "MSC" label, and Fair Trade USA's "Fair Trade Certified" labels have all proven particularly successful.

The idea of a sustainable fish label started in 1997, when Unilever, the world's largest buyer of seafood, and the World Wide Fund for Nature formed the MSC. Unilever made this move after realizing that the future of its fish finger and cod fillet businesses relied on a sustainable source of white fish. In 2012, more than 14,000 products with an estimated retail value of $3 billion in 80 countries carried an MSC label. Fair Trade USA, the leading third-party certifier of Fair Trade products in North America, announced in April 2013 that Fair Trade Certified coffee imports hit an all-time high in 2012: 163 million pounds were imported into the United States and Canada, representing an 18 percent increase over 2011.

Environmental labels are an indicator that companies are addressing increasing consumer concerns about the environmental impact of numerous products. Although many labeling efforts are voluntary and facilitated by nongovernmental organizations, governments are becoming more involved. The EU Ecolabel is a voluntary certification scheme in which the European Commission assesses products' environmental impact based on a rigorous set of criteria established by a panel of experts from consumer organizations and industry. Labels are not the solution to every negative environmental externality, in

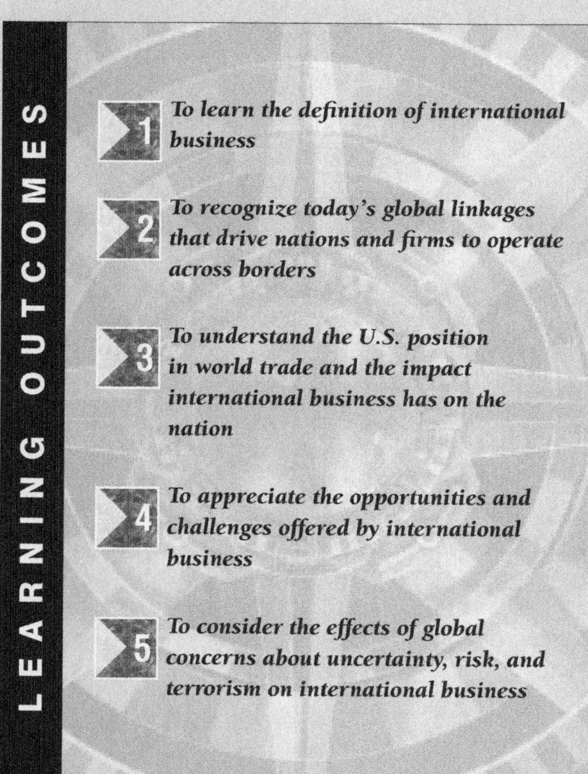

LEARNING OUTCOMES

1. *To learn the definition of international business*
2. *To recognize today's global linkages that drive nations and firms to operate across borders*
3. *To understand the U.S. position in world trade and the impact international business has on the nation*
4. *To appreciate the opportunities and challenges offered by international business*
5. *To consider the effects of global concerns about uncertainty, risk, and terrorism on international business*

the absence of established governance, but good labels do provide an incentive for change.

SOURCES: "Ecological labelling takes off," *The Economist*, January 28, 2008; "Fair Trade Certified™ Coffee Imports Hit Record High in 2012," **www.fairtrade.org**, press release, April 10, 2013; Marine Stewardship Council, "Commitments from our commercial partners," **http://ec.europa.eu/environment/ecolabel/**, April 2012; **http://www.msc.org**, accessed May 21, 2013; The European Commission, accessed 5/21/13

As You Read This Chapter

1. Think of the ways in which globalization creates links between nations. How beneficial are such linkages?
2. Considering the criticisms of globalization, is its growth likely to continue as it has in the past 30 years?

WELCOME TO THE WORLD OF GLOBAL BUSINESS

You are about to set out on an exciting journey in which you will explore the world through new eyes: from the unique perspective of international business. While you will learn much about why and how businesses operate on a global scale, you will also encounter many other disciplines, including economics, politics, geography, history, language, anthropology, demography, jurisprudence, and statistics. You will discover why it is imperative for nations to participate in the global marketplace, for failure to do so leads inexorably to declining economic influence and deteriorating standards of living. **Globalization**—defined as awareness, understanding, and response to global developments and linkages—holds the promise of improved quality of life and a better society, even leading, some believe, to a more peaceful world.

GLOBALIZATION
Awareness, understanding, and response to global developments and linkages

On an individual level, as a student of international business, at some point in your career you are likely to work either for a multinational organization or a smaller firm that engages in international activities. Manufacturing and service companies across the entire spectrum of industry are going global. In an era of open borders, global supply chains, and burgeoning technology that enables instant communication and virtually free ways of reaching millions of people, an unprecedented opportunity emerges for individuals to enter the international business arena. It has become easier for start-up firms to challenge even giant competitors.

As hundreds of examples in this book will reveal, speed, flexibility, creativity, and innovation—all enabled by advances in technology—are as important as size to international success. Understanding international business is a crucial part of career development, not just for future business managers but for budding entrepreneurs as well.

International business offers companies new markets. For the last five decades, international trade and investment have grown at a faster rate than domestic economies. Today and in the future, only a combination of domestic and international activities will allow for expansion, growth, and increased income. International business enables the flow of ideas, services, and capital across the world. The results are higher levels of innovation, faster dissemination of goods and information worldwide, more efficient use of human capital, and improved access to financing. International business facilitates the mobility of factors of production—except land—and provides challenging employment opportunities.[1]

International business benefits consumers by offering new choices. Consumers not only have a wider variety of goods to choose from, but international competition leads to improved quality and reduced prices. The car you drive may well have been made by Germany's Volkswagen or by one of several Japanese or Korean automakers. The Amoco station where you fill up with gas belongs to British oil company BP, while the competition, Shell, is a Dutch company. A majority of Burger King is owned by 3G Capital of Brazil, which also owns Heinz's Ketchup, always a good topping for a burger. Britain's beverage giant Diageo owns Mexican tequila José Cuervo, the American rum Captain Morgan, and Crown Royal Canadian whiskey, among other famous global brands. Retail chains Brooks Brothers and Casual Corner are part of an Italian conglomerate. Universal Studios is a subsidiary of the French media company, Vivendi, which is also a major operator of pay-per-view television in the United States. The AMC theater where you see the latest blockbuster movie is owned by Dalian Wanda Group from China. Even Budweiser, the quintessential American beer, is owned by Anheuser-Busch InBev, a Belgian brewer.[2]

But all this does not just apply to products. Management and managers are just as well affected.

International business is not without its challenges. Because it opens up markets to competition, it can—just like Janus, the two-faced Roman god—deliver benefits and opportunity to some, while causing others to falter. Because of its ability to impact citizens, firms, and economies negatively as well as positively, international business and the ways in which it is conducted are of vital concern to countries, companies, and individuals.

What Is Global Business?

IMPORT-EXPORT TRADE
The sale and purchase of tangible goods and services to and from another country

FOREIGN DIRECT INVESTMENT (FDI)
The establishment or expansion of operations of a firm in a foreign country; like all investments, a transfer of capital is assumed

Global business consists of transactions that are devised and carried out across national borders to satisfy the objectives of individuals, companies, and organizations. These transactions take on various forms, which are often interrelated. Primary types of international business are **import-export trade** and **foreign direct investment (FDI)**. The latter is carried out in varied forms, including wholly owned subsidiaries and joint ventures. Additional types of international business are licensing, franchising, and management contracts.

As the definition indicates, and as for any kind of domestic business, "satisfaction" remains a key tenet of global business. Beyond this, because transactions are across national borders, participating firms are subject to a new set of macro-environmental factors, to different constraints, and quite frequently to conflicts resulting from different laws, cultures, and societies. The basic principles of business still apply, but their application, complexity, and intensity vary substantially. To operate outside national borders, firms must be ready to incorporate international considerations into their thinking and planning, making decisions related to questions such as these:

- How will our idea, good, or service fit into the international market?
- Should we enter the market through trade or through investment?
- Should I obtain my supplies domestically or from abroad?
- What product adjustments are necessary to be responsive to local conditions?
- What threats from global competition should be expected, and how can these threats be counteracted?

When management integrates these issues into each decision, international markets can provide growth, profit, and needs satisfaction not available to businesses that limit their activities to the domestic marketplace. The aim of this book is to prepare you, as a student of international business, to participate in this often-complex decision process.

Global Links Today

Today, world trade and investment are central to the well-being of the global community. In centuries past, trade was conducted internationally but not at the level or with the impact on nations, firms, and individuals that it has recently achieved. From 1970 to 2012, the volume of international trade in goods and services has expanded from $200 billion to more than

Quick Take *Controlling the Dark Side of Globalization*

Labor abuse is one of the most public drawbacks of globalization. During the past 15 years, the U.S. media has publicized numerous stories of unhealthy working conditions, 20-hour shifts, and minimal pay. From Nike in Vietnam to Kathy Lee Gifford in Honduras to Apple in China, plenty of companies have found themselves in the midst of sweatshop scandals. Providing consumers the brands they want at low prices often involves companies hiring contract manufacturers that may not respect the rights of their workers. This often has tragic consequences, as in the May 2013 Rana Plaza factory collapse that killed more than 1,100 people in Bangladesh.

What is a conscientious consumer to do? Students at campuses around the United States have banded together in the search for a solution. What began as largely disjointed protests, letter-writing campaigns, and various other forms of student activism centered around individual cases has gradually evolved into a coordinated large-scale effort called United Students Against Sweatshops. It is active on campuses around the country. The organization has successfully advocated a "designated suppliers program" that requires companies producing the apparel sold on campuses to establish long-term relationships with garment factories, so workers can be guaranteed a "living wage." The consolidated power of student consumers is ensuring manufacturing accountability on a national scale. Industry leaders have responded with the Fair Labor Association (FLA)—a nonprofit organization dedicated to ending sweatshop conditions in factories worldwide and eradicating abusive labor conditions. Apple called in the Fair Labor Association in 2012 to investigate labor conditions at Foxconn, its contract manufacturer in China.

The power of unified consumer action is not to be underestimated. Putting an end to labor abuses around the world is good, right? "Wrong," says Harvard economist Jeffrey Sachs. He is not concerned that there are too many sweatshops but that there are too few. Sachs' opinion is based on the theory of comparative advantage, which states that international trade will, in the long run, make most parties better off. According to this theory, poor countries can develop by doing something that they do "better" than rich countries (in this case, provide cheap labor). Eventually, as the developing country becomes wealthier, its people come to enjoy higher living standards. Indeed, in response to the Walt Disney Company announcing that it was pulling out of Bangladesh and several other countries, many workers' rights advocates argued that companies should remain in the countries and use their influence to improve working conditions. Could the "dark" side of globalization be a blessing in disguise?

SOURCE: Allen Meyerson, "In Principle, A Case for More Sweatshops," *The New York Times*, June 22, 1997; [**http://en.wikipedia.org/wiki/ Sweatshop#accessed 5/31/2007**]; Andrew North, "Dhaka Rana Plaza collapse: Pressure tells on retailers and government," BBC News, **http://www.bbc.co.uk/news/world-asia-22525431**, accessed May 21, 2013; Peter Grier, "The Walt Disney Company pulls out of Bangladesh: Will that make workers safe?," *The Christian Science Monitor*, May 3, 2013.

$22.5 trillion.[3] As Figure 1.1 shows, the growth in the value of trade has greatly exceeded the growth level of overall world output. By comparison, in 2011, total foreign direct investment stocks in the world amounted to more than $21.6 trillion.[4]

The sheer volume and value of international trade has led to the forging of a network of global links around the world that binds us all—countries, institutions, and individuals—much closer than ever before. These links tie together trade, financial markets, technology, and living standards in unprecedented ways. The 2001 collapse of Argentina's currency following its divorce from the U.S. dollar resonated throughout South America and affected trade in the United States, Europe, and the Far East. The economic turmoil in Asia influenced

FIGURE 1.1 Growth of World International Direct Investment, 1992–2010

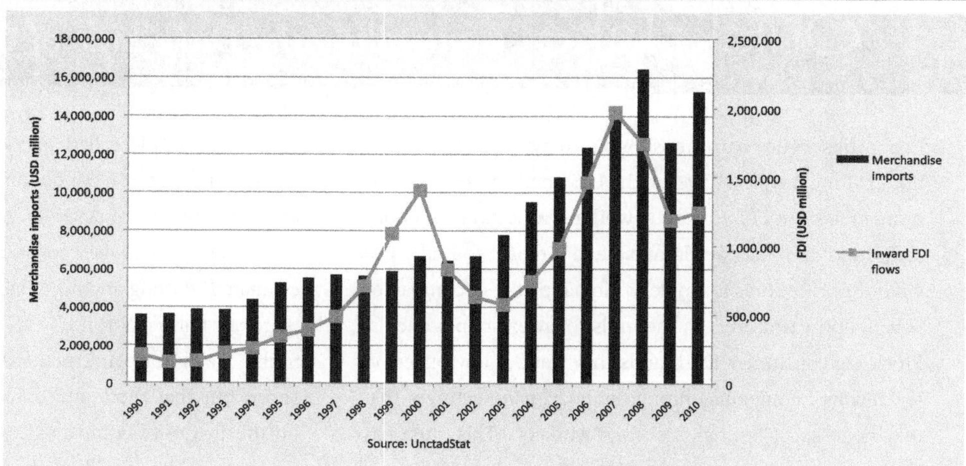

SOURCE: "A New Era for Transatlantic Trade Leadership", The German Marshall Fund, February 2012, **http://www.gmfus.org/wp-content/blogs.dir/1/files_mf/tatf_report_2012.pdf**, accessed May 22, 2013.

stock markets, investments, and trade flows around the world. A 2007 announcement by the U.S. Federal Reserve that it was lowering a key interest rate reverberated throughout the world stock markets, pushing the Japanese NIKKEI into bear-market territory (defined as a fall of 20 percent from its high). Terrorist attacks and the resulting wars in Afghanistan and Iraq affected stock markets, investments, and trade flows in all corners of the globe. The European sovereign debt crisis combined with corrupt accounting practices by U.S.-based multinationals have sent world stock markets into shock.[5]

Global linkages have also become more intense on an individual level. Communication has built new international bridges, be it through music or through international programming transmitted by CNN or MTV. New products have attained international appeal and encouraged similar activities around the world: We carry colorful cell phones; we dance the same dances; we eat hamburgers and drink double lattes. Transportation links and Internet access allow individuals from different countries to meet or otherwise interact with unprecedented ease. Common cultural pressures result in similar social phenomena and behavior—for example, more dual-income families are emerging around the world, which leads to higher levels of spending.

International business has also brought a global reorientation in production strategies. Only a few decades ago, for example, it would have been thought impossible to produce car parts in more than one country, assemble the cars in another, and sell them in countries around the world. Today, such global strategies, coupled with production and distribution sharing, are common. Consumers, union leaders, policymakers, and sometimes even the firms themselves are finding it increasingly difficult to define where a particular product was made because subcomponents may come from many different nations. Firms are also linked to each other through global supply agreements and joint undertakings in research and development.

Figure 1.2 gives an example of how such links result in a final consumer product. How many consumers are aware of the multiple countries of origin for the ingredients in a Big Mac?

Firms and governments are recognizing production's worldwide effects on the environment common to all. For example, high sulfur emissions in one area may cause acid rain in another. Pollution in one country may result in water contamination in another.

FIGURE 1.2 Global Components of a Big Mac®

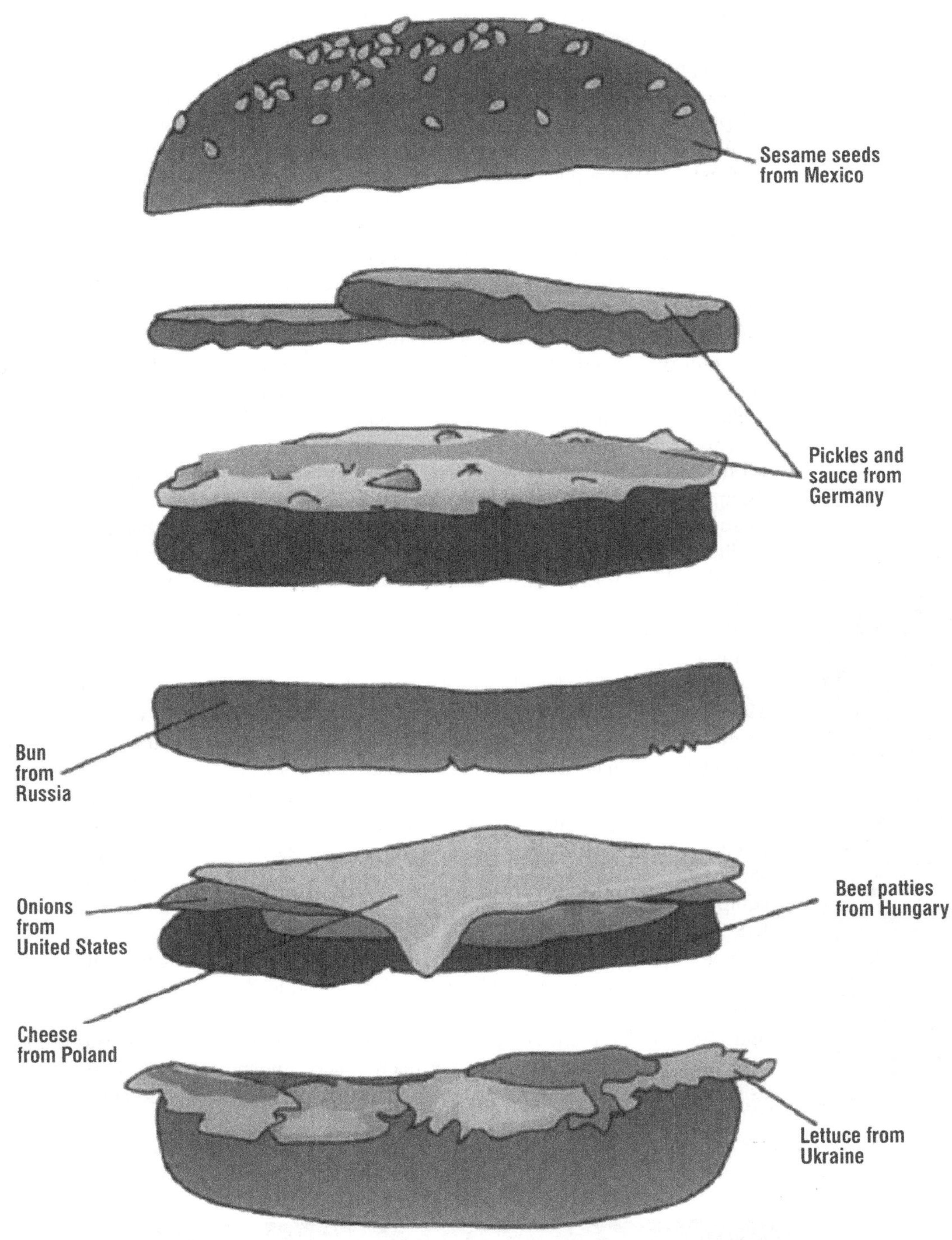

SOURCE: Used with permission from McDonald's Corporation.

It is not just the production of goods that has become global. Increasingly, service firms are part of the global scene. Consulting firms, insurance companies, software firms, and universities are participating to a growing degree in the international marketplace.

Service activities can have cross-national impacts as well. For example, currency weaknesses due to problems in a country's banking sector can quickly spill over and affect the currency values of other nations. The deregulation of some service industries, such as air transport or telephony, can have a ripple effect on the structure of these industries around the world.

All these changes have affected the international financial position of countries and the ownership of economic activities. For example, the United States, after being a net creditor to the world for many decades, has been a world debtor since 1985. This means that the nation owes more to foreign institutions and individuals than to U.S. entities. The shifts in financial flows have had major effects on international direct investment into plants as well. U.S.-owned investments abroad in 2012 were $20,760 billion, while foreign-owned assets in the United States were $25,176 billion.[6]

MULTINATIONAL CORPORATIONS
Companies that invest in countries around the globe

Though the U.S. holds the world's largest gold reserves (8,133.5 tons, as of June 2013),[7] the country is also the largest debtor in the world. In today's era of **multinational corporations**, countless people around the world toil for foreign bosses. All of these developments make nations more dependent on one another than ever before.

This interdependence, however, is not static. On an ongoing basis, realignments take place on both micro and macro levels that make past orientations at least partially obsolete. For example, for its first 200 years, the United States looked to Europe for markets and sources of supply. But today, the picture has shifted. In 2012, U.S. merchandise trade across the Pacific (to the top ten trading partners) totaled $1,190 billion, while U.S. merchandise trade with the EU 27 was $645,890 billion.[8] Furthermore, the relative participation of countries in world trade is shifting. The market share of Western Europe in trade, for example, has been on the decline. Concurrent with this shift, the global market shares of Japan, Southeast Asian countries, and China have increased dramatically.

The composition of trade has also been changing. For example, from the 1960s to the 1990s, the trade role of primary commodities has declined sharply, while the importance of manufactured goods has increased. This has meant that those countries and workers who had specialized in commodities such as *caoutchouc* (rubber plantations) or mining were likely to fall behind those who had embarked on strengthening their manufacturing sector. With sharply declining world market prices for their commodities and rising prices for manufactured goods, commodity producers were increasingly unable to catch up. More recently, a shift has occurred from manufacturing to services—perhaps presaging a similar shift of trade composition for the future. Currently, U.S. service exports represent about 30 percent of all U.S. exports.[9]

Not only are the environment and composition of trade changing, but the pace of that change is accelerating. Atari's Pong was first introduced in the early 1980s; today, action games and movies are amazingly sophisticated. The first office computers emerged in the mid-1980s; today, home computers have become commonplace. E-mail was introduced to a mass market only in the 1990s; today, many college students hardly ever send personal notes using a stamp and an envelope.[10] The first text message, or SMS, was sent in 1992. In 2010,

Fast Facts

Which world organization states its key objectives as follows?

- To save succeeding generations from the scourge of war
- To reaffirm faith in fundamental human rights, in the dignity and worth of the human person, in the equal rights of men and women, and of nations large and small
- To establish conditions under which justice and respect for the obligations arising from treaties and other sources of international law can be maintained
- To promote social progress and better standards of life in larger freedom

The United Nations

Culture Clues

When attending your first meeting with a prospective business partner in Russia, especially one with whom you hope to establish a long-term relationship, it is perfectly acceptable and even expected to bring a gift.

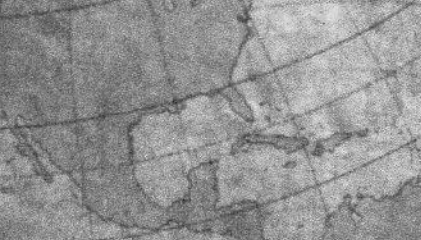

200,000 text messages were sent every minute, and 6.1 trillion texts were sent worldwide.[11] In 2012, however, SMS messaging in countries around the world has been declining because Internet-based alternatives, like Facebook messaging and Apple's iMessage, are becoming popular.[12]

As we shall see in coming chapters, all these changes and the speed with which they come about significantly affect countries, companies, and individuals, altering almost every aspect of the global marketplace.

U.S. International Trade Position

From a global perspective, the United States has gained in prominence as a market for the world but has lost some of its importance as a supplier. In spite of the decline in the global market share of U.S. exports, the nation's international activities have not been reduced. On the contrary, exports have grown rapidly and successfully. However, many new participants have entered the international market. Competitors from both Europe and Asia have aggressively won a share of the growing world trade, resulting in U.S. export growth not keeping pace with total growth of world exports.

U.S. exports, as a share of the **gross domestic product (GDP)** have grown substantially in recent years, representing 14 percent in 2011. However, this increase pales in comparison to the international trade performance of other nations. For example, German exports of goods and services were 50 percent of that nation's GDP and Canada's and China's exports amounted to 31 percent of GDP for each in 2011.[13]

GROSS DOMESTIC PRODUCT (GDP)
Total monetary value of goods produced and services provided by a country over a one-year period

Table 1.1 shows the degree to which the U.S. comparatively "underparticipates" in international business on a per capita basis, particularly on the export side.

TABLE 1.1 Merchandise Trade as a Share of GDP for Selected Countries (U.S.$) (2011)

Country	Merchandise *Exports and Imports as a Percentage of GDP*
Brazil	21.1%
Canada	51.0
China	47.0
Denmark	63.4
France	47.6
India	42.5
Indonesia	43.1
Korea	94.5
Japan	28.3
Mexico	63.8
Netherlands	161.4
United Kingdom	47.2
United States	24.8

SOURCE: The World Bank, **http://data.worldbank.org/indicator/TG.VAL.TOTL.GD.ZS**, accessed September 12, 2013

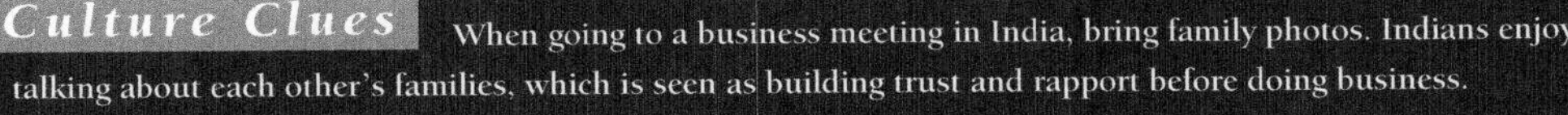

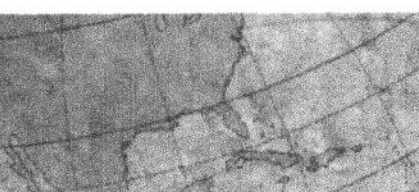

Global Business Imperative

MACROECONOMIC LEVEL
Level of business concerns at which trading relationships affect individual markets

Why should one worry about this underparticipation in trade? Why not simply concentrate on the large domestic market and get on with it? Who should it bother that the largest portion of U.S. exports is attributed to only 2,500 companies?

U.S. international business outflows are important on the **macroeconomic level** in terms of balancing the trade account. Macroeconomic means an analysis of a national economy with a focus on overall perspectives and workings. Lack of export growth has resulted in long-term trade deficits. In 1983, imports of products exceeded exports by more than $70 billion. Although exports increased at a rapid rate in ensuing years, import growth also continued. As a result, in 2012, the U.S. total trade deficit was estimated to be at $540 billion.[14] Ongoing annual trade deficits in this range are not sustainable in the long run. Such deficits add to the U.S. international debt, which must be serviced and eventually repaid. Exporting is not only good for the international trade picture but also a key factor in increasing employment. Indeed, exports have a major influence on employment. The $2.1 trillion in U.S. exports of goods and services in 2011 supported 9.7 million jobs (about 4,600 jobs per billion dollars of exports).[15]

Imports, in turn, bring a wider variety of products and services into a country. They exert competitive pressure on domestic firms to improve. Imports, therefore, expand consumers' choices and improve their standard of living. Typically, the sale and maintenance of imports also increases the domestic job number.

MICROECONOMIC LEVEL
Level of business concerns that affect an individual firm or industry

On the **microeconomic level**, participation in international business allows firms to achieve economies of scale that cannot be achieved in domestic markets. Addressing a global market greatly adds to the number of potential customers. Increasing production lets firms ride the learning curve more quickly and therefore makes goods available more cheaply at home. Finally, and perhaps most importantly, international business permits firms to hone their competitive skills by meeting the challenge of foreign products. By going abroad, firms can learn from their foreign competitors, challenge them on their home turf, and translate the absorbed knowledge into productivity improvements back home. U.S. multinationals of all sizes and in all industries typically outperform their strictly domestic counterparts—growing more than twice as fast in sales and earning significantly higher returns on equity and assets. Workers also benefit because exporting firms of all sizes typically pay significantly higher wages compared to nonexporting firms. In fact, nine of the ten most-admired U.S. companies in the world, as shown in Table 1.2, are substantial exporters and international investors. All ten of them are U.S. firms.

TABLE 1.2 World's Most-Admired U.S. Companies

2013 Rank	Company
1	Apple
2	Google
3	Amazon.com
4	Coca-Cola Company
5	Starbucks
6	IBM
7	Southwest Airlines
8	Berkshire Hathaway
9	Walt Disney
10	FedEx

SOURCE: **http://money.cnn.com/magazines/fortune/most-admired/2013/list/?iid=wma_sp_full**

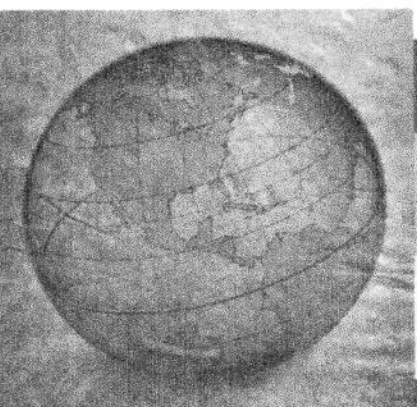

WORLD VIEW
Trade-Offs in Trade Policy

The whole notion of reducing trade barriers is in serious trouble. Some sources of this trouble include the slow growth of most of the world's economies, increased competition from developing countries, global excess capacity in most industries, and, as a result of all of these forces, the politically disruptive weakness of job markets around the world. A heightened perception of risk connected to operating across national borders exacerbates these problems.

In the face of risk, nations desire to unite on a political front, which forces an uneasy alliance between economic policy and international politics. Recently, Pakistan, a crucial U.S. ally, pressed for the reduction of tariffs on its textiles to allow clothing made in Pakistan to enter the United States at below-market prices. U.S. manufacturers immediately protested that any change in tariffs would severely damage the already-beleaguered textile industry of South Carolina. Around the same time, under constant pressure from U.S. steelmakers, the government raised tariffs to effectively block imported steel. The tariffs went into effect despite strenuous objections from political advisors that the move would adversely affect relationships with such countries as Kazakhstan, another key partner on the Afghan border, and Russia, which may prove the most important U.S. ally in the war against terror.

Different perspectives require different trade-offs. While Senator Ernest "Fritz" Hollings (D-South Carolina) believes in the need for full protection of the textile manufacturers in his state, U.S. trade representative Robert Zoellick favors the use of trade to ease political frictions. "If we want to support countries over the long term in a conflict with terror," he says, "we'll have to pay attention to the economic problems they have."

SOURCES: Helene Cooper, "Pakistan's Textile Bind Presents Bush Team with a Tough Choice" and "Trade Craft Is Employed on War's Economic Front," *The Wall Street Journal*, October 29, 2001; "At Daggers Drawn," *The Economist*, May 8, 1999, **http://www.economist.com**.

focused on the customs and products that make them different from one another and possibly separate them. Now we think more of the issues that make us behave alike and strengthen the bonds between us.

These five features of common sense bode well for a future of international negotiations, policy directives, and formulation of joint approaches to the progress of globalization.

Structure of the Book

This book is intended to enable you to become a better, more successful participant in the global business arena. Other than doing a "book by committee," the three of us have developed this book over thirty years to bring a consistent, harmonious, and non-overlapping perspective to those who simply want to know more about what is going on in international markets and to those who want to translate their knowledge into successful business transactions. The text melds theory and practice to balance conceptual understanding with knowledge of day-to-day

Migration Flow and Population

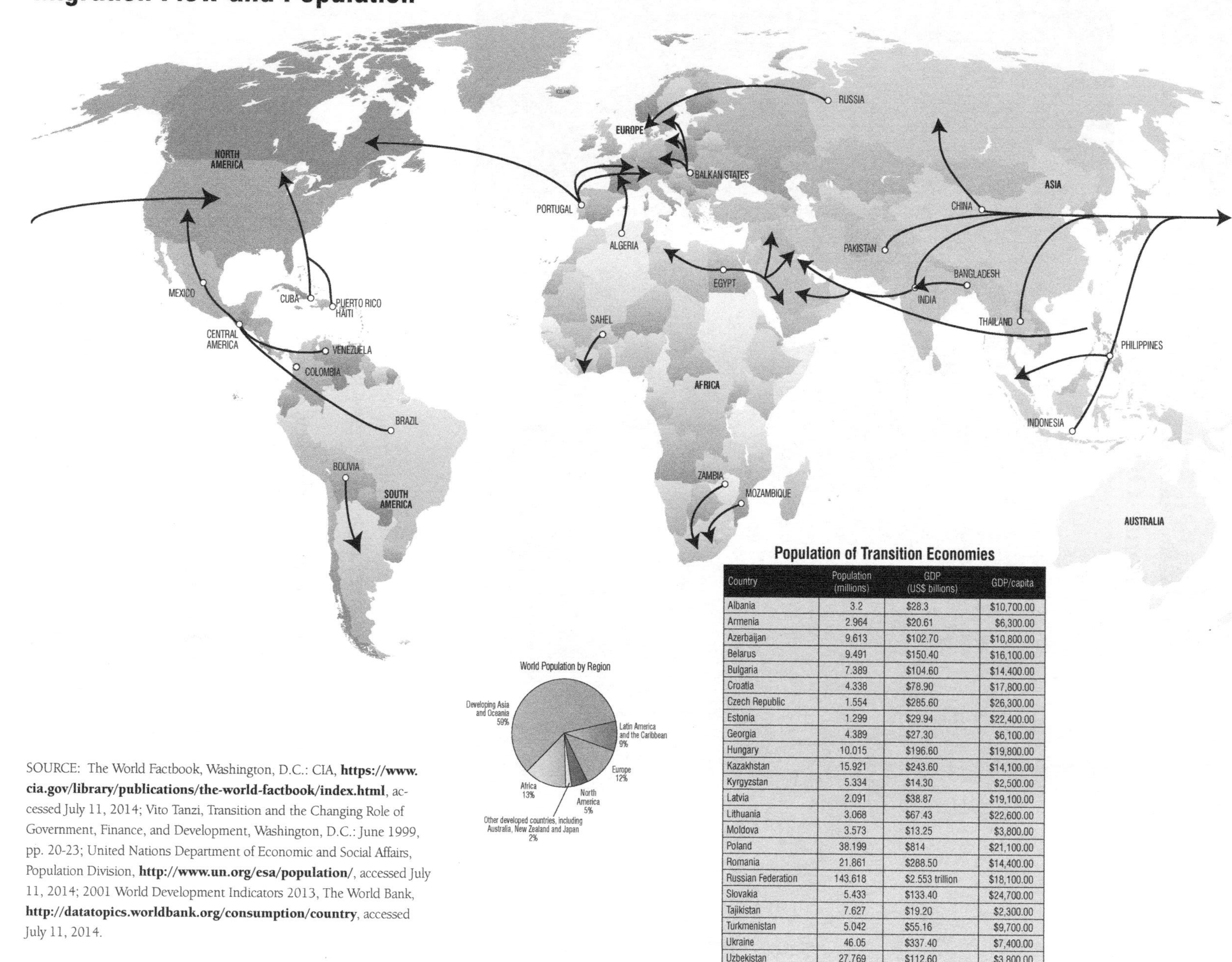

Population of Transition Economies

Country	Population (millions)	GDP (US$ billions)	GDP/capita
Albania	3.2	$28.3	$10,700.00
Armenia	2.964	$20.61	$6,300.00
Azerbaijan	9.613	$102.70	$10,800.00
Belarus	9.491	$150.40	$16,100.00
Bulgaria	7.389	$104.60	$14,400.00
Croatia	4.338	$78.90	$17,800.00
Czech Republic	1.554	$285.60	$26,300.00
Estonia	1.299	$29.94	$22,400.00
Georgia	4.389	$27.30	$6,100.00
Hungary	10.015	$196.60	$19,800.00
Kazakhstan	15.921	$243.60	$14,100.00
Kyrgyzstan	5.334	$14.30	$2,500.00
Latvia	2.091	$38.87	$19,100.00
Lithuania	3.068	$67.43	$22,600.00
Moldova	3.573	$13.25	$3,800.00
Poland	38.199	$814	$21,100.00
Romania	21.861	$288.50	$14,400.00
Russian Federation	143.618	$2.553 trillion	$18,100.00
Slovakia	5.433	$133.40	$24,700.00
Tajikistan	7.627	$19.20	$2,300.00
Turkmenistan	5.042	$55.16	$9,700.00
Ukraine	46.05	$337.40	$7,400.00
Uzbekistan	27.769	$112.60	$3,800.00

SOURCE: The World Factbook, Washington, D.C.: CIA, **https://www.cia.gov/library/publications/the-world-factbook/index.html**, accessed July 11, 2014; Vito Tanzi, Transition and the Changing Role of Government, Finance, and Development, Washington, D.C.: June 1999, pp. 20-23; United Nations Department of Economic and Social Affairs, Population Division, **http://www.un.org/esa/population/**, accessed July 11, 2014; 2001 World Development Indicators 2013, The World Bank, **http://datatopics.worldbank.org/consumption/country**, accessed July 11, 2014.

realities. To do so effectively, we address the interests of both beginning internationalists and multinational corporations.

The beginning international manager will need to know the answers to basic, yet important questions: How can I find out whether demand for my product exists abroad? What must I do to get ready to market internationally? These issues are also relevant for managers in multinational corporations, but the questions they consider are often much more sophisticated. Of course, the resources available to address them are also much greater.

Throughout the book, public policy concerns are included in discussions of business activities. In this way, you are exposed to both macro and micro issues. Part 1 introduces the concept of globalization and underlines the critical importance of international activities to the future survival and growth of firms.

Part 2 describes the macroenvironment for international business and explores the cultural, political, legal, and economic forces that drive globalization. Part 3 presents the theoretical dimensions of international trade and investment, exploring the effect of international economic activities on a nation. Part 4 explains the role of the international monetary system, showing how fluctuations in foreign exchange impact the conduct of business. It also presents strategies for international financial management. Part 5 describes how firms initiate and develop a global business strategy and lays out the options for market entry and the steps essential to success—from planning to research to marketing to logistics and operations management.

Part 6 looks to the future, anticipating changes that will continue to affect the dynamics of the international business environment as it exists today and as it develops tomorrow.

We hope that upon finishing the book, you will not only have completed another academic subject but also will be well-versed in the theoretical, policy, and strategic aspects of international business and therefore will be able to contribute to improved international competitiveness and a better global standard of living.

Fast Facts

This, the world's fifth most populous nation with a total of 201 million people, covers a vast area of 3,287,612 square miles comprised of tropical forest, plains, and mountains. (Hint: Virtually, the whole country lies east of Savannah, Georgia.) Source: CIA - The World Factbook, accessed May 22, 2013.

Brazil

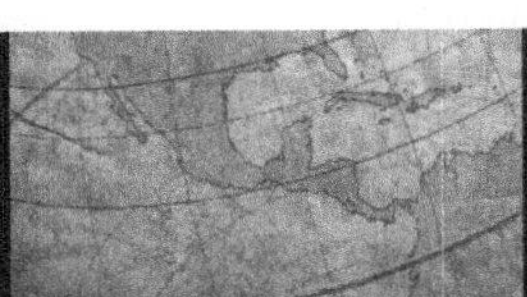

SUMMARY

International business has been conducted ever since national borders were formed and has played a major role in shaping world history. Growing in importance during the past three decades, it has shaped an environment that, due to economic linkages, today presents us with a global marketplace.

Global business involves transactions across borders, primarily through export-import trade and foreign direct investment (FDI).

From 1970 to 2012, the volume of international trade in goods and services has expanded from $200 billion to more than $22.5 trillion, while international investment has grown to $21.6 trillion. Both outpace the growth of most domestic economies, increasing the importance of international business. Global links have made possible investment strategies and business alternatives that offer tremendous opportunities. Yet these changes and the speed of change can also represent threats to nations, firms, and individuals.

During the past 30 years, the dominance of the U.S. international trade position has gradually eroded. The United States has gained in prominence as a market and has decreased in importance as a producer of goods. New participants in international business compete fiercely for world market share.

Individuals, corporations, and policymakers around the globe have awakened to the fact that international business is a major imperative and offers opportunities for future growth and prosperity. International business provides access to new customers, affords economies of scale, and permits the honing of competitive skills.

A heightened awareness of the risks—both to firms and individuals—connected to business across borders has led to a changed global environment best characterized on five key dimensions: vulnerability, outrage, collaboration, politics, and connection.

Key Terms and Concepts

globalization	multinational corporation	microeconomic level
import-export trade	gross domestic product (GDP)	macroeconomic level
foreign direct investment (FDI)		

Review Questions

1. Will future expansion of international business be similar to that in the past?
2. Does increased international business mean increased risk?
3. What areas of business decision making are affected by changes in the global business environment?
4. Explain the rise in Chinese exports to the United States and other parts of the world.
5. With wages in some countries at one-tenth of those in developed nations, how can highly paid workers expect to compete?
6. Compare and contrast domestic and international business.
7. Why do more firms in other countries enter international markets than do firms in the United States?
8. Explain the effect of terrorism on risk and uncertainty in the conduct of cross-border transactions?

Critical Skill Builders

1. Is it beneficial for nations to become dependent on one another? Why or why not? Prepare your arguments for and against and participate in a class debate on this topic.
2. China joined the World Trade Organization in 2001. How has membership affected the Chinese world trade market share? How has it affected the Chinese domestic market? Research and discuss.
3. Select a business in your area. Find out how the company is currently involved in international activities, either in the procurement of supplies or the marketing of finished products. How might this firm take further advantage of ongoing shifts in the global business environment? Prepare a report on past activities and future opportunities.
4. Using your library and Internet resources, research such issues as global equity, sustainable development, and the forgiving of debt of the poorest countries. What are the arguments for and against forgiving the debt of countries that borrow money and then can't afford to repay it?
5. Do you believe that terrorism furthers the cause of globalization or drives a wedge between nations? Prepare your arguments and discuss in small groups.

On the Web

1. Using World Trade Organization data (shown on the International Trade page of its web site, **http://www.wto.org**), determine the following information: (a) the fastest-growing traders; (b) the top ten exporters and importers in world merchandise trade; and (c) the top ten exporters or importers of commercial services.

2. Foreign factories to which U.S. companies outsource manufacturing are under continued criticism for poor working conditions and unfair wages. Using the case studies available on Nike's web site (see **http://www.nikebiz.com**) and other Internet sources you find, assess the criticisms and the ability of a company to address them.

3. Visit **http://www.worldbank.org** to review the discussion of the reconstruction of Afghanistan. Discuss the responsibility of developed nations to provide funding for the reconstruction.

Endnotes

1. Louise Blouin MacBain, "Doha: No Hostage to American Politics," *Forbes*, January 3, 2008.
2. Elizabeth Weise, "Buying American? It's not in the bag." *USA Today*, **http://usatoday30.usatoday.com/news/health/2007-07-10-buying-american_N.htm**, accessed April 30, 2014.
3. UNCTAD, **http://unctadstat.unctad.org/TableViewer/tableView.aspx?ReportId=25116**, accessed May 21, 2013.
4. OECD, "FDI in Figures," April 2013, **http://www.oecd.org/daf/inv/FDI%20in%20figures.pdf**, accessed May 22, 2013.
5. Michael R. Czinkota, Illka Ronkainen, and Bob Donath, *The New Trade Globalist* (Cincinnati: Thomson, 2003); "Nikkei hits a 19-month low as nervous investors worry about U.S. slowdown," *International Herald Tribune*, January 11, 2008.
6. U.S. Department of Commerce, Bureau of Economic Analysis, **http://www.bea.gov/newsreleases/international/intinv/intinvnewsrelease.htm**, accessed May 21, 2013.
7. "Gold Demand Trends first half Year 2013," World Gold Council, **http://www.gold.org/investment/research/regular_reports/gold_demand_trends/**, accessed September 12, 2013.
8. "Top Trading Partners – March 2013," U.S. Department of Commerce, International Trade Administration, May 2013, **http://www.trade.gov/mas/ian/build/groups/public/@tg_ian/documents/webcontent/tg_ian_003364.pdf**, accessed May 22, 2013.
9. J. Bradford Jensen, "Global Trade in Services—Fear, Facts, and Offshoring," Peterson Institute for International Economics, Washington, D.C., 2011, p. 40.
10. Michael R. Czinkota and Sarah McCue, The STAT-USA Companion to International Business, Economics and Statistics Administration (Washington, D.C.: U.S. Department of Commerce, 2007).
11. Joanna Stern, "Happy 20th Birthday, Text Message, But You're Past Your Prime,"ABC News, December 3, 2012.
12. Brian X. Chen, "Text Messaging Declines in U.S. for First Time, Report Says," *New York Times*, November 12, 2012.
13. World Bank, **http://data.worldbank.org/indicator/NE.EXP.GNFS.ZS**, accessed May 22, 2013.
14. U.S. Department of Commerce International Trade Administration, Top U.S. Trade Partners, **http://www.trade.gov/mas/ian/build/groups/public/@tg_ian/documents/webcontent/tg_ian_003364.pdf**, accessed January 2, 2014.
15. 2012 National Export Strategy, **http://www.trade.gov/publications/pdfs/nes2012.pdf**, accessed May 22, 2013.
16. This section is based on Michael Czinkota, "Terrorism and International Business: A Research Agenda, (with G. Knight, P. Liesch, J. Steen), *Journal of International Business Studies*, 45, 1, 2010.

PART 2

GLOBALIZATION DRIVERS

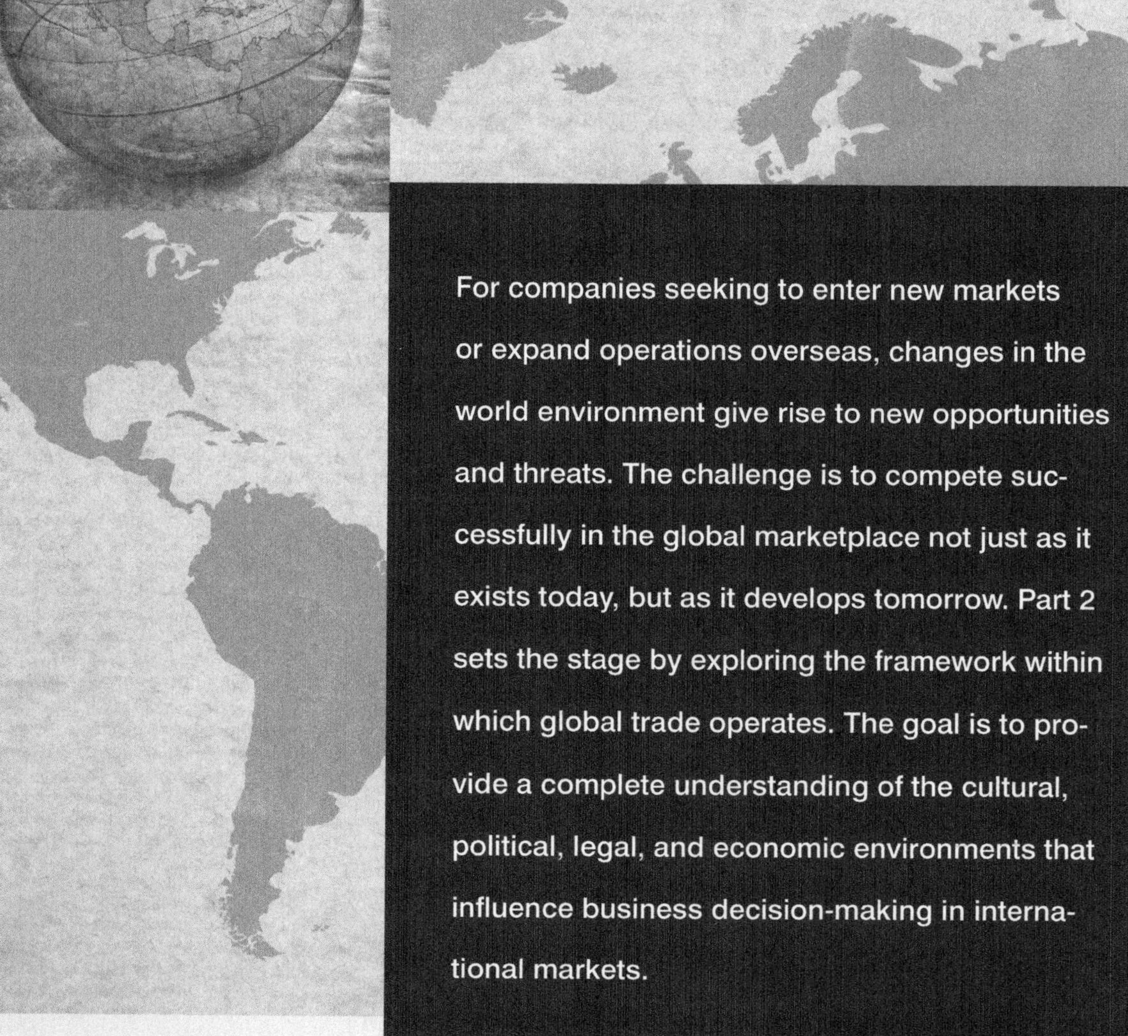

For companies seeking to enter new markets or expand operations overseas, changes in the world environment give rise to new opportunities and threats. The challenge is to compete successfully in the global marketplace not just as it exists today, but as it develops tomorrow. Part 2 sets the stage by exploring the framework within which global trade operates. The goal is to provide a complete understanding of the cultural, political, legal, and economic environments that influence business decision-making in international markets.

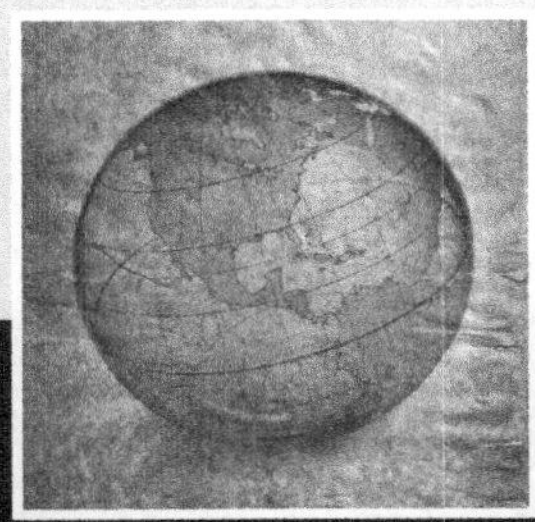

CHAPTER 2

CULTURAL ENVIRONMENT

Not Just Cream Filling

OREO is the world's favorite cookie in more than 100 countries worldwide. The Nabisco division of Mondeléz International had more than $2 billion in global annual revenues for its OREO brand. OREO just celebrated its 100th birthday in 2012. The traditional black and white cookie continues to be the most popular in the United States, but new exotic flavors are sweeping the globe. OREO's Facebook page has more than 27 million followers from around the globe. More than 50 percent of all OREO cookie eaters confirm that "Twist, Lick and Dunk" is the best way to eat an OREO. One thing that transcends continents and cultures is the desire to celebrate the kid inside of all of us.

Mondeléz's ability to adapt to local tastes is important as it continues to look for overseas growth. In 2014, Mondeléz's international revenues more than doubled compared to the U.S. revenues. OREO's biggest markets ranking in order are United States, China, Venezuela, Canada, Indonesia, Mexico, Spain, Central America and the Caribbean, United Kingdom, and Argentina.

Global companies face a critical question when considering entering a new market: How far should they go to localize their offerings and should they adapt just enough to appeal to the local consumer? Mondeléz introduced OREO cookies to Central and Latin America in 1928 and then to Canada in 1949. In 2006, Mondeléz offered only a wafer cookie to Chinese consumers to familiarize them with the brand. Three years later, Mondeléz worked with a Chinese consumer panel to determine the right combination of color, crunchiness, and bitterness to appeal to their tastes, so the company reengineered the traditional OREO to be smaller and not so sweet. When Mondeléz noticed their sales lagging, they introduced a green tea OREO flavor in China that evokes eating ice cream by featuring a cooling sensation in the cream. OREO is now the top-selling cookie in China with a market share of 13 percent.

Asia also has fruit duo OREO cream fillings, which include the side-by-side flavors of raspberry and blueberry, orange and mango, and peach and grape. In Indonesia, OREO is offering a chocolate and strawberry duo cookie. Meanwhile, in Argentina, OREO has introduced cookies with a dulce de leche and banana cream filling, both of which are traditional ice cream toppings in that country.

In Mexico, OREO offers three different combinations of chocolate with different chocolate flavored wafers, as well as a cocoa cream filling.

LEARNING OUTCOMES

1. *To understand the effects of cultural differences on international business*
2. *To illustrate the possibilities involved in cross-cultural business communications and transactions*
3. *To suggest ways in which international businesses act as change agents in the diverse cultural environments in which they operate*
4. *To examine how cultural knowledge is acquired and how individuals and organizations prepare for cross-cultural interaction*

For its 100th birthday celebration, OREO launched a "Global Spirit of Childhood" campaign with Ipsos Public Affairs conducting the research. The report indicates that from China to Poland and Portugal to Venezuela, the spirit of childhood, the chance to enjoy simple, carefree moments, may soon be extinct. Parents believe that children are growing up faster than previous generations, and parents desire more time and chances for their kids to be kids. Sheeba Philip, Global Brand director for OREO, says, "We believe this sentiment is more important now than ever before, so we conducted this research to learn more about the spirit of childhood worldwide."

SOURCES: **http://www.kraftfoodscompany.com/sitecollectiondocuments/pdf/Oreo-Global-Fact-Sheet-100th-Birthday.pdf**; and Sanette Tanaka, "Style & Travel: What's Selling Where/OREO Cookies," *Wall Street Journal*, August 2012, D2.

As You Read This Chapter

1. Consider whether the following statement is accurate: "The more the world becomes global, the more people want their own culture."
2. Assess the degree to which international business is a cultural change agent both for the good and the bad.

As new markets open up for world trade and as global competition intensifies, businesses of all sizes and in all sectors are expanding their operations overseas at unprecedented rates. In fact, business across borders has become so much the norm that distinctions between domestic and global markets and operations have blurred.[1] Yet while advances in communications and transportation have made the business world a smaller place, the cultural differences that divide nations and govern international interactions are as complex as ever. Culture should not be viewed as a challenge, but rather as an opportunity that can be exploited.

This chapter explores how cultural differences manifest themselves in business situations. Success in new markets requires smooth adaptation to unfamiliar cultural environments, best achieved through patience, flexibility, and appreciation of the values and beliefs of potential business partners. This means recognizing cultural competence as a key management skill that directly affects both revenues and profitability in new markets.

What is Culture?

1 LEARNING OUTCOME

Culture is the unique combination of learning and experience that gives an individual an anchoring point, an identity, as well as codes of conduct. Scholars have defined culture in more than 164 ways, but all of the definitions share some key common elements.[2] Culture is learned, shared, and transmitted from one generation to the next. It is primarily passed on from parents to their children but also transmitted by social organizations, special-interest groups, governments, schools, and religious institutions. Culture affects not only the way people behave but also the ways they think. For this reason, it has been termed "the collective programming of the mind."[3] Through cultural influences, common ways of thinking and behaving are developed and then reinforced through social pressure. Within the same national borders, intercultural differences, based on religion, race, or geographic region, have resulted in the emergence of distinct subcultures, such as the Hispanic subculture in the United States.

CULTURE
An integrated system of learned behavior patterns that are characteristic of the members of any given society

For the purposes of this text, **culture** is defined as an integrated system of learned behavior patterns that are characteristic of the members of any given society. It includes not just everything a group thinks, says, does, and makes—its customs, language, and material artifacts—but the group's shared systems of attitudes and feelings, too. The definition, therefore, encompasses a wide variety of elements from the materialistic to the spiritual. Culture is inherently conservative, resisting change and fostering continuity. Every person is brought up in a particular culture, learning the "right way" of doing things. Problems may arise when a person from one culture has to adjust to another one. The process of **acculturation**—adjusting and adapting to a specific culture other than one's own—is one of the keys to success in international business operations.

ACCULTURATION
The process of adjusting and adapting to a specific culture other than one's own

Figure 2.1 distinguishes between high- and low-context cultures. In **high-context cultures**, such as Japan and Saudi Arabia, the context of a communication is at least as important as what is actually said. The speaker and the listener rely on a common understanding of the context. In **low-context cultures**, however, most of the information is contained explicitly in the words. North American cultures engage in low-context communications. Unless one is aware of this basic difference, messages and intentions can easily be misunderstood. Consider, for example, the different approaches to as simple a business communication as the exchange of business cards. A Chinese or Japanese businessperson carefully presents the card with both hands. Etiquette requires that recipients study the card when it is handed to them and place it on the table before them. An executive who proffers a travel-worn card or—worse still—makes notes on a card he or she is given is considered offensive, even insulting.[4]

HIGH-CONTEXT CULTURE
Culture in which behavioral and environmental nuances are an important means of conveying information

LOW-CONTEXT CULTURE
Culture in which most information is conveyed explicitly rather than through behavioral and environmental nuances

FIGURE 2.1 Context Orientation in Major Cultures

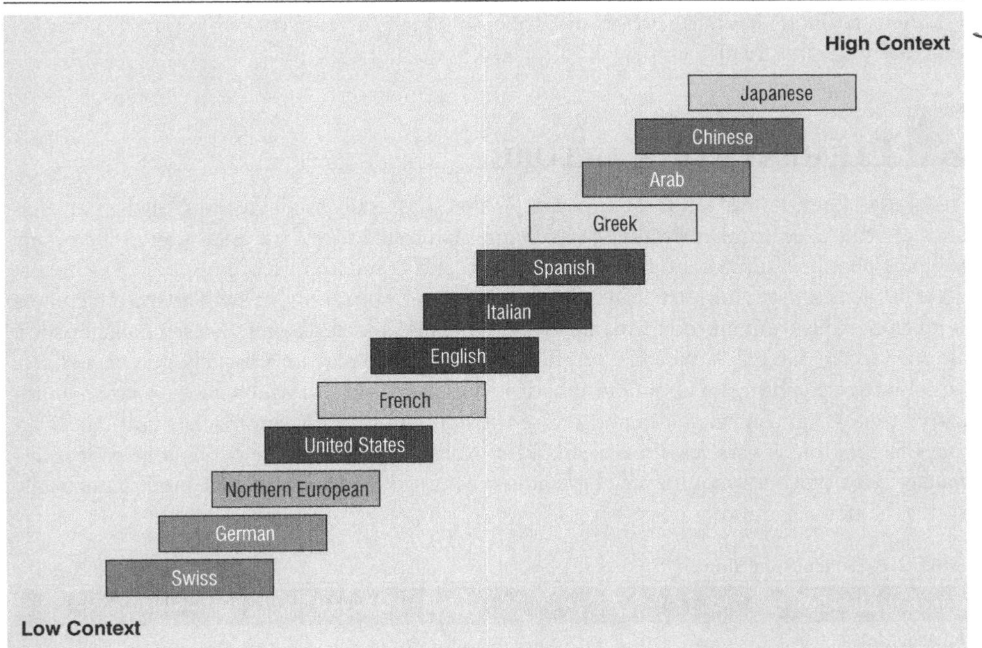

SOURCE: Adapted from E. T. Hall, and Mildred Reed Hall, *Understanding Cultural Differences* (Yarmouth, ME: Intercultural Press, 1990).

Borrowing and interaction among cultures often serve to narrow the gaps between them. It is not uncommon, for instance, for products or brands to act as **change agents**, able to alter commonly held values or behavior patterns that eventually result in the blurring of cultural

CHANGE AGENT
An institution or person who facilitates change in a firm or in a host country

Culture Clues A booming economy and flourishing development have made India a lot more business-friendly in recent years. The influence of the West is being felt across most cities with supermarkets and shopping malls coming up everywhere. India's middle class is growing and has more money to spend. Most people now have mobile phones. Many have computers and access to the Internet. Cities such as Mumbai and Delhi have become quite cosmopolitan, with an increasing number of modern restaurants, bars, and clubs.

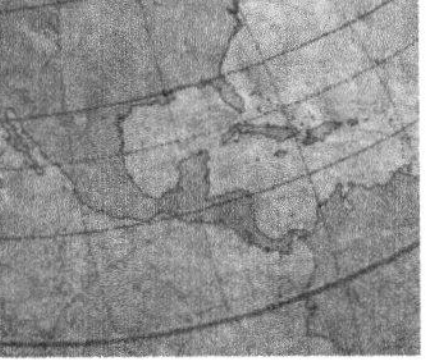

distinctions. In China, for example, the Kentucky Fried Chicken menu features its signature "Original Recipe" fried chicken, but it also includes products that appeal to local tastes, such as the Spicy Dragon Twister, Pi Dan Congee (rice porridge), Fu Young Vegetable Soup, and Egg Tart (signature dessert). Although this may consist of no more than shifting consumption from one product brand to another, it may lead to massive social change in the manner of consumption, the type of products consumed, and social organization.

CULTURAL IMPERIALISM
Promoting Western behaviors and values along with products and into other cultures, encouraging homogeneous demand across markets

In bringing about change or in encouraging increasingly homogeneous demand across markets, global businesses open themselves to charges of **cultural imperialism**. They are sometimes accused of pushing Western behaviors and values—along with products and promotions—into other cultures. Coca-Cola and Disney, for example, have all drawn the ire of anti-American demonstrators. Some countries, such as Brazil, Canada, France, and Indonesia, use restrictive rules and subsidies to protect their "cultural industries," including music and movies. Similar measures have been taken to protect geographic indications, such as labels on goods that have a specific geographic origin and possess qualities or a reputation due to that place of origin (Parma ham from Italy, Stilton cheese from the United Kingdom, and Vidalia for onions from Georgia, United States). Some countries have started taking measures to protect their traditions in areas such as medicine, in which the concern is bio-piracy of natural remedies (e.g., in Africa).[5]

Elements of Culture

CULTURAL UNIVERSALS
Manifestations of the total way of life of any group of people, including concrete elements such as language, infrastructure, social institutions, education, or abstract elements such as religion, values and attitudes, manners and customs, and aesthetics

The study of culture has led to generalizations that may apply to all cultures. Such characteristics are called **cultural universals**, which are manifestations of the total way of life of any group of people. Cultures are typically described and compared according to such concrete elements as language, infrastructure, social institutions, education, or such abstract elements as religion, values and attitudes, manners and customs, and aesthetics. These characteristics, summarized in Table 2.1, which occur across all cultures, may be uniquely manifested in a particular society, bringing about cultural diversity. The ease with which an international firm adapts to cultural characteristics and the sensitivity with which it approaches cultural differences factors into its success in new markets. Naturally, while some goods and services or management practices require very little adjustment, others have to be adapted dramatically to suit the new environment.

TABLE 2.1 Elements of Culture

Concrete Elements	Abstract Elements
• Language	• Religion
Verbal	• Values and attitudes
Nonverbal	• Manners and customs
• Infrastructure	• Aesthetics
• Education	
• Social institutions	

Language

Language has been described as the mirror of culture. Language itself is multidimensional. This is true not only of the spoken word but also of the nonverbal language of international business. Messages are conveyed not just by the words used but by how those words are spoken and through such nonverbal means as gestures, body position, and eye contact. In addition, with the global use of new technologies, such as texting, micro-blogging sites like

Quick Take *Twtr!*

Micro-blogging is a broadcast medium form of blogging. Micro-blogs allow users to exchange small elements of content, such as short sentences, individual images, or video links. Which tongues work best for micro-blogs?

This 24–character tweet in Chinese would be 78 characters in English: **这条七十八个字的英语句子如果写成中文只有二十五个字**. That makes Chinese ideal for micro-blogs, which typically restrict messages to 140 symbols. Though Twitter, with 140 million active users, is the world's best-known micro-blogging service, it is blocked in China; Sina Weibo, a local variant, has more than 368 million users. Chinese is so succinct that most messages never reach the 140 symbol limit.

Romance tongues generally tend to be more verbose. So Spanish and Portuguese, the two most frequent European languages in the Twitterverse, after English, have tricks to reduce the number of characters. Brazilians use "abs" for *abracos* (hugs) and "bjs" for *beijos* (kisses); Spanish speakers need never use personal pronouns ("I go" is denoted by the verb alone: *voy*).

Twitter's growth around the world has reduced the proportion of total global tweets in English from two-thirds in 2009 to 39 percent now, but polyglot tweeters still often favor the language because of its ubiquity.

SOURCE: "Twtr," *The Economist*, March 31, 2012, 71.

Twitter, and video cameras on computers, research must be conducted on how those tools affect virtual cross-cultural communication and what the impact could be of non-face-to-face communication.

Very often, mastery of the language is required before a person is acculturated. Language mastery must go beyond technical competency because every language has words and phrases that can be readily understood only in context. Such phrases are carriers of culture; they represent special ways a culture has developed to view some aspect of human existence.

Language capability serves four distinct roles in international business:[6]

1. Language aids in information gathering and evaluation efforts. Rather than rely completely on the opinions of others, the manager is able to see and hear personally what is going on. People are far more comfortable speaking their own language, and this should be treated as an advantage. The best intelligence on a market is gathered by becoming part of the market rather than observing it from the outside.
2. Language provides access to local society. Although English may be widely spoken, and may even be the official company language, speaking the local language may make a dramatic difference. For example, firms that translate promotional materials and information are seen as being serious about doing business in that country.
3. Language capability is increasingly important in company communications, whether within the corporate family or with channel members. Imagine the difficulties encountered by a country manager who must communicate with employees through an interpreter.
4. Language provides more than the ability to communicate. It extends beyond mechanics to the interpretation of contexts. Realize that in several cultures, "yes" will not mean "I agree," but rather only signals "I hear what you're saying," so it does not convey consent.

Table 2.2 lists the populations who speak the world's top ten languages. While some 328 million people speak English as their first language and about a billion speak it as their second, English as an international language has met much resistance. The French have sought to banish English expressions from such documents as legal contracts and to restrict its use in public signage (as referenced in World View, France vs. the Internet). Following in French footsteps, the Germans have founded a society for the protection of the German language from the spread of "Denglis(c)h." In Hong Kong, the Chinese government is promoting the use of Mandarin and Cantonese rather than English as the language of commerce, while some people in India—with its 800 dialects—scorn the use of English as a lingua franca because it is a reminder of British colonialism.[7]

TABLE 2.2 Top Ten World Languages

Language	Number of Speakers
1. Chinese (Mandarin)	1,213,000,000
2. Spanish	329,000,000
3. English	328,000,000
4. Arabic	221,000,000
5. Hindi	182,000,000
6. Bengali	181,000,000
7. Portuguese	178,000,000
8. Russian	144,000,000
9. Japanese	122,000,000
10. German	90,000,000

SOURCE: *Ethnologue*, 16th Edition, 2009.

Despite the fact that English is encountered daily by those on the Internet, the "e" in e-business does not translate into "English." Companies that tend to do the best job at Web globalization are those that strive to treat customers in all markets equally. Instead of viewing themselves as domestic companies with foreign customers, they view themselves as global companies with local customers. This way of thinking permeates the design, functionality, and content of the web sites, ensuring that a Web user in South Korea has the same experience as a Web user in Florida. Hotels.com, which is owned by Expedia, is the best travel web site. It supports more than 35 languages in addition to English. Hotels.com not only meets language needs but also branding and design. Each of their international Hotels.com sites has the same core design.[8]

Internet slang refers to a variety of everyday languages used by different communities on the Internet. Slang seems to be commonly sourced, however, from online games, video games, and general pop culture. In the English-speaking world, examples include the word "bazinga" from *The Big Bang Theory*, and in Japanese, the term "moe" has come into common use among slang users to mean something appealing.

BACKTRANSLATION

The retranslation of text to the original language by a different person from the one who made the first translation, useful for finding translation errors

When translation is required, as when communicating with suppliers or customers, care should be taken in selecting the localization or translation software. One of the simplest methods of control is **backtranslation**—the translating of a foreign language version back to the original language by a different person from the one who made the first translation. International search engine marketing (SEM) can be difficult on any given day with multiple languages and locations and complicated cultural voices and tones. The goal is to achieve consistent branding across cultures while crafting communications that are meaningful for Web surfers in each micro-market. Finding the right language service provider with the cultural and linguistic expertise to guide you through the process can make the path smoother.[9]

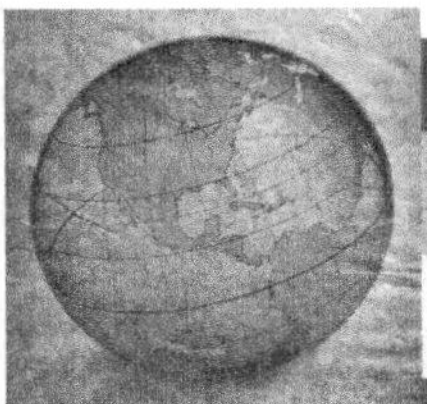

WORLD VIEW

France vs. the Internet

As the Internet continues to evolve, new uses for digital communication tools like Facebook, MySpace, Twitter, Badoo, Skyrock, and YouTube continue to increase beyond expectations, creating large global communities acting in concert for social, environmental, and even political change. Although a direct affront to authoritarian governments, this explosion of international online communities raises questions for nations like France and its policies to protect its own unique culture from outside invasion. Yet as part of a trend toward globalization, scores of participating citizens are transcending France's cultural borders to join these powerful online communities and in turn, bypassing established policies concerning the free flow of information, isolation, and protectionism.

Cultural convergence theorists would see a potential fusion of cultures here that would not bode well for cultural protectionists, especially since the American culture would be predominant. American-centered Google and Microsoft sites are the most visited in France. Google's YouTube was the top ranked video site in France with 25 million people watching 2.3 billion videos online—in spite of concerns by French government officials who claim these particular sites have the strongest potential for American dominance and imperialism. Recent polls indicate that a majority of today's youth—often referred to as "digital natives" for whom laptops and wireless Internet connections are a given—are creating and consuming online content on an international scale.

SOURCE: Hazel G. Warlaumont, Social Networks and Globalization: Facebook, YouTube and the Impact of Online Communities on France's Protectionist Policies, *French Politics*, July 2010, 204–214. **http://www.comscore.com/Press_Events/Presentations_Whitepapers/2011/2010_Europe_Digital_Year_in_Review**.

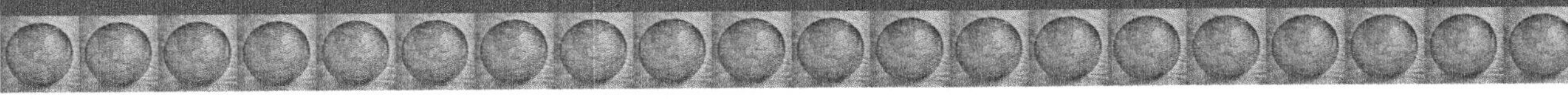

Nonverbal Language

Language goes beyond the spoken word, encompassing nonverbal actions and behaviors that reveal hidden clues to culture. Five key topics—time, space, body language, friendship patterns, and business agreements—offer a starting point from which managers can begin to acquire the understanding necessary to do business in foreign countries.

Understanding national and cultural differences in the concept of time is critical for an international business manager. In many parts of the world, time is flexible and is not seen as a limited commodity; people come late to appointments or may not come at all. In Mexico, for instance, it is not unusual to show up at 1:45 p.m. for a 1:00 p.m. appointment. Although a late afternoon siesta cuts apart the business day, businesspeople will often be at their desks until 10 o'clock at night. In Hong Kong, too, it is futile to set exact meeting times because getting from one place to another may take minutes or hours, depending on traffic. Showing indignation or impatience at such behavior would astonish an Arab, Latin American, or Asian. Perception of time also affects business negotiations. Asians and Europeans tend to be more interested in long-term partnerships, while Americans are eager for deals that will be profitable in the short term, meaning less than a year.

Individuals vary in their preferences for personal space. Arabs and Latin Americans like to stand close to people when they talk. If an American, who may not be comfortable at such close range, backs away from an Arab, this might incorrectly be perceived as a negative reaction. An interesting exercise is to compare and contrast the conversation styles of different nationalities. Northern Europeans are quite reserved in using their hands and maintain a good amount of personal space, whereas Southern Europeans involve their bodies to a far greater degree in making a point.

International body language, too, can befuddle international business relations. For example, an American manager may, after successful completion of negotiations, impulsively give a finger-and-thumb "okay" sign. In southern France, this would signify that the deal was worthless, and in Japan it would mean that a little bribe had been requested. The gesture would be grossly insulting to Brazilians. Misunderstanding nonverbal cues can undermine international negotiations. While Eastern and Chinese negotiators usually lean back and make frequent eye contact while projecting negativity, Western negotiators usually avert their gaze for the same purpose.[10]

In some countries, extended social acquaintance and the establishment of appropriate personal rapport are essential to conducting business. The feeling is that one should know one's business partner on a personal level before transactions can occur.

Therefore, rushing straight to business will not be rewarded because deals are made on the basis of not only the best product or price, but also the entity or person deemed most trustworthy. Contracts may be bound on handshakes, not lengthy and complex agreements—a fact that makes some, especially Western, businesspeople uneasy.

Infrastructure

A culture's infrastructure is directly related to how society organizes its economic activity. The basic **economic infrastructure** consists of transportation, energy, and communications systems. **Social infrastructure** refers to housing, health, and educational systems. **Financial** and **marketing infrastructures** provide the facilitating agencies for the international firm's operation in a given market—for example, banks and research firms. In some parts of the world, the global firm may have to be a partner in developing the various infrastructures before it can operate, whereas in others it may greatly benefit from their high level of sophistication.

ECONOMIC INFRASTRUCTURE
The transportation, energy, and communication systems in a country

SOCIAL INFRASTRUCTURE
The housing, health, education, and other social systems in a country

FINANCIAL INFRASTRUCTURE
Facilitating financial agencies in a country, such as banks

MARKETING INFRASTRUCTURE
Facilitating marketing agencies in a country, such as market research firms, channel members

The level of infrastructure development can be used to aid segmentation in international markets. Companies like General Electric, for example, may see a demand for basic energy generating products in developing countries, while markets with sophisticated infrastructures are ripe for such goods as time-saving home appliances.

While infrastructure is often a good indicator of potential demand, goods sometimes discover unexpectedly rich markets due to the informal economy at work in developing nations. In Kenya, for example, where most of the country's 41 million people live on between $2 and $20 dollar a day, more than 22,000,000 people have signed up for mobile phone service.[11] Leapfrogging older technologies, mobile phones are especially attractive to Kenya's thousands of small-business entrepreneurs—market stall owners, taxi drivers, and even hustlers who sell on the sidewalks. For most, income goes unreported, creating an invisible wealth on the streets. Mobile phones outnumber fixed lines in Kenya, as well as in Uganda, Venezuela, Cambodia, South Korea, and Chile. The advent of new technologies must be culturally calibrated (as seen in World View: Telecommunication).

Culture Clues Hoping to become the global leader in electric vehicles, the Chinese government wants 500,000 electric and plug-in hybrid vehicles on China's roads by 2015, and more than 5 million by 2020. It is already backing these aspirations with a range of subsidies, including up to $8,800 for every electric vehicle purchased by taxi companies and local governments.

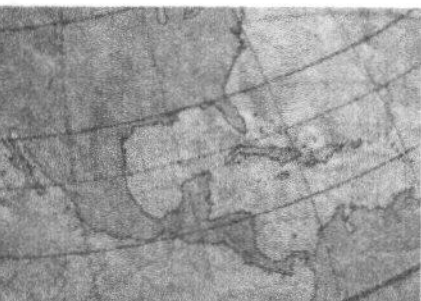

WORLD VIEW

Telecommunication: Mobile Payments Across the Globe?

Mobile payment services enable consumers to pay for goods and services from their bank account using their mobile phone. M-payments have taken off in Japan and Korea but failed to reach estimated potential within the European Union and the United States. Reasons for this can be found in the lack of readiness in existing technology, unwillingness of the various stakeholders (banks, credit card issuers, handset makers, and telecommunication companies) to collaborate, as well as cultural variables in terms of existing usage patterns and perceptions of risk and relative advantage of a new technology. The combined market for all types of mobile payments is expected to reach more than $600 billion globally by 2013.

Mobile financial services are experiencing a global surge, especially in emerging markets. Arthur D. Little outlines how players in each country must consider specific local requirements to succeed:

- *Mexico*—the best option for fast market entry, as regulations are already in place to facilitate entry of nonbanks, enhancing the chances of mobile network operator (MNOs) and third-party providers
- *Brazil*—banks will take the lead and should identify the most valuable potential key accounts for bulk payments and money collection services.
- *Russia*—the country is well positioned to develop mobile bill and utility payments, and MNOs have the potential to strengthen their market position by focusing on business-to-consumer (B2C) transactions in cooperation with banks and nonbank payment operators.
- *India*—m-payments will be bank-led, with banks offering this service to regions where ATMs and/or branches are not in reasonable distance. Over the next two years, players should focus their attention on top-ups and bill payments services.
- *China*—existing technology can be used to reach China's rural areas both quickly and cheaply to provide a short message services (SMS)-based m-payments system.

SOURCE: **http://www.adlittle.com/downloads/tx_adlreports/ADL_2010_M_Payments_in_M_BRIC.pdf** and **http://cellular-news.com/story/4451.php**.

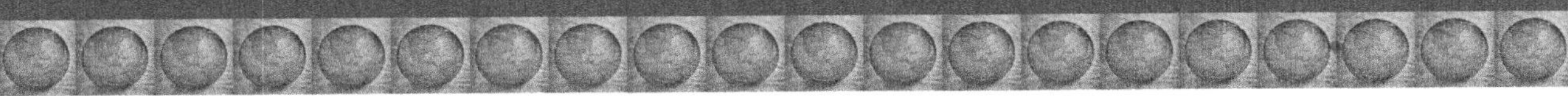

Developed, emerging, and developing markets will require different adjustments by marketers. As several markets have achieved greater than 100 percent penetration, handset vendors and network operators have to provide new features such as cameras, MP3 music, and mobile TV. When exposure to foreign cultures is accelerated by technological advances, the result is **cultural convergence**. New growth will come from markets such as China, India, Eastern Europe, Latin America, and Africa. By the end of 2011, China had 952 million subscribers, and India's growth reached 865 million. Brazil's telecoms regulator has announced that there are now more mobile phones in the country in use than there are people. The number of active mobile subscriptions in Africa crossed the half-billion mark to reach 506 million in 2011. Africa accounted for 10 percent of the world's mobile subscriptions and was one of the world's fastest-growing regions.[12]

CULTURAL CONVERGENCE
Increasing similarity among cultures accelerated by technological advances

The diffusion of Internet technology into core business processes and into the lifestyles of consumers has been rapid, especially in industrialized countries. The number of Internet hosts (computers through which users connect to the network) has increased to 2,095.0 mil-

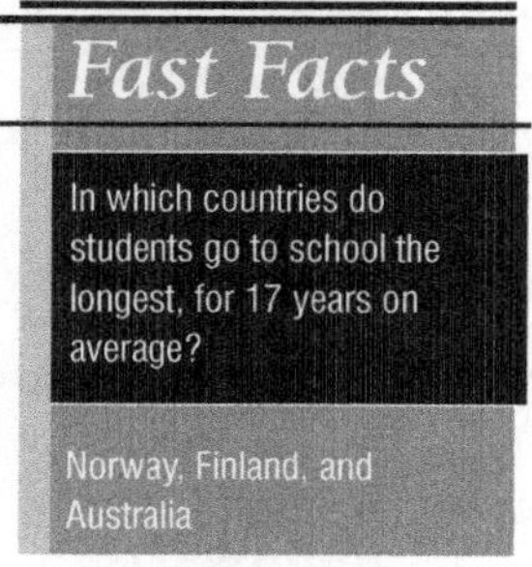

lion by 2011, up from 56.2 million in 1999.[13] Naturally, significant differences exist within regions as well; for example, within the European Union, the Nordic countries have penetration rates of 85.2 percent, while new members, such as Romania, are at less than 30 percent.[14]

Education

Education, either formal or informal, plays a major role in the passing on and sharing of culture. Educational levels of a culture can be assessed using literacy rates, enrollment in secondary education, or enrollment in higher education available from secondary data sources. International firms also need to know about the qualitative aspects of education, namely varying emphasis on particular skills and the overall level of the education provided. Japan and South Korea, for example, emphasize the sciences, especially engineering, to a greater degree than Western countries do.

Educational levels also affect the types of new products introduced and the manner in which they are sold and marketed. For example, a high level of illiteracy suggests the use of visual aids rather than printed manuals. Successful marketing of sophisticated technologies depends greatly upon the educational level of prospective users. Product adaptation decisions are often influenced by the extent to which targeted customers are able to—or can be educated to—use the good or service properly.

Education also affects other business functions. Recruitment of local sales personnel, for example, depends on the availability of adequately educated people. In some cases, international firms routinely send locally recruited personnel to headquarters for training. In recent years, U.S. manufacturing companies have outsourced multiple operational tasks, from customer service to software design, to India. The highly educated Indian population, with fluency in English, is sought after for its skills as well as its comparatively low costs.

The international marketing manager may also have to be prepared to fight obstacles in recruiting a suitable sales force or support personnel. For example, highly skilled Chinese professionals prefer working for Western multinationals. Attracting talent in emerging markets has always been a challenge for Western multinationals, but historically they did enjoy an advantage. Now, with Western firms and their brands taking a significant financial hit—reducing hiring, cutting expenses, and laying off employees—there has been shrinkage in Chinese professionals seeking these jobs. International marketing managers are finding that these highly skilled candidates prefer to stay domestically, potentially optimizing their immediate and long-term career development opportunities in one of the world's fastest growing economies.[15]

As testimony to the value of educational systems overseas, the number of U.S. students seeking to attend colleges abroad is at an all-time high. The rapid rise in applications to top-ranked schools in the United Kingdom, France, Spain, Japan, and China reveals a desire for international experience that schools at home fall short in providing.

Social Institutions

Social institutions affect the ways people relate to one another. The family unit, which in Western industrialized countries consists of parents and children, is extended in a number of cultures to include grandparents and other relatives. This affects consumption patterns and must be taken into account, for example, when conducting market research.

The concept of kinship, or blood relations between individuals, is defined in a very broad way in societies such as those in sub-Saharan Africa. Family relations and a strong obligation to family are important factors to consider in human resource management in those regions. Understanding tribal politics in countries such as Nigeria may help the manager avoid unnecessary complications in executing business transactions.

The division of a particular population into classes is termed **social stratification**. Stratification ranges from the situation in Northern Europe, where most people are members of the middle class, to highly stratified societies such as India, in which the higher strata control most of the buying power and decision-making positions.

SOCIAL STRATIFICATION
The division of a particular population into economic classes

Reference groups are an important part of the socialization process of consumers worldwide. These groups provide the values and attitudes that influence behavior. Primary reference groups include the family and co-workers and other intimate acquaintances. Secondary reference groups are social organizations where less continuous interaction takes place, such as professional associations and trade organizations. In addition to providing socialization, reference groups develop a person's concept of self, which is manifested, for example, through the choice of products used. Reference groups also provide a baseline for compliance with group norms, giving the individual the option of conforming to or avoiding certain behaviors.

REFERENCE GROUP
A group, such as the family, co-workers, and professional and trade associations, that provides the values and attitudes that influence and shape behavior, including consumer behavior

Social organization also determines the roles of managers and subordinates and how they relate to one another. In some cultures, managers and subordinates are separated explicitly and implicitly by various boundaries ranging from social class status to separate office facilities. In other cultures, cooperation is elicited through equality. However, Nissan and Toyota plants in the United States found only positive results from the implementation of Japanese human resource practices. The Japanese approach of trust, building employee loyalty, investing in training, treating employees as resources, recognizing employee accomplishments, and consensual decision-making positively influenced the behaviors of U.S. employees. Japanese and U.S. managers and subordinates have developed cross-cultural partnerships that allowed them to share ideas and solutions.[16]

Although Western business has impersonal structures for channeling power and influence—primarily through reliance on laws and contracts—the Chinese emphasize *guanxi*, or personal relationships. For instance, while legal contracts form a useful agenda and are a symbol of progress, business obligations come from relationships, not formalized agreements. Unilever's corporate web site in China meets these criteria nearly perfectly by highlighting its long-term commitment to the country, its contribution to the Chinese economy, its charitable activities, and the evidence of its commitment to corporate social responsibility.[17]

Quick Take *Lots of Stuff to Do*

Women in the United States use about three to four skin-care routines per day, while women in Asia typically use eleven different products, and European women use seven to eight. U.S. women are known for brevity when it comes to skin-care routines, and the beauty and skin-care industry wants its products used correctly. Consumers want immediate results, so products are offering some immediate results, with the real results taking months to achieve. Beauty brands are offering "how to" videos on their Web sites and YouTube.

Skin care is a strong segment of the beauty industry. U.S. sales reached $10.3 billion in 2011, a 3.6 percent increase over 2010 and a nearly 11 percent rise over 2006, according to market research firm Euromonitor International. Sales of anti-aging products rose 6.9 percent in 2011, reaching nearly $2.9 billion.

SOURCE: "When Skin Creams Gets Bossy," *The Wall Street Journal*, August 23, 2012, D1.

Religion

In cultures the world over, people turn to religion in search of a reason for being and legitimacy in the belief that they are part of a larger context. Religion both acknowledges the existence of a higher power and defines certain ideals for life, which in turn are reflected in the values, attitudes, and behaviors of societies and individuals. As well as providing insight into the differences between cultures, religion provides a basis for transcultural similarities as peoples from different nations share similar beliefs and behaviors.

Religion provides the basis for transcultural similarities under shared beliefs and behavior. The impact will vary depending on the strength of the dominant religious tenets. While religion's impact may be quite indirect in Protestant Northern Europe, its impact in countries where Islamic fundamentalism is on the rise may be profound. The influence of these similarities will be assessed in terms of the dominant religions of the world. Other religions may have smaller numbers of followers, such as Judaism with 13.6 million followers around the world, but their impact is still significant due to the many centuries during which they have influenced world history. While some countries may officially have secularism, such as Marxism-Leninism, as a state belief (e.g., China, Cuba, and Vietnam), traditional religious beliefs still remain a powerful force in shaping behavior.

Within the context of international business, the influence of religion is evident, for example, in attitudes toward entrepreneurship, consumption, and social organization. Global managers must be aware of the differences not only *among* the major religions but also *within* them. In Hinduism, for example, people are divided into subgroups that determine their status and to a large extent their ability to consume.

CHRISTIANITY. With more than 2 billion people in diverse nations, Christianity is the world's largest religion. Although there are many subgroups, the major division is between Catholicism and Protestantism. A prominent difference is attitudes toward making money. While Catholicism questions the value of personal gain, the Protestant ethic emphasizes the importance of work and the accumulation of wealth for the glory of God. At the same time, Protestantism encourages frugality—hard work leads to accumulation of wealth, which, in turn, forms the basis for investment. Some scholars, in fact, believe that the Protestant work ethic is responsible for the development of capitalism in the Western world and the rise of predominantly Protestant countries into world economic leadership.

Major holidays are often tied to religion and are observed differently from one culture to the next. Firms operating in foreign cultures are advised to keep this in mind when planning marketing events or in operating local offices. Christian cultures observe Christmas and exchange gifts on either December 24 or December 25, with the exception of the Dutch, who exchange gifts on St. Nicholas Day, December 6. Tandy Corporation (e.g., RadioShack Corporation), in its first year in the Netherlands, targeted its major Christmas promotion for the third week of December with less than satisfactory results. During Mexico's *Día de los Muertos* (Day of the Dead) festivities from November 1 and 2, it is pointless to attempt to keep local offices open because the culture gives priority to observing the holiday.

ISLAM. Islam, which reaches from the west coast of Africa to the Philippines and across a broad band that includes Tanzania, central Asia, western China, India, and Malaysia, has more than 1.2 billion followers. Islam is also a significant minority religion in many parts of the world, including Europe. Islam has a pervasive role in the life of Muslims, its adherents. *Sharia*, the law of Islam, for example, requires five daily periods of prayer, fasting during the holy month of Ramadan, and that each Muslim make a pilgrimage to Mecca, Islam's holy city.

Some people believe that Islam's basic fatalism (that is, nothing happens without the will of Allah) and traditionalism have deterred economic development in countries observing the religion. Although Islam has proven supportive of entrepreneurship, it nevertheless strongly discourages acts that may be interpreted as exploitation.

Religions of the World: A Part of Culture

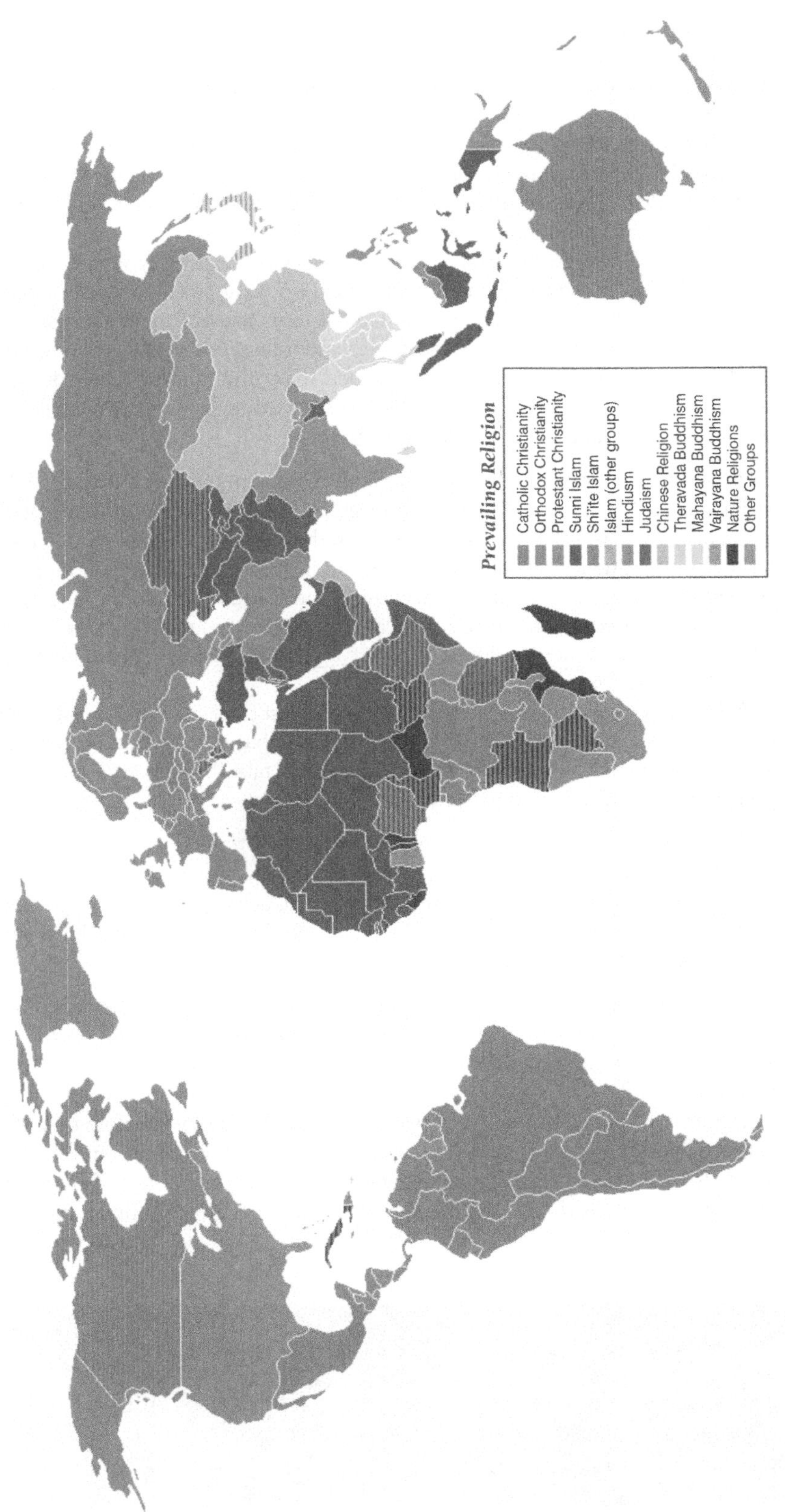

Fast Facts

What cities have Europe's largest Muslim population?

Moscow has 2.5 million Muslims. London and Paris have 607,000 and 1.7 million, respectively.

Given that Islam considers interest payments usury, bankers and Muslim scholars have worked to create interest-free banking that relies on lease agreements, mutual funds, and other methods to avoid paying interest. Banks and other financial companies have been successful in creating numerous Islamic finance instruments that have been judged as satisfying the Koran's concept of a just transaction. The market for Islamic finance has been growing at a rate of 15 percent annually and is becoming a competitive arena for Islamic banks and funds as well as global financial players. Currently there are more than 250 Islamic financial institutions managing funds of more than $250 billion.[18]

The role of women in business is tied to religion, especially in the Middle East, where women are not allowed to function as they would in the West. The effects of this are numerous; for example, a firm may be limited in its use of female managers or personnel in these areas, and women's role as consumers and influencers in the consumption process may be different. Except for food purchases, men make the final purchase decisions. Access to women in Islamic countries may only be possible through the use of female sales personnel, direct marketing, and women's specialty shops.[19]

HINDUISM. Hinduism has 980 million followers, mainly in India, Nepal, Malaysia, Guyana, Suriname, and Sri Lanka. As well as a religion, Hinduism is a way of life predicated on the caste, or class, to which one is born. Although the caste system has produced social stability, it has negative influences on business. For example, because it is difficult for individuals to rise above their caste, there is limited incentive for individual effort. The caste system also limits integration and coordination in a mixed-caste workforce, raising severe problems. Because Hinduism places value on spiritual rather than materialistic achievement, it may hamper individual drive for business success.

The family is an important element of Hindu society, with extended families being the norm. The extended family structure affects the purchasing power and consumption of Hindu families, and market researchers, in particular, must take this into account in assessing market potential and consumption patterns.

BUDDHISM. Buddhism, which extends its influence throughout Asia from Sri Lanka to Japan, has 520 million followers. Although it is an offspring of Hinduism, it has no caste system. Life is seen as filled with suffering, and the solution is to achieve nirvana—a spiritual state marked by an absence of desire. The central theme of Buddhism is spiritual achievement rather than accumulation of worldly goods.

CONFUCIANISM. Confucianism has more than 150 million followers throughout Asia, especially among the Chinese, and has been characterized as a code of conduct rather than a religion. Its teachings, which stress loyalty and relationships, have been broadly adopted, however.

Loyalty to central authority and placing the good of a group before that of the individual may explain the economic success of Japan, South Korea, Singapore, and the Republic of China. It also has led to cultural misunderstandings: Western societies often perceive the subordination of the individual to the common good as a violation of human rights. The emphasis

Culture Clues

McDonald's opened two new vegetarian restaurants in the Indian cities that are pilgrimage sites for Hindus and Sikhs. The meat-free outlets are a first for the world's biggest chain, which also hopes that catering to this population will boost revenues. Menus at the restaurants in Amrisar and Katra include the McAloo Tikki (a burger with an aloo tikki-inspired patty made out of potatoes, peas, and spices), the McVeggie burger (the vegetarian equivalent of the McChicken). McDonald's has more than 271 outlets in India where the majority of the population are practicing Hindus and Muslims.

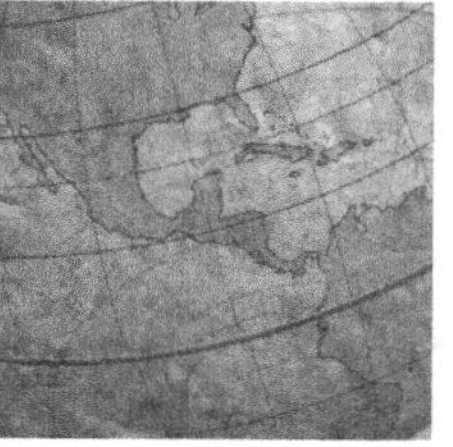

on relationships is very evident in developing business ties in Asia. Preparation may take years before understanding is reached and actual business transactions can take place.

Values and Attitudes

Values are shared beliefs or group norms that have been internalized by individuals.[20] **Attitudes** are evaluations of alternatives based on these values. Differences in cultural values affect the way business planning is executed, decisions are made, strategy is implemented, and personnel are evaluated.

VALUES
Shared beliefs or group norms internalized by individuals

ATTITUDES
Evaluation of alternatives based on values

The more rooted values and attitudes are in central beliefs (such as religion), the more cautious international companies have to be. Whereas Western nations tend to view change as basically positive, tradition-bound societies treat it with an attitude of suspicion—especially when change is driven by a foreign entity. The Japanese culture, for example, raises an almost invisible—and often unscalable—wall against all *gaijin* (outsiders). Many middle-aged bureaucrats and company officials believe that buying foreign products is downright unpatriotic. The resistance is not so much to foreign products as to those who produce and market them.

Cultural attitudes are not always a deterrent to foreign business practices or foreign goods. Japanese youth, for example, display extremely positive attitudes toward Western goods, from popular music to Nike sneakers to Louis Vuitton haute couture to Starbucks lattes. Similarly, attitudes of U.S. youth toward Japanese "cool" have increased the popularity of authentic Japanese "manga" comics and animated cartoons. Pokémon cards and the popular cooking show *Iron Chef* are examples of Japanese products that caught on in the United States almost as quickly as in Japan.[21]

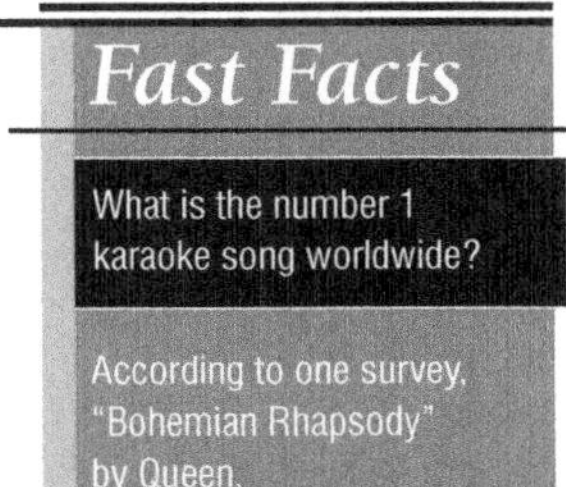

While products that hit the right cultural buttons can be huge successes in markets, not all top brands will translate easily from one culture to another. For example, although the Disneyland concept worked well in Tokyo, it had a tougher time in Paris. One of the main reasons was that, while the Japanese have positive attitudes toward American pop culture, the Europeans are quite content with their own cultural values and traditions. To fix its Euro Disney mistakes, the Euro-centric resort now features restaurants, rides, and theaters targeted to appeal to the indigenous cultures throughout Europe. Disney's theme park in Hong Kong, which opened in 2005, and the Shanghai park, which should open in 2016, continues Disney's goal of cross-pollination and using regional programs to "Asianize" or even globalize their product more quickly.[22]

Manners and Customs

Manners and customs provide clues to culture and are influenced by religion, values, and attitudes. Although the pervasive success of global brands like McDonald's and IKEA may seem to indicate a narrowing of differences, this does not mean that cultural distinctions are blurring or that other nations are becoming "Westernized." Modernization and Westernization are not at all the same, as can be seen in Saudi Arabia, for example. When the Swedish-based retailer, IKEA, shipped its annual catalog to the religiously conservative Islamic kingdom, images of women were airbrushed out.[23] Both views are superficially right, and both miss the most significant uniformity generated by globalization: in our ways of thinking and living. Globalization cannot be rejected because it represents a transformation that we ourselves have brought about—and which has already transformed us.

Understanding manners and customs is especially important in business negotiations because interpretations based on one's own frame of reference may lead to incorrect conclusions. Americans, for instance, tend to interpret inaction or silence as negative signs, while the Japanese use silence to get business partners to sweeten a deal. Even a simple agreement may take days to negotiate in the Middle East because the Arab party may want to talk about unrelated issues or do something else for a while. The aggressive style of Russian negotiators, who often make requests for last-minute changes, astonishes ill-prepared negotiators. Even within Europe, there are stark differences. Whereas an Italian might open negotiations by providing detailed background information on the company, German counterparts—who typically do extensive research before approaching the negotiating table—may interpret this as idle boasting and a waste of their time. Southern Europe, with its Catholic background and open-air lifestyle, tends to favor personal networks and social context. In contrast, the Protestant tradition of Northern Europe emphasizes numerical and technical detail.

Preparation is needed not only in the business sense but in a cultural sense as well. Some of the potential areas in which marketers may not be prepared include the following: (1) insufficient understanding of different ways of thinking; (2) insufficient attention to the necessity of saving face; (3) insufficient knowledge and appreciation of the host country—history, culture, government, and image of foreigners; (4) insufficient recognition of the decision-making process and the role of personal relations and personalities; and (5) insufficient allocation of time for negotiations.[24]

The questions to ask are the same central issues that inform business strategies: "What are we selling?" "What are the benefits we are providing?" and "Who or what are we competing against?" In addition, sound research techniques—including such methods as focus-group research that test the potential acceptance of new products, along with consumer usage and attitude studies—must precede market entry. **In-depth studies** are also used to study consumer needs across markets. Intel, for example, has a team of ten ethnographers traveling the world to find out how to redesign existing products or to come up with new ones to fit different cultures and demographic groups.

IN-DEPTH STUDIES
A market research tool that is used for gathering detailed data after studying consumer needs across markets

Aesthetics

Each culture makes a clear statement concerning good taste, as expressed in the arts and in the particular symbolism of colors, form, and music. What is and what is not acceptable may vary dramatically in otherwise highly similar markets. Sex in advertising is an example. In an apparent attempt to preserve the purity of Japanese womanhood, Japanese advertisers frequently turn to blonde, blue-eyed foreign models to make a point. When Henkel introduced the shower soap Fa from the European market to the Middle East, Africa, Asia Pacific, and Latin America, Henkel extended its European advertising campaign to the new market. The main difference was to have the young woman in the waves don a bathing suit rather than be naked, as in the original German campaign.

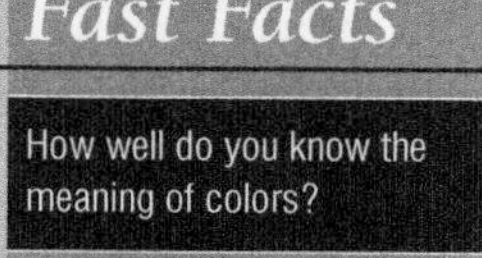

Blue is thought to be the best universal color, with the most positive—and fewest negative—cultural associations.

Color is often used as a mechanism for brand identification, feature reinforcement, and differentiation. In international markets, colors may have symbolic meanings that differ from domestic markets. Black, for example, is considered the color of mourning in the United States and Europe, whereas white has the same symbolic value in China, India, and most of the Far East. LG invested in local research and development and staffed its operations with top-notch Indian designers and engineers in their Bangalore product innovation center when it wanted to enter the Indian markets. LG entered the Indian marketplace with brighter color refrigerators and smaller freezers; big, family-size washing machines; and one-touch "Indian menu" function microwaves.[25]

History may also play a role. The Shanghai World Financial Center (developed largely by Japanese Mori Building Corporation) became the second tallest structure in China at 492 meters (1,641 feet). The building had an opening at the peak (allowing airflow). The Chinese saw it resembling the rising sun design of the Japanese flag rather than the designer's circular moon gate. It was replaced by a trapezoidal hole featuring an observation deck on the hundredth floor.

Artists also have to be aware of multiple cultural segments. U.S. entertainers, such as Britney Spears, 50 Cent, Akon, and Enrique Iglesias, turned to Desi Hits to crack the India markets with a new hybrid pop sound. Desi Hits not only wants to help artists reach the South Asian markets but to offer a platform for South Asian artists to promote themselves globally.

UNDERSTANDING CULTURAL DIFFERENCES

Any analysis of culture is incomplete without the basic recognition of cultural differences. Adjusting to differences requires putting one's own cultural values aside. It has been suggested that natural **self-reference criterion**—the unconscious reference to one's own cultural values—is the root of most international business problems.

SELF-REFERENCE CRITERION
The unconscious reference to one's own cultural values

However, recognizing and admitting this are often quite difficult. The following analytical approach is recommended to reduce the influence of cultural bias:

1. Define the problem or goal in terms of the domestic cultural traits, habits, or norms.
2. Define the problem or goal in terms of the foreign cultural traits, habits, or norms. Make no value judgments.
3. Isolate the self-reference criterion influence in the problem and examine it carefully to see how it complicates the problem.
4. Redefine the problem without the self-reference criterion influence.

Let's see how this approach is applied to a product introduction. Breakfast around the world is probably the meal that is most rooted in tradition. Kellogg's, Pepsi, and Cereal Partners Worldwide control roughly 52 percent of the nearly $30 billion worldwide hot- and cold-cereal market. U.S. style grain-based breakfasts, both hot and cold, are becoming popular in other countries. Indians usually snack first thing in the morning with breakfast occurring later. One popular breakfast choice is *halwa*, which is made from ground wheat, butter, sugar, and almonds. The standard breakfast in Brazil includes bread and a hot milk and coffee mixture. Fresh fruit, cereal, and cheese are sometimes added in wealthier households. Breakfast begins earlier in China than most countries, usually between 6:00 a.m. and 7:00 a.m. The traditional choice is congee, watery rice gruel sometimes served with deep-fried dough and vegetables, meat, or fish. Western brands are trusted but can also be very expensive. Kellogg's is testing less-expensive products, Corn Flakes Porridge, in South Africa as the bridge poorer consumers aspire to buy when they can afford it.[26]

Understanding cultural differences requires constant monitoring of changes caused by outside events as well as changes caused by the business entity itself. Controlling **ethnocentrism**—the tendency to consider one's own culture superior to other cultures—can be achieved only by acknowledging it and properly adjusting to its possible effects in managerial decision-making.

ETHNOCENTRISM
Regarding one's own culture as superior to other cultures

Osman Sultan, the CEO of Emirates Integrated Telecommunications Company, explains, "I come from a country where you always live at the borders of different worlds. Every day, from very early in my life, I crossed borders between languages, between religions, between cultures. Understanding this made me very aware that there is a certain way you do business in different organizations and different cultures. This perspective is necessary to reach certain phases of leadership in a more and more globalized world."[27]

It has been argued that differences among cultures can be explained according to dimensions of culture:

1. Individualism—"I" consciousness versus "we" consciousness
2. Power distance—levels of equality in society
3. Uncertainty avoidance—need for formal rules and regulations

4. Masculinity—attitude toward achievement, roles of men and women
5. Long-term versus short-term orientation—virtues oriented toward future rewards
6. Indulgence versus restraint—life and having fun

Figure 2.2 presents a summary of twelve countries' positions along these dimensions. Japan, for example, displays the highest uncertainty avoidance and might therefore be receptive to such risk-reducing marketing programs as return privileges and extended warranties. Because individualism is highly regarded in the United States, promotional appeals that promise empowerment are likely to be effective. In Arab countries, power distance scores high, indicating that consumers may respond well to promotions that imply status in society. Understanding the implications of the dimensions helps the marketer prepare for encounters. When negotiating in Germany, one can expect a counterpart who is thorough, systematic, very well prepared, but also rather dogmatic and therefore lacking in flexibility and compromise. Great emphasis is placed on efficiency. In Mexico, however, the counterpart may prefer to address problems on a personal and private basis rather than on a business level. This means more emphasis on socializing and conveying one's humanity, sincerity, loyalty, and friendship. Also, the differences in pace and business practices of the region have to be accepted.

FIGURE 2.2 Culture Dimension Scores for Twelve Countries (0 = Low; 100 = High)

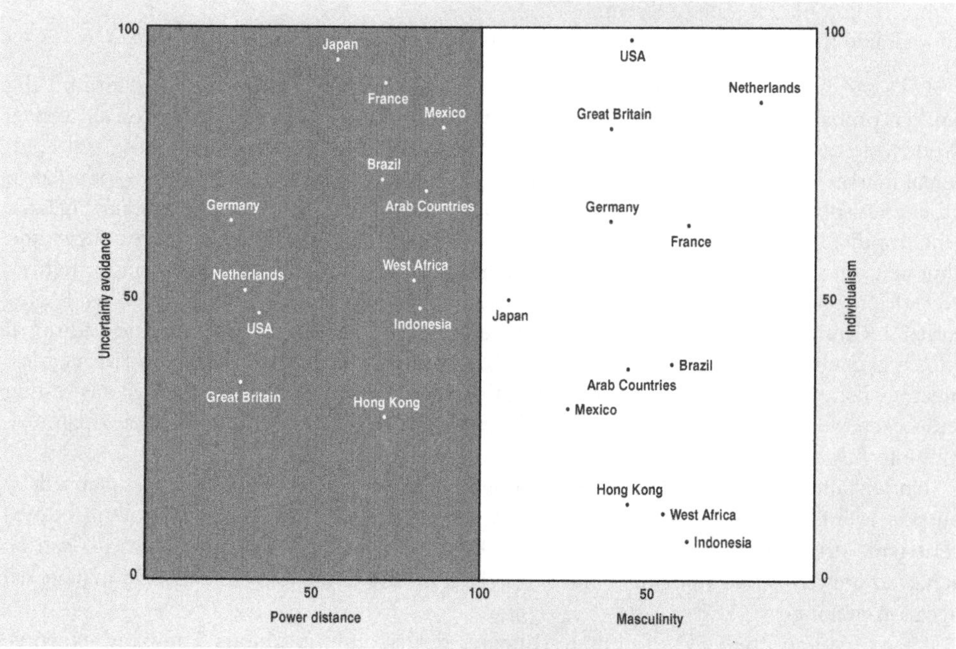

SOURCE: Data for the figure derived from Geert Hofstede, "Management Scientists Are Human," *Management Science* 40 (no. 1, 1994): 4–13.

A fifth dimension—long-term versus short-term orientation—has also been considered. Asian countries—China, Hong Kong, Taiwan, Japan, and South Korea—score high on the long-term axis of this dimension, while Australia, Canada, and the United States do not. This may help explain why the Japanese tend to evaluate marketing decisions based on long-term market share rather than short-term profit motivations.[28]

A sixth dimension needs to be added to measure life control and importance of leisure as the best predictors of happiness across more than 93 nations. At one end of the spectrum, indulgence or extravagance stands for a social value related to enjoying life and having fun. At the other end, restraint stands for a society that suppresses gratification of needs and regulates it by means of strict social norms.[29] Extravagance countries—New Zealand, Australia, and the United Kingdom— score high on this dimension, while Russia, China, and India do not.

GAINING CULTURAL KNOWLEDGE

EXPERIENTIAL KNOWLEDGE
Acquisition of cultural competence through personal involvement

Knowledge of a culture is generally acquired in one of two ways, and both are essential for developing the level of cultural competence required for doing business in foreign markets. Objective or factual information is obtained from others through communication, research, and education. **Experiential knowledge**, on the other hand, can be acquired only by being involved in a culture other than one's own. Global capability is developed through assignments, networking across borders, and the use of multicountry, multicultural teams to develop strategies and programs.

Various sources and methods are available to managers to extend both their factual and experiential knowledge of cultures other than their own. Specific-country studies, for example, are published by the government, private companies, and universities. The U.S. Department of Commerce's Country Commercial Guides cover more than 133 countries, while the Economist Intelligence Unit's Country Reports offer intelligence on 180 countries. CultureGrams, published by the Center for International Area Studies at Brigham Young University, detail the customs of people of 187 countries. Organizations such as advertising agencies, banks, consulting firms, and transportation companies often offer clients background information on the markets they serve. These range from AIRINC international reports on site selections and cost of living for 125 countries, and the Hong Kong and Shanghai Banking Corporation's *Business Profile Series* (Dubai, Hong Kong, Singapore, South Africa, and the United Kingdom).[30]

Most country newspapers are available online and for home delivery. These overseas newspapers can be translated into native languages, providing extensive knowledge of foreign markets as well giving access to the homeland for executives abroad. *Sing Tao Daily* offers sixteen overseas editions published at nine overseas bureaus and circulated in 100 cities worldwide. Consider the *Sing Tao Daily* advertisement (Figure 2.3), celebrating twenty-three years in business by giving its Chinese customers twenty-three flowers.

FIGURE 2.3 Overseas Communication in Clients

Courtesy: interTrend Communications, Inc.

Developing Cultural Competence

Managers face a dilemma in terms of global and intercultural competence. The lack of adequate foreign language and international business skills has resulted in lost contracts, weak negotiations, and ineffectual management. The race is on among nations to create knowledge-fueled innovation economies. In Singapore, Germany, China, Brazil, Korea, and other countries around the world, educational improvement is viewed as a critical part of that mission. Nations and states are therefore working hard to benchmark their education systems to establish a solid foundation for economic development in the twenty-first century. Some are finding innovative ways to measure their students' progress internationally. Others are examining high-performing and fast-improving nations to learn about best practices that they then adapt or adopt to improve their own systems.[31]

Some companies try to avoid the training problem by hiring only nationals or well-traveled executives for their global operations. This makes sense for the management of overseas operations but will not solve the training need, especially if transfers to a culture unfamiliar to the manager are likely. Global experience may not necessarily transfer from one market to another.

The increase in overall international activity of firms has increased the need for cultural sensitivity training at all levels of the organization. Today's training must take into consideration not only outsiders to the firm but interaction within the corporate family as well. However inconsequential the degree of interaction may seem, it can still cause problems if proper understanding is lacking.

Formal Training Programs

The most effective way to foster cultural sensitivity and acceptance of new ways of doing things within the organization is through internal education programs. The objective of formal training programs is to foster in managers and other personnel four critical characteristics: preparedness, sensitivity, patience, and flexibility. Of course, such programs vary dramatically in terms of their rigor, involvement, and cost. Figure 2.4 summarizes their scope.

FIGURE 2.4 Cross-Cultural Training Methods

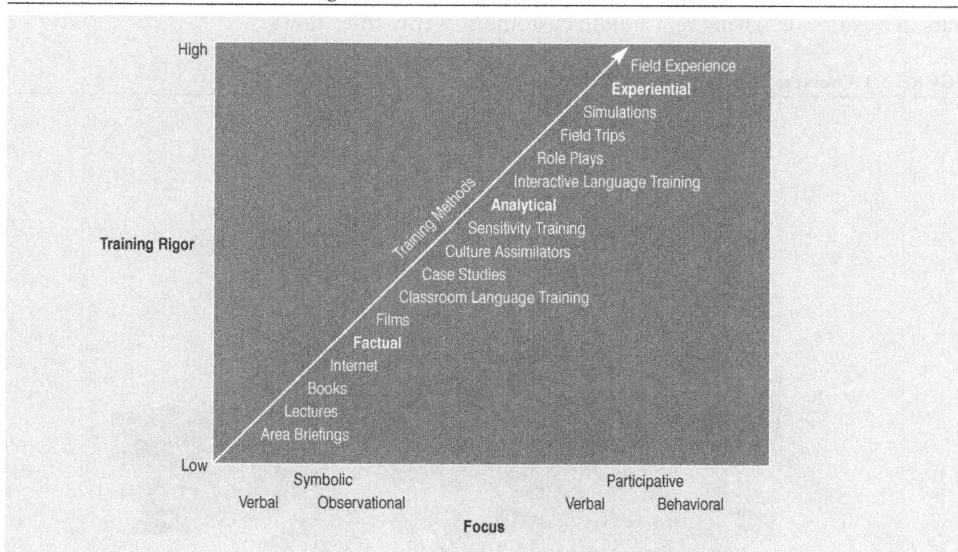

SOURCE: J. Stewart Black and Mark Mendenhall, "A Practical but Theory-Based Framework for Selecting Cross-Cultural Training Methods," in *International Human Resources Management*, eds. Mark Mendenhall and Gary Oddou, 1991, 188.

Area briefings are the simplest and least expensive form of cultural training, providing factual preparation on specific countries prior to an overseas assignment. However, their practical purpose is limited because, alone, they provide little context in which factual information can be understood or applied; i.e., action learning is key.[32] Far more effective are training programs that also include general cultural information (values, practices, and assumptions about countries other than one's own) and self-specific information (training that allows managers to identify their own cultural paradigms, including their values, assumptions, and perceptions about others).

AREA BRIEFINGS
Training programs that provide factual preparation prior to an overseas assignment

As well as area briefings and factual information gained through such methods as reading, research, case studies, and time permitting, classroom language training, comprehensive programs include cultural assimilation training. For example, by using a **cultural assimilator**—a program in which trainees respond to scenarios of specific situations in particular countries—trainers are able to evaluate a manager's preparedness for an overseas assignment. Programs like these are particularly useful in cases of transfers abroad at short notice. Programs have been developed for the Arab countries, China, Japan, and Central America.

CULTURAL ASSIMILATOR
Training program in which trainees for overseas assignments must respond to scenarios of specific situations in a particular country

Sensitivity training focuses on enhancing a manager's flexibility in situations that are quite different from those at home. It assumes that understanding and accepting oneself is critical to understanding people from other cultures. Role-playing and other face-to-face settings are particularly effective for sensitivity training, but Web-based methods are also gaining popularity, particularly in time-strapped situations.

SENSITIVITY TRAINING
Human relations training that focuses on personal and interpersonal interactions; training that focuses on enhancing an expatriate's flexibility in situations quite different from those at home

The most comprehensive training model includes **field experience**, which exposes a manager to a different cultural environment for a limited amount of time. Because the expense of placing and maintaining an expatriate within a foreign culture is high and success is not guaranteed, field experience is rarely used in training. As a halfway measure, some companies have experimented by placing trainees and sometimes their families within a domestically located host family from the culture to which the trainee is to be assigned.

FIELD EXPERIENCE
Experience acquired in actual rather than laboratory settings; training that exposes a corporate manager to a cultural environment

To foster cultural sensitivity and acceptance of new ways of doing things within the organization, management must institute internal education programs. Samsung has several shorter-term assignments to try to allow people to gain global experience earlier in their careers. Also available is a Region Expert program for assistant managers, who take a one-year foreign assignment to do regional research, business analysis, and networking. Samsung offers a Field Expert program, which lasts six months to one year and allows selected employees to experience working in an overseas branch and living in a foreign culture. To give high-performing foreign employees more global experience, Samsung offers a two-year opportunity to work in South Korea for up to two years. This gives employees the chance to observe the business style at headquarters and have the Korean culture experience.[33]

Cultural similarities and differences are vital to successful interactions.

Culture Shock

The effectiveness of orientation training can be measured only after managers begin their assignments overseas. Once there, a unique phenomenon they face is **culture shock**, a pronounced reaction to the psychological disorientation people feel when they move for an extended time into a markedly different culture. Although they all experience it, individuals differ widely in how they allow themselves to be affected by culture shock.

CULTURE SHOCK
Pronounced reactions to the psychological disorientation that most people feel when they move for an extended period of time into a markedly different culture

Although the severity of culture shock may be a function of the individual's lack of adaptability, it may equally be a result of the firm's lack of understanding of the situation into which the manager was sent. Often, goals set for a subsidiary or a project may be unrealistic, or the means by which they are to be reached may be inadequate. Situations like these can lead to the external manifestations of culture shock, such as bitterness and even physical illness. In extreme cases, they can lead to hostility toward anything in the host environment.

Quick Take *Cultural Awareness Online*

Managers heading abroad to negotiate a deal, relocating to a foreign environment, or multicultural teams working within large organizations are just some of the scenarios that benefit from cross-cultural training. Skimping on training in this area can be potentially hazardous. For example, those going unprepared for high levels of etiquette and ceremony risk offending valuable clients. Employees who move to Hong Kong are often responsible for working with multiple countries and, therefore, require the know-how to work in a variety of cultural settings.

Many of the programs use the following elements:

1. Expatriates prepare for moves abroad.
2. Global teams work more effectively together.
3. Employees better understand and work with diverse peers, suppliers, and customers.
4. Executives build their culture savvy before business trips to other cultures.

Argonaut, a cultural learning system that aims to enable international teams to work efficiently together, was conceptualized by Coghill and Beery International, U.K. A user can take the entire course—choosing the relevant culture from the base of fifty-four cultures—and finish it in about fifteen hours. Naturally nobody would do it over that period; normally, it would take about a month with breaks.

SOURCE: **http://www.coghillbeery.com/consulting-training/train-the-trainer-for-argonautonline/** and Bently Ross, "It Pays to Be a Cross-Cultural Vulture," *Personnel Today*, January 23, 2007, 8.

Managers typically go through five distinct stages when adapting to a new culture. The duration of each stage is highly individual.

1. *Preliminary stage*—events that occur before departure
2. Initial *euphoria*—enjoying the novelty of living in the host culture, largely from the perspective of a spectator
3. *Irritation and hostility*—experiencing cultural differences as participation in the culture increases
4. *Adjustment*—adapting to the situation, which in some cases leads to biculturalism and even accusations of "going native"
5. *Re-entry*—returning home[34]

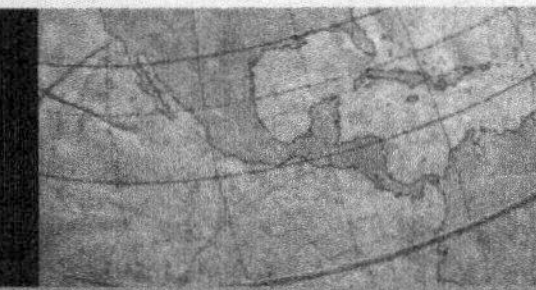

SUMMARY

Most companies, recognizing cultural differences, tailor their business approaches to individual cultures and can only be successful with lots of patience. They do not rush into new situations but rather build their operations carefully by following the most basic business principles. These principles are to know your adversary, know your audience, and know your customer with an overriding awareness of culture.

Culture is a system of learned behavior patterns characteristic of the members of a given society. It is constantly shaped by a set of dynamic variables, both concrete and abstract. 1

Concrete influences on culture include language, infrastructure, education, and social institutions. Abstract or spiritual influences encompass religion, values and attitudes, manners and customs, and aesthetics.

The tendency is to view other cultures from the perspective of the individual's own cultural influences. Global managers can reduce this cultural bias, with a thorough understanding of and sensitivity toward cultural differences.

To cope in new cultural environments, a global manager needs both factual and interpretive knowledge of culture. To some extent, the factual knowledge can be learned; its interpretation comes only through experience. Cultural training must include experiential knowledge as well as factual knowledge with an emphasis on both the concrete and abstract cultural influences.

The most complicated problems in dealing with the cultural environment stem from the fact that one cannot learn culture but must live it.

Key Terms and Concepts

culture
acculturation
high-context culture
low-context culture
change agent
cultural imperialism
cultural universals
backtranslation
economic infrastructure
social infrastructure
financial infrastructure
marketing infrastructure
cultural convergence
social stratification
reference group
values
attitudes
in-depth studies
self-reference criterion
ethnocentrism
experiential knowledge
area briefings
cultural assimilator
sensitivity training
field experience
culture shock

Review Questions

1. What is culture? Suggest some of the ways in which it influences the conduct of international business.
2. Language can be a mirror of culture. What does this mean?
3. Language has both verbal and nonverbal elements. Which is more important?
4. Early in your business relationships, you may want to make your gift selections. How?
5. What is the self-reference criterion?
6. What is the difference between factual cultural knowledge and experiential cultural knowledge?
7. What are the requirements of an effective cross-cultural training program?
8. Describe culture shock and explain why it occurs.

Critical Skill Builders

1. Culture risk is just as important as commercial or political risk in the international business arena. Why?
2. You are on your first business visit to Germany. You feel confident about your ability to speak the language (you studied German in school and have taken a refresher course), and you decide to use it. During introductions, you want to break the ice by asking "Wie geht's?" and insisting that everyone call you by your first name. Speculate as to the reaction.
3. A helpful approach to increase one's options in negotiating across culture is to carry out a cultural review or a cultural audit of the relevant cultures in advance as part of your preparation. What you should consider reviewing, both from the viewpoint of one's own culture and that of the other culture?
4. What can be learned about a culture from reading and attending to factual materials?
5. The ability of an individual to influence, motivate, and enable others contributes to the effectiveness and success of the organization of which the person is a member. Uncertainty avoidance and gender are important dimensions of culture. You might consider how other dimensions of culture, such as individualism/collectivism, femininity/masculinity, power distance, uncertainty avoidance, and long term/ short term orientation, might affect your understanding of another culture.
6. As Hollywood has become dependent on world markets, the more it produces generic blockbusters that are made to play from Pisa to Peoria to Penang. What changes has the entertainment industry made to make itself more global?

On the Web

1. A combination of attitudes, expectations, and habitual behavior influences negotiation style. Although some of the following recommendations may go against the approach commonly used at home, they may allow the negotiator to adjust to the style of the host-country negotiators. Using **http://www.globalnegotiator.com/country-guides-how-to-negotiate-in-70-countries.html**, what can you learn to help you in negotiations?
2. The European Union is home to more than 500 million consumers. As firms contemplate selling goods in the European Union, they conduct research using secondary data. An excellent source of secondary data and for learning about the European Union is **http://europa.eu/index_en.htm**. Visit the various links at this site.
3. A total of 75 percent of all international ventures fail due to cross-cultural issues. Many companies, such as InterCultural Group, provide cross-cultural consulting, coaching, and training. Using the company's site (**http://www.interculturalgroup.com**), assess the different ways such consultants can play an important role in mastering cultural competency.

Endnotes

1. Pankaj Ghemawat, "Remapping Your Strategic Mind-set," *McKinsey Quarterly*, no. 3 (2011), 56–67.
2. Alfred Kroeber and Clyde Kluckhohn, *Culture: A Critical Review of Concepts and Definitions* (New York: Random House, 1985), 11.
3. Geert Hofstede, Gert Jan Hofstede, and Michael Minkov, *Cultures and Organizations: Software for the Mind* (New York: McGraw-Hill, 2010), 3–27.
4. Robin Hicks, "A Rough Guide to Asian Business Etiquette," Campaign, November 2, 2007, 24–25.
5. Oduor Ong'wen, "Biopiracy, the Intellectual Property Regime and Livelihoods in Africa," *The Monitor*, October 25, 2010, 4.
6. David A. Ricks, *Blunders in International Business* (Malden, MA: Wiley-Blackwell Publishers, 2006), Chapter 1.
7. "A World Empire by Other Means," *The Economist*, December 22, 2001, 65.
8. John Yunker, "Well-Traveled Websites: Global Lessons from the Leading Travel Websites," *UX Magazine*, December 11, 2011.
9. Michael Kriz, "Global SEM: A Story in Three Acts," Marketing News, September 30, 2011. **www.acclaro.com**.
10. Zhalech Semnami-Azad and Wendi L. Adair, "Reading the Body Language in International Negotiations," *Strategy+Business*, September 16, 2011.
11. Answers, "List of mobile network operators of the Middle East and Africa, **http://www.answers.com/topic/list-of-mobile-network-operators-of-the-middle-east-and-africa#Kenya**. 2010 data.
12. Ian Mansfield, "Africa Crosses 500 Million Mobile Subscriptions Mark," *Cellular-News*, November 11, 2010.
13. Miniwatts Market Group, "Internet World Stats," **http://internetworldstats.com/stats.htm**.
14. Miniwatts Market Group, "Internet World Stats," **http://www.internetworldstats.com/stats9.htm**.
15. Conrad Schmidt, "The Battle for China's Talent," *Harvard Business Review*, March 2011, 25–27.
16. Fredric William Swierczek, "Culture and Conflict: Japanese Managers and Thai Subordinates," *Personnel Review*, June 2003, 187–210. Phillip Marksberry, "The Toyota Way," *International Journal of Lean Six Sigma*, February 2011, 132–150.
17. **www.unilever.com.cn** and Ying Fan, "Guanxi, Government and Corporate Reputation in China: Lessons for International Companies," *Marketing Intelligence & Planning*, no. 25, 2007, 499–510.
18. Carla Power, "Faith in the Market," *Foreign Policy*, January/February 2009, 70–5; "Profit versus the Prophet: Islamic Law has Transformed Some Muslims into Creative Bankers" *Los Angeles Times*, February 10, 2008, M11.
19. "Out from Under," *Marketing News*, July 21, 2003, no. 1, 9.
20. Frank Kardes, Maria Cronley, and Thomas Cline, *Consumer Behavior* (Stamford, CT: Cengage, 2010), 10.
21. Amelia Newcomb, "Japan Cracking US Pop Culture Hegemony," *The Christian Science Monitor*, December 15, 2008.
22. "World News: Chinese Village Hopes for a Disney Windfall," *The Wall Street Journal*, August 24, 2009, A8.
23. Joe Sterling, "Images of Women Shelved in IKEA's Saudi Catalog," *CNN*, October 10, 2012.
24. Sergey Frank International, "About Us," **http://www.sergey-frank.com/en/about/about-us-sfi**.
25. Todd Guild, "Think Regionally, Act Locally: Four Steps to Reaching the Asian Consumer," *McKinsey Quarterly*, no.4, 2009, 24–25.
26. E. J. Schultz, "Cereal Marketers Race for Global Bowl Domination," *Advertising Age*, August 20, 2012, 12–13.
27. Joe Saddi, Karim Sabbagh, and Richard Shediac, "Measures of Leadership," *Strategy+Business*, May 25, 2010 and **http://www.du.ae/en/default**.
28. Harry Triandis, "The Made Dimensions of Culture," *The Academy of Management Executive*, 18, 2004, 88–93.
29. Michael Minkov and Geert Hofstede, "The Evolution of Hofstede's Doctrine," *Cross Cultural Management*, 18, 1, 2011, 10–20.
30. **www.ita.doc.gov, www.eiu.com**, **www.culturegrams.com**, **www.air-inc.com**, and **www.hsbc.com**.
31. **http://www.unesco.org/new/en/unesco/**.
32. Maureen Lewis, "Why Cross-Cultural Training Simulations Work," *Journal of European Industrial Training* 29, no. 7, 2005, 593–8.
33. Siegfried Russwurm, Luis Hernández, Susan Chambers, and Keumyong Chung, "Developing Your Global Know-How," *Harvard Business Review*, March 2011, 89–98 and "Special Interest Group Operations," available at **http://www.samsung.com**.
34. Li Dongfeng, "Culture Shock and Its Implications for Cross-Cultural Training and Culture Teaching," *Cross-Cultural Communication*, 8, no. 4, 2012, 70–4.

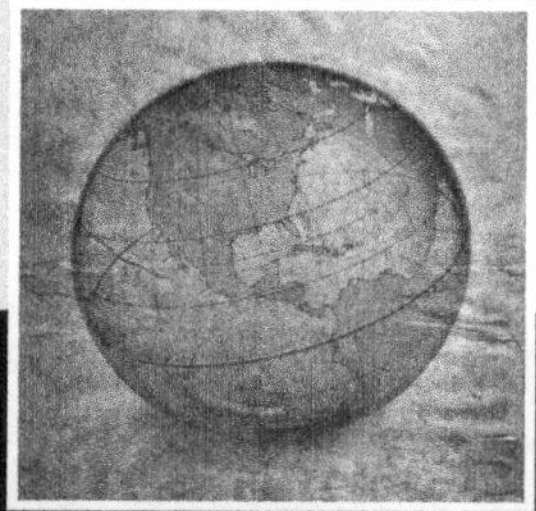

CHAPTER 3

GLOBAL TRADE ENVIRONMENT

Yes, Virginia, the Ham is Chinese

For many Americans, Virginia ham is a long established part of a festive family dinner. But good old American traditions like that can carry new meaning in a global economy. The news that Smithfield Foods, owner of leading pork brands like Smithfield Ham, Eckrich sausages, Armour meatballs, and Farmland bacon, was acquired by Chinese company Shuanghui International Holdings Ltd. caused indigestion for some in the United States.

The $4.7 billion deal, announced on May 30, 2013, was the largest acquisition of a U.S. company by a Chinese firm. It is another of a series of recent significant global acquisitions by Chinese business. Other examples include the 2012 purchase of the AMC movie chain by Dalian Wanda Group Corp. of Beijing and the 2013 acquisition of Canada's Nexen by China National Offshore Oil Corporation (CNOOC). At year's mid-point, 2013 promised to be a record year for Chinese foreign direct investment in the United States. It is also indicative of a new focus for Chinese investment: branded consumer businesses. Previous investment attempts by Chinese companies have not always gone smoothly. A big obstacle has been that many deals have touched on national security sensitivity. The Committee on Foreign Investment in the United States (CFIUS) is a U.S. interagency government panel that reviews foreign deals for national security issues. CFIUS approved the Smithfield acquisition in September 2013. China may well be approaching a tipping point for an economic transition from being export-focused to becoming consumption-driven. After improving the world by manufacturing good basic products, Chinese businesses must now learn how to succeed through marketing and excellence.

Marketing guru Philip Kotler defines marketing as both an art and a science. Chinese firms have mainly concentrated on science, via price. Now they must become better at creating higher quality products, placing them in distribution outlets that Western consumers prefer and promoting them with a direct appeal to Western emotions. The best way to accomplish all this quickly is through

LEARNING OUTCOMES

1. *To see how trade and investment policies have historically been a subset of domestic policies*
2. *To see how global links in trade and investment have made policymakers less able to focus solely on domestic issues*
3. *To understand the challenges of international trade institutions*
4. *To gain a broad perspective on conflicts between emerging and industrialized nations*
5. *To examine policy responses to changing conditions, including import and export restrictions and promotion*
6. *To examine the positive and negative impacts of foreign direct investments on both the host nation and the home nation*
7. *To understand the purpose of investment policies, including investment restrictions and promotion*

the acquisition of Western firms with already established bases of consumer preference. Therefore, in addition to the establishment of new brands, we are likely to see a significant expansion of Chinese acquisitions of U.S. and European consumer brand goods in the coming years.

Is this a good thing? Acquisitions by foreigners tend to be accompanied by concerns. When U.S. giant Kraft acquired British Cadbury, there was worry in the United Kingdom about diminished chocolate quality. Now Americans (accompanied with much hamming it up by master comic Jay Leno) state that the Smithfield acquisition could lead to diminished quality and loss of American jobs.

Far from it! The Chinese are not just obtaining products—imports and exports would have done that. Rather, the acquisition helps integrate China into the global economy and contributes to its future branding success by delivering new connections, experience, capabilities, and trust. The key benefits will be in learning both quality and marketing. Of even more interest is the reverse flow, where international investments have a spillover effect on home country markets. Why not eat Hunan pork with Smithfield ham during a picnic at the Yangtze River? What pork other than Smithfield's should be specified when planning the Chinese government-subsidized opening of restaurant chains in Africa? The Smithfield acquisition opens new markets both for the Chinese investors as well as for American ham. Such is the path of true globalization.

The emerging middle class in China represents enormous opportunity not only for Smithfield but also for many American companies. But such market expansion must be a two-way street. For more American firms to be able to have access to the Chinese marketplace, Chinese firms must be allowed and encouraged to compete in the United States.

SOURCES: Michael Czinkota and Charles Skuba, "Yes, Virginia, the Ham Is Chinese," *Marketing News*, July 2013.

As You Read This Chapter

1. Will the acquisition of Smithfield make the U.S. firm more Chinese, or the new Chinese owner more American?
2. Does it make a difference whether the buyer is from abroad or a domestic firm? How about Canadian versus U.S.?

Every nation has its own international trade and investment policies. The policies may be publicly pronounced or kept secret; they may be disjointed or coordinated. They may be applied consciously or determined by a laissez-faire attitude, which means that government does not intervene in market activities. Whatever form they take, trade policy actions come into play when measures taken by governments affect the flow of trade and investment across national borders. This chapter explores trade and investment issues from both the host country and the home country perspectives, with a focus on what happens when the interests of multiple nations come into conflict.

What Are Trade and Investment Policies?

Government policies are designed to regulate, stimulate, direct, and protect national activities. The exercise of these policies is the result of **national sovereignty**, which provides a government with the right and responsibility to shape the environment of the country and its citizens. Because they are border-bound, governments focus mainly on domestic policies. Nevertheless, many policy actions have repercussions on other nations, firms, and individuals abroad and are therefore a component of a nation's trade and investment policy.

NATIONAL SOVEREIGNTY
The supreme right of nations to determine national policies; freedom from external control

Influence of Domestic Policy

Domestic policy can be subdivided into two groups of actions that affect trade and investment. The first affects trade and investment indirectly, the second directly.

DOMESTIC POLICY
Public policy concerned with national issues but that may have direct or indirect bearing on foreign trade and investment

QUALITY OF LIFE
The standard of living combined with environmental and cultural factors; determines the level of well-being of individuals

STANDARD OF LIVING
The level of material affluence of a group or nation, measured as a composite of quantities and qualities of goods

The **domestic policy** actions of most governments aim to increase the standard of living of the country's citizens, to improve the quality of life, to stimulate national development, and to achieve full employment. Clearly, all of these goals are closely intertwined. For example, an improved standard of living is likely to contribute to national development. Similarly, **quality of life** and **standard of living** are interlinked. Also, a high level of employment plays a major role in determining standard of living. Yet all of these policy goals also indirectly affect international trade and investment. For example, if foreign industries become more competitive and rapidly increase their exports, employment in importing countries may suffer. Likewise, if a country accumulates large quantities of debt, which at some time must be repaid, present and future standards of living may be threatened.

Policy affects trade and investment in more direct ways, too. A country may pursue policies of increased development that mandate either technology transfer from abroad or the exclusion of foreign industries to the benefit of domestic firms. Also, government officials may believe that imports threaten the culture, health, or standards of living of the country's citizens and thus the quality of life. As a result, nations develop regulations aimed at protecting their citizens.

Influence of Foreign Policy

FOREIGN POLICY
The area of public policy concerned with relationships with other countries

Nations also institute **foreign policy** measures that, while designed with domestic concerns in mind, are explicitly aimed at exercising influence abroad. One major goal of foreign policy is national security. For example, nations may develop alliances, coalitions, and agreements to protect their borders or their spheres of interest.

Similarly, nations may take measures to enhance their national security preparedness in case of international conflict. They may even take action to restrict or encourage trade and investment flows in order to preserve or enhance the capability of industries that are important to national security.

Another goal of foreign policy may be to improve trade and investment opportunities. To develop new markets abroad and increase their sphere of influence, for instance, nations may give foreign aid to other countries. Such aid may be long term, such as the generous Marshall Plan funds awarded by the United States for the reconstruction of Europe following World War II, or may serve as emergency measures.

The United States is the world's largest single-country donor of foreign aid, providing more than $50 billion in various forms of aid in 2012. In recent years, debt forgiveness has played a major role in helping developing countries make advanced repayment of external public debt.[1]

Conflicting Policies

Each country develops its own domestic and foreign policies, and therefore, policy aims vary from nation to nation. Inevitably, conflicts arise. For example, full employment policies in one country may directly affect employment policies in another. Similarly, the development aims of one country may reduce the development capability of another. Even when health issues are concerned, disputes arise. One nation may argue that its regulations are in place to protect its citizens, while other nations interpret domestic regulations as market barriers.

Disagreement between the United States, Europe, and China regarding the safety of Chinese-produced toys is one example. Whereas the U.S. claims that levels of lead found in toys make them too dangerous for children to play with, China counters that the United States uses overly stringent safety standards to restrict imports.[2]

Quick Take *May I Please Have Some Congee with My Breakfast?*

Reflecting China's rapid economic rise, Chinese overseas travelers are now the most numerous and the largest spenders in international tourism. The United Nations World Tourism Organization (UNWTO) reported that Chinese travelers spent a record $102 billion on international tourism in 2012, an increase of 40 percent from the previous year. Chinese tourists overtook their counterparts from Germany and the United States in 2012 to become the world's largest spenders.

This has been a very rapid development. In 2000, only 10 million Chinese traveled abroad, but this had grown to 83 million in 2012 and is projected to reach 100 million in 2015. The UNWTO reports that Chinese tourists' expenditures have increased almost eight times since 2000. Recently, this has been amplified by easier visa requirements and an appreciating Chinese currency that makes shopping abroad, especially for luxury goods, a relative bargain.

Where are they traveling to? Although France and Spain remain the leading tourism destinations in the world, many Chinese tourists stay relatively close to home, traveling to Hong Kong and Macau to relax and shop.

Russians are also traveling more. Russia's tourists spent $43 billion in 2012. Russia jumped from seventh to fifth place in international tourism spending. And it is not that Germans and Americans are not traveling. In fact, spending on international tourism from Germany and the United States grew by 6 percent in 2012.

Smart businesses are moving to capitalize on the opportunities this trend presents. Chinese tourists will naturally seek some of the comforts of home in their travels. For example, the New York's Carlyle Hotel is now owned by New World Group from Hong Kong. Large American hotel chains like Marriott and Hilton now have Mandarin-speaking employees at key hotels. Marriott even offers several regional Chinese breakfasts that include congee, salted duck eggs, pickled vegetables, and sliced pig's liver, depending upon the regional preferences of the Chinese traveler.

TABLE 3.1 Top International Tourism Spenders in 2012 (U.S. Dollars)

1 China	$102 billion
2 Germany	$83.8 billion
3 United States	$83.7 billion
4 United Kingdom	$52.3 billion
5 Russian Federation	$42.8 billion
6 France	$38.1 billion
7 Canada	$35.2 billion
8 Japan	$28.1 billion
9 Australia	$27.6 billion
10 Italy	$26.2 billion
11 Singapore	$22.4 billion
12 Brazil	$22.2 billion
13 Belgium	$21.7 billion
14 Hong Kong (China)	$20.5 billion
15 Netherlands	$20.2 billion

SOURCES: Katie Cripps, "Chinese travelers the world's biggest spenders," CNN, April 12, 2013; Paul J. Davies, "Hotels check in to Chinese tourism," *Financial Times*, May 21, 2013; Associated Press, "Mandarin-speaking staff, congee breakfasts and no rooms on the fourth floor: How U.S. hotels are cashing in on Chinese tourists," June 21, 2012.

Conflicts among national policies have always existed but have come into prominence only in recent decades. The reason lies in the changes that have taken place in the world trade and investment climate. These changes are discussed next.

Post-War Global Trade Regulation

LEARNING OUTCOME 1

GENERAL AGREEMENT ON TARIFFS AND TRADE (GATT)
An international code of tariffs and trade rules signed by 23 nations in 1947; headquartered in Geneva, Switzerland; 159 members currently; now part of the World Trade Organization

MOST-FAVORED NATION (MFN)
A term describing a GATT clause that calls for member countries to grant other member countries the same most favorable treatment they accord any country concerning imports and exports, now also known as normal trade relations

WORLD TRADE ORGANIZATION (WTO)
The institution that supplanted GATT in 1995 to administer international trade and investment accords (see **http://www.wto.org**)

GENERAL AGREEMENT ON TRADE IN SERVICES (GATS)
A legally enforceable pact among GATT participants that covers trade and investments in the services sector

The **General Agreement on Tariffs and Trade (GATT)** started out in 1947 as a set of rules to ensure nondiscrimination, transparent procedures, the settlement of disputes, and the participation of the lesser developed countries in international trade. To increase trade, GATT used tariff concessions, through which member countries agreed to limit the level of tariffs they would impose on imports from other GATT members. An important tool is the **most-favored nation (MFN)** clause, recently renamed as "normal trade relations." It called for member countries to grant each other the same treatment accorded any other nation with respect to imports and exports. MFN is, in effect, an equal-opportunity clause.

In time, GATT became the governing set of regulations for settling international trade disputes. It evolved into an institution that sponsored various successful rounds of international trade negotiations with an initial focus on the reduction of high tariffs that restricted cross-border trade. Headquartered in Geneva, Switzerland, the GATT Secretariat conducted its work as instructed by the representatives of its member nations. Even though the GATT had no independent enforcement mechanism and relied entirely on moral suasion and on frequently wavering membership adherence to its rules, it achieved major progress for world trade.

Early in its history, the GATT accomplished the reduction of duties for trade in 50,000 products, amounting to two-thirds of the value of the trade among its participants.

In subsequent years, special GATT negotiations, such as the Kennedy Round—named after John F. Kennedy—and the Tokyo Round, further reduced trade barriers and improved dispute-settlement mechanisms. The GATT also developed better provisions for dealing with subsidies and more explicit definitions of roles for import controls.

In early 1995, the GATT was supplanted by a new institution, the **World Trade Organization (WTO)**, which now administers international trade and investment accords. Through the **General Agreement on Trade in Services (GATS)**, an entire new set of rules was designed to govern the service area. Agreement also was reached on new rules to encourage international investment flows.

In 2001, a new round of international trade negotiations was initiated. Because the agreement to embark on a new round was reached in the city of Doha (Qatar), the negotiations are known as the Doha Round or Doha Development Agenda (DDA). The aim was to further hasten implementation of liberalization to help developing and impoverished nations in particular. Another goal was to expand the role of the WTO to encompass more trade activities where rules were deemed insufficient, due either to purposeful exclusion by governments in earlier negotiations or to new technology changing the global marketplace. Regulations covering trade in agricultural goods, anti-dumping, and electronic commerce are all examples. In the agriculture sector, signs of compromise have not been seen on major issues, such as the reduction of customs duties, the handling of sensitive products, and the reduction of domestic subsidies, although substantial progress has been made in the levels of communication among participating nations.

The Doha negotiations have been the longest running round in the history of the GATT and WTO. The talks have been at an impasse since 2008 as diverging interests between developed and developing nations presented obstacles. Claims by developing countries that the United States and the European Union unfairly subsidize agriculture and impose import duties on agricultural products while the wealthy nations pressed for lower duties on manufactured goods and improved customs procedures by developing nations have been at the heart of the conflict. In December 2013, the Ninth Ministerial Conference of the WTO is scheduled to be held in Bali, Indonesia, with the objective of reinvigorating the Doha round negotiations. WTO President Roberto Azevêdo stated in his inaugural address, "The multilateral trading system remains the best defense against protectionism and the strongest force for growth, recovery and development."[3]

The World Trade Organization

The WTO is the only international body dealing with the rules of trade between and among nations. At the heart of the WTO are agreements, negotiated and signed by most of the world's trading nations. These documents provide the legal ground rules for international commerce. Their goal is to help producers of goods and services, exporters, and importers conduct business in the global marketplace.

The WTO has three main purposes:

1. To help trade flow as freely as possibly as long as there are no undesirable side effects. In part, this means removing obstacles to trade. It also means making rules transparent and predictable so that individuals, companies, and governments know their scope of influence.
2. To serve as a forum for trade negotiations among the community of trading nations.
3. To settle trade disputes among member nations. Recent cases have included heated disputes regarding steel tariffs. Other contentious issues include trade in U.S. cotton and South Korean-made semiconductors.

© VANDERWOLF IMAGES

Cattle in Europe are raised without hormones. Since 1989 hormone-fed beef has been banned in European countries, effectively restricting imports of U.S. beef. A WTO review of the hormones found the ban was not based on scientific evidence. Despite threats of sanctions, the ban has not been lifted.

The GATT and now the WTO have made major contributions to improved trade and investment flows around the world. Their successes have resulted in improvements in the economic well-being of nations around the world.

To understand both the benefits and the challenges of entering the WTO, consider the case of China, which joined the organization in 2001. WTO accession provided China not only with easier access to global markets, but with the opportunity to reform its inefficient industries and farms. By 2013, it had become the world's second largest economy and trader. China's limited economic reform during the last 30 years has allowed its businesses to flourish and the standard of living for millions of people to rise slowly but steadily.

During this period China has shown exponential economic growth even during the financial crisis that began in 2008. Due to increased opening and reform, its political and social stability have increased, and labor productivity has improved. In 2013, the United Nations Conference on Trade and Development identified China as the most promising host nation for multinational foreign direct investment.[4] Reflecting the importance of WTO membership, Russia was finally able to join the WTO in 2012 after an accession process that had lasted for more than 19 years. Russia was the only G-20 and UN Security Council member that had not been a WTO member. In order to qualify for WTO membership, Russia was required to make important concessions and commitments. For example, at the end of the implementation period, the average tariff ceiling for all imported products in Russia will be reduced from 10 percent to 7.8 percent. The average tariff ceiling for manufactured products will be reduced from 9.5 percent to 7.3 percent, while the average tariff ceiling for agriculture will go down from 13.2 percent to 10.8 percent. In addition, the Russian government has committed to improving market access opportunities for foreign companies in certain areas of goods and in many services sectors.[5]

Changes in the Global Policy Environment

Three major changes have occurred over time in the global policy environment: a reduction of domestic policy influence, a weakening of traditional international institutions, and a sharpening of the conflict between industrialized and developing nations. These three changes in turn have had a major effect on policy responses in the international trade and investment field.

Reduction of Domestic Policy Influences

The effects of growing global influences on domestic economies have been significant. Policymakers have increasingly come to recognize that it is very difficult to isolate domestic economic activity from international market events. Again and again, domestic policy measures are vetoed or counteracted by the activities of global market forces. Decisions that were once clearly in the domestic purview now have to be revised due to influences from abroad. At the same time, the clash between the fixed geography of nations and the nonterritorial nature of many of today's problems and solutions continues to escalate. Nation-states may simply no longer be the natural problem-solving unit. Local government may be most appropriate to address some of the problems of individuals, whereas transnational or even global entities are required to deal with larger issues such as economics, resources, or the environment.

Agricultural policies, for example—historically a domestic issue—have been thrust into the international realm. Any time a country or a group of nations such as the European Union contemplates changes in agricultural subsidies, quantity restrictions, or even quality regulations, international businesses and interest groups are quick to speak up against the resulting global effects of such changes. Quick Take: Agricultural Subsidies: Sacred Cows or Political Necessities? demonstrates how product safety and quality measures are influenced by global concerns.

When countries contemplate specific industrial policies that encourage, for example, industrial innovation or collaboration, they often encounter major opposition from trading partners who believe that their own industries are jeopardized by such policies. Those reactions and the resulting constraints are the result of growing interdependencies among nations and closer links between industries around the world.

TABLE 3.2 The Global Benefits of Trade

The WTO identifies ten core benefits of trade:

- The system helps promote peace.
- Disputes are handled constructively.
- Rules make life easier for all.
- Freer trade cuts the costs of living.
- It provides more choice of products and qualities.
- Trade raises incomes.
- Trade stimulates economic growth.
- The basic principles make life more efficient.
- Governments are shielded from lobbying.
- The system encourages good government.

SOURCE: **http://www.wto.org/english/res_e/doload_e/10b_e.pdf**

Consider, too, that some of today's products would be nearly impossible to build if manufacturers were unable to source supplies from and sell resulting goods into multiple global markets. Figure 3.1, for instance, shows how essential multinational links are to the automotive industry. Further, with so many product components being sourced from so many countries around the world, it becomes increasingly difficult to decide what constitutes a domestic product. In light of this uncertainty, policy actions against foreign products become more difficult as well.

CURRENCY FLOWS
The flow of currency from nation to nation, which in turn determines exchange rates

To some extent, the complex links that trade fosters between nations have turned the economic world inside out. For example, trade flows once determined **currency flows** and, therefore, exchange rates. In the more recent past, currency flows have taken on a life of their own, increasing from an average daily trading volume of $18 billion in 1980 to a record $5 trillion in 2011.[6] As a result, currency flows have begun to set the value of

FIGURE 3.1 Who Builds a Volvo?

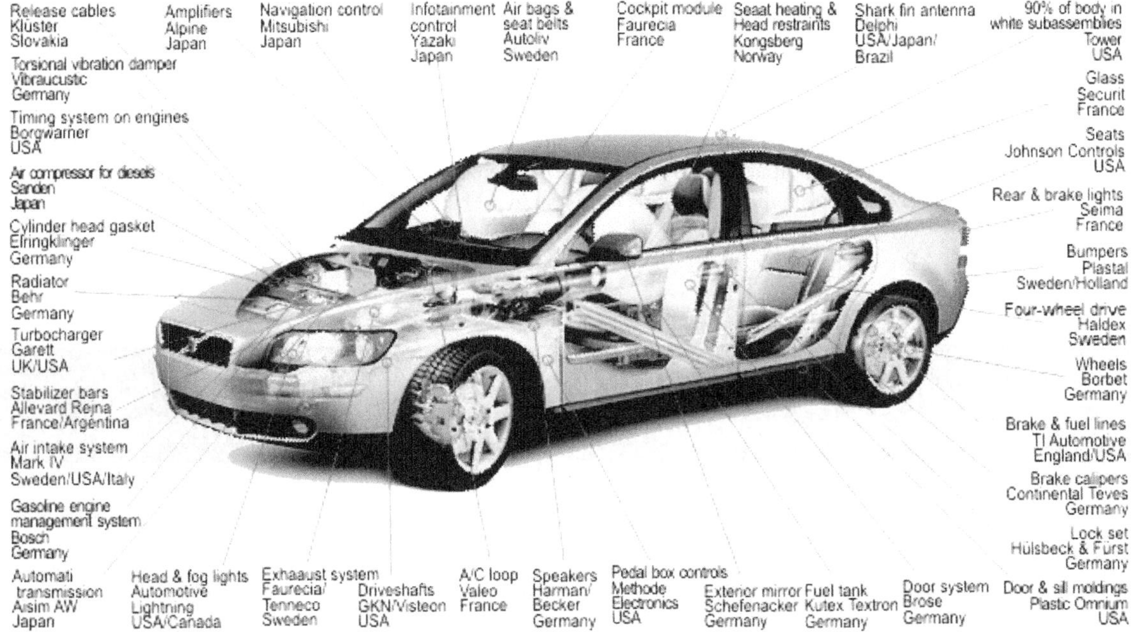

SECONDARY SOURCE: "A New Era for Transatlantic Trade Leadership", The German Marshall Fund, February 2012, **http://www.gmfus.org/wp-content/blogs.dir/1/files_mf/tatf_report_2012.pdf**, accessed May 22, 2013.

exchange rates, independent of trade. These exchange rates, in turn, have now begun to determine the level of trade. Governments that want to counteract these developments with monetary policies find that currency flows vastly outnumber the financial flows that can be marshaled by governments, even when acting in concert. The interactions between global and domestic financial flows have severely limited the freedom for governmental action. For example, if the European Central Bank, the Bank of Japan, or the U.S. Federal Reserve changes interest-rate levels or implements other forms of monetary policy, these changes not only influence domestic activities but also trigger international flows of capital that may reduce, enhance, or even negate domestic effects. In 2013, the Bank of Japan implemented a policy of "quantitative easing" to increase the money supply and complement the Japanese government's fiscal stimulus policies to revitalize the deflationary economy that has troubled Japan for nearly fifteen years. Although the new policy created a quick increase in the stock market, an unintended consequence was a highly volatile Japanese government bond market that increased borrowing costs for Japanese companies.[7]

Governments also find that domestic regulations often have major international repercussions. Consider, for example, that purchases or mergers with non-U.S. companies are subject to review by the **Committee on Foreign Investment in the United States (CFIUS)**. In 2013, CFIUS cleared the way for the proposed purchase of Sprint by Japanese company SoftBank with certain conditions. SoftBank and Sprint agreed to the U.S. government having an ongoing right to review and approve certain network vendors and to appoint a government-approved independent member of the board to serve as security director and oversee the agreement. The CFIUS clearance does not guarantee the deal going through because the U.S. Federal Communications Commission and Justice Department still must approve telecom

COMMITTEE ON FOREIGN INVESTMENT IN THE UNITED STATES (CFIUS)

A federal committee, chaired by the U.S. Treasury, with the responsibility to review major foreign investments to determine whether national security or related concerns are at stake

deals.[8] In October 2012, the U.S. House of Representatives Permanent Select Committee on Intelligence issued a report on "the counterintelligence and security threat posed by Chinese telecommunications companies doing business in the United States" that recommended that "CFIUS must block acquisitions, takeovers, or mergers" involving Chinese companies Huawei and ZTE, "given the threat to U.S. national security interests" and legislation providing for an "expanded role for the CFIUS process to include purchasing agreements."[9]

Chinese companies get close attention in the CFIUS process. In 2012, CFIUS ordered Chinese company Ralls, which had purchased four Oregon wind farm companies, to cease construction and operations to install wind turbine generators made in China by Sany Electric on wind farm sites adjacent to a sensitive U.S. Navy flight area. Based on a CFIUS report, President Obama issued an executive order that declared Ralls' purchase of the wind farms to

Quick Take *Agricultural Subsidies: Sacred Cows or Political Necessities?*

From the perspective of developing nations like Brazil and India, subsidies by the European Union and the United States to domestic agricultural sectors are perceived as inherently unfair to global trade competitiveness and remain the largest obstacle to a Doha Round agreement. Yet, from the perspective of politicians from developed nations, their agricultural sectors are vital to their nations' economic competitiveness and their political lives. The political lobbies of the various farming industries are far too powerful for many politicians to go against, so vast subsidy programs are regularly approved by the U.S. Congress and the European Commission despite strong economic arguments against them. Consequently, the U.S. Farm Bill and the EU Common Agricultural Policy allocate large portions of their governments' budgets to agricultural subsidies.

The Common Agricultural Policy is a common policy for all of member states in the European Union to ensure Europe's food security and to support its 14 million farmers. In the European Union, despite a reduction of 13 percent as of 2013 to address budget austerity demands, farm subsidies will consume 38 percent of the total EU budget for 2014–20 at a rate of approximately 50 billion euros per year. Southern European countries, led by France, which is the leading recipient of agricultural payments, are strong supporters of these subsidies and fight against reductions and reforms proposed by the United Kingdom and northern European nations.

In the United States, Congress sets U.S. agricultural policy every five years through the Farm Bill. Although originally due in 2012, the new Farm Bill is expected to be passed in 2013. The expected omnibus farm bill will allocate approximately $500 billion over ten years to various programs constituting support for U.S. farmers and agricultural producers, including the corn, soybean, wheat, cotton, sugar, peanuts, and rice businesses. These subsidies have their roots in programs that were designed to help farmers through the Great Depression in the 1930s and appear outdated to many. Critics of these programs call for reform, arguing that the subsidies distort competition and often result in higher prices for manufacturers and consumers. "But if such changes occur, they'll have to surmount a formidable obstacle on Capitol Hill. Representatives from any farming region that benefits from one subsidy often vote with members from another region that profits from a different subsidy. Alone, the regional interests carry little power. Together, they wield the kind of influence that has distorted market prices for more than eighty years."

SOURCES: Doug McKelway, "What to Cut: Striking Subsidies Could Save Billions," **Foxnews.com**, March 29, 2013; Marcella S. Kreiter, **UPI.com**, "The Issue: The 2013 Farm Bill, May 19, 2013; Charlie Dunmore, **Reuters.com**, "Farm Subsidies Still Get Top Share of EU Austerity Budget," February 8, 2013.

be prohibited on national security grounds and required divestiture within ninety days. Ralls subsequently sued the U.S. government.[10]

Legislators around the world are continuously confronted with such international links. In some countries, the implications are understood, and new legislation is devised with an understanding of its international consequences. In other nations, legislators often ignore the international repercussions. Given the ties between economies, this threatens to place firms at a competitive disadvantage in the international marketplace, or it may make it easier for foreign firms to compete in the domestic market.

Even when policymakers want to take decisive steps, they are often unable to do so. In 2013, the European Commission announced its plan to impose **punitive tariffs** on Chinese solar panels to combat **dumping** practices by Chinese companies, which are accused of selling the panels in Europe at less than the cost of producing them in China. The European Commission is also investigating dumping practices by Chinese mobile telecommunications companies Huawei and ZTE. Despite the firm intentions of the European Commission, the German government, concerned about its own trade relations with China, and other EU member states have announced their opposition to the measures and called for an end to the dispute.[11] It is hard to herd the coop if all the chickens are running loose.

In situations like this, policymakers find themselves with increasing responsibilities, yet with fewer and less effective tools to carry out those responsibilities. More segments of the domestic economy are vulnerable to international shifts at the same time that they are becoming less controllable. To regain some power to influence policies, some governments have sought to restrict the influence of world trade by erecting barriers, charging tariffs, and implementing import regulations. However, these measures too have been restrained by the existence of international agreements forged through institutions such as the WTO or by bilateral negotiations. World trade has therefore changed many previously held notions about the sovereignty of nation-states and extraterritoriality. The same interdependence that made us all more affluent has also left us more vulnerable.

Fast Facts

Where is the world's largest rain forest?

The Amazon region in South America is the world's largest rain forest. It is an area almost as big as 48 of the 50 U.S. states and contains more plant and animal species than any other place on Earth. It is being burned and cleared at a rate of about 4 percent each year, contributing to global warming.

PUNITIVE TARIFF
A tax on imported goods or services intended to punish a trading partner

DUMPING
An unfair international trade practice involving the selling of a product in an importing country at a price less than the price in an exporting country or below the cost of production

WEAKENING INTERNATIONAL INSTITUTIONS

The intense links among nations and the new economic environment resulting from new market entrants with different economic systems are weakening the traditional international institutions and are therefore affecting their roles.

The formation of the WTO has provided the former GATT with new impetus. However, the organization is confronted with many difficulties. One of them is the result of the organization's success. Historically, a key focus of the WTO's predecessor was on reducing tariffs. With tariff levels at an unprecedented low level, however, attention now has to rest with areas such as **nontariff barriers**, which are much more complex and indigenous to nations. As a consequence, any emerging dispute is likely to be more heatedly contested and more difficult to resolve. A second traditional focus rested with the right to establishment in countries. Given today's technology, however, the issue has changed. Increasingly, firms will clamor for the right to operate in a country without seeking to establish themselves there. For example, given the opportunities offered by telecommunications, one can envision a bank becoming active in a country without establishing a single office or branch.

NONTARIFF BARRIERS
Barriers to trade, other than tariffs; examples include buy-domestic campaigns, preferential treatment for domestic bidders, and restrictions on market entry of foreign products, such as involved inspection procedures

Another key problem results from the fact that many disagreements were set aside for the sake of concluding negotiations. Disputes in such areas as agriculture or intellectual property rights protection continue to cause a series of trade conflicts among nations. If the WTO's dispute settlement mechanism is then applied to resolve the conflict, outcries in favor of national sovereignty may cause nations to withdraw from the agreement whenever a country loses in a dispute.

WORLD VIEW

World View: Waging War with Currencies

The warning shot of the currency wars was fired in 2010 when Brazilian Finance Minister Guido Mantega announced "we're in the middle of an international currency war…this threatens us because it takes away our competitiveness." Mr. Mantega was referring to monetary policies of advanced economies that have pursued weakening their currencies in order to make their exports more attractively priced, improve trade balances, and create domestic jobs. With the more wealthy nations experiencing prolonged economic doldrums, devaluing currencies became attractive as developing countries sought solutions to their domestic economic woes. These policies have destructive effects on other economies as traders and investors seek cheaper costs and better returns. Some rapidly growing developing markets have been the major victims of depreciating currencies in the advanced economies as capital has flowed to them. These large capital flows result in their currencies rising dramatically, thus making their exports less competitive and potentially leading to inflation and currency crises.

Some point to China as the main culprit of the currency wars because of its long policy of keeping the *renminbi* undervalued to promote its exports. Others, including Mr. Mantega, have seen the U.S. Federal Reserve Bank's policy of "quantitative easing" as being a thinly veiled effort to weaken the U.S. dollar. German Finance Minister Wolfgang Schäuble stated that "it's inconsistent for the Americans to accuse the Chinese of manipulating exchange rates and then to artificially depress the dollar exchange rate by printing money."

What's a developing market finance minister or central banker to do in the face of a weaker dollar or yen? Countries like Brazil, Colombia, Peru, and New Zealand have tried to slow their currencies' appreciation by intervening directly in foreign exchange markets to buy dollars and imposing capital controls, such as increasing deposit requirements on bank accounts and taxing foreign investment.

More recently, in 2013, finance ministers in some emerging markets, like India, Indonesia, and Brazil, have been implementing policies to curb the depreciation of their currencies. At the same time, increased active currency manipulation by multiple nations with existing current account surpluses, such as China, Korea, Taiwan, Japan, and Switzerland, has a serious negative impact upon the current account deficit of the United States, driven in part by the role of the dollar as the primary international currency.

SOURCES: *The Telegraph*, "Brazil Warns of World Currency War," September 28, 2010, **http://www.telegraph.co.uk/finance/economics/8029560/Brazil-warns-of-world-currency-war.html**; Andre Soliani and Joshua Goodman, "Mantega Says Currency War He Named Eases as Brazil Recovers," Bloomberg, February 27, 2013; Ian Talley, "Bergsten Warns of Currency Wars in Peterson Valedictory Speech," *The Wall Street Journal*, May 16, 2013.

A final major weakness of the WTO may result from the desire of some of its members to introduce "social causes" into trade decisions. It is debatable, for example, whether the WTO should also deal with issues such as labor laws, competition, and emigration freedoms. Other issues, such as freedom of religion, provision of health care, and the safety of animals have been raised as well. It will be difficult for the WTO to remain a viable organization if too many non-trade-related issues are loaded onto its trade and investment mission. The 159 governments participating in the WTO have diverse perspectives, histories, relations, economies, and ambitions. Many of them fear that social causes can be used to devise new rules of protectionism against their exports. Then there is also the question of how much companies—which, after all, are the ones doing the trading and investing—should be burdened with concerns outside of their scope.

Similar problems have befallen international financial institutions. For example, although the **International Monetary Fund (IMF)** functions effectively, it is currently under a severe challenge by new substantial financial requirements. So far, the IMF has been able to smooth over the most difficult problems but has not found ways to solve them. For example, since the beginning of the financial crisis in 2008 to 2012, the IMF has committed $540 billion and disbursed $157 billion in 126 lending programs to different countries to help with varying problems.[12]

INTERNATIONAL MONETARY FUND (IMF)
A specialized agency of the United Nations established in 1944; an international financial institution for dealing with Balance of Payment problems; the first international monetary authority with at least some degree of power over national authorities (see **http://www.imf.org**)

Yet, given the financial needs of many other nations, the IMF simply may not have enough funds to satisfy the needs of all. In cases of multiple financial crises, it is unable to provide its traditional function of calming financial markets in turmoil.

Apart from its ability to provide funds, the IMF must also rethink its traditional rules of operations. For example, it is quite unclear whether stringent economic rules and benchmark performance measures are equally applicable to all countries seeking IMF assistance. New economic conditions not experienced to date may require different types of approaches. The link between economic and political stability also may require different considerations, possibly substantially changing the IMF's mission.

Former **World Bank** President Robert Zoellick set out a vision for the bank to act as a "catalyst" for private and public action, extending the benefits of global integration to the poor and making globalization more "inclusive and sustainable." The World Bank successfully met its goal of aiding the reconstruction of Europe but has been less successful in furthering the economic goals of the developing world. Some even claim that instead of alleviating poverty, misguided bank policies may have created poverty.[13]

WORLD BANK
An international financial institution created to facilitate trade (see **http://www.worldbank.org**)

The pressures upon the WTO, the IMF, and the World Bank demonstrate that at a time when domestic policy measures are becoming less effective, international institutions that could help to develop substitute international policy measures have been weakened by new challenges to their traditional missions and insufficient resources to meet such challenges.

Conflict between Industrialized and Developing Nations

In the 1960s and 1970s, it was hoped that the developmental gap between industrialized nations and many countries in the less-developed world could gradually be closed. This goal was to be achieved with the transfer of technology and the infusion of major funds. Even though the 1970s saw vast quantities of petrodollars available for recycling and major growth in borrowing by some developing nations, the results have not been as expected. Although several less-developed nations have gradually emerged as newly industrialized countries (NICs), even more nations are facing grim economic futures.

In Latin America, many nations are still saddled with enormous amounts of debt, rapidly increasing populations, and very fragile economies. The developing countries of Africa also face major debt and employment problems. In view of their shattered dreams, policymakers in these nations have become increasingly aggressive in their attempts to reshape the ground rules of the world trade and investment flows. Although many policymakers share the view that major changes are necessary to resolve the difficulties that exist, no clear-cut solutions have emerged.[14]

Lately, individual national fiscal and monetary policies have led to international disputes over currency valuation. World View: Waging War with Currency demonstrates that developing countries are particularly vulnerable to the domestic economic policies of developed nations.

Policy Responses to Changing Conditions

The word *policy* conjures up an image of a well-coordinated set of governmental activities. Unfortunately, in the trade and investment sector, as in most of the domestic policy areas, this is rarely the case. Policymakers too often need to respond to short-term problems; they need to worry too much about what is politically salable to multiple constituencies; and in some countries, they are in office too short a time to formulate a guiding set of long-term strategies. Because of public and media pressures, policymakers must also be concerned with current events—such as monthly trade deficit numbers and investment flow figures—that may not be meaningful in the larger picture. In such an environment, actions may lead to extraordinarily good tactical measures but fail to achieve long-term success.

Import Restrictions

5 LEARNING OUTCOME

Worldwide, most countries maintain at least a surface-level conformity with international principles. However, many exert substantial restraints on free trade through import controls and barriers. Some of the more frequently encountered barriers are listed in Table 3.3. They are particularly common in countries that suffer from major trade deficits or major infrastructure problems, causing them to enter into voluntary restraint agreements with trading partners or to selectively apply trade-restricting measures such as tariffs, quotas, or nontariff barriers against trading partners.

TABLE 3.3 Trade Barriers

How many ways are there to raise a barrier? The likely answer is hundreds. Here are just a few of the obstacles that exporters encounter.

• Advance import deposits	• Global quotas	• Selected purchases licenses
• Barter and countertrade licenses	• Health and sanitation prohibitions	• Service charges
• Consular invoice fees	• Industry group fees	• Special import authorization
• Consumption taxes	• Licensing fees	• Stamp taxes
• Country quotas	• Local content rules	• Transportation taxes
• Customs surcharges	• Re-expat requirements	• Turnover taxes
• Excise duties	• Restrictive licensing	• Value-added taxes
• Foreign exchange licensing	• Seasonal prohibitions	• Voluntary export restraints
• Foreign exchange trade taxes		

SOURCE: Adapted and updated 2014 by Michael Czinkota from original list by Mark Magnier.

TARIFFS
Taxes on imported goods and services, instituted by governments as a means to raise revenue and as barriers to trade

QUOTAS
Legal restrictions on the import quantity of particular goods, imposed by governments as barriers to trade

VOLUNTARY RESTRAINT AGREEMENTS
Trade-restraint agreements resulting in self-imposed restrictions that are used to manage or distort trade flows but do not violate existing international trade rules

Tariffs are taxes on imports based primarily on the value of imported goods and services. **Quotas** are restrictions on the number of foreign products that can be imported. Nontariff barriers consist of a variety of measures such as testing, certification, or simply bureaucratic hurdles that have the effect of restricting imports. All of these measures tend to raise the price of imported goods. They therefore constitute a transfer of funds from the buyers (or, if absorbed by them, the sellers) of imports to the government, and—if accompanied by price increases of competing domestic products—to the domestic producers of such products.

Voluntary restraint agreements are designed to help domestic industries reorganize, restructure, and recapture production prominence. Even though officially voluntary, these agreements are usually implemented through severe threats against trading partners. Due to

Culture Clues *Connections* is a key word in conducting business in Saudi Arabia. Well-connected people find that progress is made much faster. Connections in the Middle East are vital to gain access to public and private decision makers.

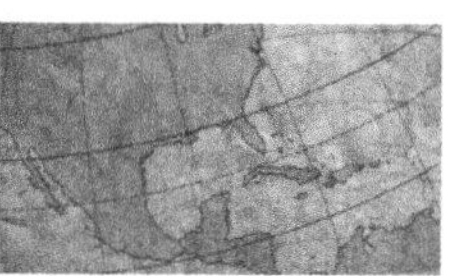

their "voluntary" nature, the agreements are not subject to any previously negotiated bilateral or multilateral trade accords.

TARIFFS AND QUOTAS Many countries use anti-dumping laws to impose tariffs on imports. Anti-dumping laws, discussed further in Chapter 4, are designed to help domestic industries that are injured by unfair competition from abroad due to products being "dumped" on them. Dumping may involve selling goods overseas at prices lower than those in the exporter's home market or at a price below the cost of production or both. The growing use of anti-dumping measures by governments around the world complicates exporters' pricing decisions. Large domestic firms, on the other hand, can use the anti-dumping process to obtain strategic shelter from foreign competitors.

In emerging markets, barriers often exist to protect small-scale domestic industries from larger-scale overseas producers. In India, for example, a stiff import tariff of 150 percent exists on foreign brands of wine. Though wine production in India has increased nearly 300 percent since 2003 to an estimated 13.5 million liters in 2010, the industry is still seen as being in its infancy.[15] Until the nation develops and implements technology needed to produce on a larger scale, industrialized producers from around the world are seen as a threat to India's wine industry. As soon as the wine industry becomes competitive enough to compete on the world market, India promises that these tariffs will be lifted.

NONTARIFF BARRIERS Nontariff barriers include buy-domestic campaigns, preferential treatment for domestic bidders compared with foreign bidders, national standards that are not comparable to international standards, and an emphasis on the design rather than the performance of products. Argentina in 2012, for example, increased the use of non-automatic import licensing, a process under which discretionary conditions must be met before a license is granted—which leads to much longer government processing times.[16] In India, major exports from neighboring Bangladesh, such as leather goods, melamine products, and cosmetics, are restricted from entering the Indian market because of stringent requirements on packaging, biosecurity, laboratory testing, sanitary and phytosanitary permits, and mandatory labeling.[17] Such nontariff barriers are often the most insidious obstacles to free trade because they are difficult to detect, hard to quantify, and demands for their removal are often stifled by the lack of economic resources to do so. Frequently, they are also blocked by resistance that results from a nation's cultural and historic heritage.

EFFECTS OF IMPORT RESTRICTIONS Policymakers are faced with several problems when trying to administer import controls. First, most of the time such controls exact a huge price from domestic consumers. Import controls may mean that the most efficient sources of supply are not available. The result is either second-best products or higher costs for restricted supplies, which in turn cause customer service standards to drop and consumers to pay significantly higher prices. Even though these costs may be widely distributed among many consumers and are not very obvious, the social cost of these controls may be quite damaging to the economy. For example, import controls may force EU citizens to pay elevated prices for agricultural products, while agricultural producers in the region benefit from higher incomes. Achieving a proper trade-off is often difficult, if not impossible, for the policymaker.

A second major problem resulting from import controls is the downstream change in the composition of imports that may result. For example, if the importation of copper ore is restricted, through either voluntary restraints or quotas, producing countries may opt to shift their production systems and produce copper wire instead, which they can export. As a result, initially narrowly defined protectionist measures may snowball in order to protect one downstream industry after another. Downstream effects can hurt domestic industries, too. Another major problem that confronts the policymaker is that of efficiency. Import controls designed to provide breathing room to a domestic industry so that it can either grow or recapture its competitive position often do not work. Rather than improve the productivity of an industry, such controls may provide it with a level of safety and a cushion of increased income, which cause it to lag even further behind in technological advancements.

It is also important to consider the corporate response to import restrictions. Corporations faced with restrictions often enlist the support of their home governments to knock down barriers to trade or to erect similar barriers to protect them in their home markets. The result of corporate influences over regulations can be a gradually escalating set of trade obstacles.

Finally, corporations can circumvent import restrictions by shifting to foreign direct investment. For example, instead of conducting trade, corporations can shift to foreign direct investment. The result may be a drop in trade inflow, yet the domestic industry may still be under strong pressure from foreign firms. The Japanese automobile manufacturer, Honda, for example, has a $14 billion capital investment in the United States and employs more than 26,000 Americans directly and 134,000 indirectly in dealerships. Nine manufacturing facilities churn out more than 1.2 million cars and light trucks as well as motorcycles, all-terrain vehicles, and engines, infusing local economies with jobs as well as spurring development in the states in which those plants are located. Ninety percent of Honda vehicles sold in the United States are now produced in North America.[18]

Despite increased competition in the home market due to the job-creation effects that result from shifting operations from the home country, policymakers who implement import controls achieve a favorable economic objective. Investments often have a variety of effects.

Fast Facts

What is the distance around the Earth at the equator?

The circumference of the Earth at the equator is 24,901.45 miles (40,074.89 km). The Earth rotates counterclockwise on its axis at approximately 1,000 miles per hour (1,609 km per hour), making one complete revolution each day.

EXPORT RESTRICTIONS In addition to imposing restraints on imports, nations also control their exports. The reasons include national security concerns. As explained in Chapter 4, for example, U.S. export legislation focuses on the control of weapons or high-technology exports that might adversely affect the safety of the nation. Exports are also controlled for reasons of foreign policy (a government's desire to send a political message to another country), short supply, or the desire to retain capital.

Export restrictions are almost never in the best interests of firms. Moreover, as explained further in Chapter 4, they rarely achieve their stated purpose. If, for example, exports from the United States are restricted, the targeted government simply obtains similar products from companies in other nations. Although perhaps valuable as a tool of international relations, such policies too often end up giving a country's firms a reputation for unreliability, with the result that orders are diverted elsewhere.

EXPORT PROMOTION The desire to increase participation in international trade and investment flows has led nations to implement export promotion programs. These programs are designed primarily to help domestic firms enter and maintain their position in international markets and to match or counteract similar export promotion efforts by other nations.

Most governments supply some support to firms participating or planning to participate in international trade. Typically, support falls into one of four categories: export information and advice, production support, marketing support, or finance and guarantees. Although such support is widespread and growing, its intensity varies by country. To help improve the international performance of U.S. firms, the Department of Commerce offers information services that provide data on foreign trade and market developments. Its **Commercial Service** posts hundreds of professionals around the world to assist business executives. In addition, a

U.S. COMMERCIAL SERVICE

A department of the U.S. Department of Commerce that gathers information and assists business executives in business abroad (see **http://www.trade.gov**)

Culture Clues

To the Japanese, almost no distinction exists between the business day and the business night. They consider it part of both their personal and professional lives to spend virtually every evening with business associates. "You get through to a man's soul at night" is a popular saying among Japanese businesspeople.

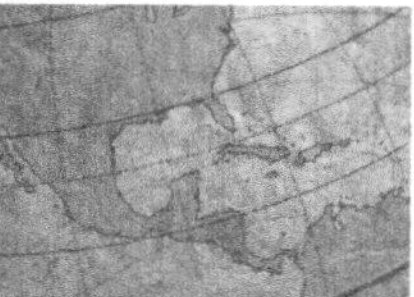

national network of export assistance centers has been created, capable of providing one-stop shops for exporters in search of export counseling and financial assistance. Also, an advocacy network helps U.S. companies win overseas contracts for large government purchases abroad. Other countries also try to help their firms through international support programs.

To assist in export financing, the Export-Import Bank of the United States provides long-term loans and loan guarantees so that U.S. firms can bid on contracts where financing is a key issue. In response to actions by foreign competitors, the bank has, on occasion, also offered **mixed aid credits**. These credits, which take the form of loans composed partially of commercial interest rates and partially of highly subsidized developmental aid interest rates, result in very low-interest loans to exporters.

MIXED AID CREDITS
Credits at rates composed partially of commercial interest rates and partially of highly subsidized developmental aid interest rates

Tax legislation also encourages exports by making the high cost of living of employees posted overseas easier to bear. A revision in the tax code now allows a substantial portion of income earned abroad to remain tax-free (up to $95,100 in 2012).[19]

Any export promotion raises several questions. One concerns the justification of the expenditure of public funds for what is essentially a for-profit activity. Companies argue that, especially for smaller firms, the start-up cost for international operations is sufficiently high to warrant some kind of government support. A second question focuses on the capability of government to provide support. Both for the selection and reach of firms as well as the distribution of support, government is not necessarily better equipped than the private sector to do a good job. A third issue concerns competitive export promotion. Countries that provide export support may well distort the flow of trade. If other countries then increase their support to counteract the effects, all that results is the same volume of trade activity, but at subsidized rates. It is therefore important to carefully evaluate export promotion activities as to their effectiveness and competitive impact. Perhaps such promotion is beneficial only when it addresses existing market gaps.

IMPORT PROMOTION Some countries have also developed import promotion measures. The measures are implemented primarily by nations that have accumulated and maintained large balance-of-trade surpluses. They hope to allay other nations' fears of continued imbalances and to gradually redirect trade flows.

Japan, for example, has completely refurbished the operations of the Japan External Trade Organization (JETRO) (**http://www.jetro.org**). This organization, which was initially formed to encourage Japanese exports, has now begun to focus on the promotion of imports to Japan. It organizes trade missions for foreign firms coming to Japan, hosts special exhibits and fairs within Japan, and provides assistance and encouragement to potential importers.

INVESTMENT POLICIES

The discussion of policy actions has focused thus far on merchandise trade. Similar actions are applicable to investment flows and, by extension, to international trade in services. In order to protect ownership, control, and development of domestic industries, many countries attempt to influence investment capital flows. Most frequently, investment-screening agencies decide on the merits of any particular foreign investment project. Investment in Canada, for example, is a government agency that scrutinizes foreign investments. Most developing nations similarly require special government permission for investment projects. This permission frequently carries with it certain conditions, such as levels of ownership permitted, levels of dividends that can be repatriated, numbers of jobs that must be created, or the extent to which management can be carried out by individuals from abroad. As noted earlier in this chapter, the United States restricts foreign investment only in instances where national security or related concerns are at stake.

Host-Country Perspective on Investment Policies

The host government is caught in a love-hate relationship with foreign direct investment. On the one hand, the host country has to appreciate the various contributions, especially economic, that foreign direct investment can make. On the other, allowing investment from abroad gives rise to fears of dominance, interference, and dependence. The major positive and negative impacts of foreign investment policies are summarized in Table 3.4 and are discussed below.

TABLE 3.4 **Pros and Cons of Foreign Direct Investment in Host-Country Economies**

Pros	Cons
• Improved capital flows • Technology transfer • Regional development • Increased competition that benefits the economy • Favorable balance of payments • Increased employment opportunities	• Low levels of research and development • Risk of increase capital outflows • Stifling of domestic competition and entrepreneurship • Erosion of host culture • Disruption of domestic business practices • Risk of interference by foreign governments

Positive Effects

TECHNOLOGY TRANSFER
The transfer of systematic knowledge for the manufacture of a product, the application of a process, or the rendering of a service

Capital inflows that result from foreign direct investment benefit all countries by making more resources available, but it particularly benefits those nations with limited domestic sources and restricted opportunities to raise funds in the world's capital markets. Another benefit of foreign direct investment is the transfer of technology from developed to developing nations. **Technology transfer** includes not only the introduction of new technologies, but also of the knowledge and skills to operate those technologies. In industries where the role of intellectual property is substantial, such as pharmaceuticals or software development, access to parent companies' research and development provides benefits that may be far greater than those gained through infusion of capital. Technology transfer explains in part the eagerness of many governments to invite multinational corporations to establish research and development facilities in their countries.

Foreign direct investment can help develop particular industry sectors or particular geographical regions, lowering unemployment levels. Furthermore, the costs of establishing an industry are often prohibitive, and the time needed is excessive for the domestic industry, even with governmental help, to try it on its own. In many developing countries, foreign direct investment may be a way to diversify the industrial base and thereby reduce the country's dependence on one or a few sectors.

At the company level, foreign direct investment may intensify competition and result in benefits to the economy as a whole, as well as to consumers, through increased productivity and, possibly, lower prices. Competition typically introduces new techniques, goods and services, and ideas. It also often improves existing patterns of how business is done.

Foreign direct investment has a long-term positive impact on the balance of payments of the host country. Import substitution, export earnings, and subsidized imports of technology and management all assist the host nation on the trade account side of the balance of payments. Not only may a new production facility substantially decrease the need to import the type of products manufactured, but it may start earning export revenue as well. Several countries, such as Brazil, have imposed export requirements as a precondition for foreign direct investment. On the capital account side, foreign direct investment may have a short-term impact in lowering a deficit as well as a long-term impact in keeping capital at home that otherwise could have been invested or transferred abroad. However, measurement is difficult because significant portions of capital flows may miss—or evade—the usual government reporting channels.

Jobs are often the most obvious reason to cheer about foreign direct investment. For example, U.S. subsidiaries of global companies employ 5.3 million Americans, about 4.7 percent of private sector employment, and support an annual payroll of $408 billion.[20] Also, such subsidiaries indirectly create opportunities for millions more. The benefits reach far beyond mere employment. Salaries paid by multinational corporations are usually higher than those paid by domestic firms. The creation of jobs translates also into the training and development of a skilled work force. Consider, for example, the situation in Indonesia, which became more attractive to foreign investors after it emerged much stronger from the 2008 financial crisis. Although Indonesia has long been interesting to investors for its abundant natural resources, today's investors are drawn by its growing middle class, which may reach 141 million by 2020. European companies like L'Oreal and American companies like GM, Apple, McDonald's and Yum Brands have been drawn to the Indonesian marketplace in recent years.[21]

The combined effects of all the benefits accruing from foreign direct investment can lead to overall improvements in the standard of living in the host country, as well as increasing its access to and competitiveness in world markets. World View: Bringing in the Money describes some of the incentives offered by nations to compete for foreign direct investment.

Negative Effects

Because foreign direct investment is most often concentrated in technology-intensive industries, research and development issues are often an area of tension. Rather than support research and development centers in all countries in which they operate, multinational corporations usually concentrate this function in just a few markets. This means that not all host countries benefit from technology transfer. Worse still, in some cases, multinational firms have withdrawn research and development from certain markets, blunting those markets' ability to acquire technological know-how. Furthermore, the multinational firm may contribute to the brain drain by attracting scientists from host countries to its central research facility. Many countries have demanded and received research facilities on their soil, where they can better control results. They do so because they are weary of the technological dominance of such countries as the United States and Japan, seeing it as a long-term threat.

From an economic perspective, capital inflows resulting from foreign direct investment are often accompanied by higher, longer term outflows that do not benefit the host government. For example, when multinational chains built hotels in the Caribbean, the shortage of local suppliers meant that much-needed foreign currency was spent on imported supplies. In other cases, multinationals simply prefer to use existing suppliers in their own countries rather than develop local supplier networks. Host countries do not look favorably on multinationals that keep the import content of a product high, especially when local suppliers are available.

Another frequent complaint is that investors fail to follow through on their promises. Rather than training local personnel for management roles, staff members are hired from overseas. Rather than stimulate local competition and encourage entrepreneurship, multinationals, with their often-superior product offerings and marketing skills, can reduce competition.

Multinational companies are, by definition, change agents. That is, welcome or not, the products and services they generate and market bring about change in the lifestyles of consumers in the host country. For example, the introduction of fast-food restaurants to Taiwan dramatically altered eating patterns, especially of teenagers, who make these outlets extremely popular and profitable. Concern has been expressed about the impact on family life and the higher relative cost of eating in such establishments.

The Global Environment: A Source of Conflict between Developed and Less-Developed Nations

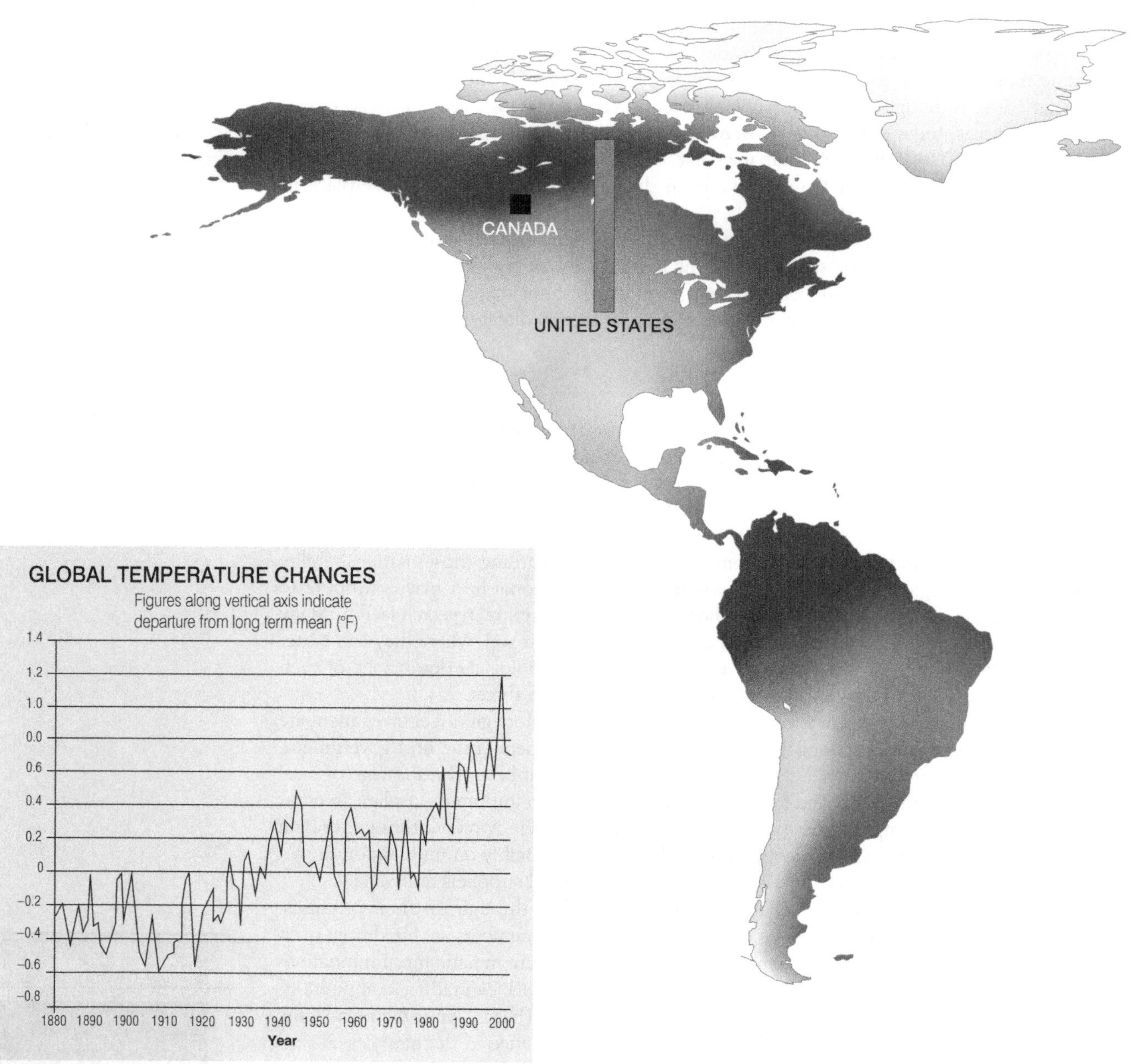

SOURCES: U.S. National Climactic Data Center, 2001; U.S. Department of Agriculture, 2001; National Geographic Society, Biodiversity map supplement, Feb. 1999; AAAS Atlas of Population and Environment, 2000; United Nations Environment Programme, 2001; World Resources Institute, World Resources, 1998–1999; Energy Information Administration, International Energy Annual, 1999.

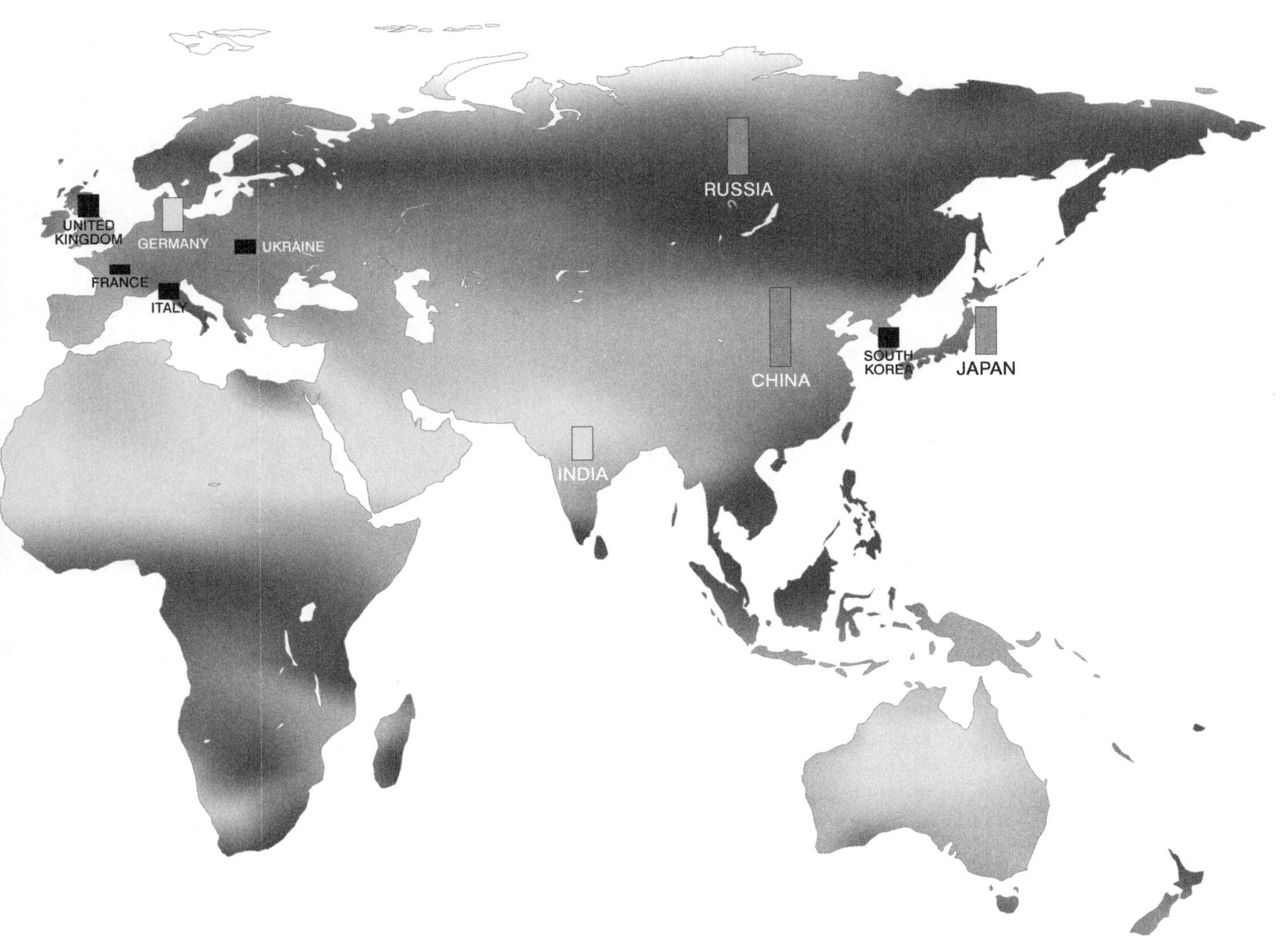

Greenhouse Gas Emissions

Million metric tons of carbon equivalent

- 100–200
- 200–400
- over 400

Color of bar indicates total emissions; height of bar per capita level of emissions

Rainforest Destruction

- Present distribution of forest area
- Areas originally forested

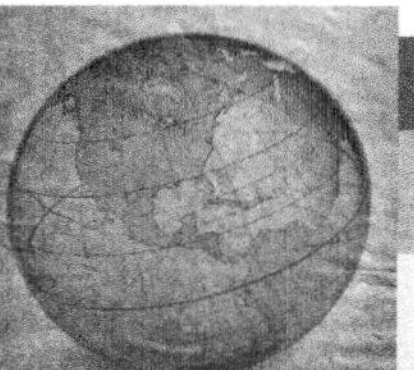

WORLD VIEW
Bringing in the Money

Global foreign direct investment (FDI) flows have still to recover from their pre-crisis peak in 2007. FDI flows declined in 2012 in terms of overall monetary value and the number of projects after a relatively strong performance in 2011. This decline was widespread in all regions of the world, although not all nations experienced a decline. It was primarily driven by poor economic growth in Europe, Japan, and Brazil as well as slower growth in China. Other contributing factors to the slowdown in FDI were the European debt crisis, political instability in the Middle East, and recovery from natural disasters, such as the earthquake, tsunami, and nuclear disaster in Japan and flooding in Thailand.

For 2012, the Organization for Economic Development (OECD), estimated an overall decline of 14 percent in global FDI. It reported that 44 percent of global FDI inflows were received by only five countries: China, the United States, Brazil, the United Kingdom, and France. China remains the leading destination for FDI. FDI Intelligence, a *Financial Times* unit that tracks FDI, identified five countries that were exceptions to the overall decline trend and experienced strong growth in inward FDI projects: Chile, Spain, Indonesia, Poland, and Oman.

In terms of outward FDI, the United States remains the largest investing nation globally, accounting for 25 percent of global outflows. Other major investing economies in 2012 were Japan, Belgium, the United Kingdom, Germany, China, and France.

SOURCES: UNCTAD, 2012 World Investment Report, *OECD FDI in Figures* April 2013; FDI Intelligence, *The FDI Report 2013*.

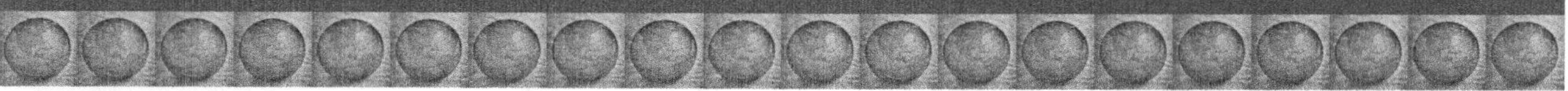

Multinational corporations also influence business practices in the host nation. Higher salaries and flexible work schedules, for example, may disrupt local practices. Some company practices may not be exportable. For example, taking older employees off production lines to make room for more productive workers—a common-enough practice in Japan—may go against the grain of local workplace ethics, not to mention trade union rules and antidiscrimination laws.

Some host nations express concerns over the possibility of interference, both economically and politically, by the home government of the multinational corporation; that is, they fear that the presence of a multinational may be used as an instrument of influence, affecting their economies in ways they cannot control.

Home-Country Perspective on Investment Policies

Most of the aspects of foreign direct investment that concern host countries apply to the home country as well. Foreign direct investment means addition to the home country's gross domestic product from profits, royalties, and fees remitted by affiliates. In many cases, intracompany transfers bring about additional export possibilities. Many countries promote foreign direct investment as a means to stimulate economic growth—an end that would expand

Quick Take Export and Investment Promotion Agencies

Although only a few countries have agencies to actively promote imports, a significant move has been to establish export promotion and inward investment promotion agencies by nations. Whereas some countries have separate offices for each function, many combine the functions in one office. As more and more developing nations seek the benefits of trade and investment, they are opening offices in other countries as well. For example, ApexBrasil has offices in Miami, Havana, Dubai, Luanda, Pequim, Moscow, and Brussels. As evidence of Colombia's very aggressive promotion activities, Proexport Colombia has a network of thirty-five offices in twenty-five countries. Here is a sampling of export and investment promotion agencies.

TABLE 3.5 Sampling of Export and Investment Promotion Agencies

Country	Agency	Web Site
Australia	Australian Trade Commission	**http://www.austrade.gov.au/**
Brazil	ApexBrasil	**http://www2.apexbrasil.com.br/en**
Canada	Canadian Trade Commissioner Service	**http://www.international.gc.ca/**
Chile	Pro/Chile (Exports)	**http://www.prochile.gob.cl/**
Chile	CIE Chile (Investment)	**http://www.foreigninvestment.cl/**
Colombia	Proexport	**http://www.investincolombia.com.co**
France	UBIFRANCE (Exports)	**http://www.ubifrance.com**
France	Invest in France (Investment)	**http://www.invest-in-france.org/us**
Germany	Germany Trade & Invest	**http://www.gtai.de**
Japan	JETRO	**http://www.jetro.go.jp**
Korea	KOTRA	**http://english.kotra.or.kr/**
South Africa	Department of Trade and Industry	**http://www.thedti.gov.za**
United Kingdom	UK Trade & Investment	**http://www.ukti.gov.uk**
United States	U.S. Foreign & Commercial Service	**http://export.gov/**
United States	SelectUSA (Investment)	**http://selectusa.commerce.gov/**

SOURCE: Adapted and updated 2014 by Michael Czinkota from original list by Mark Magnier.

export markets and possibly serve political motives as well. Japan and China, for example, have attempted to gain preferential access to raw materials by purchasing firms that own the deposits. China is also aggressively pursuing investments in the oil industries of developing countries, such as Sudan, in an effort to ensure future supply security. Other factors of production can be obtained through foreign direct investment as well. Companies today may not have the luxury of establishing research and development facilities wherever they choose but must locate them where human resources are available or where either policy restrictions or market dynamics make it advantageous. Global electronics giant Siemens, for example, employs 250,000 employees outside of its headquarters country Germany, where it employs another 119,000. The company has "290 major production and manufacturing plants worldwide" as well as other facilities in "nearly every country around the globe."[22] Siemens' major competitor, GE, has global research and development locations outside of the United States in Bangalore, India, Shanghai, China, and Munich, Germany, as it seeks new ideas from different parts of the world. GE Global Research employs more than 1,000 Ph.D.s globally.[23]

The biggest negative against foreign investment from the home-country perspective centers on employment. Many unions point not only to outright job loss but also to ripple effects on imports and exports. For example, when manufacturing plants are developed overseas, products often find their way back to the domestic market as low-priced imports. The result is more job losses when local companies can no longer compete. Electronics manufacturers who have moved plants to Southeast Asia and Mexico have justified their decisions as cost-cutting competitive measures.

Another critical issue is that of technological advantage. Some critics claim that, by establishing plants abroad or forming joint ventures with foreign entities, the country may in time risk its competitive lead in the world marketplace. The argument is that developing nations, which have saved the time and expense involved in developing new technologies, are then able to leapfrog over companies that brought the technologies to them.

Restrictions on Investment

Many nations restrict exports of capital because outward capital flows can severely damage their economies. Particularly in situations where countries lack necessary foreign exchange reserves, governments are likely to place restrictions on capital outflow. In essence, government claims to have higher priorities for capital than its citizens do. Citizens, in turn, often believe that the return on investment or the safety of their capital is not sufficiently ensured in their own countries, either due to governmental measures or domestic economic factors, such as inflation. These holders of capital want to invest abroad. By doing so, however, they deprive their domestic economy of much-needed investment funds.

CAPITAL FLIGHT
The flow of private funds abroad because investors believe that the return on investment or the safety of capital is not sufficiently ensured in their own countries

Once governments impose restrictions on the export of funds, the desire to transfer capital abroad only increases. Because companies and individuals are ingenious in their efforts to practice **capital flight**, governments, particularly in developing countries, continue to suffer. In addition, few new outside investors will enter the country because they fear that dividends and profits will not be remitted easily.

Investment Promotion

FISCAL INCENTIVES
Incentives used to attract foreign direct investment that provide specific tax measures to attract the investor

FINANCIAL INCENTIVES
Monetary offers intended to motivate; special funding designed to attract foreign direct investors that may take the form of land or buildings, loans, or loan guarantees

NONFINANCIAL INCENTIVES
Nonmonetary offers designed to attract foreign direct investors that may take the form of guaranteed government purchases, special protection from competition, or improved infrastructure facilities

Many countries implement policy measures to attract foreign direct investment. These policies can result from the need of poorer nations to bring in foreign capital without taking out more loans that call for fixed schedules of repayment. In industrialized nations, investment promotion usually arises from the pressure to provide jobs: Foreign direct investment can serve to increase employment and income. Nations around the world have government agencies to promote investment. For example, the United States agency charged with leading the drive to attract investment is Select USA, (**http://selectusa.commerce.gov/**); it originally opened in 2007 as InvestInAmerica. Increasingly, even state and local governments are participating in investment promotion. Many U.S. states send out investment missions on a regular basis. Some have opened offices abroad to inform local businesses about their state's beneficial investment climate. An example is the Georgia Department of Economic Development, which has ten international offices.

Incentives offered by policymakers to facilitate foreign investments are mainly of three types: fiscal, financial, and nonfinancial. **Fiscal incentives** are specific tax measures designed to attract foreign investors. They typically consist of special depreciation allowances, tax credits or rebates, special deductions for capital expenditures, tax holidays, and the reduction of tax burdens. **Financial incentives** offer special funding for the investor by providing, for example, land or buildings, loans, and loan guarantees. **Nonfinancial incentives** include guaranteed government purchases; special protection from competition through tariffs, import quotas, and local content requirements; and investments in infrastructure facilities.

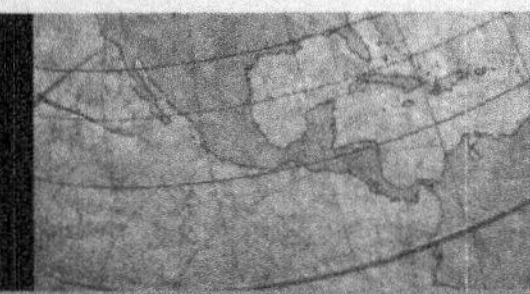

SUMMARY

All countries have international trade and investment policies. The importance and visibility of these policies have grown dramatically as international trade and investment flows have become more relevant to the well-being of most nations. Given the growing links among nations, it will be increasingly difficult to consider domestic policy without looking at international repercussions. To enhance international trade and investment in the future, nations must cooperate closely and view domestic policymaking in a global context.

International trade and investment policies have evolved as a subset of domestic policies. 1
Increasingly, however, the ability of policymakers to focus primarily on domestic issues is reduced because of global links in trade and investment. First the GATT and now the WTO seek to improve trade investment flows around the world by establishing rules that ensure nondiscrimination, transparent procedures, and a forum for the settlement of trade disputes.

Policymakers have shifted their focus from domestic issues to broader international issues due 2
to a general reduction of domestic policy influence, the weakening of traditional global institutions, and the accelerated conflict between industrialized and developing nations.

International trade institutions face many challenges stemming from strengthening links and 3
interdependence among nations' policies, economies, and legal systems. Several international agencies facilitate mediation and negotiation.

Efforts continue to close the gap between industrialized and emerging nations. These efforts 4
include technology, financial resources, and policy changes in international interactions. The motives behind equalizing a nation's status are not always pure, and arguments have been made that industrialized nations ultimately act in their own self-interest.

Many nations seek to restrict imports and, thereby, protect domestic industries by creating tariff barriers, such as quotas on imports, voluntary restraint agreements, and anti-dumping laws. In addition, a variety of nontariff barriers are used, including buy domestic campaigns, preferential treatment for domestic bidders, and the imposition of national rather than international standards. All these restrictions have repercussions that negatively affect industries and consumers.

Several nations seek to restrict exports, often for reasons of foreign policy, national security, short supply, or the desire to retain capital.

Nations attempt to promote exports though dissemination of information, production and marketing support, and financial assistance.

Through foreign direct investment, governments are able to receive needed products or to attract economic activity. Although restricting such investments may permit more domestic control over industries, it also denies access to foreign capital. This, in turn, can result in a tightening up of credit markets, higher interest rates, and a decreased impetus for innovation.

Investment policies aim to benefit both parties, while at the same time protecting each country's interests. Restrictions on outflow of foreign investment aim to protect a country's economy, primarily in the employment sector, while promotions to increase FDI are the result of poorer nations' desire to garner capital without potentially incurring further debt.

Key Terms and Concepts

Committee on Foreign Investments in the United States (CFIUS)
national sovereignty
domestic policy
quality of life
standard of living
foreign policy
General Agreement on Tariffs and Trade (GATT)
Most-Favored Nation (MFN)
World Trade Organization (WTO)
General Agreement on Trade in Services (GATS)
currency flows
punitive tariff
dumping
nontariff barriers
International Monetary Fund (IMF)
World Bank
tariffs
quotas
voluntary restraint agreements
U.S. Commercial Service
mixed aid credits
technology transfer
capital flight
fiscal incentives
financial incentives
nonfinancial incentives

Review Questions

1. Explain the relationship between domestic and international trade policies.
2. Summarize the role of the GATT and WTO in international trade regulation.
3. Explain changes that have occurred in the global policy environment due to increased international trade.
4. Outline the major benefits and drawbacks of trade restrictions.
5. What methods do nations use to discourage imports?
6. What methods can nations use to promote exports?
7. Summarize the positive and negative effects of foreign direct investment on trade from the host-country perspective.
8. How does foreign investment impact the home-country's economy?

Critical Skill Builders

1. Why would policymakers sacrifice major international progress for minor domestic policy gains? In teams, prepare arguments for and against protecting domestic industries. Present your arguments in a class debate.
2. Discuss the impact of import restrictions on consumers in both the home country and international markets.
3. Consider the conflict between industrialized and developing nations. What are its root causes and how might international trade policies alleviate them?
4. Do investment promotion programs of state (or provincial) governments make sense from a national perspective? Why or why not? Discuss in groups.
5. Consider why Japanese, German, and Korean automakers have set up manufacturing plants in the United States. How do their U.S. operations enhance their performance in both the home country and the host nation? Research specific examples to support your arguments.

On the Web

1. The Bureau of Economic Analysis (**http://www.bea.gov**) and Stat-USA (**http://www.stat-usa.gov**) provide a multitude of information about the current state of the U.S. economy. Look under the International subtitle on the Bureau of Economic Analysis main page and click on Operations of Multinational Companies. Go to the International Investment

Tables (D-57) to find the current market value of direct investment abroad as well as the value of direct investment in the United States.

2. Check the U.S. Department of Commerce web site (**http://www.export.gov**) to determine the assistance available to exporters. Which programs do you find most helpful to firms?
3. Go to the World Bank web site (**http://www.worldbank.org**) to obtain an overview of the bank's purpose and programs. Search for criticism of bank programs on other web sites and prepare a two-page report on key issues.

Endnotes

1. "Can't Afford Foreign Aid, or Can't Afford to Cut It?," *New York Times*, August 15, 2012.
2. Michael Sasso, "China Says It's Cleaning Up Products, Pollution," *Tampa Tribune*, Tampa, Florida: December 7, 2007; "Huge Energy Subsidies Bolster China's Steel Export," Comtex News Network, Inc., January 11, 2008, **http://www.lexisnexis.com/clients/senate/**, January 14, 2008.
3. Shawn Donnan, "Roberto Azevêdo urges WTO to reach $1tn global trade deal in Bali," *Financial Times*, September 9, 2013.
4. UNCTAD World Investment Report 2013, accessed March 12, 2014.
5. Pascal Lamy, "WTO accession puts Russia in a better position to address its domestic challenges," January 18, 2013, **http://www.wto.org/english/news_e/sppl_e/sppl263_e.htm**, accessed May 28, 2013.
6. Morten Bech, "FX Volume During the Financial Crisis and Now," *BIS Quarterly Review March 2012*, Bank for International Settlements.
7. Rocky Swift, "Bass Sees BOJ Bond Purchases Overwhelmed as Investors Dump Debt," Bloomberg, May 23, 2013, **http://www.bloomberg.com/news/2013-05-23/boj-bond-buying-to-be-overwhelmed-by-investor-sales-bass-says.html**, accessed January 21, 2014.
8. John Eggerton, "SoftBank/Sprint Deal Clears CFIUS Review," *Broadcasting & Cable*, May 29, 2013.
9. James K. Jackson, "The Committee on Foreign Investment in the United States (CFIUS), Congressional Research Service, March 29, 2013.
10. John Villasenor, "If You Want to Buy an American Company, Ask Permission, Not Forgiveness," *Forbes*, November 14, 2012.
11. Angelo Young, "European Commission Wants Punitive Tariffs Place on Solar Panels Made in China, But At Least 15 Member States Oppose the Measure," *International Business Times*, May 28, 2013.
12. Christine Lagarde, "Annual Meetings Speech: The Road Ahead—A Changing Global Economy, A Changing IMF," October 12, 2012, **http://www.imf.org/external/np/speeches/2012/101212a.htm**, accessed March 13, 2014.
13. Anup Shah, "Structural Adjustment—a Major Cause of Poverty, July 2, 2007, **http://www.globalissues.org/TradeRelated/SAP.asp**, accessed January 18, 2008; Krishna Guha, "Tackling Poverty A Priority for Zoellick," *Financial Times*, October 11, 2007.
14. Gumisai Mutume, "Wanted: Jobs for Africa's young people," Africa Renewal, United Nations, **http://www.un.org/ecosocdev/geninfo/afrec/newrels/203-jobs.html**, accessed January 18, 2008.
15. USDA Foreign Agricultural Service, "The Indian Wine Market," April 7, 2011.
16. Bernard Hoekman, "Trade Policy: So Far So Good?," International Monetary Fund, Finance and Development, June 2012, **http://www.imf.org/external/pubs/ft/fandd/2012/06/hoekman.htm**.
17. World Trade Organization, **http://www.wto.org/english/news_e/news12_e/good_30mar12_e.htm**, accessed June 12, 2013.
18. **http://www.hondainamerica.com/**, accessed May 29, 2013.
19. U.S. Internal Revenue Service, **http://www.irs.gov/Individuals/International-Taxpayers/Foreign-Earned-Income-Exclusion**, accessed June 12, 2013.
20. Organization for International Investment, **http://ofii.org/resources/insourcing-facts.html**, accessed May 29, 2013.
21. Joe Cochrane, "Multinationals Hasten to Invest in Indonesia," *New York Times*, April 23, 2013.
22. **http://www.siemens.com/about/en/worldwide.htm**, accessed May 29, 2013.
23. **http://www.ge.com/about-us/research/factsheet**, accessed May 29, 2013.

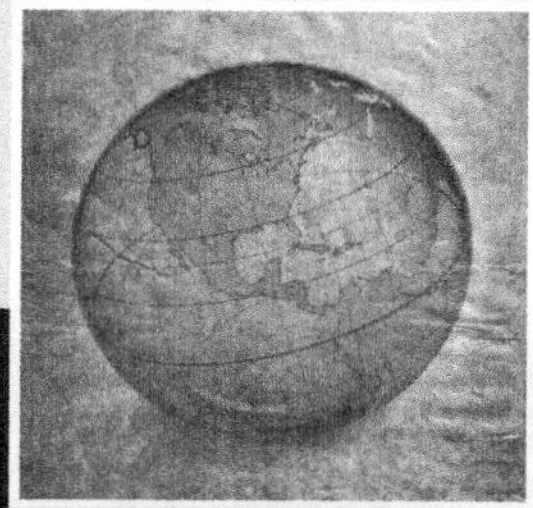

CHAPTER 4

POLITICS AND LAWS

Finding Safe Harbor in Data Privacy

When information was leaked in 2013 that the U.S. National Security Agency was obtaining data from telecom carriers and Internet companies about global phone calls and e-mails as part of a secret program called Prism, a debate about privacy rights was immediately created in the press. This debate became an international brouhaha when the German magazine *Der Spiegel* reported on the NSA bugging the offices of European governments. Although precise details on the veracity of the information and the extent of the programs are lacking, the public debate may signal a need for international cooperation on tighter rules for the collection of data about private individuals.

LEARNING OUTCOMES

1. *To understand the importance of the political and legal environments in both domestic and overseas markets*
2. *To learn how governments affect business through legislation, regulations, and monitoring*
3. *To see how the political actions of countries expose firms to international risks*
4. *To examine the differing laws regulating international trade in different countries*
5. *To understand how international political relations, agreements, and treaties affect international business*

Along with the explosion in the availability of "big data" for governments and businesses to use for various purposes come increasing concerns about the rights of citizens to privacy. New advancements in Web-based data acquisition, storage, management, and marketing allow organizations to better understand the habits and preferences of consumers and to customize programs to better serve their needs. At the same time, a thin line exists between monitoring consumer data and invading their privacy. It is one thing for a retailer to use scanner tracking data to provide shoppers with coupons or incentives to purchase items based on their shopping habits. It is far different for that retailer to use the data in predictive modeling on highly personal issues. For example, the U.S. giant retailer Target developed a pregnancy-prediction model that allowed them to develop lists of women who had been purchasing products that signaled a likelihood of pregnancy and even to estimate their due dates. With this information, Target could send coupons timed to very specific stages of a woman's pregnancy. When Target learned how negatively consumers reacted to the idea of this kind of invasion of privacy, they terminated the program.

Governments are still deliberating on what constitutes a reasonable use of personal data and what constitutes an invasion of privacy. Significantly different approaches to privacy are taken in the United States compared to Europe. Companies need to understand these differences and carefully adjust their practices to avoid violating different legal frameworks. These are dangerous waters for companies to navigate.

In order to help businesses work with these differences, the U.S. Department of Commerce and the European Commission developed a "Safe Harbor" framework and a web site to provide a streamlined means to comply with different requirements. (See **http://export.gov/safeharbor/index.asp**.) A separate U.S.-Switzerland Safe Harbor Framework was also developed.

The U.S.-EU Safe Harbor Framework is a voluntary program, but once an entity elects to participate in the program, it is legally required to comply with the Safe Harbor Privacy Principles. In the United States, this program is administered by the Office of Technology and E-Commerce at the U.S. International Trade Administration (ITA). ITA reviews every Safe Harbor certification and annual recertification submission that it receives to ensure that these include all of the elements required by the Frameworks. When a company's Safe Harbor submission does not meet the standards, ITA contacts the company to explain what is lacking and what steps must be taken before the company's certification or recertification may be finalized. By their very nature, the Safe Harbor Frameworks are technical. International firms need good legal counsel in order to truly find safe harbor in these very dangerous waters.

SOURCES: Charles Duhigg, "How Companies Learn Your Secrets," *The New York Times*, February 6, 2012; "Listening in on Europe Isn't a Good Strategy," *The International Herald Tribune*, July 4, 2013; U.S.-EU & U.S.-Swiss Safe Harbor Frameworks, **http://export.gov/safeharbor/index.asp**, accessed July 4, 2013.

As You Read This Chapter

1. Risk is the price of opportunity. Do you agree?
2. Should multinational firms do business in potentially unstable environments if it means they are fueling an invisible, illegal economy?
3. Where do you personally see the borderline between governments and firms gathering data and invasion of privacy?

Politics and laws play a critical role in international business. Unexpected political or legal influences can send the best-laid plans awry. Failure to anticipate or factor in these elements frequently proves the undoing of otherwise-successful business ventures.

Of course, a single international political and legal environment does not exist. This means that business executives must be aware of political and legal factors on several, often conflicting, dimensions. Although it is useful, for example, to understand the complexities of the host country's legal system, such knowledge may not protect against sanctions imposed by the firm's home country.

This chapter will examine politics and laws from the manager's point of view. The two subjects are considered together because laws generally are the result of political decisions. The chapter explores the international political and legal environment in three segments: the politics and laws of the home country, those of the host country, and the bilateral and multilateral agreements, treaties, and laws governing the relations among host and home countries.

Home-Country Perspective

No manager can afford to ignore the rules and regulations of the country from which he or she conducts international business transactions. Many of these regulations do not specifically address international business issues, but they can have a major impact on a firm's opportunities abroad. Consider, for example, how minimum-wage legislation in the home country affects international competitiveness. If the cost of adhering to domestic safety regulations forces a firm to price its goods higher than those of overseas competitors, the firm risks losing international market share. Moving manufacturing to regions of the world where labor costs are lower may be the solution. In the trade of commodity-type products such as steel or chemicals, where few significant differences exist between one firm's output and another's, competitiveness is an even greater factor. For example, U.S. legislation requires chemical manufacturers to pay into the Environmental Superfund, thereby increasing costs. Overseas competitors are not required to make similar payments in their home countries. As a result, U.S. chemical firms are at a cost disadvantage when competing in international markets. At the same time, all companies doing business in the EU must comply with Registration, Evaluation, Authorization, and Restriction of Chemical substances (REACH) regulations. Although many large foreign firms have adjusted to the information reporting and registration requirements of REACH, the costs of compliance can be a serious competitiveness issue for smaller businesses.[1]

Other legal and regulatory measures single out international operations. In the United States, following a widely publicized scandal involving U.S.-based Pfizer testing an experimental meningitis medication on Nigerian children, an amendment to the Export Administration Act was passed, restricting the export of potentially dangerous experimental drugs to developing countries. There is some debate about the effectiveness of this measure, considering that companies are still able to conduct such trials through foreign-based subsidiaries. Currently, the majority of clinical tests are conducted outside of highly developed nations, which might be explained with a simple issue of supply. Even though the average American buys ten prescriptions per year, fewer than one in twenty is willing to take part in a drug trial.[2] Other laws address standards by regulating product content and quality. Frequently, such standards favor national firms and exclude imports that fail to satisfy them. Still other regulations aim to protect a citizenry from outside influences that its culture deems unacceptable. Quick Take: Caught in the Web explains how governments attempt to control Internet content considered offensive or illegal.

Quick Take *Caught in the Web*

Use of the Internet in China is subject to Chinese government surveillance and censorship and requires sensitivity to Chinese political issues. Beginning in 2001, the Chinese government created the "Great Firewall of China," a part of what is called the "Golden Shield Project," a complex system that monitors and filters multiple forms of information flow in China. This system censors the Web by blocking access to sites and preventing searches for specific information and designated terms. In order to do business in China, search engines are required to self-censor searches. This led to Google's decision in 2010 to withdraw from direct Chinese search operations. Access to YouTube, Facebook, and Twitter have been blocked since 2009. In 2012, Bloomberg and the *New York Times* were temporarily blocked after publishing stories about the finances of family members of Chinese leaders.

Most Web users in China use China-specific sites for information and e-commerce. Baidu is the search engine of choice for most Chinese, while Youku serves as China's top video sharing site. However, international business operations require access to information from a variety of sources. Some try to circumvent the Great Firewall through the use of virtual private networks, but such networks are not immune to government intervention.

Although this may seem to affect only political issues, it has an indirect effect on business operations by impeding access to information and slowing digital information flows. In the 2013 Business Climate survey, the American Chamber of Commerce in Beijing reported that 55 percent of the business respondents found China's Internet restrictions "as negatively or somewhat negatively affecting their capacity to do business there." In addition, 62 percent said "the disruption of search engines (*sic*) made it more difficult to obtain real-time market data, share time-sensitive information, or collaborate with colleagues outside China," and 72 percent found "that slow and unstable Internet speeds impede their ability to efficiently conduct business in China." So, businesses can become caught in the Web in China.

SOURCES: Christina Larson, "Chinese Censors Slow the Net and U.S. Businesses," *Bloomberg Business Week*, April 1, 2013; Beibei Bao, "How Internet Censorship Is Curbing Innovation in China," *The Atlantic*, April 22, 2013; "The Art of Concealment," *The Economist*, April 6, 2013.

In most countries, the political environment tends to support the international business efforts of firms headquartered there. For example, a government may work to reduce trade barriers and thereby increase trade opportunities through bilateral and multilateral negotiations. Sometimes, however, political decisions can restrict the practice of international business. Six European Union member states, Austria, France, Germany, Greece, Hungary, and Luxembourg, have invoked a "safeguard clause" to restrict the use and/or sale of genetically modified organisms (GMO), which they believe may have health risks. This not only restricts the ability of Monsanto, which sells GMO crop seeds, but also U.S. agricultural growers, to access these markets.

Three main areas of governmental activity are of concern to the international business manager. They are embargoes and trade sanctions, export controls, and the regulation of international business behavior.

Embargoes and Sanctions

The terms **sanction** and **embargo** refer to governmental actions that distort the free flow of trade in goods, services, or ideas for decidedly adversarial and political (rather than economic) purposes. Sanctions tend to consist of specific coercive trade measures, such as the cancellation of trade financing or the prohibition of high-technology trade. Embargoes are usually much broader in that they prohibit trade entirely. For example, the United States imposes sanctions against some countries by prohibiting the export of weapons to them, and the decades-long embargo against Cuba bans all but humanitarian trade in food and medicines. To better understand sanctions and embargoes, it is useful to examine the auspices and legal justifications under which they are imposed.

SANCTION

A governmental action, usually consisting of a specific coercive trade measure, that distorts the free flow of trade for an adversarial or political purpose rather than an economic one

EMBARGO

A governmental action, usually prohibiting trade entirely, for a decidedly adversarial or political rather than economic purpose

Trade embargoes have been used quite frequently and successfully in times of war or to address specific grievances. In 1284, when a German ship was pillaged by Norwegians, the Hansa, an association of north German merchants, instigated an economic blockade against Norway. The export of grain, flour, vegetables, and beer was prohibited on pain of fines and confiscation of goods. The blockade was a complete success. Deprived of grain from Germany, the Norwegians were unable to obtain it from England or elsewhere. As a contemporary chronicler reports: "Then there broke out a famine so great that they were forced to make atonement." Norway was made to pay indemnities for the financial losses caused and to grant the Hansa extensive trade privileges.[3]

Over time, economic sanctions and embargoes have become a principal tool of foreign policy. They are often imposed unilaterally in the hope of changing a country's government or at least changing its policies. Reasons for imposing sanctions and embargoes have varied: They range from upholding human rights to attempts to promote nuclear nonproliferation or anti-terrorism.

A fundamental problem with sanctions is that their unilateral imposition frequently fails to produce the desired results. Sanctions may make obtaining goods more difficult or expensive for the sanctioned country, yet their purported objective is almost never achieved.

However, such unilateral measures often fall short. For example, the United States is relatively alone in its stance toward Cuba; Europeans, Canadians, and others from around the world do business in Cuba, so the costs of the embargo are mainly felt by American businesses and citizens. The annual cost of the embargo to the U.S. economy is estimated to range from $1.2 billion to $3.6 billion, according to the U.S. Chamber of Commerce.[4] However, the sanctions also exact a steep price from the Cubans in terms of insufficient growth and economic well-being.

In order to work, sanctions need to be imposed multilaterally and affect goods that are vital to the sanctioned country—goals that are clear, yet difficult to implement. Consider, for example, the international sanctions that have been imposed on Iran because of its persistent efforts to develop nuclear capabilities. After the European Union and Japan joined the United States in sanctions on Iranian petroleum exports and international financial transactions, Iran has found it more difficult to earn revenue and conduct business. The U.S. Treasury Department estimates that Iran's economy has been seriously affected by the international efforts with its GDP having fallen by some 5 percent to 8 percent in 2012.[5]

Sanctions usually mean significant loss of business. A 2012 study by the Iran Project highlights the benefits of international sanctions on Iran but also identifies the disadvantages, such as the opportunity cost of business lost to U.S. and European firms as well as those from other allied countries like Japan and the Gulf Cooperation Council states. China and India have continued to do business with Iran by bartering goods for oil. This has disruptive effects on long-term patterns of commerce. The study describes other negative effects such as disputes with allies and other countries like Russia, China, India, Turkey, and South Korea, increased corruption and control of the economy by unaccountable and repressive factions that have control over financial resources, empowering antireform voices and disempowering civil society, long-term alienation between the United States and Iran, negative humanitarian effects on the Iranian people, and the increased potential for conflict. Because of the sanctions, Iran has threatened to retaliate by closing the Strait of Hormuz, a vital strategic chokepoint in the global commercial system.[6]

The international business manager is often caught in this political web and loses business as a result. Frequently, firms try to anticipate sanctions based on their evaluations of the international political climate. Nevertheless, even when all reasonable precautions are taken, firms still suffer substantial losses due to contract cancellations once sanctions or embargoes are put in place.

Export Controls

EXPORT-CONTROL SYSTEMS
A system designed to deny or at least delay the acquisition of strategically important goods to adversaries: in the United States, based on the Export Administration Act and the Munitions Control Act

DUAL-USE ITEM
Good or service that is useful for both military and civilian purposes

EXPORT LICENSE
A license obtainable from the U.S. Department of Commerce Bureau of Industry and Security, which is responsible for administering the Export Administration Act

CRITICAL COMMODITIES LIST
A U.S. Department of Commerce file containing information about products that are either particularly sensitive to national security or controlled for other purposes

Many nations have **export-control systems** designed to deny or at least delay the acquisition of strategically important goods by political adversaries. The legal basis for export controls varies from nation to nation. For example, in Germany, armament exports are governed by the War Weapons Control Law. The exports of other goods are covered by the German Export List. **Dual-use items**, which are goods useful for both military and civilian purposes, are then controlled by the Joint List of the European Union. The U.S. export-control system is based on the Export Administration Act and the Munitions Control Act. These laws control all export of goods, services, and ideas. The determinants for controls are national security, foreign policy, short supply, and nuclear nonproliferation. World View: Bullets, Bugs, and Bytes explores how the U.S. makes decisions regarding export controls.

Export licenses are issued by the Department of Commerce, which administers the Export Administration Act. In consultation with other government agencies—particularly the departments of State, Defense, and Energy—the Commerce Department has drawn up a list of commodities whose export is considered particularly sensitive. In addition, a list of countries differentiates nations according to their political relationship with the United States. Finally, a list exists of individual firms in each country that are considered to be unreliable trading partners because of past trade-diversion activities.

After an export license application has been filed, specialists in the Department of Commerce match the commodity to be exported with the **critical commodities list,** a file containing information about products that are either particularly sensitive to national security or controlled for other purposes. The product is then matched with the country of destination and the recipient company. If no concerns regarding any of the three steps exist, an export license is issued. Control determinants and the steps in the decision process are summarized in Figure 4.1.

FIGURE 4.1 U.S. Export Control System

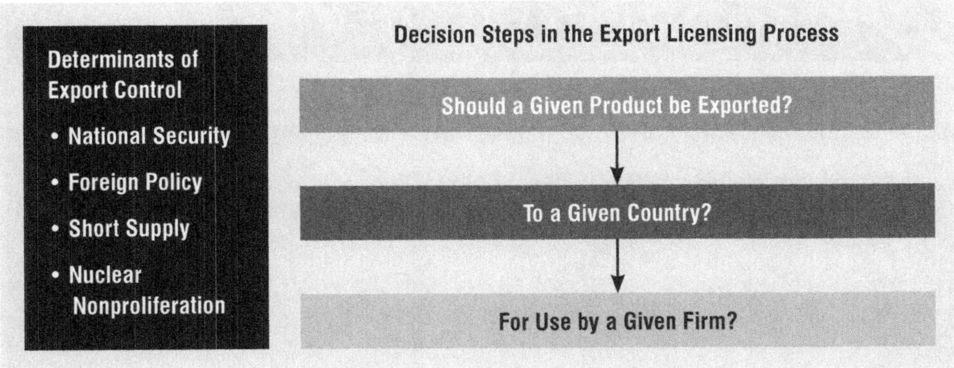

This process may sound overly cumbersome, but it does not apply in equal measure to all exports. Most international business activities can be carried out under "no license required" (NLR) conditions. NLR provides blanket permission to export to most trading partners, provided that neither the end user nor the end use is considered sensitive. It therefore pays to check out the denied persons list published by the U.S. government (**http://www.bis.doc.gov/DPL**) to ensure that one's trading partner is not a prohibited one. However, the process becomes more complicated when it involves products incorporating high-level technologies and unfriendly nations. The exporter must then apply for an export license, which consists of written authorization to send a product abroad. In most cases, license applications can be downloaded and submitted over the Internet.

Export controls are increasingly difficult to implement and enforce for several reasons. First, the number of countries able to manufacture products of strategic importance, such as advanced weaponry, has increased. Industrializing nations, which only a decade ago were seen as poor imitators at best, are now at the forefront of cutting-edge technology. Second, products that are in need of control are developed and disseminated very quickly. Product life cycles are so short that even temporary delays in distribution may result in a significant setback for a firm. Third, because of advances in miniaturization, products that need to be controlled are shrinking in size. The smuggling and diversion of such products have become easier because they are easier to conceal. Finally, the transfer of technology and know-how has increasingly taken on major strategic significance. Because such services are often invisible, performed by individuals, and highly personalized, they are easy to transship and therefore difficult to trace and control.

Regulating International Business Behavior

Home countries of international businesses may implement special laws and regulations to ensure that the behavior of those firms is conducted within appropriate moral and ethical boundaries. The definition of appropriateness shifts from country to country and from government to government. Therefore, the content, enforcement, and impact of such regulations on firms may vary substantially. As a result, the international manager must walk a careful line, balancing the expectations held in different countries.

BOYCOTT
An organized effort to refrain from conducting business with a particular seller of goods or services; used in the international arena for political or economic reasons

BOYCOTTS One method nations and sometimes localities or individuals use in an attempt to affect international business activities is **boycotts**. A boycott is a collaboration to prevent a country from carrying on international trade by deterring or obstructing other countries from dealing with it. The ongoing boycott by Arab nations that blacklists firms that deal with Israel

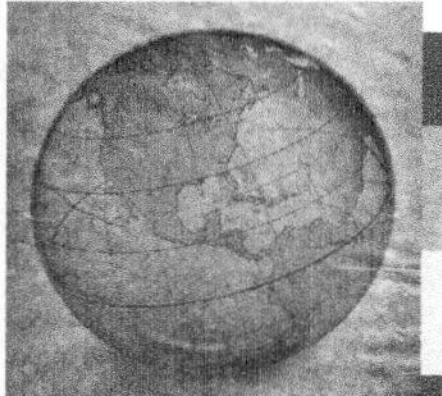

WORLD VIEW

Bullets, Bugs, and Bytes

To keep the world a safe place, nations must ensure that the promotion of trade is carefully balanced with responsible foreign policy. Clearly, arms embargoes that keep advanced weaponry out of countries like Iran and North Korea, which support worldwide terrorism, are necessary export controls. But what about supercomputer exports to India or Pakistan? Will the supercomputers be used to advance the nations' economies or to speed development of nuclear weapons? In a delicate balancing act, U.S. export policy is swayed by manufacturers, the national political climate, shifts in the geopolitical map, and rapid technology advances.

Across a range of industries, companies that trade internationally are subject to scrutiny by the Commerce Department's Bureau of Industry and Security (BIS). Penalties imposed in 2012 included judgments against FedEx Corporation for provision of freight forwarding services to unlicensed exporters of electronic components to Dubai, flight simulation software to China, and printer components to Syria; Ericsson de Panama for routing items from Cuba through Panama for repair and replacement in the United States and return to Cuba; and a California company for illegal exports of computer-related goods to Iran.

In 2012, ING Bank N.V., headquartered in Amsterdam, agreed to pay a penalty of $619 million to the U.S. Department of Justice and the New York County District Attorney's Office for moving more than $2 billion illegally through the U.S. financial system in more than 20,000 transactions on behalf of Cuban and Iranian entities subject to U.S. economic sanctions. Fears of chemical and biological warfare have increased the urgency of developing international inspection protocols to monitor the development of technologies behind biological weaponry. The Australia Group is an informal forum of countries, including the United States, that works to harmonize export controls to protect against the development chemical or biological weapons. In 2012, members of this group agreed to subject exports to Syria to "particular scrutiny" in light of suspected use of these weapons in the civil war in that country.

Even more difficult to control may be how foreign governments use powerful computer technologies. Recently, a particular area of challenge for export controls is in the area of cloud computing. Although BIS has found that the provision of cloud computing services and "computational capacity" do not require export licenses, it has also advised that cloud service providers need to ensure that "export-controlled user data will not be stored on servers located outside of the U.S. or be accessible by any foreign national employed by the provider."

Export controls extend beyond sensitive products to encompass technological know-how. U.S. companies must obtain an export license before a non-U.S. individual can work on a technology that would require an export license. The reach of the so-called "**deemed export**" regulation even affects foreign nationals attending universities or conferences in the United States. In effect, foreign engineers, scientists, and students are treated as though they are foreign countries.

While high-tech firms claim that this measure constitutes "bureaucratic overkill" and stalls the hiring of high-demand specialists, the BIS insists that it helps keep sensitive information out of dangerous hands.

SOURCES: U.S. Department of Justice, Press Release, June 12, 2012, **http://www.bis.doc.gov/news/2012/doj06122012.htm**, accessed June 28, 2013; U.S. Bureau of Industry and Security, press release, January 4, 2012, **http://www.bis.doc.gov/news/2012/bis_press01042012.htm**, accessed June 28, 2013; U.S. Bureau of Industry and Security, press release, May 25, 2012, **http://www.bis.doc.gov/news/2012/bis_press05252012.htm**, accessed June 28, 2013; U.S. Department of Justice, press release, May 12, 2013, **http://www.bis.doc.gov/news/2012/doj05162012.htm**, accessed June 28, 2013; The Australia Group, **http://www.australiagroup.net/en/index.html**, accessed June 28, 2013; Burt Braverman and Brian Wong, "Cloud Computing: U.S. Export Controls Reach for the Sky," Davis Wright Tremaine advisory, May 20, 2013, **http://www.dwt.com/Cloud-Computing-US-Export-Controls-Reach-for-the-Sky-05-20-2013/**, accessed June 28, 2013.

is just one example. It has led to anti-boycott laws in the United States through which the government denies foreign income tax benefits to companies that comply with the boycott.

Caught in a web of governmental activity, firms may be forced either to lose business or to pay substantial fines. This is especially true if the firm's products are competitive but not unique, so that the supplier can opt to purchase the products elsewhere. The heightening of such conflict can sometimes force companies to search for new, and possibly risky, ways to circumvent the law or to totally withdraw operations from a country.

DEEMED EXPORT
Addresses people rather than products where knowledge transfer could lead to a breach of export restrictions

ANTITRUST LAWS
Laws that prohibit monopolies, restraint of trade, and conspiracies to inhibit competition

ANTITRUST LEGISLATION **Antitrust laws** are another area of regulatory activity that affects international business. Antitrust laws prohibit monopolies, restraint of trade, and conspiracies that inhibit competition. Google, which has about 95 percent of the European search market in 2013, has been working to settle with European competition regulators who have been investigating complaints by competitors that it promotes its own specialist search services at the expense of others, that it copies rivals' travel and restaurant reviews, and that it uses agreements with web sites and software developers to stifle competition for advertising. Google is also facing antitrust investigations in other countries, such as South Korea and Argentina.[7]

While antitrust laws apply to international operations as well as domestic firms, the United States has taken steps to protect from antitrust legislation any firm cooperating in the development of foreign markets. For example, the Webb-Pomerene Act of 1918 and the Export Trading Company Act of 1982 both sought to aid export efforts by limiting the international scope of antitrust laws. However, this legislation does not help the firm battle charges of antitrust actions overseas. In 2012, the European Commission ruled against the planned merger between Deutsche Börse and the New York Stock Exchange on the grounds that it "would lead to a quasi-monopoly in the market for European financial derivatives traded globally on exchanges."[8]

BRIBERY AND CORRUPTION In many countries, payments or favors to grease the wheels of business or government are a way of life, forcing international companies to make payments to foreign officials in order to conduct business. Although most countries forbid the exchange of money or other favors in order to gain competitive contracts, some—like the United States—allow what are known as "facilitation payments" or payments made to expedite routine needs such as processing paperwork, obtaining permits, or gaining customs clearance. In some countries, facilitation payments are even tax deductible.

India has been plagued by this mixture of bureaucracy and corruption. In his 2012 book "India Grows at Night," former head of P&G in India, Gurcharan Das, lamented the levels of bad governance that hinder Indian economic development. He reported that to build a new power station in India requires 118 permits, or "corruption opportunities," in Das's words.[9] The Organization for Economic Cooperation and Development (OECD) took steps to stamp out corruption by adopting a treaty that criminalizes the bribery of foreign public officials. Working industry-by-industry and enlisting the voluntary participation of top corporations, the OECD seeks to crack down on the world's worst offenders. Transparency International conducts an annual survey that tracks perceptions of corruption across the globe. Figure 4.2 shows the corruption perceptions index of 2012. Backing OECD efforts, the World Bank is compiling a blacklist of bribers and encourages even poorer states to prosecute the offenders. On January 19, 2013, Colombia became the fortieth signatory to the OECD's Anti-Bribery Convention.[10]

Regulations governing bribery and corruption leave managers operating in international environments with the tough choice of either adhering to home-country laws or following foreign business practices. To compete internationally, executives argue, they must be free to use the most common methods of competition in host countries. In time, the emerging consensus among international organizations that bribery should be outlawed may level the playing field.

FIGURE 4.2 Corruption Perception Index 2012

RANK	COUNTRY/TERRITORY	SCORE
1	Denmark	90
1	Finland	90
1	New Zealand	90
4	Sweden	88
5	Singapore	87
6	Switzerland	86
7	Australia	85
7	Norway	85
9	Canada	84
9	Netherlands	84
11	Iceland	82
12	Luxembourg	80
13	Germany	79
14	Hong Kong	77
15	Barbados	76
16	Belgium	75
17	Japan	74
17	United Kingdom	74
19	United States	73
20	Chile	72
20	Uruguay	72
22	Bahamas	71
22	France	71
22	Saint Lucia	71
25	Austria	69
25	Ireland	69
27	Qatar	68
27	United Arab Emirates	68
29	Cyprus	66
30	Botswana	65
30	Spain	65
32	Estonia	64
33	Bhutan	63
33	Portugal	63
33	Puerto Rico	63
36	Saint Vincent and the Grenadines	62
37	Slovenia	61
37	Taiwan	61
39	Cape Verde	60
39	Israel	60
41	Dominica	58
41	Poland	58
43	Malta	57
43	Mauritius	57
45	Korea (South)	56
46	Brunei	55
46	Hungary	55
48	Costa Rica	54
48	Lithuania	54
50	Rwanda	53
51	Georgia	52
51	Seychelles	52
53	Bahrain	51
54	Czech Republic	49
54	Latvia	49
54	Malaysia	49
54	Turkey	49
58	Cuba	48
58	Jordan	48
58	Namibia	48
61	Oman	47
62	Croatia	46
62	Slovakia	46
64	Ghana	45
64	Lesotho	45
66	Kuwait	44
66	Romania	44
66	Saudi Arabia	44
69	Brazil	43
69	FYR Macedonia	43
69	South Africa	43
72	Bosnia and Herzegovina	42
72	Italy	42
72	Sao Tome and Principe	42
75	Bulgaria	41
75	Liberia	41
75	Montenegro	41
75	Tunisia	41
79	Sri Lanka	40
80	China	39
80	Serbia	39
80	Trinidad and Tobago	39
83	Burkina Faso	38
83	El Salvador	38
83	Jamaica	38
83	Panama	38
83	Peru	38
88	Malawi	37
88	Morocco	37
88	Suriname	37
88	Swaziland	37
88	Thailand	37
88	Zambia	37
94	Benin	36
94	Colombia	36
94	Djibouti	36
94	Greece	36
94	India	36
94	Moldova	36
94	Mongolia	36
94	Senegal	36
102	Argentina	35
102	Gabon	35
102	Tanzania	35
105	Algeria	34
105	Armenia	34
105	Bolivia	34
105	Gambia	34
105	Kosovo	34
105	Mali	34
105	Mexico	34
105	Philippines	34
113	Albania	33
113	Ethiopia	33
113	Guatemala	33
113	Niger	33
113	Timor-Leste	33
118	Dominican Republic	32
118	Ecuador	32
118	Egypt	32
118	Indonesia	32
118	Madagascar	32
123	Belarus	31
123	Mauritania	31
123	Mozambique	31
123	Sierra Leone	31
123	Vietnam	31
128	Lebanon	30
128	Togo	30
130	Côte d'Ivoire	29
130	Nicaragua	29
130	Uganda	29
133	Comoros	28
133	Guyana	28
133	Honduras	28
133	Iran	28
133	Kazakhstan	28
133	Russia	28
139	Azerbaijan	27
139	Kenya	27
139	Nepal	27
139	Nigeria	27
139	Pakistan	27
144	Bangladesh	26
144	Cameroon	26
144	Central African Republic	26
144	Congo Republic	26
144	Syria	26
144	Ukraine	26
150	Eritrea	25
150	Guinea-Bissau	25
150	Papua New Guinea	25
150	Paraguay	25
154	Guinea	24
154	Kyrgyzstan	24
156	Yemen	23
157	Angola	22
157	Cambodia	22
157	Tajikistan	22
160	Democratic Republic of the Congo	21
160	Laos	21
160	Libya	21
163	Equatorial Guinea	20
163	Zimbabwe	20
165	Burundi	19
165	Chad	19
165	Haiti	19
165	Venezuela	19
169	Iraq	18
170	Turkmenistan	17
170	Uzbekistan	17
172	Myanmar	15
173	Sudan	13
174	Afghanistan	8
174	Korea (North)	8
174	Somalia	8

INTERNATIONAL BUSINESS ETHICS Differences in ethical standards around the world divide nations on such issues as environmental protection, global warming, pollution, and moral behavior. What may be frowned upon or even illegal in one country is often customary or at least acceptable in others. China, for example, may use prison labor in producing products for export, but U.S. law prohibits their import. Similarly, low safety standards are too common in the sweatshops of Bangladesh, but they may outrage potential buyers of low-cost apparel in foreign markets. While other nations push for a moratorium on commercial whaling, Japan, Iceland, and Norway—whose people consider whaling a tradition and whale blubber a delicacy—have fought for exemptions from International Whaling Commission (IWC) rulings to allow them to kill and sell whales. In 2013, Australia, with the support of New Zealand, asked the International Court of Justice to withdraw all permits for future whale hunts from the Japanese fleet, disputing the Japanese exemption that their whaling is being conducted as "scientific research."[11] As a truly global example, cutting down the Brazilian rain forest may be acceptable to the government of Brazil, but scientists and consumers the world over vehemently object because it factors into climate changes and global warming.

When it comes to ethical issues like these, international managers have an opportunity to act as change agents, asserting leadership in implementing change. Keep in mind that not everything should be exploited for profit, even if such exploitation is legal in the country of operation. If they choose to adhere to ethical standards, firms not only benefit in the long term from consumer goodwill but avoid the possibility of later recrimination. It may well be that the concept of the "honorable merchant" will bear major fruit in international business in the future.

WORLD VIEW

The Honorable Merchant

As we have witnessed scandals, corruption, and inequities in international business, there have been growing calls for new thoughts on both education and training, as well as the maintenance of recognition for what business actions are right, which ones are wrong, and what basic protective considerations one should have about one's business partners. Not all that can be done should be done. It is also insufficient for the long term if one sees business relations strictly on a transaction basis. For educators, rather than running the risk of developing a reputation for the creation of greedy graduates without a moral compass, the conferment of a degree should signify not just the passing of courses but also the exposure to and acceptance of rules of virtue and honor.

Going even further, one can extend the perspective of responsibility beyond the manager and include the corporation as well. One can argue that because the corporation has all the rights and responsibilities of a citizen, it also has the moral responsibility to act in the best interest of society and society's future.

Of great help here is the historic concept of the "Honorable Merchant." The guidelines of the Honorable Merchant stem as far back as 1340, during the Middle Ages, in Italy where it was first spoken of the "truthful and honest merchant."[12] This model was also adapted by Germany.

In Germany, the Honorable Merchant stems from the Hanseatic merchants in Hamburg dating back to 1517 where the "Versammlung Eines Ehrbaren Kaufmanns zu Hamburg e.V. (VEEK)" was created (assembly of honorable merchants of Hamburg).[13] These rules prepared merchants on how to conduct business with other international parties and soon became ingrained into their regular proceedings.[14] Table 4.1 lists the key rules for the honorable merchant.

The core of these principles is centered on trust. Your word is a deal, your handshake the symbol of trust. Even if the handshake cannot be completed due to a deal constructed on paper or nowadays telephonically or online, this bond of trust is never broken. It solidifies the ethical code the merchants live by.[15]

The fall of the Hanseatic League and the end of the Thirty Years War (1618–48) crippled Germany's economy, and the merchant class lost its importance, yet the principles remained instilled with merchants.[16]

As global markets began to develop rapidly, the principles were replaced by a more laissez-faire way of conducting business. Profit maximization soon became the central goal of the firm, and new managers aimed to achieve this new goal regardless of the costs or whether it violated the guidelines of the honorable merchant.[17] Today may well be the opportunity to take the timeless principles of honor, trust, and collaboration of the "honorable merchant" and use them as an integral part, if not the foundation, of our teaching and learning.

TABLE 4.1 The Guiding Principles of the Honorable Merchant

The Honorable Merchant as a Person	The Honorable Merchant in His/Her Company	The Honorable Merchant in Society and the Economy
Commitment to value compliance	*Creating the conditions for honorable behavior*	*Comprehending and creating the framework for honorable behavior*
• The honorable merchant has a tolerant and liberal attitude. • The honorable merchant keeps his/her word with the handshake as a binding act. • The honorable merchant develops commercial judgment capabilities.	• The honorable merchant acts as a role model through all actions. • The honorable merchant promotes honorable behavior in his business. • The honorable merchant aims at long-term and sustainable business objectives.	• The honorable merchant heeds the principle of equity and good faith. • The honorable merchant recognizes and takes responsibility for the economic and social order. • The honorable merchant always advocates his values both in domestic and foreign trade.

SOURCE: **http://www.ihk-nuernberg.de/de/media/PDF/Zentrale-Dienste/ekaufmann**

HOST-COUNTRY PERSPECTIVE

The political and legal environment at work in the host country affects the conduct of international business in a variety of ways. To be effective, the international manager needs to work within the scope of local laws and policies, anticipating and planning for changes that may affect operations today and in the future.

Political Action and Risk

POLITICAL RISK
The risk of loss by an international corporation of assets, earning power, or managerial control as a result of political actions by the host country

OWNERSHIP RISK
The risk inherent in maintaining ownership of property

OPERATING RISK
The danger of interference by governments or other groups in one's corporate operations abroad

TRANSFER RISK
The danger of having one's ability to transfer profits or products in and out of a country inhibited by governmental rules and regulations

Ideally, business is best conducted in countries with stable and friendly governments. But this does not describe the reality of today's global business environment. Particularly in nations where government stability is in question, it is critical to monitor policies, practices, and current events that could adversely affect corporate operations.

Every nation faces **political risk**, but the range of risks varies widely from country to country. In general, political risk is highest in countries that do not have a history of stability and consistency. Even in countries that seem stable, however, popular movements arising from civil unrest have been known to sweep away ruling parties and cause major setbacks in the operation of business. There are three major types of political risk:

1. **Ownership risk.** Companies with foreign subsidiaries, for example, are exposed to the risk of losing properties. In some political situations, loss of life is also a serious possibility.
2. **Operating risk.** Any company dealing with partners in politically unstable environments risk interference or setbacks to ongoing operations, including loss of contracts or disruption of local manufacturing facilities.
3. **Transfer risk.** The difficulty of shifting funds from troubled countries leads to potential losses.

Firms can be exposed to political risk not only because of government actions but due to actions outside the control of governments. Figure 4.3 summarizes some of these risks.

FIGURE 4.3 Exposure to Political Risk

	Loss May Be the Result of:	
Contingencies May Include:	The actions of legitimate government authorities	Events caused by factors outside the control of government
The involuntary loss of control over specific assets without adequate compensation	• Total or partial expropriation • Forced divestiture • Cancellation or unfair calling of performance bonds	• War • Revolution • Terrorism • Strikes • Extortion
A reduction in the value of a stream of benefits expected from the foreign-controlled affiliate.	• Nonapplicability of "national treatment" • Restriction in access to financial, labor, or material markets • Currency and remittance restrictions • Value-added and export performance requirements	• Nationalistic buyers or suppliers • Threats and disruption to operations by hostile groups • Externally induced financial constraints • Externally imposed limits on imports or exports

SOURCE: José de la Torre and David H. Neckar, "Forecasting Political Risks for International Operations," in H. Vernon-Wortzel and L. Wortzel, *Global Strategic Management: The Essentials*, 2nd ed, p. 195. Copyright © 1990. This material is used by permission of John Wiley & Sons, Inc.

Fast Facts

What would happen if the Earth's polar ice caps were to melt, let's say as a result of extreme global warming?

If they melt, the average sea level would rise by about 60 feet, a catastrophe that would submerge half of the world's most populated areas.

Quick Take *Fake Foods Defy European Regulators*

Branded labels can be deceiving. In the economic downturn that affected much of the world since 2008, food counterfeiters expanded the range of fake products from luxury items to everyday consumer goods and food products. Often, organized criminal networks are involved, and some counterfeit brands are not only fake but dangerous. For instance, some foods may be tainted or contain high levels of dangerous ingredients like bleach, nitrates, and arsenic. In response, European governments have been increasing efforts to enforce intellectual property rights laws.

Police in England discovered a large-scale counterfeit spirits operation called Moscow Farms selling tens of thousands of liters of fake Glen's vodka across the country. The fake vodka was distributed in real vodka bottles with forged labels and duty stamps, but it was "spiked with bleach to lighten its color, and contained high levels of methanol, which in large doses can cause blindness." In one week in 2012, "French authorities seized 100 tons of fish, seafood, and frogs legs whose origin was incorrectly labeled; 1.2 tons of fake truffle shavings; 400 kilograms, or 1,100 pounds, of inedible pastries; false Parmesan cheese from America and Egypt; and liquor from a Dutch company marketed as tequila."

Have you ever purchased a fake designer apparel product? Is counterfeiting a victimless crime as some claim?

SOURCE: Stephen Castle and Doreen Carvajal, "Food fraud proliferates as byproduct of fiscal crisis," *International Herald Tribune*, June 27, 2013.

VIOLENCE AND CONFLICT Violence and conflict—often directed at overseas interests—pose the most dangerous of political risks to international businesses. Guerrilla warfare, civil disturbances, and terrorism all expose global corporations as potential targets. International terrorists have frequently targeted U.S. and European corporate facilities, operations, and personnel abroad. In 2013, more than three-dozen foreign hostages were killed by terrorists at the In Aménas gas plant in the Algerian Sahara desert in response to a French military intervention in Mali. The victims included ten Japanese and three Americans as well as other civilians from the United Kingdom, France, Romania, and other countries.[18]

PHOTO SOURCE: AP

Aménas gas plant attacked by terrorists in 2013

International terrorists have frequently targeted U.S. corporate facilities, operations, and personnel abroad. Since the September 11 attacks on the World Trade Center and the Pentagon, it is realistic to expect that future attacks can take place anywhere. American companies, which account for nine out of ten of the world's most powerful brands, have proven particularly vulnerable. Bombings, arson, hijacking, and sabotage, as well as extortion of funds through the kidnapping of business executives, are all a reality of international business. A cruel irony, however, is that many of the businesses on the receiving end of anti-Western attacks are locally owned franchises of global businesses. Therefore, the ones suffering most from such attacks are the local owners, managers, and employees. The horrors of 9/11 have shown the omnipresence of terrorism to the world. Given the symbolism attributed to the United States, U.S. firms have to be particularly aware of some of the risks incurred when doing business abroad.

Culture Clues Confucianism and the importance it places on status differences remain influential in South Korea. Acknowledging differences in rank and showing respect for symbols of authority are important to Koreans. Most foreign business executives are perceived as belonging to the upper-middle or higher class.

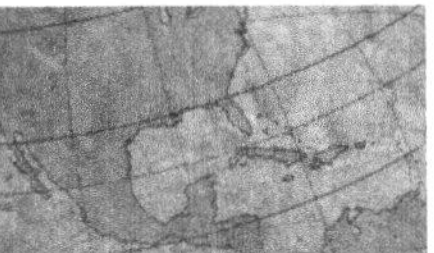

McDonald's franchises, both within and outside the United States, have been the targets of international terrorists around the world, from Canada to France to Moscow to Seattle.

In many countries, particularly in the developing world, coups d'état can result in drastic changes in government. The new government often will attack foreign firms as remnants of a Western-dominated colonial past, as has happened in Cuba, Nicaragua, and Iran. Even if such changes do not represent an immediate physical threat, they can lead to drastic policy changes that threaten the survival of foreign businesses in those regions. The past few decades have seen coups in Venezuela, Ghana, Ethiopia, Iran, Nigeria, and Egypt, for example, each of which seriously impeded the conduct of international business.

Not as drastic, but still worrisome, are changes in government policies that are not caused by changes in the government itself. These occur when, for one reason or another, a government feels pressured to change its policies toward foreign businesses. The pressure may be the result of nationalist or religious factions or widespread nationalist feeling. Consider, for instance, the problems that Japanese companies experienced in China in 2012–13 as a result of the dispute over ownership of the islands in the East China Sea known as the Senkaku in Japan and the Diaoyu in China. After Japan purchased several of the islands from a private Japanese owner, the Chinese government protested that the islands were Chinese territory. Following this, Chinese consumers organized a boycott of Japanese products and attacked some Japanese-owned retail stores. Also, Chinese firms began to steer orders away from Japanese component suppliers. Japanese automakers' share of the Chinese market slumped to 14 percent in November from about 23 percent before the dispute began, with Toyota and Nissan reporting steep declines.[19]

EXPROPRIATION, CONFISCATION, AND DOMESTICATION Less extreme than the risk of violence or conflict, political unrest can lead to changes that nevertheless damage business operations. Through **expropriation**, for example, a host government may transfer ownership of an international business to a domestic entity. In December 2012, Bolivian President Evo Morales announced the expropriation of four subsidiaries of the Spanish power company Iberdrola, accusing the companies of overcharging consumers in rural areas. Earlier that year, Bolivia expropriated Transportadora de Electricidad, a subsidiary of Red Eléctrica de España.[20]

EXPROPRIATION
The government takeover of a company with compensation frequently at a level lower than the investment value of the company's assets

CONFISCATION
The forceful government seizure of a company without compensation for the assets seized

DOMESTICATION
Government demand for partial transfer of ownership and management responsibility from a foreign company to local entities, with or without compensation

LOCAL CONTENT REGULATION
Regulation to gain control over foreign investment by ensuring that a large share of the product is locally produced or a larger share of the profit is retained in the country

Although compensation is paid under expropriation, the settlements are usually far from satisfactory to the foreign companies who have lost ownership. In recent years, the use of expropriation as a policy tool has declined sharply, suggesting that governments have come to recognize that the damage they inflict on themselves through expropriation exceeds the benefits they receive. When Canada signed the North American Free Trade Agreement, for example, one of the clauses exposed its government to lawsuits from foreign investors who objected to some of Canada's controversial environmental regulations, including bans on gasoline additives and restrictions on the cross-border trade of toxic waste. Objectors claimed that these constituted expropriations and unfairly restricted free trade.[21]

Similar to expropriation, **confiscation** also results in a transfer of ownership from the firm to the host country. It differs in that it does not involve compensation for the firm. Some industries are more vulnerable than others to confiscation and expropriation because of their importance to the host country's economy and their lack of ability to shift operations. For this reason, such sectors as mining, energy, public utilities, and banking have frequently been targets of such government actions.

More subtle in approach than either confiscation or expropriation but equally devastating for international businesses is the attempt to gain control over foreign investment through **domestication**. In these cases, the local government demands transfer of ownership and management responsibilities. It can impose **local content regulations** to ensure that a large share of the product is locally produced or demand that a larger share of profits is retained in the country. Changes in labor laws, patent protection, and tax regulations are also used for purposes of domestication.

Domestication can have profound effects on an international business operation for a number of reasons. If a firm is forced to hire nationals as managers, poor cooperation and communication can result. If domestication is imposed within a very short time span, corporate operations overseas may have to be headed by poorly trained and inexperienced local managers. Domestic content requirements may force a firm to purchase its supplies and parts locally, resulting in increased costs, decreased efficiency, and lower-quality products. Export requirements imposed on companies may create havoc for their international distribution plans and force them to change or even shut down operations in third countries.

INTELLECTUAL PROPERTY RIGHTS A potentially damaging outcome of local government action is the lack of enforcement or weakening of **intellectual property rights (IPR)**. Without protection, companies run the risk of losing their core competitive edge because domestic firms are able to imitate their products and offer them for sale at lower prices, often with lower performance. Of key concern is also the systematic exploitation of progress made by other firms or industries, often within the context of industrial espionage.[22]

INTELLECTUAL PROPERTY RIGHTS (IPR)
Legal right resulting from industrial, scientific, literary, or artistic activity

A World Trade Organization agreement sets minimum standards of protection to be provided for copyrights, trademarks, **geographical indications**, industrial designs, patents, layout designs of integrated circuits, and undisclosed information, such as trade secrets and test data.[23] Although not all-encompassing, these standards provide substantial assurances of protection that—after an implementation delay for the poorest countries—will apply to virtually all parts of the world.

GEOGRAPHICAL INDICATIONS
Place names (in some countries also words associated with a place) used to identify products that come from that place

Poor IPR legislation and enforcement in newly industrialized countries illustrate a clash between international business interests and developing nations' political and legal environments. In 2013, the Office of the United States Trade Representative designated Ukraine as a Priority Foreign Country (PFC), "a designation reserved by statute for countries with the most egregious IPR-related acts, policies and practices with the greatest adverse impact on relevant U.S. products, and that are not entering into good faith negotiations or making significant progress in negotiations to provide adequate and effective IPR protection." This was the first time in seven years that this designation was made for any country. Other countries that the United States designated for its "Priority Watch List" for IPR issues were Algeria, Argentina, Chile, China, India, Indonesia, Pakistan, Russia, Thailand, and Venezuela.[24] To counter accusations of IPR violations, newly industrialized countries argue that the laws discriminate against them because they impede the diffusion of technology and artificially inflate prices. Furthermore, although these nations are becoming increasingly aware that strong IPR protection will encourage technology transfer and foreign investment, their legislative structures often fail to keep pace with the needs of their rapidly transforming economies. For IPR to act as a catalyst for innovation rather than as a barrier to trade, developing nations need to be vigilant against new forms of piracy, particularly those that arise because of the Internet. Francis Gurry, the Director General of the World Intellectual Property Organization, stated in 2013 that "counterfeiting and piracy remain major problems worldwide, fuelled by socio-economic variables such as poverty, ambivalent consumer attitudes towards intellectual property rights, the involvement of criminal networks and easy-access to illegal goods, particularly through digital media. Despite solid legal and institutional frameworks, more needs to be done to achieve better compliance with the existing intellectual property systems, to ensure that these systems fulfill their role as a force for innovation and creativity. Building respect for intellectual property will underpin efforts in this regard."[25]

Culture Clues Russians are renowned for their negotiating ability. As related by an experienced international negotiator, they will stall for time if they do not think they can win. They are famous for unnerving negotiators by continuously delaying the proceedings and trying for a better deal.

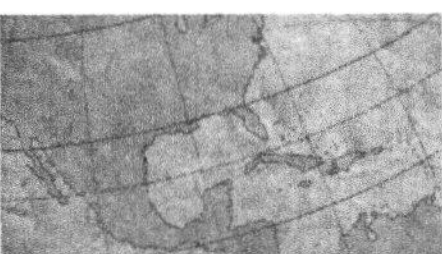

Economic Risk

Most businesses operating abroad face a number of other risks that are less dangerous but probably more common than those explored so far. A host government's political situation or desires may lead it to impose economic regulations or laws that restrict or control international business activities.

EXCHANGE CONTROLS
Controls on the movement of capital in and out of a country, sometimes imposed when the country faces a shortage of foreign currency

EXCHANGE CONTROLS Nations facing foreign currency shortages, for example, sometimes impose **exchange controls** that restrict the movement of capital into and out of the country, making it difficult to remove business profits from or make investments in the host country. Sometimes exchange controls are levied selectively against certain products or companies in an effort to reduce the importation of goods that are either sufficiently available through domestic production or that are considered to be luxuries and therefore not considered valid expenditure of foreign currency resources. Exchange controls often affect the importation of parts, components, or supplies that are vital to production operations in the country. They may force a firm either to alter its production program or shut down its entire plant.

Argentina introduced various exchange control measures in 2011–13 to reduce high capital outflows and improve central bank reserves. For example, Argentina imposed a 20 percent tax on credit- and debit-card purchases made abroad and on foreign shopping over the Internet. Taxes were also applied to purchases of tickets for international travel and package tours and to hotel and restaurant bills overseas. The Argentine central bank issued a list of acceptable reasons to justify foreign currency purchases and suspended all dollar purchases for any reason other than those on the list. Also, individuals were only allowed to buy a limited amount of dollars for foreign travel and overseas mortgage payments. Restrictions were also applied to ATM withdrawals for Argentines with peso-denominated accounts.[26]

TAX POLICY
A fiscal means by which countries may control foreign investors

TAX POLICY Countries may also use **tax policy** in their efforts both to invite foreign investment and to control multinational corporations and their capital. For example, Hong Kong cites low taxes as the number one reason why foreign companies have set up regional operations in its city. Beyond inviting investors, tax policies may raise much-needed revenue for the host country. However, tax increases can severely damage the operations of foreign investors. This damage, in turn, frequently results in decreased income for the host country in the long run. Raising tax rates needs to be carefully differentiated from increased tax scrutiny of foreign investors. Many governments believe that multinational firms may be tempted to shift tax burdens to lower-tax countries by using artificial pricing schemes between subsidiaries. In such cases, governments are likely to take measures to obtain their fair contribution from multinational operations.

PRICE CONTROL
Government regulation of the prices of goods and services; control of the prices of imported goods or services as a result of domestic political pressures

ANTI-DUMPING LAW
Legislation that allows the imposition of tariffs on foreign imports, designed to help domestic industries injured by unfair competition from abroad in cases where imported products are sold at less than fair market value

PRICE CONTROLS In many countries, domestic political pressures can force governments to control the prices of imported products or services, particularly in sectors considered highly sensitive from a political perspective, such as food or health care. A foreign firm involved in these areas is vulnerable to **price controls** because the government can play on citizens' nationalistic tendencies to enforce the controls. Particularly in countries that suffer from high inflation, frequent devaluations, or sharply rising costs, the international executive may be forced to choose between shutting down operations or continuing production at a loss in the hope of recouping profits when the government loosens or removes its price restrictions.

Price controls can also be administered to prevent prices from being too low. As explained in more detail in Chapter 3, governments have enacted **anti-dumping laws**, which prevent foreign competitors from pricing their imports unfairly low in order to drive domestic competitors out of the market. Because dumping charges depend heavily on the definition of "fair" price, a firm can sometimes become the target of accusations quite unexpectedly. Proving that no dumping took place can become quite onerous in terms of time, money, and information disclosure.

WORLD VIEW

Use of Secret Bank Accounts Can Be Risky Business

Governments tend to look for fairness and equity when looking for new sources of revenue. As a result of the financial crisis and recession, the United States, the United Kingdom, Germany, France, and other OECD nations began to pressure well known tax haven countries like Switzerland, Luxembourg, Austria, Hong Kong, Singapore, Andorra, Liechtenstein, and Monaco for information on secret bank accounts held in their banks and foundations. The United States, for example, wanted banks in these countries to pay fines and release the names of Americans who may be using secret accounts to evade taxes owed to the United States.

Some countries responded quickly to the pressure to adopt international bank information standards set by the OECD. In 2009, the Principality of Liechtenstein agreed to the new, more limited standards in bank secrecy, and Prime Minister Otmar Hasler stated: "We are aware of our responsibility as part of a globally integrated economic area. With today's declaration, we are making our contribution to a joint solution that will make an effective enforcement of foreign tax claims possible and takes account of the legitimate interests of the clients of our financial center at the same time." Later, Liechtenstein agreed to additional changes in an existing tax treaty with the United States, allowing U.S. authorities to access to more banking information.

Other countries, notably Switzerland where bank secrecy has been protected by law since the 1930s, resisted the pressure. Their perspective was that the nondisclosure of funds to a depositor's government did not represent a violation of Swiss law. Switzerland is the world's biggest offshore financial center and is home to global banks such as UBS and Credit Suisse as well as smaller, private banks. However, Swiss banks cut their own deals with the United States and other nations. In 2009, UBS agreed to a $780 million settlement with U.S. authorities to avoid an indictment. In 2012, Wegelin & Co., the oldest private Swiss bank, founded thirty-five years before the U.S. Declaration of Independence, pleaded guilty to conspiring to help hide more than $1.2 billion in secret accounts for more than 100 U.S. citizens. The bank, which paid $58 million to resolve the investigation, had to close its doors after 272 years. The U.S. Department of Justice is investigating more than a dozen banks including Credit Suisse, Julius Baer, and the Swiss arm of Britain's HSBC regarding the hiding of funds. The United States and Switzerland have been negotiating a tax treaty, similar to the agreement reached with Germany and the United Kingdom.

U.S. authorities have become more aggressive in searching for fraud cases involving more complex structures. For example, some accounts had multiple layers of secrecy: a bank account in Switzerland, which was held by a corporation in Panama or the British Virgin Islands, which in turn was owned by a Liechtenstein foundation, which was created by "fiduciaries," lawyers, accountants, financial advisers, and asset managers for U.S. clients.

How far can countries like Switzerland and Liechtenstein be pressed for banking information? What are the respective rights of tax authorities and banks in different sovereign countries? Banking secrecy has helped to build strong financial businesses and institutions, the future of which may now be threatened. Patrick Odier, chairman of the Swiss Bankers Association makes this case: "The U.S. must comprehend that a solution must be found within the existing Swiss legal framework...Bank secrecy protects assets; it doesn't hide them."

SOURCES: John Letzing, "U.S. Presses Liechtenstein on Tax Havens," *The Wall Street Journal* June 14, 2013; Matthew Saltmarch, "Tax Havens Likely to Be Target of G-20 Nations," *The New York Times*, March 12, 2009; Goran Mijuk and Anita Greil, "U.S. Pushes on Banks, Switzerland Pushes Back," *The Wall Street Journal*, September 6, 2011; *BBC News*, "Swiss Bank Wegelin to Close After US Tax Evasion Fine," January 4, 2013; Dylan Griffiths, "U.S. Seeks Answers in Liechtenstein on Tax Cheats," *Bloomberg*, March 25, 2013.

Managing Risk

Considering the many types of risks discussed so far, one might ask why companies choose to do business in risky markets. The answer lies in the connection between risk and reward. If the returns are high, risk becomes acceptable. The poorest and most war-torn of African nations, for example, pose extremely high levels of risk. In some, the risks are so great that firms tend to invest only in projects that promise quick returns. Yet, historically, average return on foreign direct investment in Africa has been higher than in any other region of the world. The World Bank reports that the continent has experienced an average growth rate of more than 5 percent during the past decade.[27] Chinese investment in Africa has been particularly aggressive as Chinese companies seek mineral resources and commodities to fuel domestic economic growth as well as African markets. This goes to show that along with risk comes opportunity—and along with opportunity come potentially rich rewards.

To make risk acceptable, companies that trade overseas can take various approaches to manage it. Obviously, in situations where a newly empowered government is dedicated to the removal of all foreign influences, there is little a firm can do. In less extreme cases, however, managers can take actions to reduce risk, provided they understand the root causes of the host country's policies.

Adverse governmental actions are usually the result of nationalism, the deterioration of political relations between home and host country, the desire for independence, or opposition to colonial remnants. If a host country's citizens feel exploited by foreign investors, government officials are more likely to take anti-foreign action. To reduce the risk of government intervention, the international firm needs to demonstrate that it is an integral part of the host country, rather than an exploitative foreign corporation. Achieving this involves intensive local hiring and training practices, better pay, contributions to charity, and investments that are both strategically important to the firm and societally useful. Chapter 6 explores this in more detail. In addition, the company can form joint ventures with local partners to demonstrate that it is willing to share its gains with nationals. Although such actions will not guarantee freedom from political risk, they will certainly lessen the exposure.

Close monitoring of political development also reduces vulnerability to political risk. Increasingly, private-sector firms offer monitoring assistance, permitting the overseas corporation to discover potential trouble spots as early as possible and to react quickly to prevent major losses.

Firms can take out insurance to cover losses due to political and economic risk. In Germany, for example, Hermes Kreditanstalt (**http://www.hermes.de**) offers insurance services to exporters. Its web site promises products adapted to the special requirements of every country it covers. In the United States, the Overseas Private Investment Corporation (OPIC) (**http://www.opic.gov**) covers three types of risk insurance: currency inconvertibility insurance, debt service, and other remittances from local currency into U.S. dollars; expropriation insurance, which covers the loss of an investment due to expropriation, nationalization, or confiscation by a foreign government; and political violence insurance, which covers the loss of assets or income due to war, revolution, insurrection, or politically motivated civil strife, terrorism, and sabotage. Usually policies do not cover commercial risks. Moreover, they cover only actual losses—not lost profits. In the event of a major political upheaval, however, risk insurance can be critical to a firm's survival.

The discussion to this point has focused primarily on the political environment. Laws have been mentioned only as they appear to be the direct result of political change. However, the laws of host countries need to be considered on their own to some extent, for the basic system of law is important to the conduct of international business.

Control Risks 2013 map of political and regional risks faced by businesses

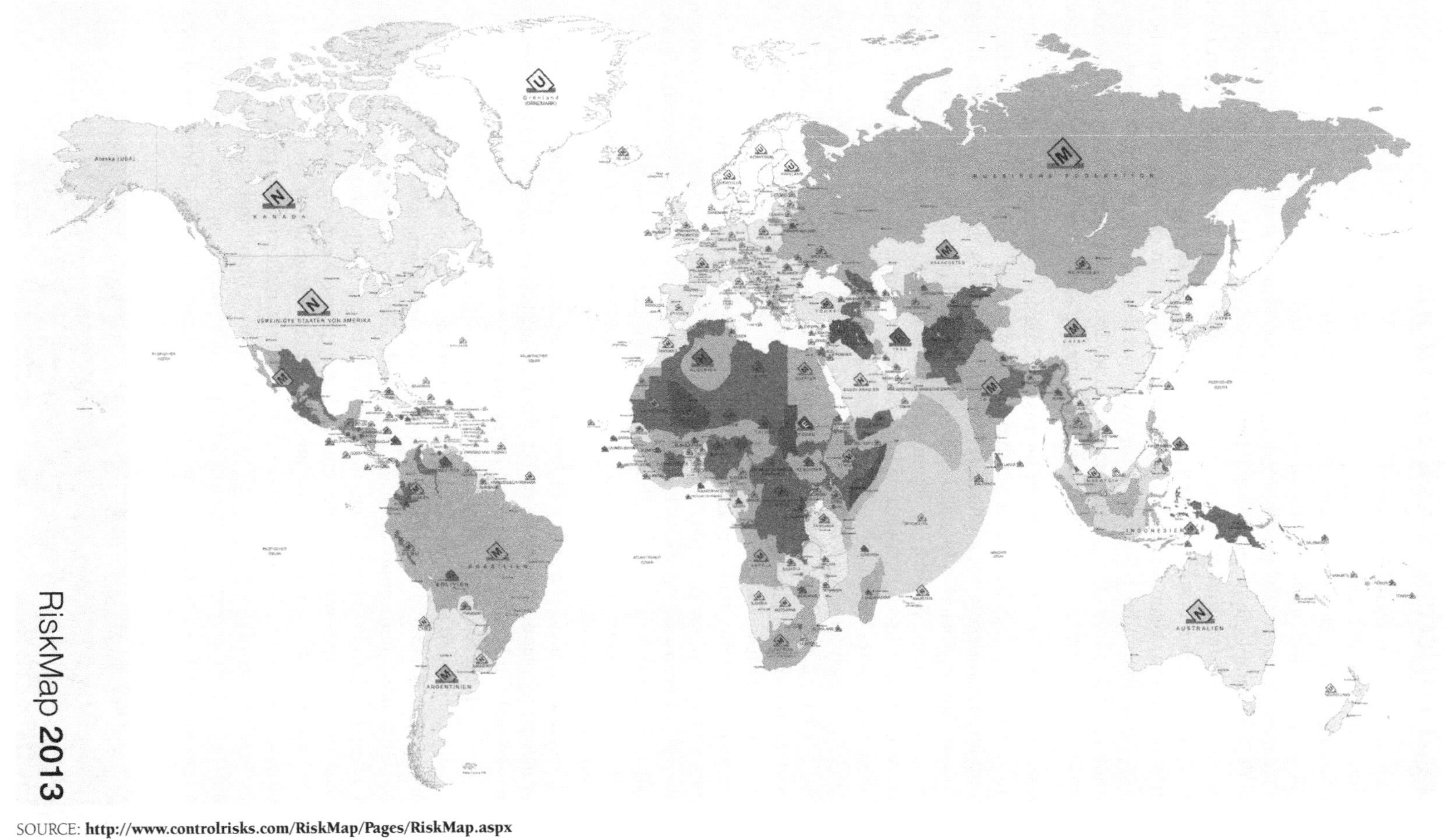

SOURCE: **http://www.controlrisks.com/RiskMap/Pages/RiskMap.aspx**

Legal Differences and Restraints

Countries differ in their laws as well as in their use of the law. Whereas in most Western cultures law is a function of society, in theocratic cultures, it is usually a mix of societal and spiritual guidance. Hebrew law and Islamic law (the Sharia) are the result of the dictates of God, scripture, and prophetic utterances and practices.

Yet even in nations where the legal systems are similar, attitudes toward the law differ greatly. For example, in recent decades, the United States has become an increasingly litigious society in which institutions and individuals are quick to initiate lawsuits. Court battles are often protracted and costly, and even the threat of a court case can reduce business opportunities. In contrast, Japan, with a fraction of the number of lawyers who practice in the United States, tends to minimize the role of the law. Japan has more than 4,500 people per lawyer, compared with 300 in the United States.[28] Litigation in Japan means that the parties have failed to compromise, which is contrary to Japanese tradition and results in loss of face.

COMMON LAW
Law based on tradition and depending less on written statutes and codes than on precedent and custom; used in the United States

CODE LAW
Law based on a comprehensive set of written statutes

BASIC SYSTEMS OF LAW From an international business perspective, the two major legal systems worldwide can be categorized into common law and code law. **Common law** is based on tradition and depends less on written statutes and codes than on precedent and custom. Common law originated in England and is the system of law in the United States. **Code law** is based on a comprehensive set of written statutes. Countries with code law try to spell out all possible legal rules explicitly. Code law is based on Roman law and is found in the majority of the nations of the world.

In general, common law tends to be less rigid than code law, but in practice, the difference does not have a major influence on international business. The reason is that many common-law countries, including the United States, have adopted commercial codes to govern the conduct of business.

Host-country laws that may affect the firm's ability to do business are many and various. Tariffs and quotas, for example, influence the entry of foreign goods. Some goods may require special licenses. Other laws restrict entrepreneurial activities. In Argentina, for example, pharmacies must be owned by pharmacists. Many European countries also limit sales of many nonprescription drugs, pharmacies, and drugstores, and sometimes require pharmacist involvement in the sale.[29]

Laws also regulate the ability of foreign enterprises to buy property on which to build manufacturing plants or overseas offices. Local regulations that have a major impact on the international firm's success are often overlooked—for example, a set of intricate regulations designed to protect local merchants used to hamper the opening of new department stores and supermarkets in Japan. The lack of large stores as conduits for the sale of imported consumer products severely restricted opportunities for market penetration of imported merchandise. Only after intense pressure from the outside did the Japanese government reconsider the regulations. India changed laws in 2012 to allow global multibrand retailers to enter the Indian market. However, the issue remains highly political and the law lacks clarity. Global firms have held off on investment because they are uncertain about many aspects of the law, including a clause that requires 30 percent of their manufactured or processed products be from small industries with less than $1 million in investment in factories and machinery.[30] Similarly, with the intent of protecting local products, seemingly innocuous laws in Switzerland decide what can be labeled as a "Swiss army knife." In 2013, China joined the United

Culture Clues Remember that every culture has its own holidays. Never schedule a business trip to Riyadh during Ramadan, to Rio during Carnival , or to Beijing during Chinese New Year. You may find that locals have other priorities.

Quick Take The Archbishop and the Law

Rowan Williams was the archbishop of Canterbury and the spiritual leader of the approximately 80 million-member global Anglican Church. He stirred up some controversy when he examined the role of Sharia in British life. Sharia is the body of Islamic religious law that is based on the Koran, the words and actions of the Prophet Mohammad, and the rulings of Islamic scholars. It typically finds its application mainly in Muslim countries.

The archbishop suggested that, with a population of more than 2 million Muslims in Great Britain, Sharia already figures prominently in the lives of many. For example, informal neighborhood councils provide rulings on family issues such as divorce, and banks, such as HSBC, already market mortgages that comply with Sharia rules of lending. Perhaps Muslims in Britain would be more comfortable and willing to build a more constructive relationship with their fellow citizens if they could choose Sharia law for the settling of civil disputes.

Many commentators, which included the former British Prime Minister Gordon Brown, strongly opposed such thinking. There was the feeling that such a move would undermine British values and laws and substantially weaken the position of women. Perhaps not since Thomas Becket ran afoul of King Henry II in 1170 was there such controversy surrounding the archbishop and the law.

SOURCES: Karla Adam, "Archbishop Defends Remarks on Islamic Law in Britain," *The Washington Post*, February 12, 2008, p. A11; "Archbishop of Canterbury: Sharia Law Unavoidable in Britain," *Christian Today*, February 7, 2008; Matthew Lynn, "Archbishop Williams Is Wrong to Back Sharia Law," **Bloomberg.com**, February 28, 2008.

States and other countries in officially recognizing "Champagne" as a protected geographical indication and has agreed to allow the name only to be used to describe sparkling wine from the Champagne region of France.[31]

Often, laws are specifically designed to protect domestic industries by reducing imports. For example, even after its WTO accession, Russia continues to impose high customs charges and fees as well as valuation procedures that result in artificially high total tariffs. Russia also has "burdensome" licensing, registration, and certification requirements.[32]

Specific legislation may regulate what does and does not constitute deceptive advertising. Many countries prohibit claims that compare products to the competition, or they restrict the use of promotional devices. Even when no laws exist, regulations may hamper business operations. For example, in some countries, firms are required to join the local chamber of commerce or become a member of the national trade association. These institutions in turn may have internal sets of rules that specify standards for the conduct of business.

Fast Facts

One of the smallest nations in the world is also the oldest country in Europe and the oldest republic in the world. Most of its citizens earn their living making and selling postage stamps. Name it.

San Marino, on the slopes of the Apennines, entirely within Italy, has been an independent republic since 1631. It covers 24 square miles.

Influencing Politics and Laws

Many areas of politics and law are not immutable. Viewpoints can be modified or even reversed, and new laws can supersede old ones. To achieve change, however, some impetus for it—such as the clamors of a constituency—must occur.

The international manager has various options. One high-risk option is to simply ignore prevailing rules and expect to get away with doing so. A second option is to provide input to trade negotiators and expect any problem areas to be resolved in multilateral negotiations. The drawbacks are that this is a time-consuming process, and issues remain outside the control of the firm.

A third option involves the development of coalitions and constituencies that can motivate legislators and politicians to implement change. Even simple changes, such as the way key terms are defined, can positively influence the business environment. Consider, for example, the change in terminology used in the United States to describe trade relations between two nations. For years, attempts to normalize relations with China by granting "most-favored nation" (MFN) status drew the ire of objectors who questioned why China deserved to be treated in a "most-favored" way. Lost in the debate was the fact that the term "most-favored nation" was taken from WTO terminology and indicated only that China would be treated like any other nation for the purposes of trade. When the term was changed to "normal trade relations," tensions eased.

Beyond the recasting of definitions, firms can effect change in other ways. A manager may, for example, explain the employment and economic effects of certain laws and regulations and demonstrate the benefits of change. The firm might also enlist the help of local suppliers, customers, and distributors to influence decision makers. The public at large can even be involved through public statements or advertisements. Developing coalitions is no easy task. Companies often turn to **lobbyists** for help, particularly when addressing narrow economic objectives or single-issue campaigns. Lobbyists are usually well-connected individuals and firms who can provide access to policymakers and legislators in order to communicate new and pertinent information. Brazilian citrus exporters and computer manufacturers, for example, use U.S. legal and public relations firms to provide them with information about relevant U.S. legislative activity. The Banco do Brasil has used lobbyists to successfully restructure Brazilian debt and establish U.S. banking regulations favorable to Brazil.

LOBBYISTS
Well-connected individuals or firms who can provide access to policymakers and legislators to communicate new and pertinent information

Although representation of the firm's interests to government decision makers and legislators is entirely appropriate, the international manager must also consider any potential side effects. Major questions can be raised if such representation becomes very overt. Short-term gains may be far outweighed by long-term negative repercussions if the international firm is perceived as exerting too much political influence.

International Relations and Laws

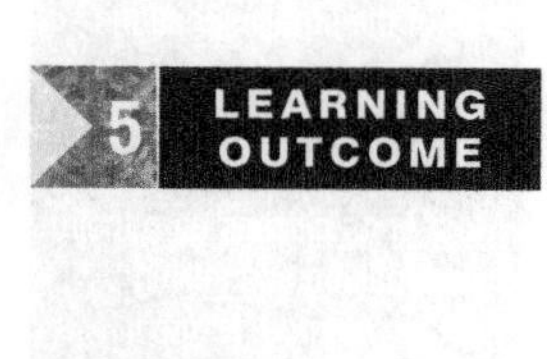

In addition to understanding the politics and laws of both home and host countries, the international manager must consider the overall international political and legal environment. This is important because policies and events occurring among countries can have a profound impact on firms trying to do business internationally.

International Politics

The effect of politics on international business is determined by both the **bilateral agreements** between home and host countries and by **multilateral agreements** governing relations among groups of countries.

BILATERAL AGREEMENT
Agreement or treaty between two nations focusing only on their interests

MULTILATERAL AGREEMENT
Trade agreement or treaty among more than two parties; the intricate relationships among trading countries

The government-to-government relationship can have a profound influence in a number of ways, particularly if it becomes hostile. For example, political tensions in the bilateral U.S.-China relationship, due to China's increased naval presence in the South China Sea, conflicts with Japan in the East China Sea. China's large bilateral trade surplus, renewed currency manipulation, and violations of intellectual property rights, could potentially jeopardize the interests of U.S. companies in that country. International political relations do not always have harmful effects. If bilateral political relations between countries improve, business can benefit. One example is the improvement in Western relations with Central Europe, Ukraine, Georgia, and Central Asia following the official end of the Cold War. The political warming opened the potentially lucrative former Eastern bloc markets to Western firms.

The overall international political environment has effects, whether good or bad, on international business. For this reason, the good manager will strive to remain aware of political currents and relations worldwide and attempt to anticipate and plan for changes.

International Law

International law plays an important role in the conduct of international business. Although no enforceable body of international law exists, certain treaties and agreements are respected by a number of countries and profoundly influence international business operations. For example, the World Trade Organization (WTO) defines internationally acceptable economic practices for its member nations. Although it does not directly deal with individual firms, it does affect them indirectly by providing some predictability in the international environment.

INTERNATIONAL LAW

The body of rules governing relationships between sovereign states; also certain treaties and agreements respected by a number of countries

The Patent Cooperation Treaty (PCT) provides procedures for filing one international application designating countries in which a patent is sought, which has the same effect as filing national applications in each of those countries. Similarly, the European Patent Office examines applications and issues national patents in any of its member countries. Other regional offices include the African Industrial Property Office (ARIPO), the French-speaking African Intellectual Property Organization (OAPI), and an office in Saudi Arabia for six countries in the Gulf region.

International organizations, such as the United Nations (UN) and the Organization for Economic Cooperation and Development (OECD), provide multilateral agreements that affect international business. These codes and guidelines, such as the UN Code of Conduct for Transnational Corporations, are general in scope. They can also be very specific, such as the Code on International Marketing of Breast-milk Substitutes, developed by the World Health Organization. Even though there are thirty-four such codes in existence, the lack of enforcement ability hampers their full implementation.

In addition to multilateral agreements, firms are affected by bilateral treaties and conventions between the countries in which they do business. For example, a number of countries have signed bilateral Treaties of Friendship, Commerce, and Navigation (FCN). The agreements generally define the rights of firms doing business in the host country. They normally guarantee that firms will be treated by the host country in the same manner in which domestic firms are treated. Although these treaties provide for some sort of stability, they can also be canceled if relations worsen.

The international legal environment also affects the manager to the extent that firms must concern themselves with jurisdictional disputes. Because no single body of international law exists, firms usually are restricted by both home- and host-country laws. If a conflict occurs between contracting parties in two different countries, a question arises concerning which country's laws are to be used and in which court the dispute is to be settled. Sometimes the contract will contain a jurisdictional clause that settles the matter with little problem. If the contract does not contain such a clause, however, the parties to the dispute have a few choices. They can settle the dispute by following the laws of the country in which the agreement was made, or they can resolve it by obeying the laws of the country in which the contract will have to be fulfilled. Which laws to use and in which location to settle the dispute are two different decisions. As a result, a dispute between a U.S. exporter and a French importer could be resolved in Paris but be based on New York State law. The importance of such provisions was highlighted by the lengthy jurisdictional disputes surrounding a 1984 gas leak at a Union Carbide chemical factory in Bhopal, India, which killed thousands and injured thousands more. Union Carbide sold the factory in 1994 and Dow Chemical completed its merger with Union Carbide in 2001. Yet, thirty years later, litigation in the case continues.

LITIGATION

To resolve disagreements and conflicts by the use of the judicial system

In cases of disagreement, the parties can choose either litigation or arbitration. **Litigation**, which is to resolve disagreements and conflicts by use of the judicial system, is usually

ARBITRATION
The procedure for settling a dispute in which an objective third party hears both sides and makes a decision; a procedure for resolving conflict in the international business arena through the use of intermediaries such as representatives of chambers of commerce, trade associations, or third country institutions

avoided for several reasons, but particularly because it often involves extensive delays and can be costly. In addition, firms may fear discrimination in foreign countries. **Arbitration** generally brings quicker, less costly results. The procedures are often spelled out in the original contract and usually provide for an intermediary who is judged to be impartial by both parties.

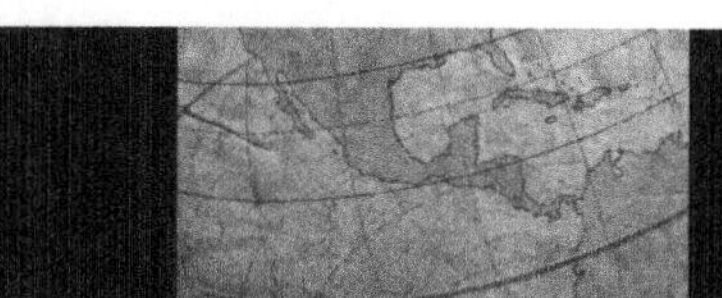

SUMMARY

The political and legal environment in the home and host countries and the laws and agreements governing relationships among nations are important to the international business executive. Compliance is mandatory in order to successfully do business abroad. To avoid the problems that can result from changes in the political and legal environment, it is essential to anticipate changes and to develop strategies for coping with them. Whenever possible, the manager must avoid being taken by surprise and letting events control business decisions.

Governments affect international business through legislation and regulations, which can support or hinder business transactions. Export sanctions, embargoes, and export controls are used both to preserve national security and improve economic conditions for domestic firms.

Governments regulate the conduct of international firms through means such as boycotts that limit its trade partners. Other methods of regulation include setting standards related to bribery and corruption and laws governing the restraint of competition. The firm's and the individual's ethical codes and beliefs influence the conduct of business overseas.

Political instability as well as government actions such as expropriation, confiscation, or domestication expose firms to international risk. In the event of a loss, firms may rely on insurance for political risk, or they may seek redress in court.

Different countries have different laws. One clearly pronounced difference is between code-law countries, where all possible legal rules are spelled out, and common-law countries such as the United States, where the law is based on tradition, precedent, and custom.

International political relations, agreements, and treaties influence international business. Arbitration, rather than litigation, is often the quickest and most effective way to resolve disagreements.

Key Terms And Concepts

sanction
embargo
export-control system
dual-use item
export license
critical commodities list
deemed export
boycott
antitrust laws
political risk
ownership risk
operating risk
transfer risk
expropriation
confiscation
domestication
local content regulation
intellectual property rights (IPR)
geographical indications
exchange controls
tax policy
price control
anti-dumping law
common law
code law
lobbyists
bilateral agreement
multilateral agreement
international law
litigation
arbitration

Review Questions

1. What are the differences between embargoes and sanctions? Give an example of each.
2. What types of products or services are typically not granted export licenses? Why are they prohibited?
3. What happens in a boycott? Are boycotts effective?
4. Describe the three types of political risk.
5. What are the differences between expropriation, confiscation, and domestication? How might each be applied?
6. What is the purpose of anti-dumping laws?
7. What is the difference between common law and code law?
8. What is arbitration? When and why is it useful?
9. Where should government draw the line between legitimate monitoring of important communications and the entitlement to privacy?
10. Is the honorable merchant simply a dated concept from the past, or can we build relationships based on this concept?

Critical Skill Builders

1. Discuss this potential dilemma: "High political risk requires companies to seek a quick payback on their investments. Striving for a quick payback, however, exposes firms to charges of exploitation and results in increased political risk."
2. In teams, debate this statement: "The national security that our export control laws seek to protect may be threatened by the resulting lack of international competitiveness of our nation's firms."
3. Discuss the advantages and disadvantages of common law and code law.
4. The United States has been described as a litigious society. How does frequent litigation affect international business?
5. After you hand your passport to the immigration officer in country X, he misplaces it. A small "donation" would certainly help him find it again. Should you give him the money? Is this a business expense to be charged to your company? Should it be tax deductible? Many business executives believe that a nation has no right to apply its moral principles to other societies and cultures. Do you agree?

On the Web

1. What are some of the countries suspected of nuclear proliferation? What types of exports might be barred from going to these countries? If your product is classified as a dual-use item, how would you go about obtaining a export license? What are some of the penalties that the U.S. government can impose on noncompliant exporters? See **http://www.bis.doc.gov**.

2. According to the anticorruption monitoring organization Transparency International, which countries have the highest levels of corruption? Which have the lowest levels? Use the Corruption Perceptions Index found at **http://www.transparency.org** to form your conclusions. What problems might an exporter have in doing business in a country with high levels of corruption?

3. The United States and European Union have reached some agreements on the use of geographical indications. Referring to **http://www.uspto.gov/ip/global/geographical/** and **http://ec.europa.eu/trade/policy/accessing-markets/intellectual-property/geographical-indications/**, answer these questions: (a) Can a Chilean wine maker produce "champagne"? (b) Can an American cheesemaker produce Cheddar? (c) Can a Kenyan diary produce Swiss cheese?

Endnotes

1. European Commission, **http://Ec.Europa.Eu/Environment/Chemicals/Reach/Reach_Intro.Htm**, accessed July 4, 2013.
2. Sonia Shah, "Body Hunting: The Outsourcing of Drug Trials," *The Globalist*, January 31, 2007.
3. Philippe Dollinger, *The German Hansa* (Stanford, CA: Stanford University Press, 1970), 49.
4. Daniel Hanson, Dayne Batten, and Harrison Ealey, "It's Time for the U.S.to End Its Senseless Embargo of Cuba," *Forbes*, January 16, 2013.
5. Toni Johnson and Robert McMahon, "The Lengthening List of Iran Sanctions," Council on Foreign Relations, June 6, 2013, **http://www.Cfr.Org/Iran/Lengthening-List-Iran-Sanctions/P20258**, accessed June 28, 2013.
6. "Weighing Benefits and Costs of International Sanctions Against Iran," The Iran Project, Released December 3, 2012, **http://www.bakerinstitute.org/News/Benefits-And-Costs-Of-Sanctions-Against-Iran**, accessed June 28, 2013.
7. Carol Matlack and Stephanie Bodoni, "Google's EU Antitrust Proposal Will Likely Be Tweaked," *Bloomberg Business Week*, April 15, 2013.
8. Gibson Dunn, "2013 Antitrust Merger Enforcement Update and Outlook," March 21, 2013, **http://www.gibsondunn.com/publications/pages/2013-Antitrust-Merger-Enforcement-Update-Outlook.aspx**, accessed June 28, 2013.
9. Edward Luce, Book review: "India Grows at Night: A Liberal Case for a Strong State" by Gurcharan Das, *Gulf Times*, February 21, 2013.
10. OECD, **http://www.oecd.org/daf/anti-bribery/antibriberyconventionratification.pdf**, accessed June 30, 2013.
11. Justin McCurry, "Australia censures Japan for 'scientific' whaling," *The Guardian*, June 26, 2013.
12. Translated from: **http://www2.uni-frankfurt.de/43516904/Ehrbarer_Kaufmann.pdf**. Gerd Kixmoeller, Thesis: Der ehrbare Kaufmann: Was haben Leitbilder von Berufsgruppen mit dem Mythos zu tun und in wiefern haben sie in der heutigen Realität Bestand? Johann Wolfgang Goethe Universitaet, March 17, 2010, accessed March 14, 2014.
13. Translated from: **http://www.veek-hamburg.de/veek/geschichte**, accessed March 14, 2014.
14. Summarized and translated from: **http://www.der-ehrbare-kaufmann.de/fileadmin/Gemeinsame_Dateien/der-ehrbare-kaufmann.de/PDFs/Leitbild_2009_VEEK.pdf**. accessed March 14, 2014.
15. Ibid.
16. Translated from: **http://www2.uni-frankfurt.de/43516904/Ehrbarer_Kaufmann.pdf**, accessed March 14, 2014.
17. Ibid.
18. Angelique Chrisafis, Julian Borger, Justin McCurry, and Terry Macalister, "Algeria hostage crisis: the full story of the kidnapping in the desert," *The Guardian*, January 25, 2013.
19. "China-Japan Dispute Takes Rising Toll on Top Asian Economies," *Bloomberg News*, January 9, 2013.
20. Mabel Azcui and Ramón Muñoz, "Bolivia announces expropriation of four Iberdrola subsidiaries," El País, December 30, 2012.
21. Charles H. Brower, II. "Structure, legitimacy, and NAFTA's investment chapter," *The Free Library*, January 01,2003; and **http://www.thefreelibrary.com/Structure, legitimacy, and NAFTA's investment chapter.-a099555207**, accessed March 17, 2014.
22. Keith Maskus, "Private Rights and Public Problems: The Global Economics of Intellectual Property in the 21st Century," September 2012, Peterson Institute for International Economics, Washington D.C.

23. See Trade Related Aspects of International Property Rights (TRIPS), **http://www.wto.org**.
24. 2013 Special 301 Report, Office of the United States Trade Representative, **http://www.ustr.gov/sites/default/files/05012013 2013 Special 301 Report.pdf**, accessed June 30, 2013.
25. "Seventh Global Congress on Combating Counterfeiting and Piracy Opens in Istanbul," World Intellectual Property Organization, press release, April 24, 2013, **http://www.wipo.int/pressroom/en/articles/2013/article_0010.html**
26. Eliana Raszewski, "Argentine President Tightens Foreign Exchange Controls: Timeline," **www.bloomberg.com**, March 20, 2013.
27. The Africa Competitiveness Report 2013, The World Bank, **http://www.afdb.org/fileadmin/uploads/afdb/Documents/Publications/The Africa Competitiveness Report 2013.pdf**, accessed 7/2/13.
28. Hiroki Ogawa, "Japan's Creaking Legal System," *The Diplomat*, April 22, 2011.
29. United States Government Accountability Office, "Nonprescription Drugs: Considerations Regarding a Behind-the-Counter Drug Class," February 2009. Washington D.C., REPORT, GAO-09-245: Published: Feb 20, 2009. Publicly Released: Mar 23, 2009, **www.GAO.gov**, accessed March 17, 2014.
30. Adi Narayan and Siddharth Philip, "India Tries to Clarify Multi-Brand Retail FDI Investment Rules," *Bloomberg News*, June 6, 2013.
31. Lucy Shaw, "China officially recognizes Champagne," *The Drinks Business*, May 13, 2013.
32. 2012 National Trade Estimate Report on Foreign Trade Barriers, Office of the United States Trade Representative, **http://www.ustr.gov/sites/default/files/Russia_0.pdf**, accessed July 2, 2013.

CHAPTER 5

ECONOMIC INTEGRATION AND EMERGING MARKETS

Worldwide Free Trade

As businesses have become increasingly dependent on exports and overseas trade, regional groupings based on economics rather than geography alone have gained in importance. Blocs are joining bigger blocs as in the case of the Asia Pacific Economic Cooperation, which brings partners together from multiple continents (including NAFTA and individual countries such as Australia, China, Japan, and Russia). The United States, Canada, Japan, and Mexico expressed interest in joining twelve countries (Australia, Brunei, Chile, Malaysia, New Zealand, Peru, Singapore, and Vietnam) in discussing a free-trade pact. Altogether, the possible members of the Trans-Pacific Partnership (TPP) produce 40 percent of world GDP—far more than the European Union. Europe and the United States are set to launch trade talks to deepen the world's largest trading relationship. With an impasse in the Doha Round of WTO negotiations, more countries are turning to bilateral agreements with 205 of them in effect.

Companies are facing ever-intensifying competition within these blocs but, at the same time, can take advantage of emerging opportunities. As new countries join blocs, fears that these blocs are nothing but protectionism on a grander scale are allayed. As governments liberalize their industrial sectors and allow for competition, they give birth to companies that are not only in competition regionally, but globally as well. A deal would be the most ambitious in a new generation of sophisticated agreements that go beyond tariffs to take in intellectual property rights, services, and regulation.

Eliminating barriers in the automotive sector, which makes up the largest chunk of EU-U.S. trade, could bring a 15 percent fall in costs for both sides. "It would be very useful for us," says Sergio Marchionne, chief executive of Fiat and Chrysler, indicating the deal could make it easier to exchange car components across the Atlantic. Businesses on both sides would like an agreement in which a car tested for safety in the United States would not have to be tested again in Europe. But both sides appear likely to leave much of the highly sensitive agricultural sector out of the agreement altogether.

LEARNING OUTCOMES

1. *To review types of economic integration among countries*
2. *To examine the costs and benefits of integrative arrangements*
3. *To suggest corporate response to advancing economic integration*
4. *To survey the vast opportunities for trade offered by emerging market economies*
5. *To illustrate growth in developing countries by encouraging potential markets*
6. *To consider the strategic challenges that economic integration presents for global managers*

As You Read This Chapter

1. What happens when the interests of one trading bloc conflict with those of another?
2. Should firms be able to trade with whomever they choose, regardless of the bloc potential customers belong to?

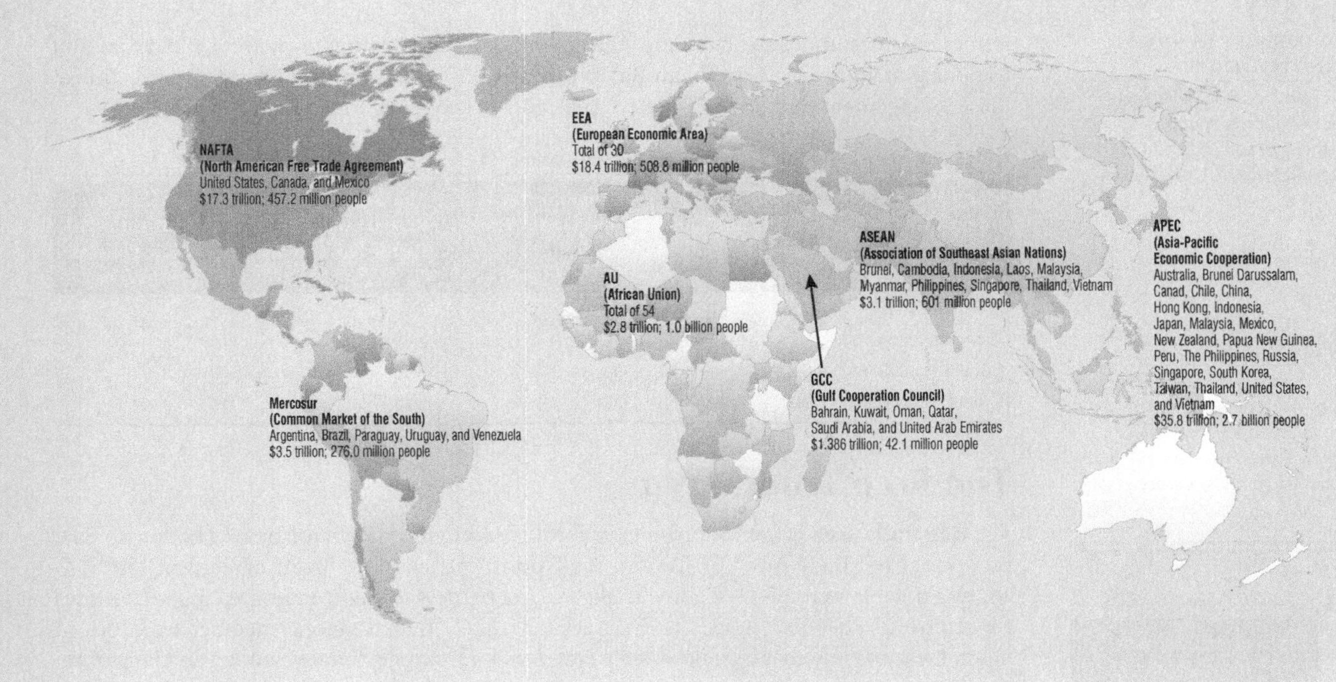

The benefits of free trade are available only if nation-states are willing to give up some measure of independence and autonomy. Agreements among countries to establish links through movement of goods, services, capital, and labor across borders have resulted in increased economic integration. Some predict, however, that the regional **trading blocs** of the new economic world order will allow the rise of a handful of protectionist super-states that, although liberalizing trade among members, may raise barriers to external trade.

Economic integration is best viewed as a spectrum. At one extreme we might envision a truly global economy in which all countries share a common currency and agree to a free flow of goods, services, and **factors of production**. At the other extreme would be a number of closed economies, each independent and self-sufficient. The various integrative agreements in effect today lie along the middle of this spectrum and are the subject of this chapter.[1]

TRADING BLOC
Formed by agreements among countries to establish links through movement of goods, services, capital, and labor across borders

FACTORS OF PRODUCTION
All inputs into the production process, including capital, labor, land, and technology

 LEVELS OF ECONOMIC INTEGRATION

Success of these blocs, from their establishment to future expansion institutionally and geographically, will depend (1) on leadership of selected countries (i.e., every bloc needs an "engine"); (2) their proximity in terms of geography, culture, administrative dimensions, and basis economic factors; and (3) their commitment to regional cooperation. For example, the biggest trading partners for any of the European Union member nations are other EU countries. Countries that have traditionally not traded with each other or have relations driven by animosities (e.g., in the South Asian Association for Regional Cooperation, SAARC) have a more challenging time in implementing economic integration.

It should be noted that countries (or groups of countries) may give preferential treatment to other countries on the basis of historic ties or due to political motivations. Examples include the European Union's granting preferential access for selected products from their

CARIBBEAN BASIN INITIATIVE (CBI)
Extended trade preferences to Caribbean countries and grants of special access to the markets of the United States

former colonies under the Cotonou Agreement, or similar treatment by the United States of Caribbean nations (the **Caribbean Basin Initiative**). Because the benefits are unidirectional, these arrangements are not considered to be part of economic integration.

TABLE 5.1 Forms of International Economic Integration

Stage of Integration	Abolition of Tariffs and Quotas Among Members	Common Tariff and Quota System	Abolition of Restrictions on Factor Movements	Harmonization and Unification of Economic Policies and Institutions
Free trade area	Yes	No	No	No
Customs union	Yes	Yes	No	No
Common market	Yes	Yes	Yes	No
Economic union	Yes	Yes	Yes	Yes

FREE TRADE AREA
An area in which all barriers to trade among member countries are removed, although sometimes only for certain goods or services

The Free Trade Area

The **free trade area** is the least restrictive form of economic integration among countries. The European Free Trade Area (EFTA) and the North American Free Trade Agreement (NAFTA) are two notable examples. In a free trade area, all barriers to trade among member countries are removed. Therefore, goods and services are freely traded among member countries in much the same way that they flow freely between, for example, South Carolina and New York. No discriminatory taxes, quotas, tariffs, or other trade barriers are allowed. Sometimes a free trade area is formed only for certain classes of goods and services. An agricultural free trade area, for example, implies the absence of restrictions on the trade of agricultural products only. The most notable feature of a free trade area is that each country continues to set its own policies in relation to nonmembers. In other words, each member is free to set any tariffs, quotas, or other restrictions that it chooses on trade with countries outside the free trade area. Members are also able to exempt other nations or groups of nations from such restrictions. NAFTA member Mexico, for instance, has a number of bilateral free trade agreements with other blocs (the European Union) and nations (Chile) to improve trade and to attract foreign direct investment.

The United States has free trade agreements in force with twenty countries: Australia, Bahrain, Canada, Chile, Colombia, Costa Rica, Dominican Republic, El Salvador, Guatemala, Honduras, Israel, Jordan, Korea, Mexico, Morocco, Nicaragua, Oman, Panama, Peru, and Singapore.[2]

Fast Facts

The European Union is the main market in the world for bananas, constituting 33.3 percent of all trade. Where are they from?

Seventy-two percent of bananas sold in Europe came from Latin America, 17 percent from African, Caribbean, and Pacific Group of States (ACP) countries and 10.5 percent from the European Union (e.g., Guadeloupe and Martinique, and Canary Islands).

CUSTOMS UNION
Collaboration among trading countries in which members dismantle barriers to trade in goods and services and also establish a common trade policy with respect to nonmembers

The Customs Union

The **customs union** is one step further along the spectrum of economic integration. Like members of a free trade area, members of a customs union dismantle barriers to trade in goods and services among themselves. In addition, the customs union establishes a common trade policy with respect to nonmembers. Typically, this takes the form of a common external tariff; imports from nonmembers are subject to the same tariff when sold to any member country.

Tariff revenues are then shared among members according to a prespecified formula. The Southern African Customs Union is the oldest and most successful example of economic integration in Africa.

COMMON MARKET
A group of countries that agree to remove all barriers to trade among members, to establish a common trade policy with respect to nonmembers, and also to allow mobility for factors of production—labor, capital, and technology

The Common Market

Still further along the spectrum of economic integration is the **common market**. Like the customs union, a common market has no barriers to trade among members and has a common external trade policy. In addition, factors of production are mobile among members. Factors of production include labor, capital, and technology. Thus restrictions on immigration, emigration, and cross-border investment are abolished. The importance of **factor mobility** for economic growth cannot be overstated. When factors of production are freely mobile, then capital, labor, and technology may be employed most productively. To see the importance of factor mobility, imagine the state of the U.S. economy if unemployed workers in Massena, New York, were prevented from migrating to the growing West Point, Georgia, in search of better opportunities.

Despite the obvious benefits, members of a common market must be prepared to cooperate closely in monetary, fiscal, and employment policies. Further, while a common market will enhance the productivity of members in the aggregate, it is by no means clear that individual member countries always benefit. Because of these difficulties, the goals of common markets have proved to be elusive in many areas of the world, notably South America and Asia. The Association of Southeast Asian Nations (ASEAN) hopes to organize its ten members into a single market and production base that is highly competitive and fully integrated into the global community by 2015. For example, procedures for trading are relatively easy to complete in Singapore, Thailand, and Malaysia but very difficult in Laos and Cambodia.

FACTOR MOBILITY

The ability to freely move factors of production across borders, as among common market countries

ECONOMIC UNION

A union among trading countries that has the characteristics of a common market and also harmonizes monetary policies, taxation, and government spending and uses a common currency

MAASTRICHT TREATY

A treaty, agreed to in Maastricht, the Netherlands, in 1991, but not signed until 1993, in which European community members agreed to a specific timetable and set of necessary conditions to create a single currency for the EU countries

ECONOMIC AND MONETARY UNION (EMU)

Umbrella term for the group of polices aimed at converging the economics of all EU states

POLITICAL UNION

A group of countries that have common foreign policy and security policy and that share judicial cooperation

The Economic Union

The creation of a true **economic union** requires integration of economic policies in addition to the free movement of goods, services, and factors of production across borders. Under an economic union, members would harmonize monetary policies, taxation, and government spending. In addition, a common currency would be used by all members. This could be accomplished de facto, or in effect by a system of fixed exchange rates. Clearly, the formation of an economic union requires nations to surrender a large measure of their national sovereignty to supranational authorities in community-wide institutions such as the European Parliament.

The ratification of the **Maastricht Treaty** by all member countries created the European Union, effective January 1, 1994. The treaty (jointly with the Treaty of Amsterdam, 1999, and the Nice Treaty, 2001) set the foundation for **economic and monetary union (EMU)** with the establishment of the euro (€) as the common currency. In addition, the treaties set the foundation for moves toward a **political union** with common foreign and security policies, as well as judicial cooperation. The Lisbon Treaty (2009) attempts to streamline EU institutions to make the enlarged bloc function better.[3]

COSTS AND BENEFITS OF ECONOMIC INTEGRATION

A number of arguments are made both for and against economic integration. The arguments center on (1) trade creation and diversion; (2) the effects of integration on import prices, competition, economies of scale, and factor productivity; and (3) the benefits of regionalism versus nationalism.[4]

Trade Creation and Trade Diversion

When trade barriers between two nations are removed, the countries and their industries are able to maximize efficient use of resources and trade for goods. The result is that both countries gain from trade—a win-win situation. But are such gains possible when free trade is limited to a single group of countries? The classic example of the entry of Spain into the European Union demonstrates not just the benefits of trade creation, but the resulting drawback of trade diversion.

TRADE CREATION
A benefit of economic integration; the benefit to a particular country when a group of countries trade a product freely among themselves but maintain common barriers to trade with nonmembers

TRADE DIVERSION
A cost of economic integration; the cost to a particular country when a group of countries trade a product freely among themselves but maintain common barriers to trade with nonmembers

In 1986, Spain formally entered the European Union. Prior to membership, Spain's trade with EU countries was restricted by the common external tariff, imposed on all nonmembers, including the United States, Canada, and Japan. A 20 percent tariff, for example, was applied to exports of agricultural products to the European Union. This meant that low-cost U.S. wheat at $3.00 a bushel and Spanish wheat at $3.20 were both hurt by the tariff, boosting their costs to $3.60 and $3.84 respectively. When Spain joined the European Union, tariffs were lifted, allowing Spain to win out on price over U.S. wheat producers by $0.40 a bushel. As a result, trade flows changed. The increased export of wheat and other products by Spain to the European Union as a result of its membership is termed **trade creation**. The elimination of the tariff literally created more trade between Spain and the European Union. At the same time, because the United States is outside the European Union, its products suffered due to the higher price that resulted from the tariff application. U.S. exports to the European Union fell. When the source of trading competitiveness is shifted in this manner from one country to another, it is termed **trade diversion**.

Whereas trade creation is a distinct positive of free trade for member nations, usually resulting in lower prices, trade diversion is inherently negative. This is because it shifts competitive advantage away from lower-cost producers to the higher-cost producers. The benefits of Spain's membership are enjoyed by Spanish farmers (greater export sales) and EU consumers (lower prices). The two major costs are reduced tariff revenues (borne by the EU) and lost sales (suffered by the United States). From the perspective of nonmembers, the formation or expansion of a customs union is obviously negative. It is particularly damaging for emerging economies that need to build overseas trade. From the perspective of members of the customs union, the formation or expansion is beneficial only if trade-creation benefits exceed trade-diversion costs.

Reduced Import Prices

When a small country imposes a tariff on imports, the price of goods typically rises because sellers increase prices to cover the cost of tariffs. In turn, such prices lead to lower demand for imports. If a bloc of countries, as opposed to a single nation, imposes tariffs, the fall in demand can be substantial, forcing exporting countries to reduce their prices. Because of its greater market power relative to that of a single country, the trading bloc is able to improve its trading position and garner such low-price benefits. Any gain in the trade position of bloc members, however, is offset by a deteriorating trade position for exporting countries. Again, unlike the win-win situation resulting from free trade, the scenario involving a trade bloc is instead win-lose.

Increased Competition and Economies of Scale

Integration increases market size and therefore may result in a lower degree of monopoly in the production of certain goods and services. This is because a larger market will tend to increase the number of competing firms, resulting in greater efficiency and lower prices for consumers. Moreover, less-energetic and less-productive economies may be spurred into action by competition from the more industrious bloc members.

INTERNAL ECONOMIES OF SCALE
Lower production costs resulting from greater production within one firm for an enlarged market

Many industries, such as steel and automobiles, require large-scale production in order to obtain economies of scale. This is why certain industries are simply not economically viable in smaller, trade-protected countries. However, the formation of a trading bloc enlarges the market so that large-scale production by a firm—and the accompanying lower per-unit cost—is justified. Lower costs resulting from greater production for an enlarged market are called **internal economies of scale**. Sometimes increased production is possible as a result of adopting common standards. Ericsson and Nokia, now global powerhouses, both benefited when the EU adopted the standard for wireless communication, allowing companies like these to build scale beyond their small domestic markets.

In a common market, **external economies of scale** may also be present at the industry level. Because a common market allows factors of production to flow freely across borders, firms may now have access to cheaper capital, more highly skilled labor, or superior technology. These factors will improve the quality of the firms' goods or services or will lower costs or both.

EXTERNAL ECONOMIES OF SCALE
Lower production costs resulting from the interaction of many firms

Higher Factor Productivity

When freely mobile, the wealth of common market countries will likely increase in aggregate. This is because factor mobility leads to the movement of labor and capital from areas of low productivity to areas of high productivity. In contrast to economic gains from factor mobility, other benefits are not so easily quantified. The free movement of labor fosters a higher level of communication across cultures. This, in turn, leads to a higher degree of cross-cultural understanding: As people move, their ideas, skills, and ethnicities move with them.

Again, however, factor mobility will not necessarily benefit each country in the common market. A poorer country, for example, may lose badly needed investment capital to a richer country, where opportunities are perceived to be more profitable. Another disadvantage of factor mobility that is often cited is the brain-drain phenomenon. A poorer country may lose its most talented workers when they are free to search out better opportunities. More developed member countries worry that companies may leave for other member countries where costs of operation, such as social costs, are lower. Now, they are outsourcing knowledge work—engineering, software, product design, and development—to such countries as China, India, and Russia, and already have as many as 250 million to 500 million knowledge workers—the kind of highly educated, technologically skilled employees who can write computer code, design sophisticated products, and manage high-end production processes.[5]

Fast Facts

Chinese companies will employ 27,000 Americans in 2012. How many are projected for 2020?

If investment from China remains on track, Chinese businesses will employ 200,000 to 400,000 Americans by 2020.

Regionalism Versus Nationalism

Economists have composed elegant and compelling arguments in favor of the various levels of economic integration. It is difficult, however, to turn these arguments into reality in the face of intense nationalism. Integration, by its very nature, requires the surrender of national power and self-determinism.

Politicians blame other member countries for the loss of investment opportunities and the jobs they represent. In France, firm labor laws protect wages and pensions and make redundancy decisions costly for employers. Mouvement des Entreprises de France (MEDEF) is the largest union of employers and insists that unless France reforms its legal and fiscal business environment, it will continue to lose jobs and wealth-creating enterprises to its competitors in Europe. Nokia's decision to close down a major production facility for mobile devices in Bochum, Germany, and to move its manufacturing to more cost-competitive regions in Europe met with a hailstorm of protests from the German government to individual citizens.

Culture Clues

The summer of 2012 saw a succession of maritime disputes involving China, Japan, South Korea, Vietnam, Taiwan, and the Philippines. The number of anti-Japanese riots increased in cities across China because of a dispute over a group of uninhabited islands known to the Japanese as the Senkakus and to the Chinese as the Diaoyus. Toyota and Honda closed down their factories in China. The government in Beijing is belatedly trying to play down the dispute, aware of the economic interests in keeping the peace.

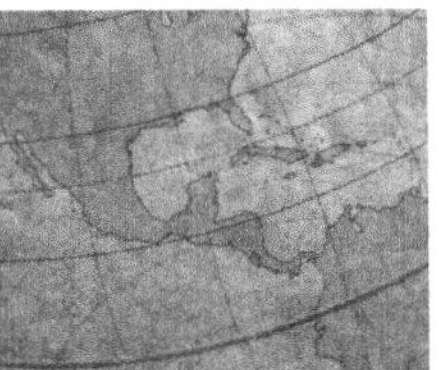

A listing of the world's major regional trade organizations is provided in Table 5.2.

TABLE 5.2 Major Regional Trade Agreements

AFTA	ASEAN Free Trade Area	Brunei, Cambodia, Indonesia, Laos, Malaysia, Myanmar, Philippines, Singapore, Thailand, Vietnam
ANCOME	Andean Common Market	Bolivia, Colombia, Ecuador, Peru
APEC	Asia Pacific Economic Cooperation	Australia, Brunei, Canada, Indonesia, Japan, Republic of Korea, Malaysia, New Zealand, Philippines, Singapore, Thailand, United States, Chinese Taipei, Hong Kong, People's Republic of China, Mexico, Papua New Guinea, Chile, Peru, Russia, Vietnam
COMESA	Common Market for Eastern and Southern Africa	Burundi, Comoros, Democratic Republic of the Congo, Djibouti, Egypt, Eritrea, Ethiopia, Kenya, Libya, Madagascar, Malawi, Mauritius, Rwanda, Seychelles, Swaziland, Sudan, Uganda, Zambia, Zimbabwe
CARICOM	Caribbean Community	Antigua and Barbuda, Bahamas, Barbados, Belize, Dominica, Grenada, Guyana, Haiti, Jamaica, Montserrat, Saint Kitts and Nevis, Saint Lucia, Saint Vincent and the Grenadines, Suriname, Trinidad and Tobago
ECOWAS	Economic Community of West African States	Benin, Burkina Faso, Cape Verde, Côte d'Ivoire, Gambia, Ghana, Guinea, Guinea-Bissau, Liberia, Mail, Niger, Nigeria, Senegal, Sierra Leone, Togo
EFTA	European Free Trade Association	Iceland, Liechtenstein, Norway, Switzerland
EU	European Union	Austria, Belgium, Bulgaria, Croatia, Cyprus, Czech Republic, Denmark, Estonia, Finland, France, Germany, Greece, Hungary, Ireland, Italy, Latvia, Lithuania, Luxembourg, Malta, Netherlands, Poland, Portugal, Romania, Slovakia, Slovenia, Spain, Sweden, United Kingdom
GCC	Gulf Cooperation Council	Bahrain, Kuwait, Oman, Qatar, Saudi Arabia, United Arab Emirates
LAIA	Latin American Integration Association	Argentina, Brazil, Chile, Cuba, Mexico, Paraguay, Peru, Uruguay, Bolivia, Colombia, Ecuador, Venezuela
MERCOSUR	Southern Common Market	Argentina, Brazil, Paraguay, Uruguay, Venezuela
NAFTA	North American Free Trade Agreement	Canada, Mexico, United States
SAARC	South Asian Association for Regional Cooperation	Bangladesh, Bhutan, India, Maldives, Nepal, Pakistan, Sri Lanka, Afghanistan
SADC	Southern African Development Community	Angola, Botswana, Democratic Republic of the Congo, Lesotho, Madagascar, Malawi, Mauritius, Mozambique, Namibia, Seychelles, South Africa, Swaziland, Tanzania, Zambia, Zimbabwe
SICA	Central American Integration System	Belize, Costa Rica, Dominican Republic, El Salvador, Guatemala, Honduras, Nicaragua, Panama

SOURCE: **http://www.aseansec.or; http://www.apec.org; http://www.caricom.org; http://www.eurunion.org; http://www.nafta.org**

REGIONAL GROUPINGS

European Union

DEVELOPMENT OF THE EUROPEAN UNION The first steps toward European integration were taken following the devastation of World War II, when a spirit of cooperation began to emerge across Europe. Established in 1948 to administer Marshall Plan aid from the United

States, the Organization for European Economic Cooperation (OEEC) set the stage for more ambitious integration programs.

Over the following years, several cooperative treaties and coalitions contributed to the eventual development of the European Union. Most notably, in 1957, the European Economic Community (EEC) was formally established by the **Treaty of Rome**. The cooperative spirit apparent throughout the treaty was based on the premise that the mobility of goods, services, labor, and capital—the "four freedoms"—was of paramount importance for the economic prosperity of the region. Founding members envisioned that the successful integration of the European economies would result in an economic power to rival that of the United States. Table 5.3 shows the founding members of the community in 1957 and members who have joined since, as well as those invited to join early in the twenty-first century.

TREATY OF ROME
The original agreement that established the foundation for the formation of the European Economic Community

TABLE 5.3 Membership of the European Union

1952	1973–1986	1995	2004		2007	2013
Belgium*	Denmark (1973)	Austria*	Czech Republic	Lithuania	Bulgaria	Croatia
France*	Ireland* (1973)	Finland*	Cyprus*	Malta*	Romania	
Germany*	United Kingdom (1973)	Sweden	Estonia*	Poland		
Italy*	Greece* (1981)		Hungary	Slovakia*		
Luxembourg*	Spain* (1986)		Latvia*	Slovenia*		
Netherlands*	Portugal* (1986)					

*Euro users

SOURCE: **http://europa.eu/about-eu/countries/index_en.htm**

The enlargement of the European Union has become one of the most debated issues. The European Union expanded to twenty-eight members, accepting eleven Central European and two Mediterranean countries to the Union. Despite some of the uncertainties about the future cohesiveness of the European Union, new nations want to join. Currently, there are five candidate countries: the former Yugoslav Republic of Macedonia (fYROM), Iceland, Montenegro, Serbia, and Turkey (World View: Turkey Versus the European Union). Potential candidates are Albania, Bosnia-Herzegovina, and Kosovo. The agreement on the European Economic Area (EEA) extends the Single Market of the European Union to three of the four EFTA countries (Iceland, Liechtenstein, and Norway, with Switzerland opting to develop its relationship with the European Union through bilateral agreements).[6]

EVOLUTION OF EUROPEAN UNION The most important implication of the freedom of movement for products, services, people, and capital within the European Union is the economic growth that is expected to result. Several specific sources of increased growth have been identified. First, there will be gains from eliminating the transaction costs associated with border patrols, customs procedures, and so forth. Second, economic growth will be spurred by the economies of scale that will be achieved when production facilities become more concentrated. Third, there will be gains from more intense competition among European companies. Firms that were monopolists in one country will now be subject to competition from firms in other member countries. The introduction of the € (euro) is expected to add to the efficiencies, especially in terms of consolidation of firms across industries and across countries. Furthermore, countries in Euroland will enjoy cheaper transaction costs and reduced currency risks, and consumers and businesses will enjoy price transparency and increased price-based competition.[7]

The European Union's Economic and Monetary Union (EMU), a single monetary policy for the seventeen euro area member states, combined with coordinated national fiscal policies, has helped foster macroeconomic stability, precipitated the economic integration of Europe, and boost cross-border trade, financial integration, and investment. EMU has also

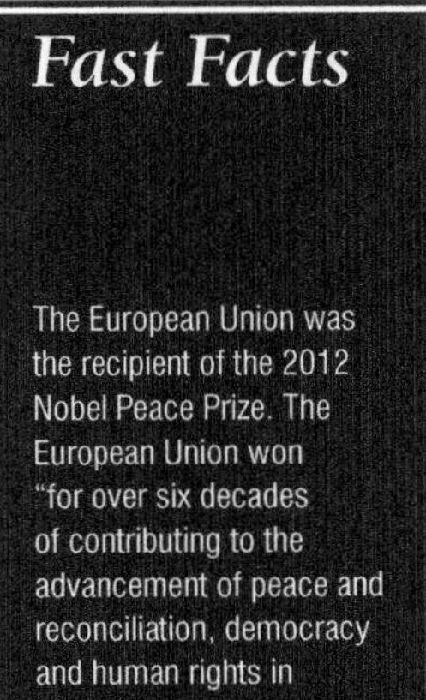

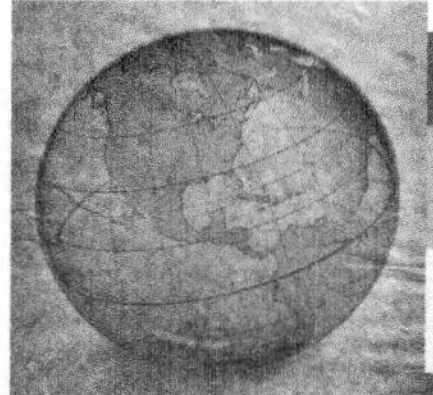

Turkey versus the European Union

Turkey has aspired to join what is today's European Union since 1959 when it applied for associate membership, which it gained in 1963. Turkey signed a customs union agreement with the EU in 1995 and was officially recognized as a candidate for full membership in 1999. Negotiations were started in 2005, and the process is likely to take at least a decade to complete. Almost immediately thereafter, the EU froze negotiations on eight policy areas because of Turkey's refusal to open its ports and airports to vessels and aircraft from Cyprus. Overall, the membership bid has become the central controversy of the enlargement of the European Union.

Institutionally and commercially, Turkey is deeply integrated into Europe. For example, nearly 60 percent of its exports and more than 50 percent of its imports are with the European Union members. Turkey's membership would bolster the EU's economy by $635 billion (ppp basis) and add a member that is part of the OECD and G-20. Arguments in favor of Turkey joining include the belief that this would bolster democratic institutions in Turkey and enable further improvements in human rights. Many fear that if Turkey is not granted membership in the EU, the winners will be the country's ultranationalists and the West would lose an important ally.

The concerns are many as well. If Turkey joined the EU in 2015, it would become its most populous state within a decade, due to strong population growth in the predominantly Muslim republic and low fertility rates in the European Union. As population size largely determines voting power in the EU, it would leapfrog Germany to become the state with the greatest political clout. Despite the fact that Europe already has more than 15 million Muslims (3.5 million of whom are Turkish), critics have argued that Turkey is "in permanent contrast to Europe." Turkey is considerably poorer than EU states, with a per capita gross domestic product equal to a quarter of the EU average. Many fear that more Turks would emigrate into European territories, which might result in tensions both on the labor side and on the level of society.

Although many of the EU member states are in favor of membership, the mood among the general population is more negative with nearly 60 percent of respondents being against and less than 30 percent in favor. Here it is important that certain EU member states, above all France and Germany, who are skeptical about Turkish entry into the bloc, show responsibility. It would be all too easy to use the collapse of the talks as an excuse to punish Turkey and bury its membership aspirations forever. Holding out the prospect of membership is one of the most important levers the EU possesses to steer Turkish domestic reforms in a positive direction. If the worst happens, and the Cyprus talks break down, the EU must still keep alive Turkey's EU accession process.

Sources: "Advice for the EU if Cyprus Talks Fail," *Financial Times* September 10, 2009, 8; "Turkey's EU Talks Inch Forward," *Financial Times*, December 20, 2007, 8; "The Slow Move Towards Accession," *Business Europe*, November 1–15, 2007, 8; "Sarkozy: Turkey Has No Place Inside the European Union," **TurkishPress.com**, January 14, 2007, **http://www.turkishpress.com/news.asp?id=159133**; "The West's Eastern Front," *The Wall Street Journal*, November 28, 2006, A14.

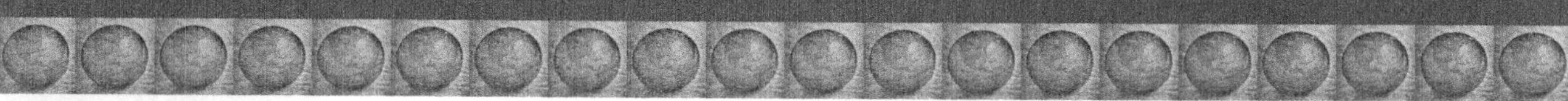

increased the European Union's resilience to adverse shocks. The EU also addressed the sovereign debt crises in several euro area countries by creating new instruments to provide financial assistance to a euro area country, should this become necessary. In 2011–13, fears about whether the governments in Greece, Portugal, Ireland, Spain, and Italy will honor their €3 trillion of borrowing while wreaking havoc on European banks, which own their debts, will further weakens the banks.[8]

Progress toward the goal of free movement of goods has been achieved largely due to the move from a "common standards approach" to a "mutual recognition approach." Under the common standards approach, EU members were forced to negotiate the specifications for literally thousands of products, often unsuccessfully. For example, because of differences in tastes, agreement was never reached on specifications for beer, sausage, or mayonnaise. Under the mutual recognition approach, the laborious quest for common standards is, in most cases, no longer necessary. Instead, as long as a product meets legal and specification requirements in one member country, it may be freely exported to any other, and customers serve as the final arbiters of success. More progress has been made in Europe toward the free movement of goods than has been made toward the free movement of people.

The primary difficulty is that EU members have been unable to agree on a common immigration policy. As long as this disagreement persists, travelers between countries must pass through border checkpoints. Some countries—notably Germany—have had relatively lax immigration policies, while others—especially those with higher unemployment rates—favor strict controls. The member states have agreed to develop a common immigration policy at the EU level by a coordinated approach that takes into account the economic and demographic situation of the EU.[9] A second issue concerning the free movement of people is the acceptability of professional certifications across countries. This means that workers' professional qualifications will be recognized throughout the EU, guaranteeing them equal treatment in terms of employment, working conditions, and social protection in the host country.

Attaining free movement of capital within the European Union entailed several measures. First, it required that citizens be free to trade in EU currencies without restrictions. Second, the regulations governing banks and other financial institutions would be harmonized. In addition, mergers and acquisitions would be regulated by the EU rather than by national governments. Finally, securities would be freely tradable across countries.

A key aspect of free trade in services is the right to compete fairly to obtain government contracts. Under the guidelines, a government should not give preference to its own citizens in awarding government contracts. However, little progress has been made in this regard. Public procurement accounts for 10 percent to 25 percent of world trade but is mostly restricted to national companies.[10]

Another source of difficulty that intensified was the administration of the community's **common agricultural policy (CAP)**. Most industrialized countries, including the United States, Canada, and Japan, have adopted wide-scale government intervention and subsidization schemes for agriculture. In the case of the European Union, however, these policies have been implemented on a community-wide, rather than national, level. The CAP includes: (1) a price-support system whereby EU agriculture officials intervene in the market to keep farm product prices within a specified range; (2) direct subsidies to farmers; and (3) rebates to farmers who export or agree to store farm products rather than sell them within the community. The implementation of these policies absorbs about 47 percent of the annual EU budget. The CAP has caused problems both within the EU and in relationships with nonmembers. Within the EU, the richer, more industrialized countries resent the extensive subsidization of the more agrarian economies.

COMMON AGRICULTURAL POLICY (CAP)
An integrated system of subsidies and rebates applied to agricultural interests in the European Union

ORGANIZATION OF THE EUROPEAN UNION The executive body of the European Union is the European Commission, headquartered in Brussels. It is composed of twenty-seven commissioners and headed by a president. The commissioners oversee directorates-general (or departments), such as agriculture, transportation, and external relations. The commissioners are appointed by the member states, their allegiance is to the community, not to their home countries. The commission's staff in Brussels number more than 25,000. Because the EU has twenty-three official languages, 20 percent of the staff are interpreters and translators.

The Council of Ministers has the final power to decide EU actions. The votes are allocated to the representatives of member countries on the basis of country size. With the reweighting of votes to accommodate new members, the United Kingdom has twenty-nine votes, while Finland has seven. Some of the most important provisions of the **Single European Act** expanded the ability of the Council to pass legislation. Most decisions are taken by qualified majority vote.

SINGLE EUROPEAN ACT
The legislative basis for the European integration

The Court of Justice is somewhat analogous to the judicial branch of the U.S. government. The court is composed of twenty-seven judges and is based in Luxembourg. The court adjudicates matters related to the European Constitution, especially trade and business disputes. Judicial proceedings may be initiated by member countries, as well as by firms and individuals.

The European Parliament is composed of 766 members elected by popular vote in the twenty-eight member countries for a five-year term. The Parliament can question the Commission and Council, amend and reject the budget, and dismiss the entire Commission. The Court of Auditors is to ensure the sound financial management of the EU. The entities and the process of decision making are summarized in Figure 5.1; not shown is the European Central Bank, which is responsible for monetary policy and the euro.

FIGURE 5.1 The Institution of the European Union

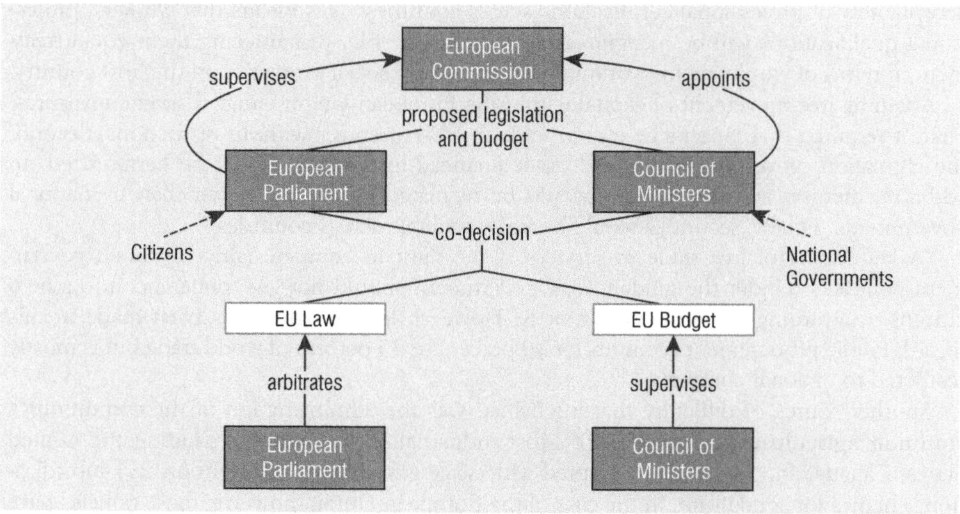

SOURCE: Web sites of the major institutions of the European Union can be found at **http://www.europarl.europa.eu/addresses/institutions/websites.htm**.

North American Economic Integration

Economic integration in North America has in recent years gained momentum. What started as a trading pact between two close and economically well-developed allies—the United States and Canada—has expanded to include Mexico, and long-term plans call for further additions.

Unlike the EU, which has political integration as one of its goals, in North America the single purpose is economic integration.

Negotiations on a North American Free Trade Agreement (NAFTA) began in 1994 to create the world's largest free market, with currently more than 460 million consumers and a total output of nearly $17.5 trillion. The pact marked a bold departure: Never before had industrialized countries created such a massive free trade area with a developing country neighbor. Because Canada stands to gain very little from NAFTA (its trade with Mexico is 1 percent of its trade with the United States), much of the controversy has centered on the gains and losses for the United States and Mexico. Proponents have argued that the agreement will give U.S. firms access to a huge pool of relatively low-cost Mexican labor at a time when demographic trends are indicating labor shortages in many parts of the United States. At the same time, many new jobs will be created in Mexico. The agreement will give firms in both countries access to millions of additional consumers, and the liberalized trade flows will result in faster economic growth in both countries. The top twenty exports and imports between Mexico and the United States are in virtually the same industries, indicating intra-industry specialization and building of economies of scale for global competitiveness.[11]

Opposition to NAFTA has risen from issues relating to labor, labor abuses, and the environment. At the outset, unions in particular worried about job loss to Mexico, given its lower wages and work standards. Some estimated that six million U.S. workers were vulnerable to job loss. The North American Agreement on Labor Cooperation (NAALC) was set up to hear complaints about worker abuse. Similarly, the Commission for Environmental Cooperation was established to act as a public advocate on the environment. The side agreements have, however, had little impact, mainly because the mechanisms they created have almost no enforcement power.

Quick Take *Sweet for the Right Price*

Kraft Foods and Nestlé have moved some operations to foreign countries, such as Mexico. This is not because of sugar prices, which are roughly the same in Mexico as here, but for savings in a host of other costs, such as wages, health insurance and other benefits, taxes, and environmental compliance. For example, one candy company fled average wages in Pennsylvania of just under $19 per hour to open a plant in Monterrey, Mexico, where average wages are a mere 51 cents per hour. Another major manufacturer that left Chicago admitted that their move "was based on lots of factors and could not be pinned specifically on sugar pricing." These companies are usually met with sugar prices that are similar to what they paid in America.

The sugar industry alleges that candy companies that relocate hide those factors and use America's efficient sugar farmers as the scapegoat.

According to the U.S. Census Bureau, U.S. production of candy and chocolate has grown nearly 9 percent since 2004, and 2.5 percent since current sugar policy took hold in 2008. To keep pace, confectioners have recently expanded domestic operations and added jobs—a far cry from the economic woes faced by many industries during the recession.

TABLE 5.4 Comparison of Costs to Produce Candy in NAFTA Countries

	United States	Mexico	Canada
Wages per hour	$18.78	$0.51	$10.20
Annual healthcare costs per employee	$7,680	$258	$1,551
Water and sewage cost per 1,000 gallons	$7.04	$1.00	$3.27

SOURCES: American Sugar Alliance, "The Confectionary Industries in the U.S., Canada, and Mexico: Trends in Structure, Domestic Production and Use, Trade and Cost Comparisons," Peter Buzzanell & Associates, Inc., August 2009; "Corporate Millionaires Likely to Spin Same Sob Story this Valentine's," American Sugar Alliance, February 8, 2006, and **http://sugaralliance.org/images/stories/Sugar_Fact_Sheets_2012/candy-companies-seek-cheap-labor.pdf**.

Trade among Canada, Mexico, and the United States has increased dramatically since NAFTA took effect, with total trade exceeding $1,139.0 billion in 2013. Reforms have turned Mexico into an attractive market in its own right. Mexico's domestic product has been expanding by more than 3 percent every year since 1989, and exports to the United States rose 20 percent a year to $226.2 billion in 2013. By institutionalizing the nation's turn to open markets, the free trade agreement has attracted considerable new foreign investment. The United States has benefited from Mexico's success. U.S. exports to Mexico are nearly double those to Japan at $138.5 billion in 2013. Although the surplus of $1.3 billion in 1994 has turned to a deficit of $54.3 billion in 2013, these imports have helped in Mexico's growth and will, therefore, strengthen NAFTA in the long term.[12]

Furthermore, U.S. imports from Mexico have been shown to have much higher U.S. content than imports from other countries. At present, cooperation between Mexico and the United States is taking new forms beyond trade and investment: For example, bi-national bodies have been established to tackle issues such as migration, border control, and drug trafficking.

Among the U.S. industries to benefit are computers, autos, petrochemicals, financial services, and aerospace. Aerospace companies such as Boeing, Honeywell, Airbus Industries, and GE Aircraft Engines have recently made Mexico a center for both parts manufacture and assembly. Aerospace is now one of Mexico's largest industries, second only to electronics, with 20,000 workers employed.[13]

In Mexico's growth toward a more advanced society, manufacturers of consumer goods will also stand to benefit. NAFTA has already had a major impact in the emergence of new retail chains, many established to handle new products from abroad.[14] Not only have U.S. retailers, such as Walmart, expanded to and in Mexico, but Mexican retailers, such as Grupo Gigante, have entered the U.S. market.

MAQUILADORAS
Mexican border plants that make goods and parts or process food for export back to the United States. They benefit from lower labor costs

U.S. companies have been moving operations to Mexico since the 1960s. The door was opened when Mexico liberalized export restrictions to allow for more so-called **maquiladoras**, plants that make goods and parts or process food for export back to the United States. The supply of labor was plentiful, the pay and benefits low, and the work regulations lax by U.S. standards. In the last three decades, maquiladoras evolved from low-end garment or small-assembly outfits to higher-end manufacturing of TVs, computers, and auto parts. However, the NAFTA treaty required Mexico to strip maquiladoras of their duty-free status in 2001. Tariff breaks formerly given to all imported parts, supplies, equipment, and machinery used by foreign factories in Mexico now could apply only to inputs from Canada and Mexico. European companies felt less of an effect because of Mexico's free trade agreement with the EU, which eliminated tariffs gradually by the end of 2007. The maquila industry faced competition due to rise of other countries with availability of cheap labor, including Malaysia, India, and Pakistan. The biggest threat came from China's Special Economic Areas. Although the Mexican government is eager to attract maquiladora investment, it is also keen to move away from using cheap labor as the central element of competitiveness. Such reasons are driving precision manufacturers like GKN Aerospace, a maker of aircraft engine components, to cluster close to the border in cities like Mexicali.

Integration pains extend to other areas as well. Approximately 85 percent of U.S.-Mexican trade moves on trucks. Under NAFTA, cross-border controls on trucking were to be eliminated by the end of 1995, allowing commercial vehicles to move freely in four U.S. and six Mexican border states. But the U.S. truckers, backed by the Teamsters Union, would have nothing of this, arguing that Mexican trucks were dangerous and exceeded weight limits. The union also worried that opening the border would depress wages because it would allow U.S. trucking companies to team up with lower-cost counterparts in Mexico. In 2001, however, the NAFTA Arbitration Panel ruled that Mexican trucks must be allowed to cross U.S. borders and the U.S. Senate approved a measure that allows Mexican truckers to haul cargo provided they meet strict inspection and safety rules. On the Mexican side, truckers are worried that if the border opens, U.S. firms will simply take over the trucking industry in Mexico.[15]

Countries dependent on trade with NAFTA countries are concerned that the agreement will divert trade and impose significant losses on their economies. Asia's continuing economic success depends largely on easy access to the North American markets, which account for more than 25 percent of annual export revenue for many Asian countries. Lower-cost producers in Asia are likely to lose some exports to the United States if they are subject to tariffs, while Mexican firms are not and may, therefore, have to invest in NAFTA. Similarly, many in the Caribbean and Central America fear that the apparel industries of their regions will be threatened, as would much needed investments.

Integration in Latin America

The Free Trade Area of the Americas (FTAA) is a policy initiative to bring together five major blocs in the Western hemisphere to compete more effectively against Europe and Asia. It was supposed to be in effect in 2005, but due to political changes in South America and disputes over agriculture and intellectual property rights, there is little chance for a comprehensive trade agreement in the foreseeable future. Mercosur members rejected the agreement and are very concerned it would lead to increased inequality in the region. Proponents of the FTAA have not been able to make progress in forging that deal since.

COMMON MARKET OF THE SOUTH—MERCOSUR Common Market of the South membership includes Brazil, Argentina, Paraguay, Uruguay, and Venezuela. The population of Mercosur's full membership totaled more than 276 million people in 2011; it has a collective GDP of $3.5 trillion and is the world's fourth-largest trading bloc after the European Union (EU), North American Free Trade Agreement (NAFTA), and the Association of South East Asian Nations (ASEAN). Mercosur has three main objectives: (1) establishment of a free-trade zone; (2) creation of a common external tariff system (i.e., a customs union); and (3) free movement of capital, labor, and services. In addition, future plans call for the harmonization of economic, fiscal, and trade policies.

Of the five Mercosur countries, Brazil is the most advanced in manufacturing and technology. São Paulo is one of the world's major industrial cities and is home to the affiliates and subsidiaries of many U.S and EU corporations. Even with its significant industrial base, vast interior areas of Brazil and their rich resources remain virtually untapped. Major infrastructure improvements are under way to permit these resources to be brought to market in a cost-efficient manner. Infrastructure and transportation improvements throughout member nations and in other parts of South America are an important outgrowth of Mercosur. Intra-Mercosur exports now account for only 13 percent of its members' total exports (intra-EU exports are 60 percent). Brazil's exports to Argentina, for example, its main partner in the Mercosur bloc, amount to only about 1 percent of its GDP. Oil-rich Venezuela can make significant economic contributions to Mercosur—its entry into the bloc adds Venezuela's $378.9 billion gross domestic product to Mercosur's overall GDP. Yet Venezuela has nationalized several industries in the country, affecting Mercosur member states.

Mercosur's internal disputes, increased protectionism, and controversy over Venezuela's membership have prompted some observers to speculate about the union's demise. To revive economic growth, Brazil needs to put more stress on competitiveness and market-opening trade diplomacy.[16] The organization is more and more political and to some degree anti-United States. The fastest-growing part of South America is the free-trading Pacific countries (Chile, Colombia, and Peru), which have shunned full membership of Mercosur.

ANDEAN COMMON MARKET—ANCOM The ANCOM was founded in 1969 and currently comprises four countries that straddle the Andes: Bolivia, Colombia, Ecuador, and Peru.

ANCOM and Mercosur leaders have discussed the possibility of allying to form a South American Community of Nations, modeled on the European Union, but those talks have not progressed quickly. The Andean Trade Preference Act (ATPA) was enacted to help four Andean countries in their fight against drug production and trafficking by expanding their economic alternatives.

BOLIVARIAN ALLIANCE FOR THE PEOPLES OF OUR AMERICA—ALBA As a matter of fact, an alternative has arisen in opposition to the U.S.-led Free Trade Area of the Americas (FTAA). ALBA, the Bolivarian Alliance for the Peoples of Our America (led by Cuba and Venezuela) focuses more on social welfare and economic aid than trade liberalization. Ideally, the larger countries would have agreed to consider giving smaller and lesser-developed countries more time to reduce tariffs, to open their economies to foreign investment, and to adopt effective laws in areas such as antitrust, intellectual property rights, bank regulation, and prohibitions on corrupt business practices. At the same time, the less-developed countries would agree to include labor and environmental standards in the negotiations. ALBA member countries approved the technical details for the introduction of the new currency, which was named SUCRE.

CENTRAL AMERICAN INTEGRATION SYSTEM—SICA Central American Integration System is the economic and political organization of Central American states since 1991. The framework of SICA included Belize, Guatemala, El Salvador, Honduras, Nicaragua, Costa Rica, and Panama. The group anticipates the eventual liberalization of interregional trade and the establishment of a free-trade zone. The SICA has often been cited as a model integrative effort for other developing countries. A continuing source of difficulty, however, is that the benefits of integration have fallen disproportionately to the richer and more developed members. Political difficulties in the area have also hampered progress.

A major change occurred in 2004 with the signing of the Central America–Dominican Republic–United States Free Trade Agreement. CAFTA-DR created the second-largest U.S. export market in Latin America, behind only Mexico, and the thirteenth-largest U.S. export market in the world. The United States exported $30.1 billion in goods to the five Central American countries (Costa Rica, El Salvador, Guatemala, Honduras, and Nicaragua) and the Dominican Republic in 2011, more than all exports to Russia, India, and Indonesia combined. At the same time, U.S. imports amounted to $28.6 billion.

CARIBBEAN COMMON MARKET—CARICOM Integration efforts in the Caribbean have focused on the Caribbean Common Market formed in 1968. Its primary mandate is to provide a framework for regional political and economic integration. The following fifteen nations make up the Caribbean community: Antigua and Barbuda, Bahamas, Barbados, Belize, Dominica, Grenada, Guyana, Haiti, Jamaica, Montserrat, St. Kitts-Nevis, St. Lucia, St. Vincent and the Grenadines, Suriname, and Trinidad and Tobago. Among CARICOM's objectives are the strengthening of the economic and trade regulations among member states, the expansion and integration of economic activities, and the achievement of a greater measure of economic independence for member states.

Integration in Asia

The development of regional integration in Asia has been quite different from that in Europe and in the Americas. Whereas European and North American arrangements have been driven by political will, market forces may compel politicians in Asia to move toward formal integration. In the meantime, however, Asian interest in regional integration is increasing for pragmatic reasons. First, European and American markets are significant for Asian producers, and some type of organization or bloc may be needed to maintain leverage and balance against the two other blocs. Second, given that much of the growth in trade for the nations in the region is from intra-Asian trade, having a common understanding and common policies will become necessary.

ASSOCIATION OF SOUTHEAST ASIAN NATIONS—ASEAN The Association of Southeast Asian Nations comprises ten member nations: Brunei, Cambodia, Indonesia, Laos, Malaysia, Myanmar, Philippines, Singapore, Thailand, and Vietnam. Under the auspices of the ASEAN Free Trade Agreement (AFTA), its objectives include reductions in tariffs to a maximum level of 5 percent among members as of 2005 and the creation of a customs union by 2015.

With a strong and diverse consumer base, ASEAN has established itself as one of the world's fastest-growing markets. Thailand is moving fast to evolve from an agricultural to a manufacturing economy and also toward a knowledge-based economy. The leading food exporter in Asia, Thailand is also a producer of electronics and automobiles and the world's top exporter of hard disk drives. ACE Group is one of the largest multiline property and casualty insurers. The company established life insurance operations in Vietnam in 2005 and in Indonesia in 2009 as the middle-class emerged and consumers accumulated assets and wealth.

Skepticism about the association's lofty targets has been raised about the group's ability to follow the example of the European Union given the widely divergent levels of economic development (e.g., Singapore versus Laos) and the lack of democratic institutions (especially in Myanmar). ASEAN has also agreed to economic cooperation with China, Japan, and South Korea (the so-called ASEAN+1 and ASEAN+3 arrangements), as well as with India. Integrating Southeast Asia, China has recently signed agreements to build new rail lines in Laos and Thailand, while it extends its reach from Kunming to the China-Laos border.[17]

ASIA PACIFIC ECONOMIC COOPERATION—APEC In 1989, Australia proposed the Asia Pacific Economic Cooperation (APEC) as an annual forum. The proposal called for ASEAN members to be joined by Australia, New Zealand, Papua New Guinea, Japan, China, Hong Kong, Taiwan, South Korea, Russia, Canada, Chile, Mexico, Peru, and the United States. It was initially modeled after the Organization for Economic Cooperation and Development (OECD), which is a center for research and high-level discussion. Since then, APEC's goals have become more ambitious. At present, APEC has members with a combined 55 percent of global GDP, 58 percent of U.S. goods exports, and nearly 43 percent of global trade. APEC is the third largest economy of the world. The key objectives of APEC are to liberalize trade by 2020, to facilitate trade by harmonizing standards, and to build human capacities for realizing the region's ambitions. The trade-driven economies of the region have the world's largest pool of savings, the most advanced technologies, and growing markets.[18]

Some individuals have publicly called for a U.S.-Japan common market. Given the differences on all fronts between the two countries, the proposal may be quite unrealistic at this time. Negotiated trade will not open Japanese markets after many rounds of negotiations with totally unsatisfactory results due to major institutional differences. The only solution, especially for the U.S. government, is to forge better cooperation between the government and the private sector to improve competitiveness.

SOUTH ASIAN ASSOCIATION FOR REGIONAL COOPERATION—SAARC Economic integration has also taken place on the Indian subcontinent. In 1985, seven nations of the region

Culture Clues One of the challenges in achieving economic integration in Asia is the resentment and suspicion felt toward the Japanese, due to their military occupation of countries such as China (in the 1930s) and Korea (1910–1945). The Japanese called their attempt to dominate the Asia-Pacific the "Co-Prosperity Sphere."

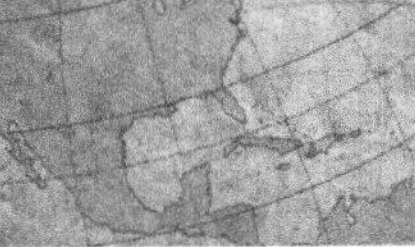

(India, Pakistan, Bangladesh, Sri Lanka, Nepal, Bhutan, and the Maldives) launched the South Asian Association for Regional Cooperation (SAARC). Cooperation has been limited to relatively noncontroversial areas, such as agriculture and regional development, and is hampered by political disagreements. India exported $2.33 billion of goods to Pakistan. In the same period, Pakistan sold goods valued at $332.5 million in India. By comparison, two-way trade between India and China is valued at more than $60 billion annually.[19]

Africa

Africa's economic groupings range from currency unions among European nations and their former colonies to customs unions among neighboring states. In addition to wanting to liberalize trade among members, African countries want to gain better access to European and North American markets for farm and textile products. Given that most of the countries are too small to negotiate with the other blocs, alliances have been the solution. In 1975, fifteen West African nations attempted to create a mega-market large enough to interest investors from the industrialized world and reduce hardship through economic integration. The objective of the Economic Community of West African States (ECOWAS) was to form a customs union and eventual common market. Although many of its objectives have not been reached, its combined population of 300 million represents the largest economic entity in sub-Saharan Africa. Other entities in Africa include the Common Market for Eastern and Southern Africa (COMESA), the Economic Community of Central African States (CEEAC), the Southern African Customs Union, the Southern African Development Community (SADC), and some smaller, less globally oriented blocs, such as the Economic Community of the Great Lakes Countries, the Mano River Union, and the East African Community (EAC). Most member countries are part of more than one bloc (for example, Tanzania is a member in both the EAC and SADC). The blocs, for the most part, have not been successful due to the small size of the members and lack of economic infrastructure to produce goods to be traded inside the blocs. Moreover, some of the blocs have been relatively inactive for substantial periods of time while their members endure internal political turmoil or even warfare amongst each other. In 2002, African nations established the African Union (AU) for regional cooperation. Eventually, plans call for a pan-African parliament, a court of justice, a central bank, and a shared currency by 2023.[20]

The Middle East

Countries in the Arab world have made some progress in economic integration. The Arab Maghreb Union ties together Algeria, Libya, Mauritania, Morocco, and Tunisia in northern Africa. The Gulf Cooperation Council (GCC) is one of the most powerful, economically speaking, of any trade groups. The per capita income of its six member states (Bahrain, Kuwait, Oman, Qatar, Saudi Arabia, and the United Arab Emirates) is at the ninetieth percentile in the world. Significant progress has already been made in regional economic integration. The GCC countries have largely unrestricted intraregional mobility of goods, labor, and capital; regulation of the banking sector is being harmonized; and in 2008, the countries established a common market. Further, most of the convergence criteria established for entry into a monetary union have already been achieved. In establishing a monetary union, however, the GCC countries must decide on the exchange rate regime for the single currency. A proposal among GCC members calls for the creation of a common currency.[21] This area has some of the fastest-growing economies in the world, mostly due to a boom in oil and natural gas revenues coupled with a building and investment boom backed by decades of saved petroleum revenues. In an effort to build a tax base and economic foundation before the reserves run out, the UAE's Abu Dhabi Investment Authority retained more than $875 billion in assets.

Quick Take *East and West*

The countries of the Gulf Cooperation Council (GCC) represent one regional powerhouse whose relationships with emerging peers can offer valuable insights into the way such alliances are forming.

More than oil. The top item on the strategic agenda for every GCC country is to diversify its economy and thus decrease its dependence on oil. Despite significant efforts, achieving this goal has so far proven challenging: Saudi Arabia's exports to the United States still revolve around oil, whereas its exports to Brazil, Russia, India, and China include chemicals, plastics, and minerals.

Rich in talent. As goods and services flow across the borders of the GCC and other emerging markets, so do people. The most significant aspect of this change is the skill level of many of the people entering the GCC. No longer do executives come from the West and laborers from the East; instead, skilled individuals from emerging markets are deepening their impact in the GCC with influential positions in the region's financial, energy, transportation, and public sectors. India, in particular, has a large community of professional expats in the region.

New sources of capital. GCC nations have long been investors in other countries—primarily in the United States and Europe—via their sovereign wealth funds and other state-owned entities. In light of the strong role that GCC governments play in determining the direction of their countries' capital investments, this trend could accelerate if GCC governments decide that other emerging markets are sent a better strategic destination. The state-owned airlines in the UAE and Qatar have quickly achieved global prominence.

Getting connected. As GCC countries seek to branch out and build relationships with other emerging markets, they have found one point of entry in the information and communications technology (ICT) sector. The nations of the Gulf and their partners in other emerging markets have collaborated to boost their ICT development in ways that they might not have been able to do alone. Chinese companies Huawei and ZTE have provided equipment for GCC telecom networks.

SOURCES: Joe Saddi, Karim Sabbagh, and Richard Shediac, "Staying on the Road to Growth," *Strategy and Business*, Issue 68, Autumn 2012, and Joe Saddi, Karim Sabbagh and Richard Shediac, "The New Web of World Trade," *Strategy and Business*, Issue 64, Autumn 2011.

Cartels and Commodity Price Agreements

An important characteristic that distinguishes developing countries from industrialized countries is the nature of their export earnings. Whereas industrialized countries depend heavily on the export of manufactured goods, technology, and services, developing nations rely chiefly on the export of primary products and raw materials, such as copper, iron ore, and agricultural products. This distinction is important for several reasons. First, the level of price competition is higher among sellers of primary goods because of the typically larger number of sellers and also because primary goods are homogeneous. This can be seen by comparing the sale of computers with, for example, copper. On average, only three or four countries are competitive forces in the computer market, whereas at least a dozen compete in the sale of copper. Furthermore, while goods differentiation and therefore brand loyalty are likely to exist in the market for computers, buyers of copper are likely to purchase on the basis of price alone. Another distinguishing factor is that supply variability is greater in the market for primary goods because production often depends on uncontrollable factors, such as weather. For these reasons, market prices of primary goods—and therefore developing country export earnings—are highly volatile.

CARTEL
An association of producers of a particular good, consisting either of private firms or of nations, formed for the purpose of suppressing the market forces affecting prices

CARTELS A **cartel** is an association of producers of a particular good. Although a cartel may consist of an association of private firms, our interest is in the cartels formed by nations. The objective of a cartel is to suppress the market forces affecting its good in order to gain greater control over sales revenues. A cartel may accomplish this objective in several ways. First, members may engage in price fixing. This entails an agreement by producers to sell at a certain price, eliminating price competition among sellers. Second, the cartel may allocate sales territories among its members, again suppressing competition. A third tactic calls for members to agree to restrict production, and therefore supplies, resulting in artificially higher prices.

The most widely known cartel is the Organization of Petroleum Exporting Countries (OPEC). It consists of twelve oil-producing and -exporting countries (Algeria, Angola, Ecuador, Iran, Iraq, Kuwait, Libya, Nigeria, Qatar, Saudi Arabia, United Arab Emirates, and Venezuela). As any cartel, OPEC has had its challenges. First, not all oil-producing countries are members of OPEC. The current OPEC members account for about 40 percent of world oil production and about two-thirds of the world's proven oil reserves. Most non-OPEC countries (e.g., United States, Norway, United Kingdom, Canada) have private oil sectors, and their governments have little control over production levels, which OPEC, on its part, controls for pricing stability. Secondly, the cohesiveness of members in a cartel may not always be complete. Sales have occurred at less than agreed upon prices, and production quotas have been violated. A third challenge is balancing the market's tolerance for high prices (with the record of $105.06 per barrel in 2012) and the need for oil revenues to support member countries' domestic spending programs. OPEC prices have stayed in the range of $85–$95 barrel for this decade, compared to potentially reaching $133 per barrel by 2035.[22]

COMMODITY PRICE AGREEMENT
An agreement involving both buyers and sellers to manage the price of a particular commodity but often only when the price moves outside a predetermined range

BUFFER STOCK
Stock of a commodity kept on hand to prevent a shortage in times of unexpectedly great demand; under international commodity and price agreements, the stock is controlled by an elected or appointed manager for the purpose of managing the price of the commodity

COMMODITY PRICE AGREEMENTS International **commodity price agreements** involve both buyers and sellers with the joint objective of managing the price of a certain commodity. The free market is often allowed to determine the price of the commodity over a certain range. However, if demand and supply pressures cause the commodity's price to move outside that range, an elected or appointed manager will enter the market to buy or sell the commodity to bring the price back into the range. The manager controls the **buffer stock** of the commodity. If prices float downward, the manager purchases the commodity and adds to the buffer stock. Under upward pressure, the manager sells the commodity from the buffer stock. This system is somewhat analogous to a managed exchange rate system, in which authorities buy and sell to influence exchange rates. International commodity agreements have been in effect for sugar, tin, rubber, cocoa, and coffee.

The tremendous pressures exerted by declining demand, falling prices, over-production, and the conflicting interests of producers have destroyed commodity price agreements.

Emerging Markets

Emerging markets are nations with social or business activity in the process of rapid growth and industrialization. Improved economies can benefit emerging-market countries through higher personal income levels and better standards of living, more exports, increased foreign-direct investment, and more stable political structures. Developed countries benefit from the development of human and natural resources in emerging markets through increased international trading.

Although opinions on which countries are emerging markets differ, the big emerging markets are Brazil, Russia, India, China, and South Africa (BRICS). South Africa has formally joined this loose political grouping but does not have the population, the growth, or the long-term economic potential of the other four. Indonesia, Mexico, and Turkey would have been other logical contenders or South Korea and Taiwan, which have comparable GDPs but much smaller populations than the original BRICS.[23] The data provided in Table 5.5 compares selected emerging markets with each other on dimensions indicating market potential. The biggest emerging markets display the factors that make them strategically important: favorable consumer demographics, rising household incomes and increasing availability of credit, as well as increasing productivity resulting in more attractive prices.[24] GE, for example, expects to get as much as 60 percent of its revenue growth from emerging markets over the next decade.

TABLE 5.5 Emerging Markets

Overall Rank	Country	Market Size	Market Growth Rate	Market Intensity	Market Consumption Capacity	Commercial Infrastructure	Economic Freedom	Market Receptivity	Country Risk	Overall Score
1	Singapore	1	100	72	65	83	80	100	100	63
2	Hong Kong	1	29	100	59	100	93	86	95	58
3	China	100	93	1	67	36	7	4	55	55
4	South Korea	10	41	59	92	88	83	16	71	49
5	Czech Republic	1	18	45	100	92	89	14	76	45
6	India	38	83	35	67	17	50	2	42	41
7	Israel	1	17	63	76	73	81	20	61	40
8	Poland	4	21	60	79	73	80	5	69	40
9	Hungary	1	4	65	83	81	83	17	47	40
10	Turkey	6	70	66	65	49	60	4	43	38
11	Brazil	20	57	47	42	51	58	1	54	36
12	Mexico	10	40	59	47	46	65	18	45	35
19	Russia	23	20	39	62	64	15	3	42	32
26	South Africa	6	23	35	1	17	68	4	47	19

SOURCE: Global Edge, available at **http://globaledge.msu.edu/resourceDesk/mpi/**.

Mere size and growth do not guarantee an emerging market's overall appeal and potential. The growth rates may be consistently higher than in developed markets, but they may also be subject to greater volatility. Each may experience deep, life-threatening crises that would catapult them onto a different road of development. Evident in the data is the role of political risk; that is, government interference in entry and market development situations. The Russian government blocked a landmark investment of German engineering company Siemens in OAO Power Machines on antitrust grounds, as the government tightened its control on industries it deemed vital to the country's interests. The Russian government has also barred foreign-owned companies from bidding for its oil and metal deposits.[25]

BRICS tapped into their vast economic potential. Their total GDP of close to $14 trillion now nearly equals the United States and is even bigger on a purchasing power parity basis. A concern, however, is the current and future competition from emerging-market companies. Chinese companies have been able to develop powerful global brands in a very short period of time (see World View: China Spree, which illustrates these concerns). Some global brands have been developed from the domestic base in a step-by-step manner (e.g., Haier in

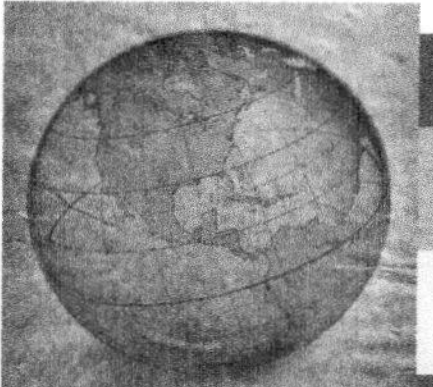

WORLD VIEW

China Spree

The world's top exporting nation amassed $2.7 trillion in aggregate domestic savings by the end of 2009, a pot likely to grow six-fold by 2020, according to the World Bank. Experts are predicting a surge of overseas takeovers by Chinese companies over the next decade. A five-year plan Beijing approved calls for establishing international sales networks and brand names.

Chinese companies' investment in European businesses, which totaled just $853 million in 2003–05, surged to $43.9 billion in 2008 through 2010. The burst gave Chinese companies control of 118 European businesses. In the latest deal, Chinese personal-computer maker Lenovo Group Ltd. agreed to buy 37 percent of Medion AG, a German computer and consumer-electronics company and will launch a public offer for enough additional shares to gain control.

Although some of the deals make headlines, such the purchase in 2010 of Volvo auto operations from Ford Motor Co. by Zhejiang Geely Holding Group, Chinese companies have also quietly acquired control of more than 100 smaller European businesses, ranging from a Czech cigarette company to a Dutch pharmaceuticals firm to a British wood producer. The frequency of these takeovers is increasing.

The Chinese government provides help to Chinese companies on their overseas shopping tours. It publishes guidebooks for individual countries on investing in those countries.

TABLE 5.6

Sector	Date	Target, Country	Acquirer	Value, in Billions
Mining	Feb. 1, 2008	Rio Tinto (9 percent), United Kingdom	Aluminum Corp. of China	$10.74
Oil and gas	June 24, 2009	Addax Petroleum, Switzerland	China Petrochemical	$7.28
Finance	July 23, 2007	Barclays (2.64 percent), United Kingdom	China Development Bank	$2.98
Chemicals	Jan. 11, 2011	Elkem, Norway	China National Chemical Corp. (CNCC)	$2.17
Auto and truck	March 28, 2010	Volvo Car, Sweden	Zhejiang Geely Holding Group, Daqing State Asset Operation	$1.5
Utility and energy	Nov. 29, 2010	InterGen (50 percent), Netherlands	China Huaneng Group	$1.23
Dining and lodging	May 10, 2011	NH Hoteles SA(20 percent), Spain	Hainan Traffic Control Holding	$0.62
Telecomm.	Jan. 23, 2011	Telefonica (0.48 percent), Spain	China United Network Communications	$0.51
Food and beverage	Oct. 21, 2005	Adisseo France, France	China National Chemical Corp. (CNCC)	$0.48

SOURCES: "China Goes Shopping for German Factories," *Bloomberg Businessweek*, June 2012, 44–45; John W. Miller, "Chinese Companies Embark on Shopping Spree in Europe," *Wall Street Journal*, June 6, 2011, 1–6, and "Being Eaten by the Dragon: Chinese Makeovers," *The Economist*, November 13, 2010, 81–83.

appliances and Geely in cars) or through acquisitions of existing global brands (such as TCL in TVs). Another concern is based on economic and national security. Companies such as GE, Microsoft, Cisco, and Intel all have established research and development operations in China, thereby training foreign scientists and possibly giving the omnipresent Chinese government access to proprietary technologies.[26]

A number of strategic choices are available, but most of them require recognizing the idiosyncrasies of the market. Whatever the strategy, the marketer has to make sure to secure the company's core competencies while being innovative.[27] Five elements of success are required for any global marketer to take advantage of and thrive in emerging markets.

Adjust Entry Strategy

GM entered the Russian market to produce SUVs in a joint venture with AvtoVAZ, Russia's largest automaker. Russia is one of the eight largest markets and is expected to grow substantially in the future. GM chose to use a joint venture to secure a local engineering source to eliminate many of the risks that lead to failure in emerging markets. GM will increase its share of locally sourced components to an average of 60 percent and grow its percentage of vehicles with locally sourced engines and transmissions to 30 percent. GM will also expand its engineering, research, and development center in Russia, which will enable it to develop products tailored for the Russian market. In exchange for these significant investments in the domestic economy, the Russian government will provide GM lower customs duties on imported components for eight years. GM will increase the production capacity at its wholly owned plant in St. Petersburg to 230,000 vehicles per year and at its GM-AutoVAZ joint venture in Togliatti to 120,000 vehicles per year, for a combined annual production capacity of 350,000 vehicles. GM's facility in St. Petersburg will continue to manufacture Chevrolet and Opel models for the Russian market. GM-AvtoVAZ will concentrate on the production of small SUVs and all-new versions of the Chevrolet Niva and Lada 4X4. Another benefit of GM's strategy is securing an existing dealer network. An added benefit for GM is its ability to export the Niva to other emerging markets using the Daewoo network (acquired by GM earlier).[28]

Manage Affordability

Companies have described how they have adapted to the new global era through a process they call **reverse innovation**. For example, in India, General Electric (GE) has developed a handheld electrocardiogram device that it sells for $1,000, about one-tenth of the price of the original (and much bulkier) U.S.-developed machine. Similarly, in China, the company has introduced a portable ultrasound machine with a price tag of $15,000, again vastly cheaper than the original model GE tried to sell to the Chinese market.[29] Both these innovations have not only been successful in emerging markets, but they have also found new customers back in the United States, with ambulance teams and in emergency rooms.[30] There is also a great need to develop new products for people with little money who aspire to a taste of the better life. Also, because fewer than one in five Indian homes has a refrigerator, corporations could attract a huge new group of consumers if they could get the price right. By keeping it small and reducing the numbers of parts to around 20 instead of 200 that go in regular refrigerators, it could sell for only $70 which is less than one third of the price of a regular bottom-of-the-line fridge.

REVERSE INNOVATION
Innovations from emerging markets and then distributed to developed markets

Invest in Distribution

In March 2011, Goldman Sachs reported that the focus on such Goliath-on-Goliath combat overlooks how the multinational "Goliaths" are increasingly overtaking emerging-market "Davids." After locally based competitors outperformed multinationals for much of the past decade, the tide has begun to turn. History has shown that you cannot just come in and beat up on the local competitors. The local rivals typically understand the local consumer better and have already mastered distribution in a complex distribution environment. The multinationals versus local players (household and personal-care products, in billions of dollars) game is changing.

An example has emerged with the increase from commuter airlines that the airlines own or contract out to connect with smaller markets hubs. Brazil's aerospace conglomerate Embraer has taken advantage of the increased demand that has challenged the market leader, Canada's Bombardier. When demand took off faster than expected, Bombardier could not meet those demands, thus opening the door for the Embraer 145 family. Currently, Brazil's lower labor costs allow Embraer to undercut its competitor on prices.

Supplier Base and Logistics

Transportation networks by land, rail, waterway, or air are essential for physical distribution. An analysis of rail traffic by freight tons per kilometer offers a possible way to begin an investigation of transportation capabilities; however, these figures may not always indicate the true state of the system. Since late 2008, when China enacted a fiscal stimulus program to avert the contagion effects of a global economic slowdown, the country embarked on a building binge, including new highways, high-speed rail lines, bridges, municipal subway systems,

Quick Take *Growth Opportunity That Lies Next Door*

Brazil's Natura is already the number one cosmetic company in Latin America. Natura focuses on its image as an eco-friendly, sustainable company (using natural products, working toward sustainable environment and social support) while building an international brand. The company also prides itself on strong research and development. Natura presents itself as the product for the "ordinary" women rather than supermodels in its advertisements. Before becoming a global brand, Natura wants to establish global quality.

It follows a successful direct-sales model, working with one million consultants (resellers) in Brazil and another 200,000 in Mexico, Colombia, Peru, Argentina, and Chile, but splurged on a concept store in Paris, plus an additional fifty-person research-and-development unit there, to take advantage of the sophisticated French consumer's knowledge of and interest in beauty products. French women's magazine *Madame Figaro* rated Natura's exfoliating cream, whose active ingredient is Brazilian fruit acai, as a "must have." "Natura always has been concerned about using natural ingredients. French consumers are highly aware, and their demands have helped us improve. Before becoming a global brand, we want to reach global quality."

SOURCE: Geoffrey Jones, "The Growth Opportunity That Lies Next Door," *Harvard Business Review*, 90 (September 2012): 141–145; and Claudia Penteado, "Brazil's Natura Building Global Brand," *Advertising Age*, 4 June 13, 2011.

terminal buildings, and nearly a hundred new airports. A new rail line cut travel time between Beijing and Shanghai to just five hours. The world's longest bridge over water opened this year in the city of Qingdao, spanning 26 miles across the Jiaozhou Bay. China is on track to soon surpass the United States in the number of highway miles built. China now has about 46,000 miles of expressways—a close second to the United States—with plans to build that out to 112,500 miles by 2030.[31]

Build Brands

A common characteristic across all emerging markets is the appeal of recognizable brands. Although it is easiest for global marketers to extend their global brands to emerging markets, some companies, such as Danone, acquire companies but continue selling the products under original names. Adding a new quality dimension to well-established brands, consumer loyalty is ensured. This strategy has generated favor among Chinese officials who may not want to see local brands go under. Brands in the packaged goods, beverages, and retail categories operate in extremely crowded spaces, where brand building can play a critical role in differentiation. Retail, sportswear, and clothing brands also stand out, such as Li Ning, Metersbonwe, Anta, and 361 Degrees. Leading corporations transformed themselves from second-rate producers of cheap goods into world-class manufacturers of smartphones, semiconductors, software, and planes. China's Lenovo took over IBM's PC business. Brazilian and South African beer companies became leading global brewers.

Labor Markets

Multinationals have trouble recruiting managers and other skilled workers because the quality of talent is hard to ascertain. There are relatively few search firms and recruiting agencies in low-income countries. The high-quality firms that do exist focus on top-level searches, so companies must scramble to identify middle-level managers, engineers, or floor supervisors. Engineering colleges, business schools, and training institutions have proliferated. For example, more than 80 percent of India's IT services exports, for instance, are to English-speaking countries. The Indian diaspora and the Commonwealth can also be tapped, and a newer possibility is afforded by "South–South" connections that leverage common interests between Indian enterprises and their counterparts in Southeast Asia, Central Asia, and Africa.

Developing Markets

The time may have come to look at the four billion people in the world who live in poverty, subsisting on less than $2,000 a year.[32] Not only is this segment a full two-thirds of the current market place, but it is expected to grow to six billion by 2040. Despite initial skepticism about access and purchasing power, marketers are finding that they can make profits while having a positive effect on the sustainable livelihoods of people not normally considered potential customers. However, it will require radical departures from the traditional business models; for example, new partnerships (ranging from local governments to nonprofits) and new pricing structures (allowing customers to rent or lease rather than buy and providing new financing choices for purchases).

Five elements of success are required for a global marketer to take advantage of and thrive in developing markets.[33]

Research

The first order of business is to learn about the needs, aspirations, and habits of targeted populations for whom traditional intelligence gathering may not be the most effective. For example, just because the demand for landlines in developing countries was low, it would have been wrong to assume that little demand for phones existed. The real reasons were that landlines were expensive, subscribers had to wait for months to get hooked up, and lines often went down due to bad maintenance, flood, and theft of copper cables. Mobile phones have been a solution to that problem. Developing countries have more than 600 million mobile-phone users—more than America or Europe. Because roads are generally dreadful, advances in communications, with mobile banking and telephonic agro-info, have triggered a huge mobile phone boom.[34]

Creating Buying Power

MICROFINANCE

A source of financial services for entrepreneurs and small business lacking access to banking services

Without credit, it is impossible for many of the developing-country consumers to make major purchases. Programs in **microfinance** have allowed consumers, with no property as collateral, to borrow sums averaging $100 to make purchases and have retail banking services available to them. Lenders such as GrameenBank in Bangladesh and Compartamos in Mexico have helped millions of families to escape poverty. Excellent payment records (e.g., only 0.56 percent of the loans are even days late at Compartamos) have started attracting companies such as Citicorp to microfinancing through underwriting microfinance bonds in markets such as Peru.[35]

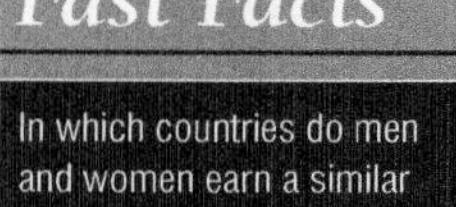

In which countries do men and women earn a similar amount?

Burundi is the only one where more women work than men; 92 percent (World Economic Forum). Burundi women made 80 percent of what men earned.

Tailoring Local Solutions

In the product area, companies must combine advanced technology with local insights. Hindustan Lever (part of Unilever) learned that low-income Indians, usually forced to settle for low-quality products, wanted to buy high-end detergents and personal care products but could not afford them in the quantities available. In response, the company developed extremely low-cost packaging material, smaller product sizes, and other innovations that allowed for a product priced in pennies instead of the $4 to $15 price of the regular containers. The same brand is on all of the product forms, regardless of packaging.[36]

Improving Access

Due to the economic and physical isolation of poor communities, providing access can lead to a thriving business. In Bangladesh (with income levels of $200), GrameenPhone Ltd. leases access to wireless phones to villagers. Every phone is used by an average of 100 people and generates $90 in revenue a month—two or three times the revenues generated by wealthier users who own their phones in urban areas.[37] Similarly, the Jhai Foundation, an American-Lao foundation, is helping villagers in Laos. One of its projects is bringing communication services to rural communities lacking electricity or telephones. To achieve this goal they have developed the Jhai PC and Communication System, a solid state, low energy-consuming computer that can be powered by a foot-crank generator built into a bicycle frame or by solar energy and uses a wireless network to provide VoIP and Internet services.

Shaping Aspirations

The biggest challenge in developing markets is to provide essential services. The emergence of these markets presents a great growth opportunity for companies. It also creates a chance for business, government, and civil society to join together in a common cause to help the aspiring poor to join the world market economy. Lifting billions of people from poverty may help avert social decay, political chaos, terrorism, and environmental deterioration that are certain to continue if the gap between the rich and poor countries continues to widen. For example, Coca-Cola has introduced "Project Mission" in Botswana to launch a drink to combat anemia, blindness, and other afflictions common in poorer parts of the world. The drink, called Vitango, is like the company's Hi-C orange-flavored drink, but it contains twelve vitamins and minerals chronically lacking in the diets of people in developing countries.[38]

ECONOMIC INTEGRATION AND THE GLOBAL MANAGER

Regional economic integration creates opportunities and challenges for the global manager. It affects, for instance, a company's entry mode by favoring direct investment because one of the basic rationales for integration is to generate favorable conditions for local production and interregional trade. By design, larger markets are created with potentially more opportunity.

Harmonization efforts may also result in standardized regulations, which can positively affect production and marketing efforts.

Effects of Change

Change in the competitive landscape resulting from moves toward integration can be dramatic, especially if scale opportunities can be exploited in relatively homogeneous demand conditions.

This could be the case, for example, for industrial goods and consumer durables, such as cameras and watches, as well as for professional services. To assess opportunities, the global manager must take into consideration the varying degrees of change readiness within the markets themselves. Consider, for example, that governments and other stakeholders, such as labor unions, may oppose the liberalization of competition, especially where national monopolies exist, such as in the airline, automobile, energy, or telecommunication industries. For example, an automaker enters the each country with distinctive consumer demand patterns, distributor networks, and regulations on imports, foreign direct investment, safety, and transportation in general.[39]

Strategic Planning

The global marketer will then have to develop a strategic response to the new environment to maintain a sustainable long-term competitive advantage. Those companies already present in an integrated market should fill in gaps in product and market portfolios through acquisitions or alliances to create a regional or global company. It is increasingly evident that even regional presence may not be sufficient, and companies need to set their sights on presence beyond that. In industries such as beer, mobile communications, and retailing, blocs in the twenty-first century may be dominated by two or three giants, leaving room only for niche players. Those with currently weak positions, or no presence at all, will have to create alliances for market entry and development with established firms. Tesco is highly flexible in its retailing format to respond to different consumer norms and tastes. Tesco entered the market not by opening hypermarkets but by acquiring a discount supermarket operator. The company's stores in Thailand seek to replicate the product selection experience of traditional street markets, with less emphasis on the neatly packaged portions found in many Western markets.

Reorganization

Whatever changes are made, they will require company reorganization. Structurally, authority will have to become more centralized to execute regional programs. In staffing, focus will have to be on individuals who understand the subtleties of consumer behavior across markets and are therefore able to evaluate the similarities and differences among cultures and markets. In developing systems for the planning and implementation of regional programs, adjustments have to be made to incorporate views throughout the organization. If, for example, decisions on regional advertising campaigns are made at headquarters without consultation with in-country operations, resentment from the local marketing staff could lead to less-than-optimal execution. Companies may even move corporate or divisional headquarters from the domestic market to be closer to the customer or centers of innovation. "Nokia Developer [Beta]," a portal available in English, Chinese, and Japanese, gives outside developers access to resources to help them design, test, certify, market, and sell their own applications, content, services, or websites to mobile uses via Nokia devices.[40]

Lobbying

International managers, as change agents, must constantly seek ways to influence the regulatory environment in which they have to operate. Economic integration will create its own powers and procedures similar to those of the EU commission and its directives. The international marketer is not powerless to influence both of them; as a matter of fact, a passive approach may result in competitors gaining an advantage, or it may put the company at a disadvantage. For example, it was very important for the U.S. pharmaceutical industry to obtain tight patent protection as part of the NAFTA agreement; therefore, substantial time and money were spent on lobbying both the executive and legislative branches of the U.S. government. Often, policymakers rely heavily on the knowledge and experience of the private sector to carry out their own work. Influencing change and protection will therefore provide industry preservation. Many marketers consider lobbying a public relations activity that can go beyond the traditional approaches.

Culture Clues Culture does play a role in lobbying in Brussels versus lobbying in Washington, D.C. One does not have to grapple with twenty-three different languages in Washington as you do in Brussels. Although English is increasingly imposing itself as the *lingua franca* in Brussels, many members of the European Parliament still value being approached in their native language. Internal political cultures are starkly different, too. Whereas U.S. style politics tend to be polarized around bi-partisanship and highly adversarial, Brussels politics draw on a wider array of parties and specific national issues, which are often deeply rooted in a country's governance culture (e.g., British laisser-faire versus French command and control).

SOURCE: "EU and US Approaches to Lobbying," **Euractiv.com**, February 15, 2005.

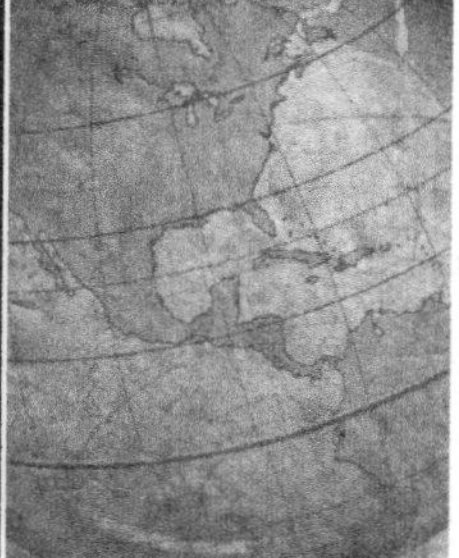

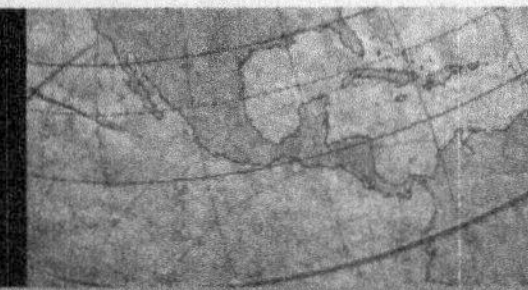

SUMMARY

Economic integration involves agreements among countries to establish links through the movements of goods, services, and factors of production across borders. These links may be weak or strong, depending on the level of integration.

The benefits derived from economic integration include trade creation, economies of scale, improved terms of trade, the reduction of monopoly power, and improved cross-cultural communication.

The emergence of economic integration in the world economy poses unique opportunities for and challenges to the global marketer. Eliminating barriers between member markets and erecting new ones vis-à-vis nonmembers will call for adjustments in past strategies to fully exploit the new situations. New trading blocs and the expansion of the existing ones will largely depend on future trade liberalization and political will within and among countries.

As developed markets have matured, marketers are looking at both emerging and developing markets for their future growth. To succeed, marketers will have to be innovative, pioneer new ways of doing business, and outmaneuver local competitors, many of them intent on becoming global players themselves.

6

Economic integration requires constant adjustment to the changes driven by the opening of markets. These adjustments include changes in the strategy to maintain competitive advantages as well as organizational modifications to implement these strategies.

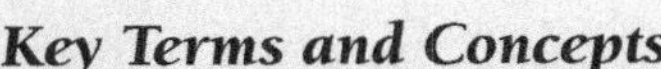

Key Terms and Concepts

trading bloc
factors of production
Caribbean Basin Initiative (CBI)
free trade area
customs union
common market
factor mobility
economic union
Maastricht Treaty
economic and monetary union
political union
trade creation
trade diversion
internal economies of scale
external economies of scale
Treaty of Rome
common agricultural policy (CAP)
Single European Act
maquiladoras
cartel
commodity price agreements
buffer stock
reverse innovation
microfinance

Review Questions

1. List the several types of trading blocs in existence around the world.
2. Are economic blocs building blocks or stumbling blocks as far as worldwide free trade is concerned?
3. What effect has the Free Trade Area of the Americas (FTAA) policy had on the United States?
4. In addition to Brazil, China, India, Russia, and South Africa, identify three other emerging markets that make sense for international business growth. Why?
5. The China-ASEAN Free Trade Area went into effect in 2010. Low wages have encouraged local and foreign manufacturers to phase out their operations in relatively

high-wage Southeast Asia and move them to China. For its Southeast Asian partners, what are the benefits of this current situation?

6. What are the advantages and disadvantages of global businesses outsourcing customer service functions to countries like India and Russia?
7. Tata Motors introduced the Nano, a fuel-efficient, two-cylinder-engine automobile that has the lowest CO_2 emission of all cars in India. What other countries might be potential markets for the Nano?
8. Almost by definition, poor people have very little money. How can microfinance work?

Critical Skill Builders

1. Explain the difference between a free trade area and a customs union. Speculate why negotiations were held for a North American Free Trade Agreement rather than for a North American Common Market.
2. What are the different barriers of culture and values to Iceland's quick membership to the European Union?
3. Discuss the Western dependence on oil reserves in the Gulf Cooperation Council (GCC) from both perspectives. Present your arguments in favor of or against policies to the rest of the class.
4. The continued rise of the BRICS is inevitable. Why?
5. The African Development Bank says a third of Africans are now "middle class," defined as having between \$2 and \$20 to spend a day. Does \$2 to \$4 a day really mean middle class?

On the Web

1. Compare and contrast two different points of view on expanding trade by accessing the web site of the Business Roundtable, an industry coalition promoting increased trade to and from world markets (**http://businessroundtable.org/**) and the AFL-CIO, American Federation of Labor-Congress of Industrial Organizations (**www.aflcio.org**).
2. Asia Pacific Economic Cooperation (APEC) proposes to bring together partners from multiple continents and blocs, linking members with such economic powerhouses as China, Russia, South Korea, and the United States. Visit the 2010 Guide to Investment Regimes of APEC Member Economies (**http://publications.apec.org/publication-detail.php?pub_id=1158**).
3. To address a chronic deficit in IT job applicants, Cisco created Network Academy, a concept whereby it contributes networking equipment to schools. The company now operates 10,000 academies in secondary schools, community colleges, and community-based organizations in 150 countries. Using their website (**http://www.cisco.com/web/learning/netacad/index.html**), see how Cisco's program is helping young deaf people learn valuable job skills and increase their economic opportunities in Kenya. Please review the programs offered by the Networking Academy, and suggest whether and how this approach might be useful.

Endnotes

1. "Free Trade in the Pacific," *The Economist*, November 19, 2011, 18; Ni Wang, "The Relationship between Regional Trading Blocs and Globalization," *International Journal of Economics and Finance*, February 2010, 171–173; Michael R. Czinkota and Ilkka A. Ronkainen, "A Forecast of Globalization, International Business and Trade: Report from a Delphi Study," *Journal of World Business*, 40 (May 2005): 111–123; and Ilkka A. Ronkainen, "Trading Blocs: Opportunity or Demise for International Trade?" *Multinational Business Review* 1 (Spring 1993): 1–9.
2. **http://www.ustr.gov/trade-agreements/free-trade-agreements**, accessed February 10, 2014.

3. *The European Union: A Guide for Americans*. (Washington, DC: Delegation of the European Commission to the United States, 2012), chapter 2. See **http://www.euintheus.org/who-we-are/what-is-the-european-union/**. Accessed February 5, 2014.
4. The discussion of economic integration is based on the pioneering work by Bela Balassa, *The Theory of Economic Integration* (Homewood, IL: Richard D. Irwin, 1961).
5. Frédéric Docquier and Hillel Rapoport, "Globalization, Brain Drain, and Development, *Journal of Economic Literature*, 50 (September 2012), 681–730.
6. Agreement on the European Economic Area, Main Part. **http://www.efta.int/media/documents/legal-texts/eea/the-eea-agreement/Main%20Text%20of%20the%20Agreement/EEAagreement.pdf**. Accessed February 5, 2014.
7. European Union, Facts and Figures. **http://europa.eu/about-eu/facts-figures/index_en.htm**. Accessed February 5, 2014.
8. "Staring into the Abyss," *The Economist*, November 12, 2011, 1–16.
9. "EU-wide Migration Policy Needed," *BBC News*, March 26, 2008.
10. "U Trade Deals Will Not Hang on Doha," *Financial Times*, July 10, 2006, 9.
11. Definition of NAFTA, The Free Dictionary, **http://encyclopedia2.thefreedictionary.com/NAFTA**, accessed February 5, 2014; full text of the North American Free Trade Agreement, **http://www.worldtradelaw.net/fta/agreements/nafta.pdf**, accessed February 5, 2014; Gary Clyde Hufbauer and Jeffrey J. Schott, *NAFTA Revisited: Achievements and Challenges*. (Washington, DC: Peterson Institute for International Economics, 2005), Chapter 1.
12. U.S. International Trade in Goods and Services (FT900), **http://www.census.gov/foreign-trade/Press-Release/current_press_release/**, accessed February 6, 2014; Exhibit 14. Exports, Imports, and Balance of Goods by Selected Countries and Areas: 2013.
13. Chris Hawley, "Aerospace Industry Migrating to Mexico in Greater Numbers," *Arizona Republic*, April 2, 2008. **http://www.azcentral.com/news/articles/2008/04/02/20080402mex-planes0402.html**, accessed February 10, 2014.
14. Dante Di Gregorio, Douglas Thomas, and Fernan Gonzalez de Castilla, "Competition Between Emerging Market and Multinational Firms: Wal-Mart and Mexican Retailers," *International Journal of Management* 25 (September 2008): 532–545.
15. David Alexander, Adriana Barrera, Mica Rosenberg, and Xavier Briand, "Obama Hopeful of Fixing Truck Dispute with Mexico," *Reuters*, April, 17, 2009.
16. "Mercosur RIP?" *The Economist*, July 14, 2012, 31–32.
17. "China Coming Down the Tracks," *The Economist*, January 22, 2011, 49.
18. About APEC: Achievements and Benefits. **http://www.apec.org/About-Us/About-APEC/Achievements-and-Benefits.aspx**, accessed February 6, 2014.
19. "Pakistan to Boost Trade With India; Rare Goodwill Gesture Shows Small Thaw in Relations Despite Tension on Kashmir, Mumbai Attacks, *Wall Street Journal*, November 3, 2011, A16.
20. Wafula Okumu, "The African Union: Pitfalls and Prospects for Uniting Africa," *Journal of International Affairs*, Spring 2009, 93–106.
21. Ibrahim El-Husseini, Fadi Majdalani, and Alessandro Borgogna, "Filling the Gulf States' Infrastructure Gap," *Strategy & Business*, September 22, 2009.
22. "World Oil Outlook 2011," *Organization of the Petroleum Exporting Countries*, Vienna, Austria, 2012, 5–22.
23. Antoine Van Agtmael, "Think Again: The BRICS," *Foreign Policy*, November 2012, 76–79.
24. Yuval Atsmon, Ari Kertesz, and Ireena Vitta, "Is Your Emerging-market Strategy Local Enough?" *McKinsey Quarterly*, April 2011.
25. "Kremlin Blocks Big Acquisition by Siemens AG," *The Wall Street Journal*, April 14, 2005, A14, A16.
26. "The High-tech Threat from China," *Business Week*, January 31, 2005, 22.
27. This section builds on Tarun Khanna, Krishna Palepu, and Jayant Sinha, "Strategies That Fit Emerging Markets," *Harvard Business Review* 83 (June 2005): 63–76; and James A. Gingrich, "Five Rules for Winning Emerging Market Consumers," *Strategy and Business* (second quarter, 1999): 19–33.
28. GM Russia Gearing Up for Annual Production of 350,000 Vehicles, **http://www.media.gm.com/content/media/us/en/gm/news.detail.html/content/Pages/news/global/en/2011/0602_russia.html**. Accessed February 6, 2014.
29. Orit Gadiesh, Philip Leung, and Til Vestring, "The Battle for China's Good-Enough Market," *Harvard Business Review* 85 (September 2007): 81–89.
30. Vijay Govindarajan, "A Reverse-Innovation Playbook," *Harvard Business Review*, 90 (April 2012): 120–125.
31. "As China Builds, Too Much 'Boom'?," *The Washington Post*, October 23, 2011, G1–G7.
32. The World Bank considers $2,000 to be the minimum to sustain a decent life.
33. This framework is adapted from C. K. Prahalad and Stuart L. Hart, "The Fortune at the Bottom of the Pyramid," *Strategy and Business*, First Quarter, 2002, 35–47.

34. "Africa rising," *The Economist*, December 3, 2011, 15.
35. "Major Victories for Micro-finance," *Financial Times*, May 18, 2005, 10. See also **http://www.planetfinancegroup.org**, accessed February 6, 2014.
36. Erik Simanis, "Reality Check at the Bottom of the Pyramid," *Harvard Business Review*, 90 (June 2012): 120–125.
37. "And the Winners Are…," *The Economist*, September 18, 2004, 17; "The Digital Village," *Business Week*, June 28, 2004, 60–62; and Arundhati Parmar, "Indian Farmers Reap Web Harvest," *Marketing News*, June 1, 2004, 27, 31.
38. "Procter & Gamble, Coca-Cola Formulate Vitamin Drinks for Developing Countries," *The Wall Street Journal*, November 27, 2001, **http://online.wsj.com/article/SB1006818282554536760.html?dsk=y**, accessed February 6, 2014; **http://tccaf.org/coca-cola-africa-foundation-partners.asp**, accessed February 6, 2014.
39. Ronald Haddock and John Jullens, "The Best Years of the Auto Industry Are Still to Come," *Strategy & Business*, May 26, 2009.
40. **http://www.developer.nokia.com/**, accessed February 6, 2014.

PART 3

GLOBAL TRADE AND INVESTMENT

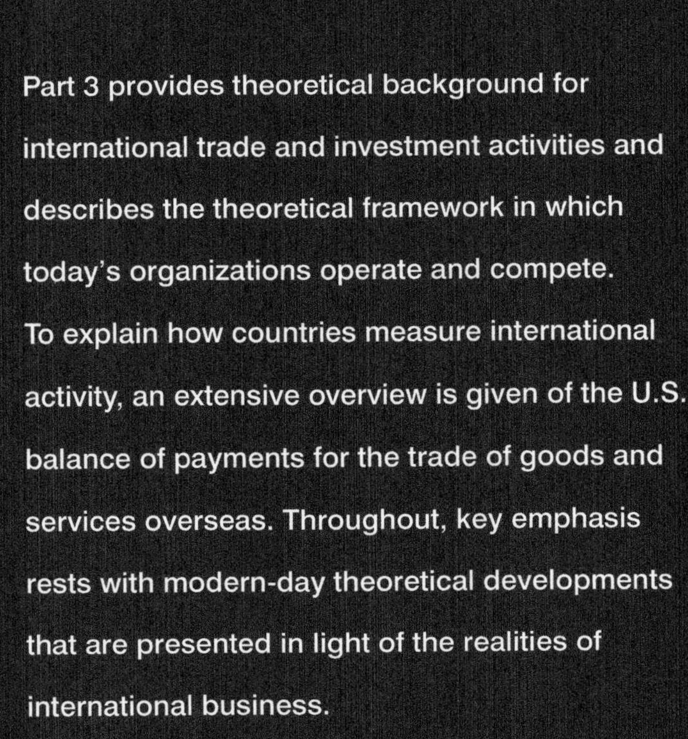

Part 3 provides theoretical background for international trade and investment activities and describes the theoretical framework in which today's organizations operate and compete. To explain how countries measure international activity, an extensive overview is given of the U.S. balance of payments for the trade of goods and services overseas. Throughout, key emphasis rests with modern-day theoretical developments that are presented in light of the realities of international business.

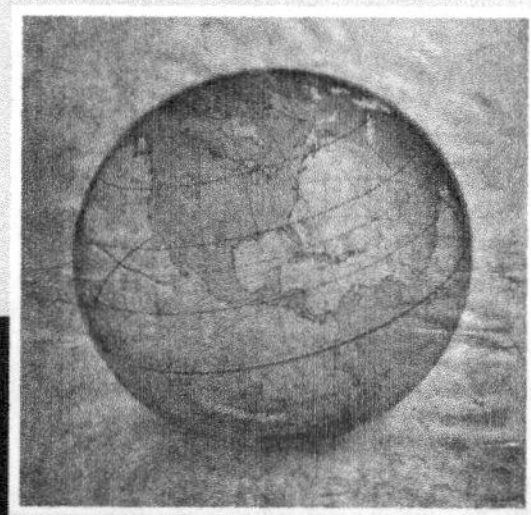

CHAPTER 6

TRADE AND INVESTMENT THEORY

Millennium Development Goals: The Role of International Trade

But though the rich by unfair combinations contribute frequently to prolong a season of distress among the poor, yet no possible form of society could prevent the almost constant action of misery upon a great part of mankind, if in a state of inequality, and upon all, if all were equal.

— An Essay on the Principle of Population by Thomas Malthus, 1798

LEARNING OUTCOMES

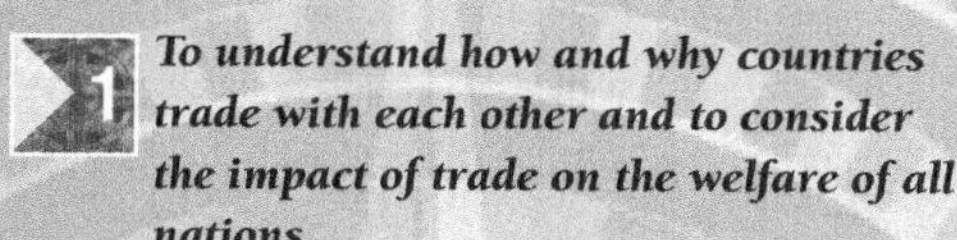

1 To understand how and why countries trade with each other and to consider the impact of trade on the welfare of all nations

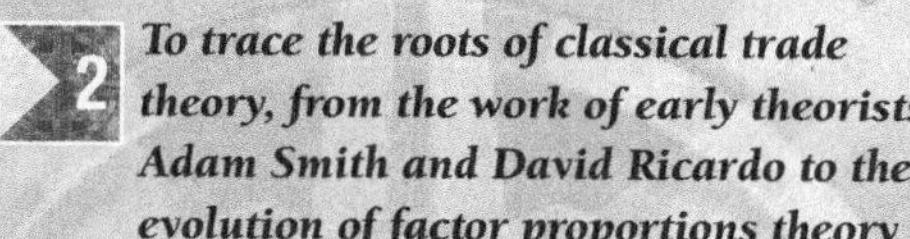

2 To trace the roots of classical trade theory, from the work of early theorists Adam Smith and David Ricardo to the evolution of factor proportions theory

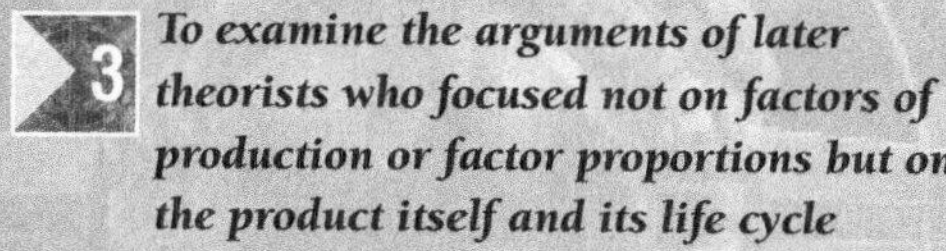

3 To examine the arguments of later theorists who focused not on factors of production or factor proportions but on the product itself and its life cycle

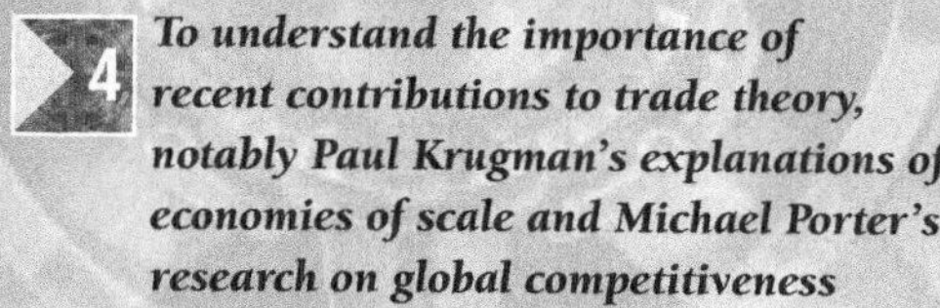

4 To understand the importance of recent contributions to trade theory, notably Paul Krugman's explanations of economies of scale and Michael Porter's research on global competitiveness

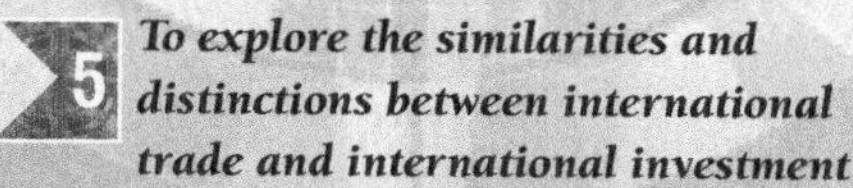

5 To explore the similarities and distinctions between international trade and international investment

6 To consider the decision process involved in foreign direct investment strategies

At the Millennium Summit in 2000, members of the United Nations agreed to a set of goals—Millennium Development Goals (MDGs)—for the health and welfare of people everywhere. As described by the U.N.:

> *"The eight Millennium Development Goals (MDGs)—which range from halving extreme poverty rates to halting the spread of HIV/AIDS and providing universal primary education, all by the target date of 2015—form a blueprint agreed to by all the world's countries and all the world's leading development institutions. They have galvanized unprecedented efforts to meet the needs of the world's poorest."*
>
> — United Nations, **http://www.un.org/millenniumgoals/**

The eight millennium development goals are as follows:

1. Eradicating extreme poverty and hunger
2. Achieving universal primary education
3. Promoting gender equality and empowering women
4. Reducing child mortality rates
5. Improving maternal health
6. Combating HIV/AIDS, malaria, and other diseases
7. Ensuring environmental sustainability
8. Developing a global partnership for development

The first, eradicating extreme poverty and hunger, was a singular and lofty goal, as poverty has always been with mankind.

But that is history. Between 1990 and 2010, in twenty years, global poverty (extreme poverty) was cut in half. To be more specific, in 1990 about 1.9 billion people, or 43 percent of the earth's population, lived on less than $1 per day. By 2010, despite the rapid growth in the world's population, 1.2 billion— or 21 percent—now lived below the extreme poverty level of a revised $1.25 per day. All things considered, a miraculous achievement.

How was this reduction in global poverty achieved? It is simple: economic growth. Was this economic growth the result of political and economic policies of governments or nongovernmental organizations across the world? Yes, some. But most of the true improvements were in countries like Brazil, India, and China, which achieved higher levels of general economic growth. And what was the most frequent driving force in those cases? International trade between nations.

"They said poverty would always be with us. Well, maybe not."

—Jim Yong Kim, President of the World Bank (2013)

As You Read This Chapter

1. Think about what factors give rise to increasing competitiveness of a nation in trade.
2. Consider the benefits of trade—exports and imports—in raising the prospects for all people.

The debates, the costs, the benefits, and the dilemmas of international trade have in many ways remained without significant change since the time when Marco Polo crossed the barren wastelands of Eurasia. At its heart, international trade is all about the gains—and the risks—to the firm and the country as a result of a seller from one country servicing the needs of a buyer in a different country. If a Spanish firm wants to sell its product to the enormous market of mainland China, whether it produces at home and ships the product from Cádiz to Shanghai (international trade) or actually builds a factory in Shanghai (international investment), the goal is still the same: to sell a product for profit in a foreign market.

This chapter provides a directed path through centuries of thought and theory on why and how trade and investment across borders occurs. Although theories and theorists come and go with time, a few basic questions have dominated this intellectual adventure:

- Why do countries trade?
- Do countries trade or do firms trade?
- Do the elements that give rise to the competitiveness of a firm, an industry, or a country as a whole arise from some inherent endowment of the country itself, or do they change with time and circumstance?
- Once identified, can these sources of competitiveness be manipulated or managed by firms or governments to the benefit of traders?

International trade is expected to improve the productivity of industry and the welfare of consumers. Let us learn how and why we still seek the exotic silks of the Far East.

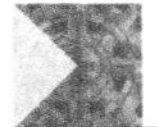

Why Countries Trade

The question of why countries trade has proven difficult to answer. Since the second half of the eighteenth century, academicians have tried to understand not only the motivations and benefits of international trade, but also why some countries grow faster and wealthier than others through trade. Figure 6.1 provides an overview of the evolutionary path of trade theory since the fall of mercantilism. Although somewhat simplified, it shows the line of development of the major theories put forward during the past two centuries. It also serves as an early indication of the path of modern theory: the shifting focus from the country to the firm, from cost of production to the market as a whole, and from the perfect to the imperfect.

FIGURE 6.1 The Evolution of Trade Theory

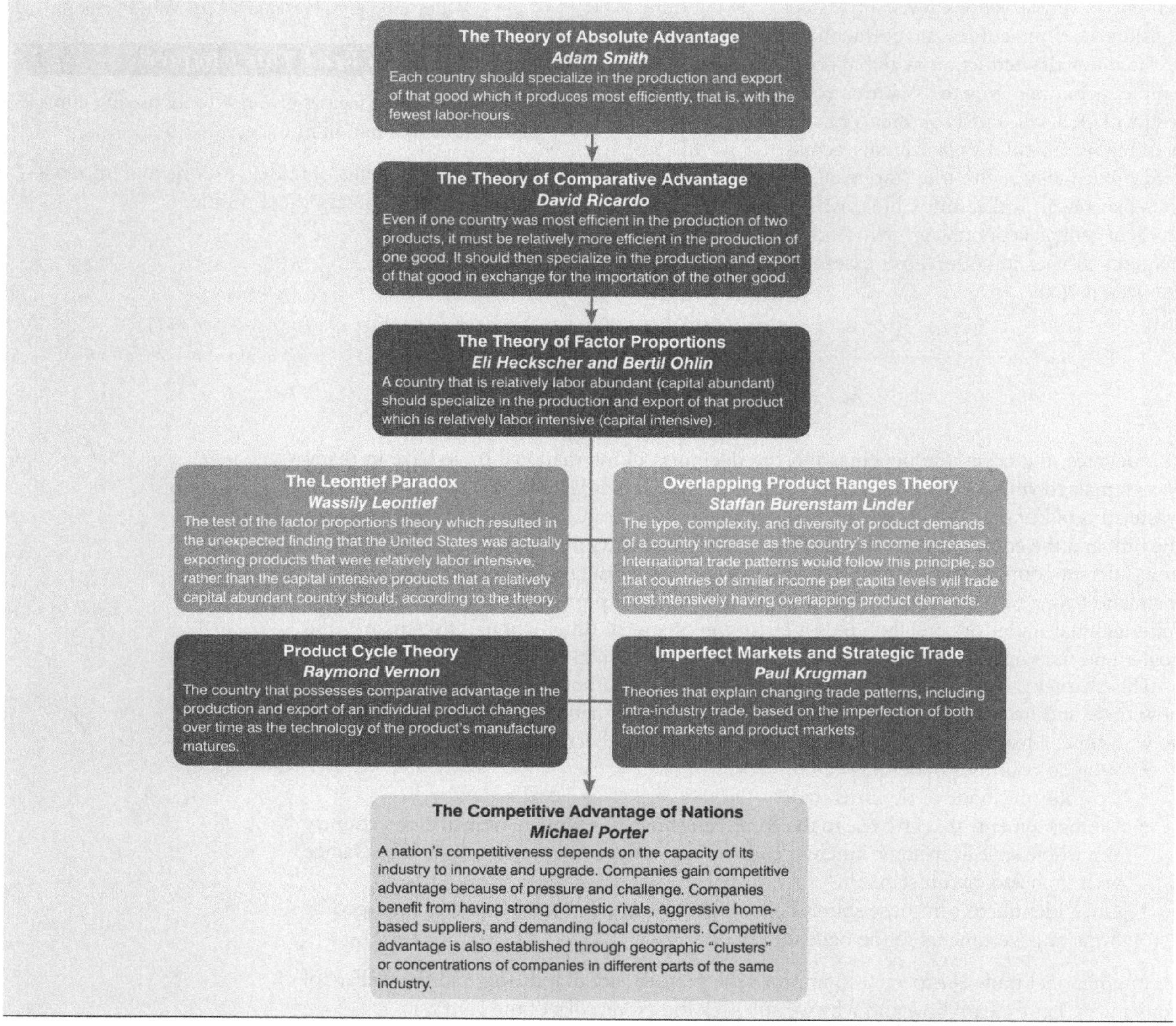

The Theory of Absolute Advantage
Adam Smith
Each country should specialize in the production and export of that good which it produces most efficiently, that is, with the fewest labor-hours.

The Theory of Comparative Advantage
David Ricardo
Even if one country was most efficient in the production of two products, it must be relatively more efficient in the production of one good. It should then specialize in the production and export of that good in exchange for the importation of the other good.

The Theory of Factor Proportions
Eli Heckscher and Bertil Ohlin
A country that is relatively labor abundant (capital abundant) should specialize in the production and export of that product which is relatively labor intensive (capital intensive).

The Leontief Paradox
Wassily Leontief
The test of the factor proportions theory which resulted in the unexpected finding that the United States was actually exporting products that were relatively labor intensive, rather than the capital intensive products that a relatively capital abundant country should, according to the theory.

Overlapping Product Ranges Theory
Staffan Burenstam Linder
The type, complexity, and diversity of product demands of a country increase as the country's income increases. International trade patterns would follow this principle, so that countries of similar income per capita levels will trade most intensively having overlapping product demands.

Product Cycle Theory
Raymond Vernon
The country that possesses comparative advantage in the production and export of an individual product changes over time as the technology of the product's manufacture matures.

Imperfect Markets and Strategic Trade
Paul Krugman
Theories that explain changing trade patterns, including intra-industry trade, based on the imperfection of both factor markets and product markets.

The Competitive Advantage of Nations
Michael Porter
A nation's competitiveness depends on the capacity of its industry to innovate and upgrade. Companies gain competitive advantage because of pressure and challenge. Companies benefit from having strong domestic rivals, aggressive home-based suppliers, and demanding local customers. Competitive advantage is also established through geographic "clusters" or concentrations of companies in different parts of the same industry.

THE AGE OF MERCANTILISM

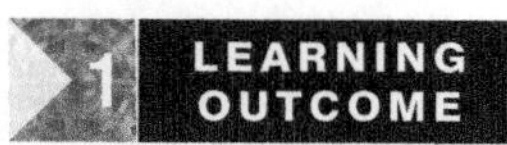

The evolution of trade into the form we see today reflects three events: the collapse of feudal society, the emergence of the mercantilist philosophy, and the life cycle of the colonial systems of the European nation-states. Feudal society was a state of **autarky**, a society that did not trade because all of its needs were met internally. The feudal estate was self-sufficient, although hardly "sufficient" in more modern terms, given the limits of providing entirely for oneself. Needs literally were only those of food and shelter, and all available human labor was devoted to the task of fulfilling those basic needs. As merchants began meeting in the marketplace, as travelers began exchanging goods from faraway places at the water's edge, the attractiveness of trade became evident.

AUTARKY
Self-sufficiency; a country that is not participating in international trade

In the centuries leading up to the Industrial Revolution, international commerce was largely conducted under the authority of governments. The goals of trade were, therefore, the goals of governments. As early as 1500, the benefits of trade were clearly established in Europe, as nation-states expanded their influence across the globe in the creation of colonial systems. To maintain and expand their control over these colonial possessions, the European nations needed fleets, armies, food, and all the other resources the nations could muster. They needed wealth. Trade was therefore conducted to fill the governments' treasuries, at minimum expense to themselves but to the detriment of their captive trade partners. Although colonialism normally is associated with the exploitation of those captive societies, it went hand in hand with the evolving exchange of goods among the European countries themselves, **mercantilism**.

MERCANTILISM
Political and economic policy in the seventeenth and eighteenth centuries aimed at increasing a nation's wealth and power by encouraging the export of goods in return for gold

Mercantilism mixed exchange through trade with accumulation of wealth. Because government controlled the patterns of commerce, it identified strength with the accumulation of specie (gold and silver) and maintained a general policy of exports dominating imports. Trade across borders—exports—was considered preferable to domestic trade because exports would earn gold. Import duties, tariffs, subsidization of exports, and outright restriction on the importation of many goods were used to maximize the gains from exports over the costs of imports. Laws were passed making it illegal to take gold or silver out of the country, even if such specie was needed to purchase imports to produce their own goods for sale. This was one-way trade, the trade of greed and power.

The demise of mercantilism was inevitable, given class structure and the distribution of society's product. As the Industrial Revolution introduced the benefits of mass production,

Quick Take *Trade, Transactions, and Accountability*

Ethical trade, fair trade, and corporate social responsibility are all concepts surrounding the social responsibility and accountability of business. International trade has long been the target of much of this debate, particularly following the growing concerns over globalization beginning in the mid-1990s. The concerns know few bounds, and the following is just one short, select list of the multitude of issues.

Many of the programs use the following elements:

- *Fair trade coffee:* An amalgam of concerns have been expressed, particularly on whether the growers of coffee in Central America, South America, South Asia, or East Africa are paid a sufficient price for their product to allow them a living wage and a sustainable existence.
- *Textiles from Bangladesh:* The horrific collapse of the textile factory in Bangladesh in 2013, in which 1,100 people lost their lives, once again highlighted the horrific working conditions in one of the world's oldest and most abusive industries, textiles. Because textile products benefit from large economies of scale, yet remain relatively labor intensive, the industry has long been a fertile field for labor abuse.
- *Conflict diamonds:* Also referred to as blood diamonds, these are diamonds mined in a variety of African war zones. The proceeds from their mining and sale are often used to sustain and support the military regimes that are conscripting citizens for the perpetuation of conflict.
- *Curse of oil:* This phrase is used to characterize the frequent result of oil and gas development in many African or South American countries. Many of these countries experience slower economic growth, more income inequality, and lower per capita incomes after the discovery and development of oil and gas than those countries without such "wealth."

lowering prices and increasing the supplies of goods to all, the exploitation of colonies and trading partners came to an end. However, governments still exercise considerable power and influence on the conduct of trade.

Absolute Advantage and the Division of Labor

ABSOLUTE ADVANTAGE
A country that is capable of producing a product with fewer labor hours

DIVISION OF LABOR
The practice of subdividing a production process into stages that can then be performed by labor repeating the process, as on a production line

Adam Smith is considered the father of economics. In *The Wealth of Nations* (1776), he attempted to explain the process by which markets and production actually operate in society. He introduced two concepts that are fundamental to trade theory: **absolute advantage** and the **division of labor**.

Production, the creation of a product for exchange, always requires the use of society's primary element of value, human labor. Smith noted that some countries, owing to the skills of their workers or the quality of their natural resources, could produce the same products as others with fewer labor-hours. He termed this efficiency absolute advantage.

Smith observed the production processes of the early stages of the Industrial Revolution in England and recognized the fundamental changes that were occurring. In previous states of society, a worker performed all stages of a production process, with resulting output that was little more than sufficient for the worker's own needs. The factories of the industrializing world were, however, separating the production process into distinct stages, each performed exclusively by one individual. This specialization increased the production of workers and industries. Smith termed it the division of labor. Smith's pin factory analogy best encapsulates one of the most significant principles of the industrial age.

> To take an example, therefore, from a very trifling manufacture; but one in which the division of labour has been very often taken notice of, the trade of the pin maker; a workman not educated to this business . . . could scarce, perhaps, with his utmost industry, make one pin in a day, and certainly could not make twenty. But in a way in which this business is now carried on, not only the whole work is a peculiar trade, but it is divided in to a number of branches, of which the greater part are likewise peculiar trades. One man draws out the wire, another straights it, a third cuts it, a fourth points it, a fifth grinds it at the top for receiving the head: to make the head requires two or three distinct operations; to put it on is a peculiar business . . . I have seen a small manufactory of this kind where ten men only were employed, and where some of them consequently performed two or three distinct operations. But though they were very poor, and therefore but indifferently accommodated with the necessary machine, they could, when they exerted themselves, make among them about twelve pounds of pins in a day. There are in a pound upwards of four thousand pins of a middling size.[1]

Smith then extended his division of labor in the production process to a division of labor and specialized product across countries. Each country would specialize in a product for which it was uniquely suited. More would be produced for less. Thus, with each country specializing in products for which it possessed absolute advantage, countries could produce more in total and exchange products—trade for goods—that were cheaper in price than those produced at home.

Comparative Advantage

Although Smith's work was instrumental in the development of economic theories about trade and production, it did not answer some fundamental questions about trade. First,

Smith's trade relied on a country possessing absolute advantage in production but did not explain what gave rise to the production advantages. Second, if a country did not possess absolute advantage in any product, could it (or would it) trade?

David Ricardo, in *On the Principles of Political Economy and Taxation* (1819), took the basic ideas set down by Smith a few steps further. Ricardo noted that even if a country possessed absolute advantage in the production of two products, it still must be relatively more efficient than the other country in one good's production than the other. Ricardo termed this the **comparative advantage**. Each country would then possess comparative advantage in the production of one of the two products, and both countries would then benefit by specializing completely in one product and trading for the other.

COMPARATIVE ADVANTAGE

The ability to produce a good or service more cheaply, relative to other goods and services, than is possible in other countries

A Numerical Example of Classical Trade

To fully understand the theories of absolute advantage and comparative advantage, consider the following example. Two countries, France and England, produce only two products, wheat and cloth (or beer and pizza, guns and butter, and so forth). The relative efficiency of each country in the production of the two products is measured by comparing the number of labor-hours needed to produce one unit of each product.

Table 6.1 provides an efficiency comparison of the two countries. England is more efficient in the production of wheat. Whereas it takes France four labor-hours to produce one unit of wheat, it takes England only two hours to produce the same unit of wheat. France takes twice as many labor-hours to produce the same output. England has absolute advantage in the production of wheat. France needs two labor-hours to produce a unit of cloth that it takes England four labor-hours to produce. England therefore requires two more labor-hours than France to produce the same unit of cloth. France has absolute advantage in the production of cloth. The two countries are exactly opposite in relative efficiency of production.

TABLE 6.1 Absolute Advantage and Comparative Advantage

Country	Wheat	Cloth
England	2*	4*
France	4*	2*

*Labor-hours per unit of output

England has absolute advantage in the production of wheat. It requires fewer labor-hours (2 being less than 4) for England to produce one unit of wheat.

France has absolute advantage in the production of cloth. It requires few labor-hours (2 being less than 4) for France to produce one unit of cloth.

England has comparative advantage in the production of wheat. If England produces one unit of wheat, it is forgoing the production of 2/4 (0.50) of a unit of cloth. If France produces one unit of wheat, it is forgoing the production of 4.2 (2.00) of a unit of cloth. England therefore has the lower opportunity cost of producing wheat.

France has comparative advantage in the production of cloth. If England produces one unit of cloth, it is forgoing the production of 4.2 (2.00) of a unit of wheat. If France produces one unit of cloth, it is forgoing the production of 2/4 (0.5) of a unit of wheat. France therefore has the lower opportunity cost of producing cloth.

David Ricardo took the logic of absolute advantage one step further to explain how countries could exploit their own advantages and gain from international trade. Comparative advantage, according to Ricardo, was based on what was given up or traded off in producing one product instead of the other. In this example, England needs only two-fourths as many labor-hours to produce a unit of wheat as France, whereas France needs only two-fourths as many labor-hours to produce a unit of cloth. England has comparative advantage in the production of wheat, while France has comparative advantage in the production of cloth. A country cannot possess comparative advantage in the production of both products, so each country has an economic role to play in international trade.

National Production Possibilities

PRODUCTION POSSIBILITIES FRONTIERS
A theoretical method of representing the total productive capabilities of a nation used in the formulation of classical and modern trade theory

If the total labor-hours available for production within a nation were devoted to the full production of either product, wheat or cloth, the **production possibilities frontiers** of each country can be constructed. Assuming both countries possess the same number of labor-hours, for example 100, the production possibilities frontiers for each country can be graphed, as in Figure 6.2.

FIGURE 6.2 Production Possibility Frontiers, Specialization of Production, and the Benefits of Trade

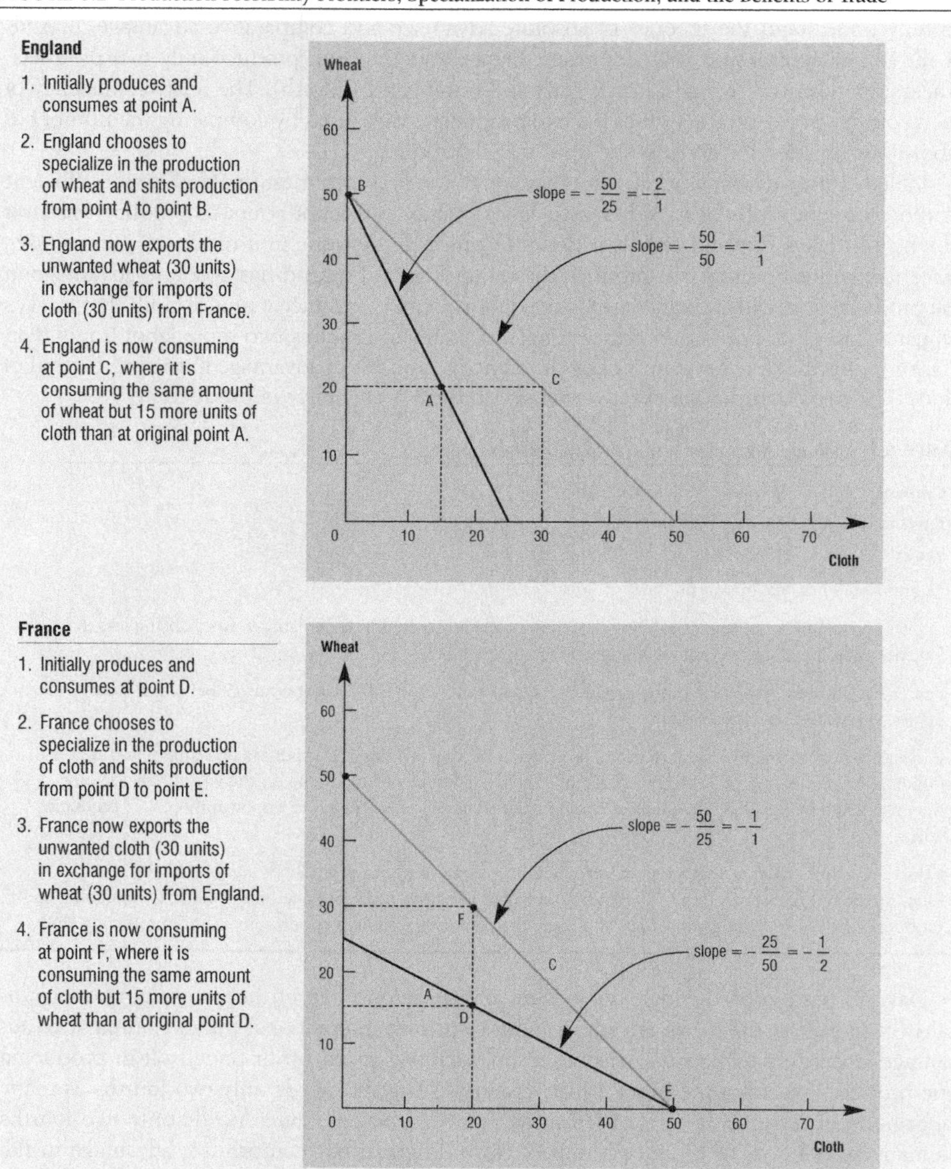

If England devotes all labor-hours (100) to the production of wheat (which requires two labor-hours per unit produced), it can produce a maximum of fifty units of wheat. If England devotes all labor to the production of cloth instead, the same 100 labor-hours can produce a maximum of twenty-five units of cloth (100 labor-hours divided by 4 hours per unit of cloth). If England did not trade with any other country, it could only consume the products that it produced itself. England would therefore probably produce and consume some combination of wheat and cloth such as point A in Figure 6.2 (fifteen units of cloth, twenty units of wheat). France's production possibilities frontier is constructed in the same way, with France producing and consuming at some point such as point D in Figure 6.2 (twenty units of cloth, fifteen units of wheat).

These frontiers depict what each country could produce in isolation—without trade. The slope of the production possibility frontier of a nation is a measure of how one product is traded off in production with the other (moving up the frontier, England is choosing to produce more wheat and less cloth). The slope of the frontier reflects the "trade-off" of producing one product over the other; the trade-offs represent prices, or opportunity costs. **Opportunity cost** is the forgone value of a factor of production in its next-best use. If England chooses to produce more units of wheat (in fact, produce only wheat), moving from point A to point B along the production possibilities frontier, it is giving up producing cloth. The "cost" of the additional wheat is the loss of cloth. The slope of the production possibilities frontier is the ratio of product prices (opportunity costs). The slope of the production possibilities frontier for England is –50/25, or –2.00. The slope of the production possibilities frontier for France is flatter, –25/50, or –0.50.

OPPORTUNITY COST

Cost incurred by a firm as a result of taking one action rather than another

The relative prices of products also provide an alternative way of seeing comparative advantage. The flatter slope of the French production possibilities frontier means that to produce more wheat (move up the frontier), France would have to give up the production of relatively more units of cloth than would England, with its steeper sloped production possibilities frontier.

The Gains from International Trade

Continuing with Figure 6.2, if originally England was not trading with France (the only other country) and it was producing at its own maximum possibilities (on the frontier and not inside the line), it would be producing at point A. Because it was not trading with another country, whatever it was producing it must also be consuming. So England could be said to be consuming at point A also. Therefore, without trade, you consume what you produce.

If, however, England recognized that it has comparative advantage in the production of wheat, it should move production from point A to point B. England should specialize completely in the product it produces best. It does not want to consume only wheat, however, so it would take the wheat it has produced and trade with France. For example, England may only want to consume twenty units of wheat, as it did at point A. It is now producing fifty units and, therefore, has thirty units of wheat it can export to France. If England could export thirty units of wheat in exchange for imports of thirty units of cloth (a 1:1 ratio of prices), England would clearly be better off than before. The new consumption point would be point C, where it is consuming the same amount of wheat as point A but is now consuming thirty units of cloth instead of just fifteen. More is better; England has benefited from international trade.

France, following the same principle of completely specializing in the product of its comparative production advantage, moves production from point D to point E, producing fifty units of cloth. If France now exported the unwanted cloth, for example thirty units, and exchanged the cloth with England for imports of thirty units of wheat (note that England's exports are France's imports), France is better off as well as a result of international trade. Each country would do what it does best, exclusively, and then trade for the other product.

But at what prices will the two countries trade? Because each country's production possibilities frontier has a different slope (different relative product prices), the two countries can determine a set of prices between the two domestic prices. England's price ratio was –2:1, while France's domestic price was –1:2. Trading thirty units of wheat for thirty units of cloth is a price ratio of –1:1, a slope or set of prices between the two domestic price ratios. The dashed line in Figure 6.2 illustrates this set of trade prices.

Are both countries better off as a result of trade? Yes. The final step to understanding the benefits of classical trade theory is to note that the point where a country produces (point B for England and point E for France in Figure 6.2) and the point where it consumes are now different. This allows each country to consume beyond its own production possibilities frontier. Society's welfare, which is normally measured in its ability to consume more wheat, cloth, or any other goods or services, is increased through trade.

Applying Classical Trade Theory

Classical trade theory contributed much to the understanding of how production and trade operates in the world economy. Although, like all economic theories, they are often criticized for being unrealistic or out of date, the purpose of a theory is to simplify reality so that the basic elements of the logic can be seen. Several of these simplifications have continued to provide insight in understanding international business.

- *Division of labor:* Smith's explanation of how industrial societies can increase output using the same labor-hours as in preindustrial society is fundamental to our thinking even today. Smith extended this specialization of the efforts of a worker to the specialization of a nation.
- *Comparative advantage:* Ricardo's extension of Smith's work explained for the first time how countries that seemingly had no obvious reason for trade could individually specialize in producing what they did best and trade for products they did not produce.
- *Gains from trade:* The theory of comparative advantage argued that nations could improve the welfare of their populations through international trade. A nation could actually achieve consumption levels beyond what it could produce by itself. To this day, this is one of the fundamental principles underlying the arguments for all countries to strive to expand and "free" world trade.

Factor Proportions Trade Theory

Trade theory changed drastically in the first half of the twentieth century. Concepts developed by Swedish economist Eli Heckscher and later expanded by his former student Bertil Ohlin formed the theory of international trade that is still widely accepted today, factor proportions theory.

Factor Intensity in Production

The Heckscher-Ohlin theory considered two factors of production: labor and capital. Technology determined how they combine to form a good. Different goods required different proportions of the factors of production.

Figure 6.3 illustrates two goods by factor proportions. The production of one unit of good X requires four units of labor and one unit of capital. At the same time, to produce one unit of good Y requires four units of labor and two units of capital. Good X therefore requires more units of labor per unit of capital (4 to 1) relative to Y (4 to 2). X is therefore classified as a relatively labor-intensive product, and Y is relatively capital intensive. These **factor intensities**, or **proportions**, are truly relative and are determined only on the basis of what product X requires relative to product Y and not to the specific numbers of labor to capital.

FACTOR INTENSITIES/ FACTOR PROPORTIONS
The proportion of capital input to labor input used in the production of a good

It is easy to see how the factor proportions of production differ substantially across goods. For example, the manufacturing of leather footwear is still a relatively labor-intensive process, even with the most sophisticated leather treatment and patterning machinery. Other goods, such as computer memory chips, however, although requiring some highly skilled labor, require massive quantities of capital for production. These large capital requirements include the enormous sums needed for research and development and the manufacturing facilities needed for clean production to ensure the extremely high quality demanded.

FIGURE 6.3 Factor Proportions in Production

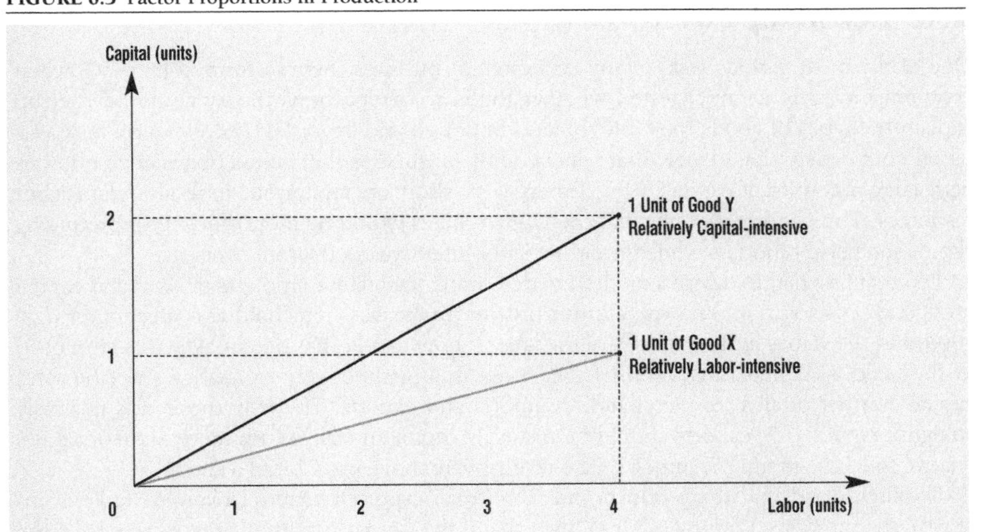

According to **factor proportions theory**, factor intensities depend on the state of technology—the current method of manufacturing a good. The theory assumed that the same technology of production would be used for the same goods in all countries. It is not, therefore, a difference in the efficiency of production that will determine trade between countries as it did in classical theory. Classical theory implicitly assumed that technology or the productivity of labor is different across countries. Otherwise, there would be no logical explanation why one country requires more units of labor to produce a unit of output than another country. Factor proportions theory assumes no such productivity differences.

FACTOR PROPORTIONS THEORY
Systematic explanation of the source of comparative advantage

Factor Endowments, Factor Prices, and Comparative Advantage

If technology or productivity of factors is not different across countries, what then determines comparative advantage in production and export? The answer is that factor prices determine cost differences. And these prices are determined by the endowments of labor and capital the country possesses. The theory assumes that labor and capital are immobile; factors cannot move across borders. Therefore, the country's endowment determines the relative costs of labor and capital as compared with other countries.

Using these assumptions, factor proportions theory stated that a country should specialize in the production and export of those products that use intensively its relatively abundant factor.

- A country that is relatively labor abundant should specialize in the production of relatively labor-intensive goods. It should then export those labor-intensive goods in exchange for capital-intensive goods.
- A country that is relatively capital abundant should specialize in the production of relatively capital-intensive goods. It should then export those capital-intensive goods in exchange for labor-intensive goods.

The Leontief Paradox

One of the most famous tests of any economic or business theory occurred in 1950, when economist Wassily Leontief tested whether the factor proportions theory could be used to explain the types of goods the United States imported and exported. Leontief's premise was based on a widely shared view that some countries, such as the United States, are endowed with large amounts of capital, while others were short on capital but have abundant labor resources. Thus, it was thought that the United States would be more efficient in producing capital-intensive products while importing labor-intensive goods from overseas.

INPUT–OUTPUT ANALYSIS
A method for estimating market activities and potential that measures the factor inflows into production and the resultant outflow of products

Leontief first had to devise a method to determine the relative amounts of labor and capital in a good. His solution, known as **input-output analysis**, is a technique of decomposing a good into the values and quantities of the labor, capital, and other potential factors employed in the good's manufacture. Leontief then used this methodology to analyze the labor and capital content of all U.S. merchandise imports and exports. The hypothesis was relatively straightforward: U.S. exports should be relatively capital intensive (use more units of capital relative to labor) than U.S. imports. The results were, however, a bit of a shock.

Leontief found that the products that U.S. firms exported were relatively more labor intensive than imported products.[2] It seemed that if the factor proportions theory was true, the United States is a relatively labor-abundant country! Alternatively, the theory could be wrong. Neither interpretation of the results was acceptable to many in the field of international trade.

LEONTIEF PARADOX
Wassily Leontief's studies that indicated that the United States was a labor-abundant country, exporting labor-intensive products; a paradox because of the general belief that the United States was a capital-abundant country that should be exporting capital-intensive products

A variety of explanations and continuing studies have attempted to solve what has become known as the **Leontief Paradox**. At first, it was thought to have been simply a result of the specific year of the data. However, the same results were found with different years and data sets. Second, it was noted that Leontief did not really analyze the labor and capital contents of imports but rather the labor and capital contents of the domestic equivalents of these imports. It was possible that the United States was actually producing the products in a more capital-intensive fashion than were the countries from which it also imported the manufactured goods. Finally, the debate turned to the need to distinguish different types of labor and capital. For example, several studies attempted to separate labor into skilled labor and unskilled labor. These studies have continued to show results more consistent with what the factor proportions theory would predict for country trade patterns.

Linder's Overlapping Product Ranges Theory

The difficulties in confirming the factor proportions theory led many in the 1960s and 1970s to search for new explanations of the determinants of trade between countries. The work of Staffan Burenstam Linder focused, not on the production or supply side, but instead on the preferences of consumers—the demand side. Linder argued that trade in manufactured goods was dictated not by cost concerns but rather by the similarity in product demands across countries. Linder based his work on two principles:

1. As per capita income rises, the complexity and quality level of the products demanded by the country's residents also rises. The range of product sophistication demanded is largely determined by the country's level of income.
2. The businesses that produce a society's needs are more knowledgeable about their domestic market than foreign markets. A logical pattern is for firms to gain success and market share at home first then expand to foreign markets that are similar in their demands or tastes.

This would mean that global trade in manufactured goods is influenced by similarity of demands. The countries that would see the most intensive trade are those with similar per-capita income levels, for they would possess a greater likelihood of overlapping product demands. For example, the United States and Canada have almost parallel sophistication ranges, implying a lot of common ground or overlapping product ranges for intensive international trade and competition. They are quite similar in their per-capita income levels. By contrast, Mexico and the United States, or Mexico and Canada, are not.

The overlapping product ranges described by Linder would today be termed **market segments**. Not only was Linder's work instrumental in extending trade theory beyond cost considerations, but it also found a place in the field of international marketing.

MARKET SEGMENT
Overlapping ranges of trade targets with common ground and levels of sophistication

Product Cycle Theory

PRODUCT CYCLE THEORY
A theory that views products as passing through four stages—introduction, growth, maturity, decline—during which the location of production moves from industrialized to lower-cost developing nations

A very different path was taken by Raymond Vernon in his creation of **product cycle theory**. Diverging significantly from traditional approaches, Vernon focused on the product rather than on the country, technology, or factor proportions. Most striking was the appreciation of the role of information, knowledge, and the costs and power that go hand in hand with knowledge. Vernon rejected the notion that knowledge is a universal free good, and introduced it as an independent variable in the decision to trade or to invest.

Using many of the same basic tools and assumptions of factor proportions theory, Vernon added two technology-based premises to the factor-cost emphasis of existing theory:

1. Technical innovations leading to new and profitable products require large quantities of capital and highly skilled labor. These factors of production are predominantly available in highly industrialized capital-intensive countries.
2. These same technical innovations, both the product itself and its manufacture, go through three stages of maturation as the product becomes increasingly commercialized. As the manufacturing process becomes more standardized and low-skill labor-intensive, the comparative advantage in its production and export shifts across countries.

Stages of the Product Cycle

Product cycle theory is both supply-side (cost of production) and demand-side (income levels of consumers) in its orientation. Each of these three stages that Vernon described combines differing elements of each.

STAGE I: THE NEW PRODUCT Innovation requires highly skilled labor and large quantities of capital for research and development. The product will normally be most effectively designed and initially manufactured near the parent firm and therefore in a highly industrialized market due to the need for proximity to information and the need for communication among the many different skilled-labor components required. In this development stage, the product is nonstandardized. The production process requires a high degree of flexibility (meaning continued use of highly skilled labor). Costs of production are, therefore, quite high.

STAGE II: THE MATURING PRODUCT As production expands, its process becomes increasingly standardized. The need for flexibility in design and manufacturing declines; therefore, the demand for highly skilled labor declines. The innovating country increases its sales to other countries. Competitors with slight variations develop, pressuring prices and profit margins. Production costs are an increasing concern.

As competitors increase, as well as their resulting pressures on price, the innovating firm faces critical decisions on how to maintain market share. Vernon argues that the firm faces a critical decision at this stage, either to lose market share to foreign-based manufacturers using lower cost labor or to invest abroad to maintain its market share by exploiting the comparative advantages of factor costs in other countries. This is one of the first theoretical explanations of how trade and investment become increasingly intertwined.

STAGE III: THE STANDARDIZED PRODUCT In this final stage, the product is completely standardized in its manufacture. Thus, with access to capital on world capital markets, the country of production is simply the one with the cheapest unskilled labor. Profit margins are thin, and competition is fierce. The product has largely run its course in terms of profitability for the innovating firm.

The country of comparative advantage therefore shifts as the technology of the product's manufacture matures. The same product shifts in its location of production. The country possessing the product during that stage enjoys the benefits of net trade surpluses. But such advantages are fleeting, according to Vernon. As knowledge and technology continually change, so does the country with that product's comparative advantage.

Trade Implications of the Product Cycle

Product cycle theory shows how specific products were first produced and exported from one country but, through product and competitive evolution, shifted their location of production and export to other countries over time. Figure 6.4 illustrates the trade patterns that Vernon visualized as resulting from the maturing stages of a specific product cycle. As the product and the market for the product mature and change, the countries of its production and export shift.

The product is initially designed and manufactured in the United States. In its early stages (from time t_0 to t_1), the United States is the only country producing and consuming the product. Production is highly capital-intensive and skilled-labor intensive. At time t_1, the United States begins exporting the product to Other Advanced Countries, as Vernon classified them. These countries possess the income to purchase the product in its still New Product Stage, in which it was relatively high priced. These Other Advanced Countries also commence their own production at time t_1 but continue to be net importers. A few exports, however, do find their way to the Less Developed Countries at this time as well.

As the product moves into the second stage, the Maturing Product Stage, production capability expands rapidly in the Other Advanced Countries. Competitive variations begin to appear as the basic technology of the product becomes more widely known, and the need for skilled labor in its production declines. These countries eventually also become net exporters of the product near the end of the stage (time t_3). At time t_2, the Less Developed Countries begin their own production, although they continue to be net importers. Meanwhile, the lower cost of production from these growing competitors turns the United States into a net importer by time t_4. The competitive advantage for production and export is clearly shifting across countries.

FIGURE 6.4 Trade Patterns and Product Cycle Theory

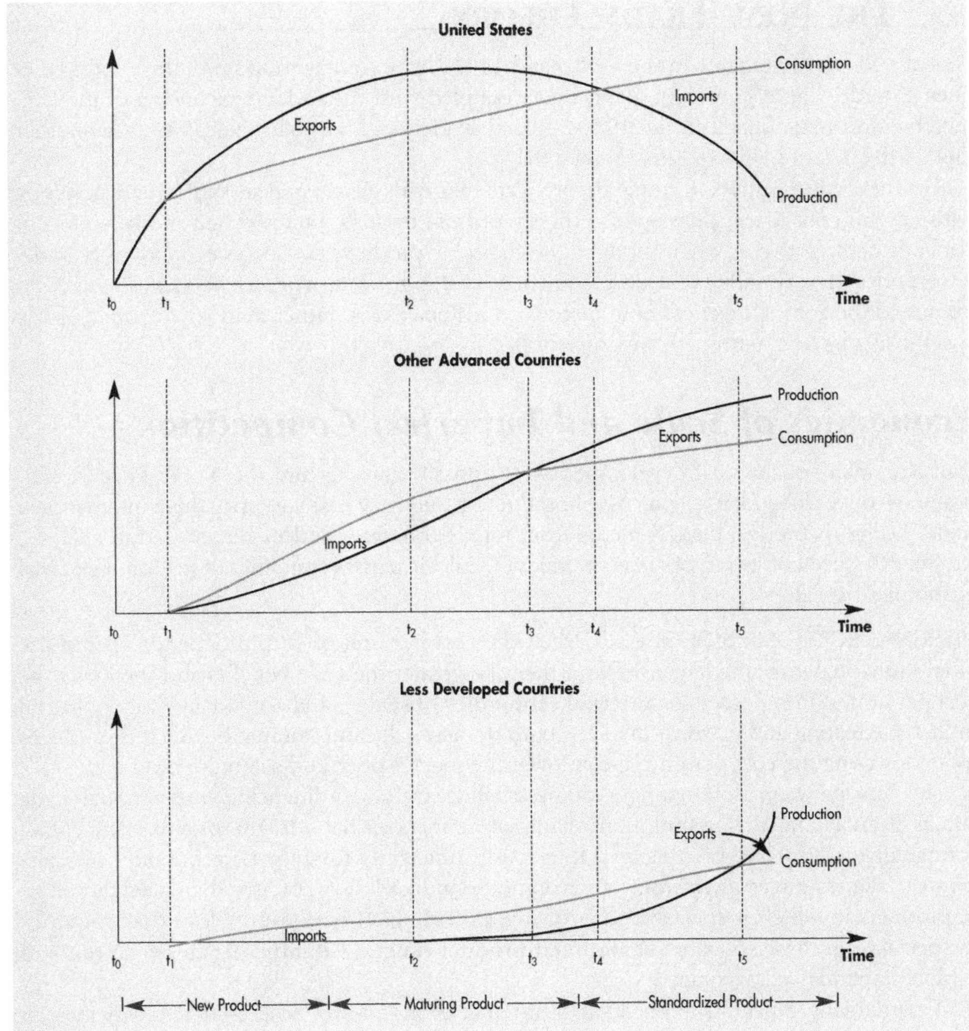

SOURCE: Raymond Vernon, "International Investment and International Trade in the Product Cycle," *Quarterly Journal of Economics* (May 1966): 199.

The third and final stage, the Standardized Product Stage, sees the comparative advantage of production and export now shifting to the Less Developed Countries. The product is now a relatively mass-produced product that can be made with increasingly less-skilled labor. The United States continues to reduce domestic production and increase imports. The Other Advanced Countries continue to produce and export, although exports peak as the Less Developed Countries expand production and become net exporters themselves. The product has run its course or life cycle in reaching time t_5.

Note that throughout this cycle, the countries of production, consumption, export, and import are identified by their labor and capital levels, not firms. Vernon noted that it could very well be firms that are moving production from the United States to other advanced countries to less developed countries. The shifting location of production was instrumental in the changing patterns of trade but not necessarily in the loss of market share, profitability, or competitiveness of the firms.

THE NEW TRADE THEORY

LEARNING OUTCOME 4

NEW TRADE THEORY
The new theoretical developments of Paul Krugman that emphasized imperfect competition's impacts on markets and of Michael Porter and his work on industry specific competitive forces that alter international competitiveness

Global trade developments in the 1980s and 1990s led to much criticism of the existing theories of trade. Rapid growth in world trade, coupled with the sudden expansion of the U.S. merchandise trade deficit in the 1980s, forced academics and policymakers to take another look at the determinants of international trade.

Two new contributions to trade theory were met with great interest. Paul Krugman, along with several colleagues, developed a theory of how trade is altered when markets are not perfectly competitive or when production of specific products possesses economies of scale. A second and very influential development was the growing work of Michael Porter, who examined the competitiveness of industries on a global basis, rather than relying on country-specific factors to determine competitiveness.

Economies of Scale and Imperfect Competition

Paul Krugman's theoretical developments—eventually earning him the Nobel Prize in economics—once again focused on cost of production and how cost and price drive international trade. Using theoretical developments from microeconomics and market structure analysis, Krugman focused on two types of economics of scale, internal economies of scale and external economies of scale.[3]

INTERNAL ECONOMIES OF SCALE
When the cost per unit of the product of a single firm continues to fall as the firm's size continues to increase

ABANDONED PRODUCT RANGES
The outcome of a firm narrowing its range of products to obtain economies of scale, which provides opportunities for other firms to enter the markets for the abandoned products

INTRA-INDUSTRY TRADE
The simultaneous export and import of the same good by a country; of interest due to the traditional theory that a country will either export or import a good but not do both at the same time

PRODUCT DIFFERENTIATION
The effort to build unique differences or improvements into products

INTERNAL ECONOMIES OF SCALE When the cost per unit of output depends on the size of an individual firm, the larger the firm then the greater the scale benefits and the lower the cost per unit. A firm possessing **internal economies of scale** could potentially monopolize an industry (creating an imperfect market), both domestically and internationally. If it produces more, lowering the cost per unit, it can lower the market price and sell more products.

The link between dominating a domestic industry and influencing international trade comes from taking this assumption of imperfect markets back to the original concept of comparative advantage. For this firm to expand sufficiently to enjoy its economies of scale, it must take resources away from other domestic industries. A country then sees the range of products in which it specializes narrowing, providing an opportunity for other countries to specialize in these so-called **abandoned product ranges**. Countries again search out and exploit comparative advantage.

A particularly powerful implication of internal economies of scale is that it provides an explanation of intra-industry trade. **Intra-industry trade** occurs when a country seemingly imports and exports the same product, an idea that is obviously inconsistent with any of the trade theories put forward in the past three centuries. According to Krugman, internal economies of scale may lead a firm to specialize in a narrow product line (to produce the volume necessary for economies of scale cost benefits); other firms in other countries may produce products that are similarly narrow, yet extremely similar: **product differentiation**. If consumers in either country wish to buy both products, they will be importing and exporting products that are, for all intents and purposes, the same.

EXTERNAL ECONOMIES OF SCALE When the cost per unit of output depends on the size of an industry, not the size of the individual firm, the industry of that country may produce at lower costs than the same industry that is smaller in size in other countries. A country can potentially dominate world markets in a particular product, not because it has one massive firm producing enormous quantities (for example, Boeing), but rather because it has many small firms that interact to create a large, competitive, critical mass (for example, semiconductors in Penang, Malaysia). No one firm need be all that large, but several small firms in total may create such a competitive industry that firms in other countries cannot ever break into the industry on a competitive basis.

Unlike internal economies of scale, external economies of scale may not necessarily lead to imperfect markets, but they may result in an industry maintaining its dominance in its field in world markets. This provides an explanation as to why all industries do not necessarily always move to the country with the lowest cost energy, resources, or labor. What gives rise to this critical mass of small firms and their interrelationships is a much more complex question.

The Competitive Advantage of Nations

The focus of early trade theory was on the country or nation. As trade theory evolved, it shifted its focus to the industry and product level, leaving the national-level competitiveness question somewhat behind. Recently, many have turned their attention to the question of how countries, governments, and even private industry can alter the conditions within a country to aid the competitiveness of its firms.

The leader in this area of research has been Michael Porter of Harvard. Porter argued innovation is what drives and sustains competitiveness. A firm must avail itself of all dimensions of competition, which he categorized into four major components of "the diamond of national advantage."[4]

1. *Factor conditions:* The nation's factors of production to compete successfully in a specific industry must be appropriate. Porter notes that although these factor conditions are important in the determination of trade, they are not the only source of competitiveness. It is the ability of a nation to continually create, upgrade, and deploy its factors (such as skilled labor) that is important, not the initial endowment.
2. *Demand conditions:* The firm must have a degree of health and competition in its original home market. Firms that can survive and flourish in highly competitive and demanding local markets are much more likely to gain the competitive edge. Porter notes that it is the character of the market—demanding customers—not its size, that is paramount in promoting the continual competitiveness of the firm.
3. *Related and supporting industries:* The competitiveness of all related industries and suppliers to the firm is important. A firm that is operating within a mass of related firms and industries gains and maintains advantages through close working relationships, proximity to suppliers, and timeliness of product and information flows. The constant and close interaction is successful if it occurs not only in terms of physical proximity but also through the willingness of firms to work at it.
4. *Firm strategy, structure, and rivalry:* The conditions in the home-nation either hinder or aid in the firm's creation and sustaining of international competitiveness. Porter notes that no one managerial, ownership, or operational strategy is universally appropriate. It depends on the fit and flexibility of what works for that industry in that country at that time.

These four points, as illustrated in Figure 6.5, constitute what nations and firms must strive to "create and sustain through a highly localized process" to ensure their success.

Porter's emphasis on innovation as the source of competitiveness reflects an increased focus on both industry and products that we have seen in the past three decades. The acknowledgment that the nation is "more, not less, important" is to many eyes a welcome return to a positive role for government in encouraging international competitiveness. Including factor conditions as a cost component, demand conditions as a motivator, and competitiveness all combine to include the elements of classical, factor proportions, product cycle, and new trade theories in a pragmatic approach to the challenges that global markets present today.

FIGURE 6.5 Determinants of National Competitive Advantage: Porter's Diamond

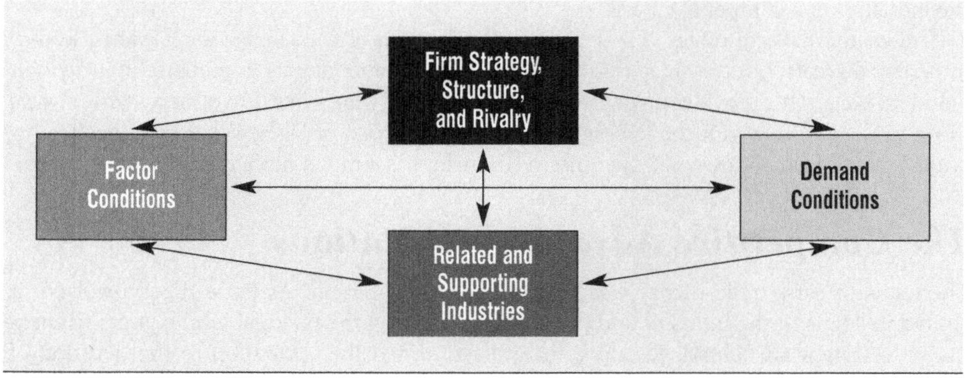

Firm Strategy, Structure, and Rivalry
Factor Conditions
Demand Conditions
Related and Supporting Industries

Theory of International Investment

Trade is the production of a good or service in one country and its sale to a buyer in another country. In fact, it is a firm (not a country) and a buyer (not a country) that are the subjects of trade, domestically or internationally. A firm needs access to markets and buyers. The producing firm wants to utilize its competitive advantage for growth and profit and can also reach this goal by international investment.

Although this sounds easy enough, consider any of the following potholes on the road to investment success. Any of the following potholes may be avoided by producing within another country.

- Sales to some countries are difficult because of tariffs imposed on your good when it is entering. If you were producing within the country, your good would no longer be an import.
- Your good requires natural resources that are available only in certain areas of the world. It is therefore imperative that you have access to the natural resources. You can buy them from that country and bring them to your production process (import) or simply take the production to them.
- Competition is constantly pushing you to improve efficiency and decrease the costs of producing your good. You therefore may want to produce where it will be cheaper—cheaper capital, cheaper energy, cheaper natural resources, or cheaper labor. Many of these factors are still not mobile, and therefore you will go to them instead of bringing them to you.

The subject of international investment arises from one basic idea: the mobility of capital. Although many of the traditional trade theories assumed the immobility of the factors of production, it is the movement of capital that has allowed **foreign direct investments** across the globe.

FOREIGN DIRECT INVESTMENTS
The establishment or expansion of operations of a firm in a foreign country; like all investments, assumes a transfer of capital

The Theory of Foreign Direct Investment

What motivates a firm to go beyond exporting or licensing? What benefits does the multinational firm expect to achieve by establishing a physical presence in other countries? These are the questions that the theory of foreign direct investment has sought to answer.

The following overview of investment theory has many similarities to the preceding discussion of international trade. The theme is a global business environment that attempts to satisfy increasingly sophisticated consumer demands, while the means of production, resources, skills, and technology needed become more complex and competitive.

Firms As Seekers

A firm that expands across borders may be seeking any of a number of specific sources of profit or opportunity.

1. *Seeking resources:* Much of the initial foreign direct investment of the eighteenth and nineteenth centuries was the result of firms seeking unique and valuable natural resources for their products.
2. *Seeking factor advantages:* The resources needed for production are often combined with other advantages that are inherent in the country of production. The same low-cost labor of classical trade theory provides incentives for firms to move production to countries possessing these factor advantages.
3. *Seeking knowledge:* Firms may attempt to acquire other firms in other countries for the technical or competitive skills they possess. Alternatively, companies may locate in and around centers of industrial enterprise unique to their specific industry, like the footwear industry of Milan.
4. *Seeking security:* Firms continue to move internationally as they seek political stability or security. For example, Mexico has experienced a significant increase in foreign direct investment as a result of the tacit support of the United States, Canada, and Mexico itself as reflected by the North American Free Trade Agreement.
5. *Seeking markets:* The ability to gain and maintain access to markets is of paramount importance to multinational firms. Whether following the principles of Linder, in which firms learn from their domestic market and use that information to go international, or the principles of Porter, which emphasize the character of the domestic market as dictating international competiveness, foreign market access is necessary.

Firms As Exploiters of Imperfections

Much of the investment theory developed in the past three decades has focused on the efforts of multinational firms to exploit the imperfections in factor and product markets created by governments. The work of Hymer, Kindleberger, and Caves noted that many government policies create imperfections. These market imperfections cover the entire range of supply and demand of the market: trade policy (tariffs and quotas), tax policies and incentives, preferential purchasing arrangements established by governments themselves, and financial restrictions on the access of foreign firms to domestic capital markets.

- Imperfections in access: Many of the world's developing countries have long sought to create domestic industry by restricting imports of competitive products in order to allow smaller, less competitive domestic firms to grow and prosper—so-called **import substitution** policies. Multinational firms have sought to maintain their access to these markets by establishing their own productive presence within the country, effectively bypassing the tariff restriction.
- Imperfections in factor mobility: Other multinational firms have exploited the same sources of comparative advantage identified throughout this chapter—the low-cost resources or factors often located in less-developed countries or countries with restrictions on the mobility of labor and capital. However, combining the mobility of capital with the immobility of low-cost labor has characterized much of the foreign direct investment seen throughout the developing world during the past fifty years.

IMPORT SUBSTITUTION
A policy for economic growth adopted by many developing countries that involves the systematic encouragement of domestic production of goods formerly imported

- Imperfections in management: The ability of multinational firms to successfully exploit or at least manage these imperfections still relies on their ability to gain an "advantage." Market advantages or powers are seen in international markets as in domestic markets: cost advantages, economies of scale and scope, product differentiation, managerial or marketing knowledge, financial resources, and strength.

All these imperfections are the things of which competitive dreams are made. The multinational firm needs to find these in some form or another to justify the added complexities and costs of international investments.

Strategic Implications of Foreign Direct Investment

Consider a firm that wants to exploit its competitive advantage by accessing foreign markets as illustrated in the decision-sequence tree of Figure 6.6.

The first choice is whether to exploit the existing competitive advantage in new foreign markets or to concentrate its resources in the development of new competitive advantages in the domestic market. Although many firms may choose to do both as resources will allow,

FIGURE 6.6 The Direct Foreign Investment Decision Sequence

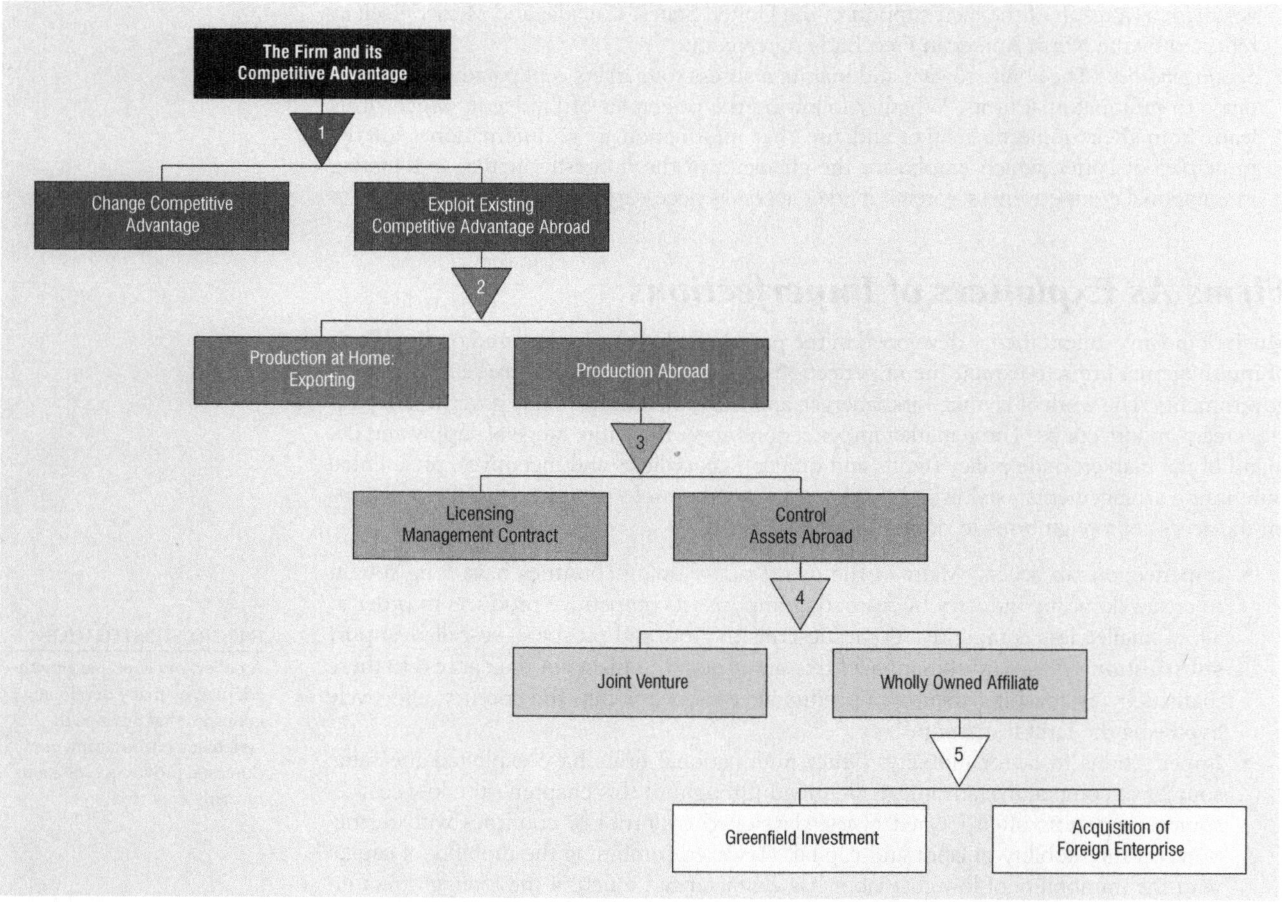

SOURCE: Adapted from Gunter Dufey and R. Mirus, "Foreign Direct Investment: Theory and Strategic Considernations" (University of Michigan, May 1985).

more and more firms are choosing to go international as at least part of their expansion strategies.

Second, should the firm produce at home and export to the foreign markets, or should it produce abroad? The firm will choose the path that will allow it to access the resources and markets it needs to exploit its competitive advantage. But it will also consider two additional dimensions of each foreign investment decision: (1) the degree of control over assets, technology, information, and operations; and (2) the magnitude of capital that the firm must risk. Each decision increases the firm's control at the cost of increased capital outlays.

After choosing to produce abroad, the firm must decide how. The distinctions among different kinds of foreign direct investment (branch 3 and downward in Figure 6.6), licensing agreements to "greenfield" construction (building a new facility from the ground up), vary by degrees of ownership. The licensing management contract is by far the simplest and cheapest way to produce abroad. Another firm is licensed to produce the product but with your firm's technology and know-how. The question is whether the reduced capital investment of simply licensing the product to another manufacturer is worth the risk of loss of control over the product and technology.

The firm that wants direct control over the foreign production process next determines the degree of equity control: to own the firm outright or as a joint investment with another firm. Trade-offs with joint ventures continue the debate over control of assets and other sources of the firm's original competitive advantage. Many countries try to ensure the continued growth of local firms and investors by requiring that foreign firms operate jointly with local firms.

The final decision branch between a greenfield investment and the purchase of an existing firm is often a question of cost. A greenfield investment is the most expensive of all foreign investment alternatives. The acquisition of an existing firm is often lower in initial cost but may also contain a number of customizing and adjustment costs that are not apparent at the initial purchase. The purchase of a going concern may also have substantial benefits if the existing business possesses substantial customer and supplier relationships that can be used by the new owner in the pursuit of its own business.

SUMMARY

As world economies have grown and the magnitude of world trade has increased, the ideas that guided international trade and investment theory have similarly evolved to higher levels of sophistication. Trade theory informs the decisions that many firms face today, requiring them to directly move their capital, technology, and know-how to countries that possess unique factors of production or market advantages that will help them keep pace with market demands.

At its root, international trade assumes that trade will improve the quality of life for the consumers, both as individuals and as a nation. The rise of mercantilism saw trade evolve for the purposes of increasing wealth and power. Other theories emerged after mercantilism's failure to help explain the costs and benefits of trade.

The classical theories of Adam Smith and David Ricardo focused on the abilities of countries to produce goods more cheaply than other countries. The earliest production and trade theories saw labor as the major factor expense that went into any product. If a country could pay that labor less, and if that labor could produce more physically than labor in other countries, the country might obtain an absolute or comparative advantage in trade.

Subsequent theoretical development led to a more detailed understanding of production and its costs. Factors of production are now believed to include labor (skilled and unskilled), capital, natural resources, and other potentially significant commodities that are difficult to reproduce or replace, such as energy.

Technology, once assumed to be the same across all countries, is now seen as one of the premier driving forces in determining who holds the competitive edge or advantage. International trade is a complex combination of thousands of products, technologies, and firms that are constantly innovating to either keep up with or get ahead of the competition.

Modern trade theory looks beyond production cost to analyze how the demands of the marketplace alter who trades with whom and which firms survive domestically and internationally. The abilities of firms to adapt to foreign markets have required international trade theory to search out new and innovative approaches to what determines success and failure.

To understand what motivates firms to invest overseas, theorists have analyzed firms from multiple perspectives: firms as seekers, not only of aspects of competitiveness, such as new markets or cheaper resources, but of knowledge or technical expertise; firms as exploiters of imperfections created by government policies; and firms as internalizers, motivated to protect knowledge that is at the core of their competitiveness.

Once a firm makes a decision in favor of some form of foreign direct investment, the options range from the relatively simple, such as the decision to manufacture abroad or license other firms to do so, to the complex, including greenfield investment or acquisition of a foreign enterprise.

Key Terms and Concepts

autarky
mercantilism
absolute advantage
division of labor
comparative advantage
production possibilities frontiers
opportunity cost
factor intensities/factor proportions
factor proportions theory
input–output analysis
Leontief Paradox
market segment
product cycle theory
new trade theory
internal economies of scale
abandoned product ranges
intra-industry trade
product differentiation
foreign direct investment
Import substitution

Review Questions

1. Explain the relationship between absolute advantage and the division of labor.
2. According to the theory of comparative advantage, why is trade always possible between two countries, even when one is inefficient compared to the other?
3. What are the flaws inherent in factor intensity theory?
4. What, in your opinion, were the constructive impacts on trade theory resulting from the empirical research of Leontief?
5. Why do you think product cycle theory has always been a very popular theory?
6. Many trade theorists argue that the primary contribution of Porter has been to popularize old ideas, in new, more

applicable ways. To what degree do you think Porter's ideas are new or old?

7. How would you analyze the statement that "international investment is an extension of classical trade"?
8. Explain why firms are motivated to move beyond exporting or licensing to more complex forms of foreign direct investment.
9. What is really "new" about new trade theory?

Critical Skill Builders

1. The factor proportions theory of international trade assumes that all countries produce the same product the same way. Would international competition cause or prevent this from happening? Discuss in small groups.
2. If the product cycle theory were accepted for the basis of policymaking, what should the U.S. government do to help its firms exploit the principles of the theory?
3. How can a crisis in Asia impact jobs and profits in Western nations? Give examples from recent world events. What obstacles and opportunities does it present?
4. We typically think of "commodities" as being relatively easy-to-manufacture goods with little product differentiation, such as paper, steel, or agricultural products. Consider the statement that Dell has made a commodity out of the personal computer. Research the company's competitive strategies, particularly its price-cutting policies. Do you think the personal computer is a commodity?
5. Research a small or mid-size business in your area that currently manufactures its product domestically and sells mainly within the domestic market. How might that company benefit from considering the decision-sequence tree illustrated in Figure 6.6? In groups, outline a foreign direct investment program for the company.

On the Web

1. The differences across multinational firms are striking. Using a sample of firms such as those listed below, look at the company web sites and find the proportions of their incomes that are earned outside their country of incorporation. Also, consider the way in which international business is now conducted using the Internet. Several of these web sites allow the user to view the site in different languages. Others, like Nestlé, report financial results in two different accounting frameworks, those used in its home country and the Generally Accepted Accounting Practices (GAAP) used in the United States.

   Walt Disney at **www.disney.com**
   Nestlé S.A. at **www.nestle.com**
   Intel at **www.intel.com**
   Mitsubishi Motors at **www.mitsubishi-motors.com**

2. Corporate governance, the way in which firms are controlled by management and ownership across countries, is the hottest topic in business today. Use the following sites to view recent research, current events and news items, and other information related to the relationships between a business and its stakeholders.

   Corporate Governance Net at **www.corpgov.net**
   Corporate Governance Research at **www.irrc.org**

3. International trade statistics between countries, as reported by each, often do not match. Go to **www.census.gov/foreign-trade/** to view a study of trade statistics discrepancies between NAFTA member nations. Isolate reasons for the discrepancies and discuss their impact on trade between the United States, Canada, and Mexico.

Endnotes

1. Adam Smith, *An Inquiry into the Nature and Causes of the Wealth of Nations* (New York: E.P. Dutton, 1937), pp. 4–5.
2. In Leontief 's own words: "These figures show that an average million dollars' worth of our exports embodies considerably less capital and somewhat more labor than would be required to replace from domestic production an equivalent amount of our competitive imports. . . . The widely held opinion that—as compared with the rest of the world—the United States' economy is characterized by a relative surplus of capital and a relative shortage of labor proves to be wrong. As a matter of fact, the opposite is true." Wassily Leontief, "Domestic Production and Foreign Trade: The American Capital Position Re-Examined," *Proceedings of the American Philosophical Society,* 97, No. 4 (September 1953), p. 86.
3. For a detailed description of these theories, see Elhanan Helpman and Paul Krugman, *Market Structure and Foreign Trade* (Cambridge: MIT Press, 1985).
4. Michael E. Porter, "The Competitive Advantage of Nations," *Harvard Business Review* (March-April 1990): pp. 73–74.

CHAPTER 7

THE INTERNATIONAL MOVEMENT OF TRADE AND CAPITAL (THE BALANCE OF PAYMENTS)

International Payments and the Migration of People

One area within the balance of payments that has received intense interest in the past decade is that of remittances. According to the International Monetary Fund (IMF), **remittances** are international transfers of funds sent by migrant workers from the country where they are working to people, typically family members, back to the country from which they originated. According to the IMF, a **migrant** is a person who comes to a country and stays, or intends to stay, for a year or more.

LEARNING OUTCOMES

1. *To understand the fundamental principles of how countries measure international business activity through the balance of payments*
2. *To examine the similarities of the current and capital accounts of the balance of payments, particularly their treatment of merchandise goods, services, and international investment activity*
3. *To provide a useful overview of the U.S. balance of payments as presented by the International Monetary Fund (IMF)*
4. *To consider the causes and effects of economic crises as reflected in the balance of payments, including the growing fears of capital mobility and capital flight*

Remittances largely reflect the income that is earned by migrant or guest workers in one country (source country) and then returned to families or related parties in their home countries (receiving countries). Therefore it is not surprising that although there are more migrant worker flows between developing countries, the high-income developed economies remain the main source of remittances. The global economic recession of 2009 resulted in reduced economic activities like construction and manufacturing in the major source countries; as a result, remittance cash flows fell in 2009 but rebounded slightly with economic conditions and employment of migrant workers in 2010 and 2011.

Most remittances are frequent small payments made through wire transfers or a variety of informal channels (some even carried by hand). The U.S. Bureau of Economic Analysis (BEA), which is responsible for the compilation and reporting of U.S. balance of payments statistics, classifies migrant remittances as "current transfers" in the current account. Wider definitions of remittances may also include capital assets, which migrants bring with them to host countries, and similar assets, which they take back with them to their home countries. These values, when compiled, are generally reported under the capital account of the balance of payments. Transfers back to their home country made by individuals who may be working in a country (for example, an expat working for a multinational enterprise, a firm that has operating subsidiaries, affiliates, or branches located in foreign countries, MNE) but not considered "residents," may also be considered global remittances under current transfers in the current account.

With the growth in global remittances has come a growing debate as to what role they do or should play in a country's balance of payments, and more importantly, economic development. In some cases, like India, there is growing resistance from the central bank and other banking institutions to allow online payment services like PayPal to process remittances. In other countries, like Honduras, Guatemala, and Mexico, there is growing debate on whether the remittances flow to families or are actually payments made to a variety of Central American smugglers—human trafficking smugglers.

In Mexico for example, remittances now make up the second largest source of foreign exchange earnings, second only to oil exports. The Mexican government has increasingly viewed remittances as an integral component of its balance of payments and, in some ways, a "plug" to replace declining export competition and dropping foreign direct investment. But evidence is also growing that remittances flow to those who need it most, the lowest income component of the Mexican population, and therefore mitigate poverty and support consumer spending. Former Mexican President Vicente Fox was quoted as saying that Mexico's workers in other countries remitting income home to Mexico are "heroes."

As You Read This Chapter

1. Consider how people working in foreign countries alter the balances on goods and services globally.
2. Given the growing debates over migrant workers and immigrant policies, how would the introduction of a guest worker program in the United States alter this important element of Mexico's balance of payments?

REMITTANCES
International transfers of funds sent by migrant workers from the country where they are working to people, typically family members, back to the country from which they originated

MIGRANT
A person who comes to a country and stays, or intends to stay, for a year or more

International business transactions occur in many different forms over the course of each year. The measurement of all international economic transactions between the residents of a country and foreign residents is called the balance of payments.[1] Government policymakers need such measures of economic activity to evaluate the general competitiveness of domestic industry, to set exchange-rate or interest-rate policies or goals, and for many other purposes. Individuals and businesses use various BOP measures to gauge the growth and health of specific types of trade or financial transactions by country and regions of the world against the home country.

This chapter largely describes the various balance of payment accounts, their meanings, and their relationships, using the United States as the example. The chapter concludes with a discussion—and a number of examples—of how different countries with different policies or levels of economic development may differ markedly in their balance of payment accounts.

International Transactions and the Balance of Payments

International transactions take many forms. Each of the following examples is an international economic transaction that is counted and captured in the U.S. balance of payments.

- The United States imports Porsche sports cars, which are manufactured in Germany.
- A U.S.-based firm, Bechtel, is hired to manage the construction of a major water-treatment facility in the Middle East.
- The U.S. subsidiary of a French firm, Saint Gobain, pays profits (dividends) back to the parent firm in Paris.
- An American tourist purchases a hand-blown glass figurine in Venice, Italy.
- The U.S. government provides grant financing of military equipment for its NATO ally, Turkey.
- A Canadian dentist purchases a U.S. Treasury bill through an investment broker in Cleveland, Ohio.

These are just a small sample of the hundreds of thousands of international transactions that occur each year. The **balance of payments (BOP)** provides a systematic method for the classification of them all. One rule of thumb will always aid in the understanding of BOP accounting: Watch the direction of the movement of money.

The BOP comprises a number of subaccounts that are watched quite closely by groups as diverse as investors on Wall Street, farmers in Iowa, politicians on Capitol Hill, and board members across corporate America. These groups track and analyze the two major subaccounts, the **Current Account** and the **Financial Account**, on a continuing basis. Before describing these two subaccounts and the BOP as a whole, it is necessary to understand the rather unusual features of how balance of payments accounting is conducted.

BALANCE OF PAYMENTS (BOP)
A statement of all transactions between one country and the rest of the world during a given period; a record of flows of goods, services, and investments across borders

CURRENT ACCOUNT
An account in the BOP statement that records the results of transactions involving merchandise, services, and unilateral transfers between countries

FINANCIAL ACCOUNT
An account in the BOP statement that records transactions involving borrowing, lending, and investing across borders

Basics of BOP Accounting

There are three main elements to the process of measuring international economic activity:

1. Identifying what is and is not an international economic transaction
2. Understanding how the flow of goods, services, assets, and money creates debits and credits to the overall BOP
3. Understanding the bookkeeping procedures for BOP accounting

Identifying International Economic Transactions

Identifying international transactions is ordinarily not difficult. The export of merchandise, goods such as trucks, machinery, computers, telecommunications equipment, and so forth, is obviously an international transaction. Imports such as French wine, Japanese electronics, and German automobiles are also clearly international transactions. But this merchandise trade is only a portion of the thousands of different international transactions that occur in the United States or any other country each year.

Many other international transactions are not so obvious. All expenditures made by American tourists around the globe, for example, that are for goods or services (meals, hotel accommodations, and so forth) are recorded in the U.S. BOP as imports of travel services. The purchase of a U.S. Treasury bill by a foreign resident is an international financial transaction and is dutifully recorded in the U.S. BOP.

BOP As a Flow Statement

The BOP is often misunderstood because many people believe it to be a balance sheet rather than a cash-flow statement. By recording all international transactions over a period of time, it tracks the continuing flow of purchases and payments between a country and all other countries. Unlike a firm's balance sheet, it does not add up the value of all assets and liabilities of a country.

Two types of business transactions dominate the BOP:

1. *Real assets:* The exchange of goods (automobiles, computers, watches, textiles) and services (banking services, consulting services, travel services) for other goods and services (barter), or for the more common type of payment, money
2. *Financial assets:* The exchange of financial claims (stocks, bonds, loans, purchases or sales of companies) in exchange for other financial claims or money

Although assets can be separated as to whether they are real or financial, it is often easier simply to think of all assets as being goods that can be bought and sold. An American tourist's purchase of a hand-woven rug in a shop in Bangkok is not all that different from a Wall Street banker buying a British government bond for investment purposes.

BOP Accounting: Double-Entry Bookkeeping

DOUBLE-ENTRY BOOKKEEPING
A method of accounting in which every transaction produces both a debit and a credit of the same amount

The BOP employs an accounting technique called **double-entry bookkeeping**. This is the age-old method of accounting in which every transaction produces a debit and a credit of the same amount simultaneously. It has to. A debit is created whenever an asset is increased, a liability is decreased, or an expense is increased. Similarly, a credit is created whenever an asset is decreased, a liability is increased, or an expense is decreased.

An example clarifies this process. A U.S. retail store imports $2 million worth of consumer electronics from Japan. A negative entry is made in the merchandise-import subcategory of the current account in the amount of $2 million. Simultaneously, a positive entry of the same $2 million is made in the financial account for the transfer of a $2 million bank account to the Japanese manufacturer. Obviously, the result of hundreds of thousands of such transactions and entries should theoretically result in a perfect balance.

That said, it is now a problem of application, and a problem it is. The measurement of all international transactions in and out of a country over a year is a daunting task. Mistakes, errors, and statistical discrepancies will occur. The primary problem is that although double-entry bookkeeping is employed in theory, the individual transactions are recorded independently. Current and financial account entries are recorded independent of one another, not together as double-entry bookkeeping would prescribe. It must then be recognized that there will be serious discrepancies between debits and credits, and the possibility in total that the BOP may not balance!

The BOP consists of two primary subaccounts: the Current Account and the Financial Capital Account.

BOP Current Account

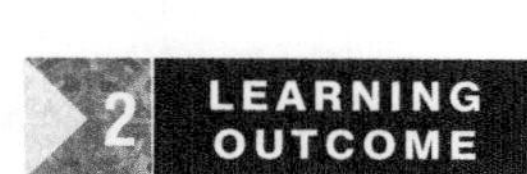

The Current Account includes all international economic transactions with income or payment flows occurring within the year, the current period. The Current Account consists of four subcategories:

GOODS TRADE ACCOUNT
An account of the BOP statement that records funds used for merchandise imports and funds obtained from merchandise exports

SERVICES TRADE ACCOUNT
An account of the BOP that records the international exchange of personal or professional services, such as financial and banking services, construction, and tourism

INCOME ACCOUNT
An account of the BOP statement that records current income associated with investments that were made in previous periods

1. **Goods trade account**: This records the export and import of goods. Merchandise trade is the oldest and most traditional form of international economic activity. Although many countries depend on imports of many goods (as they should according to the theory of comparative advantage), they also normally work to preserve either a balance of goods trade or even a surplus.
2. **Services trade account**: This records the export and import of services. Some common international services are financial services provided by banks to foreign importers and exporters, travel services of airlines, and construction services of domestic firms in other countries. For the major industrial countries, this subaccount has shown the fastest growth in the past decade.
3. **Income account**: This category is predominantly current income associated with investments that were made in previous periods. If a U.S. firm created a subsidiary in South Korea to produce metal parts in a previous year, the proportion of net income that is paid back to the parent company in the current year (the dividend) constitutes current investment income. In addition, wages and salaries paid to nonresident workers are also included in this category.

4. **Current transfers account**: Transfers are the financial settlements associated with the change in ownership of real resources or financial items. Any transfer between countries that is one-way, a gift, or a grant is termed a current transfer. A common example of a current transfer would be funds provided by the U.S. government to aid in the development of a less-developed nation.

CURRENT TRANSFERS ACCOUNT

A current account on the BOP statement that records gifts from the residents of one country to the residents of another

All countries possess some amount of trade, most of which is merchandise. Many smaller and less-developed countries have little in the way of service trade, or items that fall under the income or transfers subaccounts.

The Current Account is typically dominated by the first component described—the export and import of merchandise. For this reason, the balance of trade (BOT), which is so widely quoted in the business press in most countries, refers specifically to the balance of exports and imports of goods trade only. For a larger industrialized country, however, the BOT is somewhat misleading because service trade is not included; it may be opposite in sign on net, and it may actually be fairly large as well.

Table 7.1 summarizes the U.S. Current Account and its components for 2002–10. As illustrated, the U.S. goods trade balance has consistently been negative but has been partially offset by the continuing surplus in services trade.

TABLE 7.1 The U.S. Current Account, 2002–10 (billions of U.S. dollars)

	2002	2003	2004	2005	2006	2007	2008	2009	2010
Goods exports	686	733	825	916	1,043	1,168	1,312	1,074	1,293
Goods imports	–1,167	–1,271	–1,486	–1,693	–1,876	–1,984	–2,139	–1,576	–1,936
Goods trade balance (BOT)	–481	–538	–661	–778	–833	–816	–827	–503	–642
Services trade credits	289	290	338	372	417	487	531	501	544
Services trade debits	–231	–243	–282	–303	–337	–367	–402	–380	–402
Services trade balance	58	47	55	69	80	119	129	121	142
Income receipts	281	322	416	537	685	834	814	600	663
Income payments	–254	–279	–351	–469	–640	–732	–667	–472	–498
Income balance	27	44	65	69	44	101	147	128	165
Current transfers, credits	12	15	20	19	27	25	26	22	16
Current transfers, debits	–77	–87	–109	–125	–118	–140	–152	–145	–152
Net transfers	–65	–72	–88	–106	–92	–115	–126	–123	–136
Current Account Balance	–461	–519	–629	–746	–801	–710	–677	–377	–471

SOURCE: Derived from Balance of Payments Statistics Yearbook, International Monetary Fund, December 2011, p. 1101.

Goods Trade

Figure 7.1 places the Current Account values of Table 7.1 in perspective over time by dividing the Current Account into its two major components: (1) goods trade and (2) services trade and investment income. The first and most striking message is the magnitude of the goods trade deficit in the 1990s (a continuation of a position created in the early 1980s). The balance on services and income, although not large in comparison to net goods trade, has generally run a surplus during the past two decades.

The deficits in the BOT of the past decade have been an area of considerable concern. Merchandise trade is the original core of international trade. It has three major components: manufactured goods, agriculture, and fuels. The manufacturing of goods was the basis of the Industrial Revolution and the focus of the theory of international trade described in the

FIGURE 7.1 U.S. Trade Balances on Goods & Services, 1985–2010

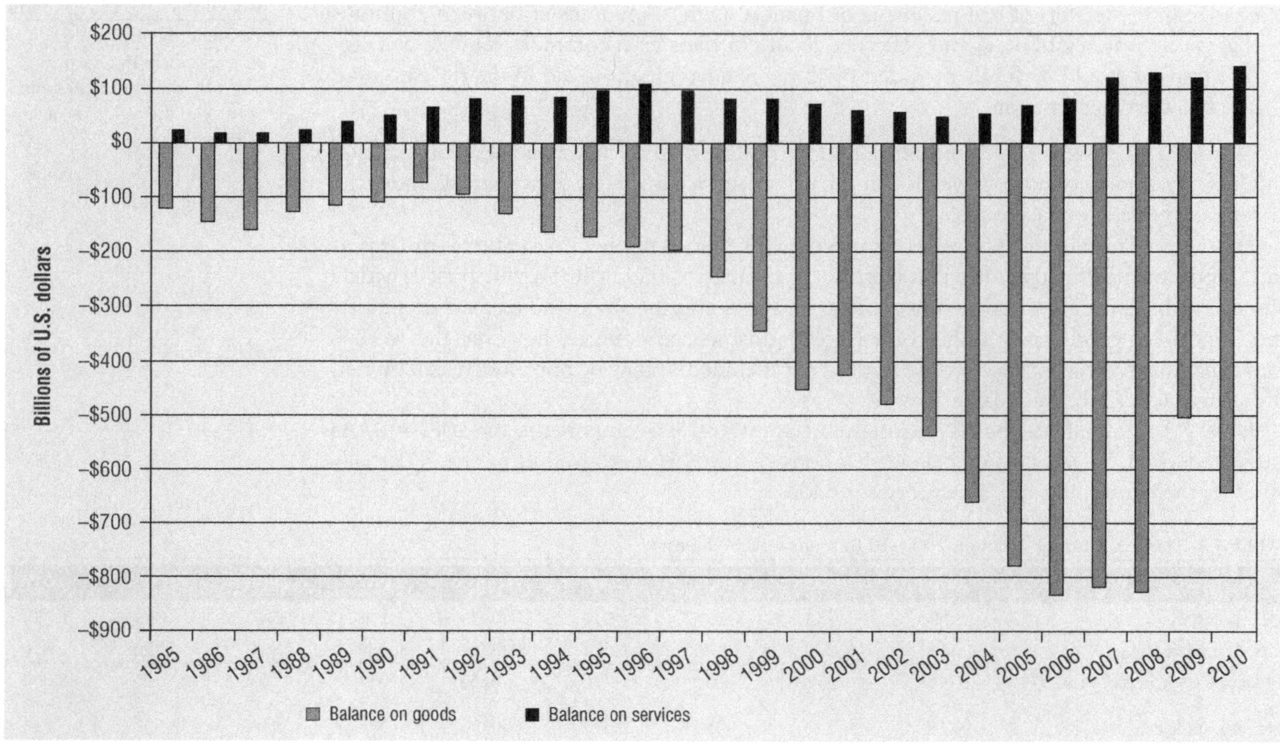

SOURCE: *Balance of Payments Statistics Yearbook*, International Monetary Fund, December 2011, p. 1101.

previous chapter. The U.S. goods trade deficit of the 1980s and 1990s was mainly caused by a decline in traditional manufacturing industries that have, during the past two centuries, employed many of America's workers. Declines in the net trade balance in areas such as steel, automobiles, automotive parts, textiles, shoe manufacturing, and others caused massive economic and social disruption. The problems of dealing with these shifting trade balances will be discussed in detail in the next chapter.

The most encouraging news for U.S. manufacturing trade is the growth of exports in recent years. A number of factors contributed to the growth in exports, such as the weaker dollar (which made U.S.-manufactured goods cheaper in relation to the currencies of other countries), more rapid economic growth in Europe, and a substantial increase in agricultural exports. Understanding merchandise import and export performance is much like understanding the market for any single product. The demand factors that drive both imports and exports are income, the economic growth rate of the buyer, and price (the price of the product in the eyes of the consumer after passing through an exchange rate). For example, U.S. merchandise imports reflect the income level and growth of American consumers and industry. As income rises, so does the demand for imports. The 2009 global financial and economic crisis made itself evident as U.S. incomes, and therefore imports, declined radically.

Exports follow the same principles but in the reversed position. U.S. merchandise exports depend not on the incomes of U.S. residents but on the incomes of the buyers of U.S. products in all other countries around the world. When these economies are growing, the demand for U.S. products will also rise. However, the recent economic crises in Asia now raise questions regarding U.S. export growth in the immediate future. The service component of the U.S. Current Account is one of mystery to many. As illustrated in both Table 7.1 and Figure 7.1, the United States has consistently achieved a surplus in services trade income. The major categories of services include travel and passenger fares, transportation services, expenditures by U.S. students abroad and foreign students in the United States, telecommunications services, and financial services.

THE BOP CAPITAL AND FINANCIAL ACCOUNT

The Capital and Financial Account of the BOP measures all international economic transactions of financial assets. It is divided into two major components, the Capital Account and the Financial Account.

- The Capital Account: The Capital Account is made up of transfers of financial assets and the acquisition and disposal of nonproduced/nonfinancial assets. The magnitude of capital transactions covered is of relatively minor amount and will be included in principle in all of the following discussions of the financial account.
- The Financial Account: The Financial Account consists of three components: direct investment, portfolio investment, and other asset investment. Financial assets can be classified in a number of different ways, including the length of the life of the asset (its maturity) and by the nature of the ownership (public or private). The Financial Account, however, uses a third way. It is classified by the degree of control over the assets or operations the claim represents: portfolio investment, where the investor has no control, or direct investment, where the investor exerts some explicit degree of control over the assets.

Table 7.2 shows the major subcategories of the U.S. Capital Account balance from 2002–10, direct investment, portfolio investment, and other long-term and short-term capital.

TABLE 7.2 The U.S. Financial Account and Components, 2002–10 (billions of U.S. dollars)

	2002	2003	2004	2005	2006	2007	2008	2009	2010
Direct Investment									
Direct investment abroad	–154	–150	–316	–36	–245	–414	–329	–304	-351
Direct investment in the United States	84	64	146	113	243	221	310	159	236
Net direct investment	–70	–86	–170	76	–2	–193	–19	–145	–115
Portfolio Investment									
Assets, net	–49	–123	–177	–258	–499	–391	280	–360	-166
Liabilities, net	428	550	867	832	1,127	1,157	524	360	707
Net portfolio investment	379	427	690	575	628	766	804	0	541
Financial Derivatives, Net					30	6	–33	49	14
Other Investment									
Other investment assets	–88	–54	–510	–267	–544	–649	386	576	-486
Other investment liabilities	283	244	50	303	695	687	–402	–183	303
Net other investment	195	190	10	36	151	38	–17	393	–184
Net Financial Account Balance	504	531	530	687	807	617	735	298	256

SOURCE: Derived from *Balance of Payments Statistics Yearbook*, International Monetary Fund, December 2011, p. 1101.

Quick Take Nonresident Indians and the Indian Current Account

India, although running a current account deficit in recent years, has seen the deficit narrow in recent years as a result of bank deposits held in India by nonresident Indians. These deposits have offered attractive interest rates to depositors in recent years as a result of deregulation, which has allowed bank interest rates to rise. These higher rates have attracted large quantities of capital from outside India, specifically by nonresident Indians living and working across the world. One of the primary risks, however, is the value of the Indian rupee itself. If it were to fall against the major currencies like the dollar, euro, or yen, it would offset some or all of the interest rate advantages offered.

DIRECT INVESTMENT ACCOUNT
An account in the BOP statement that records investments with an expected maturity of more than one year and an investor's ownership position of at least 10 percent.

PORTFOLIO INVESTMENT ACCOUNT
An account in the BOP statement that records investments in assets with an original maturity of more than one year and where an investor's ownership position is less than 10 percent.

1. ***Direct investment account***: This is the net balance of capital dispersed out of and into the country for the purpose of exerting control over assets. For example, if a U.S. firm either builds a new automotive parts facility in another country or actually purchases a company in another country, this would fall under direct investment in the U.S. BOP accounts. When the capital flows out of the United States, it enters the BOP as a negative cash flow. If, however, foreign firms purchase firms in the United States, it is a capital inflow and enters the BOP positively. Whenever 10 percent or more of the voting shares in a U.S. company is held by foreign investors, the company is classified as the U.S. affiliate of a foreign company, and a foreign direct investment. Similarly, if U.S. investors hold 10 percent or more of the control in a company outside the country, that company is considered the foreign affiliate of a U.S. company.
2. ***Portfolio investment account***: This is net balance of capital that flows in and out of the country but does not reach the 10 percent ownership threshold of direct investment. If a U.S. resident purchases shares in a Japanese firm but does not attain the 10 percent threshold, it is considered a portfolio investment (and in this case an outflow of capital). The purchase or sale of debt securities (like U.S. Treasury bills) across borders is also classified as portfolio investment because debt securities by definition do not provide the buyer with ownership or control.
3. *Other investment assets/liabilities:* This final category consists of various short-term and long-term trade credits, cross-border loans from all types of financial institutions, currency deposits and bank deposits, and other accounts receivable and payable related to cross-border trade.

Direct Investment

Figure 7.2 shows how the major subaccounts of the U.S. capital account, net direct investment, portfolio investment, and other investment have changed since 1993.

As seen in earlier chapters, foreign investment into any country raises two major concerns—control and profit. Most countries possess restrictions on what foreigners may own, largely based on the premise that domestic land, assets, and industry in general should be held by residents of the country. For example, until 1990 it was not possible for a foreign firm to own more than 20 percent of any company in Finland. This rule is the norm rather than the exception. The United States has traditionally had few restrictions on what foreign residents or firms can own or control; most that remain today are related to national security

FIGURE 7.2 The United States Financial Account, 1985–2010

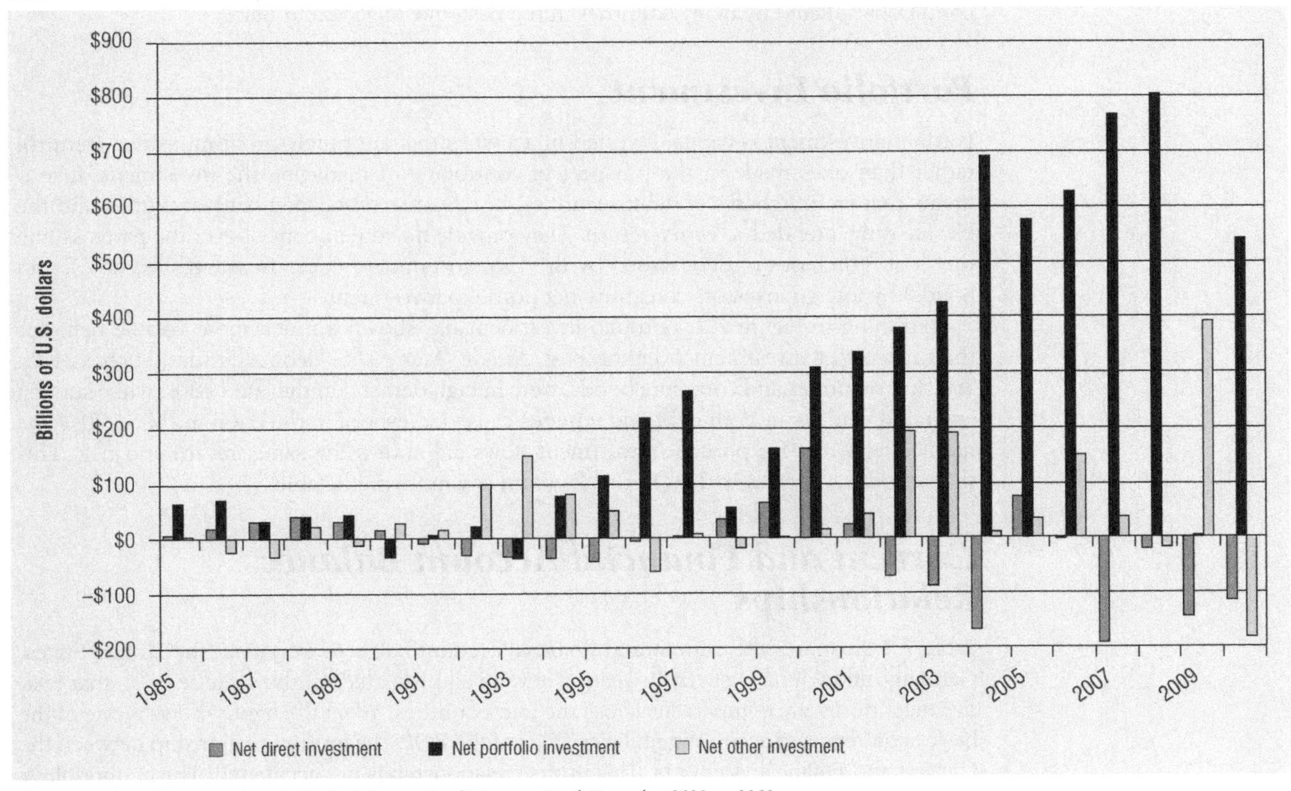

SOURCE: *Balance of Payments Statistics Yearbook*, International Monetary Fund, December 2011, p. 1101.

concerns. As opposed to many of the traditional debates over whether international trade should be free or not, there is not the same consensus that international investment should necessarily be free.

The second major source of concern over foreign direct investment is who receives the profits from the enterprise. Foreign companies owning firms in the United States ultimately profit from the activities of the firms, or put another way, from the efforts of American workers. In spite of evidence that foreign firms typically reinvest most of their profits in the United States (in fact, at a higher rate than domestic firms), the debate on possible profit drains has continued. Regardless of the actual choices made, workers of any nation feel the profits of their work should remain in the hands of their own citizens.

The choice of words used to describe foreign investment can also influence public opinion. If these massive capital inflows are described as "capital investments from all over the world showing their faith in the future of American industry," the net capital surplus is represented as decidedly positive. If, however, the net capital surplus is described as resulting in "the United States as the world's largest debtor nation," the negative connotation is obvious. Both are essentially spins on the economic principles at work. Capital, whether short-term or long-term, flows to where it believes it can earn the greatest return for the level of risk. Although in an accounting sense that is "international debt," when the majority of the capital inflow is in the form of direct investment and a long-term commitment to jobs, production, services, technological, and other competitive investments, the impact on the competitiveness of American industry (an industry located within the United States) is increased. The "net debtor" label is misleading in that it inappropriately invites comparison with large-debt crisis conditions suffered by many countries in the past, like Mexico and Brazil.

Portfolio Investment

Portfolio investment is capital invested in activities that are purely profit-motivated (return), rather than ones made in the prospect of controlling or managing the investment. Investments that are purchases of debit securities, bonds, interest-bearing bank accounts, and the like are only intended to earn a return. They provide no vote or control over the party issuing the debt. Purchases of debt issued by the U.S. government (U.S. Treasury bills, notes, and bonds) by foreign investors constitute net portfolio investment.

Returning to Figure 7.2, portfolio investment has shown a much more volatile behavior than net direct investment over the past decade. Many U.S. debt securities, such as U.S. Treasury securities and corporate bonds, were in high demand in the late 1980s, while surging emerging markets in both debt and equities caused a reversal in direction in the 1990s. The motivating forces for portfolio investment flows are always the same, return and risk. This theoretical fact, however, does not make them any more predictable.

Current and Financial Account Balance Relationships

Table 7.3 illustrates the current and financial account balances for Japan, the United States, Germany, and China over recent years. They are all presented on the same scale so that relative magnitudes are comparable across the four countries. What the figure shows is one of the basic economic and accounting relationships of the BOP: the inverse relationship between the Current and Financial accounts. This inverse relationship is not accidental. The methodology of the BOP, if markets work, exchange rates adjust, and double-entry bookkeeping is used, requires that the current and financial accounts be offsetting. Countries experiencing large current account deficits "finance" these purchases through equally large surpluses in the financial account and vice versa.

TABLE 7.3 Current and Financial Account Balances of Selected Countries

	1990–99		2000–10	
Country	**Current Account**	**Financial Account**	**Current Account**	**Financial Account**
United States	Deficit	Surplus	Deficit	Surplus
Japan	Surplus	Deficit	Surplus	Deficit
Germany	Deficit	Surplus	Surplus	Deficit
China	Surplus	Surplus	Surplus	Surplus

Most countries consistently run a Current Account deficit (surplus) while simultaneously running a Financial Account surplus (deficit). Regardless of the combination, they nearly always demonstrate an inverse relationship. Most, but not all. China has over the past two decades generated a twin surplus, a surplus in both the current and financial accounts.

Note that Germany has indeed experienced an inverse relationship, but the accounts have reversed in the most recent decade.

But, China is different. As illustrated in Figure 7.3, China has run twin surpluses—a surplus in both the current account and financial account—for many years. The Chinese economy has been able to sustain the surpluses because the Chinese government has not allowed the Chinese currency, the *yuan*, to appreciate versus other foreign currencies, but instead the government regulates all foreign exchange and accumulates the excess euros, dollars, and yen it has earned in exchange in the country's massive foreign exchange reserves.

FIGURE 7.3 Current and Combined Financial/Capital Account Balances for the United States, 1992-2010

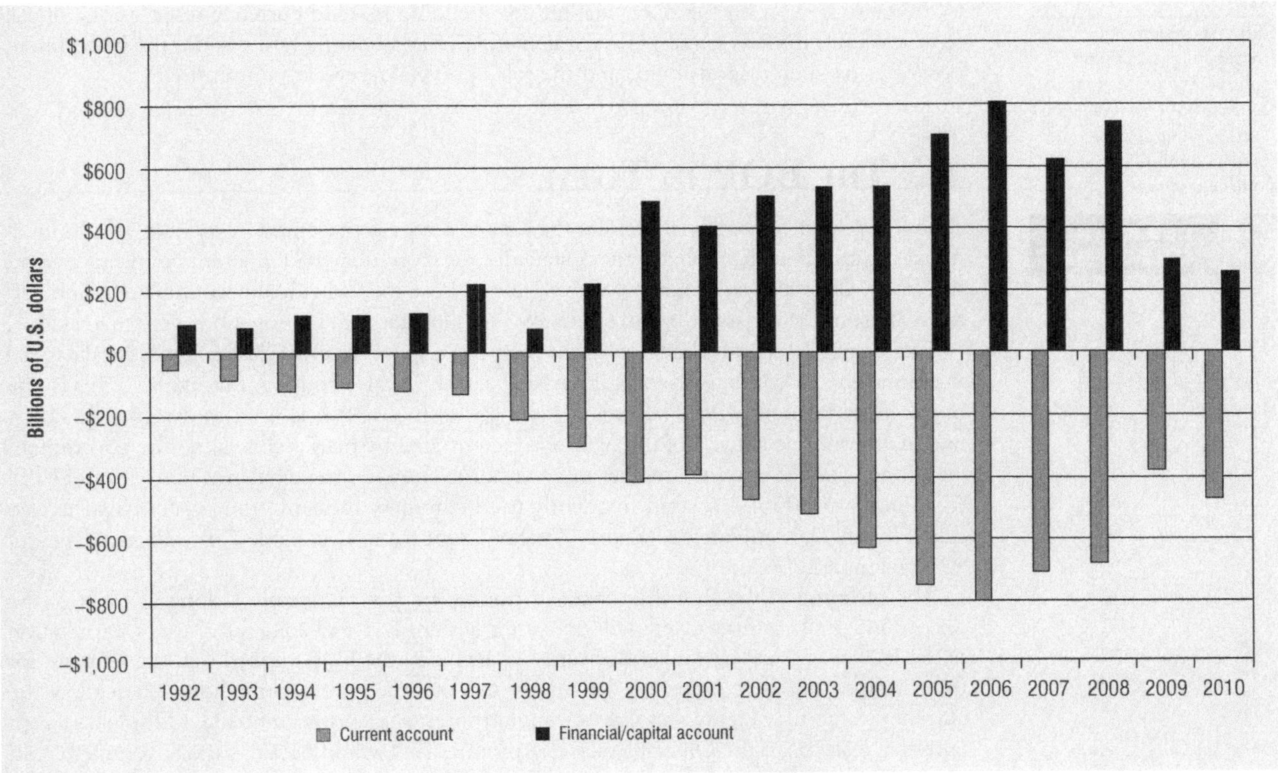

SOURCE: *Balance of Payments Statistics Yearbook*, International Monetary Fund, December 2011, p. 1101.

Net Errors and Omissions

As noted before, because Current Account and Financial Account entries are collected and recorded separately, errors or statistical discrepancies will occur. The **net errors and omissions account** (this is the title used by the International Monetary Fund [IMF]) makes sure that the BOP actually balances.

NET ERRORS AND OMISSIONS ACCOUNT
Makes sure the BOP actually balances

Official Reserves Account

The **official reserves account** is the total currency and metallic reserves held by official monetary authorities within the country. These reserves are normally composed of the major currencies used in international trade and financial transactions (so-called "hard currencies" such as the U.S. dollar, German mark, and Japanese yen) and gold.

The significance of official reserves depends generally on whether the country is operating under a **fixed exchange rate** regime or a **floating exchange rate** system. If a country's currency is fixed, this means that the government of the country officially declares that the currency is convertible into a fixed amount of some other currency.

For example, for many years the South Korean won was fixed to the U.S. dollar at 484 won equal to one U.S. dollar. It is the government's responsibility to maintain this fixed rate. If for some reason there is an excess supply of Korean won on the currency market, then to prevent

OFFICIAL RESERVES ACCOUNT
An account in the BOP statement that shows (1) the change in the amount of funds immediately available to a country for making international payments and (2) the borrowing and lending that has taken place between the monetary authorities of different countries either directly or through the IMF

FIXED EXCHANGE RATE
The government of a country officially declares that its currency is convertible into a fixed amount of some other currency

FLOATING EXCHANGE RATE
Under this system, the government possesses no responsibility to declare that its currency is convertible into a fixed amount of some other currency; diminishes the role of official reserves

the value of the won from falling, the South Korean government must support the won's value by purchasing won on the open market (by spending its hard currency reserves, its official reserves) until the excess supply is eliminated. Under a floating rate system, the government possesses no such responsibility, and the role of official reserves is diminished.

THE BOP IN TOTAL

Table 7.4 provides the official BOP for the United States as presented by the IMF, the multinational organization that collects these statistics for more than 160 different countries around the globe. It gives a comprehensive overview of how the individual accounts are combined to create some of the most useful summary measures for multinational business managers.

The Current Account (line A in Table 7.4), the Capital Account (line B), and the Financial Account (line C) combine to form the basic balance (Total, Groups A through C). This is one of the most frequently used summary measures of the BOP. It is used to describe the international economic activity of the nation as determined by market forces, not by government decisions (such as currency market intervention). The U.S. basic balance totaled a deficit of $13 billion in 2006. A second frequently used summary measure, the overall balance, also called the official settlements balance (Total of Groups A to D in Table 7.4), was at a deficit of $31 billion in 2006.

The meaning of the BOP has changed during the past 50 years. As long as most of the major industrial countries were still operating under fixed exchange rates, the interpretation of the BOP was relatively straightforward. A surplus in the BOP implied that the demand for the country's currency exceeded the supply and that the government should then allow the currency value to increase (revalue) or should intervene and accumulate additional foreign currency reserves in the Official Reserves Account. This would occur as the government sold its own currency in exchange for other currencies, thus building up its stores of hard currencies. A deficit in the BOP implied an excess supply of the country's currency on world markets, and the government would then either devalue the currency or expend its official reserves to support its value.

The transition to floating exchange-rate regimes in the 1970s (described in the chapter on global finance), however, changed the focus from the total BOP to its various subaccounts like the Current and Financial Account balances. These are the indicators of economic activities and currency repercussions to come. The crises in Mexico (1994), Asia (1997), Russia (1998), Turkey (2001), and Argentina and Venezuela (2002) highlight the continuing changes in the role of the BOP.

The BOP and Economic Crises

The sum of cross-border international economic activity—the BOP—can be used by international managers to forecast economic conditions and, in some cases, the likelihood of economic crises. The mechanics of international economic crisis often follow a similar path of development:

1. A country that experiences rapidly expanding current account deficits will simultaneously build financial account surpluses (the inverse relationship noted previously in this chapter).
2. The capital that flows into a country, giving rise to the financial account surplus, acts as the "financing" for the growing merchandise/services deficits—the constituent components of the current account deficit.

TABLE 7.4 The United States Balance of Payments, Analytic Presentation, 2000–2010 (billions of U.S. dollars)

	2000	2001	2002	2003	2004	2005	2006	2007	2008	2009	2010
A. Current Account	**–417**	**–385**	**–461**	**–523**	**–625**	**–729**	**–804**	**–718**	**–677**	**–377**	**–471**
Goods exports fob	775	722	686	717	811	898	1020	1164	1312	1074	1293
Goods imports fob	–1227	–1148	–1167	–1264	–1477	–1682	–1863	–1985	–2139	–1576	–1936
Balance on Goods	–452	–426	–481	–548	–666	–783	–844	–820	–827	–503	–642
Services: credit	296	283	289	301	350	385	432	484	531	501	544
Services: debit	–224	–222	–231	–250	–291	–314	–349	–366	–402	–380	–402
Balance on Goods & Services	–380	–365	–424	–497	–608	–712	–760	–702	–698	–381	–500
Income: credit	351	291	281	320	414	535	682	830	814	600	663
Income: debit	–330	–259	–254	–275	–347	–463	–634	–730	–667	–472	–498
Balance on Goods, Services, & Income	–359	–333	–396	–452	–541	–639	–712	–603	–551	–253	–335
Current transfers: credit	11	9	12	15	20	19	26	24	26	22	16
Current transfers: debit	–69	–60	–77	–87	–105	–109	–117	–140	–152	–145	–152
B. Capital Account	**–1**	**–1**	**–1**	**–3**	**–2**	**–4**	**–4**	**0**	**6**	**0**	**0**
Capital account: credit	1	1	1	1	1	1	1	0	6	0	0
Capital account: debit	–2	–2	–2	–4	–3	–5	–5	0	0	0	0
Total, Groups A Plus B	**–418**	**–386**	**–463**	**–527**	**–627**	**–733**	**–807**	**–718**	**–671**	**–377**	**–471**
C. Financial Account	**–1**	**–1**	**–1**	**–3**	**–2**	**–4**	**–4**	**0**	**6**	**0**	**0**
Direct investment	162	25	–70	–86	–170	76	–2	–143	–19	–145	–115
Direct investment abroad	–159	–142	–154	–150	–316	–36	–245	–414	–329	–304	–351
Direct investment in United States	321	167	84	64	146	113	243	271	310	159	236
Portfolio investment assets	–128	–91	–49	–123	–177	–258	–499	–391	280	–360	–166
Equity securities	–107	–109	–17	–118	–85	–187	–147	–148	39	–64	–79
Debt securities	–21	18	–32	–5	–93	–71	–362	–243	242	–296	–86
Portfolio investment liabilities	437	428	428	550	867	832	1127	1157	524	360	707
Equity securities	194	121	54	34	62	89	145	276	127	221	172
Debt securities	243	307	374	516	806	743	981	881	397	139	535
Financial derivatives, net	0	0	0	0	0	0	30	6	–33	49	14
Other investment assets	–273	–145	–88	–54	–510	–267	–544	–671	386	576	–486
Monetary authorities	0	0	0	0	0	0	0	–24	–530	543	10
General government	–1	0	0	1	2	6	5	2	0	–2	–3
Banks	–133	–136	–38	–36	–359	–151	–343	–500	456	–192	–427
Other sectors	–139	–9	–50	–29	–153	–121	–207	–148	460	226	–67
Other investment liabilities	280	187	283	244	520	303	695	680	–402	–183	303
Monetary authorities	–11	35	70	11	13	8	2	–11	29	60	28
General government	–2	–2	0	–1	0	0	3	5	9	11	12
Banks	123	88	118	136	347	232	344	468	–357	–257	207
Other sectors	171	66	96	98	160	62	346	217	–83	4	55
Total, Groups A Through C	**60**	**19**	**41**	**5**	**–98**	**–46**	**–1**	**–79**	**64**	**–79**	**–215**
D. Net Errors and Omissions	**–59**	**–14**	**–38**	**–6**	**95**	**32**	**–2**	**80**	**85**	**163**	**217**
Total, Groups A Through D	**0.31**	**4.88**	**3.71**	**–1.33**	**–2.8**	**–14.1**	**–2**	**0**	**149**	**84**	**2**
E. Reserves and Relates Items	**0**	**–5**	**–4**	**2**	**3**	**14**	**2**	**0**	**–5**	**–52**	**–2**

SOURCE: International Monetary Fund, *Balance of Payments Statistics Yearbook*, December 2011, p. 1101. Note: Totals may not match original source due to rounding.

3. Some event, be it a report, a speech, an action by a government or business inside or outside the country, raises the question of the country's economic stability. Investors of many kinds, portfolio and direct investors in the country, fearing economic problems in the near future, may withdraw capital from the country rapidly to avoid any exposure to this risk. This is prudent for the individual, but catastrophic for the whole if all individuals move similarly.
4. The rapid withdrawal of capital from the country, so-called "capital flight," results in the loss of the financial account surplus, creating a severe deficit in the country's overall BOP. This is typically accompanied by rapid currency depreciation (if a floating-rate currency) or currency devaluation (if a fixed-rate currency).

International debt and economic crises have occurred for as long as there has been international trade and commerce. And they will occur again. Each crisis has its own unique characteristics, but all follow the economic fundamentals described previously. (The one additional factor that differentiates many of the crises is whether inflation is a component.) The recent Asian economic crisis was a devastating reminder of the tenuous nature of international economic relationships.

CAUSES OF ECONOMIC CRISIS The Asian economic crisis (when major currencies throughout Asia collapsed in the summer of 1997) was more than just a currency collapse. It had many roots besides the traditional BOP difficulties. The causes are different in each country, yet there are specific underlying similarities that allow for comparison: corporate socialism, corporate governance, and banking stability and management.

Corporate Socialism. Although Western markets have long known the cold indifference of the free market, the countries of post–World War II Asia have known mostly the good. Because of the influence of government and politics in the business arena, even in the event of failure, governments would not allow firms to fail, workers to lose their jobs, or banks to close. When the problems reached the size seen in 1997, the business liability exceeded the capacities of governments to bail businesses out. Practices that had persisted for decades without challenge, such as lifetime employment, were now no longer sustainable. The result was a painful lesson in the harshness of the marketplace.

Quick Take *India Borrows Its Way Out of Trouble*

In October 2000, India hit on a not-so-novel idea to shield an economy made vulnerable by high international oil prices. The government floated a scheme for State Bank of India, the country's largest bank, to sell five-year foreign currency deposits to expatriate Indians to help tackle a worsening BOP situation. By October 2001, SBI, whose largest owner is the Indian Central Bank, had collected $5.5 billion from the sale of India Millennium Deposits (IMD).

India's oil import bill was also expected to double to about $18 billion. A widening trade deficit and a sell-off by foreign portfolio investors put the BOP in the red by about $1 billion in the quarter that ended June 2000, as compared with a surplus of $3.32 billion in the previous quarter. The rupee had lost around 6 percent of its value against the dollar.

SOURCES: "An Incredible Shrinking Government," *The Economist*, February 7, 2002, **http://www.economist.com**; Niharika Bisaria, "Going on a Millennium Hunt," October 18, 2001, **http://www.hometrade.com**; Kala Rao, "India Tries to Borrow Its Way Out of Trouble," *Euromoney*, London, November 2000.

Corporate Governance. An expression largely unused until the 1990s, corporate governance refers to the complex process of how a firm is managed and operated, to whom it is accountable, and how it reacts to changing business conditions. There is little doubt that many firms operating within the Far Eastern business environments mainly were controlled by either families or groups related to the governing party or body of the country. The interests of stockholders and creditors were often secondary at best to the primary motivations of corporate management. Without the motivation to focus on "the bottom line," the bottom line deteriorated.

Banking Liquidity and Management. Banking is one of the sectors that have fallen out of fashion in the past two decades. Bank regulatory structures and markets have been deregulated nearly without exception around the globe. The central role played by banks in the conduct of business, however, was largely ignored and underestimated.

As firms across Asia collapsed, as government coffers were emptied, as speculative investments made by the banks themselves failed, banks closed. Without banks, the "plumbing" of business conduct was shut down. Firms could not obtain the necessary working capital financing they needed to manufacture their products or provide their services. This pivotal role of banking liquidity was the focus of the International Monetary Fund's bailout efforts.

CAPITAL MOBILITY

The degree to which capital moves freely cross-border is critically important to a country's BOP. We have already seen how the United States has suffered a deficit in its current account balance over the past twenty years while running a surplus in the financial account, and how China has enjoyed a surplus in both the current and financial accounts over the last decade. But these are only two country cases and may not reflect the challenges that changing balances in trade and capital may mean for many countries, particularly smaller ones or emerging markets.

Current Account Versus Financial Account Capital Flows

Capital inflows can contribute significantly to an economy's development. Capital inflows can increase the availability of capital for new projects, new infrastructure development, and productivity improvements. All of which may stimulate general economic growth and job creation. For domestic holders of capital, the ability to invest outside the domestic economy may reap greater investment returns, portfolio diversification, and extend the commercial development of domestic enterprises.

That said, the free flow of capital in and out of an economy can potentially destabilize economic activity. Although the benefits of free capital flows have been known for centuries, so have the negatives. For this very reason, the creators of the Bretton Woods system were very careful to promote and require the free movement of capital for **current account transactions**—foreign exchange, bank deposits, money market instruments—but not require such free transit for **capital account transactions**—foreign direct investment and equity investments.

Experience has shown that current account-related capital flows can be more volatile, capital flowing in and out of an economy and a currency on the basis of short-term interest rate differentials and exchange rate expectations. But in some ways this same volatility is somewhat compartmentalized, not directly impacting real asset investments, employment, or long-term economic growth. Longer-term capital flows often reflect more fundamental economic expectations, including growth prospects and perceptions of political stability.

CURRENT ACCOUNT TRANSACTION

Any international economic transaction with income or payment flows occurring within the year, the current period

CAPITAL ACCOUNT TRANSACTION

Any international transfer of a financial asset or the acquisition and disposal of a nonfinancial asset

IMPOSSIBLE TRINITY

The theoretical structure that states that no country can have all three of the following: (1) maintain fixed exchange rates; (2) allow the free movement of capital; and (3) conduct independent monetary policy. The political and economic leadership of a country must pick two of the three but cannot have all three at the same time.

The complexity of issues, however, is apparent when you consider the plight of many emerging market countries. The **Impossible Trinity** is the theoretical structure that states that no country can have all three of the following: (1) maintain fixed exchange rates; (2) allow the free movement of capital; and (3) conduct independent monetary policy. The political and economic leadership of a country must pick two of the three but cannot have all three at the same time.

Many emerging market countries have continued to develop by maintaining a near-fixed (soft peg) exchange rate regime, a strictly independent monetary policy, while restricting capital inflows and outflows. With the growth of current account business activity (exports and imports of goods and services), more and more current account-related capital flows are deregulated. If, however, the country experiences significant volatility in these short-term capital movements, capital flows potentially affecting either exchange rate pegs or monetary policy objectives, authorities are often quick to reinstitute capital controls.

The growth in capital openness in the 1970s, 1980s, and first half of the 1990s resulted in a significant increase in political pressures for more countries to open up more of their financial account sectors to international capital. But the devastation of the Asian financial crisis of 1997–98 brought much of that to a halt. Smaller economies, no matter how successful their growth and development may have been under export-oriented trade strategies, found themselves still subject to sudden and destructive capital outflows in times of economic crisis and financial contagion.

Historical Patterns of Capital Mobility

Before leaving our discussion of the BOP, we need to gain additional insights into the history of capital mobility and the contribution of capital outflows—capital flight—to BOP crises. Has capital always been free to move in and out of a country? Definitely not. The ability of foreign investors to own property, buy businesses, or purchase stocks and bonds in other countries has been controversial.

Figure 7.4 is helpful in categorizing the last 150 years of economic history into five distinct exchange rate eras and their associated implications for capital mobility (or lack thereof). These exchange rate eras reflect the evolution of cross-border political economy beliefs and policies of both industrialized and emerging market nations over this period.

THE GOLD STANDARD (1860–1914) Although an era of growing capital openness in which trade and capital began to flow more freely, it was an era dominated by industrialized nation economies that were dependent on gold convertibility to maintain confidence in the system.

THE INTER-WAR YEARS (1914–45) The years between World War I and World War II were a period of retrenchment, in which major economic powers returned to policies of isolationism and protectionism, restricting trade and nearly eliminating capital mobility. The devastating results included financial crisis, a global depression, and rising international political and economic disputes that drove nations into the Second World War.

THE BRETTON WOODS ERA (1945–71) The dollar-based fixed exchange rate system under Bretton Woods gave rise to a long period of economic recovery and growing openness of both international trade and capital flows in and out of more and more countries. Many researchers (for example Obstfeld and Taylor, 2001) believe it was the rapid growth in the speed and volume of capital flows that ultimately led to the failure of Bretton Woods—global capital could no longer be held in check.

THE FLOATING ERA (1971–97) The Floating Era saw the rise of a growing schism between the industrialized and the emerging market nations. The industrialized nations (primary currencies) moved to—or were driven to—floating exchange rates by capital mobility. The

FIGURE 7.4 The Evolution of Capital Mobility

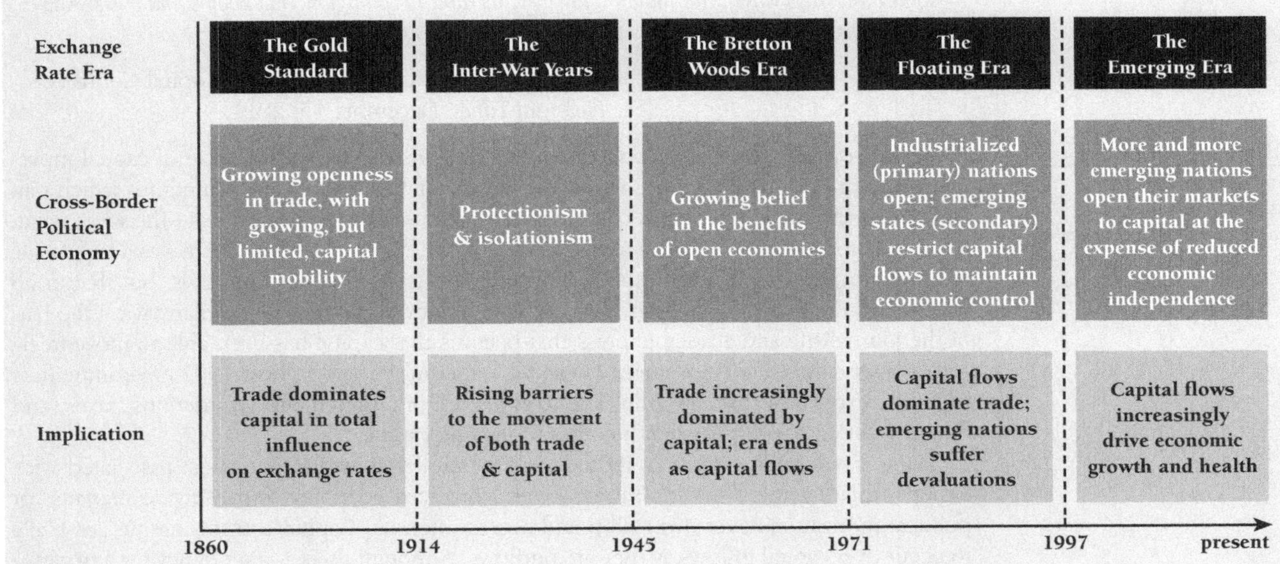

The last 150 years has seen periods of increasing and decreasing political and economic openness between countries. Beginning with the Bretton Woods Era, global markets have moved toward increasing open exchange of goods and capital, making it increasingly difficult to maintain fixed or even stable rates of exchange between currencies. The most recent era, characterized by the growth and development of emerging economies is likely to be even more challenging.

emerging markets (secondary currencies), in an attempt to both promote economic development but maintain control over their economies and currencies, opened trade but maintained restrictions on capital flows. Despite these restrictions, the era ended with the onslaught of the Asian Financial Crisis in 1997.

THE EMERGING ERA (1997–PRESENT) The emerging economies, led by China and India, attempt to gradually open their markets to global capital. But, as the Impossible Trinity taught the industrial nations in previous years, the increasing mobility of capital now requires that they give up either the ability to manage their currency values or conduct independent monetary policies. By 2011 and 2012 more and more emerging market currencies "suffer" appreciation (or fight appreciation) as capital flows grow in magnitude and speed.

The 2008–11 period reinforced what some call the double-edged sword of global capital movements. The credit crisis of 2008, beginning in the United States, quickly spread to the global economy, pulling and pushing down industrial and emerging market economies alike. But in the post–credit crisis period, global capital now flowed toward the emerging markets. Although funding and fueling their rapid economic recoveries, it came—in the words of one journalist—"with luggage." The increasing pressure on emerging market currencies to appreciate is partially undermining their export competitiveness.

Capital Controls

Back in the halcyon pre-crisis days of the late 20th and early 21st centuries, it was taken as self evident that financial globalisation was a good thing. After all, free capital should enable money to flow to where it is most needed, at the best price; or so the theory goes.

But the subprime crisis and eurozone dramas are shaking that belief. Never mind the fact that imbalances amid globalisation can stoke up bubbles; what is the bigger risk now—particularly in the eurozone—is that financial globalisation has created a system that is interconnected in some dangerous ways. This makes it highly vulnerable to contagion, and booms and busts. And if globalisation increases, these swings could potentially get worse.

— Gillian Tett, "Crisis Fears Fuel Debate on Capital Controls," *The Financial Times*, December 15, 2011.

CAPITAL CONTROL
Any government imposed restriction that limits or prevents the free movement of capital in and out of a country

A **capital control** is any restriction that limits or alters the rate or direction of capital movement into or out of a country. Capital controls may take many forms, sometimes which parties may undertake which types of capital transactions for which purposes—the who, what, when, where, and why of investment. As noted in the previous section, there was a large-scale reduction of capital controls in the years leading up to the 1997 Asian Crisis, but that in no way means the controls had gone away or were minor in nature. It is in many ways the bias of the journalistic and academic press that believes that capital has been able to move freely across boundaries. Free movement of capital, either in the pre- or post-1997 environment, is more the exception than the rule. The world is full of requirements, restrictions, taxes, and documentation approvals when it comes to moving capital.

There is a wide spectrum of motivations for capital controls, with most associated with either insulating the domestic monetary and financial economy from outside markets, or political motivations over ownership and access interests. Capital controls are just as likely to occur over capital inflows as they are outflows. Although there is a tendency for a negative connotation to accompany capital controls (possibly the bias of the word "control" itself), the Impossible Trinity requires that capital flows be controlled if a country wishes to maintain a fixed exchange rate and an independent monetary policy.

Capital controls may take a variety of forms, which mirror restrictions on trade. They may simply be a tax on a specific transaction, may limit the quantity or magnitudes of specific capital transactions, or may prohibit them altogether. The controls themselves have tended to follow the basic dichotomy of the BOP—current account related transactions versus financial account transactions.

In some cases, capital controls are intended to stop or thwart capital outflows and currency devaluation or depreciation. The case of Malaysia during the Asian Crisis of 1997–98 helps explain both the logic of the controls, the forms of implementation, and the relationship between capital controls and currency controls in a falling currency case. As the Malaysian currency came under attack and capital started to exit the Malaysian economy, the government imposed a series of capital controls that were intended to stop short-term capital movements, in or out, but not hinder trade and not restrict long-term inward investment. All trade-related requests for access to foreign exchange were granted, allowing current account-related capital flows to continue. But access to foreign exchange for inward or outward money market or capital market investments was restricted. Foreign residents wishing to invest in Malaysian assets—real assets, not financial assets—had ready access to exchange and capital movements.

Capital controls can be implemented in the opposite case, in which the primary fear is that large rapid capital inflows will both cause currency appreciation (and therefore harm export competitiveness) and complicate monetary policy (capital inflows flooding money markets and bank deposits). Chile in the 1990s is one such case, in which a new found political and economic soundness started attracting international capital. The Chilean government responded with its *encaje* program, which imposed taxes and restrictions on short-term (less than one year) capital inflows, as well as restricting the ability of domestic financial institutions to extend credits or loans in foreign currency. Although credited with achieving its goals of maintaining domestic monetary policy and preventing a rapid appreciation in the Chilean peso, it came at substantial cost to Chilean firms, particularly smaller ones.

CAPITAL FLIGHT:
The rapid outflow of capital from a country when owners of the capital, whether they be domestic or foreign residents, fear for the preservation of the capital's value

CAPITAL FLIGHT An extreme problem that has raised its ugly head a number of times in international financial history is **capital flight**, one of the extremes that capital controls hope

Quick Take Capital Controls and Dutch Disease

One use of capital controls to prevent domestic currency appreciation is the so-called case of *Dutch Disease* (a term coined by the *Economist* magazine). With the rapid growth of the natural gas industry in the Netherlands in the 1970s, there was growing fear that massive capital inflows would drive up the demand for the Dutch guilder and cause a substantial currency appreciation. A more expensive guilder would then reduce the international competitiveness of other Dutch manufacturing industries, causing their relative decline to that of the natural resource industry. This is a challenge faced by a number of resource rich economies of relatively modest size and relatively small export sectors in recent years, including oil and gas development in Azerbaijan, Kazakhstan, and Nigeria, or copper in Chile or Ghana, to name but a few.

to control. Although no single accepted definition of capital flight exists, the most common is when capital transfers by residents of a country (usually capital flowing out) conflicts with the country's political objectives (of keeping the capital in the country).

A number of mechanisms are used for moving money from one country to another—some legal, some not. Transfers using the usual international payments mechanisms (regular bank transfers) are obviously the easiest and lowest cost and are legal. Most economically healthy countries allow free exchange of their currencies, but of course for such countries "capital flight" is not a problem. The opposite, transfer of physical currency by bearer (the proverbial smuggling out of cash in the false bottom of a suitcase) is more costly and, for transfers out of many countries, illegal. Such transfers may be deemed illegal for balance of payments reasons or to make difficult the movement of money from the drug trade or other illegal activities.

There are a number of more creative solutions. One is to move cash using collectibles or precious metals, which are then transferred across borders. **Money laundering** is the cross-border purchase of assets that are then managed in a way that hides the movement of money and its ownership. And finally, **false invoicing** of international trade transactions occurs when capital is moved through underinvoicing exports or overinvoicing imports, where the difference between the invoiced amount and the actual agreed upon payment is deposited in banking institutions in a country of choice.

MONEY LAUNDERING
The process of transforming the proceeds of some criminal or illegal activities into legitimate money or other assets

FALSE INVOICING
The illegal practice of falsifying or altering the amount of an international transaction in order to move funds in or out of a country

Globalization of Capital Flows

Traditionally, the primary concern over the inflow of capital is that they are short term in duration, may flow out with short notice, and are characteristics of the politically and economically unstable emerging markets. But as described in the recent quote, two of the largest capital flow crises in recent years have occurred within the largest, most highly developed, mature capital markets—the United States and Western Europe.

The 2008 global credit crisis which had the United States as its core, and the current 2011–12 Greece/European Union sovereign debt crisis, both occurred within the markets that have long been considered the most mature, the most sophisticated, and the "safest." The next chapter will explore the causes and implications these recent financial crises have caused for the structure and operations of the world's multinational enterprises.

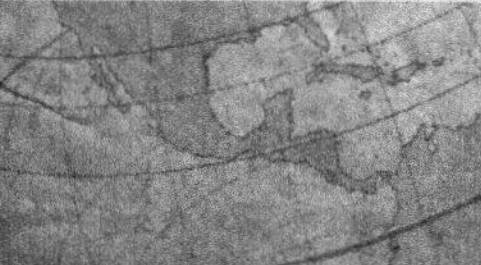

SUMMARY

The BOP is the summary statement of all international transactions between one country and all other countries.

The BOP is a flow statement, summarizing all the international transactions that occur across the geographic boundaries of the nation over a period of time, typically a year.

Although in theory the BOP must always balance, in practice substantial imbalances result due to statistical errors and misreporting of current account and financial/capital account flows.

The two major subaccounts of the BOP, the current account and the financial/capital account, summarize the current trade and international capital flows of the country respectively.

The current account and financial/capital account are typically inverse on balance, one in surplus and the other in deficit.

Although most nations strive for current account surpluses, it is not clear that a balance on current or capital account, or a surplus on current account, is either sustainable or desirable.

Although merchandise trade is more easily observed (e.g., goods flowing through ports of entry), today, the growth of services trade is more significant to the BOP for many of the world's largest industrialized countries.

Monitoring of the various subaccounts of a country's balance of payment activity is helpful to decision makers and policymakers on all levels of government and industry in detecting the underlying trends and movements of fundamental economic forces driving a country's international economic activity.

A devaluation results initially in a further deterioration in the trade balance before an eventual improvement—the path of adjustment taking on the shape of a flattened "j."

The ability of capital to move instantaneously and massively cross-border has been one of the major factors in the severity of recent currency crises. In cases such as Malaysia in 1997 and Argentina in 2001, the national governments concluded that they had no choice but to impose drastic restrictions on the ability of capital to flow.

Although not limited to heavily indebted countries, the rapid and sometimes illegal transfer of convertible currencies out of a country poses significant economic and political problems. Many heavily indebted countries have suffered significant capital flight, which has compounded their problems of debt service.

Key Terms and Concepts

remittances
migrant
balance of payments (BOP)
Current Account
Financial Account
double-entry bookkeeping
goods trade account
services trade account
income account
current transfers account
direct investment account
portfolio investment account
net errors and omissions account
official reserves account
fixed exchange rate
floating exchange rate
current account transaction
capital account transaction
Impossible Trinity
capital control
capital flight
money laundering
false invoicing

Review Questions

1. Why must a country's balance of payments always be balanced in theory?
2. What is the difference between the merchandise trade balance (BOT) and the current account balance?
3. What is service trade?
4. What is the difference between the Current Account and the Capital Account?
5. While the United States "suffered" a current account deficit and a capital account surplus in the 1980s, what were the respective balances of Japan doing?
6. How do exchange-rate changes alter trade so that the trade balance actually improves when the domestic currency depreciates?
7. How did trade balances in Asia contributed to the cause of the 1997 Asian crisis?
8. Summarize the effects of the Asian crisis on the global economy.

Critical Skill Builders

1. Why is foreign direct investment so much more controversial than foreign portfolio investment? How did this relate to Mexico in the 1990s?
2. What does it mean for the United States to be one of the world's most-indebted countries? Should this be a concern for government policymakers?
3. In pairs or small groups, use your library's resources or the Internet to find an up-to-date balance-of-payments report for an emerging economy. Discuss any patterns you see that may be considered red flags for companies exporting to or investing in that nation. Present your findings to the rest of the class.
4. In groups, discuss the causes and effects of a currency crisis. Refer to recent events in Asia and South America.
5. How might businesses in a developing nation benefit or suffer from an ongoing economic crisis in a neighboring emergent economy? Discuss.

On the Web

1. The IMF, the World Bank, and the United Nations are only a few of the major world organizations that track, report, and aid international economic and financial development. Using these web sites and others that may be linked to them, briefly summarize the economic outlook for the developed and emerging nations of the world. For example, the full text of Chapter 1 of the World Economic Outlook published annually by the World Bank is available through the IMF's web site.
   - International Monetary Fund **http://www.imf.org**
   - United Nations **http://www.unsystem.org**
   - The World Bank **http://www.worldbank.org**
   - Europa (EU) Homepage **http://www.europa.eu.int**
   - Bank for International Settlements **http://www.bis.org**
2. Current economic and financial statistics and commentaries are available using the IMF's web site under "What's New," "Fund Rates," and the "IMF Committee on Balance of Payments Statistics." For an in-depth examination of the IMF's ongoing initiative on the validity of these statistics, termed metadata, visit the IMF's Dissemination Standards Bulletin Board listed below.
   - International Monetary Fund **http://www.imf.org**
   - IMF's Dissemination Standards Bulletin Board **http://www.dsbb.imf.org**
3. Visit Moody's sovereign ceilings and foreign-currency ratings service site on the Internet to evaluate what progress is being made in the nations of the Far East on recovering their perceived creditworthiness.
   - Moody's Sovereign Ceilings **http://www.moodys.com**

Endnotes

1. The official terminology used throughout this chapter, unless otherwise noted, is that of the International Monetary Fund (IMF). Because the IMF is the primary source of similar statistics for BOP and economic performance worldwide, it is more general than other terminology forms, such as that employed by the U.S. Department of Commerce.

PART 4

GLOBAL FINANCE

Operating internationally requires managers to be aware of a highly complex environment that is constantly in flux. Part 4 explores the workings of the international monetary system and its influence on the conduct of business. By understanding international currency exchange—its guiding principles and its operations—it is possible to identify vital linkages between exchange rates and interest rates. Part 4 concludes with a strategic investigation of financial management, accounting, and taxation as they affect the conduct of business across borders.

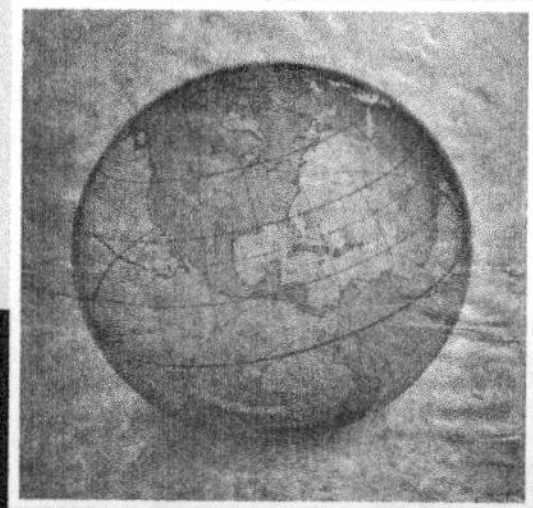

CHAPTER 8

GLOBAL FINANCE

Venezuela Fights a Currency War Against ... Itself

During the entire regime of President Hugo Chávez in Venezuela (1997–2013), Venezuela devalued its currency—the bolívar fuerte (translated "strong bolívar") —six times. The latest devaluation in February 2013 was considered huge, a 32 percent reduction in its purchasing value against the U.S. dollar, from Bfs4.30/$ to Bfs6.29/$.

Trading in the bolívar is regulated by the Venezuelan government and may only occur at the official exchange rate set by the government. The result, however, is that many individuals and businesses in Venezuela have not been able to exchange bolívars for dollars for all their commercial needs, creating a black market of trading. The black market rates typically are at rates of exchange for a much weaker bolívar, putting additional downward pressure on the already inflation-suffering Venezuelan currency.

Venezuelan Bolivars fuertes (Bfs or VEF) per US dollar

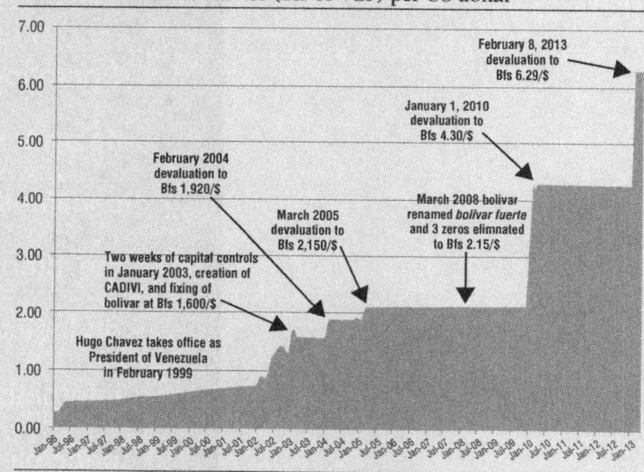

President Chávez had a very specific motivation for the recent devaluation: higher government spending. The Chávez government was spending at a very rapid rate, creating a government fiscal deficit. Because Venezuela's primary export is crude oil, after the devaluation every barrel of crude oil will generate more Venezuelan bolívars. With Chávez's passing, it remains to be seen what path Venezuela will take for its currency, continued devaluation or a movement toward market-based trading.

LEARNING OUTCOMES

1. *To understand exchange rates and find out how currencies are traded and quoted on world financial markets*
2. *To examine how the international currency-exchange system evolved and to understand the difference between fixed and floating rates of exchange*
3. *To realize the value of eurocurrency accounts—accounts that are free of governmental interference—to the conduct of international business*
4. *To explore the similarities and differences between domestic sources of capital and international sources of capital*
5. *To explain how international bond and equities markets meet the diverse borrowing and investing needs of corporations that trade overseas*

As You Read This Chapter

1. Consider how basic economic and political forces can influence the value of a country's currency.
2. Consider how trade, exports and imports, is both driven by and a driver of a currency's value.

Global financial markets serve as links between the financial markets of individual countries and as independent markets outside the jurisdiction of any one country. The market for currencies is at the heart of this international financial market. International trade and investment transactions are often denominated in a foreign currency, so the purchase of the currency precedes the purchase of goods, services, or assets.

This chapter begins by providing a detailed guide to the structure and functions of the foreign currency markets. It then explores the international financial markets and the securities markets that connect the financial markets of individual nations. All firms striving to attain or preserve competitiveness in the global arena must work with and within the frameworks of these markets, which operate independently of the jurisdiction or supervision of governmental authorities.

The Purpose of Exchange Rates

If countries are to trade, they must be able to exchange currencies. To buy wheat, or corn, or DVD players, the buyer must first have the currency in which the product is sold. An American firm purchasing consumer electronic products manufactured in Japan must first exchange its U.S. dollars for Japanese yen, then purchase the products. The exchange of one country's currency for another should be a relatively simple transaction, but as we shall see, it is not.

What Is a Currency Worth?

At what rate should one currency be exchanged for another? For example, what should the exchange rate be between the U.S. dollar and the Japanese yen? The simplest answer is that the exchange rate should equalize purchasing power. For example, if the price of a movie ticket in the United States is \$6, the "correct" exchange rate would be one that exchanges \$6 for the amount of Japanese yen it would take to purchase a movie ticket in Japan. If ticket prices are ¥540 (¥ is a common symbol for the yen) in Japan, then the exchange rate that would equalize purchasing power would be

$$\frac{¥540}{\$6} = \frac{¥90}{\$}$$

Therefore, if the exchange rate between the two currencies is ¥90/\$, moviegoers can purchase tickets, regardless of which country they are in. This is the theory of **purchasing power parity (PPP)**, generally considered the definition of what exchange rates ideally should be. The purchasing power parity exchange rate is simply the rate that equalizes the price of the identical product or service in two different currencies:

Price in Japan = Exchange rate × Price in the United States

PURCHASING POWER PARITY (PPP)
A theory that the prices of tradable goods will tend to equalize across countries, and hence the exchange rate between the two currencies should be the ratio of prices in the two countries

If the price of the same product in each currency is $P^¥$ and $P^\$$, and the spot exchange rate between the Japanese yen and the U.S. dollar is S¥/$, the price in yen is simply the price in dollars multiplied by the spot exchange rate:

$$P^{¥} = S^{¥/\$} \times P^{\$}$$

If this is rearranged (dividing both sides by $P^\$$), the spot exchange rate between the Japanese yen and the U.S. dollar is the ratio of the two product prices:

$$S^{¥/\$} = \frac{P^{¥}}{P^{\$}}$$

These prices could be the price of just one good or service, such as the movie ticket mentioned previously, or they could be price indices for each country that cover many different goods and services. Either form is an attempt to find comparable products in different countries (and currencies) in order to determine an exchange rate based on purchasing power parity. The question then is whether this logical approach to exchange rates actually works in practice.

LAW OF ONE PRICE
The theory that the relative prices of any single good between countries, expressed in each country's currency, is representative of the proper or appropriate exchange rate value

Foreign exchange traders at banks can move millions of dollars, yen, or marks around the world with a few keystrokes on their networked computers. The deregulation of international capital flaws contributes to faster, cheaper transactions in the currency markets.

The Law of One Price

The version of purchasing power parity that estimates the exchange rate between two currencies using just one good or service as a measure of the proper exchange for all goods and services is called the **Law of One Price**. To apply the theory to actual prices across countries, we need to select a product that is identical in quality and content in every country. To be truly theoretically correct, we would want such a product to be produced entirely domestically, so no import factors are used in its construction.

Where would one find such a perfect product? McDonald's. Table 8.1 presents what *The Economist* magazine calls "the golden-arches standard." What McDonald's provides is a product that is essentially the same the world over and is produced and consumed entirely domestically.

TABLE 8.1 Selected Rates from the Big Mac Index

Country and Currency		(1) Big Mac Price in Local Currency	(2) Actual Dollar Exchange Rate on July 25th	(3) Big Mac Price in Dollars	(4) Implied PPP of the Dollar	(5) Under/over Valuation Against Dollar**
United States	$	4.07	—	4.07	—	—
Britain	£	2.39	1.63	3.90*	1.70*	–4%
Canada	C$	4.73	0.95	4.98	1.16	22%
China	Yuan	14.70	6.45	2.28	3.61	–44%
Denmark	DK	28.50	5.20	5.48	7.00	35%
Euro area	€	3.44	1.43	4.92*	1.18*	21%
Japan	¥	320.00	78.40	4.08	78.60	0%
Peru	Sol	10.00	2.74	3.65	2.46	–10%
Russia	Rouble	75.00	27.80	2.70	18.40	–34%
Switzerland	SFr	6.50	0.81	8.02	1.60	97%
Thailand	Baht	70.00	29.80	2.35	17.20	–42%

* These exchange rates are stated in US$ per unit of local currency, $/£ and $/€.

** Percentage under/over valuation against the dollar is calculated as (Implied–Actual)/(Actual), except for the Britain and Euro area calculations, which are (Actual–Implied)/(Implied).

SOURCE: Data for columns (1) and (2) drawn from "The BigMac Index," *The Economist*, July 28, 2011.

The *Big Mac Index* compares the actual exchange rate with the exchange rate implied by the purchasing power parity measurement of comparing Big Mac prices across countries. For example, say the average price of a Big Mac in the United States on a given date is \$4.07. On the same date, the price of a Big Mac in Canada, in Canadian dollars, is C\$4.73. These prices can be used to calculate the PPP exchange rate as before:

$$\frac{\text{C\$4.73 per Big Mac}}{\text{\$4.07 per Big Mac}} = \text{C\$1.1622/\$}$$

The exchange rate between the Canadian dollar and the U.S. dollar should be C\$1.1622/\$, according to a PPP comparison of Big Mac prices. The actual exchange rate on the date of comparison was C\$0.95/\$. This means that each U.S. dollar was actually worth 0.95 Canadian dollars, when the index indicates that each U.S. dollar should have been worth 1.16 Canadian dollars. Therefore, if one is to believe the Big Mac index, the Canadian dollar was overvalued by 22 percent.

The Market for Currencies

The price of any one country's currency in terms of another country's currency is called a **foreign currency exchange rate**. Table 8.2 lists selected foreign currency exchange rates for Thursday, February 14, 2013. For example, the exchange rate between the U.S. dollar (\$ or USD) and the European euro (€ or EUR) may be "1.3342 dollars per euro," or simply abbreviated as \$1.3342/€. This is the same rate as when stated "EUR1.00 = USD 1.3342." Because most international business activities require at least one of the two parties to first purchase the country's currency before purchasing any good, service, or asset, a proper understanding of exchange rates and exchange-rate markets is very important to the conduct of international business.

FOREIGN CURRENCY EXCHANGE RATE
The price of any one country's currency in terms of another country's currency

A word about currency symbols: As already noted, the letters USD and EUR are often used as the symbols for the U.S. dollar and the European Union's euro. These letters are the computer symbols (ISO-4217 codes). The field of international finance suffers, however, from a lack of agreement when it comes to currency abbreviations. This chapter uses the more common symbols used in the financial press—\$ and € in this case. As a practitioner of international finance, however, stay on your toes. Every market, every country, and every firm may have its own set of symbols. For example, the symbol for the British pound sterling can be £ (the pound symbol), GBP (Great Britain pound), STG (British pound sterling), ST£ (pound sterling), or UKL (United Kingdom pound).

Exchange-Rate Quotations and Terminology

Most of the quotations listed in Table 8.2 are **spot exchange rates**. A spot transaction is the exchange of currencies for immediate delivery. Although it is defined as immediate, in actual practice, settlement typically occurs two business days following the agreed-upon exchange. The other time-related quotations listed in Table 8.2 are the **forward exchange rates**. Forward exchange rates are contracts that provide for two parties to exchange currencies on a future date at an agreed-upon exchange rate.

SPOT EXCHANGE RATES
Contracts that provide for two parties to exchange currencies, with delivery in two business days

FORWARD EXCHANGE RATES
Contracts that provide for two parties to exchange currencies on a future date at an agreed-upon exchange rate

Forwards are often quoted on major world currencies for maturities of one month, three months, and one year (from the present date). The forward, like the basic spot exchange, can be for any amount of currency. Forward contracts serve a variety of purposes, but their primary purpose is to allow a firm to lock in a future rate of exchange. This is a valuable tool in a world of continually changing exchange rates.

TABLE 8.2 Selected Global Currency Exchange Rates February 14, 2013

Country	Currency	Symbol	Code	Dollar	Euro	Pound
Argentina	peso	Ps	ARS	5.0055	6.6781	7.7716
Australia	dollar	A$	AUD	0.9655	1.2882	1.4991
Bolivia	boliviano	Bs	BOB	6.9100	9.2190	10.7285
Brazil	real	R$	BRL	1.9594	2.6142	3.0422
Canada	dollar	C$	CAD	1.0011	1.3356	1.5542
Chile	peso	$	CLP	470.750	628.051	730.886
China	yuan	¥	CNY	6.2325	8.3151	9.6766
Egypt	pound	£	EGP	6.7304	8.9793	10.4496
India	rupee	Rs	INR	53.8950	71.9041	83.6774
Japan	yen	¥	JPY	93.0600	124.156	144.485
One month				93.0420	124.156	144.430
Three month				92.9961	124.144	144.311
One year				92.6692	123.922	143.655
Mexico	new peso	$	MXN	12.6871	16.9265	19.698
Nigeria	naira	?	NGN	157.330	209.902	244.271
Norway	krone	NKr	NOK	5.5096	7.3506	8.5542
Russia	ruble	R	RUB	30.0878	40.1416	46.7143
Saudi Arabia	riyal	SR	SAR	3.7502	5.0033	5.8226
Singapore	dollar	SDR	SGD	1.2354	1.6482	1.9180
South Africa	rand	R	ZAR	8.8231	11.7713	13.6987
Switzerland	franc	Fr.	CHF	0.9221	1.2302	1.4317
Thailand	baht	B	THB	29.8300	39.7977	46.3141
Tunisia	dinar	DT	TND	1.5584	2.0792	2.4196
United Kingdom*	pound	£	GBP	1.5526	0.8593	—
One month				1.5523	0.8596	—
Three month				1.5518	0.8603	—
One year				1.5502	0.8626	—
United States	dollar	$	USD	—	1.3342	1.5526
Venezuela	bolivar fuerte	Bs	VEB	6.2921	8.3946	9.7691
Vietnam	dong	d	VND	20,835.00	27,797.00	32,348.40
Euro	euro	€	EUR	1.3342	—	1.1637
One month				1.3344	—	1.1633
Three month				1.3349	—	1.1625
One year				1.3373	—	1.1592
Special Drawing Right	—	—	SDR	0.6551	0.8739	1.017

Note that a number of different currencies use the same symbol (for example both China and Japan have traditionally used the ¥ symbol, yen or yuan, meaning round or circle). That is one of the reasons why most of the world's currency markets today use the three-digit currency code for clarity of quotation. All quotes are mid-rates, and are drawn from the *Financial Times*, February 15, 2013.

* The British pound is quoted as $/£ and €/£ consistent with market convention.

DIRECT EXCHANGE QUOTATION

A foreign exchange quotation that specifies the amount of home country currency needed to purchase one unit of foreign currency

The order in which the foreign exchange rate is stated is sometimes confusing to the uninitiated. For example, when the rate between the U.S. dollar and the European euro was stated as $1.3342/€, a **direct exchange quotation** on the U.S. dollar was used. This is simultaneously an **indirect exchange quotation** on the European euro. The direct quote on any currency refers to the currency stated first; an indirect quotation refers to the subject currency that is stated second.

Most of the world's markets and businesses use common conventions of quoting currencies versus the U.S. dollar—Japanese yen per dollar, Mexican pesos per dollar, Thai baht per dollar, Chinese yuan or renminbi per dollar, Swiss francs per dollar, etc. There are a few exceptions, however. The two most important are the euro and the British pound. Traditionally, the British pound is quoted as "U.S. dollars per British pound." In Table 8.2, the spot rate is shown as 1.5526, meaning $1.5526 = £1.00 (despite the fact that the column heading even says "Dollar"). Similarly, the European euro is quoted as 1.3342, or $1.3342 = €1.00. Our advice is simply to be very careful when quoting rates!

INDIRECT EXCHANGE QUOTATION
Foreign exchange quotation that specifies the units of foreign currency that could be purchased with one unit of the home currency

Regardless of the quotation convention, one can always find the inverse quotation form. For example, in Table 8.2 the dollar/pound exchange rate is quoted as $1.5526 to equal £1.00. The inverse of this spot rate, 1/1.5526, will give us the number of pounds to equal one U.S. dollar, £0.6441 = $1.00. It's just math.

Cross Rates

Although it is common among exchange traders worldwide to quote currency values against the U.S. dollar, it is not necessary. Any currency's value can be stated in terms of any other currency. When the exchange rate of a currency is stated without using the U.S. dollar as a reference, it is referred to as a **cross rate**.

CROSS RATE
Exchange rate quotations that do not include the U.S. dollar as one of the two currencies quoted

For example, if the Japanese yen and European euro are both quoted versus the U.S. dollar, they would appear as ¥93.06/$ and $1.3342/€. But if the Japanese yen per euro (¥/€) cross rate is needed, it is simply a matter of multiplication:

¥93.06/$ × $1.3342/€ = ¥124.16/€

Our calculation, ¥124.16/€, is the same value quoted for the Japanese yen in the column labeled Euro in Table 8.2 (although they do list one more decimal place, ¥124.156/€).

This yen-per-euro cross rate is the third leg of any triangle of currency calculation, which must be true if the first two exchange rates are known. If one of the exchange rates changes due to market forces, the others must adjust for the three exchange rates again to align. If they are out of alignment, it would be possible to make a profit simply by exchanging one currency for a second, the second for a third, and the third back to the first. This is known as **triangular arbitrage**. Besides the potential profitability of arbitrage that may occasionally occur, cross rates have become increasingly common in a world of rapidly expanding trade and investment.

TRIANGULAR ARBITRAGE
The exchange of one currency for a second currency, the second for a third, and the third for the first in an effort to make a profit

Foreign Currency Market Structure

The market for foreign currencies is a worldwide market that is informal in structure. This means that it has no central place, pit, or floor (like the floor of the New York Stock Exchange) where the trading takes place. The "market" is actually the thousands of telecommunications links among financial institutions around the globe, and it is open twenty-four hours a day. Someone, somewhere, is nearly always open for business.

The Bank for International Settlements (BIS), in conjunction with central banks around the world, conducts a survey of currency trading activity every three years. The most recent survey, conducted in April 2010, estimated daily global net turnover in the foreign exchange market to be $3.2 trillion. The BIS data for surveys between 1989 and 2010 is shown in Figures 8.1 and 8.2.

Figure 8.1 shows the proportionate share of foreign exchange trading for the most important national markets in the world between 1992 and 2010. (Note that although the data is collected and reported on a national basis, "United States" should largely be interpreted as "New York" because the majority of foreign exchange trading takes place in the major financial city. This is also true for "United Kingdom" and "London.")

FIGURE 8.1 Top 10 Geographic Trading Centers in the Foreign Exchange Market, 1992-2010 (average daily turnover in April)

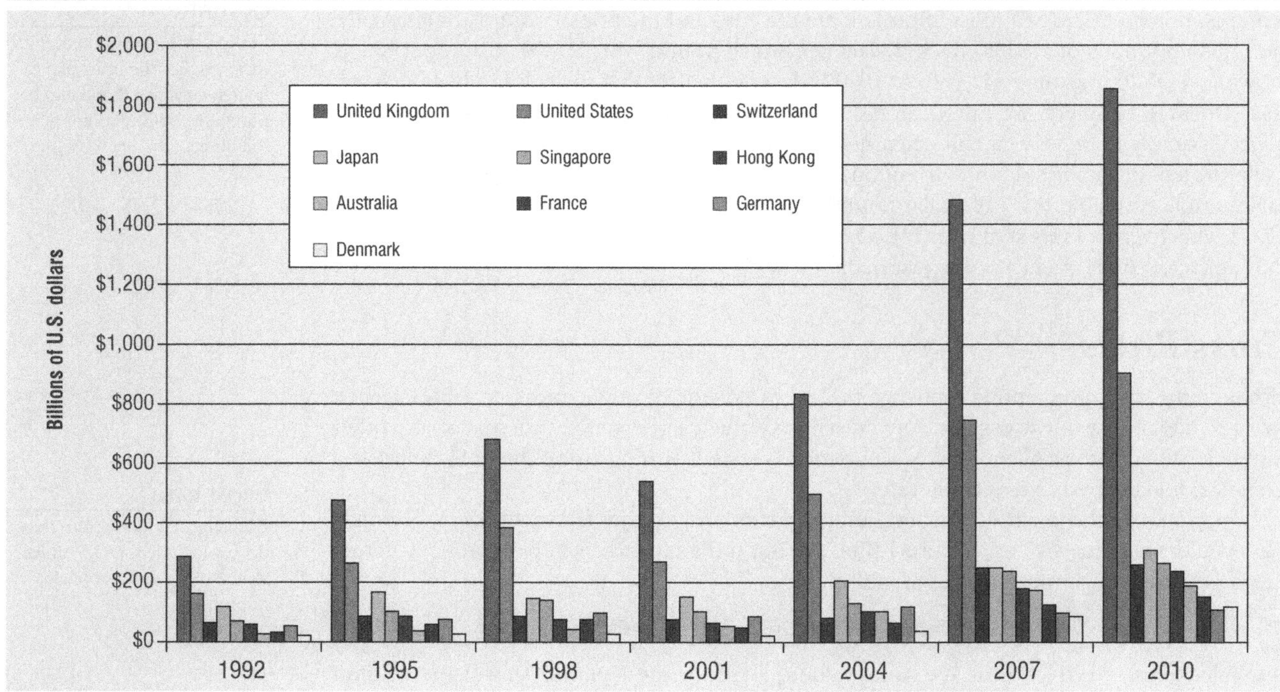

SOURCE: Bank for International Settlements, "Triennial Central Bank Survey: Foreign Exchange and Derivatives Market Activity in April 2010," September 2010, **www.bis.org**.

FIGURE 8.2 Foreign Exchange Market Turnover by Currency Pair (Daily averages in April)

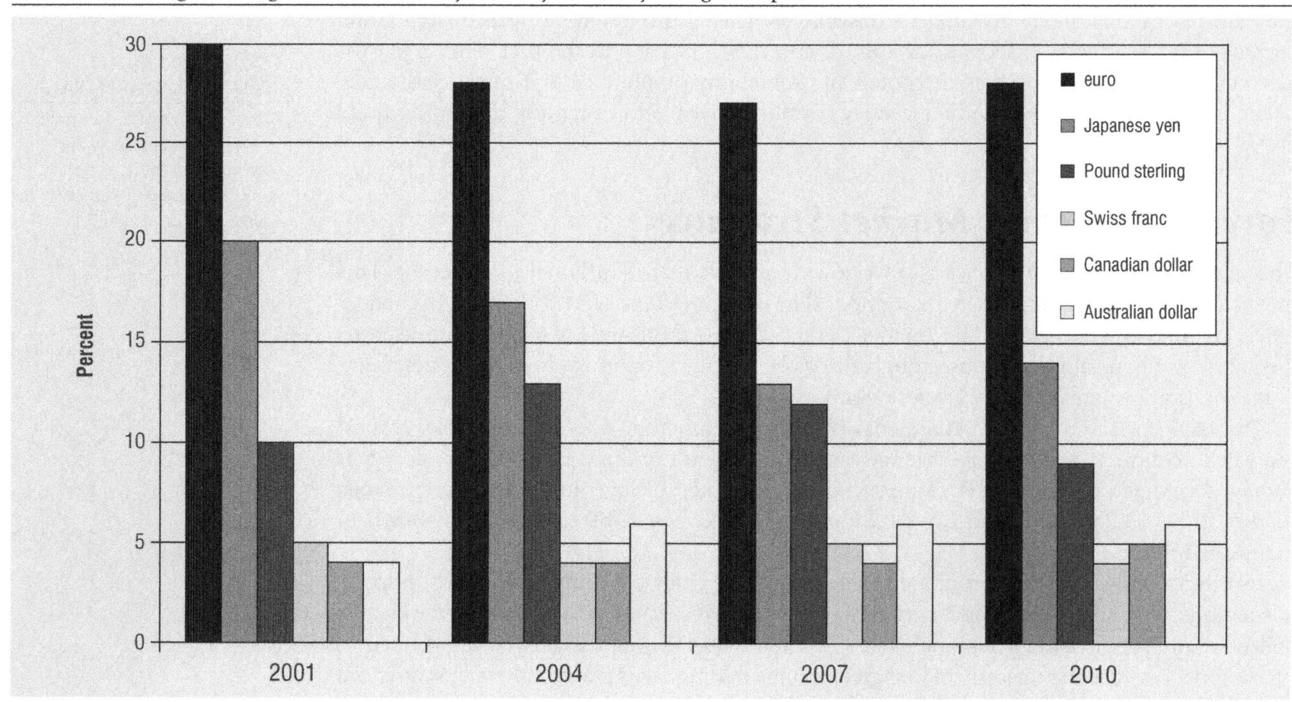

SOURCE: Bank for International Settlements, "Triennial Central Bank Survey: Foreign Exchange and Derivatives Market Activity in April 2010," September 2010, **www.bis.org**.

Evolution of the Global Monetary System

The mixed-fixed/floating exchange rate system operating today is only the latest stage of a continuing process of change. The systems that have preceded the present system varied between gold-based standards (the gold standard) and complex systems in which the U.S. dollar largely took the place of gold (the Bretton Woods Agreement). To understand why the dollar, the mark, and the yen are floating today, it is necessary to return to the (pardon the pun) golden oldies.

The Gold Standard

Although there is no recognized starting date, the **gold standard** as we understand it today began sometime in the 1880s and lasted up through the outbreak of World War I. The gold standard was premised on three basic ideas:

GOLD STANDARD
A standard for international currencies in which currency values were stated in terms of gold, for example, \$20.67 per ounce of gold

1. A system of fixed rates of exchange existed between participating countries.
2. "Money" issued by member countries had to be backed by reserves of gold.
3. Gold would act as an automatic adjustment, flowing in and out of countries, and automatically altering the gold reserves of that country if imbalances in trade or investment did occur.

Under the gold standard, each country's currency would be set in value per ounce of gold. For example, the U.S. dollar was defined as \$20.67 per ounce, while the British pound sterling was defined as £4.2474 per ounce. Once each currency was defined versus gold, the determination of the exchange rate between the two currencies (or any two currencies) was simple:

$$\frac{\$20.67/\text{ounce of gold}}{£4.2472/\text{ounce of gold}} = \$4.8665/£$$

The use of gold as the pillar of the system was a result of historical tradition and not anything inherently unique to the gold metal itself. It was shiny, soft, rare, and generally acceptable for payment in all countries.

Interwar Years, 1919–39

The 1920s and 1930s were a tumultuous period. The British pound sterling, the dominant currency prior to World War I, survived the war but was greatly weakened. The U.S. dollar returned to the gold standard in 1919, but gold convertibility was largely untested across countries throughout the 1920s, as world trade took a long time to recover from the destruction wrought by the war. With the economic collapse and bank runs of the 1930s, the United States was forced, once again, to abandon gold convertibility.

The economic depression of the 1930s was worldwide. As countries came under increasingly desperate economic conditions, many (including the United States) resorted to isolationist policies and protectionism. World trade slowed to a trickle and with it the general need for currency exchange. It was not until the latter stages of World War II that international trade and commerce once again demanded a system for currency convertibility and stability.

The Bretton Woods Agreement, 1944–71

The governments of forty-four of the Allied powers gathered together in Bretton Woods, New Hampshire, in 1944, to plan for the postwar international monetary system. The delegates labored long, and in the end, all parties agreed that a postwar system would be stable and sustainable only if it was able to provide sufficient liquidity to countries during periods of crisis. Any new system had to have facilities for the extension of credit for countries to defend their currency values.

BRETTON WOODS AGREEMENT
An agreement reached in 1944 among finance ministers of forty-four Western nations to establish a system of fixed exchange rates

After weeks of debate, the **Bretton Woods Agreement** was reached. The plan called for the following:

1. Fixed exchange rates between member countries, termed an "adjustable peg."
2. The establishment of a fund of gold and currencies available to members for stabilization of their respective currencies (the International Monetary Fund).
3. The establishment of a bank that would provide funding for long-term development projects (the World Bank).

Like the gold standard at the turn of the century, all participants were to establish par values of their currencies in terms of gold. Unlike the prior system, however, there was little, if any, convertibility of currencies to gold expected. Instead, convertibility was against the U.S. dollar ("as good as gold"). In fact, the only currency officially convertible to gold was the U.S. dollar (pegged at $35/ounce). This reliance on the value of the dollar and on the stability of the U.S. economy led to twenty-five years of relatively stable currency. But, alas, nothing lasts forever.

Times of Crisis, 1971–73

On August 15, 1971, U.S. President Richard M. Nixon announced, "I have instructed [Treasury] Secretary [John B.] Connally to suspend temporarily the convertibility of the dollar into gold or other assets." With this simple statement, President Nixon effectively ended the fixed exchange rates established at Bretton Woods. In the weeks and months following the August announcement, world currency markets devalued the dollar, although the United States had only ended gold convertibility and had not officially declared the dollar's value to be less. In late 1971, the Group of Ten finance ministers met at the Smithsonian Institution in Washington, D.C., to try to piece together a system to keep world markets operational. First, the dollar was officially devalued to $38/ounce of gold (as if anyone had access to gold convertibility). Secondly, all other major world currencies were revalued against the dollar, and all would now be allowed to vary from their fixed parity rates by plus/minus 2.25 percent (rather than the previous 1.00 percent).

Without convertibility of at least one of the member currencies to gold, the system was doomed from the start. Within weeks, currencies were surpassing their allowed deviation limits, revaluations were occurring more frequently, and the international monetary system no longer worked as a "system." It was chaos. Finally, world currency trading nearly ground to a halt in March 1973. The world's currency markets closed for two weeks. When they reopened, major currencies like the U.S. dollar were allowed to float in value. In January 1976, the Group of Ten once again met, this time in Jamaica, and the Jamaica Agreement officially recognized what the markets had known for years—the world's currencies were no longer fixed in value.

Floating Exchange Rates, 1973–Present

Since March 1973, the world's major currencies have floated in value versus each other. This flotation poses many problems for the conduct of international trade and commerce, problems that are themselves the subject of entire courses of study (currency risk management for one). The inability of a country's government to control the value of its currency on world markets has been a harsh reality for most.

Throughout the 1970s, if a government wished to alter the current value of its currency, or even slow or alter a trending change in the currency's value, the government would simply buy or sell its own currency in the market, using its reserves of other major currencies. This process of **direct intervention** was effective as long as the depth of the government's reserve pockets kept up with the volume of trading on currency markets. For these countries—both then and now—the primary problem is maintaining adequate foreign exchange reserves.

DIRECT INTERVENTION
The process used by governments to alter the current value of their own currency by buying or selling their own currency in the market using their reserves of other major currencies

By the 1980s, however, the world's currency markets were so large that the ability of a few governments (the United States, Japan, and Germany, for example) to move a market

Quick Take *The Yuan Goes Global*

The Chinese *renminbi* (RMB) or *yuan* (CNY) is going global. (Formally, the term *yuan* is used in reference to the unit of account, while the physical currency itself is termed the *renminbi*.) Trading in the RMB is closely controlled by the People's Republic of China (PRC), the Chinese government, with all trading inside China between the RMB and foreign currencies, primarily the U.S. dollar, being conducted only according to Chinese regulations. The Chinese government, however, is now starting to relax restrictions, releasing the yuan to move toward prominence as a truly global currency.

The first and foremost RMB/USD traditional role for currency trading is through its use in the settlement of trade transactions—the denomination of exports (which generate foreign currency inflows traditionally) and imports (which use up foreign currency reserves traditionally) in the currency—and that is already changing rapidly. In 2009, of the $1.2 trillion of Chinese exports, only about 1 percent were denominated in RMB. By the end of the first quarter of 2011, in a little more than one year, that percentage had risen to 7 percent. The Chinese government was now encouraging exporters to convert to RMB invoicing.

RMB/USD

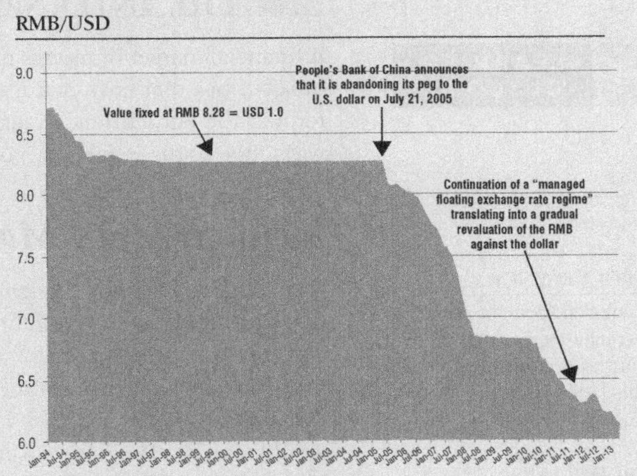

Inevitably, the currency of an economy of China's size and scope will result in more and more of its currency leaving China. Although it has restricted the flow of yuan out of China for many years, ultimately more and more will find its way beyond the reach of the onshore authorities. Once out of the reach of Chinese authorities, the yuan will be traded freely without government intervention. China knows this all too well and has therefore adopted a gradual policy of developing the trading in the yuan—but through its own onshore offshore market, Hong Kong.

simply through direct intervention was over. The major tool now left was for a government (at least when operating alone) to alter economic variables, such as interest rates; that is, to alter the motivations and expectations of market participants for capital movements and currency exchange. During periods of relatively low inflation (a critical assumption), a country that wishes to strengthen its currency versus others might raise domestic interest rates to attract capital from abroad. Although relatively effective in many cases, the downside of this policy is that it raises interest rates for domestic consumers and investors alike, possibly slowing the domestic economy. The result is that governments today must often choose between an external economic policy action (raising interest rates to strengthen the currency) and a domestic economic policy action (lowering interest rates to stimulate economic activity).

COORDINATED INTERVENTION
A currency-value management method whereby the central banks of the major nations simultaneously intervene in the currency markets, hoping to change a currency's value

There is, however, one other method of currency-value management that has been selectively employed in the past fifteen years: **coordinated intervention**. After the U.S. dollar had risen in value dramatically during the 1980 to 1985 period, the Group of Five, or G5 nations (France, Japan, West Germany, the United States, and the United Kingdom), met at the Plaza Hotel in New York in September 1985 and agreed to a set of goals and policies called the Plaza Agreement. These goals were to be accomplished through coordinated intervention among the central banks of the major nations. With the central banks of all five countries intervening in the currency markets simultaneously, they hoped to reach the combined level of strength needed to push the dollar's value down. Their actions were met with some success in that case, but there have been few occasions since then of coordinated intervention.

The International Money Markets

A financial market or money market is traditionally defined as a market for deposits, accounts, or securities that have maturities of one year or less. The international money markets, often termed the eurocurrency markets, constitute an enormous financial market that is, in many ways, free of the regulatory constraints of financial and government authorities.

Eurocurrency Markets

EUROCURRENCY
A bank deposit in a currency other than the currency of the country where the bank is located; not confined to banks in Europe

EURODOLLARS
U.S. dollars deposited in banks outside the United States; not confined to banks in Europe

A **eurocurrency** is any foreign-currency-denominated deposit or account at a financial institution outside the country of the currency's issuance. For example, U.S. dollars that are held on account in a bank in London are termed **eurodollars**. Similarly, Japanese yen held on account in a Parisian financial institution are classified as euroyen. The euro prefix does not mean these currencies or accounts are only European, as Japanese yen on account in Singapore would also be classified as a eurocurrency.

Eurocurrency Interest Rates

What is the significance of these foreign-currency-denominated accounts? Simply put, it is the purity of value that comes from no governmental interference or restrictions with their use. Eurocurrency accounts are not controlled or managed by governments (for example, the Bank of England has no control over eurodollar accounts); therefore, the financial institutions pay no deposit insurance, hold no reserve requirements, and normally are not subject to any interest rate restrictions with respect to such accounts. Eurocurrencies are one of the purest indicators of what these currencies should yield in terms of interest. Sample eurocurrency interest rates are shown in Table 8.3.

INTERBANK INTEREST RATES
The interest rate charged by banks to banks in the major international financial centers

There are hundreds of different major interest rates around the globe, but the international financial markets focus on a very few, the **interbank interest rates**. Interbank rates charged

TABLE 8.3 Exchange Rates and Eurocurrency Interest Rates

Maturity	Eurodollar Interest Rate	Europound Interest Rate	Exchange Rate (US$/£)
Spot	—	—	1.5526
1-month	3.600%	3.850%	1.5523
3-months	3.825%	4.040%	1.5518
6-months	4.000%	4.260%	1.5506
12-months	4.485%	4.650%	1.5502

by banks to banks in the major international financial centers, such as London, Frankfurt, Paris, New York, Tokyo, Singapore, and Hong Kong, are generally regarded as "the interest rate" in the respective market. The interest rate that is used most often in international loan agreements is the eurocurrency interest rate on U.S. dollars (eurodollars) in London between banks: the London interbank offer rate (LIBOR). Because it is a eurocurrency rate, it floats freely without regard to governmental restrictions on reserves or deposit insurance or any other regulation or restriction that would add expense to transactions using this capital. The interbank rates for other currencies in other markets are often named similarly: PIBOR (Paris interbank offer rate), MIBOR (Madrid interbank offer rate), HIBOR (either Hong Kong or Helsinki interbank offer rate), SIBOR (Singapore interbank offer rate). Although LIBOR is the offer rate—the cost of funds "offered" to those acquiring a loan—the equivalent deposit rate in the **euromarkets** is LIBID, the London interbank bid rate, the rate of interest other banks can earn on eurocurrency deposits.

EUROMARKETS
Money and capital markets in which transactions are denominated in a currency other than that of the place of the transaction; not confined to Europe

How do these international eurocurrency and interbank interest rates differ from domestic rates? Not by much. They generally move up and down in unison, by currency, but often differ by the percentage by which the restrictions alter the rates of interest in the domestic markets. For example, because the euromarkets have no restrictions, the spread between the offer rate and the bid rate (the loan rate and the deposit rate) is substantially smaller than in domestic markets. This means the loan rates in international markets are a bit lower than domestic market loan rates, and deposit rates are a bit higher in the international markets than in domestic markets.

However, this is only a big-player market. Only well-known international firms, financial or nonfinancial, have access to the quantities of capital necessary to operate in the euromarkets. But, as described in the following sections on international debt and equity markets, more and more firms are gaining access to the euromarkets to take advantage of deregulated capital flows.

Linking Eurocurrency Interest Rates and Exchange Rates

Eurocurrency interest rates also play a large role in the foreign exchange markets. They are, in fact, the interest rates used in the calculation of the forward rates noted earlier. Recall that a forward rate is a contract for a specific amount of currency to be exchanged for another currency at a future date, usually 30, 60, 90, 180, or even 360 days in the future. Forward rates are calculated from the spot rate in effect on the day the contract is written, along with the respective eurocurrency interest rates for the two currencies.

For example, to calculate the ninety-day (three-month) forward rate for the U.S. dollar-British pound cross rate, \$1.5518/£ (as shown in Table 8.2), the spot exchange rate is multiplied by the ratio of the two eurocurrency interest rates—the eurodollar and the europound rates. Note that it is important to adjust the interest rates for the actual period of time needed, ninety days (three months) of a 360-day financial year:

$$\text{Ninety-day forward rate} = \$1.5526/\pounds \times \frac{1 + \left(i_{90}^{\$} \times \frac{90}{360}\right)}{1 + \left(i_{90}^{\pounds} \times \frac{90}{360}\right)}$$

Quick Take *The Trouble with LIBOR*

The global financial markets use many different interest rates for their daily activity, but no single interest rate is more fundamental than the *London Interbank Offered Rate (LIBOR)*. LIBOR is used in loan agreements, financial derivatives, swap agreements, in different maturities and different currencies, every day—globally. It is the single most important and common parameter in global finance. Beginning as early as 2007, a number of participants in the interbank market feared that there was trouble with LIBOR.

How LIBOR Is Calculated

LIBOR is published under the auspices of the British Bankers Association (BBA). Daily, a panel of sixteen major multinational banks are requested to submit their *estimated borrowing rates* in the unsecured interbank market; the rates are then collected, massaged, and published in three steps.

Step 1. The banks on the LIBOR panels must submit their estimated borrowing rates by 11:10 a.m. London time. The submissions are directly to Thomson Reuters, which executes the process on behalf of the BBA.

Step 2. Thomson Reuters discards the lowest 25 percent and highest 25 percent of interest rates submitted, then calculates an average rate by maturity and currency using the remaining 50 percent of borrowing rate quotes.

Step 3. The BBA publishes that day's Libor rates 20 minutes later, by 11:30 a.m. London time.

The process is used to publish LIBOR for ten different currencies across fifteen different maturities. The three-month and six-month maturities are the most significant due to their widespread use in various loan and derivative agreements, with the dollar and the euro being the widest used currencies.

The Trouble with LIBOR

The LIBOR calculation process is relatively simple and clear and is not the source of the problem. The problem has been the rates submitted by the banks—the origin of the values they report.

First, bank reports are not limited to actual rates at which borrowing occurred, meaning they are not market transaction rates. As a result, the origin of the rate submitted by each bank becomes discretionary.

Secondly, banks—specifically money-market and derivative traders within the banks—have a number of interests or concerns about what is reported. For example, during the financial crisis of 2008–09 many banks did not want to report that they were paying higher LIBOR rates, fearing it would be interpreted as the market's pessimism on their credit quality. In the words of one analyst, "the issue is Lie More, not LIBOR."

A third and final issue was when individual traders in individual banks attempted to increase their own profits on current positions or investments by reporting a higher or lower LIBOR rate. It was also rumored that traders at different banks may have colluded in these rate-rigging maneuvers.

Now, plugging in the spot exchange rate of \$1.5526/£ and the two ninety-day (three-month) eurocurrency interest rates from Table 8.3 (3.825 percent for the dollar and 4.040 percent for the pound), the ninety-day forward exchange rate is:

$$\text{Ninety-Day Forward Rate} = \$1.5526/£ \times \frac{\left[1 + \left(0.03825 \times \frac{90}{360}\right)\right]}{\left[1 + \left(0.0404 \times \frac{90}{360}\right)\right]} = \$1.5518/£$$

The forward rate of \$1.5518/£ is a "weaker rate" for the British pound than the current spot rate. This is because one British pound will yield \$1.5526 in the spot market but only \$1.5518 in the forward market (at ninety days). The British pound would be said to be "**selling forward** at a discount," while the dollar would be described as "selling forward at a premium" because its value is stronger at the ninety-day forward rate.

SELLING FORWARD
A market transaction in which the seller promises to sell currency at a certain future date at a prespecified price

Why is this the case? The reason is that the ninety-day eurocurrency interest rate on the U.S. dollar is lower than the corresponding eurocurrency interest rate on the British pound. If it were the other way around—if the U.S. dollar interest rate were higher than the British pound interest rate—the British pound would be selling forward at a premium. The forward exchange rates quoted in the markets, and used so frequently in international business, simply reflect the difference in interest rates between currencies.

Businesses frequently use forward exchange rate contracts to manage their exposure to currency risk. Corporations use many other financial instruments and techniques beyond forward contracts to manage currency risk, but forwards are still the mainstay of industry.

International Capital Markets

Just as with money markets, international capital markets serve as links among the capital markets of individual countries, as well as a separate market of their own—the capital that flows into the euromarkets. In the international capital markets, firms can now raise capital, with debit or equity, with fixed or floating interest rates, in any of a dozen currencies, for maturities ranging from one month to thirty years. Although the international capital markets traditionally have been dominated by debt instruments, international equity markets have shown considerable growth in recent years.

Defining International Financing

The definition of what constitutes an international financial transaction is dependent on two fundamental characteristics: (1) whether the borrower is domestic or foreign, and (2) whether the borrower is raising capital denominated in the domestic currency or in a foreign currency. These two characteristics form four categories of financial transactions, as illustrated in Figure 8.3.

CATEGORY 1: DOMESTIC BORROWER/DOMESTIC CURRENCY. This is a traditional domestic financial-market activity. A borrower who is a resident within the country raises capital from domestic financial institutions denominated in local currency. All countries with basic market economies have their own domestic financial markets, some large and some quite small. This is still, by far, the most common type of financial transaction.

CATEGORY 2: FOREIGN BORROWER/DOMESTIC CURRENCY. This is when a foreign borrower enters another country's financial market and raises capital denominated in the local

FIGURE 8.3 Categorizing International Financial Transactions: Issuing Bonds in London

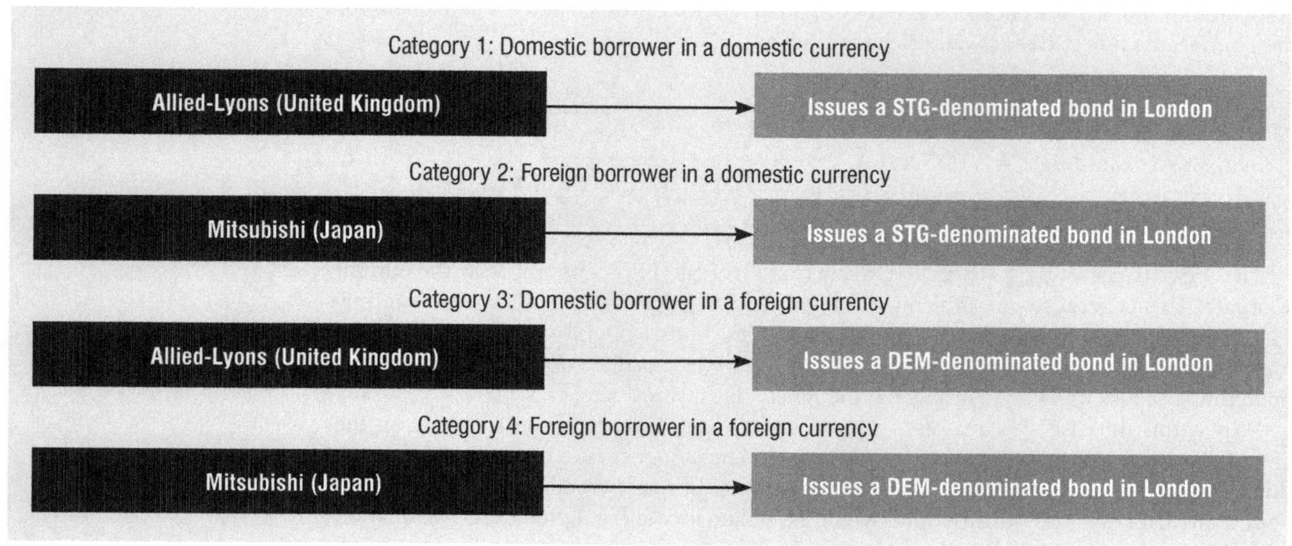

currency. The international dimension of this transaction is based only on who the borrower is. Many borrowers, both public and private, increasingly go to the world's largest financial markets to raise capital for their enterprises. The ability of a foreign firm to raise capital in another country's financial market is sometimes limited by that government's restrictions on who can borrow, as well as the market's willingness to lend to foreign governments and companies that it may not know as well as domestic borrowers.

CATEGORY 3: DOMESTIC BORROWER/FOREIGN CURRENCY. Many borrowers in today's international markets need capital denominated in a foreign currency. A domestic firm may actually issue a bond to raise capital in its local market where it is known quite well but raise the capital in the form of a foreign currency.

This type of financial transaction occurs less often than the previous two types because it requires a local market in foreign currencies, a eurocurrency market. A number of countries, such as the United States, tightly restrict the amount and types of financial transactions in foreign currency. International financial centers, such as London and Zurich, have been the traditional centers of these types of transactions.

CATEGORY 4: FOREIGN BORROWER/FOREIGN CURRENCY. This is the strictest form of the traditional eurocurrency financial transaction, a foreign firm borrowing foreign currency. Once again, this type of activity may be restricted as to which borrowers are allowed into a country's financial markets and which currencies are available. This type of financing dominates the activities of many banking institutions in the **offshore banking** market.

OFFSHORE BANKING
The use of banks or bank branches located in low-tax countries, often Caribbean islands, to raise and hold capital for multinational operations

Using this classification system makes it possible to categorize any individual international financial transaction. For example, the distinction between an international bond and a eurobond is simply that of a Category 2 transaction (foreign borrower in a domestic currency market) and a Category 3 or 4 transaction (foreign currency denominated in a single local market or many markets).

International Banking

Banks have existed in different forms and roles since the Middle Ages. Bank loans have provided nearly all of the debt capital needed by industry since the start of the Industrial Revolution. Even in this age, in which securitized debt instruments (bonds, notes, and other types of tradable paper) are growing as sources of capital for firms worldwide, banks still perform a critical role by providing capital for medium-sized and smaller firms, which dominate all economies.

Similar to the direct foreign investment decision sequence discussed in Chapter 6, banks can expand their cross-border activities in a variety of ways. A bank can conduct business with clients in other countries without opening a banking operation in that country through **correspondent banks** or representative offices. A correspondent bank is a bank (unrelated by ownership) based in a foreign country. By the nature of its business, it has knowledge of the local market and access to clients, capital, and information, which a foreign bank does not.

A second way that banks may gain access to foreign markets without actually opening an overseas banking operation is through **representative offices**. A representative office is basically a sales office for a bank. It provides information regarding the financial services of the bank, but it cannot deliver the services itself: It cannot accept deposits or make loans. The foreign representative office of a U.S. bank will typically sell the bank's services to local firms that may need banking services for trade or other transactions in the United States.

If a bank wants to conduct banking business within the foreign country, it may open a branch banking office, a banking affiliate, or even a wholly owned banking subsidiary. A branch office is an extension of the parent bank but is not independently financed or independently incorporated and, therefore, is commonly restricted in the types of banking activities that it may conduct.

CORRESPONDENT BANKS
Banks located in different countries and unrelated by ownership that have a reciprocal agreement to provide services to each other's customers

REPRESENTATIVE OFFICES
An office of an international bank established in a foreign country to serve the bank's customers in the area in an advisory capacity; does not take deposits or make loans

International Security Markets

Although banks continue to provide a large portion of the international financial needs of government and business, it is the international debt securities markets that have experienced the greatest growth in the past decade. The international security markets include bonds, equities, and private placements.

The International Bond Market

The **international bond** market provides the bulk of financing. The four categories of international debt financing discussed previously apply particularly to the international bond markets. Foreign borrowers have been using the large, well-developed capital markets of countries such as the United States and the United Kingdom for many years. These issues are classified generally as **foreign bonds**, as opposed to **eurobonds**. Each market has developed its own pet name for foreign bonds issued in that market. For example, foreign bonds issued in the United States are called Yankee bonds; in the United Kingdom, bulldogs; in the Netherlands, Rembrandt bonds; and in Japan, samurai bonds. When bonds are issued by foreign borrowers in these markets, they are subject to the same restrictions that apply to all domestic borrowers.

Bonds that fall into Categories 3 and 4 are termed eurobonds. The primary characteristic of these instruments is that they are denominated in a currency other than that of the country where they are sold. For example, many U.S. firms may issue euroyen bonds on world markets. These bonds are sold in international financial centers, such as London or Frankfurt, but they are denominated in Japanese yen. Because these eurobonds are scattered about the global markets, most are a type of bond known as a **bearer bond**. A bearer bond is owned

INTERNATIONAL BOND
A bond issued in domestic capital markets by foreign borrowers (foreign bonds) or issued in the eurocurrency markets in currency different from that of the home currency of the borrower (eurobonds)

FOREIGN BOND
Bonds issued by a foreign corporation or government for sale in a country different from its home country and denominated in the currency of the country in which it is issued

EUROBOND
A bond that is denominated in a currency other than the currency of the country in which the bond is sold

BEARER BOND
A bond owned officially by whoever is holding it

Quick Take *The European Union's Sovereign Debt Crisis*

When the government of a country borrows capital on global financial markets it creates *sovereign debt*. That debt must obviously be repaid over time. A number of the member countries of the European Union, namely Ireland, Italy, Portugal, Spain, and particularly Greece, have been accumulating ever-increasing burdens of sovereign debt.

Greece has been the focus of much of this concern in recent years. The Greek economy has been in recession (or depression depending on definitions) since 2008. This extended economic downturn has had a twofold impact on growing the government deficit and adding to its growing sovereign debt needs. First, with negative economic growth, the government generates fewer and fewer tax revenues. Second, with continuing economic hardships, Greek society needs more and more government spending. The result of both forces is an accumulation of debt, which the government of Greece may not be able to repay—at least not without the aid of the European Union.

As illustrated in the graphic, Greece's debt-to-GDP ratio, at more than 160 percent, is by far the highest within the European Union. The EU's average, at 90 percent, is considered barely sustainable. With a total debt burden of $259 billion dollars (U.S. dollar equivalent), Greece will need more and more subsidies, financial aid, debt restructurings, and possibly debt forgiveness to survive the onslaught of its creditors.

European Sovereign Debt

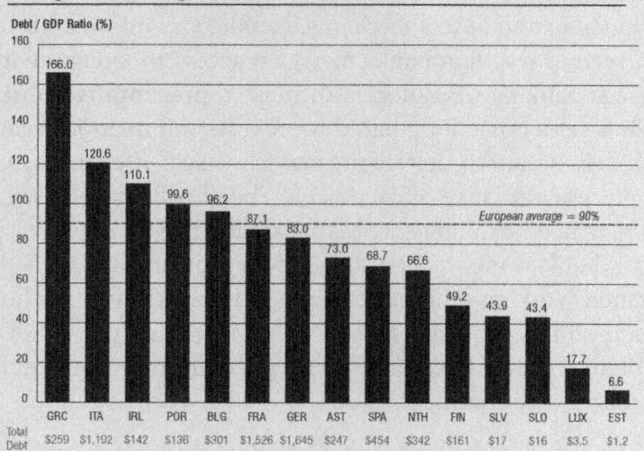

SOURCE: Debt-to-GDP ratios from "Sovereign Default in the Eurozone: Greece and Beyond," UBS Research Focus, October 2011, p. 10. Total public debt, in billions of U.S. dollars, from the World Bank Group's Joint External Debt Hub (JEDH).

officially by whoever is holding it, with no master registration list being held by government authorities, who might then track who is earning interest income from bond investments.[1] Bearer bonds have a series of small coupons that border the bond itself. On an annual basis, one of the coupons is cut or "clipped" from the bond and taken to a banking institution that is one of the listed paying agents. The bank will pay the holder of the coupon the interest payment due; usually, no official records of payment are kept.

International Equity Markets

Firms are financed with both debt and equity. Although the debt markets have been the center of activity in the international financial markets during the past three decades, there are signs that international equity capital is becoming more popular.

Again, using the same categories of international financial activities, the Category 2 transaction of a foreign borrower in a domestic market in local currency is the predominant international equity activity. Foreign firms often issue new shares in foreign markets and list their stock on major stock exchanges, such as those in New York, Tokyo, or London. The purpose of foreign issues and listings is to expand the investor base in the hope of gaining access to capital markets where demand for shares of equity ownership is strong.

A foreign firm that wants to list its shares on an exchange in the United States does so through **American Depository Receipts (ADRs).** These are the receipts to bank accounts that hold shares of the foreign firm's stock in that firm's country. The equities are actually in a foreign currency, so by holding them in a bank account and listing the receipt on the account on the American exchange, the shares can be revalued in dollars and redivided so that the price per share is more typical of that of the U.S. equity markets ($20 to $60 per share frequently being the desired range).

AMERICAN DEPOSITORY RECEIPTS (ADRS)
Receipts to bank account that holds shares of a foreign firm's stock in that firm's country

There was considerable growth in the 1990s in the euroequity markets. A euroequity issue is the simultaneous sale of a firm's shares in several different countries, with or without listing the shares on an exchange in that country. The sales take place through investment banks. Once issued, most euroequities are listed at least on the Stock Exchange Automated Quotation System (SEAQ), the computer-screen quoting system of the International Stock Exchange (ISE) in London.

Gaining Access to Global Financial Markets

Although the global markets are large and growing, this does not mean they are for everyone. For many years, only the largest of the world's multinational firms could enter another country's capital markets and find acceptance. The reasons are lack of information and unknown reputation.

Financial markets are by definition risk-averse. This means they are very reluctant to make loans to or buy debt issued by firms that they know little about. Therefore, the ability to gain access to the international markets is dependent on a firm's reputation, its ability to educate the markets about what it does, how successful it has been, and its patience. The firm must, in the end, be willing to expend the resources and effort required to build a credit reputation in the international markets. If successful, the firm may enjoy the benefits of new, larger, and more diversified sources of the capital it needs.

The individual firm, whether it be a chili-dog stand serving the international tastes of office workers at the United Nations Plaza or a major multinational firm, such as McDonald's or Honda of Japan, is affected by the workings of the international financial markets. Although the owner of the chili-dog stand probably has more important and immediate problems to deal with, it is clear that firms such as Honda see the movements in these markets as critically important to their long-term competitiveness.

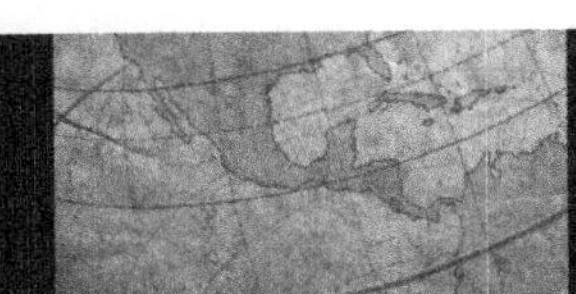

SUMMARY

This chapter has explored the operations of world currency markets and their influence on the conduct of international business. It is estimated that more than $1 trillion worth of currencies changes hands daily, and the majority of it is in one of the world's three major floating currencies: U.S. dollars, euros, or Japanese yen.

The purpose of exchange rate systems is to provide a free and liquid market for the world's currencies while ensuring some degree of stability and predictability to currency values.

The theory of purchasing power parity (PPP) defines what exchange rates ideally should be by equalizing the price of an identical product or service in two different currencies.

Currency quotations on the world's stock markets include both spot rates and forward rates of exchange. Cross rates allow for indirect quotations from any currency into any other currency.

The world's currency markets have experienced rapid growth in recent years, followed by a brief period of decline during global recession.

The global monetary system has seen periods of success and failure as exchange rates, once fixed to the value of gold, became fixed to the value of the dollar, then evolved into the floating exchange system that prevails today.

Eurocurrencies allow for the easy transfer of funds around the world without interference or restrictions imposed by governments. For this reason, eurocurrency interest rates float freely and are not subject to frequent transaction expenses.

There are four ways to categorize international financing, depending on whether the borrower is domestic or foreign and whether the capital raised is in a domestic or foreign currency.

The international securities market includes bonds, equities, and private placements.

International bond markets provide most business financing. Equity markets allow foreign firms to expand their investor base by listing their stocks on major foreign exchanges.

Key Terms and Concepts

purchasing power parity (PPP)
Law of One Price
foreign currency exchange rate
spot exchange rates
forward exchange rates
direct exchange quotation
indirect exchange quotation
cross rate
triangular arbitrage
gold standard
Bretton Woods Agreement
direct intervention
coordinated intervention
eurocurrency
eurodollars
interbank interest rates
euromarkets
selling forward
offshore banking
correspondent banks
representative offices
international bond
foreign bond
eurobond
bearer bond
American Depository Receipts (ADRs)

Review Questions

1. Why are exchange rates necessary?
2. Distinguish between spot and forward currency rates.
3. Why was it so important that the U.S. dollar be convertible to gold for the Bretton Woods system to operate efficiently?
4. Why did the major world currencies move from a fixed to a floating exchange rate system in the 1970s? Are fixed exchange rates preferable to floating exchange rates?
5. What is a eurocurrency? What is a eurocurrency interest rate? Is it different from LIBOR?
6. Summarize the four ways of categorizing international capital markets.
7. What is the difference between an international bond and a eurobond?
8. Explain why it is sometimes difficult for firms to gain access to global financial markets.

Critical Skill Builders

1. Your company imports Christmas decorations from Korea. In March, you receive a quote from a new manufacturer who will supply 50,000 glass Christmas-tree ornaments for a total of 100,000 Korean won. The won currently trades at 2.20 won to the dollar, but your banker advises you that its value is likely to fall as much as 15 percent by the time you take delivery of the ornaments in September. To gain the best possible price, what are your options?
2. Consider how the debt crises in recent decades are linked to exchange rates. Discuss.
3. For each situation described below, discuss which rate (bid or offer) would apply:
   a. A Pakistani importer wishes to convert rupees to U.S. dollars to pay for a shipment. His bank is quoting R/$ R48.51–48.61.
   b. Assume that in the example above the required U.S. dollar payment is $75,000. How many rupees would be required?
   c. An exporting firm in Singapore has just received payment in U.S. dollars and wants to convert it to Singapore dollars. The bank is quoting S$/$ 1.8366–1.8375.
   d. A Japanese manufacturing firm must make a payment in U.S. dollars. The bank has made its quotation in American terms as follows: $/¥0.009430–0.009436.
4. What is the difference between debt financing and equity financing? Discuss situations in which a company expanding overseas may need both.
5. Why have international financial markets grown so rapidly in the past decade? Is this rate of growth likely to continue? What changes do you see in the international financial markets in the coming decade? Consider the influences of both developed and emerging economies.

On the Web

1. Although major currencies, such as the U.S. dollar and the Japanese yen, dominate the headlines, there are nearly as many currencies as countries in the world. Many of these currencies are traded in extremely thin and highly regulated markets, making their convertibility suspect. Finding quotations for these currencies is sometimes very difficult. Using the Internet, see how many African currency quotes you can find.

2. Visit **http://www.nyse.com/international/**. Review the activities of the New York Stock Exchange that relate to the expansion of emerging markets, such as China. What are the benefits for companies in developing economies of listing on the NYSE? How is a non-U.S. company treated differently from a U.S. company?

3. What is the difference between the European Central Bank and the European Investment Bank? Visit their respective web sites to review the role and objectives of each. Why is each bank an essential resource for companies operating in Europe?

Endnotes

1. Bearer bonds were issued by the U.S. government up until the early 1980s, when they were discontinued. Even though they were called bearer bonds, a list of bond registration numbers was still kept and recorded in order to tax investors holding the bearer instruments

CHAPTER 9

GLOBAL FINANCIAL MANAGEMENT

Korres Natural Products of Greece

"Bringing owls to Athens"—in other words, doing something useless. In 414 B.C., when Aristophanes coined this expression in his comedy, The Birds, *people commonly referred to Athens' self-minted silver drachmas as "owls" since they had a picture of the bird on their reverse side. Athens' wealth at the time was legendary—and hence, it was pointless to bring any more money to the city-state. Yet, only a few decades later, the situation had changed dramatically. Expensive wars had wrecked the budget, and 10 out of 13 Athenian communities eventually defaulted on loans that they had taken out from the temple of Delos— the first recorded sovereign debt defaults in history.*

— "Sovereign Default in the Eurozone: Greece and Beyond," *UBS Research Focus*, 29 September 2011, p. 14.

LEARNING OUTCOMES

1. ***To understand the objectives of the various corporate stakeholders in the pursuit of profit and sustainability in the conduct of global business***
2. ***To understand how the public, private, and state-owned firms differ in terms of their specific financial goals***

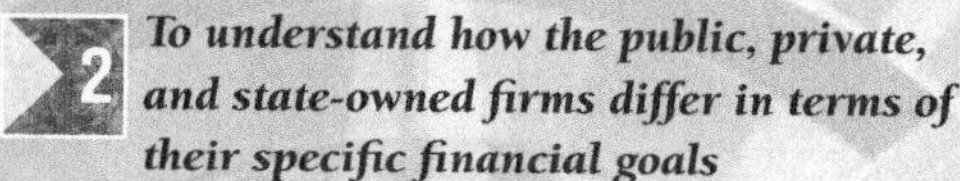

3. ***To understand how international business and investments are funded and how their cash flow is managed***
4. ***To understand the three primary currency exposures that confront the multinational firm***
5. ***To understand how accounting practices differ across countries and how these differences may alter the competitiveness of firms in international markets***
6. ***To understand the problems faced by many U.S.-based multinational firms that experience taxation liabilities at home and in foreign countries***
7. ***To examine the mechanics of financing import-export operations***

It was January 2013, and Korres Natural Products, a publicly traded natural cosmetics manufacturer, continued to suffer the throes of the Greek economic crisis. Before the Greek debt crisis, now five years running, Korres had faced little trouble securing the capital it needed for expanding its global business. But the past five years had been filled with turmoil and one challenge after another. Although the company was considered one of the true gems in the Greek business environment, it was still Greek, and that carried with it a lot of credit quality baggage.

With its emphasis on creating natural products from organic sources, Korres was well positioned to compete in the global market. Consumer consciousness in sustainable products and a growing backlash against animal testing had helped drive demand. This same consciousness stimulated new regulations on ingredients, component and product testing, and manufacturing. Consumers now demanded more information on the source of ingredients used in the products they used. Combined with a renewed emphasis on healthy living, natural product producers—like Korres—were well positioned for the future.

Korres focused on utilizing pharmaceutical experience in more than 3,000 herbs to create natural products for use in skin care, hair care, and other cosmetics. With more than 400 natural and certified organic products, the company used pharmacies as their main means of distribution (5,600 in Greece alone). Korres had expanded rapidly from 2003 to 2008, gaining a presence in more than thirty countries. The company had gone public in 2007 (Athens: Korres). But group sales had peaked in 2008, falling the next two years in step with the Greek economy. The company needed to grow, and that growth would require more capital—or a substitute for capital.

Despite the growing Greek economic and financial crisis, Korres had found a number of different paths to growth. First, the company went to a private investor for a special capital injection. Second, in order to penetrate the Americas at a faster rate but without the use of its own capital, Korres signed a global marketing agreement with Johnson & Johnson (USA). J&J would distribute Korres products throughout the Americas in return for paying a royalty to Korres on all sales. J&J would then put its own capital and operational capabilities to work on behalf of Korres.

As You Read This Chapter

1. How does a financial and economic crisis like the Greek crisis change the behavior of both equity investors and credit providers?
2. Does a global firm like Korres really pose the same risks to investors as a purely domestic firm operating in a market in crisis like that of Greece?

What does the leadership of any firm operating in global business attempt to achieve? What is the purpose of corporate governance, and what ultimately are the financial objectives of a business operating in the global marketplace? Although all management teams will claim they are pursing the creation of value in a high context, how is that actually executed in practice? Internally, within the walls of the firm, what exactly is management focusing on in the pursuit of profitability?

This chapter first describes who the primary stakeholders are in the corporation and how corporate governance is structured and conducted in the pursuit of fairness and transparency. The second section discusses how the global firm trades off complex goals in order to preserve and create shareholder value and how the financial management activities of the firm differ from domestic management. The chapter then provides an overview of the major differences between accounting practices and corporate taxation philosophies among major industrial countries.

Corporate Stakeholders and Governance

The legal existence of a business and its ownership are, however, very different concepts. The creation of the **corporation** solved a number of fundamental dilemmas faced by small businesses created by individuals.

CORPORATION

A separate legal entity organized under law which possesses legal rights and responsibilities separate from those of its owners and employees

- A corporation is legally separated from its owners (or owner because it can be just one person). If it loses money, acquires debts, or incurs legal liabilities, the individual owners can lose no more than what they have invested in the company. The owners are therefore not legally liable for debts or obligations to creditors beyond their ownership investment. This is what is meant by the oft-used phrase "limited liability."
- A corporation is perpetual. As opposed to individuals or families who may die, a corporation cannot die in the normal human sense of the word. A corporation may go bankrupt, it may be acquired, or it may be intentionally closed. But it can continue to operate in perpetuity, beyond the lives of its creators or immediate owners.
- A corporation is a legal creation but is deemed to have rights and responsibilities like a person, sometimes described as having a "legal personality." As such, a corporation can buy or sell, sue or be sued, borrow and lend, conduct business, all as a member

STAKEHOLDERS
An individual or entity which has an interest, financial or nonfinancial in nature, in the prospects and activities of some organization

STAKE
An interest or a share in some organization or undertaking

INTEREST
When a person or group is potentially affected by the actions of an organization or firm

RIGHTS
When a person or group has a legal claim, a contract, or some other existing arrangement to be treated in a certain way or have a particular right protected

of society. With these legal rights, it has the responsibility to follow all the laws of the state,and can be held accountable for failing to act in a legal manner. But unlike human beings, it has no moral conscience. The creation of the corporation had an enormously powerful influence on the growth of global commerce. The creation of a legally separate but legally responsible entity allowed the organization to raise capital independent of the financial health of any of the individual owners, to contract for purchasing and sale, and to survive the working life spans of its human creators. But it also may have freed the business entity to act as if it were a machine, devoid of the multitude of social, cultural, and moral concerns of the human individual.

Corporate Stakeholders

So who are the **stakeholders** in the corporation, and what is the nature of their interests? A **stake**, in theory, is an interest or a share in some organization or undertaking. Stakes themselves may be differentiated as to whether they are **interests**, **rights**, or **ownership stakes**. An interest is when a person or group is potentially affected by the actions of an organization or firm. The community in which a company operates, employing many of the people in the community, frequently opposes the closing of the firm citing its interest. A right is when a person or group has a legal claim, a contract, or some other existing arrangement to be treated in a certain way or have a particular right protected. This may be expressed in a variety of ways, including a right to be treated fairly, or an expectation that a firm will stand

Quick Take *Stockholder Wealth or Stakeholder Capitalism?*

There are two major schools of thought on what the firm's primary objective should be as described by the **shareholder wealth maximization model (SWM)** and the **stakeholder capitalism model (SCM)**.

The Anglo-American markets follow the SWM model: The firm should strive to maximize the return to shareholders, as measured by the sum of capital gains and dividends. The primary stakeholder is the stockholder, and all other stakeholders come second. SWM assumes that stock markets are efficient and that share prices quickly capture all new information and expectations of return and risk as perceived by investors. Share prices, in turn, are deemed the best allocators of capital in the macro economy.

In the non-Anglo-American markets, efforts to provide maximum returns to shareholders are constrained by powerful other stakeholders. Stakeholder groups such as labor unions, governments, communities, and various environmental and social interest groups carry greater weight in SCM. The SCM model does not assume that equity markets are either efficient or inefficient. It does not really matter because the firm's financial goals are not exclusively shareholder-oriented because they are constrained by the other stakeholders. In any case, the SCM model assumes that long-term "loyal" shareholders, typically controlling shareholders, rather than the transient portfolio investor should influence corporate strategy.

Although both models have their strengths and weaknesses, in recent years two trends have led to an increasing focus on the shareholder wealth form. First, as more of the non-Anglo-American markets have increasingly privatized their industries, the SWM focus is seemingly needed to attract international capital from outside investors, many of whom are from other countries. Second, and still quite controversial, many analysts believe that shareholder-based firms are increasingly dominating their global industry segments. Nothing attracts followers like success.

behind the quality of a product purchased from it. Ownership, the strongest form of stake, is when a person or group holds legal title to an asset such as a firm. Of course this then raises the question of whether the owner of a firm has dictatorial power, or must also consider the interests of nonowners?

Any analysis of corporate stakeholders must include all three levels of stakeholder interest. Depending on the country and culture of the firm itself, however, they may have very different voices in the vision, strategy, and operation of the firm. As described in the following sections, the power and influence of those who have an *interest* versus a *right* versus *legal title* (ownership) often serves to differentiate the business environments of countries. Figure 9.1 provides an overview of the potential stakeholders in the firm.

OWNERSHIP STAKE
The strongest form of stake is when a person or group holds legal title to an asset such as a firm

SHAREHOLDER WEALTH MAXIMIZATION MODEL (SWM)
The theoretical model where the primary objective of the business organization is to create and grow value for the owners of the organization

STAKEHOLDER CAPITALISM MODEL (SCM)
The theoretical model where the business organization is to maximize the wealth of all stakeholders in the business or corporation, including owners, employees, creditors, as well as community, customers, and suppliers

FIGURE 9.1 Stakeholders in the Firm

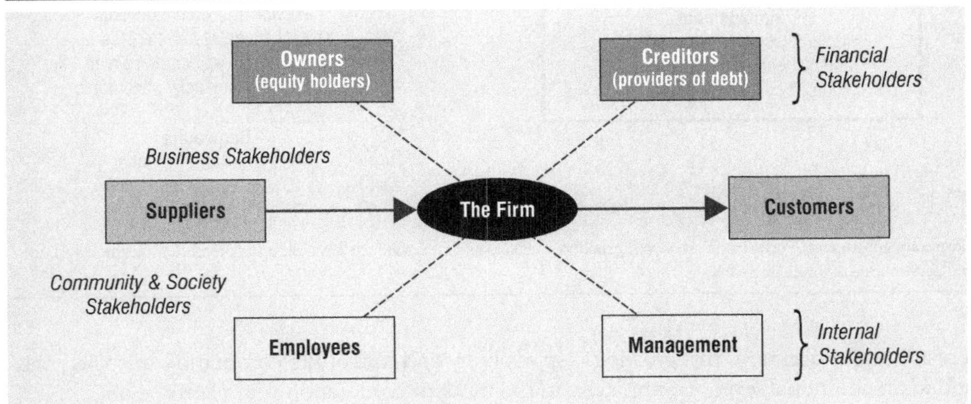

Differences in ownership, law, country of incorporation and activity, and culture lead to differences in interest and power among stakeholder groups (business, financial, internal, and society).

Although the governance structure of any company, domestic, international, or multinational, is fundamental to its very existence, this subject has become the lightning rod of political and business debate in the past few years as failures in governance in a variety of forms has led to corporate fraud and failure. Abuses and failures in corporate governance have dominated global business news in recent years. Beginning with the accounting fraud and questionable ethics of business conduct at Enron culminating in its bankruptcy, failures in corporate governance have raised issues about the very ethics and culture of business conduct.

Figure 9.2 provides an overview of the structure of any business's governance. The primary internal parties, the board of directors and the management team, are often the focus of most scrutiny. However, market economies today also rely on the external parties from the marketplace—the equity and debt markets, auditors, legal advisors, and regulators—who are expected to fill the gaps and failures which may arise from the internal parties.

Corporate Responsibility and Sustainability

> *Sustainable development is development that meets the needs of the present without compromising the ability of future generations to meet their own needs.*
>
> — Brundtland Report, 1987, p. 54.

What is the purpose of the corporation? It is increasingly accepted that the purpose of the corporation is certainly to create profits and value for its stakeholders, but the responsibility of the corporation is to do so in a way that inflicts no costs on the environment and society. As

FIGURE 9.2 The Structure of Corporate Governance

Corporate governance represents the *relationship* among stakeholders that is used to determine and control the strategic direction and performance of the organization.

a result of globalization, this growing responsibility and role of the corporation in society has added an additional level of complexity to the modern corporation never seen before.

The discussion has been somewhat hampered to date by a lot of conflicting terms and labels—*corporate goodness, corporate responsibility, corporate social responsibility (CSR), corporate*

Quick Take *Good Governance and Corporate Reputation*

Does good corporate governance matter? This is actually a difficult question, and the realistic answer has been largely dependent on outcomes historically. For example, as long as Enron's share price continued to rise dramatically throughout the 1990s, questions over transparency, accounting propriety, and even financial facts were largely overlooked by all of the corporation's stakeholders. Yet, eventually, the fraud, deceit, and failure of the multitude of corporate governance practices resulted in the bankruptcy of the firm. It not only destroyed the wealth of investors but the careers, incomes, and savings of so many of its basic stakeholders—its own employees. Ultimately, *yes,* good governance does matter. A lot.

Good corporate governance depends on a variety of factors, one of which is the general governance reputation of the country of incorporation and registration. Studies by many different organizations and academics have continued to show a number of important linkages between good governance (at both the country and corporate levels) and the cost of capital, returns to shareholders, and corporate profitability. An added dimension of interest is the role of country governance as it may influence the country in which international investors may choose to invest. Early studies indicate that good governance does indeed attract international investor interest.

philanthropy, and *corporate sustainability,* to list but a few. To put it simply, *sustainability* is often described as a goal, while *responsibility* is an obligation of the corporation. The obligation is to pursue profit, social development, and the environment—but to do so using sustainable principles.

Nearly two decades ago a number of large corporations began to refine their publicly acknowledged corporate objective as "the pursuit of the triple bottom line." This triple bottom line—*profitability, social responsibility,* and *environmental sustainability*—was considered an enlightened development of modern capitalism. What some critics referred to as a softer and gentler form of market capitalism was a growing acceptance on the part of the corporation to do something more than generate a financial profit. One way to explain this development of an expanded view of corporate responsibilities divides the arguments along two channels, the **economic channel** and the **moral channel**.

The economic channel argues that, by pursuing corporate sustainability objectives, the corporation is actually still pursuing profitability but is doing so with a more intelligent longer-term perspective—"enlightened self-interest." It has realized that a responsible organization must assure that its actions over time, whether or not required by law or markets, do not reduce future choices. Alternatively, the moral channel argues that the corporation has the rights and responsibilities of a citizen, including the moral responsibility to act in the best interests of society, regardless of its impacts on profitability.

ECONOMIC CHANNEL
The principle that if an organization pursues corporate sustainability objectives it is still pursuing profitability and is therefore still aligned with the objectives of maximizing profit and pursuing business growth; actions, while legal, are defined by self-interest, and not morality

MORAL CHANNEL
The principle that the corporation, regardless of whether it is required to by law or not, should pursue business activities which are aligned with and in support of both socially and environmentally responsible and moral outcomes

GLOBAL FINANCIAL GOALS

The financial goals of an enterprise depend first upon who owns it. The first distinction is between **public ownership**, where the state or government or civil society owns the organization, and **private ownership**, which includes individuals, partners, families, or the modern publicly traded organization. It is critical that ownership and ownership's specific financial interests be understood from the very start if we are to understand the strategic and financial goals and objectives of management.

Public ownership is a very common organizational form across the globe today. Those organizations are formed and owned by governments, on behalf of their people, and are termed *State Owned Enterprises* (SOEs). Today in many countries, SOEs are the dominant form of

PUBLIC OWNERSHIP
An organization in which any individual or citizen has the right to purchase a share of ownership

PRIVATE OWNERSHIP
An organization that is owned exclusively by a private party (individual, family, organization of some kind) with ownership extended only to other parties at the exclusive owner's permission

FIGURE 9.3 Ownership of Commercial Enterprises

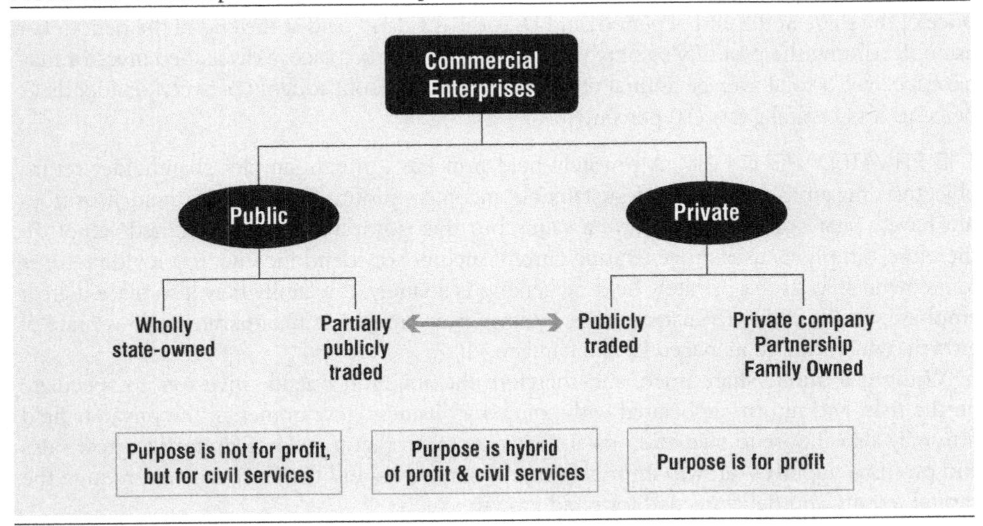

business entity. One example would be the Saudi Arabian Oil Company, Saudi Aramco, the national oil company of Saudi Arabia and the world's largest oil and gas company, which is owned by the Saudi Arabian Government.

Private ownership includes all those organizations formed for business or commercial activities. These are companies created by entrepreneurs who are typically either individuals, partners, or families. (Do not forget that even Microsoft started as the brain-child of two partners, Bill Gates and Paul Allen.)

Regardless of origins—public or private—today's global marketplace has both organizational forms traded in the public market. In addition to the usual suspects of ExxonMobil and IBM, private enterprises that are widely publicly traded and held, there are many other SOEs that are also publicly traded. For example, China National Petroleum Corporation (CNPC), the government parent company to PetroChina, has shares listed and traded on stock exchanges in Shanghai, Hong Kong, and New York.

Operational Goals

An introductory course in business usually states that leadership of the enterprise is expected to maximize shareholder value. Unfortunately, the statement is a bit simplistic considering at least two major challenges: (1) It is not necessarily the accepted goal of management across countries to maximize the wealth of shareholders—other stakeholders like government, civil society, or creditors, may also carry substantial weight; and (2) creating value is, like so many lofty goals, much easier said than done.

It is one thing to say "maximize value," but it is another to actually do it. The management objective of maximizing profit is not as simple as it sounds because the measure of profit used by ownership and management differs between the privately held firm and the publicly traded firm. In other words, is management attempting to maximize current income (accounting profits), capital appreciation (changes in share price), or both?

PUBLICLY HELD FIRMS The return to a shareholder in a publicly traded firm combines current income in the form of dividends and capital gains from the appreciation of share price:

$$\text{Shareholder Return} = \frac{P_2 - P_1 + D_2}{P_1} = \frac{P_2 - P_1}{P_1} + \frac{D_2}{P_1}$$

where the initial price, P_1, is equivalent to the initial investment by the shareholder, P_2 is the price of the share at the end of period, and D_2 is the dividend paid at the end of the period. For example, during the past fifty or sixty years in the U.S. marketplace, a diversified investor may have received a total average annual return of 12 percent, split roughly between dividends (2 percent) and capital gains (10 percent).

THE PRIVATELY HELD FIRM A privately held firm has a much simpler shareholder return objective: maximize current and sustainable income—profit. The privately held firm does not have a share price (it does have a value, but this is not a market-determined value). It, therefore, simply focuses on generating current income, dividend income, to provide returns to its ownership. If the privately held ownership is a family, the family may also place a great emphasis on the ability to sustain those earnings over time while maintaining a slower rate of growth, which can be managed by the family itself.

Without a public share price, and therefore the ability of outside investors to speculate on the risks and returns associated with company business developments, the privately held firm may also choose to take fewer risks. This may mean that it will not attempt to grow sales and profits as rapidly—growth impresses markets mostly—and therefore may not require the capital (equity and debt) needed for rapid growth.

OPERATIONAL GOALS FOR MNES The MNE must be guided by operational goals suitable for various levels of the firm. Even if the firm's goal is to maximize shareholder value, the manner in which investors value the firm is not always obvious to the firm's top management. Therefore, most firms hope to receive a favorable investor response to the achievement of operational goals that can be controlled by the way in which the firm performs, and then hope—if we can use that term—that the market will reward their results. The MNE must determine the proper balance between three common operational financial objectives:

1. Maximization of consolidated after-tax income (profit)
2. Minimization of the firm's effective global tax burden (minimize taxes)
3. Correct positioning of the firm's income, cash flows, and available funds as to country and currency (position cash and profits to protect against major risks)

These goals are frequently incompatible, in that the pursuit of one may result in a less desirable outcome in regard to another. Management must make decisions about the proper trade-offs between goals (which is why people, rather than computers, are employed as managers).

CONSOLIDATED PROFITS The primary operational goal of the MNE is to maximize consolidated profits, after tax. Consolidated profits are the profits of all the individual units of the firm originating in many different currencies expressed in the currency of the parent company. This is not to say that management is not striving to maximize the present value of all future cash flows. The leaders of the MNE, the management team that is implementing the firm's strategy, must think far beyond current earnings.

International Corporate Investment

Multinational firms follow a disciplined and deliberate process in the evaluation of potential foreign investments.

International Capital Budgeting

Any investment, whether it is the purchase of stock, the acquisition of real estate, or the construction of a manufacturing facility in another country, is financially justified if the present value of expected cash inflows is greater than the present value of expected cash outflows—in other words, if it has a positive **net present value (NPV)**. The construction of a capital budget is the process of projecting the net operating cash flows of the potential investment to determine if it is indeed a good investment.

NET PRESENT VALUE (NPV)
The sum of the present values of all cash inflows and outflows from an investment project discounted at the cost of capital

CAPITAL BUDGET
The financial evaluation of a proposed investment to determine whether the expected returns are sufficient to justify the investment expenses

Capital Budget Components and Decision Criteria

Capital budgets are only as good as the accuracy of the cost and revenue assumptions on which they are based. Adequately anticipating all of the incremental expenses that the individual project imposes on the firm is critical to a proper analysis. A capital budget is composed of three primary cash flow components:

1. *Capital outlays*: Initial expenses and capital outlays are normally the largest net cash outflow occurring over the life of an investment. Because they occur up front, they have a substantial impact on the net present value of the project.
2. *Operating cash flows*: These are the net cash flows the project is expected to yield, once production is under way. The primary positive net cash flows of the project are realized in this stage; net operating cash flows will determine the success or failure of the investment.

CAPITAL OUTLAYS
Upfront costs and expenses of a proposed investment

OPERATING CASH FLOWS
Cash flows arising from the firm's everyday business activities

TERMINAL CASH FLOWS
Salvage value or resale value of the project at its termination

3. *Terminal cash flows*: These represent the salvage value or resale value of the project at its end. The terminal value will include whatever working capital balances can be recaptured, once the project is no longer in operation (at least by this owner). The decision criterion for an individual investment is whether the net present value (NPV) of the project is positive or negative. The net cash flows in the future are discounted by the average cost of capital for the firm (the average of debt and equity costs). The purpose of discounting is to capture the fact that the firm has acquired investment capital at a cost, where that same capital has an opportunity cost. If the NPV of a proposed investment is positive, then the project is an acceptable investment. If the project's NPV is negative, then the cash flows expected to result from the investment are insufficient to provide an acceptable rate of return, and the project should be rejected.

Evaluating a Proposed Project in Singapore

The capital budget for a manufacturing plant in Singapore serves as a basic example. Coyote, a U.S. manufacturer of household consumer products, is considering constructing a plant in Singapore in 2014. It would cost S$1,660,000 to build and would be ready for operation on January 1, 2015. Coyote would operate the plant for three years and then sell it to the Singapore government.

To analyze the proposed investment, Coyote must estimate annual sales revenues, production costs, overhead expenses, depreciation allowances for the new plant and equipment, and the Singapore tax liability on corporate income. The estimation of all net operating cash flows is very important to the analysis of the project. Often the acceptability of a foreign investment may depend on the sales forecast for the project.

But Coyote needs U.S. dollars, not Singapore dollars. The only way the stockholders would be willing to undertake the investment is if it would be profitable in terms of their own currency, the U.S. dollar. This is the primary theoretical distinction between a domestic capital budget and a multinational capital budget. The evaluation of the project in the viewpoint of the parent company will focus on whatever cash flows, either operational or financial, will find their way back to the parent firm in U.S. dollars. Coyote must therefore forecast the movement of the Singapore dollar (S$) over the four-year period. The spot rate on January 1, 2014, is S$1.6600/US$. Coyote concludes that the rate of inflation will be roughly 5 percent higher per year in Singapore than in the United States. If the theory of purchasing power parity holds, as described in Chapter 8, it should take roughly 5 percent more Singapore dollars to buy a U.S. dollar per year. Using this assumption, Coyote forecasts the exchange rate from 2014 to 2017.

After considerable study and analysis, Coyote estimates that the net cash flows of the Singapore project, in Singapore dollars, would be those on line 1 in Table 9.1. Line 2 lists the expected exchange rate between Singapore dollars and U.S. dollars over the four-year period, assuming it takes 5 percent more Singapore dollars per U.S. dollar each year (the Singapore dollar is expected to depreciate versus the U.S. dollar). Combining the net cash flow forecast in Singapore dollars with the expected exchange rates, Coyote can now calculate the net cash flow per year in U.S. dollars. Coyote notes that although the initial expense is sizable, S$1,660,000 (US$1,000,000), the project produces positive net cash flows in its very first year of operations (2015) of US$172,117, and remains positive every year thereafter.

Coyote estimates that the cost to the company of capital, both debt and equity combined, is about 12 percent per year. Using this as the rate of discount, the discount factor for each of the future years can be calculated. Finally, the net cash flow in U.S. dollars multiplied by the present value factor yields the present values of each net cash flow. The net present value of the Singapore project is a negative US$7,900; Coyote may now decide not to proceed with the project because it is financially too risky.

TABLE 9.1 Multinational Capital Budgeting: Singapore Manufacturing Facility

Line #	Description	2014	2015	2016	2017
1	Net cash flow in Singapore dollars (S$)	(1,660,000)	300,000	600,000	1,500,000
2	Exchange rate, S$/US$ (@ 5%)	1.6600	1.7430	1.8302	1.9217
3	Expected net cash flow (US$)	(1,000,000)	172,117	317,842	780,576
4	Present value factor (@12%)	1.0000	0.8929	0.7972	0.7118
5	Present value of cash flow in US$	(1,000,000)	153,676	261,354	555,599
6	Net present value (US$)	(29,372)			
7	Net present value (S$)	153,844			

Notes:

a. The spot exchange rate of S$1.6600/$ is assumed to change by 5 percent per year. S$1.660/S × 1.05 = S$1.7430/$.

b. The present value factor assumes a weighted average cost of capital, here used as the discount rate, of 12 percent. The present value discount factor is found using the standard formula of $1/(1+.2)^t$, where t is the number of years in the future (1, 2, or 3).

Risks in International Investments

How is the Coyote capital budget different from a similar project constructed in San Diego? It is riskier, at least from the standpoint of cross-border risk. The higher risk of an international investment arises from the different countries—their laws, regulations, potential for interference with the normal operations of the investment project, and, obviously, currencies, all of which are unique to international investment.

The risk of international investment is considered greater because the proposed investment will be within the jurisdiction of a different government. Governments have the ability to pass new laws, including the potential nationalization of the entire project. The typical problems that may arise from operating in a different country are changes in foreign tax laws, restrictions placed on when or how much in profits may be repatriated to the parent company, and other restrictions that hinder the free movement of merchandise and capital among the proposed project, the parent company, and any other country relevant to its inputs or sales.

The other major distinction between a domestic investment and a foreign investment is that the perspective of the parent company and the project are no longer the same. The two perspectives differ because the parent values only cash flows it derives from the project. So, for example, in Table 9.1 the project generates sufficient net cash flows in Singapore dollars that the project is acceptable from the project's viewpoint, but not from the parent's viewpoint.

Assuming the same 12 percent discount rate, the NPV in Singapore dollars is S$153,844, while the NPV to the U.S. parent is negative US$7,900, as noted previously. But what if the exchange rate did not change at all, remaining fixed for the 2014–2017 period? The NPV would then be positive from both viewpoints (the project NPV remains at S$153,844; the parent's NPV is now US$109,888). Or what if the Singapore government were to restrict the payment of dividends back to the U.S. parent firm or somehow prohibit the subsidiary from exchanging Singapore dollars for U.S. dollars (capital controls)? Without cash flows in U.S. dollars, the parent would have no way of justifying the investment. And all of this could occur while the project itself is sufficiently profitable when measured in local currency. This split between project and parent viewpoints is a critical difference in international investment analysis.

CAPITAL STRUCTURE: INTERNATIONAL DIMENSIONS

CAPITAL STRUCTURE
The proportions of owner's equity (own-capital) and debt (capital provided by external creditors) that fund the organization

EQUITY
The capital provided by the owner of a company

DEBT
The capital provided by a creditor, like a bank, that will be eventually repaid and that has no rights or responsibilities associated with ownership of the organization

DEBT-EQUITY STRUCTURE
A firm's combination of capital obtained by borrowing from others, such as banks (debts), and capital provided by owners (equity)

The way a firm is funded is referred to as its **capital structure**. Capital is needed to open a factory, build an amusement park, or even start a hot-dog stand. If capital is provided by owners of the firm, it is called **equity**. If capital is obtained by borrowing from others, such as commercial banking institutions, it is termed **debt**.

Any firm's ability to grow and expand is dependent on its ability to acquire additional capital as it grows. The net profits generated over previous periods may be valuable but are rarely enough to provide needed capital expansion. Firms therefore need access to capital markets, both debt and equity. Chapter 8 provided an overview of the major debt and equity markets available internationally, but it is important to remember that the firm must have access to the markets to enjoy their fruits.

The Capital Structure of Foreign Subsidiaries

The choice of what proportions of debt and equity to use in international investments is usually dictated by either the **debt-equity structure** of the parent or the debt-equity structure of competitive firms in the host country. The parent firm sees equity investment as capital at risk; therefore, it would usually prefer to provide as little equity capital as possible. Although funding the foreign subsidiary primarily with debt would still put the parent's capital at risk, debt service provides a strict schedule for cash flow repatriation to the lender. Equity capital's return—dividends from profits—depends on managerial discretion.

The sources of debt, listed in Table 9.2, are not always available because many countries have relatively small capital markets. The parent firm is then often forced to provide not only the equity but also a large proportion of the debt to its foreign subsidiaries.

TABLE 9.2 Financing Alternatives for Foreign Subsidiaries

Foreign Subsidiary Can Raise Equity Capital:	Foreign Subsidiary Can Raise Debt Capital:
1. From the parent company	1. From the parent company
2. From a joint venture partner's parent	2. From a bank loan or bond issue in home country
3. From a third-country market like Euromarkets	3. From a third-country bank loan or bond issuance like the Euromarkets (Euro-syndicated loan or bond)

International Working Capital

WORKING CAPITAL MANAGEMENT
The management of a firm's current assets (cash, accounts receivable, inventories) and current liabilities (accounts payable, short-term debt)

Working capital management is the financing of short-term or current assets, but the term is used here to describe all short-term financing and financial management of the firm. Even a small multinational firm will have a number of different cash flows moving throughout its system at one time. The maintenance of proper liquidity, the monitoring of payments, and the acquisition of additional capital when needed—all of these require a great degree of organization and planning in international operations.

Operating and Financing Cash Flows

Firms possess both operating cash flows and financing cash flows. Operating cash flows arise from the everyday business activities of the firm, such as paying for materials or resources (accounts payable) or receiving payments for items sold (accounts receivable) or licenses granted.

Financing cash flows arise from the funding activities of the firm. The servicing of existing funding sources, interest on existing debt, and dividend payments to shareholders constitute potentially large and frequent cash flows. Periodic additions to debt or equity through new bank loans, new bond issuances, or supplemental stock sales may also add to the volume of financing cash flows in the multinational firm.

FINANCING CASH FLOWS
The cash flows arising from the firm's funding activities

Cash Flow Management

The structure of the firm dictates how cash flows and financial resources can be managed. The trend in the past decade has been toward the increasing centralization of most financial management activities. The centralized treasury often is responsible for both funding operations and cash flow management. It may enjoy significant economies of scale, offering more services and expertise to the various units of the firm worldwide than the individual units themselves could support. However, regardless of whether the firm follows a centralized or decentralized approach, there are a number of operating structures that help the multinational firm manage its cash flows.

NETTING Netting, or cash flow coordination between units, can occur between each subsidiary and the parent and between the subsidiaries themselves. Coordination simply requires some planning and budgeting of interfirm cash flows in order that two-way flows are netted against one another. Netting is particularly helpful if the two-way flow is in two different currencies, as each would otherwise suffer currency exchange charges for intrafirm transfers.

NETTING
Cash flow coordination between a corporation's global units so that only one smaller cash transfer must be made

CASH POOLING A large firm with a number of units operating both within an individual country and across countries may be able to economize on the amount of firm assets needed in cash if one central pool is used for cash pooling. With one pool of capital and up-to-date information on the cash flows in and out of the various units, the firm spends much less in terms of forgone interest on cash balances, which are held in safekeeping against unforeseen cash flow shortfalls.

CASH POOLING
Used by multinational firms to centralize individual units' cash flows, resulting in less spending or foregone interest on unnecessary cash balances

LEADS AND LAGS The timing of payments between units of a multinational is somewhat adjustable. Again, this allows the management of payments between a parent firm and its subsidiaries to be much more flexible, allowing the firm not only to position cash flows where they are needed most, but also to help manage currency risk. A foreign subsidiary that is expecting its local currency to fall in value relative to the U.S. dollar may try to speed up, or lead, its payments to the parent firm. Similarly, if the local currency is expected to rise versus the dollar, the subsidiary may want to wait, or lag, payments until exchange rates are more favorable.

LEADS
Paying a debt early to take advantage of exchange rates.

LAGS
Paying a debt late to take advantage of exchange rates

RE-INVOICING Multinational firms with a variety of manufacturing and distribution subsidiaries scattered over a number of countries within a region may often find it more economical to have one office or subsidiary taking ownership of all invoices and payments between units. The subsidiary literally buys from one unit and sells to a second unit, thereby taking ownership of the goods and re-invoicing the sale to the next unit. Once ownership is taken, the sale/purchase can be redenominated in a different currency, netted against other payments, hedged against specific currency exposures, or re-priced in accordance with potential tax benefits of the re-invoicing center's host country.

RE-INVOICING
The policy of buying goods from one unit, selling them to a second unit, and re-invoicing the sale to the next unit, to take advantage of favorable exchange rates

INTERNAL BANKS Some multinational firms have found that their financial resources and needs are becoming either too large or too sophisticated for the financial services that are available in many of their local subsidiary markets. One solution to this has been the establishment of an internal bank within the firm that buys and sells payables and receivables from

INTERNAL BANK
A multinational firm's financial management tool that actually acts as a bank to coordinate finances among its units

the various units, which frees the units of the firm from struggling for continual working-capital financing and lets them focus on their primary business activities.

COMBINING METHODS All of these structures and management techniques are often combined in different ways to fit the needs of the individual firm. Some techniques are encouraged or prohibited by laws and regulations (for example, many countries limit the ability to lead and lag payments), depending on the host-country's government and stage of capital market liberalization. Multinational cash flow management requires flexibility in thinking—artistry in some cases—as much as technique on the part of managers.

FOREIGN EXCHANGE EXPOSURE

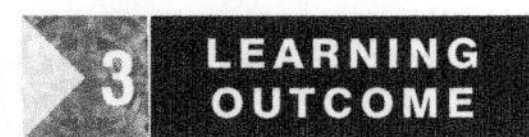

Companies today know the risks of international operations. They are aware of the substantial risks to balance sheet values and annual earnings that interest rates and exchange rates may inflict on any firm at any time. Financial managers, international treasurers, and financial officers of all kinds are expected to protect the firm from such risks. Firms have, in varying degrees, three types of foreign currency exposure as described in Table 9.3: transaction exposure, economic exposure, and translation exposure:

TABLE 9.3 The Three Types of Foreign Exchange Exposure

- *Transaction exposure*—the changing value of a foreign currency denominated obligation of the firm occurring at a future point in time.
- *Economic exposure*—the change in the value of a firm arising from unexpected changes in exchange rates.
- *Translation exposure*—the change in the reported value of a company's financial results from the translation of foreign currency financial statements into the home or reporting currency of the firm.

Managing Transaction Exposure

Only two conditions are necessary for a transaction exposure to exist: (1) a cash flow that is denominated in a foreign currency, and (2) the cash flow that will occur at a future date. For example, a U.S. firm that exports products to France will receive a guaranteed (by contract) payment in French francs in the future. Any contract, agreement, purchase, or sale that is denominated in a foreign currency that will be settled in the future constitutes a transaction exposure.

The risk of a transaction exposure is that the exchange rate might change—for better or worse—between the present date and the settlement date. Suppose that an American firm signs a contract to purchase heavy rolled-steel pipe from a South Korean producer for 21,000,000 Korean won. The payment is due in 30 days upon delivery. The 30-day account payable, so typical of international trade and commerce, is a **transaction exposure** for the U.S. firm—a foreign currency denominated payable at a future date. If the spot exchange rate on the date the contract is signed is Won 700/$, the U.S. firm would expect to pay:

TRANSACTION EXPOSURE
The potential for losses or gains when a firm is engaged in a transaction denominated in a foreign currency

$$\frac{\text{Won } 21{,}000{,}000}{\text{Won } 700/\$} = \$30{,}000$$

But the firm is not assured of what the exchange rate will be in thirty days. If the spot rate at the end of thirty days is Won 720/$, the U.S. firm would actually pay less. The payment would then be $29,167. If, however, the exchange rate changed in the opposite direction, for example to Won 650/$, the payment could just as easily increase to $32,308.

Management of transaction exposures usually is accomplished by **hedging.** Hedging activities fall into two broad categories: (1) operational hedging, a structural strategy of the firm; and (2) contractual hedging, also termed financial hedging, where the firm uses a financial instrument or derivative to manage the exposure. **Operational hedging** is when a firm arranges to have foreign currency cash flows coming in and going out at roughly the same times and same amounts. The exposure is managed by matching offsetting foreign currency cash flows. **Contractual hedging** occurs when a firm uses financial contracts, either loan agreements or financial derivatives, to hedge the transaction exposure. The most common foreign currency derivative hedge is the forward contract, as explained in Chapter 8, although other financial instruments and derivatives, such as currency futures and options, are also used.

HEDGING

Taking an investment position, for example by using a financial derivative, to offset the gains or losses associated with an underlying position of the investor.

OPERATIONAL HEDGING

When a firm arranges to have foreign currency cash flows coming in and going out at roughly the same times and same amounts and exposure is managed by matching offsetting foreign currency cash flows

CONTRACTUAL HEDGING

A multinational firm's use of contracts to minimize its transaction exposure

ECONOMIC EXPOSURE

The potential for long-term effects on a firm's value as the result of changing currency values

Managing Economic Exposure

Economic exposure, also called operating exposure, is the change in the value of a firm arising from unexpected changes in exchange rates. Economic exposure emphasizes that there is a limit to a firm's ability to predict either cash flows or exchange rate changes in the medium to long term. All firms, either directly or indirectly, have economic exposure—even domestic concerns.

The effects of economic exposure are as diverse as are firms in their international structure. Take the case of a U.S. corporation with a successful British subsidiary. The British subsidiary manufactures and then distributes the firm's products in Great Britain, Germany, and France. The profits of the British subsidiary are paid out annually to the American parent corporation. What would be the impact on the profitability of the British subsidiary and the entire U.S. firm if the British pound suddenly fell in value against all other major currencies? If the British firm had been facing competition in Germany, France, and its own home market from firms in those other two continental countries, it would instantly become more competitive. If the British pound is cheaper, so are the products sold internationally by British-based firms. The British subsidiary of the American firm would, in all likelihood, see rising profits from increased sales.

But what of the value of the British subsidiary to the U.S. parent corporations? The same fall in the British pound that allowed the British subsidiary to gain profits would also result in substantially fewer U.S. dollars when the British pound earnings are converted at the end of the year. It seems that it is nearly impossible to win in this situation. Actually, from the perspective of economic exposure management, the fact that the firm's total value—subsidiary and parent together—is roughly a wash as a result of the exchange rate change is desirable. Sound financial management assumes that a firm will profit and bear risk in its line of business, not in the process of settling payments on business already completed.

Management of economic exposure means being prepared for the unexpected. A firm that is highly dependent on its ability to remain cost-competitive in markets both at home and abroad, may choose to take actions now that would allow it to passively withstand any sudden unexpected rise of the dollar. This could be accomplished through diversification of operations and of financing.

Managing Translation Exposure

TRANSLATION EXPOSURE

The potential effect on a firm's financial statements of a change in currency values

Translation exposure, or *accounting exposure,* results from the conversion (translation) of foreign currency denominated financial statements of foreign subsidiaries and affiliates into the home currency of the parent firm. This is necessary to prepare consolidated financial statements for all firms, as country law requires. The purpose is to have all operations, worldwide, stated in the same currency terms for comparison purposes. Management often uses the translated statements to judge the performance of foreign affiliates and their personnel on the same currency terms as the parent firm itself.

However, a problem often arises from the translation of balance sheets in foreign currencies into the domestic currency. Which assets and liabilities are to be translated at current exchange rates (at the current balance sheet date) versus historical rates (those in effect on the date of the initial investment)? Or should all assets and liabilities be translated at the same rate? The answer is somewhere in between, and the process of translation is dictated by financial accounting standards. At present in the United States, the proper method for translating foreign financial statements is given in Financial Accounting Standards Board statement No. 52. If a foreign subsidiary is operating in a functional foreign currency environment, most assets, liabilities, and income statement items of foreign affiliates are translated using current exchange rates (the exchange rate in effect on the balance sheet date). For this reason, it is often referred to as the *current-rate method.*

Translation exposure under FASB 52 results in no cash flow impacts under normal circumstances. Although consolidated accounting can result in some translation losses or gains on the parent's consolidated balance sheet, the accounting entries are not ordinarily realized. Unless liquidation or sale of the subsidiary is anticipated, neither the subsidiary nor the parent firm should expend real resources on the management of an accounting convention.

International Accounting

Accounting standards and practices are, in many ways, no different in their origins from any other legislative or regulatory statutes. Laws reflect the people, places, and events of their time. Most accounting practices and laws are linked to the objectives of the parties who will use the financial information, including investors, lenders, and governments.

The fact that accounting principles differ across countries is not, by itself, a problem. However, because the accounting and taxation structures of countries are influenced by lenders, investors, and government policymakers, difficulties arise. Two firms, for instance, with identical structures, products, and strategies but based in different countries can look entirely different on paper, depending upon the accounting standards applied. In extreme cases, one may seem profitable while the other is clearly operating at a loss. Global **accounting diversity** can lead to any of the following: (1) poor or improper business decision making; (2) difficulties in raising capital in different or foreign markets; and (3) difficulty in monitoring competitive factors across firms, industries, and nations.

ACCOUNTING DIVERSITY
The range of differences in national accounting practices

- Preparation of consolidated financial statements
- Access to foreign capital markets
- Comparability of financial statements
- Lack of high-quality accounting information

Worldwide Accounting Standards

The International Accounting Standards Committee (IASC), with representatives from nine countries worldwide, seeks to create a single set of high-quality, understandable, and enforceable accounting standards. The standards would allow for transparent and comparable information in general-purpose financial statements across all countries worldwide. At present, governments limit access to capital to those companies that comply with local accounting practices, as opposed to international standards, which depend upon companies raising capital across borders. U.S. corporations and accounting firms have long resisted the move toward international accounting standards (IAS), insisting that no standards are as rigorous as their own Generally Accepted Accounting Principles (GAAP). However, the Enron debacle and the collapse of the Big Five accounting group gave supporters of international standards an unexpected boost. The energy trader Enron and its auditors allegedly colluded to hide off-balance-sheet transactions from investors, disguising the real financial performance of the company. Under IAS, Enron's accounting irregularities would have been spotted.

Principal Accounting Differences Across Countries

National accounting systems and practices can be classified and grouped a number of different ways. Figure 9.4 illustrates one of the most widely accepted classification systems, the Nobes Judgmental Classification.

FIGURE 9.4 Judgmental Classification of Financial Reporting

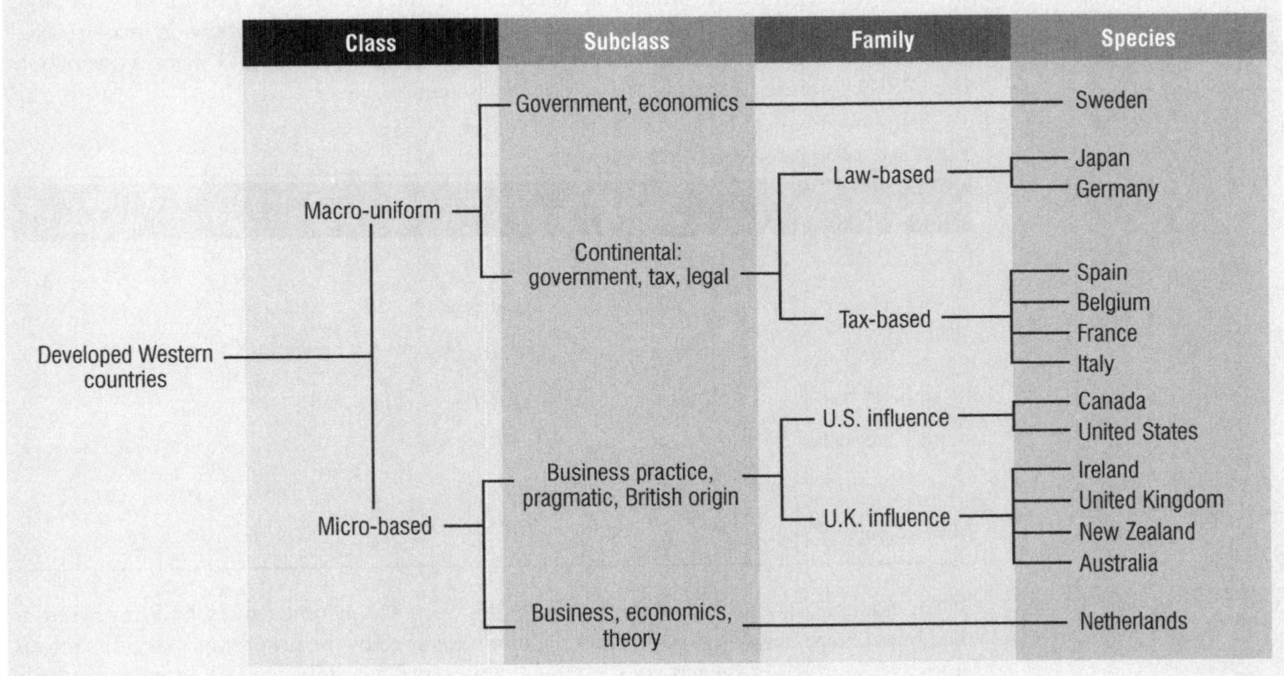

SOURCE: Based on the original work of Christopher W. Nobes, "A Judgmental International Classification of Financing Reporting Practices," *Journal of Business Finance and Accounting*, Spring 1983, p. 7.

Here, accounting systems are first subdivided into *micro-based* (characteristics of the firms and industries) and *macro-uniform* (following fundamental government or economic factors per country). The micro-based national accounting systems are then broken down into those that follow a theoretical principle or issues of pragmatic concern. The macro-uniform category includes the national accounting systems of countries as diverse as the United States, Canada, Japan, the United Kingdom, and Mexico. The macro-based system is further sub-divided into law-based and tax-based systems.

International Taxation

Governments, alone, have the power to tax. Each government wants to tax all companies within its jurisdiction without placing burdens on domestic or foreign companies that would restrain trade. Each country states its jurisdictional approach formally in the tax treaties that

it signs with other countries. One of the primary purposes of tax treaties is to establish the boundaries of each country's jurisdiction to prevent double taxation of international income.

Tax Jurisdictions

Nations structure their tax systems along two basic approaches: the worldwide approach or the territorial approach. Both are attempts to determine which firms, foreign or domestic by incorporation, or which incomes, foreign or domestic in origin, are subject to the taxation of host country tax authorities.

WORLDWIDE APPROACH TO TAXATION
The principle that taxes are levied on the income earned by firms that are incorporated in a host country, worldwide, regardless of where the income was earned (e.g., in other countries)

WORLDWIDE APPROACH The **worldwide approach**, also referred to as the residential or national approach, levies taxes on the income earned by firms that are incorporated in the host country, regardless of where the income was earned (domestically or abroad). An MNE earning income both at home and abroad would therefore find its worldwide income taxed by its host-country tax authorities. As illustrated by Table 9.4, the United States is one of only five OECD countries that utilizes a worldwide system.

TABLE 9.4 Tax Regimes of the OECD Thirty

Territorial Taxation				Worldwide Taxation
Australia	France	Japan	Slovak Republic	Ireland
Austria	Germany	Luxembourg	Spain	Korea
Belgium	Greece	Netherlands	Sweden	Mexico
Canada	Hungary	New Zealand	Switzerland	Poland
Czech Republic	Iceland	Norway	Turkey	United States
Denmark	Italy	Portugal	United Kingdom	
Finland				

For example, a country like the United States taxes the income earned by firms based in the United States regardless of whether the income earned by the firm is domestically sourced or foreign sourced. In the case of the United States, ordinary foreign-sourced income is only taxed by the U.S. authorities when the foreign profits are remitted to the United States. As with all questions of tax, however, numerous conditions and exceptions exist. The primary problem is that this does not address the income earned by foreign firms operating within the United States. Countries like the United States apply the principle of territorial taxation to foreign firms within their legal jurisdiction, taxing all income earned by foreign firms in the United States.

TERRITORIAL APPROACH TO TAXATION
The principle that taxes are levied on the income earned by firms within the legal jurisdiction of the host country, and not on income earned in any other legal jurisdiction outside the host country

TERRITORIAL APPROACH The **territorial approach** focuses on the income earned by firms within the legal jurisdiction of the host country, not on the country of firm incorporation. Countries like Germany that follow the territorial approach apply taxes equally to foreign or domestic firms on income earned within the country, but not on income earned outside the country.

The territorial approach, like the worldwide approach, results in a major gap in coverage if resident firms earn income outside the country, but are not taxed by the country in which the profits are earned. In this case, tax authorities extend tax coverage to income earned abroad if it is not currently covered by foreign tax jurisdictions. Once again, a mix of the two tax approaches is necessary for full coverage of income.

Quick Take Google's Double Irish/Dutch Sandwich Global Tax Strategy

Google, the dominant Internet search engine that is famous for encouraging all employees to *Do no evil* in the company code of conduct, has been the subject of much scrutiny over its global tax strategy in recent years. Google's effective overseas tax rate (average effective tax on all foreign income) was 2.4 percent in 2010 on more than $13 billion in sales. Google's overall tax rate, taxes paid in total globally on pre-tax earnings, has averaged roughly 22 percent in recent years. Google's tax strategy is executed through a complex structure shown in the exhibit.

Google's structure is one used by a multitude of U.S. multinationals today. It is based on repositioning the ownership of many of its patents, copyrights, and other intellectual property to a subsidiary in a low-tax environment like Ireland, and then establishing high transfer prices on various forms of services and overheads to other units, leaving most of the profits in a near-zero tax environment like Bermuda. There is nothing inherently illegal about Google's tax strategy. The company negotiated with the U.S. tax authority, the Internal Revenue Service (IRS) for years, eventually gaining IRS consent in what is known as an *advanced pricing agreement*.

Google's Global Tax Strategy: The Double Irish and Dutch Sandwich

Double Irish. **Google books nearly 90 percent of its non-US sales through Google Ireland, which then pays billions in royalties to Google Ireland Holdings – which has its effective management centre in Bermuda.**

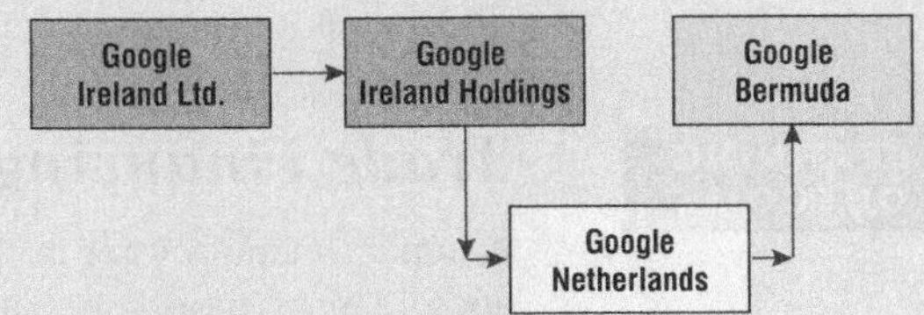

Dutch Sandwich. **To avoid withholding taxes on the payments by Ireland to Bermuda, the money is first passed through the Netherlands, taking advantage of intra-European tax treaties. Bermuda does not impose a corporate income tax on foreign-source income as earned by Google Bermuda here.**

The predominance of territorial systems has grown rapidly, as more than half of these same OECD countries used worldwide systems only ten years ago. In 2009 alone, both Japan and the United Kingdom switched from worldwide to territorial.

Tax Types

Taxes are generally classified as direct and indirect. **Direct taxes** are calculated on the actual income of an individual or a firm. **Indirect taxes**, such as sales taxes, severance taxes, tariffs, and value-added taxes, are applied to purchase prices, material costs, quantities of natural resources mined, and so forth. Although most countries still rely on income taxes as the primary method of raising revenue, tax structures vary widely.

A **value-added tax (VAT)** is the primary revenue source for the European Union. A VAT is applied to the amount of product value added by the production process. The tax is calculated as a percentage of the product price, less the cost of materials and inputs used in its manufacture, which have been taxed previously. Through this process, tax revenues are collected literally on the value added by that specific stage of the production process. Under the existing General Agreement on Tariffs and Trade (GATT), the legal framework under which international trade operates, value-added taxes may be levied on imports into a country or group of countries (such as the European Union) in order to treat foreign producers entering the domestic markets on a par with firms within the country paying VAT. Similarly, VAT may

DIRECT TAXES
Taxes applied directly to income

INDIRECT TAXES
Taxes applied to nonincome items, such as value-added taxes, excise taxes, tariffs, and so on

VALUE-ADDED TAX (VAT)
A tax on the value added at each stage of the production and distribution process; a tax assessed in most European countries and also common among Latin American countries

be refunded on export sales or sales to tourists who purchase products for consumption outside the country or community.

Financing Import/Export Operations

Unlike most domestic business, international business often occurs between two parties that do not know each other well and may be physically separated from each other by thousands of miles. Yet, in order to conduct business, a large degree of financial trust must exist.

An order from a foreign buyer may, for instance, constitute a degree of *credit risk* (the risk of not being repaid) that the producer (the exporter) cannot afford to take. Other factors that tend to intensify this problem include the increased lag times necessary for international shipments and the potential risks of payments in different currencies. For this reason, arrangements that provide guarantees for exports are important to countries and companies wanting to expand international activities. This can be accomplished through a sequence of documents surrounding the **letter of credit (L/C)**.

LETTER OF CREDIT (L/C)
Undertaking by a bank to make payment to a seller upon completion of a set of agreed-on conditions

Trade Financing Using a Letter of Credit

A lumber manufacturer in the Pacific Northwest, Vanport, receives a large order from a Japanese construction company, Endaka, for a shipment of old-growth pine lumber. Vanport has not worked with Endaka before and therefore seeks some assurance that payment will actually be made. Vanport ordinarily does not require any assurance of the buyer's ability to pay (sometimes a small down payment or deposit is made as a sign of good faith), but an international sale of this size is too large a risk. If Endaka could not or would not pay, the cost of returning the lumber products to the United States would be prohibitive. Figure 9.5 illustrates the following sequence of events that will complete the transaction.

1. Endaka Construction (Japan) requests a letter of credit (L/C) to be issued by its bank, Yokohama Bank.
2. Yokohama Bank determines whether Endaka is financially sound and capable of making the payments as required. This is a very important step because Yokohama Bank simply wants to guarantee the payment, not make the payment.
3. Yokohama Bank, once satisfied with Endaka's application, issues the L/C to a representative in the United States or to the exporter's bank, Pacific First Bank (U.S.). The L/C guarantees payment for the merchandise if the goods are shipped as stipulated in the accompanying documents. Customary documents include the commercial invoice, a customs clearance and invoice, the packing list, a certification of insurance, and a bill of lading.
4. The exporter's bank, Pacific First, assures Vanport that payment will be made, after evaluating the letter of credit. At this point, the credit standing of Yokohama Bank has been substituted for the credit standing of the importer itself, Endaka Construction.
5. When the lumber order is ready, it is loaded onboard the shipper (called a common carrier). When the exporter signs a contract with a shipper, the signed contract, or the bill of lading, serves as the receipt that the common carrier has received the goods.
6. Vanport draws a draft against Yokohama Bank for payment. The draft is the document used in international trade to effect payment and explicitly requests payment for the merchandise, which is now shown to be shipped and insured, consistent with all requirements of the previously issued L/C. (If the draft is issued to the bank issuing the L/C, Yokohama Bank, it is termed a bank draft. If the draft is issued against the importer, Endaka Construction, it is a trade draft.) The draft, L/C, and other appropriate documents are presented to Pacific First Bank for payment.

7. If Pacific First has confirmed the letter of credit from Yokohama Bank, it will immediately pay Vanport for the lumber and then collect from the issuing bank, Yokohama. If Pacific First has not confirmed the letter of credit, it only passes the documents to Yokohama Bank for payment (to Vanport). The confirmed, as opposed to unconfirmed, letter of credit obviously speeds up payment to the exporter. If the trade relationship continues over time, both parties will gain faith and confidence in the other.

FIGURE 9.5 Trade Financing with a Letter of Credit (L/C)

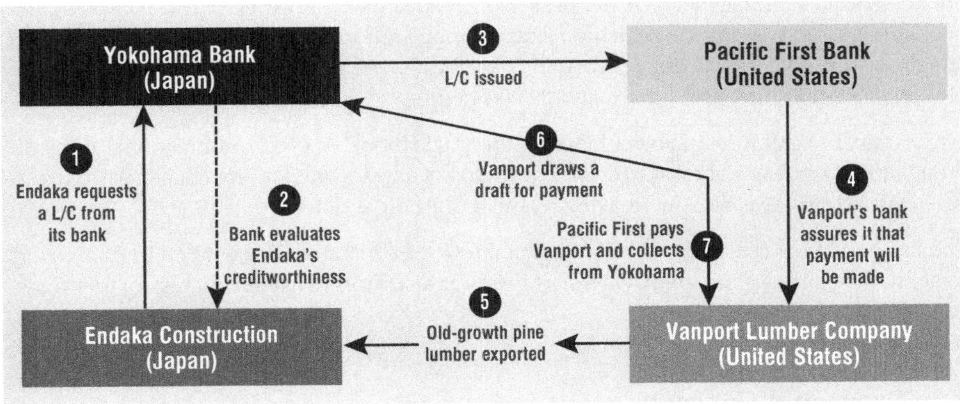

With this strengthening of financial trust, the trade financing relationship will loosen. Sustained buyer-seller relations across borders eventually end up operating on an open account basis similar to domestic commerce.

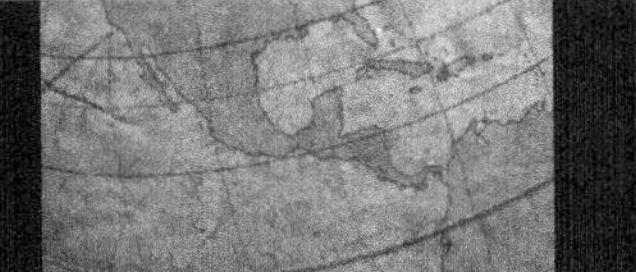

SUMMARY

The corporation is a legal entity, which poses both opportunities and challenges when conducting global business similar to that of a person. The corporation is governed by a series of structures, parties, and practices, which are expected to drive it to operate in the best interests of key stakeholders. Who those key stakeholders are—either shareholders or shareholders plus other vested interests—dictates how it will operate and generate returns to those interests. 

All traditional functional areas of financial management are affected by the internationalization of the firm. Capital budgeting, firm financing, capital structure, working capital, and cash flow management, as well as all traditional accounting and taxation functions, are made more difficult by business activities that cross borders and oceans, not to mention currencies and markets. 

Capital budgeting allows firms to predict the likely profitability of projects before any foreign investment is made. Due to currency fluctuations, a project that appears profitable to a local subsidiary may not seem so to the parent company. The choice among various cash flow 

management methods depends on the host-country government and stage of capital market liberalization.

In addition to the traditional areas of financial management, international financial management must deal with the three types of currency exposure: (1) transaction exposure, (2) economic exposure, and (3) translation exposure. Each presents serious choices regarding its exposure analysis and its degree of willingness to manage the inherent risks.

Accounting practices differ substantially across countries. The efforts of a number of international associates and agencies in the past two decades have, however, led to increasing cooperation and agreement among national accounting authorities. Real accounting differences remain, and many of these differences still contribute to the advantaged competitive position of some countries' firms over international competitors.

International taxation is a subject close to the pocketbook of every multinational firm. Although the tax policies of most countries are theoretically designed to not change or influence financial and business decision making by firms, they often do.

The letter of credit provides a system of guarantees for companies engaging in import-export trade, reducing the risk of nonpayment for goods and services delivered in cross-border transactions.

Key Terms and Concepts

corporation
stakeholders
stake
interest
rights
ownership stake
Shareholder Wealth Maximization Model (SWM)
Stakeholder Capitalism Model (SCM)
economic channel
moral channel
public ownership
private ownership
net present value (NPV)
capital budget
capital outlays
operating cash flows
terminal cash flows
capital structure
equity
debt
debt-equity structure
working capital management
financing cash flows
netting
cash pooling
leads
lags
re-invoicing
internal bank
transaction exposure
hedging
operational hedging
contractual hedging
economic exposure
translation exposure
accounting diversity.
worldwide approach to taxation
territorial approach to taxation
direct taxes
indirect taxes
value-added tax (VAT)
letter of credit (L/C)

Review Questions

1. Why is it important to identify the cash flows of a foreign investment from the perspective of the parent firm rather than from just the project?
2. How would the capital structure of a purely domestic firm differ from that of a firm with multiple international subsidiaries?
3. Which type of firm do you believe is more "naturally hedged" against exchange-rate exposure, the purely domestic firm (the barber) or the multinational firm (subsidiaries all over the world)?
4. What is the nature of the purported benefit that accounting principles provide British firms over American firms in the competition for mergers and acquisitions?
5. Why do you think foreign subsidiaries in which U.S. corporations hold more than 50 percent voting power are classified and treated differently for U.S. tax purposes?

6. Why do the U.S. tax authorities want U.S. corporations to charge their foreign subsidiaries for general and administrative services? What does this mean for the creation of excess foreign tax credits by U.S. corporations with foreign operations?
7. What is value-added tax and what benefits or drawbacks does it entail for European companies?
8. How can an exporter of goods or services protect itself against nonpayment? Describe the process.

Critical Skill Builders

1. As a manufacturer and marketer of hard candies, your company has decided to relocate its operations to Mexico, where the costs of raw materials—i.e., sugar—and labor will increase efficiency. At the same time, your company plans to develop new markets in South America and China. What aspects of capital structure and risk exposure must be taken into consideration?
2. In small groups, discuss this potential dilemma: "High political risk requires companies to seek a quick payback on their investments. Striving for a quick payback, however, exposes firms to charges of exploitation and results in increased political risk."
3. Do you think all firms, in all economic environments, should operate under the same set of accounting principles? Name two major indications that progress is being made toward standardizing accounting principles across countries.
4. After you hand your passport to the immigration officer in country X, he misplaces it. A small "donation" would certainly help him find it again. Should you give him the money? Is this a business expense to be charged to your company? Should it be tax deductible?
5. As a company expands into the global business arena and establishes wholly owned subsidiaries abroad, new financial challenges appear. These include managing cash flow across international borders and financing the subsidiary using international security markets. Subsidiaries abroad also require a new perspective on such issues as accounting practices and taxation. Create a brief financial plan of action for a company making its first moves in foreign markets.

On the Web

1. Using the following major periodicals as starting points, find a current example of a firm with a substantial operating exposure problem. To aid in your search, you might focus on businesses that have major operations in countries with recent currency crises, either through devaluation or major home-currency appreciation. Sources include the *Financial Times*, *The Economist*, and *The Wall Street Journal*.
2. In the World Trade Organization's Agreement on Government Procurement, how are offsets defined and what stance is taken toward them? Refer to the government procurement page on the WTO's web site.
3. The Financial Accounting Standards Board (FASB) promulgates standard practices for the reporting of financial results by U.S. companies. However, it also often leads the way in the development of new practices and emerging issues around the world. One such major issue today is the valuation and reporting of financial derivatives and derivative agreements by firms. Use the FASB's web site and sites for major accounting firms and other interest groups around the world to see current proposed accounting standards and reactions to them.

PART 5

GLOBAL OPERATIONS

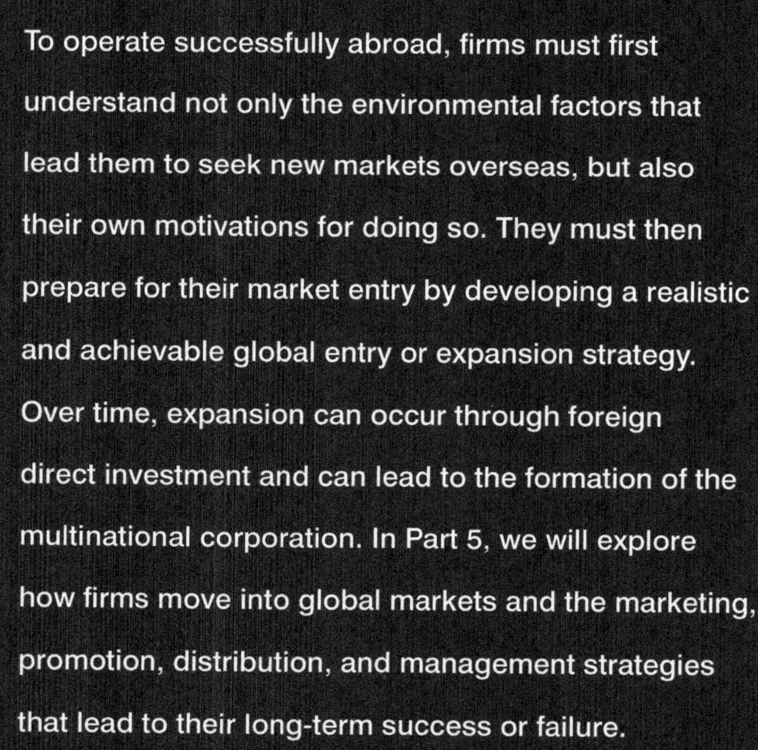

To operate successfully abroad, firms must first understand not only the environmental factors that lead them to seek new markets overseas, but also their own motivations for doing so. They must then prepare for their market entry by developing a realistic and achievable global entry or expansion strategy. Over time, expansion can occur through foreign direct investment and can lead to the formation of the multinational corporation. In Part 5, we will explore how firms move into global markets and the marketing, promotion, distribution, and management strategies that lead to their long-term success or failure.

CHAPTER 10

EXPORTING AND GLOBAL EXPANSION

Apples Go International

What are apples from the state of Virginia doing in Cuba? Well, for one thing, they're making a profit. The Virginia Apple Growers Association (VAGA) decided to take its products, eleven different varieties of apples, overseas. To do so, the VAGA created an export trading company (ETC) called the Virginia Apple Trading Company (VATC). By sharing the costs of finding clients, marketing their products abroad, and shipping and transportation, an international presence became possible for Virginia apple growers. Furthermore, because of U.S. ETC antitrust legislation, participating growers can act jointly to set export prices and share product and market information, enabling them to act more like a large company than many small ones. VAGA eventually awarded the management contract for the ETC to GIC Group, a U.S. agribusiness consulting and investment advisory firm.

Today, Virginia growers ship apples and processed apple products, such as applesauce and apple juice, to more than twenty countries and regions including: Central America, Caribbean, Cuba, Mexico, Brazil, Russia, Scandinavia, United Kingdom, and India. In Virginia, apple growing is an important economic activity. Apple orchards cover more than 16,000 acres of the landscape, and apple growers contribute an estimated $235 million to the economy. The United States produces about 250 million bushels of apples annually—that's enough for almost one bushel for every person! (1 bushel = approximately 42 pounds). However, the average American consumer only eats about nineteen pounds of fresh apples, four pounds of canned apples, and 1.7 gallons of apple juice. This excess capacity is an obvious motivation for going international.

However, for a small private business, going international is a daunting task. Therefore, for these apple growers an ETC arrangement became not only practical, but also necessary. Although relatively few export trading companies exist in the United States, their services have enabled thousands of small- and medium-sized business to tap the potential of the international marketplace.

SOURCES: **www.virginiaapples.org**, accessed July 23, 2014; **www.vermontapples.org** accessed July 23, 2014; **http://www.gicgroup.com/gc_exportpromo.html**, accessed July 23, 2014; **http://www.vdacs.virginia.gov/international/vatc-english.shtml**, accessed July 23, 2014.

LEARNING OUTCOMES

1. ***To understand ways in which changes in the global environment encourage globalization of businesses and consider why firms begin international activities***
2. ***To examine external and internal factors that determine global strategy formulation and resources allocation***
3. ***To gain an understanding of the need for international research and learn how information is gathered and interpreted***
4. ***To evaluate the various modes of entering the international market without setting up local operations, including importing/exporting, management contracts, licensing, and franchising***
5. ***To explore the implications of various levels of ownership in overseas operations***

As You Read This Chapter

1. How can a producer from a high-cost country (e.g., the United States) compete in a low-cost nation, such as Cuba?
2. What can governments do to encourage smaller firms to expand their operations abroad?

Rapid transformation of the world marketplace forces companies both large and small to look outward from their domestic markets, not only for future growth, but also for survival. This chapter begins by exploring the motivations that drive companies to enter new markets, thus leading them to formulate global strategies that take advantage of underlying market, cost, competitive, and environmental factors—a knowledge that is gained by thorough international business research. The chapter then shows the various options open to companies that are preparing to begin or expand their international activities. Even though new markets are constantly emerging, firms cannot simply jump into the international marketplace and expect to be successful. They must recognize and adjust to needs and opportunities abroad; have quality, in-demand products; understand their customers; and do their homework.

This chapter begins by providing a detailed guide to the structure and functions of the foreign currency markets. It then explores the international financial markets and the securities markets that connect the financial markets of individual nations. All firms striving to attain or preserve competitiveness in the global arena must work with and within the frameworks of these markets, which operate independently of the jurisdiction or supervision of governmental authorities.

Globalization Drivers

Several external and internal factors drive the development of a global marketplace. These can be divided into market, cost, environmental, and competitive factors.

1. *Market factors*: Similarities in demand conditions across multiple countries encourage the development of single global strategies. For example, in markets as far-flung as North America, Europe, and the Far East, consumer groups share similar educational backgrounds, income levels, lifestyles, use of leisure time, and aspirations. With approximately two billion people reaching middle class status in emerging markets, segments of these consumers can in many ways be treated as a single market with the same spending habits.[1] Global distribution channels, as well as advances in technology, also serve to ease the process of conducting business on a global scale.
2. *Cost factors*: Avoiding cost inefficiencies and duplication of effort are two of the most powerful globalization drivers. Often, single-country populations are simply not large enough for a firm to achieve meaningful economies of scale. In pharmaceuticals, for example, the cost of developing a new blockbuster drug can exceed $4 billion. Only a global market can offset the risks of escalating R&D costs.[2] The same is true in the consumer goods sector, where a new brand launch from P&G or Unilever can cost up to $100 million.
3. *Environmental factors*: As explored in Chapter 3, the falling of government and fiscal barriers to trade has facilitated the globalization of markets and the activities of companies

within them. Rapid technological advances also contribute to the process. Newly emerging markets, in particular, benefit from technological advances that allow them to leapfrog over stages of economic development.

4. *Competitive factors*: Global strategies are often necessary to prevent competitors from gaining undue advantage, not only overseas but also in the home market. If a competitor manufactures on a global scale and therefore achieves global economies of scale, it can undercut prices in the home market. When McAfee lowered its prices to lure customers from its competitor, Symantec, the world's largest security software developer responded in kind by dropping prices on like products by as much as 70 percent. Similarly, global strategies can be used to thwart the growth potential of competitors. Caterpillar faced mounting global competition from Komatsu but found that strengthening its products and operations was not enough to meet the challenge. Although Japan was a small part of the world market, as a secure home base (no serious competitors), it generated 80 percent of Komatsu's cash flow. To put a check on its major global competitor's market share and cash flow, Caterpillar formed a joint venture with Mitsubishi to serve the electric truck market in Japan.[3]

A Comprehensive View of International Expansion

The central driver of internationalization is the level of managerial commitment to overseas expansion. Commitment grows gradually from an awareness of the potential of foreign markets and eventually leads to the company embracing international business as a strategic imperative. Management commitment triggers various international business activities, ranging from indirect exporting and importing to direct involvement in the global market. Eventually, the firm may expand further through measures such as strategic alliances, joint ventures, or foreign direct investment.

All of the processes and decisions involved in developing the commitment to go international are linked to one another. A comprehensive view of these links is presented schematically in Figure 10.1.

FIGURE 10.1 A Comprehensive Model of International Market Entry and Development

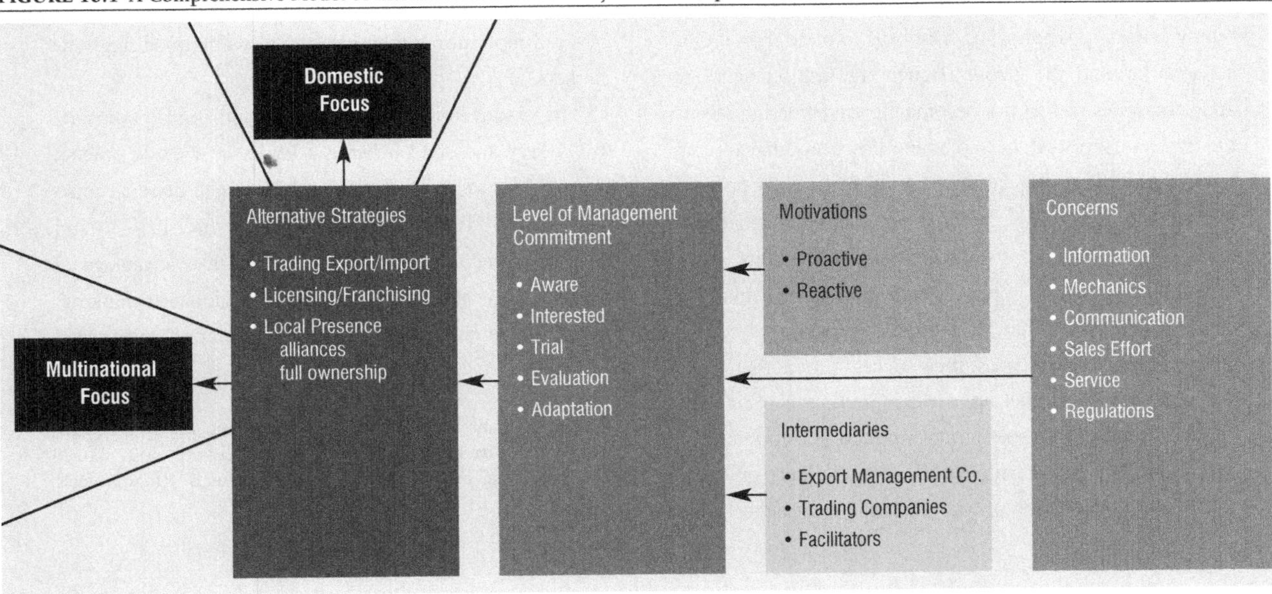

Why Go Global?

The four globalization drivers described so far explain why globalization has emerged as a business strategy. Table 10.1 summarizes the major reasons that prompt small and mid-size firms to make their first moves into overseas markets. These are divided into proactive motivations (or why companies *want* to go global) and reactive motivations (or why they *have* to do so).

PROACTIVE MOTIVATIONS Profits are the major proactive motivation. In order to increase profits, companies may look either to increase sales volume by selling into new markets or to reduce costs by producing overseas. However, the expectation of higher profits may not occur right away. Particularly in start-up operations, the cost of setting up often reduces initial profitability. Even with thorough planning, unexpected influences—such as shifts in exchange rates, for example—can change the profit picture substantially.

Unique products or technological advantage are another major stimulus, assuming, of course, that the product is in demand in foreign markets and is not available from competitors. The firm must consider, too, how long any unique product advantage will last. The fast pace of technology, the creativity of competitors, and the lack of adequate international patent protection all shorten product life-spans in foreign markets.

Special knowledge about foreign customers or market situations may be another proactive stimulus. It is usually short term because competitors quickly catch up with the information advantage.

Quick Take *Mininationals Leap into Global Markets*

Only a short time ago, Cheryl Schaefer Alves was creating and selling handbags out of her home. Today her company, Sunny Hawaii, is wholesaling handbags to more than 4,000 accounts around the globe. Though the fashion handbag and accessories market has become more crowded in recent times, Alves says that her company has been able to stay on top of fast-moving fashion trends with its "tropically inspired" handbags. By moving her manufacturing process to China, she has cut costs and increased profitability.

Sunny Hawaii is a prime example of the small to medium-sized firms that are reinventing the global corporation. Termed *mininationals*, their success proves that sheer size is no longer a buffer against competition, especially in markets that demand specialized products. Electronic process technology allows mininationals to compete on price and quality—often with greater flexibility than larger rivals can manage. In today's open trading regions, they are able to serve the world from a handful of manufacturing bases. Less red tape means they can move swiftly in seizing new markets.

The lessons from these new-generation global players are to (1) keep focused on being a leader in a market niche; (2) stay lean to save on costs and accelerate decision making; (3) take ideas and technologies international—to and from wherever they can be found; (4) take advantage of employees, regardless of nationality, to globalize thinking; and (5) solve customers' problems by creating customized solutions.

SOURCES: Frank Meyer, "How Can Small Agencies Land the Big Fish," **emailwire.com**, February 19, 2008, accessed July 22, 2014; Nina Wu, "Small firm goes global by staying focused" *Pacific Business News*, March 5, 2006.

Tax benefits also motivate overseas sales. If government uses preferential tax treatment to encourage exports, firms either are able to compete by offering low prices in foreign markets or are able to accumulate higher profits.

A final proactive motivation involves economies of scale. International activities may enable a firm to increase output and therefore rise more rapidly on the learning curve. Increased production for international markets can help reduce the cost of production for domestic sales and make the firm more competitive at home, too.

TABLE 10.1 Motivations for International Business

Proactive	Reactive
Profit advantage	Competitive pressures
Unique products	Overproduction
Technological advantage	Declining domestic sales
Exclusive information	Excess capacity
Tax benefit	Saturated domestic markets
Economies of scale	Proximity to customers and ports

REACTIVE MOTIVATIONS Reactive motivations influence firms to seek out new markets due to change or pressures in the domestic economy. Competitive pressures are one example. A company may fear losing domestic market share to competing firms that have benefited from economies of scale gained through international business activities. Further, it may fear losing foreign markets permanently by literally missing the boat when competitors expand overseas.

Overproduction is another reactive motivation. During downturns in the domestic business cycle, foreign markets can provide an ideal outlet for excess inventories. A mistake some firms make is to withdraw from foreign markets once domestic demand bounces back. International customers may prove "once bitten, twice shy"—they are not interested in temporary or sporadic business relationships.

Declining domestic sales, whether measured in sales volume or market share, are a key motivator. A product at the end of its domestic life cycle may find new markets overseas. High-tech products outmoded by the latest innovation are a good example. Some hospitals, for instance, may be much better off acquiring lower cost, "just-dated" MRI equipment than waiting until they have funding for the latest state-of-the-art technologies.

Excess capacity is a powerful motivator. If equipment is not fully utilized, firms may see expansion abroad as an ideal way to achieve broader distribution of fixed costs. Alternatively, if all fixed costs are assigned to domestic production, the firm can—at least in the short term—penetrate foreign markets with a pricing scheme that focuses mainly on variable cost. In the longer term, however, such pricing may lead to charges of dumping.

The reactive motivation of a saturated domestic market has similar results to that of declining domestic sales. Again, firms in this situation can use the international market to prolong the life of their goods and even of their organization.

A final reactive motivation is proximity to customers and ports. A firm located near a border may sell into the neighboring country without even thinking of itself as international.

Strategic Planning for Global Expansion

Taking advantage of the global marketplace requires long-term planning. Figure 10.2 summarizes the stages decision-makers go through when formulating a global strategy. The planning process starts with a complete assessment of the business. Although a later section in this chapter explores the critical role of research in selecting markets and launching products in those selected, this section provides an overview of the self-assessment process a firm must undergo before developing global entry or expansion strategies. In practice, analysis focuses on three areas: (1) level of management commitment, (2) internal organizational factors, and (3) market and competition.

FIGURE 10.2 Global Strategy Formulation

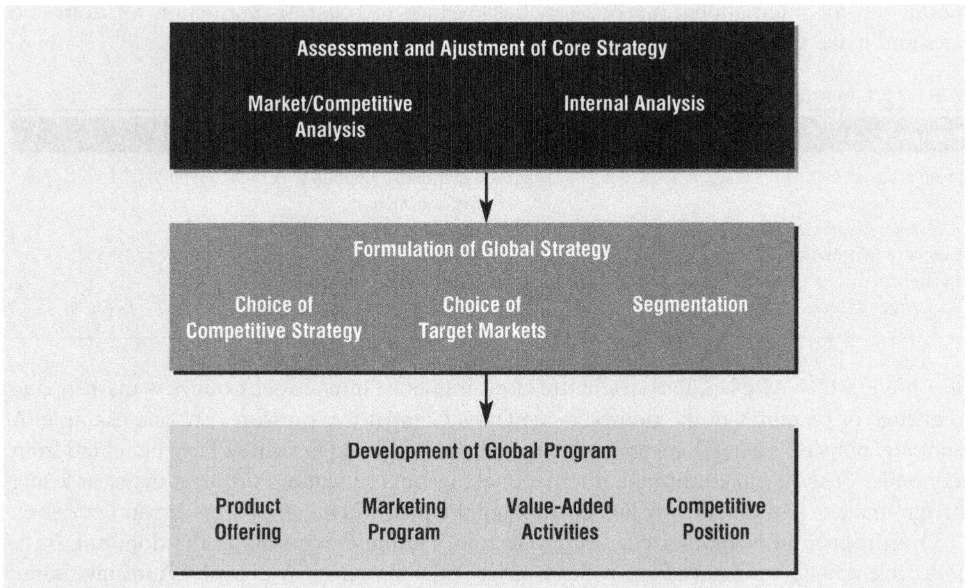

The authors appreciate the contributions of Robert M. Grant in the preparation of this figure.

Management Commitment

MANAGERIAL COMMITMENT
The desire and drive on the part of management to act on an idea and to support it in the long run

The issue of **managerial commitment** is a critical one because foreign market penetration requires a vast amount of market development activity, sensitivity toward foreign environments, research, and innovation. All of this takes time, resources, and expertise. To nurture commitment, it is important to involve all levels of management early on in the international planning process and to impress on all players that the effort will succeed only if the entire firm is behind it.

The first step in developing commitment is to become aware of international business opportunities. Management must then determine the degree and timing of the firm's internationalization. For example, a German corporation that expands its operation to the neighboring countries of Austria, Switzerland, or Belgium is less international than one that launches operations in Japan and Brazil. Further, a company that enters markets selectively is less international than one that attempts to enter multiple global markets from the outset. With regard to timing, immediate market entry might be a priority because clients are waiting for the product or because competitors are moving in on the same market. A successful global strategy hinges on management agreement and support regarding both degree and timing of international activities.

Company-wide international orientation does not develop overnight but rather needs time to grow. It is a matter of learning, of acquiring experiential knowledge. A firm must learn about foreign markets and institutions but also about its own internal resources in order to know what it is capable of when exposed to new and unfamiliar conditions. Planning and execution of an export venture must be incorporated into the firm's strategic management process, which become increasingly crucial as markets around the world become more linked and more competitive.

Internal Organizational Factors

A thorough assessment of internal organizational resources is a critical early step in determining a company's capacity for establishing and sustaining competitive advantage within global markets. Expansion may require a prolonged period of financial investment before returns are realized. In terms of human resources, expansion requires experienced and culturally wise managers, often in short supply. In many cases, commitment to expand internationally means depriving other areas of the organization of valuable resources. When Starbucks acquired La Boulange, it was moving to improve the quality of its food offerings after deliberately focusing on the global coffee business for years rather than focusing peripheral products, like baked goods and sandwiches.[4]

Market and Competition Analysis

Market and competition analysis usually starts with an overview of different regions and then further splits into analysis by country. Regional groupings are particularly helpful if they help identify similarities in demographic and behavioral traits. For example, dividing Europe into northern, central, and southern regions provides for easier analysis than treating it as a single market. An important consideration is that data may be more readily available if existing structures and frameworks are used.[5] In general, as a later section on international business research explains more fully, factors to consider when analyzing markets and competition include market size, growth potential, the number and type of competitors, government regulations, and economic and political activity.

Competitive Strategy Formulation

The firm has three general choices of strategies: (1) cost leadership, (2) differentiation, and (3) focus.[6] Any one of these can be pursued on a global or regional basis, or the firm may decide to mix and match strategies as a function of market or product dimensions.

In pursuing **cost leadership strategy**, the company offers an identical product or service at a lower cost than its competitors do. This often means investment in scale economies and strict control of costs, such as overhead, research and development, and logistics. A **differentiation strategy**, whether it is industry-wide or focused on a single segment, takes advantage of the product's real or perceived uniqueness on elements such as design or after-sales service. Starbucks brand, for example, is a standout among Japan's coffee-shop culture, largely due to brand and taste, but also because of the spacious and smoke-free store environment. Differentiation strategies do not, however, ignore the critical importance of containing costs or offering competitive prices. IKEA, for example, built a clear positioning and unique brand image around products aimed at "young people of all ages"—low price for quality goods was central to IKEA's appeal.

Through a **focus strategy**, a firm concentrates on a single industry segment, like Starbucks in the earlier example. A focus strategy may be oriented toward either low cost or differentiation.

Most global companies combine high differentiation with cost containment to enter markets or expand their market shares. As discussed further in Chapter 12, flexible manufacturing systems, standard components, and tight supply chains allow companies to customize an increasing amount of their production while at the same time saving on costs. Global activi-

COST LEADERSHIP STRATEGY
The ability of a firm to price its output lower than the competition due to efficiencies in production

DIFFERENTIATION STRATEGY
Takes advantage of the company's real or perceived uniqueness on elements such as design or after-sales service

FOCUS STRATEGY
A deliberate concentration on a single industry segment

ties permit the exploitation of scale economies not only in production but also in marketing activities.

INTERNATIONAL BUSINESS RESEARCH

The single most important cause for failure in international business is insufficient preparation and information. Failure to comprehend cultural disparities, failure to remember that customers differ from country to country, and failure to investigate whether or not a market exists prior to entry has made international business a high-risk activity.[7] International business research is instrumental to international business success because it permits the firm to take into account different environments, attitudes, and market conditions.

Why Conduct Research?

Many firms do little research before they enter a foreign market. Often, decisions concerning entry and expansion or selection of distributors are made after a cursory, subjective assessment. Research is all too often far less rigorous, less formal, and less quantitative than for domestic activities.

The reasons are many and begin with a lack of sensitivity to differences in cultures, consumer tastes, and market demands. Further, many firms—perhaps in an effort to close their eyes to potential difficulties—are unwilling to accept that a country's labor rules, distribution systems, availability of media, or advertising regulations may be entirely different from those in the home market. Often, a lack of familiarity with national and international data sources, the perceived expense of data collection (despite the growing number of low-cost Internet sources), and an inability to apply data obtained explain why firms neglect research. In many cases, research is overlooked simply because firms tend to build their international business activities gradually, often based on unsolicited orders. Over time, experience is used as a substitute for organized research.

Despite such reservations, research is as (or more) important globally than it is domestically. It not only shines a spotlight on new opportunities, but it exposes risk. It is vital in strategy development, as it is the means of identifying all the requirements of market entry, penetration, and expansion. On a continuing basis, research provides the feedback needed to fine-tune business activities, anticipate future events, and prepare for change.

Pre-Entry Research

Figure 10.3 provides a summary of the various stages through which companies research and assess the potential of export markets. The research process begins with a cursory analysis of general variables of a country, including total and per capita gross national product (GNP), mortality rates, and population figures. These factors enable the researcher to determine whether corporate objectives might be met in the market. For example, high-priced consumer products might not succeed in China, as their price may be equal to the customer's annual salary, customer benefits may be minimal, and the government is likely to prohibit importation of the product. A preliminary screening helps reduce the number of markets to be considered to a manageable number.

The next step is to amass information on promising country markets, including rate of growth, governmental or other restrictions, and demand trends within the targeted industry. Although precise data on individual products may not be obtainable, general product or service category information usually is. Although this overview is still cursory, it serves to quickly evaluate markets and further reduce their number.

FIGURE 10.3 A Sequential Process of Researching Foreign Market Potentials

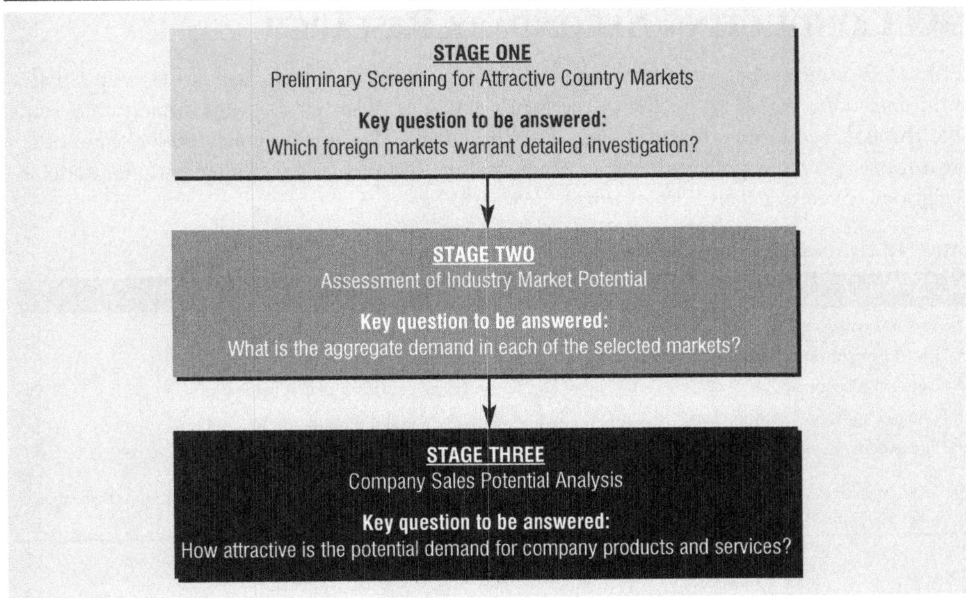

SOURCE: S. Tamer Cavusgil, "Guidelines for Export Market Research," *Business Horizons* 28 (November–December 1985): 29. Copyright 1985 by the Foundation for the School of Business at Indiana University. Reprinted by permission.

Next, it is time to select appropriate markets for in-depth evaluation. The focus is now on opportunities for a specific type of service, product, or brand, and research includes an assessment as to whether demand already exists or can be stimulated. Aggregate industry data alone may not suffice. For example, the demand for sports equipment should not be confused with the market potential for a specific new brand. The research should identify demand-and-supply patterns and evaluate any regulations and standards. This final stage also requires a competitive assessment, matching markets to corporate strengths and providing an analysis of the best potential for specific offerings.

Market Expansion Research

After initial market entry, research plays a critical role in global success. It allows firms to amass detailed information for possible business expansion. It also allows them to monitor the political climate so that the firm successfully can maintain its international operation. Research data enables international managers to evaluate new business partners or assess the impact of a technological breakthrough on future operations. The better defined the research objective is, the better the researcher will be able to determine information requirements and thus conserve the time and financial resources of the firm.

Culture Clues Note and observe national religious holidays. In parts of southern Spain, the summer heat has a major effect on daily work patterns and schedules.

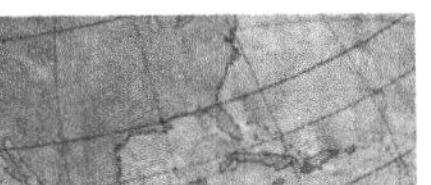

Conducting Secondary Research

SECONDARY RESEARCH
The collection and analysis of data originally collected to serve another purpose rather than the specific objectives of the firm

Table 10.2 demonstrates that firms require both macro data, related to countries and trade, and micro data, which is specific to the firm's activities. Both kinds of information are available through **secondary research**—that is, the use of data already collected by some other organization, such as governments, international institutions, service organizations, trade associations, directories, and other firms.

TABLE 10.2 Critical International Information

Macro Data	Micro Data
• Tariff information	• Local laws and regulations
• U.S. export/import data	• Size of market
• Nontariff measures	• Local standards and specifications
• Foreign export and import data	• Distribution system
• Data on government trade policy	• Competitive activity

SOURCE: Michael R. Czinkota, "International Information Needs for U.S. Competitiveness," *Business Horizons* 34, 6 (November–December 1991): 86–91.

Government Sources

Governments typically collect information on such macro issues as population trends, general trade flows among countries, and world agriculture production. They are also good sources of micro information, including data on specific industries, their growth prospects, and the extent and direction to which goods or servcies are traded. Although such information is often offered only in the local language, the fact that much of the data is numerical aids in the translation task. Embassies and consulates, as well as government-sponsored web sites or fee-based data libraries, are good places to start. The user should be cautioned, however, that the printed information is often dated and that the industry categories used abroad may not be compatible with industry categories used at home.

International Organizations

The *Statistical Yearbook* produced by the United Nations contains international trade data on products and provides information on exports and imports by country.

Because of the time needed for worldwide data collection, the information is often quite dated. Other more specialized sources include the following:

- United Nations Conference on Trade and Development (**http://www.unctad.org**): provides information on issues surrounding developing nations, such as debt and market access
- World Bank (**http://www.worldbank.org**): publishes the World Atlas, with general data on population, growth trends, and GNP figures; region- or country-specific economic data
- World Trade Organization (**http://www.wto.org**) and Organization for Economic Cooperation and Development (**http://www.oecd.org**): publish quarterly and annual trade data on member countries
- International Monetary Fund (**http://www.imf.org**): publishes summary economic data and occasional staff papers that evaluate region- or country-specific issues in depth

Electronic Information Services

International online computer database services, numbering in the thousands, are an excellent and not-too-expensive source of information external to the firm, such as exchange rates, international news, and import restrictions. Several databases offer product- and market-specific data, gleaned from systematic searches through a wide range of periodicals, reports, and books in different languages. Many of the main news agencies make market-specific information available through online databases. Some, like the Economist Intelligence Unit (**http://www.eiu.com**) provide extensive data on companies in given countries and the products they buy and sell. Of course, in many cases, the international organizations listed previously are the same ones that have been provided by countries. Therefore, these data are duplicative rather than offering a new accumulation or dissemination of data from individual nations.

Online databases are easier than ever to access and can provide valuable insights. For example, the U.S. Department of Commerce offers Global Business Opportunities (GLOBUS), which provides daily trade leads and international procurement opportunities. Over time, one can expect that most information will be delivered on an electronic basis. One example of an excellent data source is represented by **http://www.commercialdiplomacy.org**.[8]

In spite of the ease of access to up-to-the-minute data over the Internet, it must be remembered that search engines cover only a portion of international sources and are heavily biased toward English-language publications. As a result, a researcher who relies solely on electronic information may lose out on valuable input.[9]

SERVICE ORGANIZATIONS A wide variety of service organizations located around the world offer data, including banks, accounting firms, freight forwarders, airlines, international trade consultants, research firms, and publishing houses. Frequently, the organizations are able to provide information on business practices, legislative or regulatory requirements, and political stability, as well as trade and financial data.

TRADE ASSOCIATIONS World trade clubs as well as domestic and international chambers of commerce provide good information on trade flows and trends in local markets. Industry associations often collect a wide variety of data from members that are then published in aggregate form.

DIRECTORIES AND NEWSLETTERS Local, national, and international directories primarily serve to identify firms and to provide brief background data, such as the name of the CEO, the level of capitalization of the firm, contact information, and product descriptions. A host of newsletters discuss specific international business issues, such as international trade finance, legislative activities, countertrade, international payment flows, and customs news. They usually cater to niche audiences but offer important information in specific areas.

Fast Facts

Which nation was forced by the United States to open its doors to foreign trade?

Japan. The end of the Shogunate era in 1868 ushered in a new age, when Western ideas and trade first influenced Japanese thinking. Now, of course, the situation is reversed, with some nations decrying Japan's trade power

Interpreting Secondary Data

Once secondary data have been obtained, the next task is to convert them into useful, task-specific information. Secondary data should be evaluated regarding the quality of the source, recency, and relevance to the task at hand. Clearly, because the information was collected without the current research requirements in mind, there may well be difficulties in coverage, categorization, and comparability. For example, market penetration of digital recorders may be useful only as a proxy variable for the potential demand for DVD players. Similarly, in an industrial setting, information about plans for new port facilities may be useful in determining future container requirements.

Interpretation of data also requires a level of creative thinking. A researcher for a shipping company, for example, may need to interpret data about a new port facility to determine the potential demand for shipping containers. This requires creative inferences, and such creativity brings risks. Therefore, once interpretation and analysis have taken place, it is necessary to crosscheck the results with other possible sources of information or with experts.

Conducting Primary Research

PRIMARY RESEARCH
The collection and analysis of data for a specific research purpose through interviews, focus groups, surveys, observation, or experimentation

Even though secondary data are useful to the researcher, on many occasions **primary research** is necessary as well. Several worldwide research firms offer primary as well as secondary research services. Typically, primary research is necessary to obtain specific answers to specific questions:

- How much does the typical Spaniard spend on entertainment?
- What is the sales potential for our measuring equipment in India?
- What effect will our new engine have on our green consumers in Germany?
- What service standards do e-commerce customers expect in Japan?

The researcher must have a clear idea of what the population under study should be and where it is located before deciding on the country or region to investigate. It may not, for example, be necessary to conduct research across an entire country if the objective is to distribute into urban areas. In other cases, if the product will penetrate nationwide, differing economic, geographic, or behavioral factors may require multiple-region research. One firm, for example, conducted its research only in large Indonesian cities during the height of tourism season but projected the results to the entire population year around. Based on the results, the company set up large production and distribution facilities to meet the expected demand but realized only limited sales to city tourists.[10]

QUALITATIVE INFORMATION
Data that have been analyzed to provide a better understanding, description, or prediction of given situations, behavioral patterns, or underlying dimension— typically based on understanding of context rather than statistical data support

QUANTITATIVE INFORMATION
Data gathered in large masses to search for statistical significance or trends

Determining Research Techniques

Once the type of data sought is determined, the researcher must choose a research technique. As in domestic research, several types of research are available. Each provides different levels of objectivity or subjectivity, and each has its own unique strengths and weaknesses. When the required information is **qualitative** in nature, allowing for an understanding of given situations, behavioral patterns, or underlying dimensions of consumer choices, the best research techniques are personal interviews, focus groups, and observation. When **quantitative** results are required with statistical validity, then surveys and experimentation are the most appropriate research instruments.

PERSONAL INTERVIEWS
Face-to-face research method, the objective of which is to obtain in-depth information from a knowledgeable individual

Interviews

Personal interviews with knowledgeable people can be of great value. Individual bias, however, can slant the findings, so the intent should be to obtain not a wide variety of data, but rather in-depth information. When specific answers are sought to very narrow questions, interviews can be particularly useful.

FOCUS GROUP RESEARCH
A research method in which representatives of a proposed target audience contribute to market research by participating in an unstructured discussion

Focus Groups

In typical **focus group research**, a group of seven to ten knowledgeable people is gathered together for a limited period of time (two to four hours) to thoroughly discuss a specific topic. Focus groups are a highly efficient means of rapidly accumulating a substantial amount of information. Because of the interaction among participants, hidden issues are sometimes raised that are difficult to detect through personal interviews. The skill of the group leader in stimulating discussion is crucial to the success of a focus group. Focus groups do not provide statistically significant data but rather provide information about perceptions, emotions, and attitudinal factors.

When planning international research using focus groups, the researcher must be aware of the importance of language and culture in the interaction process. Even before the session begins, special preparation may be necessary. For example, in some countries, offering a fee is sufficient motivation for participants to open up in discussion. In other countries, it may be necessary to host a luncheon or dinner for the group so that members get to know each other and are willing to interact.

Once the session is under way, it is important to remember that not all societies encourage frank and open exchange and disagreement among individuals. Status consciousness may mean that the opinion of one participant is reflected by all others. Disagreement may be seen as impolite, or certain topics may be taboo. Unless a native focus group leader is used, it also is possible to completely misread the interactions among group participants and to miss nuances and constraints participants feel when making comments in a group setting.

Observation

Observation research requires the researcher to play the role of a nonparticipating observer of activity and behavior. In an international setting, observation can be extremely useful in shedding light on practices not previously encountered or understood. For example, Toyota sent a group of its engineers and designers to southern California to observe how women get into and operate cars. They found that women with long fingernails have trouble opening doors and operating various knobs on the dashboard. Toyota was then able to redesign some of its automobile exteriors and interiors, producing more desirable cars.[11]

OBSERVATION RESEARCH

A research method in which the subject's activity and behavior are watched

Survey Research

Survey research is useful in quantifying concepts. Surveys are usually conducted using questionnaires administered personally, by mail, or by telephone. Use of the survey technique presupposes that the population under study is accessible and able to comprehend and respond to questions posed. For mail surveys, a major precondition is the feasibility of using the postal system, which is not a given in all countries. Similarly, telephone or Web-based surveys may be inappropriate if telephone ownership or Internet access is rare. In such instances, even if the researcher randomized the calls, the results would be highly biased.

SURVEY RESEARCH

A research method involving the use of questionnaires delivered in person, by mail, telephone, or online to obtain statistically valid, quantifiable research information

Because surveys deal with people who, in an international setting, display major differences in culture, preference, education, and attitude, to mention just a few factors, the use of the survey technique must be carefully examined. For example, in some regions of the world, recipients of letters may be illiterate. Others may be very literate but totally unaccustomed to standard research-scaling techniques. Figure 10.4 provides an example of a rating scale

FIGURE 10.4 The Funny Faces Scale[12]

WORLD VIEW

Excellence in International Research

The Church of Jesus Christ of Latter-day Saints, commonly known as the Mormon Church, was organized by Joseph Smith in 1830 in New York. It has grown into an organization with 15 million members and congregations throughout the world, and is currently increasing at an average rate of about one million new members every three years. It generates close to $6 billion in annual income from its non-church-related businesses and enterprises and has $30 billion in assets. One of its key growth strategies is to send many of its 15 million worshipers abroad as missionaries. Therefore, the church has thousands of young and experienced travelers returning with foreign language skills and intercultural understanding. Indeed Utah, where the Mormon population is highly concentrated, has speakers fluent in 90 percent of the world's written languages, and 30 percent of its U.S.-born adult males speak a second language. Due to its large and globally educated work force, Utah is successfully attracting businesses such as Intel, eBay, American Express, and Goldman Sachs.

Young Mormon followers, nineteen to twenty-two years of age, are expected to go on a mission abroad for eighteen to twenty-four months. Currently, approximately 86,000 full-time missionaries serve in more than 405 mission districts around the world. Most missionaries learn new languages during their brief stay at the Missionary Training Centers, where about fifty different languages are taught, and become fully proficient during their stay abroad. In any country in which they are located, missionaries go door to door, promoting their religion and indirectly developing their sales skills. Young individuals are completely immersed in the culture, live among local families, and therefore have a personal understanding of the people of the country. Individuals with such extensive experience abroad can be great resources to companies as sources of global knowledge. Their personal insight into local cultures can help enlighten employers about marketing abroad.

CEOs in Utah note the diverse foreign language experience, high ethics, and family-oriented attitudes of the Mormon workforce as significant factors in the success of their businesses. Employers look for individuals who are not only well rounded but have a specific area of expertise. Having a workforce that knows foreign languages and has the experience of living abroad adds to a company's ability to research international markets.

SOURCES: "Utah CEOs Cite Cost Advantages, Ethics and Local Workforce as Top Reasons to Locate Companies Here," *PR Newswire US*, November 3, 2005; Earl Fry, and Wallace McCarlie, "Mapping Globalization along the Wasatch Front," Pacific Council on International Policy, , accessed February 19, 2008; "Mormon Missionary Numbers to rise—and then fall," *Salt Lake Tribune*, July 3, 2014; and The Church of Jesus Christ Latter-Day Saints, Newsroom, Facts and Statistics, **http://www.mormonnewsroom.org/facts-and-stats**, accessed March 16, 2014.

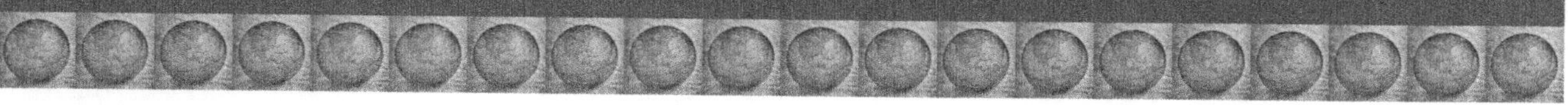

developed by researchers to work with a diverse population with relatively little education. In its use, however, it was found that the same scale aroused negative reactions among better-educated respondents, who considered the scale childish and insulting to their intelligence. Sometimes, recipients of a survey may be reluctant to respond in writing, particularly when sensitive questions are asked. In some nations, for example, information about income, even when requested in categorical form, is considered highly proprietary; in others, the purchasing behavior of individuals is not readily divulged.[13]

Experimentation

Experimental techniques determine the effect of an intervening variable and help establish precise cause-and-effect relationships. However, **experimentation** is difficult to implement in international research. The researcher faces the daunting task of designing an experiment in which most variables are held constant or are comparable across cultures. For example, an experiment to determine a causal effect within the distribution system of one country may be very difficult to transfer to another country because the distribution system may be quite different. For this reason, experimental techniques are only rarely used, even though their potential value to the international researcher is recognized.

EXPERIMENTATION
A research method capable of determining the effects of a variable on a situation

Ongoing Research

As stated earlier, many firms gradually build on their international activities without conducting any purposeful market-entry or expansion research. No matter what its stage of internationalization, however, any firm can benefit from creating what is known as an **information system** for collecting and centralizing timely, accurate, and accessible information on specific markets or on specific international activities. One type of information system that is particularly useful for international managers is the **export complaint system**, which allows customers to contact the original supplier abroad in order to inquire about products, make suggestions, or present complaints. Firms are finding that about 5 percent of customers abroad are dissatisfied with the product. By establishing direct contact using e-mail, a toll-free telephone number, or a web site, firms do not need to rely on the filtered feedback from channel intermediaries and can learn directly about product failures, channel problems, or other causes of customer dissatisfaction. The development of such an export complaint system requires substantial resources, intensive planning, and a high degree of cultural sensitivity. Customers abroad must be informed about how to complain, and their cost of complaining must be minimized—for example, by offering an interactive web site. The response to complaints must also be tailored to the culture of the complainant. Very important is the firm's ability to aggregate and analyze complaints and to make use of them internally. Complaints are often the symptom of underlying structural problems for a product or a process. If used properly, an export complaint system can become a rich source of information for product improvement and innovation.

INFORMATION SYSTEM
Can provide the decision maker with basic data for most ongoing decisions

EXPORT COMPLAINT SYSTEMS
Efforts of the firm to encourage international customers to allow final customers to contact the original supplier of a product in order to inquire about products, make suggestions, or present complaints

To build an information system, corporations use one or a combination of three mechanisms to obtain data: environmental scanning, Delphi studies, or scenario analyses.

1. *Environmental scanning*: Valuable for long-term strategic planning, **environmental scanning** involves the ongoing search and collection of political, social, and economic issues internationally. Data collected may also include information on changes or anticipated changes in the attitudes of public institutions and private citizens.
2. *Delphi studies*: To enrich the information obtained from factual data, corporations and governments frequently use creative and highly qualitative data-gathering methods. One approach is through **Delphi studies**. These studies are particularly useful in the international environment because they allow for the aggregation of information from experts who most likely cannot come together physically. Typically, Delphi studies are carried out with groups

ENVIRONMENTAL SCANNING
Obtaining ongoing data about a country, region, or condition

DELPHI STUDIES
A research tool using a group of participants with expertise in the area of concern to interact long term in order to predict and rank major future developments

Culture Clues Western managers in China joint ventures should take advantage of their positions as representatives of a prestigious entity to store up capital with local decision makers through *guanxi*, or relationships. These are a potent instrument in protecting one's interests. In fact, they are more powerful than written documents, which are seen as a necessary ritual when dealing with Westerners.

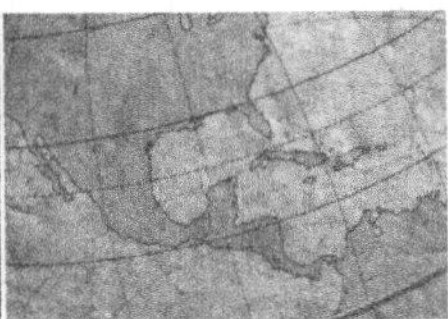

of about thirty well-chosen participants who possess expertise in an area of concern, such as future developments of the international trade environment. The participants are asked to identify major issues and to rank their statements on each according to importance. The aggregated information and comments are sent to all participants, who are then able to agree or disagree with the various rank orders and the comments. This allows statements to be challenged. In another round, the participants respond to the challenges. Several rounds of challenges and responses result in a reasonably coherent consensus. Increasingly conducted over the Internet, Delphi studies are able to bridge large distances and therefore make experts quite accessible at a reasonable cost. When carried out on a regular basis, the studies can provide crucial augmentation of the factual data. For example, a large portion of Chapter 15 is based on an extensive Delphi study carried out by the authors.

SCENARIO ANALYSIS
The identification of crucial variables and the investigation of the effects of their variations on business conditions

3. *Scenario analysis*: One approach to **scenario analysis** involves the development of a series of plausible scenarios that are constructed from trends observed in the environment. Another method consists of formally reviewing assumptions built into existing business plans and positions. Subsequently, some of these key assumptions, such as economic growth rates, import penetration, speed of international transportation, and political stability, can be varied. By projecting variations for medium- to long-term periods, completely new environmental conditions can emerge. The conditions can then be analyzed for their potential domestic and international impact on corporate strategy. For scenarios to be useful, management must analyze and respond to them by formulating contingency plans. Such planning will broaden horizons and may prepare managers for unexpected situations. Through the anticipation of possible problems, managers hone their response capability and in turn shorten response times to actual problems.

Target Country Selection

DIVERSIFICATION
A market expansion policy characterized by simultaneous entry and expansion growth in a relatively large number of markets or market segments

The choice of countries into which to expand depends on the firm's competitive strategy and the extent of market entry desired. The selection also involves decisions relating to market attractiveness, current company position, and allocation of resources. The basic alternatives are concentration on a small number of markets and **diversification**, which is characterized by growth in a relatively large number of markets. Perhaps the best example of diversification is provided by the Coca-Cola Company, which sells its branded products in 206 countries.[14]

In many cases, the choice of market is spurred by the convenience provided by geography. For a Canadian company looking to expand outside of Canada, the United States is an obvious consideration. In other cases, ease of access provided by government agreements makes certain countries attractive. For example, a company in a member country of the European Union will have numerous advantages in expanding to another member country. Or a U.S. company may look to countries with which the United States has a Free Trade Agreement, like Canada, Mexico, Colombia, or South Korea. Smart consumer companies look for countries with similar demographics or with similar commercial environments. The Spanish retail firm Inditex, parent company of Zara, seeks out countries that have shopping districts similar to New York's Soho or Brooklyn and Tokyo's Shibuya.[15]

Target Market Segmentation

MARKET SEGMENTATION
Grouping of consumers based on common characteristics such as demographics, lifestyles, and so on

Effective **market segmentation** recognizes that groups within markets differ sufficiently to warrant individual approaches. It allows global companies to take advantage of the benefits of standardization (such as economies of scale and consistency in positioning) while addressing the unique needs and expectations of specific target groups. The best example of a segment that spans country markets is the teen segment, which is converging as a result of common tastes in sports and music fueled by computer literacy, travels abroad, and in many countries, financial independence. Today's social media platforms like Facebook, Instagram, Flickr, and the Chinese WeChat, along with satellite TV and global network concepts such as MTV, not only help create the segment, but provide global companies access to the teen audience around the world.[16]

The greatest challenge for the global company is the choice of an appropriate basis for segmentation. The objective is to arrive at groupings that are not only substantial enough to merit the segmentation effort (for example the purchase power of global teens between the ages of twelve and nineteen was estimated to have reached $819 billion in 2012), but who are also reachable by the marketing effort. The possible bases for segmentation are summarized in Figure 10.5. Managers have traditionally used a combination of bases.

FIGURE 10.5 Bases for Global Market Segmentation

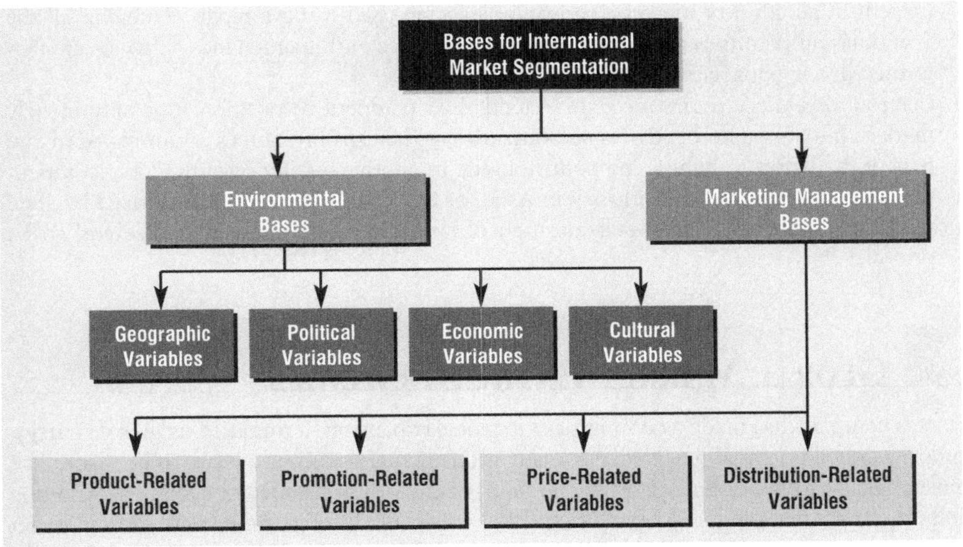

SOURCE: Imad B. Baalbaki and Naresh K. Malhotra, "Marketing Management Bases for International Market Segmentation: An Alternate Look at the Standardization/Customization Debate," International Marketing Review 10, 1 (1993): 19–44.

Global Program Development

Once target countries and segments have been identified, the firm must determine the parameters of its global program. This involves four key decisions:

1. *Degree of standardization in the product offering*: Although globalization involves some level of standardization in order to achieve economies of scale, different markets still demand some product customization. The need for localization varies by product and intended consumer segment. Fashion products can either focus on uniqueness or develop an appeal to sameness. Information technology products are susceptible to power requirements, keyboard configurations (e.g., Europe alone may require twenty different keyboards), instruction-manual language, and warning labels compliant with local regulations.
2. *Marketing program*: Nowhere is the need for the local touch as critical as in the execution of the marketing program. Although uniformity is important for strategic elements (for example, positioning), most firms take care to localize necessary tactical elements of the marketing program, such as advertising, pricing, and distribution. Sometimes, however, even the brand name can vary across countries. For example, P&G's leading cleaning liquid is sold

GLOCALIZATION
A term coined to describe the networked global organization approach to an organizational structure that also includes consideration of regional or local issues

under the brand name Mr. Clean in the United States, Mr. Propre in France, Meister Proper in Germany, and Don Limpio in Spain. This approach has been called **glocalization**.[17]

3. *Value-adding activities*: Globalization strives for cost reductions by pooling production or other activities or exploiting factor costs or capabilities. Rather than duplicating activities, a firm concentrates them in a single location. Many global companies, for example, establish R&D centers to serve multiple markets from one or more central bases. Some global companies are locating R&D centers in key emerging markets to seek innovative ideas that will be competitive in the unique conditions of these markets as well as in global markets. GE has located R&D centers in India and China to pursue what its CEO, Jeffrey Immelt, terms as "reverse innovation," when new ideas developed in emerging markets can be transferred globally.

   The quest for cost savings and improved transportation and transfer methods has allowed some marketers to concentrate customer service activities rather than having them present in all country markets. For example, Sony used to have repair centers in all the Scandinavian countries and Finland; today all service and maintenance activities are performed in a regional center in Stockholm, Sweden.

CROSS-SUBSIDIZATION
The use of resources accumulated in one part of the world to fight a competitive battle in another

4. *Competitive strategy*: Firms need to defend their competitive position, not only in new markets but also at home. **Cross-subsidization**—the use of resources accumulated in one part of the world to fight a competitive battle in another—is a powerful global competitive strategy. The telecom industry in Asia, for example, has been characterized by state monopoly with heavy cross-subsidization of tariffs to meet universal service and social priorities.[18]

Global Market Entry Strategies

Once a company has made a commitment to global expansion, formulated its global strategy, and researched potential new markets, many fundamental decisions are still to be made. The most critical is to decide among several methods of entry. Typical entry strategies are exporting and importing, licensing, and franchising, all of which allow access to markets without direct investment or ownership. More extensive methods of developing foreign markets include expansion through alliances and joint ventures as well as foreign direct investment.

Exporting and Importing

Firms can be involved in exporting and importing either indirectly or directly. Indirect involvement means that the firm participates through an intermediary and does not deal with foreign customers or firms. Direct involvement means that the firm works with and develops a relationship with foreign customers, suppliers, or markets. In both cases, goods and services either go abroad or come to the domestic market from abroad, and goods may have to be adapted to suit the targeted market. However, the less direct its involvement, the less likely the firm is to build its knowledge and experience of how to do business abroad, hampering further expansion.

Firms that export or import directly have the opportunity to learn more quickly the competitive advantages of their products and can therefore expand more rapidly. Direct exporting or importing affords them better control over international activities, and they are able to forge relationships with trading partners, leading to further international growth and success. Of course, there are hurdles, including the difficulty of identifying and targeting foreign suppliers or customers and finding the right marketing channels space, all of which can be costly and time consuming. Some firms overcome such barriers through the use of "storeless" distribution networks, such as mail-order catalogs or e-commerce. In Japan, for example, the complexity of traditional distribution systems, high retail rental rates, and crowded shelves have led many firms to launch new products using direct marketing and e-commerce.[19]

As a firm and its managers gather experience with exporting, they move through different levels of commitment, ranging from awareness, interest, trial, evaluation, and finally, adaptation of an international outlook as part of corporate strategy. Of course, not all firms progress with equal speed. Some will do so very rapidly, perhaps encouraged by success with an e-commerce approach, and move on to other forms of international involvement, such as foreign direct investment. Others may withdraw from exporting, due to disappointing experiences or as part of a strategic resource allocation decision.[20]

INTERNATIONAL INTERMEDIARIES Both direct and indirect importers and exporters frequently make use of intermediaries that can assist with troublesome yet important details, such as documentation, financing, and transportation. Intermediaries also can identify foreign suppliers and customers and help the firm with long- or short-term market penetration efforts. Together with export facilitators, intermediaries can bring the global market to the domestic firm's doorstep and help overcome financial and time constraints. Figure 10.6 shows the range of expertise they offer. Major types of international intermediaries are export management companies and trading companies.

FIGURE 10.6 Multiple Roles of International Intermediaries

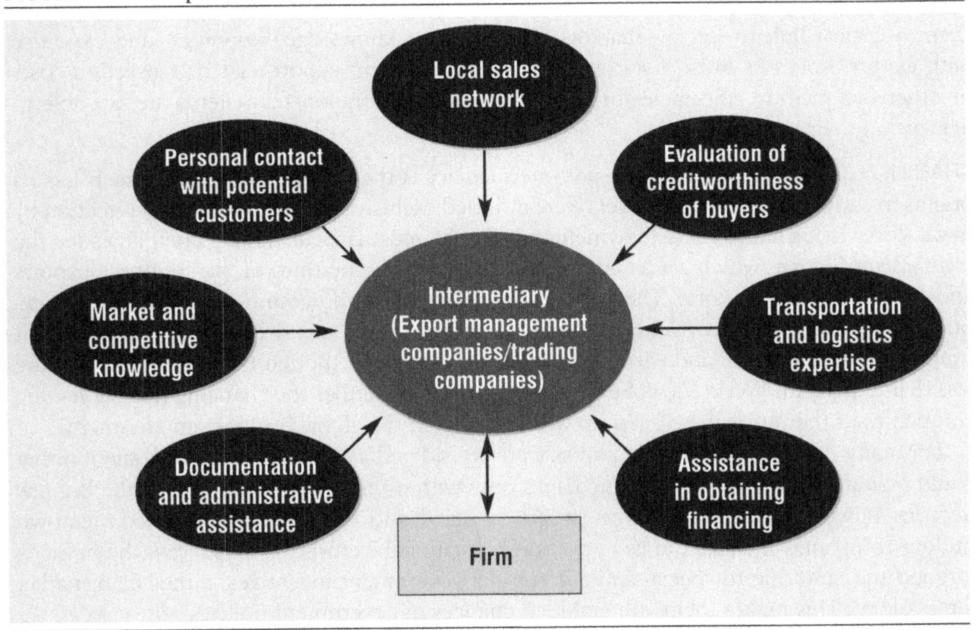

EXPORT MANAGEMENT COMPANIES (EMCS)
Domestic firms that specialize in performing international business services as commission representatives or as distributors

INTERNATIONAL AGENT
A representative or intermediary for the firm that works to develop business and sales strategies and that develops contacts

EXPORT MANAGEMENT COMPANIES Firms that represent others for a commission or that work as distributors performing specific international business services are known as **export management companies (EMCs)**. Most EMCs focus on a particular geographic area where their expertise enables them to offer specialized services. EMCs have two primary forms of operation: They perform services as agents, or they take title to goods and operate internationally on their own account.

When working as an **international agent**, the EMC is primarily responsible for developing foreign business and sales strategies and establishing contacts abroad. Because the EMC does not share in profits, it depends heavily on high sales volumes, on which it is paid commissions. An EMC may therefore be tempted to take on as many products and as many clients as possible to obtain high sales volumes. As a result, the EMC may spread itself too thin and may be unable to represent adequately all the clients and products it carries.

INTERNATIONAL DISTRIBUTOR
A representative or intermediary for the firm that purchases products from the firm, takes title, and assumes the selling risk

When operating as an **international distributor**, the EMC purchases products from the domestic firm, takes title, and assumes the trading risk. Selling in its own name, it has the opportunity to reap greater profits than when acting as an agent. The potential for greater profit is appropriate because the EMC has drastically reduced the risk for the domestic firm while increasing its own risk. The burden of the merchandise acquired provides a major motivation to complete an international sale successfully. The domestic firm selling to the EMC is in the comfortable position of having sold its merchandise and received its money without having to deal with the complexities of the international market. On the other hand, it is less likely to gather much international business expertise.

In addition to its compensation, an EMC may require the producing firm to pay market development expenses, including, for example, the cost of product samples, promotional activities such as trade show attendance or trade advertising, or even costs associated with contacting customers. Sometimes this takes the form of an annual retainer, whereas in other cases, direct expenses are passed along to the firm.

For an EMC relationship to work, both parties must fully recognize the delegation of responsibilities, the costs associated with those activities, and the need for information sharing, cooperation, and mutual reliance. As technology continues to ease the conduct of business across borders, EMCs must ensure that they deliver true value-added services that make them a critical link to foreign markets. Their market knowledge, resources, and expertise with export processes must, for example, lower their client export-related transaction costs or otherwise provide efficiencies or levels of market penetration that clients are not able to achieve on their own.

TRADING COMPANY
A company, such as the sogoshosha of Japan, that acts as an intermediary for multiple companies in such areas as import-export, countertrade, investing, and manufacturing

TRADING COMPANIES Another major intermediary is the **trading company**, which has its origins in early Europe. There, traders were awarded exclusive trading rights and protection by naval forces in exchange for tax payments. Today the most famous trading companies are the *sogoshosha* of Japan, which act as intermediaries for about one-third of the country's exports and two-fifths of its imports. They play a unique role in world commerce by importing, exporting, countertrading, investing, and manufacturing. Their vast size allows them to benefit from economies of scale and earn high rates of return, even though their profit margins are less than 2 percent. World View: Survival of the Fittest describes the changing roles of trading companies as they struggle to keep up with changes in the global business environment.

For many decades, trading companies were considered a Japan-specific phenomenon that could operate successfully as intermediaries only within the Japanese culture. In the last few decades, however, countries as diverse as Korea, Brazil, and Turkey have established their own trading companies that handle large portions of national exports. Their success, however, is in good measure due to special and preferential government incentives, rather than market forces alone. This makes them vulnerable to changes in government policies.

EXPORT TRADING COMPANY (ETC)
The result of 1982 legislation to improve the export performance of small and medium-sized firms that allow businesses to band together to export or offer export services; bank participation in trading companies and relaxes antitrust provisions permitted under law

In 1982, legislation designed to improve the export performance of small and middle-size firms facilitated the creation of U.S. **export trading companies (ETCs)**.

Antitrust laws were relaxed to permit companies to band together in joint export efforts, thus sharing the costs of international market penetration. Further, banks were allowed to participate in trading companies, providing better access to capital and therefore permitting more trading transactions and easier receipt of title to goods. The trading company concept offers a one-stop shopping center for both the firm and its foreign customers. The firm can be assured that all international functions will be performed efficiently by the trading company and yet the foreign customer will only have to deal with a few individual firms.

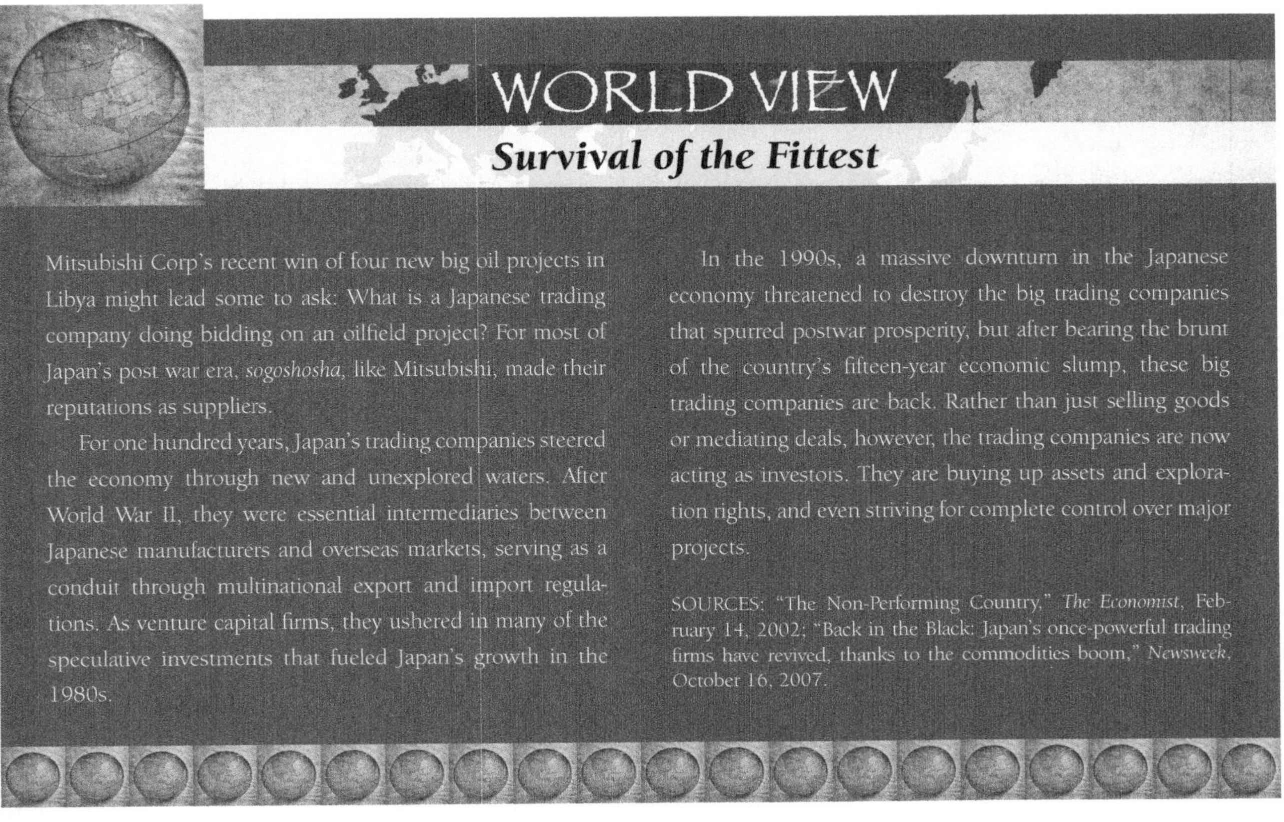

WORLD VIEW

Survival of the Fittest

Mitsubishi Corp's recent win of four new big oil projects in Libya might lead some to ask: What is a Japanese trading company doing bidding on an oilfield project? For most of Japan's post war era, *sogoshosha*, like Mitsubishi, made their reputations as suppliers.

For one hundred years, Japan's trading companies steered the economy through new and unexplored waters. After World War II, they were essential intermediaries between Japanese manufacturers and overseas markets, serving as a conduit through multinational export and import regulations. As venture capital firms, they ushered in many of the speculative investments that fueled Japan's growth in the 1980s.

In the 1990s, a massive downturn in the Japanese economy threatened to destroy the big trading companies that spurred postwar prosperity, but after bearing the brunt of the country's fifteen-year economic slump, these big trading companies are back. Rather than just selling goods or mediating deals, however, the trading companies are now acting as investors. They are buying up assets and exploration rights, and even striving for complete control over major projects.

SOURCES: "The Non-Performing Country," *The Economist*, February 14, 2002; "Back in the Black: Japan's once-powerful trading firms have revived, thanks to the commodities boom," *Newsweek*, October 16, 2007.

Although ETCs seem to offer major benefits to U.S. firms wishing to penetrate international markets, they have not been used very extensively. By 2008, only ninety-three individual ETCs were certified by the U.S. Department of Commerce. Yet these certificates covered more than 5,000 firms, mainly because various trade associations had applied for certification for all of their members.[21]

International Licensing

Licensing can be an extremely effective way to achieve penetration in international markets, either as a sole export strategy or in conjunction with other international activities. Under a licensing agreement, one firm permits another to use its intellectual property for compensation designated as **royalty**. The property licensed might include patents, trademarks, copyrights, technology, technical know-how, or specific business skills.

LICENSING
A method through which one firm allows another to produce or package its product or use its intellectual property in exchange for compensation

ROYALTY
The compensation paid by one firm to another under a licensing agreement

Licensing has intuitive appeal to many would-be international managers. As an entry strategy, it requires neither capital investment nor detailed involvement with foreign customers. By generating royalty income, licensing provides an opportunity to exploit research and development already conducted. After initial costs, the licensor can reap benefits until the end of the license contract period. Licensing also reduces the risk of expropriation because the licensee is a local company that can provide leverage against government action.

Licensing may help to avoid host-country regulations applicable to equity ventures. Licensing also may provide a means by which foreign markets can be tested without major involvement of capital or management time. Similarly, licensing can be used as a strategy to preempt a market before the entry of competition, especially if the licensor's resources permit full-scale involvement only in selected markets.

TRADEMARK LICENSING
The licensing of instantly recognizable logos, names, or images for use on unrelated products such as gifts, toys, or clothing

A special form of licensing, **trademark licensing**, permits the names or logos of designers, sports teams, or movie stars to appear on a multitude of products including clothing, games, gifts, and novelties. Licensors can make millions of dollars with little effort, while licensees can produce a brand or product that consumers will recognize immediately.

Licensing is not without disadvantages. It leaves most international marketing functions to the licensee. As a result, the licensor gains only limited expertise. Moreover, the initial toehold in the foreign market may not be a foot in the door. In exchange for the royalty, the licensor may create its own competitor not only in the markets for which the agreement was made but also in third markets.

Licensing has come under criticism from supranational organizations, such as the United Nations Conference on Trade and Development (UNCTAD). It has been alleged that licensing lets multinational corporations (MNCs) capitalize on older technology. Such technology, however, may be in the best interest of the recipient. Guinness Brewery, for example, in order to produce Guinness Stout in Nigeria, licensed equipment that was used in Ireland at the turn of the twentieth century. This equipment had additional economic life in Nigeria because it presented a good fit with local needs.[22]

International Franchising

FRANCHISING
A form of licensing that allows a distributor or retailer exclusive rights to sell a product or service in a specified area

Franchising is the granting of the right by a parent company to another independent entity to do business in a prescribed manner. The right can take the form of selling the franchisor's products, using its name, production, and marketing techniques or its general business approach. The major forms of franchising are manufacturer-retailer systems (such as car dealerships), manufacturer-wholesaler systems (such as soft-drink companies), and service-firm retailer systems (such as lodging services and fast-food outlets). Typically, to be successful in international franchising, the firm must be able to offer unique products or unique selling propositions. A franchise must offer a high degree of standardization in order to provide instant recognition.

From a franchisee's viewpoint, buying into a franchise reduces risk by implementing a proven concept. From a governmental perspective, franchises are favored because they require little outflow of foreign exchange, and the bulk of the profits—as well as jobs—remain in the country.

Global Market Development Strategies

5 LEARNING OUTCOME

The world is too large and the competition too strong for even the largest companies to do everything independently. The convergence of technologies and the integration of markets increase not just the costs but also the risks of manufacturing and marketing goods on a global scale. Partly as a reaction to increased risk and partly to better exploit opportunities, multinational corporations often join forces to achieve global goals. Strategic alliances with suppliers, customers, companies in other industries, and even competitors help to control both the costs and the risks of conducting business at the international level.

Strategic Alliances

STRATEGIC ALLIANCES
A term for collaboration among firms, often similar to joint ventures, but not necessarily involving joint capital investment

A **strategic alliance** (or partnership) is an informal or formal arrangement between two or more companies that match complementary strengths to achieve common business objec-

Quick Take *International Television Programming*

American television programming and adaptations of American shows have historically dominated the world market. The growth of television and the number of channels created a worldwide demand for programming. Many countries licensed American television shows in the 1980s and 1990s in addition to creating local content. For example, the soap opera *Santa Barbara* ran for more than ten years in Russia, until 2002, even though NBC had cancelled the show in the United States in 1992.

However, television has not been spared from globalization. Today, domestic stations have become more experienced in creating their own programming and audiences demand shows more reflective of their own cultural preferences. What do the American TV shows *American Idol*, *The Office*, and *House of Cards* have in common? They are all adaptations of popular British shows. Shows created outside of the United States are increasingly being licensed for a worldwide television market. Although the concept is the same, it is important to provide for local content adaptations. In India, *Who Wants to be a Millionaire?* is hosted by a Bollywood legend; in Russia, the "Ask the Audience Life-Line" is not very helpful as the studio audience tries to give the wrong answers to contestants.

Licensing television shows and moves creates the potential for a tremendous growth in revenue. The costs of exporting a television show vary. Some shows, like *Epitafios*, are low-cost product extension into new markets. In contrast to other programs, entire local shows are created, usually by local companies with royalties going back to the parent company. In most instances, costs such as advertising and translation are the responsibility of the licensee, thus contributing to a higher profit margin for the licensor.

SOURCES: Edward Jay Epstein, "Hollywood's Profits, Demystified," *The Slate*, August 8, 2005, **http://www.slate.com/id/2124078/fr**, accessed May 9, 2014.

tives. It is something more than the traditional customer-vendor relationship but something less than an outright acquisition. Alliances can take a variety of forms ranging from informal cooperation to joint ownership of worldwide operations.

Alliances can range from information cooperation in the market development area to joint ownership of worldwide operations. For Example, Texas Instruments has reported agreements with companies such as IBM, Hyundai, Fujitsu, Alcatel, and L. M. Ericsson, using such terms as "joint development agreement," "cooperative technical effort," "joint program for development," "alternative sourcing agreement," and "design/ exchange agreement for cooperative product development and exchange of technical data."[23]

Market development is one reason for the growth in such alliances. In Japan, Motorola is sharing chip designs and manufacturing facilities with Toshiba to gain greater access to the Japanese market. Another focus is spreading the cost and risk inherent in production and development efforts. Texas Instruments and Hitachi have teamed up to develop the next generation of memory chips.[24] The costs of developing new jet engines are so vast that they force aerospace companies into collaboration; one such consortium was formed by United Technologies' Pratt & Whitney division, Britain's Rolls-Royce, Motoren-und-Turbinen Union from Germany, Fiat of Italy, and Japanese Aero Engines.[25] Some alliances are also formed to block or co-opt competitors. For example, Caterpillar formed a heavy equipment joint venture with Mitsubishi in Japan to strike back at its main global rival, Komatsu, in its home market.

Informal Alliances

In informal cooperative deals, partners work together without a binding agreement. Typically, partners who are not direct competitors in each other's markets may exchange information on new products, processes, or technologies. They may even exchange personnel for limited periods of time. Informal arrangements often exist among small to mid-size companies, where collaboration benefits both parties.

Contractual Agreements

Through contractual agreements, alliance partners join forces for joint R&D, marketing, production, licensing, cross-licensing, or cross-marketing activities. To gain a stronghold in China's potentially vast auto market, Toyota recently formed a contractual agreement with China's largest automaker, First Automotive (FAW), to build large-scale production of a wide range of models. Toyota, which will have no equity stake, will provide management expertise, technology, marketing assistance, and cash, while FAW will provide workers, factories, and equipment.[26] Firms also can have a reciprocal arrangement whereby each partner provides the other access to its market. The New York Yankees and Manchester United, for instance, sell each other's licensed products and develop joint sponsorship programs. International airlines share hubs, coordinate schedules, and simplify ticketing. Alliances such as The Star Alliance network (joining airlines such as United and Lufthansa), Oneworld (British Airways and American Airlines), and SkyTeam (Delta and Air France) provide worldwide coverage for their customers in both the travel and shipping communities.

International licensing is another area where contractual agreements are common. For example, television networks like ABC and NBC, as described in Quick Take: International Television Programming, use contract licensing to import popular television programs.

Management Contracts

MANAGEMENT CONTRACT
The firm sells its expertise in running a company while avoiding the risks or benefits of ownership

In countries where governments insist on complete or majority ownership of firms, **management contracts** are a viable option for foreign expansion. Here, a firm sells its expertise and builds a market presence without either the risks or benefits of ownership. In time, local managers are trained to take over operations. Management contracts have clear benefits for the client or client government, who gain access to skills, resources, and support services that would be difficult and costly to build up locally. Consider, for example, the benefits available to hotels managed by the Sheraton Corporation, which include instant access to Sheraton's worldwide reservation system. Management contracts also offer distinct advantages to the supplier. They lower the risk of participating in an international venture while providing the opportunity to gain expertise in new markets. They also allow firms to leverage existing skills and resources commercially.

TURNKEY OPERATION
A specialized form of management contract between a customer and an organization to provide a complete operational system together with the skills needed for unassisted maintenance and operation

One specialized form of management contract is the **turnkey operation**, whereby the client acquires a complete international system, together with skills sufficient to operate and maintain it. Companies like AES, for example, are part of a consortium that builds electric power facilities around the world, operates them, and, in some cases, even owns parts of them.

Equity Participation

Multinational corporations that seek a measure of control in companies that are strategically important to them frequently acquire minority ownership. Ease of market entry is another attraction of equity participation and explains why Ford, Mercedes-Benz, and BMW are all pursuing opportunities in China.[27]

Joint Ventures

A **joint venture** is the long-term participation of two or more companies in an enterprise in which each party contributes assets, has some equity, and shares risk. The reasons for establishing a joint venture can be divided into three groups: (1) government suasion or legislation; (2) one partner's needs for other partners' skills; and (3) one partner's needs for other partners' attributes or assets.

JOINT VENTURE
Formal participation of two or more companies in an enterprise to achieve a common goal

The key to a joint venture is the sharing of a common business objective, which makes the arrangement more than a customer-vendor relationship but less than an outright acquisition. The partners' rationales for entering into the arrangement may vary. An example is New United Motor Manufacturing, Inc. (NUMMI), a joint venture between Toyota and GM. Toyota needed direct access to the U.S. market, while GM benefited from the technology, management expertise, and quality standards of its Japanese partner.[28]

Joint ventures are valuable when the pooling of resources results in a better outcome for each partner than if each were to conduct its activities individually. This is particularly true when each partner has a specialized advantage in areas that benefit the venture. For example, a firm may have new technology yet lack sufficient capital to carry out foreign direct investment on its own. Through a joint venture, market penetration is achieved more easily. Similarly, one partner may have a distribution system already in place, which leads to high-volume sales of the other partner's product in a shorter period of time. Another key benefit of joint ventures is the ability of foreign firms to minimize the risks involved in investing and operating in emerging, potentially unstable economies.

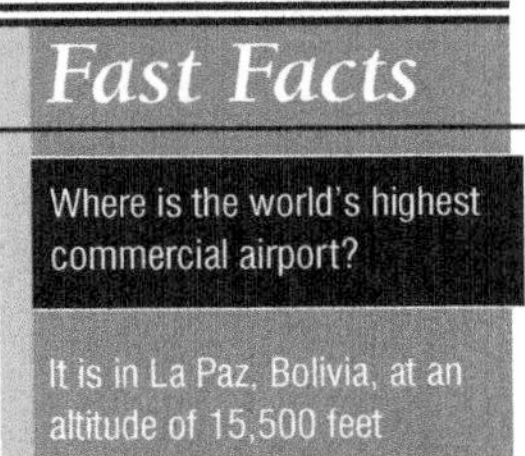

In some markets, joint ventures may be the only means through which a firm can operate profitably at all. Import restrictions or tariff barriers, for instance, are often avoided through joint-venture relationships with domestic companies. India restricts equity participation in local operations by foreigners to 40 percent, so joint ventures are a viable alternative for international firms who wish to operate there. Recently, several Western firms have used joint ventures to gain access to markets in eastern and central Europe. In markets like these, joint ventures can ease relationships between foreign firms and local governments or such organizations as trade unions. Negotiations for certifications or licenses are often easier, simply because authorities may not perceive themselves as dealing with a foreign firm. Access to local capital markets, too, may be possible. In some cases, joint ventures even make foreign companies eligible for tax incentives, grants, or government support.

Despite their many advantages, joint ventures all too frequently fall short of expectations or are disbanded. The reasons typically include conflicts of interest or differences in management styles, problems with disclosure of sensitive information, or disagreement over how profits are to be shared.

Consortia

A new drug, computer, or telecommunications switch can cost more than $1 billion to develop and bring to market. To combat the high costs and risks of research and development, research **consortia** have emerged in the United States, Japan, and Europe. Since the passage of the Joint Research and Development Act of 1984 (which allows both domestic and foreign firms to participate in joint basic research efforts without the fear of antitrust action), more than 100 consortia have been registered in the United States. These consortia pool their resources for research into technologies ranging from artificial intelligence and electric car batteries to semiconductor manufacturing.

CONSORTIUM/ CONSORTIA
A partnership among multiple companies in the same industry, usually with the aim of conducting costly research and development work and with costs and the results shared among participating companies

The European Union has several megaprojects to develop new technologies, under the names BRITE, COMET, ESPRIT, EUREKA, RACE, and SOKRATES. Japanese consortia have worked on producing the world's highest capacity memory chip and other advanced computer technologies. On the manufacturing side, the formation of Airbus Industries secured European production of commercial jets. The consortium, now backed by the European Aeronautic Defense and Space Company (EADS), which emerged from the link-up of the German Daimler-Benz Aerospace AG, the French Aerospatiale Matra, and CASA of Spain has become a prime global competitor.[29]

Elements of Successful Alliances

Table 10.3 summarizes what it takes for interfirm alliances of any kind to be beneficial for each partner. Strategic alliances operate in a dynamic business environment and must therefore adjust to changing market conditions. The agreement between partners should provide for changes in the original concept so that the venture can flourish and grow. The trick is to have a prior understanding as to which party will take care of which pains and problems so that a common goal is reached.

TABLE 10.3 Key Provisions of Successful Interfirm Alliances

1. Clear definitions of the interfirm relationship, its objectives, and its duration
2. Agreement on ownership, control, and management
3. Agreement on protection of sensitive or proprietary information
4. Policies on financial structure, including allocation of costs and profits
5. Clarity on taxation and fiscal obligations
6. Guidelines on employment, training, and skills transfer
7. Agreement on government assistance, if any
8. Plans for transfer of technology
9. Marketing and distribution arrangements
10. Environmental protection and ethics policies
11. Clear guidelines for record keeping and inspection
12. Mechanism for the settlement of disputes
13. Mechanism for dissolution of relationship

SOURCE: Michael R. Czinkota, "International Information Needs for U.S. Competitiveness," *Business Horizons* 34, 6 (November–December 1991): 86–91.

Full Ownership

For some firms, the decision to invest overseas is, initially at least, considered only in the context of 100 percent ownership. Ethnocentricity may explain this bias—management may believe that no outside entity should have an impact on corporate decision-making. Starbucks, for example, limits its global expansion strategies to licenses, joint ventures, and company operations, believing that local ownership in the form of franchising will dilute the Starbucks brand. Quick Take: Starbucks Teas Up in Japan demonstrates that the company's success hinges on its ability to recreate the entire Starbucks experience outside the United States.

In order to make a rational decision about the degree of ownership, management must evaluate the extent to which total control is critical to the success of international marketing activities. Although full ownership may be desirable, it may not be a prerequisite for success. In other cases, the corporate culture may be such that full ownership is essential. If strong interdependencies between headquarters and local operations factor into the firm's success,

Quick Take: Environment and Sustainability: Starbucks Teas Up In Japan

For decades, Japan's neighborhood *kissaten* were the place to be when it came to coffee. In a nation of tea drinkers, young people who once sipped coffee from tiny cups in smoky, dimly lit shops now flock to Starbucks for double espressos and giant lattes. By 2013, the Seattle-based company had more than a thousand stores in Japan. Initially drawn to Japan by its large market, consumer's high disposable income, and affinity for Western brands, the coffee giant further enticed customers by tailoring some of its drinks to fit the tastes of the Japanese customer. Stepping away from its standard indulgently sweet menu, Starbucks added a number of green tea beverages, which are now available at stores around the globe.

The company's strategy of maintaining its identity and its environmental leadership posture suits Japanese consumers well. According to a Starbucks international manager, "It's very easy to get swept up in this desire to localize a brand. The Japanese consumer is probably one of the most discerning consumers in the world. But if anything, they want the same experience that they've had in Los Angeles, Hawaii, Europe, or wherever."

Because Starbucks does no advertising in Japan, its success is even more dazzling. With its comfy couches and its American rock or hip-hop music, the chain has quickly become a household name—as well as the number-one ranked chain in Japan's restaurant sector. Unlike its competitors, the chain is not a franchise—Starbucks currently uses three business structures in international markets: licenses, joint ventures, and company-owned operations.

Ownership allows the company to protect its brand and duplicate those aspects of it that set Starbucks apart from the other coffee house chains. It also permits easier and quicker introduction of environmentally responsive policies. For example, Starbucks is now using recycled content for hot beverage cups, which is estimated to reduce the dependence on tree fiber by more than five million pounds annually. The firm is also committed to reducing its environmental footprint through preservation in places where coffee is grown and by recycling coffee grounds into nutrient-rich soil.

SOURCES: **http://www.starbucks.co.jp/en/**, accessed July 23, 2014. "Starbucks' green tea success with Japanese consumers leads to worldwide popularity," Japan External Trade Organization, April 2006, **www.jetro.org**, accessed February 17, 2008; "Starbucks Corporation," McGraw-Hill Higher Education, **http://www.mhhe.com/business/management/thompson/11e/case/starbucks-2.html**, accessed February 17, 2008; "environmental affairs" **www.starbucks.com**, accessed July 23, 2014.

perhaps nothing short of total coordination achieved through ownership will guarantee acceptable performance.

As explained in Chapter 3, however, the current international environment is hostile to full ownership by multinational firms. Indeed, government actions through legal restrictions or discriminatory policies lessen the attraction of ownership. The Venezuelan government, for example, recently made moves to nationalize the country's telecommunications and electric industries. Many companies in both industries are owned, in part, by foreign firms.[30] Volatility in the political or economic environment also makes full ownership a risky proposition. In many countries, the choice is either to abide by existing restraints and accept a reduction in control or to lose the opportunity to operate there at all.

SUMMARY

Firms do not become experienced in international business overnight but rather progress gradually through an internationalization process.

The convergence of several factors—market, cost, environmental, and competitive—has led to the globalization of business, presenting new opportunities and challenges.

Motivations to expand overseas are either proactive (initiated by aggressive management) or reactive (defensive responses to environmental changes or pressures).

Thorough strategic planning allows firms to increase their chances of success overseas. It involves external and internal analysis, target country selection and segmentation, and global program development.

Constraints of time, resources, and expertise are the major inhibitors to international research. Nevertheless, firms need to carry out secondary and often primary research in order to explore foreign market opportunities and challenges successfully. To provide ongoing information to management, an information system is also essential.

The most frequently used entry strategies include importing or exporting, often with the aid of international intermediaries or facilitators, and licensing and franchising. These methods do not require ownership or foreign direct investment in target markets.

Interfirm alliances, including management contracts, joint ventures, and consortia, allow firms a presence in foreign markets while minimizing costs and risks. Full ownership, while allowing total control, is a risky proposition, especially in politically unstable economies.

Key Terms and Concepts

managerial commitment
cost leadership strategy
differentiation strategy
focus strategy
secondary research
primary research
qualitative information
quantitative information
personal interviews
focus group research
observation research
survey research
experimentation
information system
export complaint systems
environmental scanning
Delphi studies
scenario analysis
diversification
market segmentation
glocalization
cross-subsidization
export management companies (EMCs)
international agent
international distributor
trading company
export trading company (ETC)
licensing
royalty
trademark licensing
franchising
strategic alliances
management contract
turnkey operation
joint venture
consortium/consortia

Review Questions

1. Summarize the four sets of factors driving globalization.
2. Explain the stages involved in formulating a global strategy. Are these processes sequential or concurrent?
3. Describe the positive and negative impacts of international expansion on domestic business activities.
4. What are the major differences between domestic and international research?
5. Discuss the possible shortcomings of secondary data. When is primary data necessary?
6. What is the purpose of export intermediaries? How can an intermediary avoid circumvention by a client or customer?
7. "Licensing is really not a form of international involvement because it requires no substantial additional effort on the part of the licensor." Comment.
8. Why is full ownership of a foreign operation a less-than-desirable goal?

Critical Skill Builders

1. Globalization is not only an imperative for survival and future growth, it is the inevitable consequence of business expansion. Prepare your arguments for and against this statement, then debate the topic in teams.
2. Select a small to middle-size business in your area. Analyze ways in which the company currently operates in the international arena. Then create a blueprint for cost-effective, profitable expansion.
3. You are employed by National Engineering, a firm that designs subways. Because you have had a course in international business, your boss asks you to spend the next week exploring international possibilities for the company. How will you go about this task?
4. The rate of expropriation has been ten times greater for a joint venture with the host government than for a 100 percent U.S.-owned subsidiary. Is this contrary to logic?
5. Comment on the observation that "a joint venture may be a combination of Leonardo da Vinci's brain and Carl Lewis' legs; one wants to fly, the other insists on running."

On the Web

1. Prepare a one-page memo to a foreign company introducing your product or service. Include a contact listing of ten businesses in foreign countries looking to import your particular product. Include the company name, address, and other contact information, along with special requirements of the company you note from its posting of an offer to buy. Cite the sources from which you prepared your list. Look at **http://www.tradematch.co/uk** or **http://www.mnileads.com**.

2. Show macro, aggregate changes in international markets by listing the total value of three commodities exported from your country to five other countries for the last four years. For each of the countries, provide a one-paragraph statement in which you identify positive or negative trends. Give your opinion on whether or not these trends are relevant or reflect the reality of today's international business environment. What are the dangers of relying on perceived trends? Use Internet sources provided in the chapter and others of your finding to conduct research on products from your hometown or region.

3. Mondélez International is one of the largest food and beverage companies in the world, marketing leading brands of chocolates, biscuits, gum, cheese, dairy products, and powdered beverages like Cadbury, Oreo's, Tang, Trident, and Philadelphia Cream Cheese in 165 countries. Based on the brand information given on its web site (**http://www.mondelezinternational.com**), what role do developing countries play in the company's growth strategies?

Endnotes

1. David Court and Laxman Narasimhan, "Capturing the world's emerging middle class," *McKinsey Quarterly*, July 2010.
2. Matthew Herper, "How Much Does Pharmaceutical Innovation Cost? A Look At 100 Companies," Forbes.com, August 11, 2013.
3. Rochelle Garner, "McAfee Margins Under Siege by Symantec, Microsoft," *Bloomberg*, December 3, 2007; Carole Vaporean, "Caterpillar to offer electric mining truck in 2008, *Reuters*, March 28, 2007.
4. Lisa Jennings, "Analysts react to Starbucks–La Boulange deal," *Nation's Restaurant News*, June 6, 2012.
5. George S. Yip, *Total Global Strategy II* (Upper Saddle River, NJ: Prentice Hall, 2002).
6. Michael Porter, *Competitive Advantage* (New York: The Free Press, 1987), chapter 1.
7. David A. Ricks, *Blunders in International Business*, 4th ed. (Hoboken, NJ: Wiley, 2006).
8. "National Trade Data Bank," **http://www.commercialdiplomacy.org**, accessed July 25, 2014.
9. Michael R. Czinkota, "International Information Cross-Fertilization in Marketing: An Empirical Assessment," *European Journal of Marketing* 34, November 12, 2000, pp. 1305–14.
10. Ricks, *Blunders in International Business*.
11. Michael R. Czinkota and Masaaki Kotabe, "Product Development the Japanese Way," in M. Czinkota and M. Kotabe, *Trends in International Business: Critical Perspectives* (Oxford: Blackwell Publishers, 1998), pp. 153–8.
12. C. K. Corder, "Problems and Pitfalls in Conducting Marketing Research in Africa," *Marketing Expansion in a Shrinking World*, ed. Betsy Gelb. *Proceedings of American Marketing Association Business Conference* (Chicago: AMA, 1978), pp. 86–90.
13. Ibid.
14. The Coca-Cola Company, **http://www.coca-colacompany.com/stories/expedition-206-revisiting-cokes-epic-quest-for-the-source-of-happiness**, September 27, 2013.
15. "Perspective on Export Withdrawal," *Journal of International Marketing* 7, 4 (1999): pp. 10–37.
16. Suzy Hansen, "How Zara Grew into the World's Largest Fashion Retailer," *New York Times*, November 9, 2012.
17. Parmy Olson, "Here's Where Teens Are Going Instead of Facebook," *Forbes*, **http://www.forbes.com/sites/parmyolson/2013/11/12/heres-where-teens-are-going-instead-of-facebook/**, November 12, 2013; Michael R. Czinkota and Ilkka A. Ronkainen, "Achieving 'Glocal' Success," *Marketing News*, April 2014.
18. Christina Sommer, "Purchase Power of Global Teens Tops $819 Billion," MasterCard Payments Perspectives Blog, November 21, 2012.
19. **http://www.enviedeplus.com/tag/mr-propre**; **http://www.pgprof.com/spain/html/don_limpio .shtml**; **http://www.pgnewsroom.de/aktuelle-presseme ldungen/meister_proper**; accessed November 17, 2013
20. Jeffrey R. Immelt, Vijay Govindarajan, and Chris Trimble, "How GE Is Disrupting Itself," *Harvard Business Review*, October 2009.
21. **http://www.nokia.com/A402785**, accessed February 17, 2008; **www.Sony.com**, accessed February 19, 2008.
22. Nigel Mukherjee, *Telecommunications International.* 39, 6, (J2005 p. S20.
23. Michael R. Czinkota and Masaaki Kotabe, "Entering the Japanese Market: A Reassessment of Foreign Firms' Entry and Distribution Perspective on Export Withdrawal," *Journal of International Marketing 7,* 4 (1999): pp. 10–37.
24. Sepia Thomson, Office of Export Trading Company Affairs, U.S. Department of Commerce, Washington, D.C., February 22, 2008.
25. Texas Instruments' homepage, **http://www.ti.com**, accessed February 22, 2008.
26. **www.unctad.org**, accessed February 19, 2008.
27. "Competition through cooperation," *Monash Business Review 3,* 3 (2007), **http://publications.epress.monash.edu/doi/abs/10.2104/mbr07041?journalCode=mbr**, accessed February 19, 2008.
28. Keith Bradsher, "Toyota and Chinese Carmaker in Venture," *The New York Times*, August 30, 2002, p. 1, 30.
29. **www.eads.com**, accessed February 10, 2008.
30. Simon Ramero, "Chaves Moves to Nationalize Two Industries," *The New York Times*, January 9, 2007.

CHAPTER 11

GLOBAL MARKETING AND SOCIAL NETWORKS

How Hollywood Conquered the World

The Hollywood movie industry is no longer profitable with what they make in the United States, but Hollywood studios need to make profits internationally to be successful. International revenue (not just North America) is up 35 percent over five years ago and accounted for 69 percent of the studios' box-office receipts in 2011. As of September 13, 2012, the studios' income from international theaters was running at $11 billion, compared with $7.6 billion domestically, per media data analyst Rentrak. Hollywood has started to take real notice; for the first time, studios have green-lighted some big-budget films based almost entirely on their foreign appeal, such as *Ice Age: Continental Drift*, which made a modest $159 million in North America but a whopping $707 million abroad as of October 2012.

Hollywood's success abroad is no accident. Blockbuster Hollywood action movies, cartoons (easy to dub), and certain hit franchises (*Skyfall* and *Indiana Jones and the Kingdom of the Crystal Skull*) translate well across cultural barriers. The spread of multiplex cinemas has increased attendance, but the multiplexes tend to show more U.S. movies.

Second, countries such as Russia and China are building state-of-the-art theaters at a staggering pace. Between 2007 and 2011, Chinese movie screens doubled to more than 6,200, and that number is projected to rise even further by 2015 to 16,500. This still leaves room for a massive increase, given that the United States, with its far smaller population, has almost 40,000 screens.

Third, China has started opening its doors for an increase in U.S. movie releases after years of restrictions. In February, the United States and China agreed to a deal allowing fourteen IMAX or 3-D films from the United States to be shown annually in China, on top of the previous quota of twenty American movies. Hollywood already has seen the benefits of this pact; China's growing appetite for American films was evident in the re-release of James Cameron's *Titanic* in 3-D.

Unsurprisingly, Hollywood is doing everything to maximize its foreign revenue. Several studios have created operations to finance local-language or "indigenous" products. Legendary Pictures, which co-financed the Batman series, has even formed a venture solely to jointly fund Chinese movies, and 20th Century Fox was one of the backers of

LEARNING OUTCOMES

1. ***To compare and contrast the merits of standardization versus localization strategies for country markets and of regional versus global marketing efforts***
2. ***To consider factors affecting the adaptation of products for launch in global markets***
3. ***To understand the variables that affect pricing in different markets and discuss various pricing methods***
4. ***To evaluate differing distribution channels, including e-commerce***
5. ***To see how marketers set about selecting the proper combination of promotional tools—advertising, personal selling, sales promotion, publicity, and sponsorship—for targeted global markets***
6.  ***To comprehend the nature of social networks and social media***

John Woo's Chinese-language epic *Red Cliff*. A recent deal between a high-profile film producer and Huayi Brothers Media led to four local language films to be presented in IMAX (*Tai Chi 0, Tai Chi Hero, Back to 1942, CZ 12*).[1]

Moviegoers may no longer be flocking to theaters in the United States, but as Hollywood is finally recognizing, foreign revenues remain a bright light for one of the great domestic industries. "We're excited that Chinese audiences will have the opportunity to experience this film in IMAX, which is the most immersive environment in cinema," says Greg Foster, chairman and president of IMAX Filmed Entertainment.

As You Read This Chapter

1. Foreign box office receipts have saved Hollywood. Why?
2. Despite globalization's damaging effect on the U.S. textile, automotive, computer industries, for movies it's still very much America's world. Are China, India, or Japan vying for second place?

Globalization reflects a business orientation based on the belief that the world is becoming more homogeneous and that distinctions between national markets are not only fading but, for some products, will eventually disappear. Even the biggest companies in the biggest home markets cannot survive on domestic sales alone if they are in global industries such as banking, automobiles, consumer electronics, entertainment, home appliances, mobile devices, pharmaceuticals, publishing, or travel services. This has meant, for example, that Chinese and Indian companies (in categories ranging from China Mobile to Tata Communications) have entered the main markets of the world, such as Europe and North America, to become global powerhouses.[2] Having a global presence ensures viability against other players, both local and global, in the home market as well.

Globalization, improving technologies, and other trends have led to the emergence of the global consumer, who is relatively sophisticated, often more demanding, and comfortable with buying global brands. Multinational firms seek to capitalize on world culture by developing global products and positioning their brands in the global consumer culture. Consumers may prefer a global brand that has been adapted to the needs of local usage conditions. Coca-Cola, for instance, uses cane sugar as sweetener in some countries and corn syrup in others. Although the approach is localized, the global resources of a marketer provide the brand with a winning edge (e.g., in terms of quality or quality perceptions).

Standardization Versus Adaptation for Global Markets

In each country, the existence of a consumer culture is characterized in relation to products and services: consumption patterns (e.g., do most consumers use the product or service for the same purpose or purposes?), psychosocial characteristics (e.g., does the symbolic content of the product or service differ from one country to another?), and general cultural criteria (e.g., does society restrict the purchase and/or use of the product or service to a particular group?).[3] Brazilians, for example, are often judged by the clothing brands they wear. In South Korea, young people typecast others based on the quality of cell phones they use. In the United States, people make inferences based on the size and location of each other's homes.

Three basic options determine what modifications in the marketing mix are needed or warranted:

1. Make no special provisions for the global marketplace but, rather, identify potential target markets and then choose products that can easily be marketed with little or no modification (the **standardization approach**).
2. Adapt to local conditions in each and every target market (the **multidomestic approach**).
3. Incorporate differences into a regional or global strategy that will allow for local differences in implementation (the **globalization approach**).

STANDARDIZATION APPROACH
Policy of making no or minimal changes to the marketing mix for the global marketplace

MULTIDOMESTIC APPROACH
Policy of adapting the marketing mix to suit each country entered

GLOBALIZATION APPROACH
Creation of a regionally or globally similar marketing mix strategy

In today's environment, standardization usually means cross-national strategies rather than a policy of viewing markets as secondary and therefore not important enough to adapt products for them. Ideally, the global marketer should "think globally and act locally," focusing on neither extreme—that is, neither full standardization nor full localization. Global thinking requires flexibility in exploiting good ideas and products on a worldwide basis, regardless of their origin. For example Yum! Brands' restaurants approached the Chinese market in this way. Pizza Hut restaurants display upscale decor to satisfy their customers' preference for "five-star service and atmosphere at a three-star price." The casual dining atmosphere is centered around an extensive menu that covers soup, salads, appetizers, and a range of pizzas such as Seafood Catch (seafood mix, crab sticks, green pepper, pineapple) and the Hot One (chili pepper, onion, tomato, beef, spicy chicken). The new East Dawning restaurant brand was designed to build on Yum!'s existing fast-food strengths: quick service, clean, brightly lit dining areas, and standardized products.[4] Factors that encourage standardization or adaptation are summarized in Table 11.1.

TABLE 11.1 Standardization versus Adaptation

Factors Encouraging Standardization	Factors Encouraging Adaptation
• Economies in product R&D	• Differing use conditions
• Economies of scale in production	• Government and regulatory influences
• Economies in marketing	• Differing buyer behavior patterns
• Control of marketing programs	• Local initiative or motivation in implementation
• "Shrinking" of the world marketplace	• Adherence to the marketing concept

Questions of adaptation have no easy answers. Marketers in many firms rely on decision-support systems to aid in program adaptation, whereas others consider every situation independently. All goods must, of course, conform to environmental conditions over which the marketer has no control. Further, the global marketer may use adaptation to enhance its competitiveness in the marketplace.

PRODUCT STRATEGIES

The core of a firm's operations is a product or service. This product or service can be defined as the complex combination of tangible and intangible elements that distinguishes it from the other entities in the marketplace and on how well the firm is able to differentiate the product from competitors' offerings.

In deciding the form in which the product is to be marketed abroad, the firm should consider three sets of factors: (1) the market(s) that have been targeted, (2) the product and its characteristics, and (3) company characteristics, such as resources and policy. Table 11.2 provides a summary of the factors that determine the need for either mandatory or discretionary product adaptation.

TABLE 11.2 Factors Affecting Product-Adaptation Decisions

Regional, Country, or Local Characteristics	Product Characteristics	Company Considerations
Government regulations	Product constituents	Profitability
Nontariff barriers	Brand	Market opportunity (market potential, product-market fit)
Customer characteristics, expectations and preferences	Packaging	Cost of adapting
Purchase patterns	Physical Form or appearance (e.g., size, styling, color)	Policies (commonality, consistency)
Culture	Function, attributes, features	Organization
Economic status of potential users	Method of operation or usage	Resources
Stage of economic development	Durability, quality	
Competitive offerings	service	
Climate and geography	Country of origin	

SOURCE: Adapted from V. Yorio, *Adapting Products for Export* (New York: Conference Board, 1983), 7.

Typically, the market environment mandates the majority of product modifications. However, the most stringent requirements often result from government regulations. Some regulations may serve no purpose other than political ones (such as protection of a domestic industry or a response to political pressures). Because of the sovereignty of nations, individual firms must comply, but they can influence the situation either by lobbying directly or through industry associations to have the issue raised during trade negotiations.

Some government regulations for adaptation may be controversial both within the company and with some of its constituents, including home governments. Google was forced by the Chinese government to establish a new site, Google.cn, the contents of which are censored by Google in accordance with government preferences. Although a warning label informs the user of the arrangement, the company was criticized for its collaboration to curtail the free flow of information.[5] Google redirects to users to its Hong Kong-based search engine but has little direct impact. Chinese users are already accustomed to using circumvention technology, which means that an uncensored, overseas version of Google remains accessible from the mainland.

The member countries of the European Economic Area are imposing standards in more than 10,000 product categories, ranging from toys to tractor seats. Overall, U.S. producers may be forced to improve product quality because some rules require adoption of an overall system approved by the International Organization for Standardization (ISO). At the end of 2010, 1,109,905 ISO 9001 certificates and 250,972 ISO 14001 certificates were issued, and the five-year period between 2005 and 2010 experienced an almost doubling of certificates worldwide.[6]

Product decisions made by marketers of consumer products are especially affected by local behavior, tastes, attitudes, and traditions—all reflecting the marketer's need to gain the customer's approval. A knowledge of cultural and psychological differences may be the key to success.

POSITIONING
The perception by consumers of a firm's product in relation to competitors' products

Often no concrete product changes are needed, only a change in the product's positioning. **Positioning** is the perception by consumers of the firm's brand in relation to competitors' brands—that is, the mental image that a brand, or the company as a whole, evokes. Coca-Cola took a risk in marketing Diet Coke in Japan because the population is not overweight by Western standards. Further, Japanese women do not like to drink anything clearly labeled as a diet product. The company changed the name to Coke Light and subtly shifted the promotional theme from "weight loss" to "figure maintenance."

Monitoring competitors' product features, as well as determining what has to be done to meet and beat them, is critical. Competitive offerings may provide a baseline against which the firm's resources can be measured—for example, what it takes to reach a critical market

Quick Take *Anyone for Flatbread?*

Food is arguably one of the most culture-sensitive categories. How is it possible for a company whose main line of business is the production of corn-flour and related products to be a player in markets beyond Mexico, where corn is plentiful and tortillas are a staple? Gruma, a company headquartered in Monterrey, Mexico, is a $2.5 billion international powerhouse transcending markets as diverse as the United States, United Kingdom, and China. Gruma's success has come in part from the realization that its product is a *carrier* of local tastes and it is the company's job to adapt that carrier to local tastes. Ultimately, Gruma's most versatile and marketable product has proven not to be a food, but a process—more specifically, the ability to roll any kind of flour, from corn to wheat to rice, into salable flatbread. Most people from India do not eat corn tortillas, but they do eat a flatbread called *naan*, made from wheat, which Gruma sells in the United Kingdom and plans to sell in India. The Chinese do not have much taste for corn tortillas either, but they buy wraps made by Gruma for Peking duck and plum sauce.

SOURCE: Jairo Senise, "Who is Your Next Customer?," *eNews of Strategy and Business*, September 28, 2007, 1–4; Alonzo Martinez and Ronald Haddock, "The Flatbread Factor," *Strategy and Business*, Spring 2007, 1–14; and **www.gruma.com**.

share in a given competitive situation. The devices have given lower income consumers—who may not have wired Internet access at home—a new path online. Huawei is expanding its device business and has found a niche with American consumers. As carriers set their sights on one of the last sources of growth in U.S. telecom-smartphone adoption among lower income consumers, Huawei has been there with some of the cheapest phones available.[7] These gains have come at the expense of companies like Samsung.

Marketing chocolate products is challenging in hot climates, which may restrict companies' option. Cadbury found opportunity in its predicament as a purveyor of chocolate in the hot climates of southern Asia, where the product melts easily. So Cadbury launched Dairy Milk Shots, ball-shaped candies that are milk with a chocolate cover. Each product has melted chocolate in its core but is not vulnerable to hot outdoor temperatures.[8]

Product Characteristics

Product characteristics are the inherent features of the product offering, whether actual or perceived. The inherent characteristics of products, and the benefits they provide to consumers in the various markets in which they are marketed, make certain products good candidates for standardization—and others not.

Culture Clues Nordic residents, accustomed to long dark winters and cold weather, are known for their coffee consumption. Finns drink an average of about 26.7 pounds of coffee a year. By way of comparison, U.S. consumers drink 9.0 pounds per year, Japanese 7.5 pounds, and British 6.7 pounds. After decades of virtually ignoring the highest coffee-consumption market in the world, Starbucks is looking for a presence in the pricey Nordic region. Expanding to open a store in the Helsinki Airport is consistent with a European growth strategy to open stores where Starbucks's customers want and expect them to be. Personnel-related costs in Finland represent 30 percent of revenue compared with the 23 percent rate that Starbucks said is typical of other European markets.
SOURCE: John D. Stoll, *Wall Street Journal*, 27 September 2012, B 8.

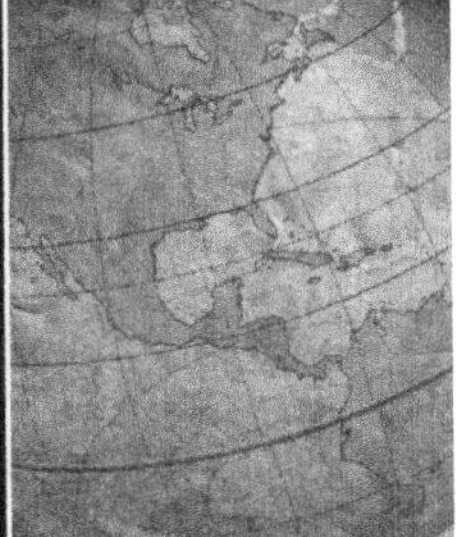

Fast Facts

Products in Asia often carry brand names that are translated from their original names. Why?

The cultural and linguistic factors must be considered in product naming as well as spelling, writing, and styling of any branding. When Frito-Lay introduced Cheetos in the Chinese market, it did so under a Chinese name that translates as "many surprises"; in Chinese *qi duo*—roughly pronounced "chee-do." Subway means "tastes better than others."

Where religion or custom determines consumption, ingredients may have to be replaced for the product to be acceptable. In Islamic countries, for example, vegetable shortening has to be substituted for animal fats. In deference to Hindu and Muslim beliefs, McDonald's Maharaja Mac is made with mutton in India. Digital technology is making it easy and inexpensive to substitute product placements in country or region-specific versions. In *Charlie's Angels: Full Throttle*, the detective character played by Lucy Liu uses her cellphone to send a clandestinely snapped photograph to a fellow detective. When he examines the photo on his computer screen, the audience clearly sees the logo for U.S. cellphone operator Cingular Wireless (AT&T). But in the movie's international release, as well as in foreign DVD releases, viewers see the logo for T-Mobile, a unit of Germany's Deutsche Telekom AG.[9]

The global marketer has a number of options in choosing a branding strategy. The marketer may choose to be a contract manufacturer to a distributor (the generics approach) or to establish national, regional, or worldwide brands. The use of standardization in branding is strongest in culturally similar markets; for example, for U.S. marketers this means Canada and the United Kingdom. Standardization of product and brand do not necessarily move hand in hand; a regional brand may well have local features, or a highly standardized product may have local brand names. PepsiCo adapts its products to the idiosyncrasies of its customers from around the world. The soda maker advertised itself as "Pecsi" in Argentina to much success. It is trying to do the same in Mexico and Spain. Many Spanish-speaking people would feel more comfortable pronouncing Pecsi or Pesi, rather than Pepsi.[10]

The consumer mandate for marketers to make products more environmentally friendly also affects the packaging dimension, especially in terms of the four Rs: redesign, reduce, recycle, and reuse. The EU has strict policies on the amounts of packaging waste that are generated and the levels of recycling of such materials.[11] Depending on the packaging materials (20 percent for plastics and 60 percent for glass), producers, importers, distributors, wholesalers, and retailers are held responsible for generating the waste. In Germany, which has the toughest requirements, all packaging must be reusable or recyclable, and packaging must be kept to the minimum needed for proper protection and marketing of the product. Exporters to the European Union must find distributors who can fulfill such requirements and agree how to split the costs.

Fast Facts

After China, which country is the top source of recalled products in the United States?

United States. Chinese products accounted for 58 percent of the recalls, while U.S. products contributed 20 percent of the total.

When a product that is sold globally requires repairs, parts, or service, the problems of obtaining, training, and holding a sophisticated engineering or repair staff are not easy to solve. If the product breaks down and the repair arrangements are not up to standard, the product image will suffer. In some cases, products abroad may not even be used for their intended purpose and thus may require not only modifications in product configuration but also in service frequency. A product recall is a request to return to the maker a batch or an entire production run of a product, usually due to the discovery of safety issues. China continues to promise to impose higher safety standards on exports, given the number of product recalls.

COUNTRY OF ORIGIN (COO)
The nation where a product is produced or branded

The **country of origin (COO)** of a product, typically communicated by the phrase "made in (country)," has considerable influence on quality perceptions. The perception of products manufactured in certain countries is affected by a built-in positive or negative assumption about quality. The international marketer must take steps to overcome, or at least neutralize, biases. For example, many consumers around the world perceive Nokia as a Japanese brand rather than as Finnish (which it is). However, this misidentification does not have a negative impact on the company despite the incorrect appropriation and has led to no action by Nokia. However, a Japanese carmaker Daihatsu suffered in the U.S. market at the time of its launch because it was perceived as a Korean brand. For this and other reasons, Daihatsu is no longer in the United States but concentrates its efforts on Latin America.[12] French and Italian trade and consumer groups are lobbying the European Union to require mandatory place-of-origin labels. The issue has become a sensitive one for high-end European fashion houses that are starting to make products overseas in low-cost countries.[13]

Company Considerations

Company policy will often determine the presence and degree of adaptation. Discussions of product adaptation often end with the question, "Is it worth it?" The answer depends on the company's ability to control costs, to correctly estimate market potential, and finally, to secure profitability. The decision to adapt should be preceded by a thorough analysis of the market. Formal market research with primary data collection and/or testing is warranted. From the financial standpoint, some companies have specific return-on-investment levels (for example, 25 percent) to be satisfied before adaptation. Others let the requirement vary as a function of the market considered and also the time in the market—that is, profitability may be initially compromised for proper market entry.

India is a country of more than a billion people with different cultures, different languages, different geographies, different food habits, different traditions, and different socio-cultural behaviors. Nobody can successfully do business in India by reading its potential from quantitative market reports. Understanding the psychological, sociological, and historical backgrounds is fundamental to hit the bull's-eye. Maggi has managed to enter Indian homes and change the traditional food habits of Indian children on the company's promise of convenience. This brand has understood the psychology of Indian mothers and positioned itself for mother-child indulgence. Nokia produced a cell phone with a dust-resistant keypad, anti-slip grip, and a built-in flash light; truck drivers and rural consumers enjoyed these simple-yet-useful features.[14]

Most companies aim for consistency in their market efforts. This means that all products must fit in terms of quality, price, and user perceptions. Consistency may be difficult to attain, for example, in the area of warranties. Warranties can be uniform only if use conditions do not vary drastically and if the company is able to deliver equally on its promise anywhere it has a presence.

Global Brand Strategy Decisions

The goal of many marketers currently is to create consistency and impact, both of which are easier to manage with a single worldwide identity.[15] **Global brands** are a key way of reaching this goal. Table 11.3 shows the fifteen most valuable global brands.

GLOBAL BRANDS
A brand/product that has worldwide recognition

TABLE 11.3 Fifteen Most Valuable Global Brands

2013 Rank	2012 Rank	Brand	Brand	2013 Brand Value (USD $billions)
1	2	Apple	Technology	$98.32
2	4	Google	Technology	$93.29
3	1	Coca-Cola	Beverages	$79.21
4	3	IBM	Business Services	$78.81
5	5	Microsoft	Technology	$59.55
6	6	GE	Diversified	$46.95
7	7	McDonald's	Restaurants	$41.99
8	9	Samsung	Technology	$39.61
9	8	Intel	Technology	$37.26
10	10	Toyota	Automotive	$35.35
11	11	Mercedes-Benz	Automotive	$31.90
12	12	BMW	Automotive	$31.84
13	14	Cisco	Technology	$29.05
14	13	Disney	Media	$28.15
15	15	HP	Technology	$25.84

SOURCE: **http://www.interbrand.com/en/news-room/press-releases/2013-09-30-d355afc.aspx**

Consumers all over the world associate global brands with three characteristics and evaluate their performance on them when making purchase decisions. Global brands carry a strong quality signal suggested by their success across markets. Part of this is that great brands often represent great ideas and leading-edge technological solutions. Second, global brands compete on emotion, catering to aspirations that cut across cultural differences. Global brands may cater to needs to feel cosmopolitan, something that local brands cannot deliver. Global brands may also convey that their user has reached a certain status both professionally and personally. This type of recognition represents both perception and reality, enabling brands to establish credibility in markets.[16] The third reason consumers choose global brands is involvement in solving social problems linked to what they are marketing and how they conduct their business. Expectations that global marketers use their monetary and human resources to benefit society are uniform from developed to developing markets.

The marketing manager must consider three main implications: (1) Don't hide globality. Given the benefits of globality, marketers should not be shy in communicating this feature of a brand. Creatively, this may mean referring to the leadership position of the brand around the world or referring to the extent of innovation or features that are possible only for a brand with considerable reach. Marketers intent on scaling down their brand portfolios and focusing on global offerings are able to invest in more marketing muscle and creative effort behind the sleeker set of offerings. (2) Tackle home-country bias. One of the marketing mantras is "being local on a global scale." Because some markets feature substantial preference for home-grown brands, it is imperative to localize some features of the marketing approach, possibly including even the brand name. One approach could be that a brand has a consistent global positioning but the name varies according to country language. An example is Mr. Clean becoming Mr. Proper in Germany/Austria/Switzerland, Mr. Propre in France, Don Limpio in Spain, and Maestro Lindo in Italy. Many global brands have already localized to neutralize the home-country effect. (3) Satisfy the basics. Global brands signal quality and aspiration. However, taking a global approach to branding is not in itself the critical factor. What is critical is creating differentiation and familiarity as well as the needed margins and growth. The greater esteem that global brands enjoy is not sufficient in itself for pursuing this strategy. However, this dimension may tip the balance in ultimate strategy choice. At the same time, it is evident that globality should not be pursued at the cost of alienating local consumers by preemptively eliminating purely local brands or converging them under a global brand.[17]

Product Counterfeiting

COUNTERFEIT GOODS
Any goods bearing an unauthorized representation of a trademark, patented invention, or copyrighted work that is legally protected in the country where it is marketed

Counterfeit goods are any goods bearing an unauthorized representation of a trademark, patented invention, or copyrighted work that is legally protected in the country where it is marketed. Companies lose a total of $657.7 billion every year because of product counterfeiting and other infringements on intellectual property.[18] Hardest hit are the most innovative, fastest growing industries, such as computer software, pharmaceuticals, and entertainment. In 2011, the software, publishing, and distribution industries lost more than $64 billion due to software theft.[19] The following percentages account for the commercial value of PC software piracy: United States (20 percent), European Union (35 percent), and BRIC countries (71 percent).

The practice of product counterfeiting has spread to high technology and services from the traditionally counterfeited products: high-visibility, strong brand-name consumer goods. In addition, management has to worry about whether raw materials and components purchased for production of counterfeit products that copycat their brand names are up to par. In general, countries with lower per capita incomes, higher levels of corruption in government, and lower levels of involvement in the international trade community tend to have higher levels of intellectual property violation.[20]

In today's environment, firms are taking more aggressive steps to protect themselves. Victimized firms are not only losing sales but also goodwill, in the longer term, if customers, believing they are getting the real product, unknowingly end up with a copy of inferior quality. In addition to the normal measures of registering trademarks and copyrights, firms are taking steps in product development to prevent the copying of trademarked goods. New authentication materials in labeling, for example, are virtually impossible to duplicate.

Pricing Strategies

Pricing is the only element in the marketing mix that is revenue generating; all of the other elements are costs. Pricing should therefore be used as an active instrument of strategy in the major areas of marketing decision-making. Pricing in the international environment is more complicated than in the domestic market, however, because of such factors as government influence, different currencies, and additional costs. Pricing situations can be divided into four general categories: export pricing, individual market pricing, price coordination, and transfer pricing.

Export Pricing

Three general price-setting strategies in global marketing are standard worldwide pricing, dual pricing, which differentiates between domestic and export prices, and market differentiated pricing. The first two are cost-oriented pricing methods that are relatively simple to establish, are easy to understand, and cover all of the necessary costs. **Standard worldwide pricing** is based on average unit costs of fixed, variable, and export-related costs. In **dual pricing**, domestic and export prices are differentiated, and two approaches are available: cost-plus and the marginal cost. The **cost-plus method** involves the actual costs, that is, a full allocation of domestic and foreign costs to the product. Although this type of pricing ensures margins, the final price may put the product beyond the reach of the customer. As a result, some exporters resort to a flexible cost-plus strategy, wherein discounts are provided when necessary as a result of customer type, intensity of competition, or size of order. The **marginal cost method** considers the direct costs of producing and selling for export as the floor beneath which prices cannot be set. Fixed costs for plants, R&D, domestic overhead, and domestic marketing are disregarded. An exporter can thus lower export prices to be competitive in markets that otherwise might have been considered beyond access.

Market-differentiated pricing calls for export pricing according to the dynamic conditions of the marketplace. For these firms, the marginal cost strategy provides a basis, and prices may change frequently due to changes in competition, exchange rate changes, or other environmental changes. The need for information and controls becomes crucial if this pricing alternative is to be attempted. Exporters are likely to use market-based pricing to gain entry or better penetration in a new market, ignoring many of the cost elements, at least in the short term.

Although most exporters, especially in the early stages of their internationalization, use cost-plus pricing, it usually does not lead to desired performance.[21] It typically leads to pricing too high in weak markets and too low in strong markets by not reflecting prevailing market conditions. But as experience is accumulated, the process allows for more flexibility and is more market-driven. Care has to be taken, however, that the cost of implementing a pricing-adaptation strategy does not outweigh the advantages of having a more adapted price.[22]

In preparing a quotation, the exporter must be careful to take into account unique export-related costs and, if possible, include them. The costs are in addition to those normally shared with the domestic side. Export-related costs include: (1) the cost incurred in modifying the

STANDARD WORLDWIDE PRICING
A price-setting strategy based on average unit costs of fixed, variable, and export-related costs

DUAL PRICING
A price-setting strategy in which the export price differs from the domestic price

COST-PLUS METHOD
A pricing policy in which there is a full allocation of foreign and domestic costs to the product

MARGINAL COST METHOD
Method that considers the direct costs of producing and selling goods for export as the floor beneath which prices cannot be set

MARKET-DIFFERENTIATED PRICING
A price-setting strategy based on market-specific demand rather than cost

good for foreign markets; (2) operational costs associated with export activities (examples are personnel, market research, additional shipping and insurance costs, communications costs with foreign customers, and overseas promotional costs; and (3) costs incurred in entering foreign markets (include tariffs and taxes, risks associated with a buyer in a different market) and dealing in other than the exporter's domestic currency—that is, foreign exchange risk. The combined effect of both clear-cut and hidden costs results in export prices far in excess of domestic prices. This is called **price escalation.**

PRICE ESCALATION
The increase in export prices due to additional marketing costs related specifically to exports

Overall, exporters see the pricing decision as a critical one, which means that it is typically taken centrally under the supervision of top-level management. In addition to product quality, correct pricing is seen as the major determinant of marketing success.

Individual Market Pricing

Pricing within the individual markets in which the firm operates is determined by (1) corporate objectives, (2) costs, (3) customer behavior and market conditions, (4) market structure, and (5) environmental constraints. All of these factors vary from country to country, and pricing policies of the multinational corporation must vary as well. Despite arguments in favor of uniform pricing in multinational markets, price discrimination is an essential characteristic of the pricing policies of firms conducting business in differing markets.

PRICE ELASTICITY OF CONSUMER DEMAND
Adjusting prices to current conditions; for example, a status-conscious market that insists on products with established reputations will be inelastic, allowing for more pricing freedom than a price-conscious market.

The global marketer must understand the **price elasticity of consumer demand** to determine appropriate price levels, especially if cost structures change. A status-conscious market that insists on products with established reputations will be inelastic, allowing for far more pricing freedom than a market where price-consciousness drives demand. Many U.S. and European companies have regarded Asia as a place to sell premium products at premium prices. Parker Pen Company found a new prestige market in China for special edition pens

QT Quick Take *Price Reset*

Fluctuations in commodity pricing can wreak havoc for companies in consumer markets when the fluctuations cause the price of some packaged brands to rise above broad consumer acceptance. With sales revenues declining, Danone initiated a program of price cuts, advertising, packaging revisions, new product introductions, and consumer promotion to boost volume growth in global markets. A key element of the price reset program was the use of advertising to create broad consumer awareness. In addition to lowered prices, the program also involved country-specific, such as switching from sampling to couponing and, in France, using hard discounts for six-packs of Danette. Procter & Gamble and Unilever found that although *selling* in small quantities, or sachets, was not the most economical way to purchase some goods, it allowed consumers to stay within their budgets. These consumers bought the products through the Philippines small sari-sari stores, which survived on high-turnover, low-value transactions. Indeed, buying goods in small amounts was part of daily life.

At $40 to $60, jeans are not affordable to the masses in developing countries. Arvind Mills, the world's fifth-largest denim maker, introduced "Ruf & Tuf" jeans—a ready-to-make kit of jeans components priced at $6 that could be assembled inexpensively by a local tailor.

SOURCES: Jamie Anderson and Costas Markides, "Strategic Innovation at the Base of the Pyramid," *MIT Sloan Management Review*, Fall 2007, 83–9; and C. K. Prahalad and Stuart L. Hart, "The Fortune at the Bottom of the Pyramid," *Strategy and Business* 7 (first quarter, 2002): 35–47.

with added Chinese characters that cost between $82 and $7,500, while its Western market has been fading.[23]

Although many global marketers emphasize nonprice methods of competition, they rank pricing high as a marketing tool overseas, even though the nondomestic pricing decisions are made at the middle management level in a majority of firms. Pricing decisions also tend to be made more at the local level, with coordination from headquarters in more strategic decision situations.[24]

Pricing Coordination

With increased trade liberalization and advanced economic integration, pricing coordination is becoming more important. However, coordination of the pricing function is necessary, especially in larger, regional markets such as the European Union. With the increasing level of integration efforts around the world, and even discussion of common currency elsewhere, control and coordination of global and regional pricing takes on a new meaning.

Subsidiaries often control the North American market (that is, a Canadian customer cannot get a better deal in the United States, and vice versa) and distances create a natural barrier against arbitrage practices that would be more likely to emerge in Europe, although even with the common currency, different rules and standards, economic disparities, and information differences may make deal-hunting difficult.[25] However, recent experience has shown that pricing coordination has to be worldwide because parallel imports will surface in any markets in which price discrepancies exist, regardless of distances.

Gray marketing, or parallel importation, refers to authentic and legitimately manufactured trademark items that are produced and purchased abroad but imported or diverted to the market by bypassing designated channels. The IT industry estimates that gray market sales of IT products account for more than $40 billion in revenue each year, collectively costing IT manufacturers up to $5 billion annually in lost profits.[26] The most important concerns are price segmentation and exchange rate fluctuations. Competitive conditions may require the international marketer to sell essentially the same product at different prices in different markets or to different customers. Because many products are priced higher in, for example, the United States, a gray marketer can purchase them in Europe or the Far East and offer discounts between 10 and 40 percent below list price when reselling them in the U.S. market. Exchange rate fluctuations can cause price differentials and thus opportunities for gray marketers. Marketers, who mainly sell to organizational customers, such as Nokia to telecommunications operators, have started using standard worldwide pricing.

GRAY MARKETING

The marketing of authentic, legally trademarked goods through unauthorized channels

Transfer Pricing

Transfer pricing, or intra-company pricing, is the pricing of sales to members of the corporate family. The overall competitive and financial position of the firm forms the basis of any pricing policy. In this, transfer pricing plays a key role. Intra-corporate sales can easily change consolidated global results because they often are one of the most important ongoing decision areas in a company.

TRANSFER PRICING

The pricing of products as sold by a firm to its own subsidiaries and affiliates

Doing business overseas requires coping with complexities of environmental peculiarities, the effect of which can be alleviated by manipulating transfer prices. Factors that call for adjustments include taxes, import duties, inflationary tendencies, unstable governments, and other regulations. For example, high transfer prices on goods shipped to a subsidiary and low transfer prices on goods imported from it will result in minimizing the tax liability of a subsidiary operating in a country with a high income tax. Tax liability thus results not only from the absolute tax rate but also from differences in how income is computed. On the other hand, a higher transfer price may have an effect on the import duty to be paid.

ARM'S LENGTH PRINCIPLE
A basis for intracompany transfer pricing; the price that an unrelated party would have paid for the same transaction

As a general rule, the best approach for the company is to follow the **arm's length principle** whereby it prices internally as it would price to a third, unrelated party. This principle is preferred by most governments and recommended by the OECD to streamline tax liabilities and to enhance transparency.

DISTRIBUTION STRATEGIES

Distribution channels provide the essential links that connect producers and customers. The channel decision is the most long term of marketing-mix decisions, in that it cannot be readily changed. In addition, it involves relinquishing some of the control the firm has over the marketing of its products. These two factors make choosing the right channel structure a crucial decision.

Channel Design

CHANNEL DESIGN
The length and width of the distribution channel

The term **channel design** refers to the length and width of the channel employed. Channel systems become more complex and enlarged as businesses acquire more customers, more distributors, more stakeholders, and more competition and become spread across more geographic boundaries. Business needs to evaluate and revaluate these channel systems for effectiveness by performing the following techniques:[27]

1. *To create new bridges between producers and customers.* At Apple's iTunes Store, consumers can choose from more than 10 million songs across every music genre, as well as movies and television shows for sale or rent. Similarly, retailers and individuals can find large international audiences for their niches using eBay's marketplace. Nokia and Grameen Foundation provide mobile access to remote village communities. The "Village Phone" program, operating in Uganda and Rwanda, involves a local entrepreneur who acquires subscribers, an operator who offers services, and a micro-financier who procures a network access point that supports seventy Nokia handsets. The program can reduce the cost of owning a mobile phone to approximately US$3 per month.
2. *To harness customers' ideas, tastes, and productive powers.* Danish toy maker Lego has launched an online customization platform—LEGO Digital Designer 4.3—where enthusiasts assemble components for their own designs, which Lego makes available to other customers.
3. *To establish new forms of business-to-business (B2B) commerce, including the emergence of specialist horizontal players.* Li & Fung, a multinational export sourcing, distribution and retail, now provides sophisticated procurement solutions and acts as a primary global sourcing agent for all Liz Claiborne labels, including Lucky Brand, Juicy Couture and Kate Spade.
4. *Offer consumer-to-consumer (C2C) activity, where participants share information in open, global online forums.* TripAdvisor's web site offers individuals the opportunity to rate and talk about their experiences in hotels and restaurants around the world, giving the traveler a voice.

Culture Clues Many market observers believed that small retail players in Latin America would be swept away by the sector's consolidation and the rapid entry of new hypermarkets and supermarkets. That had been the case in the United States and Europe, where small retailers have retained only 10 to 20 percent of the consumer packaged-goods market as large retailers have grown. So far, this has not occurred in Latin America. Small-scale independent supermarkets and traditional stores together still account for between 45 and 60 percent of consumer goods retailing in Latin American countries.

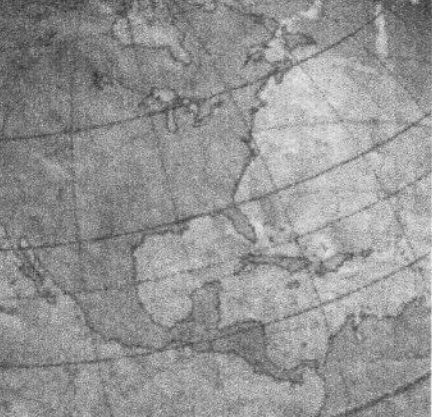

5. *To establish peer-to-peer (P2P) cooperative interaction among individuals rather than traditional sources of experience and trust.* Zopa, a U.K.-based company provides online money exchange services, allowing people who have money to lend to those who wish to borrow it instead of a traditional bank or lending institution.
6. *To encourage cooperative consumption by groups of end-consumers.* Shanghai-based Liba.com, sells items mainly for young families, everything from building materials to baby products. It has more than four million members and 30,000 transactions on average every month.

Managing the Channel Relationship

A channel relationship can be likened to a marriage in that it brings together two independent entities that have shared goals. For the relationship to work, each party must be clear about its expectations and openly communicate changes perceived in the other's behavior that might be contrary to the agreement. The closer the relationship is to a distribution partnership, the more likely marketing success will materialize. Conflict will arise, ranging from small grievances (such as billing errors) to major ones (rivalry over channel duties), but it can be managed to enhance the overall channel relationship. In some cases, conflict may be caused by an outside entity, such as gray markets, in which unauthorized intermediaries compete for market share with legitimate importers and exclusive distributors. Nevertheless, the international marketer must solve the problem.

The relationship has to be managed for the long term. In some countries, an exporter may have a seller's market situation that allows it to exert pressure on its intermediaries for concessions, for example. However, if environmental conditions change, the exporter may find that the channel support it needs to succeed is not there because of the manner in which it managed channel relationships in the past.[28] Firms with harmonious relationships are typically those with more experience abroad and those that are proactive in managing the channel relationship. Harmonious relationships are also characterized by more trust, communication, and cooperation between the entities and, as a result, by less conflict and perceived uncertainty.

As a firm's operations expand, the need for coordination across markets may grow. Therefore, the firm may want to establish distributor advisory councils to help in reactive measures (e.g., how to combat parallel importation) or proactive measures (e.g., how to transfer best practices from one distributor to another). It is for this reason that Dell formed the Customer Experience Council, a group that is scrutinizing every aspect of how Dell interacts with customers. A framework for managing channel relationships is shown in Table 11.4.

TABLE 11.4 Performance Problems and Remedies When Using Overseas Distributors

High Performance Inhibitors	Bring	Remedy Lies in
Separate ownership	Divided royalties Seller-buyer atmosphere Unclear future intentions Communication blocks	Offering good incentives, helpful support schemes, discussing plans frankly, and interacting in a mutually beneficial way
Geographic and cultural separation	Negative attitudes Physical distribution strains	Making judicious use of two-way visits, establishing a well-managed communication program
Different rules of law	Vertical trading restrictions Dismissal difficulties	Complying fully with the law, drafting a strong distributor agreement

SOURCE: Philip J. Rosson, "Source Factors in Manufacture—Overseas Distributor Relationships in International Marketing," in *International Marketing Management*, ed. Erdener Kaynak (New York: Praeger, 1984), 95.

E-Commerce as a Distribution Channel

M-COMMERCE
The exchange of goods and services using mobile devices that allow Web browsing

Various marketing constituents see the Web as more than a communication tool; they see it as a builder of interactive relationships and as a device to sell products and services—e-commerce. Global Internet penetration grew at a rate of 566 percent from 2000 to 2012 with further penetration projected as relatively inexpensive mobile 3G devices allow more access in developing countries. This in turn, has facilitated the growth of **m-commerce**, the exchange of goods and services using smart mobile handheld devices that allow Web browsing. In 2012, world Internet penetration rate in North America exceeded all other regions at 78.6 percent, followed by Oceania/Australia at 67.6 percent, Europe at 63.2 percent, Latin America at 42.9 percent, and Asia at 27.5 percent with Africa lagging behind at 15.6 percent. Asia exceeded all other regions in the number of Internet users with 34.3 percent worldwide.[29] As shown in Table 11.5, worldwide e-commerce revenue is projected to grow at an average rate of 20.2 percent between 2014 and 2017, with the fastest rates of growth occurring in Japan, Asia/Pacific, and in parts of the world outside of the United States and Western Europe. The United States, however, is projected to remain the largest market for e-commerce, followed by Western Europe.

TABLE 11.5 Business to Consumer E-Commerce Sales Worldwide, by Region (in $billions)

	2013	2015	2017
Asia-Pacific	$383.90	$681.20	$1,052.90
North America	$431.00	$538.30	$660.40
Western Europe	$312.00	$382.70	$445.00
Central & Eastern Europe	$49.50	$64.40	$73.10
Latin America	$48.10	$64.90	$74.60
Middle East & Africa	$27.00	$39.60	$51.40
Worldwide	$1,251	$1,771	$2,357

SOURCE: "Global B2C Ecommerce Sales to Hit $1.5 Trillion This Year Driven by Growth in Emerging Markets," *eMarketer*, February 3, 2014.

To fully serve the needs of its customers using e-commerce and to further development of the business relationship, the company itself must be prepared to provide twenty-four-hour order taking and customer service, have the regulatory and customs-handling expertise to deliver internationally, and have an in-depth understanding of marketing environments, as well as customer habits and preferences. The instantaneous interactivity users experience will also be translated into an expectation of expedient delivery of answers and products ordered.

Many companies entering e-commerce choose to use marketplace sites, like eBay, that bring together buyers, sellers, distributors, and transaction payment processors in one single marketplace, making convenience the key attraction. Amazon.com has broadened its offerings from books and music to include tools, clothing, television shows, jewelry, health and beauty, and electronics, among others. Walmart.com has one million products available online and continues to develop new online services such as music downloads and photo developing. For companies that choose to operate their own e-commerce sites, transaction payment processors like PayPal offer services to facilitate payments around the world. PayPal opened its global payments platform with capabilities that include currency conversion and mobile applications.

The challenges faced in terms of response and delivery capabilities can be overcome through outsourcing services or by building international distribution networks. Air express carriers such as DHL, FedEx, and UPS offer full-service packaging systems that leverage their own Internet infrastructure with customs clearance and e-mail shipment notification. If a company needs help in order fulfillment and customer support, logistics centers offer warehousing and inventory management services as well as same-day delivery from in-country stocks.

Each transaction collects information about the buyer, which allows for more customization and service by region, market, or individual customer. Dell Computer does 30 percent of its business over the Web; this adds up to be $18 million worth of hardware, software, and accessories per day. Dell offers thousands of their corporate customers a Premier site offering procurement and support designed to save these customers money by using Dell's IT process.

The marketer has to be sensitive to the governmental role in e-commerce in regard to local regulations and taxation implications. Although some countries require businesses to have a "permanent establishment" or taxable entity established before the country will hold the company responsible for taxes, there are often exceptions and requirements for payments from customers to be taxable.

Privacy issues have grown exponentially as a result of e-business as businesses collect and process personally identifiable information. Many countries, including the United States and the member states of the European Union, have specific privacy laws requiring strict compliance by online businesses.

Promotional Strategies

The international marketer must choose a proper combination of the various promotional tools—advertising, personal selling, sales promotion, publicity and sponsorship—to create images among the intended target audience. The choice will depend on the target audience, company objectives, the product or service marketed, the resources available for the endeavor, and the availability of promotional tools in a particular market. Increasingly, the focus is not a product or service but the company's image.

Advertising

The key decision-making areas in advertising are (1) media strategy, (2) creative strategy, and (3) organization of the promotional program.

MEDIA STRATEGY
Strategy applied to the selection of media vehicles and the development of a media schedule

MEDIA STRATEGY **Media strategy** is applied to the selection of media vehicles and the development of a media schedule. Media spending varies dramatically around the around the world, as seen in Table 11.6. Media spending, which totaled $504.7 billion in 2013, varies dramatically around the world. In absolute terms, the United States spends more money on advertising than most of the other major advertising nations combined. Other major spenders are Japan, China, Germany, the United Kingdom, and Brazil.[30] The mature U.S. market anticipates slower growth in the future, but the Asian markets in particular are expected to witness robust growth. The top five corporate advertisers in 2012 were Procter & Gamble ($10.61 billion), Unilever ($7.41 billion), L'Oreal ($5.64 billion), Toyota ($3.31 billion), and General Motors ($3.20 billion).

Geographic differences exist in spending; for example, while Procter & Gamble spent 38 percent of its budget in the United States, Unilever's U.S. spending was only 15 percent. The top 100 advertisers incurred one-third (33.4 percent) of their spending in the United States, with Europe second at 27.8 percent. Asia-Pacific was a distant third, commanding only 26 percent of measured media bought.[31]

Today, the Internet is well on the way to establishing itself as a complementary advertising medium worldwide. The projection is that the Internet may have a 21.2 percent market share in world advertising by 2014. Internet advertising constitutes 97 percent of advertising in Ice-

TABLE 11.6 Expenditure by Medium (in $ millions)

	2012	2013	2014
Newspapers	89,868	88,785	88,446
Magazines	42,681	42,464	42,186
Television	193,735	203,608	215,737
Radio	33,667	34,827	35,923
Cinema	2,564	2,732	2,916
Outdoor	32,928	34,559	36,350
Internet	84,267	97,764	113,281
Total	479,710	504,738	534,839

SOURCE: **http://www.zenithoptimedia.com**

land and 94.4 percent in Norway. China accounts for half of the Asia-Pacific region's Internet advertising and will constitute 52 percent of its projected growth. In addition to PCs, mobile phones and interactive television are becoming delivery mechanisms for the Internet.[32] The rapid spread of Internet connectivity is making Facebook accessible to ever more people. The Boston Consulting Group estimates that around three billion people will be online by 2016, up from 1.6 billion in 2010.

GLOBAL MEDIA

Media vehicles that have target audiences on at least three continents and have a central buying office for placements

Global media vehicles have been developed that target audiences on at least three continents and for which the media buying takes place through a centralized office. These media have traditionally been publications that, in addition to the worldwide edition, have provided advertisers the option of using regional editions.

For example, *Time* publishes regional editions for the United States, Asia, the South Pacific, Europe, the Middle East, and Africa. For each region, *Time* publishes subregional editions. In Asia, for example, nineteen geographic subeditions are available for advertisers to reach country-specific audiences. Other global publications include the *International Herald Tribune*, the *Wall Street Journal* (as well as the *Asian Wall Street Journal*), *National Geographic*, the *Financial Times*, and the *Economist*. The Internet provides the international marketer with an additional global medium.

Web exposure is often achieved through cooperation with Internet service providers. In broadcast media, pan-regional radio stations have been joined by television as a result of satellite technology. More than half of the households in Europe have access to additional television broadcasts, either through cable or direct satellite, and television is no longer restricted by national boundaries. As a result, marketers need to make sure that advertising works not only within markets but across countries as well. The launch of Star TV, featured in the ad in Figure 11.1, has increased the use of regional advertising in Asia.

Media regulations vary. Some regulations include limits on the amount of time available for advertisements; in Italy, for example, the state channels allow a maximum of 12 percent of advertising per hour and 4 percent over a week, and commercial stations allow 18 percent per

Culture Clues Product placement in television shows, movies, games, or web sites has grown to a $6.97 billion business according to PQ Media. The basic drivers of this phenomenon are the success of reality shows and the more-empowered consumer who can skip traditional ads with the touch of a button. In addition, governments (e.g., the European Union) have relaxed their restrictions on product placement. In some markets, product placement may be an effective method of attracting attention due to constraints on traditional media. The United States is the largest digital out-of-home (DOOH) market among the twenty-eight countries tracked for this report, with $2.05 billion in revenues in 2011. China ranks second with $1.44 billion in revenues, followed by Japan with $759 million.

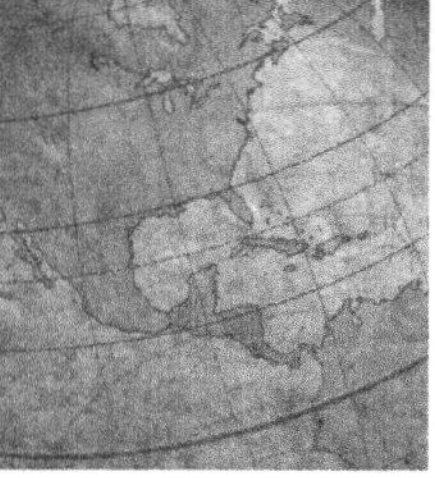

FIGURE 11.1 Broadcast Media in Asia

SOURCE: STAR USA

hour and 15 percent per week. Furthermore, the leading Italian stations do not guarantee audience delivery when spots are bought. Strict separation between programs and commercials is almost a universal requirement, preventing U.S.-style sponsored programs. Restrictions on items, such as comparative claims and gender stereotypes, are prevalent; for example, German courts can find comparative advertising to be illegal if as little as 15 percent of consumers are "misled" by the advertising.

CREATIVE STRATEGY
Development of the content of a promotional message such as an advertisement, publicity release, sales promotion activity, or Web-based promotion

CREATIVE STRATEGY Developing the promotional message is referred to as **creative strategy**. The marketer must determine what the consumer is really buying—that is, the consumer's motivations. They will vary, depending on the following:

1. *The diffusion of the product, service, or concept into the market.* For example, to enter China with online sales requires an understanding of the variances in Internet penetration and online shopping by region. With overall Internet penetration, half of Beijing and Shanghai Internet users are online shoppers, while only 35 percent of users in Guangzhou and 29 percent in Chengdu shop online.[33]
2. *The criteria on which the consumer will evaluate the product.* After determining that Indian consumers most valued the lifetime ownership cost of a vehicle, Hyundai implemented this criterion in its Santro automobile with a reduced engine output, keeping the car fuel-efficient. Hyundai also considered India's less-than-optimum road conditions when designing the car. Hyundai also priced its spare parts reasonably and tailored dozens more product specifications to the Indian market.[34]
3. *The product's positioning.* For example, Parker Pen's upscale image may not be profitable enough in a market that is more or less a commodity business. FIJI Water has been committed to doing business in responsible ways and ensuring that both the environment and society are better off as a result of its actions. In 2008, FIJI Water was recognized by *Elle* magazine's "Empower the Green Enterprise" Award.[35]

Fast Facts

Where are the world's top twenty-five agencies and agency groups located?

Twelve are based in the United States, six in the European Union, four in Japan and Korea, two in Australia, and one in Latin America.

The ideal situation in developing message strategy is to have a world brand—a product that is manufactured, packaged, and positioned the same around the world. However, a number of factors will force companies to abandon identical campaigns in favor of recognizable campaigns. The factors are culture, of which language is the main manifestation, economic development, and lifestyles. Itaú is an example of corporate image advertising; the company wants to show its vision of Latin America to the world, reinforcing its Latin roots and demonstrating that it is the bank that understands this region best (see Figure 11.2). Itaú is an

FIGURE 11.2 Corporate Image Campaign

SOURCE: Courtesy of Itaú Unibanco

international bank with operations in the Americas, Europe, and Asia, providing services in a wide range of business segments.

ORGANIZATION OF THE PROMOTIONAL PROGRAM Many multinational corporations are staffed and equipped to perform the full range of promotional activities. In most cases, however, they rely on the outside expertise of advertising agencies and other promotions-related companies, such as media-buying companies and specialty marketing firms. One of the largest world holding groups, WPP Group, includes such entities as Ogilvy & Mather, J. Walter Thompson, Young & Rubicam, and Grey. Smaller advertising agencies have affiliated local agencies in foreign markets. In a study of 40 multinational marketers, 32.5 percent are using a single agency worldwide, 20 percent are using two, 5 percent are using three, 10 percent are using four, and 32.5 percent are using more than four agencies.[36]

Personal Selling

Personal selling can be defined as a two-way flow of communication between a potential buyer and a salesperson and is designed to accomplish at least three tasks: (1) identify the buyer's needs; (2) match these needs to one or more of the firm's products; and (3) on the basis of this match, convince the buyer to purchase the product. This is part of the firm's perceived need for increased **customer relationship management**, where the sales effort is linked to call-center technologies, customer-service departments, and the company's web site. Advancements in 4G networks, voice-over-Internet protocol (VoIP), and dual-mode handsets will bring new opportunities to account management, and real-time reporting tools will enable managers to gain insight into the sales process.

PERSONAL SELLING
Marketing efforts focusing on one-on-one efforts with customers

CUSTOMER RELATIONSHIP MANAGEMENT
The collecting, storing, and analyzing of customer data to develop and maintain two-way relations

Sales Promotion

Sales promotion refers to short-term inducements that provide extra value and incentives to sales personnel, intermediaries, and consumers. The Internet lends itself well to facilitating sales promotion activities, which include offering coupons, discounts, rebates, product sampling, contests, and premiums. Firms may offer any or some combination of these to entice buyers to act immediately, such as by visiting a web site, registering online, or making a purchase. For example, Hertz offers coupon deals at its various web sites for car rentals in 146 countries worldwide. Offering coupons online significantly lowers the costs of development, distribution, and database creation. Unlike traditional coupons, the firm incurs no printing costs. Many consumers prefer to obtain coupons online because of the time savings in searching for and organizing them.

SALES PROMOTION
Short-term inducements that provide extra value and incentives to sales personnel, intermediaries, and consumers

Global marketers are well advised to take advantage of local regional opportunities. In Brazil, gas delivery people are used to distribute product samples to households by companies such as Nestlé, Johnson & Johnson, and Unilever. The delivery people are usually assigned to the same district for years and have, therefore, earned their clientele's trust. For the marketers, distributing samples this way is not only effective, it is very economical: Marketers are charged five cents for each unit distributed. The gas companies benefit as well in that their relationship with customers is enhanced through these "presents."

After sales-force costs, trade shows are one of the most significant cost items in marketing budgets. Although they are usually associated with industrial firms, some consumer products firms are represented as well. Typically, a trade show is an event at which manufacturers, distributors, and other vendors display their products or describe their services to current and prospective customers, suppliers, other business associates, and the press. The Consumer Electronics (Las Vegas) and Consumer and Industry Products (Guangzhou) trade shows, for example, run eight hours a day for three days, plus one or two preview days, and register 200,000 attendees.

Public Relations

Public relations is the marketing communications function charged with executing programs to earn public understanding and acceptance, which means both internal and external communication. Internal communication is important, especially in multinational companies, to create an appropriate corporate culture. External campaigns can be achieved through the use of corporate symbols, corporate advertising, customer relations programs, the generation of publicity, as well as getting a company's view to the public using the Internet. Some material on the firm is produced for special audiences to assist in personal selling.

Cause-related marketing is a combination of public relations, sales promotion, and corporate philanthropy. This activity should not be developed merely as a response to a crisis, nor should it be a fuzzy, piecemeal effort to generate publicity; instead, marketers should have a social vision and a planned long-term social policy. For example, in Casanare, Colombia, where it is developing oil interests, British Petroleum invests in activities that support its business plan and contribute to the region's development. This has meant an investment of $10

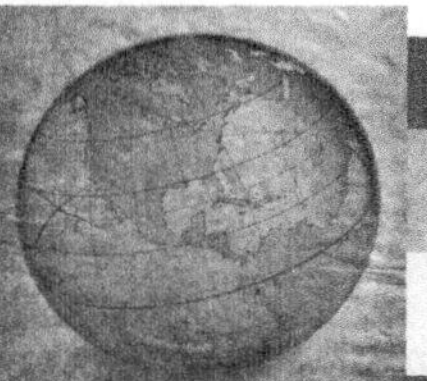

WORLD VIEW
Global Sponsorship

In any given country, the majority of corporate sponsorship goes to sports. Of the $51.0 billion spent worldwide for sponsorships in 2012, 69 percent was allocated to sports. Within sports, the two flagship events are the World Cup in soccer and the Olympic Games (both summer and winter). Sponsors want to align themselves with—and create—meaningful sports-related moments for consumers. At the same time, consumers associate sponsors of sports events with leadership, teamwork, and pursuit of excellence, as well as friendship.

Sponsorships have been a cornerstone of the Coca-Cola Company's marketing efforts for 100 years. Presently, the company is the world's biggest sports sponsor, with total sponsorship-related expenses at $1 billion annually. These activities span different types of sports and various geographies. Each country organization within Coca-Cola decides which programs it wants to use during sponsorship, depending on its goals, which are jointly set by local managers and headquarters.

SOURCE: Shutterstock.com

Although measurement of the return on such investments is challenging, Coca-Cola evaluates such dimensions as the number of new corporate customers that sell Coke in their stores, the incremental amount of promotional and display activity, and new vending placement. The influence on the brand is the most difficult to establish. The World Cup sponsorship has been suggested to have boosted Coca-Cola's presence, especially in the emerging and developing markets.

SOURCES: *FIFA*, **http://www.fifa.com**; Coca-Cola, **http://www.coca-cola.com/en/index.html**; and IEG, **http://www.sponsorship.com**.

million in setting up a loan fund for entrepreneurs, giving students technical training, supporting a center for pregnant women and nursing mothers, working on reforestation, building aqueducts, and helping to create jobs outside the oil industry.[37]

Sponsorship Marketing

Sponsorship involves the marketer's investment in events or causes. Sponsorship funds worldwide are directed for the most part at sports events (both individual and team sports) and cultural events (both in the popular and high-culture categories). World View: Global Sponsorship highlights one of the leading programs.

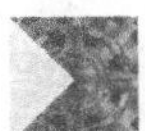

SOCIAL NETWORK AND MEDIA

Businesses can use **social networks** to directly communicate, collaborate, and understand their customer base. Social networks help raise brand awareness, increase market penetration, maintain customer loyalty, create user advocates, conduct market research, develop viral word-of-mouth advertising, create online buzz, drive customers to company web sites, and generally increase sales.

SOCIAL NETWORKS

A communal structure consisting of individuals or organizations connected with each other through friendship, common interest, commercial transactions, information exchange, or other types of relationships

SOCIAL MEDIA

The use of communications technology to facilitate meaningful interaction among individuals and organizations

A social network is among people and organizations who, for example, share interests, activities, backgrounds, or real-life connections. **Social media** employ Web- and mobile-based technologies to support interactive dialogue and the creation and exchange of user-generated content. The intent of a company that uses social media is to promote its brand and connect with customers by creating web sites, profiles, and advertising. Content reflects the expansion of media through new technologies that are accessible and affordable to the general public.

Table 11.7 lists the most popular social networking sites, applications, and tools. Social media became one of the most powerful sources for news updates through global platforms. Facebook, Twitter, and Google+ have the most users worldwide, while QQ and Qzone, both developed by Tentcent, are only available in China at this time but may be introduced into the United States to compete with Facebook. The World View highlights the problems Facebook and other social media have in China.

TABLE 11.7 How Many People Use the Top Social Media, Apps, and Tools?

Facebook	1.28 billion	Line	400 million
Youtube	1 billion	WeChat/WeiXin	396 million
Tinder	1 billion	Tagged	330 million
Baidu Tieda	1 billion	Alipay	300 million
QQ	848 million	Google+	300 million
Google Chrome	750 million	iCloud	300 million
Qzone	644 million	LinkedIn	300 million
Weibo	600 million	Skype	300 million
Tmall	500 million	Wandoujia	300 million
Whats App	500 million	Viber	280 million
Youku Tudou	450 million	Yahoo! Mail	273 million
Shazam	450 million	Trip Advisor	260 million
Gmail	425 million	Twitter	500 million
Outlook	400 million		

SOURCE: Craig Smith, "How Many People Use the Top Social Media, Apps and Tools?" *DMR*, April 2, 2014.

WORLD VIEW

Facebook Versus China

Facebook would like to reach China's 513 million Internet users, who are a very powerful consumer block. Facebook is on a mission to connect the entire world, but a third of the globe's population cannot be reached. The Chinese government has blocked its citizens from Facebook since 2009 and limits free speech and allows officials access to company data. Local social media entrepreneurs such as QQ, Qzone, Weibo, Weixin, and Renran have beaten Facebook to these consumers. Most people believe that Facebook's executives are waiting until after the government changeover to reopen conversations about a China strategy in hopes that new leaders may have a more relaxed attitude toward social-networking services.

TABLE 11.8 Synopsis of Online Chinese Media Companies and Users

Service	Company	No. of Users	Who They Are	What Users Do
QQ	Tencent	823 million	Teens, second-tier cities	Basic instant messaging; users IM and play games, and Tencent relies on QQ to cross-promote services
Qzone	Tencent	611 million	Popular with young teens and rural users	Write blogs, share photos, listen to music
Weibo	Tencent	503 million	Second-tier cities	Read and share celebrity-news snippets
Weixin (WeChat)	Tencent	400 million	Educated users in first-tier cities	Chat with friends via mobile location-based group-messaging application
Weibo	Sina	368 million	Educated user base, first-tier cities	Publish and share short bursts of celebrity gossip and breaking news
Renren	Oak Pacific Interactive	170 million	University students	Update profiles, share photos and videos

SOURCE: Jessi Hempel, " Facebook's China Problem," *Fortune*, September 24, 2012, 106.

Opportunities and Challenges

Social media are Internet-based communication media in which extensive conversations and interactions take place among people online. Social media allow people to share and feel connected with each other using brands and organizations they like and trust (see Table 11.9).[38]

ONLINE PROJECTS A wiki is a web site developed and maintained by a community of users who add informative content on a variety of topics. Wikipedia has grown rapidly into one of the largest reference web sites, attracting 470 million unique visitors monthly. More than 77,000 active contributors work on over 22,000,000 articles in 285 languages. On a smaller scale, many firms use wikis as a form of collaborative software, allowing employees and customers to interact and enhance group learning. Unilever achieved breakthrough innovations with its "disruptive technology"—technology that makes a big impact on the market by meeting consumer needs better and faster than alternatives.[39]

TABLE 11.9 Classification Social Media

		Social Presence and Media Richness		
		Low	Medium	High
Self-Presentation and Self-Disclosure	High	Blogs	Social networking sites (e.g., Facebook)	Virtual social worlds (e.g., Second Life)
	Low	Collaborative projects (e.g., Wikipedia)	Content communities (e.g., YouTube)	Virtual game worlds (e.g., World of Warcraft)

SOURCE: Andreas Kaplan and Michael Haenlein, "Users of the World, Unite! The Challenges and Opportunities of Social Media," *Business Horizons*, 53 (January/February 2010): 63.

BLOGS A typical blog combines text, images, and links to other blogs, web sites, and other media related to its topic. Readers' ability to leave comments in an interactive format is an important contribution to many blogs' popularity. Most blogs are primarily textual, although some focus on art, photographs, videos, music (iPod and MP3), and audio (podcasting). Micro-blogging is another type of blogging, featuring very short posts. Around 216 million Tumblr and 79 million WordPress blogs are in existence worldwide. Bloggers also write about global brands, such as Nokia Blog, Blog Ford, jackiechan.com/blog, and bx.businessweek.com/jack-welch/blogs.

CONTENT COMMUNITIES Content covers a range of media content available in a range of modern communications technologies. Different media exist: text (e.g., BookCrossing), photos (e.g., Flickr), videos (e.g., YouTube), and PowerPoint presentations (e.g., Slideshare). From a corporate viewpoint, content communities carry the risk of being used as platforms for sharing copyright-protected materials. Although major content communities have rules in place to ban and remove such illegal content, it is difficult to avoid popular videos being uploaded to YouTube only hours after they have been aired on television. On the positive side, the high popularity of content communities makes them a very attractive contact channel for many firms; this is easy to believe when one considers that YouTube serves more than 4 billion videos per day. Fiat commercials for the Fiat 500 featured Jennifer Lopez at the American Music Awards, where the car was seen by 120 million viewers. The Fiat 500 was also featured in Carly Rae Jepsen's video "Call Me Maybe," which has received views on YouTube, targeting the perfect audience: teenagers who are starting to drive. [40]

SOCIAL NETWORKING SITES Users are able to connect by creating personal information profiles, inviting friends and colleagues to have access to those profiles, and sending e-mails and instant messages. Every month, Facebook users share more than 30 billion pieces of content, including web links, news stories, blog posts, notes, photos, and video. The personalization aspect of social media sites such as Facebook and Twitter are powerful because it reveals what your friends and your friends' friends are buying and the companies they admire most. If you need to buy a new Nokia Lumia 920, for example, you probably care little about what smartphones are advertised on television. However, if your Facebook friends "like" a particular brand, your preference to purchase will increase. Social media succeed as a marketing tool because people usually trust the recommendations of the friends they know, particularly over those of companies they do not know. Many firms leverage the power of online opinion leaders and trendsetters to create buzz and accelerate product adoption.

Thinking about social media as digital word-of-mouth enables salespeople to appreciate just how crucial it is. Many U.S. companies claim to have a social media strategy, but only 27 percent of U.S. salespeople say their company trains or educates them on the use of social media for sales. This stands in stark contrast to Brazil, where 65 percent of salespeople surveyed received training on social media usage. Seventy-three percent of the salespeople surveyed in

Fast Facts

AOL's goviral's Social Video Equity Report explores how video content is being used by global brands as part of their marketing strategy. What are the top five?

The goviral Social Video Equity Report 2012 (**http://beon.aolnetworks.com/download/sve100.pdf**):

1. Red Bull
2. Google
3. Disney
4. Nike
5. Samsung

Quick Take *Interactive Story*

Grey Goose Cherry Noir launched a fully integrated, multi-million dollar marketing campaign including national print, out of home, radio, digital, social, and experiential "Hotel Noir" private events. Starting new conversations in social media and inviting their audience to participate in them, Grey Goose is changing the way consumers speak about the brand. Grey Goose's web site immersed visitors in the plot of Hotel Noir, a seductive six-chapter story that promoted the spirits brand's latest vodka, Cherry Noir. Created by the R/GA Chicago office to be fully integrated with the agency's worldwide network, the campaign was one of the first to leverage both Instagram and Pinterest to increase awareness of a liquor product. In addition to its initial Hotel Noir music video, a fashion-forward montage set in swanky bars and hotel rooms, Grey Goose announced a weekly theme for the story. Chapters included titles such as "If Looks Could Kill" and "Behind Room 205," and integrated fashion, music, and mysterious characters. Grey Goose commissioned a team of four popular smartphone photographers to capture shots for each chapter's Instagram stream and share the images with their personal followers. Photographers were chosen for their specific artistic styles, and the overall breadth of styles in this campaign conveyed the state and feeling associated with Grey Goose Cherry Noir vodka to its consumers.

SOURCE: Marguerite McNeal, "Campaign Corner: Grey Goose #HotelNoir," *Marketing Thought Leaders*, October 10, 2012.

China use personal blogs in their selling process.[41] Many have accelerated marketing activities by skipping less efficient or more expensive approaches, such as television and market research firms, and embracing cost-effective social media to achieve marketing goals.

Wireless technology is changing the world landscape in communications in many ways. ABI Research estimates more than five billion mobile subscriptions were active worldwide in 2011. It expects mobile subscriptions to reach 6.4 billion by 2015, of which 169 million will be subscribed to 4G technologies.[42] Consumers now spend around 20 percent of their total time online using social networks on their personal computers, and 30 percent of their time online visiting social networks on mobile devices.[43] Numerous social media applications have gone mobile, and new entrants are constantly appearing:

1. Exchange of messages with relevance for one specific location at one specific point-in-time (e.g., Facebook Places, Foursquare)
2. Exchange of messages, with relevance for one specific location, which are tagged to a certain place and read later by others (e.g., Yelp, Qype)
3. Transfer of traditional social media applications to mobile devices to increase immediacy (e.g., posting Twitter messages or Facebook status updates)
4. Transfer of traditional social media applications to mobile devices (for example, watching a YouTube video or reading a Wikipedia entry) [44]

VIRTUAL GAME WORLDS A virtual world is an online community that takes the form of a computer-based simulated environment through which users can interact with one another and use and create objects. Blizzard Entertainment is a premier developer of entertainment software since 1994. Blizzard's popular game, World of Warcraft (WoW), has more than 10 million active subscribers currently. WoW was launched in November 2004 in North America,

Australia, and New Zealand and subsequently in mainland China and in Russia in 2008. It is available in eight different languages based on the regions in which it is played. The high popularity of virtual game worlds can also be leveraged in more traditional communication campaigns. Two Mountain Dew Battle Fuel flavors were made available virtually to U.S. WoW players to promote the real world flavors. The two new Mountain Dew flavors were given WoW-based packaging and sported the newly updated "MTN Dew" logo. Mountain Dew officially announced another return of the Game Fuel promotion on their Facebook page.

VIRTUAL SOCIAL WORLDS Virtual social worlds allow inhabitants to behave more freely and essentially live virtual lives similar to their real lives. The users, or Residents, interact with each other through mobile avatars, providing an advanced level of social network services. They can explore, meet other Residents, socialize, participate in educational and social activities both individually and in groups, and create and trade virtual property and services with one another. Virtual social worlds offer a multitude of opportunities for companies in marketing (advertising/ communication, virtual product sales, marketing research). An example of this would be Apple creating an online store within Second Life. This allows the users to browse the latest and innovative products. Users cannot actually purchase a product but having these virtual stores is a way of accessing a different clientele and customer demographic. The use of advertising within virtual worlds is a relatively new idea.[45]

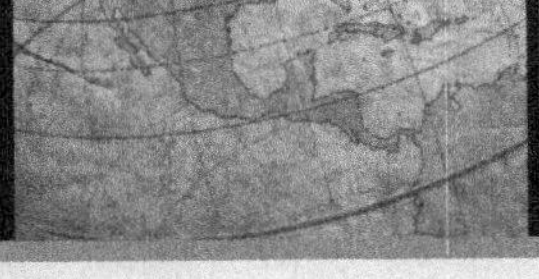

SUMMARY

The task of the global marketer is to seek new opportunities in the world marketplace and satisfy emerging needs through creative management. By its very nature, marketing is the most sensitive of business functions to environmental effects and influences.

A critical decision in international marketing concerns the degree to which the overall marketing program should be standardized or localized.

The ideal is to standardize as much as possible without compromising the basic task of marketing: satisfying the needs and wants of the target market.

Several issues affect the pricing of products for markets, including the cost of the operation, market conditions, and environmental constraints. Companies with multinational subsidiaries must also determine transfer prices for goods moved between sister companies.

Each foreign market offers its own mix of distribution channels, including e-commerce channels, which must be evaluated in terms of the company's objectives and competitive strategy.

The global marketer must choose a proper combination of the various promotional tools—advertising, personal selling, sales promotion, and publicity—to create the desired brand image within its target markets.

Firms increasingly leverage the power of social networks, communal structures of individuals or organizations connected with each other friendship, common interests, commercial transactions, and information exchange.

Key Terms and Concepts

standardization approach
multidomestic approach
globalization approach
positioning
country of origin (COO)
global brands
counterfeit goods
standard worldwide pricing
dual pricing
cost-plus method
marginal cost method
market-differentiated pricing
price escalation
price elasticity of consumer demand
gray marketing
transfer pricing
arm's length principle
channel design
m-commerce
media strategy
global media
creative strategy
personal selling
customer relationship management
sales promotion
social networks
social media

Review Questions

1. What is the danger in oversimplifying the globalization approach? Would you agree with the statement that "if something is working in a big way in one market, you better assume it will work in all markets"?
2. Are standards like those promoted by the International Organization for Standardization a hindrance or an opportunity?
3. Comment on the pricing philosophy, "Sometimes price should be wrong by design."
4. How effective is e-commerce as a global distribution channel? For what types of goods or services is it best suited?
5. What type of adjustments must advertising agencies make as more companies want "one sight, one sound, one sell" campaigns?
6. What is the role of community relations for a global marketer?
7. Describe the relationship between social networks and social media.
8. How do consumers create content using social media?

Critical Skill Builders

1. As one consumer put it: "Local brands are who I am; global brands are who I want to become." Why?
2. Smaller exporters often do not have the luxury that big corporations have to weigh risks of doing business abroad and to investigate the creditworthiness of customers. Why?
3. The international marketer and the distributor will have different expectations concerning the relationship. Why should these expectations be spelled out and clarified in the contract?
4. The world's premier mobile event, Mobile World Congress, has nearly 1,700 marketers showcasing their latest mobile products, services, and solutions. Will industry and public opinion (from fitness bands to highly secure phones) solve the current and future issues while pushing new boundaries well or not?
5. Word-of-mouth and grassroots brand advocacy can have a powerful effect, particularly for the launch of new products and services or a new marketing push. Why?

On the Web

1. The software industry is the hardest hit by piracy. Using the web site of the Business Software Alliance (**http://www.bsa.org**), assess how this problem is being tackled.
2. The FIFA World Cup is a marketing platform from which a company can create awareness, enhance its image, and foster goodwill. FIFA offers sponsors a multitude of ways to promote themselves and their products in conjunction with the FIFA World Cup as well

as other FIFA Events. Using FIFA's web site (**www.fifa.com**), assess the different ways a sponsor can benefit from this association.

3. Will using The Cools (**http://thecools.tumblr.com/**) or Motilo (**http://www.motilo.com**) give you the social shopping experience? Are there any better social shopping sites? Which are better for fashion shopping, Amazon or eBay? In assessing broad range sites versus store sites, such as H&M, would personal shopper's sites, such as Stylist Fashion Network or Vogue Stylist, serve a purpose?

Endnotes

1. Stephen Galloway, "Hollywood, Who Won the Great Recession," *Foreign Policy*, November 2012, 55–6; Stephen Galloway, "Foreign Policy: How Hollywood Conquered the World," *Foreign Policy*, February 2012, 1–2; Claudia Eller, "Studios Struggle to Rein in Movie Marketing Costs," *Los Angeles Times*, April 20, 2009; Ibsen Martinez, "Romancing the Globe," *Foreign Policy*, (November/December2005), 48–56, **www.mpaa.org; http://www.rentrak.com/downloads/info/Rentrak_BoxOffice_Factsheet.pdf,and www.imax.com**.
2. George Stalk and David Michael, "What the West Doesn't Get About China," *Harvard Business Review*, 89 (June 2011), 25–7; and "Leaders: Building India Inc; Business in India," *The Economist*, October 22, 2011, 14.
3. Steuart Henderson Britt, "Standardizing Marketing for the International Market," *Columbia Journal of World Business* 9 (Winter 1974): 32–40; and Russell Belk, "Global Consumerism and Consumption," in *International Marketing*, D. Bello and D. Griffith, eds. (West Sussex, UK: John Wiley, 2011), 67–72.
4. "Taking a Bite Out of China, *Nation's Restaurant News*, October 15, 2007, S20–2.
5. Lara Farrar, "Google.cn: R.I.P or Good Riddance? *CNN*, January 12, 2011; and "Here Be Dragons," *The Economist*, January 28, 2006, 59.
6. Daniel I. Prajogo, "The Roles of Firms' Motives in Affecting the Outcomes of ISO 9000 Adoption," *International Journal of Operations & Production Management* , 31(no. 1, 2011): 78–100 and **http://www.iso.org/iso/news.htm?refid=Ref1491**.
7. Anton Troianovski, "Can You Say 'WAH-wey'? Low-Cost Phones Find Niche,"*The Wall Street Journal*, January 11, 2012, B1–2.
8. Bhaskar Chakravorti, "Finding Competitive Advantage in Adversity," *Harvard Business Review*, 88 (November 2010): 102–8.
9. "Dubbing in Product Plugs," *The Wall Street Journal*, December 6, 2004, B1, B5.
10. "Pepsi Mexico's 'Pecsi' Campaign Recognized for Innovation and Strong Results," *PEPSICO*, Wednesday, November 30, 2011.
11. European Commission, reports on the environment and waste, **http://ec.europa.eu/environment/waste/index.htm**.
12. Peter Magnusson, Stanford A. Westjohn, and Srdan Zdravkovic, "'What? I Thought Samsung Was Japanese': Accurate or Not, Perceived Country of Origin Matters," *International Marketing Review* 28, 2011, 454–72.
13. "Push for 'Made In' Tags Grows in EU," *The Wall Street Journal*, November 7, 2005, A6; and "Breaking a Taboo, High Fashion Starts Making Goods Overseas," *The Wall Street Journal*, September 27, 2005, A1, A10.
14. Edwin Colyer, "India: A Hot Brand Climate?" *Business Week*, May 31, 2006.
15. Johny K. Johansson and Ilkka A. Ronkainen, "Are Global Brands the Right Choice for Your Company?" *Marketing Management*, March/April, 2004, 53–6.
16. Douglas B. Holt, John A. Quelch, and Earl L. Taylor, "How Global Brands Compete," *Harvard Business Review* 82 (September 2004): 68–75.
17. Johny K. Johansson and Ilkka A. Ronkainen,"The Esteem of Global Brands," *Journal of Brand Management* 12 (no. 5, 2005): 339–54.
18. **http://www.havocscope.com/market-value/**: $1,638.9 billion.
19. BSA: The Software Alliance, Anti-Piracy, "What is software piracy?," **http://www.bsa.org/country/Anti-Piracy.aspx**.
20. Ilkka A. Ronkainen and Jose-Luis Guerrero-Cusumano, "Correlates of Intellectual Property Violation," *Multinational Business Review* 9 (no. 1, 2001): 59–65.
21. Joseph Zale, Thomas T. Nagle, and Reed K. Holden, *The Strategy and Tactics of Pricing: A Guide to Profitable Decision Making* (Englewood Cliffs, NJ: Prentice-Hall, 2011), chapter 3.
22. Luis Felipe Lages and David B. Montgomery, "Effects of Export Assistance on Pricing Strategy Adaptation and Export Performance," *MSI Reports*, issue 3, 2004, 67–88.
23. Cameron McWhirter and Laurie Burkitt, "In China, the Pen Is Mightier When It's Pricier," *The Wall Street Journal*, November 2, 2011 B12.

24. Ranjay Gulati and James B. Oldroyd, "The Quest for Customer Focus," *Harvard Business Review*, 83 (April 2005), 92–101.
25. "Not What It Was: European Business Has Improved out of Recognition," *Economist*, February 8, 2007.
26. AGMA Global: Advancing Intellectual Property Protection, **www.agmaglobal.org**.
27. Accenture: From Global Connection to Global Orchestration, **http://www.accenture.com/SiteCollectionDocuments/PDF/Accenture_From_Global_Connection_to_Global_Orchestration.pdf**.
28. Maggie Chuoyan Dong, David K. Tse, and Kineta Hung, "Effective Distributor Governance in Emerging Markets: The Salience of Distributor Role, Relationship Stages, and Market Uncertainty," *Journal of International Marketing*, 18, 2010, 1–17.
29. Internet World Stats, Internet Users in the World: Distribution by World Regions—2012, Q. 2, **http://www.internetworldstats.com/stats.htm**.
30. Bradley Johnson, "Where's the Growth in Marketing? Follow the BRIC Road," *Advertising Age*, December 05, 2011, 1, 8.
31. Data Center, Global Marketers 2011, *Ad Age*, December 5, 2011, 5.
32. "The Media Issue: Content is King," *Advertising Age*, October 3, 2011, 1–52.
33. Rocky Fu, "China Online Shopping Statistics 2009 Part 1 – Penetration Rate by City," *Online Shopping*, December 9, 2009.
34. Raghavan, Lulu, "Lessons from the Maharaja Mac," *Landor*, December 2007.
35. Anna Lenzer, "Fiji Water: Spin the Bottle," *Mother Jones*, **http://motherjones.com/politics/2009/09/fiji-spin-bottle**.
36. "Agency Networks," *Ad Age Insights*, December 6, 2010, 3.
37. Bradley K. Googins, "Why Community Relations Is a Strategic Imperative," *Strategy and Business* 2 (third quarter, 1997): 64–67.
38. Andreas Kaplan and Michael Haenlein, "Users of the World, Unite! The Challenges and Opportunities of Social Media," *Business Horizons*, 53 (January/February 2010): 59–66.
39. Unilever, Overview of Research and Development, **http://www.unilever.com/innovation/innovationinunilever/Overviewofresearchanddevelopmentinunilever/default.aspx**.
40. Julie Halpert, "Chrysler Group Is Ad Age's Marketer of the Year," *Ad Age*, November 26, 2012.
41. "Future of Selling," *OgilvyOne*, October 2010, 8.
42. "Worldwide Mobile Subscriptions Number More than Five Billion," October 24, 2010, **http://www.cellular-news.com/story/46050.php**
43. Sarah Perez, "Mobile Drives Adoption of Social Media in 2012: Apps & Mobile Web Account for Majority of Growth; Nearly Half of Social Media Users Access Sites on Smartphones," *Nielsen*, December 3, 2012.
44. Andreas M. Kaplan, "If You Love Something, Let it Go Mobile: Mobile Marketing and Mobile Social Media 4x4," *Business Horizons*, 55 (March/April 2012): 129–39.
45. Michael Rose, "Visit the Virtual Apple Store in Second Life," *TUAW*, February 14, 2007.

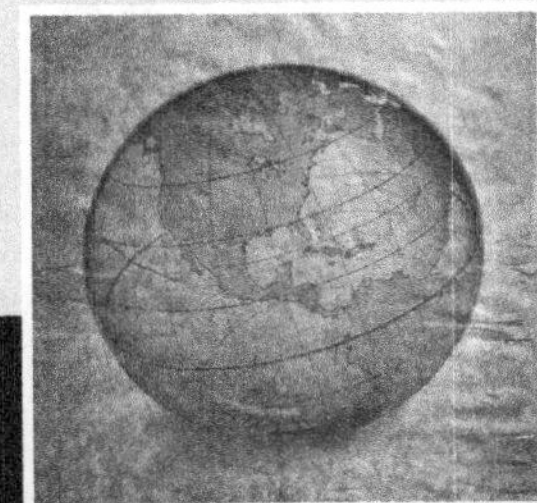

CHAPTER 12

THE GLOBAL SUPPLY CHAIN

Tracking the International Shipment

Radio-frequency identification (RFID) technology permits new levels of cost savings, efficiency, and business intelligence. The technology attaches small electronic tags to products. Transmitters or readers of the tags at several locations then are able to track the products. These tags can signal market demand and allow for real-time production and delivery.

Companies like IKEA, FedEx, Fujitsu, and Walmart have been RFID technology's main proponents. Walmart initially rolled out RFID in 2004 with its top 100 suppliers and later requiring all of its suppliers to comply by 2006. The cost savings from employing RFID technology are astronomical through reduced stock-outs, theft, and inventory, and lower labor costs.

RFID technology can alter the supply chain management process in any organization that produces, moves, or sells physical goods. Hospitals, for instance, would be able to place tags on all patients, thus knowing their exact location and all their medical information.

RFID technology offers many advantages not limited to cost savings. In comparison to traditional barcodes, more data can be stored with RFID in real time and the information can be read from a distance without a clear line of sight.

Nestlé is just one company that utilizes this technology. It manufactures its candy bars through a complex process that involves storing the confectionaries on trays throughout the production period. For quality control purposes, it is crucial that these trays undergo constant cleaning. Serious problems could arise if a few trays miss their scheduled cleaning sessions. Escort Memory Systems offered Nestlé a solution involving adhesive tags. The tags are attached to Nestlé's trays until the end of the production cycle. At the beginning of the process, as the trays are first filled, information about weight and time is recorded on the tags. When the trays pass through Nestlé's scales, the actual weight is compared with the desired weight to reduce overfills. As this information is instantly linked to Nestlé's system by RFID readers, it is possible to track the locations of trays at all times. Len Woods, senior control system supervisor, commented, "If problems arise, we are notified, enabling us to take remedial action well before any quality control issues arise."

SOURCES: "Escort Memory Systems Provides Material Handling Solution at Nestlé," courtesy of Escort Memory Systems, **http://www.ems-rifd.com/pr/nestlepr.html**, accessed February 23, 2008; Ayman Abouseif,

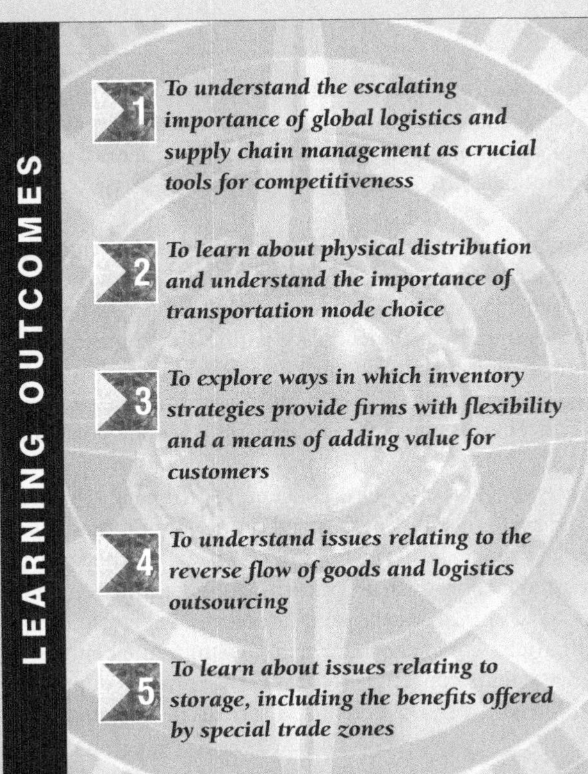

LEARNING OUTCOMES

1. *To understand the escalating importance of global logistics and supply chain management as crucial tools for competitiveness*
2. *To learn about physical distribution and understand the importance of transportation mode choice*
3. *To explore ways in which inventory strategies provide firms with flexibility and a means of adding value for customers*
4. *To understand issues relating to the reverse flow of goods and logistics outsourcing*
5. *To learn about issues relating to storage, including the benefits offered by special trade zones*

"How RFID can help optimize supply chain management," **www.ameinfo.com**, posted on February 22, 2008; "Radio Silence," *The Economist*, June 7, 2007; Edmund W. Schuster, Stuart J. Allen, David L. Brock, *Global RFID*, Springer, Heidelberg 2007; "RFID News: Looking Back at the Wal-Mart RFID Time Line," SCDigest.com. *Supply Chain Digest*, February 23, 2009, **http://www.scdigest.com/assets/On_Target/09-02-23-1.php**, accessed October 14, 2013; and "RFID Technology Boosts Walmart's Supply Chain Management." **USanFranOnline.com**. University of San Francisco, 2013, **http://www.usanfranonline.com/rfid-technology-boosts-walmarts-supply-chain-management/**, accessed July 23, 2014.

As You Read This Chapter

1. Consider how advances in technology have revolutionized the logistics function.
2. Can any firm afford not to invest in improving its supply chain?

For the international firm, customer locations and sourcing opportunities are widely dispersed. The firm can attain a strategically advantageous position only if it is able to manage successfully the complex international network known as the **supply chain**, which consists of its vendors, suppliers, other third parties, and its customers. Neglect of links inside and outside the firm not only brings higher costs but also the risk of eventual loss of noncompetitiveness because of diminished market share, more expensive supplies, or lower profits.

SUPPLY CHAIN
A complex global network created by a firm to connect its vendors, suppliers, other third parties, and its customers in order to achieve greater cost efficiencies and to enhance competitiveness

Global Logistics

Global logistics is the design and management of a system that controls the flow of materials into, through, and out of the international corporation. It encompasses the total movement concept by covering the entire range of operations concerned with the movement of goods, including both exports and imports simultaneously. Figure 12.1 shows an overview of the international supply chain.

There are two major phases in the movement of materials. The first is **materials management**, or the timely movement of raw materials, parts, and supplies into and through the firm. The second is **physical distribution**, which involves the movement of the firm's finished product to its customers. In both phases, movement takes place within the context of the entire process. Stationary periods (storage and inventory) are therefore included. The basic goal of logistics management is the effective coordination of both phases and their various components to result in maximum cost effectiveness while maintaining service goals and requirements.

MATERIALS MANAGEMENT
The timely movement of raw materials, parts, and supplies into and through the firm

PHYSICAL DISTRIBUTION
The movement of finished products from suppliers to customers

Business logistics has three key concepts: (1) the systems concept, (2) the total-cost concept, and (3) the trade-off concept. The **systems concept** is based on the notion that materials-flow activities inside and outside the firm are so extensive and complex that they can be considered only in the context of their interaction. Instead of each corporate function, supplier, and customer operating with the goal of individual optimization, the systems concept stipulates that some components may have to work suboptimally to maximize the benefits of the system as a whole. The intent of the systems concept is to provide the firm, its suppliers, and its customers, both domestic and foreign, with the benefits of synergism expected from the coordinated application of size.

SYSTEMS CONCEPT
A concept of logistics based on the notion that materials-flow activities are so complex that they can be considered only in the context of their interaction

FIGURE 12.1 The International Supply Chain

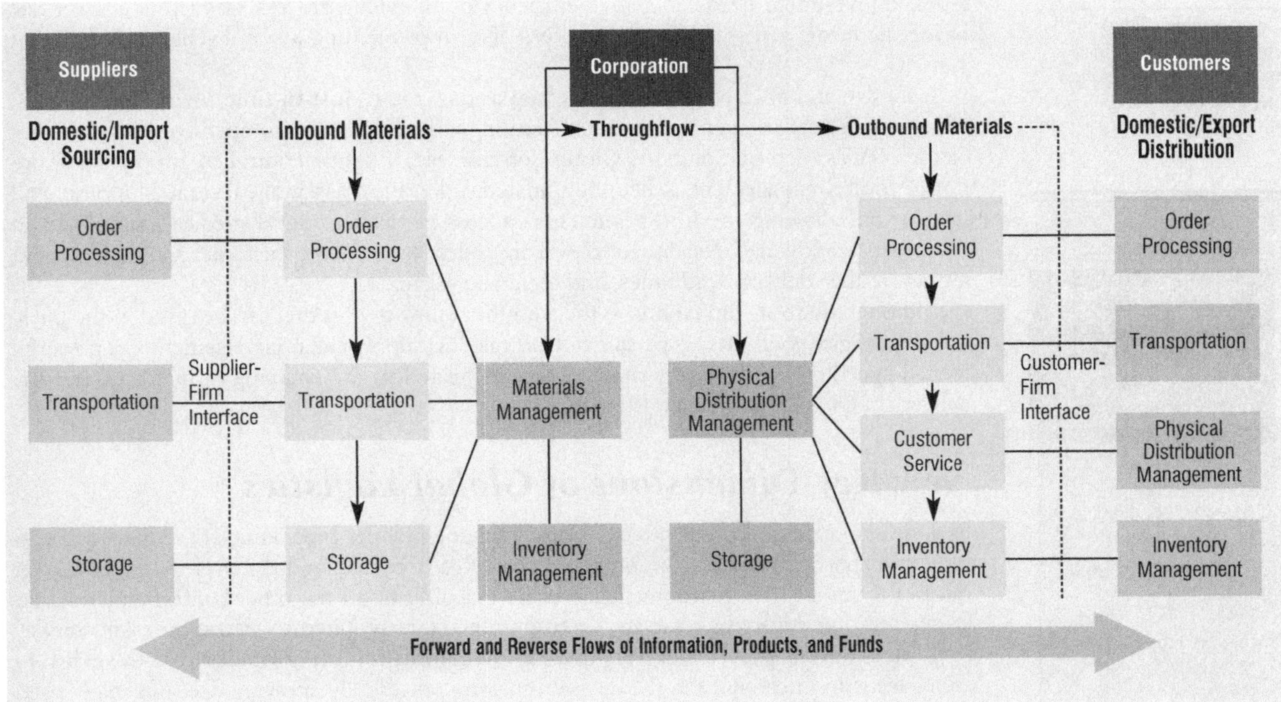

A logical outgrowth of the systems concept is the development of the **total-cost concept**. To evaluate and optimize logistical activities, cost is used as a basis for measurement. The purpose of the total-cost concept is to minimize the firm's overall logistics cost by implementing the systems concept appropriately.

TOTAL-COST CONCEPT
A decision concept that identifies and links expenditures in order to evaluate and optimize logistical activities

The third logistics concept, the **trade-off concept**, recognizes the links within logistics systems that result from the interaction of their components. For example, locating a warehouse near the customer may reduce the cost of transportation. However, additional costs are associated with new warehouses. Similarly, a reduction of inventories will save money but may increase the need for costly emergency shipments. Managers can maximize performance of logistics systems only by formulating decisions based on the recognition and analysis of such trade-offs.

TRADE-OFF CONCEPT
A decision concept that recognizes interactions within the decision system

Supply-Chain Management

The integration of these three concepts has resulted in the new paradigm of **supply-chain management**, which encompasses the planning and management of all activities involved in sourcing and procurement, conversion, and logistics. It also includes coordination and collaboration with channel partners, which can be suppliers, intermediaries, third-party service providers, and customers. In essence, supply-chain management integrates supply and demand management within and across companies.[1]

SUPPLY-CHAIN MANAGEMENT
Connecting the value-adding activities of a company's supply side with its demand side.

Advances in information technology have been crucial to progress in supply-chain management. Consider the example of Gestamp (Spain's leading supplier of metal components for car manufacturers, known for acquiring the German firm ThyssenKrupp in 2011), which used electronic data interchange technology to integrate inbound and outbound logistics be-

JUST-IN-TIME INVENTORY SYSTEMS
Materials scheduled to arrive precisely when they are needed on a production line; minimizes storage requirements

tween suppliers and customers. The company reports increased manufacturing productivity, reduced investment needs, increased efficiency of the billing process, and led to a lower rate of logistic errors across the supply process after implementing a supply-chain-management system.[2]

Cohesive and effective supply chains are at the core of **just-in-time inventory systems**, which are crucial to maintaining manufacturing costs at globally competitive levels. Within Siemens AG's Medical Solutions Group, for example, a tightly controlled supply chain optimizes order management, scheduling, materials logistics, assembly, testing, shipping, and installation, allowing the firm a seamless process to deliver critical medical equipment to customers worldwide. Efficient supply-chain design can increase customer satisfaction, save money, reduce delivery lead times, and eliminate waste.

Although there are limitations to the amount of time or cost that can be saved in the physical shipping of goods across oceans or land masses, supply-chain management is a powerful tool in speeding up the many other processes related to the sourcing of materials and the delivery of goods to ultimate customers.

Fast Facts

In most countries, obtaining space at an existing distribution center is a simple matter of paying rent. In what country is the process a good deal more complicated than this?

Japan. To obtain space, tenants often need to pay a number of charges. First, they need to pay into a construction contribution fund—typically, a one-time payment of about eighteen months' rent, refundable—without interest—after ten years. Second, a security deposit of three years' rent is refundable only at the end of the lease—again with no interest. Third is the monthly rent. On top of all that are various administrative charges.

New Key Dimensions of Global Logistics

In domestic operations, logistics decisions are guided by the experience of the manager, possible industry comparisons, an intimate knowledge of trends, and discovered heuristics—or rules of thumb. The logistics manager in the global firm, on the other hand, frequently has to depend on educated guesses to determine the steps required to obtain a desired service level. Variations in locale mean variations in environment. Lack of familiarity with such variations leads to uncertainty in the decision-making process. By applying decision rules based only on the environment encountered at home, the firm will be unable to adapt well to new circumstances, and the result will be inadequate profit performance. The long-term survival of international activities depends on an understanding of the differences inherent in the international logistics field.

Global Transportation Issues

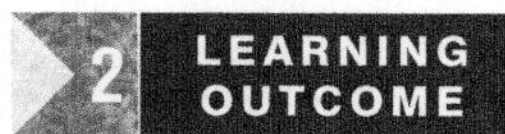

Transportation determines how and when goods will be received. The transportation issue can be divided into three components: infrastructure, the availability of modes, and the choice of modes among the given alternatives.

Transportation Infrastructure

In industrialized countries, firms can count on an established transportation network. Around the globe, however, major variations in infrastructure will be encountered. Some countries may have excellent inbound and outbound transportation systems but weak internal transportation links. This is particularly true in former colonies, where the original transportation systems were designed to maximize the extractive potential of the countries. In such instances, shipping to the market may be easy, but distribution within the market may be difficult and time-consuming. Infrastructure problems also exist in countries where transportation

Culture Clues Green or white packaging will be unsuccessful in many Asian countries, where these colors connote either disease or mourning.

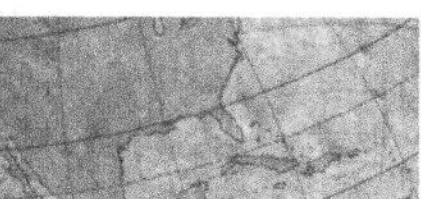

Quick Take *Changing Logistics in China*

China is a developing country when it comes to logistics, but one that is opening up to foreigners and expanding rapidly. China's economic health largely depends on trade. The expansion of trade signals a need for increased improvements in transportation and logistics. The vice minister of the National Development and Reform Commission, Ou Xinqian, stated that China's logistics industry will soon be transformed from its current "initial" state to a more "well-developed" one.

The Chinese government is pouring money into the process and encourages investors to do the same. The growing improvement in China's logistics is not only attracting local companies but the big international corporations as well.

The year 2009 marked the first time China beat out Germany as the world's leading exporter at a total of $1.2 trillion. No wonder DHL, UPS, and FedEx are looking to China as a place for increased revenue! Foreign companies are having a good impact on local logistics providers (currently more than 18,000 are registered in China) by forcing local firms to compete and therefore offer global quality standards. Options such as temperature-controlled warehouses and outsourced parts distribution are increasingly standard.

China's logistics expense is 21 percent of its GDP, which is twice that percentage in developed post-industrial countries. Much of this can be attributed to poor means of transportation in China, namely inadequate roads and railways. A second drawback is corruption, as many of the transactions are handled by several middlemen, who often demand something extra in order to speed up the transaction process. This problem became highly visible when the former deputy director of Beijing's transport department was convicted of bribery and embezzlement. Yet many international companies look at China as a place with opportunity for growth, development, and—most importantly—revenue.

SOURCES: Helen Atkinson, "China's New Logistics Choices," *Journal of Commerce*, May 9, 2005; "Logistics Industry Moving Forward," *China Daily*, May 19, 2005.

networks were established between major ports and cities in past centuries. The areas outside of the networks typically encounter problems in bringing their goods to market.

With the easing of barriers around the world, new trade opportunities await successful internationalists. Yet access to suppliers and customers is often fraught with difficulties. The firm's **logistics platform**, determined by a location's ease and convenience of market reach under favorable cost circumstances, is a key component of its competitive position. Because different countries and regions offer alternative logistics platforms, the firm must recognize that infrastructure issues are an important component of target market selection.

LOGISTICS PLATFORM
Vital to a firm's competitive position, determined by a location's ease and convenience of market reach under favorable cost circumstances

In some countries, for example, railroads may be an excellent transportation mode, far surpassing the performance of trucking, whereas in others, rail freight is a gamble at best. If the product is amenable to pipeline transportation, it pays to investigate any future routing of pipelines before committing to a particular location. Transportation of cargo from the place of manufacture to seaports or airports is another essential consideration. Mistakes can prove costly. Consider the case of the food-processing firm that built a pineapple cannery at the delta of a river in Mexico. Because the pineapple plantation was located upstream, the plan was to float the ripe fruit on barges down to the cannery on barges. To the firm's dismay, however, come harvest time, the river current was far too strong for barge traffic. Because no other feasible alternative method of transportation existed, the plant was closed, and the new equipment was sold for a fraction of its original cost.[3]

Frequency of transportation is another important issue, and extreme variations exist. For example, a particular port may not be visited by a ship for weeks, or even months. Sometimes only small carriers, which are unable to move large equipment, will serve a given location.

Business strategist Michael Porter underlines the importance of infrastructure as a determinant of national competitive advantage, highlighting the capability of governmental efforts to influence this critical issue.[4] For that reason, infrastructure is a critical issue for any governments seeking to attract new industries or retain existing firms.

Availability of Modes

Global business frequently requires transportation of cargo using ocean or airfreight, two modes that most domestic corporations rarely use. In addition, combinations such as **land bridges** or **sea bridges** may permit the transfer of freight among various modes of transportation, resulting in **intermodal movements**. The international logistics manager must understand the specific properties of the different modes to be able to use them intelligently.

LAND BRIDGE
Transfer of ocean freight among various modes of land-based transportation

SEA BRIDGE
The transfer of freight among various modes of ocean freight

INTERMODAL MOVEMENTS
The transfer of freight from one type of transportation to another

Ocean Shipping

Water transportation is a key mode for international freight movement. Three types of ocean shipping vessels can be distinguished by their service: liner service, bulk service, and tramp or charter service. **Liner service** offers regularly scheduled passage on established routes. **Bulk service** mainly provides contractual services for individual voyages or for prolonged periods of time. **Tramp service** is available for irregular routes and is scheduled only on demand.

LINER SERVICE
Ocean shipping characterized by regularly scheduled passage on established routes

BULK SERVICE
Ocean shipping provided on contract, either for individual voyages or for prolonged periods of time

TRAMP SERVICE
Ocean shipping using irregular routes, scheduled only on demand

In addition to the services offered by ocean carriers, the type of cargo a vessel can carry is also important. The most common types are conventional (break-bulk) cargo vessels, container ships, and roll-on-roll-off vessels. Conventional cargo vessels are useful for oversized and unusual cargo but may be less efficient in their port operations. Container ships carry standardized containers that greatly facilitate the loading and unloading of cargo and inter-modal transfers. As a result, the time the ship has to spend in port is reduced, as are port charges. **Roll-on-roll-off (RORO)** vessels are essentially oceangoing ferries. Trucks can drive onto built-in ramps and roll off at the destination. Another vessel similar to the RORO vessel is the **lighter aboard ship (LASH) vessel**. LASH vessels consist of barges stored on the ship and lowered at the point of destination. The individual barges can then operate on inland waterways, a feature that is particularly useful in shallow water.

ROLL-ON-ROLL-OFF (RORO)
Transportation vessels built to accommodate trucks that can drive on in one port and drive off at their destinations

LIGHTER ABOARD SHIP (LASH) VESSEL
Barge stored on a ship and lowered at the point of destination to operate on inland waterways

The availability of a certain type of vessel, however, does not automatically mean that it can be used. The greatest constraint in international ocean shipping is the lack of ports and port services. For example, modern container ships keep growing in terms of constantly improving their container capacity. By 2012, ships could typically transport an average of 12,500 containers, considering a mix of both loaded and empty containers. Developments in 2013 lead to estimates that loads of 18,000 containers could be available in just a few more years. A severe constraint on all this innovation is that some ports cannot serve these large ships because the local equipment cannot handle the resulting traffic. The problem is often found in developing countries, where local authorities lack the funds to develop facilities. In some instances, nations may purposely limit the development of ports to impede the inflow of imports. Increasingly, however, governments have begun to recognize the importance of an appropriate port facility structure and are developing such facilities in spite of the large investment necessary.

Air Shipping

Airfreight is available to and from most countries. This includes the developing world, where it is often a matter of national prestige to operate a national airline. The tremendous growth in international airfreight is shown in Figure 12.2. The volume of airfreight in relation to the total volume of shipping in international business remains quite small. Yet 40 percent of the world's manufactured exports by value travel by air.[5] Clearly, high-value items are more likely to be shipped by air, particularly if they have a high density—that is, a high weight-to-volume ratio.

FIGURE 12.2 International Airfreight, 1960–2025

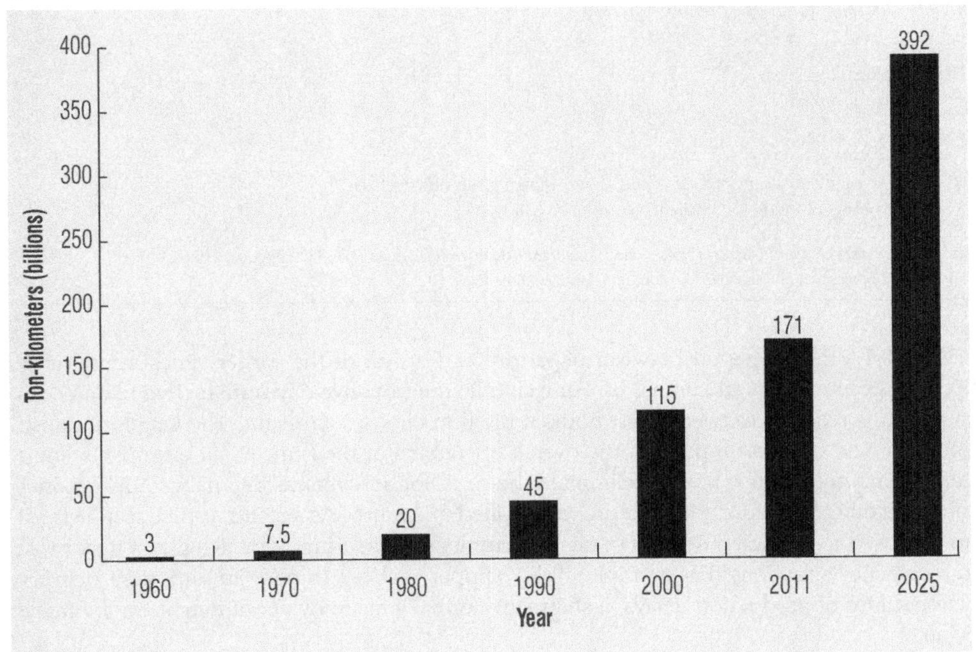

SOURCE: *Civil Aviation Statistics of the World* (Montreal: ICAO), **http://www.icao.org** and Airbus Industries Global Market Forecast, 2006-2025, **http://www.airbus.com**, accessed July 23, 2014.

Airlines make major efforts to increase the volume of airfreight by developing better and more efficient ground facilities, introducing airfreight containers, and marketing a wide variety of special services to shippers. In addition, some airfreight companies have specialized and become partners in the international logistics effort.

From the shipper's perspective, the products involved must be appropriate for air shipment, both in terms of their size and weight. In addition, the market situation for any given product must be evaluated. Airfreight may be needed for a perishable product or if the product requires a short transit time for other reasons. The level of customer service needs and expectations can also play a decisive role. For example, the shipment of an industrial product that is vital to the ongoing operations of a customer may be much more urgent than the shipment of packaged consumer products.

UPS, the world's largest package distribution company, transports more than 3.1 billion parcels and documents annually. To transport packages most efficiently, UPS has developed an elaborate network of "hubs" or central sorting facilities located throughout the world.

Selecting a Mode of Transport

The international logistics manager must make the appropriate selection from the available modes of transportation. The decision will be heavily influenced by the needs of the firm and its customers. The manager must consider the performance of each mode in four dimensions: transit time, predictability, cost, and non-economic factors. A useful overview of different modes of transportation and their comparative strengths is provided in Table 12.1.

TABLE 12.1 Evaluating Transportation Choices

	Mode of Transportation				
Characteristics of Mode	**Air**	**Pipeline**	**Highway**	**Rail**	**Water**
Speed (1 = fastest)	1	4	2	3	5
Cost (1 = highest)	1	4	3	4	5
Loss and Damage (1 = least)	3	1	4	5	2
Frequency[1] (1 = best)	3	1	2	4	5
Dependability (1 = best)	5	1	2	3	4
Capacity[2] (1 = best)	4	5	3	2	1
Availability (1 = best)	3	5	1	2	4

[1]Frequency: number of times mode is available during a given time period.
[2]Capacity: ability of mode to handle large or heavy goods

SOURCE: Ronald H. Ballou, *Business Logistics and Supply Chain Management*, 5th ed., p. 143. Copyright © 2004. Reprinted by permission of Pearson Education, Inc., Upper Saddle River, NJ.

TRANSIT TIME
The period between departure and arrival of a shipment

TRANSIT TIME The period between departure and arrival of the carrier varies significantly between ocean freight and airfreight. For example, the forty-five-day **transit time** of an ocean shipment is reduced to twenty-four hours if the firm chooses airfreight. The length of transit time can have a major impact on the overall operations of the firm. As an example, a short transit time may reduce or even eliminate the need for an overseas depot. Also, inventories can be significantly reduced if they are replenished frequently. As a result, capital can be freed up and used to finance other corporate opportunities. Transit time can also play a major role in emergency situations. For example, if the shipper is about to miss an important delivery date because of production delays, a shipment normally made by ocean freight can be made by air.

Perishable products require shorter transit times. Transporting them rapidly prolongs the shelf life in the foreign market. Air delivery may be the only way to enter foreign markets successfully with products that have a short life-span. International sales of cut flowers have reached their current volume only as a result of airfreight.

At all times, the logistics manager must understand the interactions between different components of the logistics process and their effect on transit times. Unless a smooth flow throughout the entire supply chain can be assured, bottlenecks will deny any benefits from specific improvements. For example, some consumer retailers have tried to offer instant gratification to their customers by providing custom services—such as body scanning for clothes measurements—and immediately transmitting the data electronically to suppliers. Even though the custom clothes are worked on right away, it may take weeks to get the finished item to the customer.

PREDICTABILITY
The degree of likelihood that a shipment will arrive on time and in good condition

PREDICTABILITY Providers of both ocean freight and airfreight service wrestle with the issue of reliability. Both modes are subject to the vagaries of nature, which may impose delays. Yet, because reliability is a relative measure, the delay of one day for airfreight tends to be seen as much more severe and "unreliable" than the same delay for ocean freight. However, delays tend to be shorter in absolute time for air shipments. As a result, arrival time using air is more predictable. This attribute has a major influence on corporate strategy. For example, because of the higher **predictability** of airfreight, inventory safety stock can be kept at lower levels. Greater predictability can also serve as a useful sales tool because it permits more precise

Quick Take — Environment and Sustainability: Organic Food Has a Carbon Footprint

Organic or not, carbon emissions are a major problem with food shipping. Mangoes, green peppers, and bananas are examples of products where the organic version needs to travel further to get to market. Many of the environmental benefits of buying organic food items are offset by the carbon emissions released to get the produce to the buyer. Companies that want to be considered green need to mitigate the effects of their carbon emissions.

ShipGreen, Greenworld LLC, has started to apply the concept of carbon offsets to the shipping industry. Using the unique weight, distance, and transportation mode of a shipment, ShipGreen is able to determine the amount of carbon dioxide emissions it produced and presents customers with several options for offsetting the impact of their shipment, such as reforestation or solar or wind power projects that prevent or remove carbon dioxide.

Currently, the majority of ShipGreen's customers are e-commerce companies that want to adopt a greener approach. By incorporating ShipGreen programs into their websites, e-commerce companies can provide their customers with the option of adding a fee to their order. The proceeds are then used to buy carbon credits for projects, certified according to the Kyoto protocol by a third party. The credits are calculated using an algorithm developed at the University of California, Berkley, which not only takes into account tailpipe emissions, but also energy used and emissions from making the fuels, manufacturing the vehicles, and constructing and operating the infrastructure for transportation.

SOURCES: Danny Bradbury, "Cutting the carbon footprint: plain sailing?" *BusinessGreen*, February 25, 2008; Greenworld LLC website, **http://www.greenworldorganics.com**, accessed February 26, 2008.

delivery promises to customers. If inadequate port facilities exist, airfreight may again be the better alternative. Unloading operations for oceangoing vessels are more cumbersome and time-consuming than for planes. Finally, merchandise shipped using airfreight is less likely to suffer loss and damage from exposure of the cargo to movement. Therefore, once the merchandise arrives, it is more likely to be ready for immediate delivery—a fact that also enhances predictability.

An important aspect of predictability is the capability of a shipper to track goods at any point during the shipment. **Tracking** becomes particularly important as corporations increasingly obtain products from and send them to multiple locations around the world. Being able to coordinate the smooth flow of a multitude of interdependent shipments can make a vast difference in a corporation's performance. Tracking allows the shipper to check on the functioning of the supply chain and to take remedial action if problems occur. Cargo can also be redirected if sudden demand surges so require. However, such an enhanced corporate response to the predictability issue is possible only if the shipper and the carrier develop an appropriate information system that is easily accessible to the user.

TRACKING
The capability of a shipper to determine the location of goods at any point during the shipment

COST International transportation services are usually priced on the basis of the cost of the service provided and the value of the service to the shipper. Due to the high value of the products shipped by air, airfreight is often priced according to the value of the service. In this case, of course, price becomes a function of market demand and the monopolistic power of the carrier.

The manager must decide whether the clearly higher cost of airfreight can be justified. In part, this will depend on the cargo's properties. The physical density and the value of the cargo will affect the decision. Bulky products may be too expensive to ship by air, whereas very

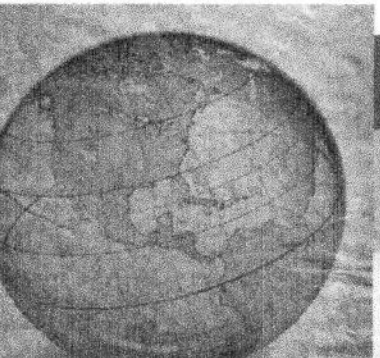

WORLD VIEW

Global Small Business: Carriers to the Rescue!

When running a small or medium-sized international enterprise (SME), it is difficult to have all required resources at hand. Yet SMEs need much information in order to become strong competitors in today's market. A variety of shipping carriers offer customized supply chain management assistance to small businesses because companies often spend more than 10 percent of their revenue just to manage their supply chain.

For a small business, it is important to focus on its core competencies, reduce costs, and improve customer service. Most of the inner workings behind supply chain management can be outsourced to a third party. FedEx offers its business clients resources and technology necessary to move products all the way through the supply chain and back if necessary. This service means FedEx touches on return management, which, in an era of shopping on the Web, takes on growing importance.

The DHL Small Business Resource Center allows SMEs to communicate with each other online. This permits business owners to share their knowledge and tips about logistics. DHL has also created an online database containing peer-to-peer knowledge, reference guides, articles, and special offers, all targeted toward SMEs.

UPS has also created a branch for small businesses where it offers improved and less time-consuming shipping technology, visibility of the supply chain process (so a business can get paid by the end-consumer faster), and dependability of the UPS Brown brand. With each of the three major global carriers offering outsourcing services to small businesses, it becomes easier for firms to take the international leap.

SOURCES: "DHL Helps Small Businesses Respond to Key Growth Challenges," *Business Wire*, August 1, 2005; **http://www.fedex.com**, accessed October 18, 2013; **http://www.ups.com**, accessed July 23, 2014.

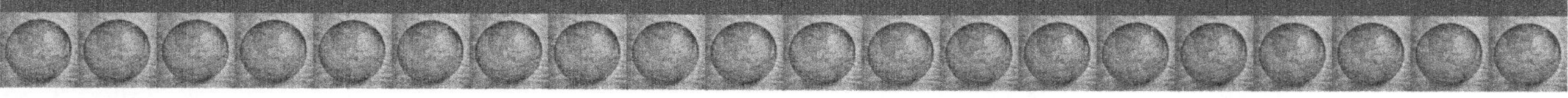

compact products may be more appropriate for airfreight transportation. The cost of transportation as a percentage of total product cost will be lower for high-priced items, so these goods can absorb transportation costs more easily than low-priced goods can. As a result, sending diamonds by airfreight is easier to justify than sending coal. Alternatively, a shipper can decide to mix modes of transportation in order to reduce overall cost and time delays. For example, part of the shipment route can be covered by air, while another portion can be covered by truck or ship.

Most important, however, are the supply-chain considerations of the firm. The manager must determine how important it is for merchandise to arrive on time. This means factoring in all corporate, supplier, and customer activities that are affected by the modal choice and exploring the full implications of each alternative. Hot fashions, for instance, obviously need very timely delivery. In some cases, a firm may want to use airfreight as a new tool for aggressive market expansion. In others, airfreight may be considered a good way to begin operations in new markets without making sizable investments into warehouses and distribution centers.

NON-ECONOMIC FACTORS The transportation sector, nationally and internationally, both benefits and suffers from government involvement. Even though transportation carriers are one prime target in the sweep of privatization around the globe, many carriers are either owned or heavily subsidized by governments. As a result, governmental pressure is exerted on shippers to use national carriers even if more economical alternatives exist. Such **preferential policies** are most often enforced when government cargo is being transported. Restrictions are not limited to developing countries. For example, the U.S. federal government requires that all travelers on government business use national flag carriers when available.

For balance of payments reasons, international quota systems of transportation have been proposed. The United Nations Conference on Trade and Development (UNCTAD), for example, has recommended that 40 percent of the traffic between two nations be allocated to vessels of the exporting country, 40 percent to vessels of the importing country, and 20 percent to third-country vessels. However, stiff international competition among carriers and the price sensitivity of customers frequently render such proposals ineffective, particularly for trade between industrialized countries.

Although many justifications are possible for such national policies, ranging from prestige to national security, they distort the economic choices of the international corporation. Yet these policies are a reflection of the international environment within which the firm must operate. Proper adaptation is necessary.

PREFERENTIAL POLICIES

Government policies that favor certain (usually domestic) firms; for example, the use of national carriers for the transport of government freight, even when more economical alternatives exist

Export Documentation

A firm must deal with numerous forms and documents when exporting to ensure that all goods meet local and foreign laws and regulations.

A bill of lading is a contract between the exporter and the carrier indicating that the carrier has accepted responsibility for the goods and will provide transportation in return for payment. The bill of lading can also be used as a receipt and to prove ownership of the merchandise. There are two types of bills, negotiable and non-negotiable. **Straight bills of lading** are non-negotiable and are typically used in prepaid transactions. The goods are delivered to a specific individual or company. **Shipper's order** bills of lading are negotiable; they can be bought, sold, or traded while the goods are still in transit and are used for letter-of-credit transactions. The customer usually needs the original or a copy of the bill of lading as proof of ownership to take possession of the goods.

A **commercial invoice** is a bill for the goods stating basic information about the transaction, including a description of the merchandise, total cost of the goods sold, addresses of the shipper and seller, and delivery and payment terms. The buyer needs the invoice to prove ownership and to arrange payment. Some governments use the commercial invoice to assess customs duties.

A variety of other export documents may be required. Some of the more common ones are summarized in Table 12.2.

STRAIGHT BILL OF LADING

A non-negotiable bill of lading usually used in prepaid transactions in which the transported goods involved are delivered to a specific individual or company

SHIPPER'S ORDER

A negotiable bill of lading that can be bought, sold, or traded while the subject goods are still in transit and that is used for letter of credit transactions

COMMERCIAL INVOICE

A bill for transported goods that describes the merchandise and its total cost and lists the addresses of the shipper and seller and delivery and payment terms

Terms of Shipment and Sale

The responsibilities of the buyer and the seller should be spelled out as they relate to what is and what is not included in the price quotation and when ownership of goods passes from seller to buyer. **Incoterms** are the internationally accepted standard definitions for terms of sale set by the International Chamber of Commerce (ICC). The Incoterms 2010 went into effect on January 1, 2010, with significant revisions to better reflect changing transportation technologies and the increased use of electronic communications.[6] Although the same terms may be used in domestic transactions, they gain new meaning in the global arena. The terms are grouped into four categories: (1) the "E"-terms, whereby the seller makes the goods available to the buyer only at the seller's own premises; (2) the "F"-terms, whereby the seller is called upon to deliver the goods to a carrier appointed by the buyer; (3) the "C"- terms, whereby the seller has to contract for carriage but without assuming the risk of loss or damage

INCOTERMS

International Commerce Terms; widely accepted terms used in quoting export prices

TABLE 12.2 Summary of Common Export Documents

Document	Issued by	General Purpose
Pro forma invoice	Seller	Quotation to buyer; used to obtain import license and letter-of-credit financing
Sales contract	Seller or buyer	Confirms all details of transaction
Export license	U.S. government	Required by U.S. law
Carrier's receipt	Truck or rail carrier	Acknowledgment that carrier has accepted cargo for transportation to pier or airport
Dock or warehouse receipt	Pier or warehouse	Acknowledgment that cargo has been received
Ocean bill of lading or airway bill	Steamship company or airline	Contract between shipper and shipping company for transport of cargo
Insurance certificate	Insurance company	Evidence that cargo is insured against stated risks
Inspection certificate	Inspection company	Confirms to financing bank and buyer that cargo meets specifications set forth in sales contract or letter of credit
Packing lists	Seller	Required by shipping company and foreign customs
Commercial invoice	Seller	Actual invoice for goods
Consular invoice	Foreign government	Used to control imports and identify goods
Certificate of origin	U.S. Chamber of Commerce	Required by foreign government
Shipper's export declaration	Seller	Required by U.S. government to control exports and compile trade statistics

EX-WORKS (EXW)
Price quotes that apply only at the point of origin; the seller agrees to place the goods at the disposal of the buyer at the specified place on a date or within a fixed period

FREE CARRIER (FCA)
Applies only at a designated inland shipping point; seller responsible for loading goods into the means of transportation; buyer responsible for all subsequent expenses

FREE ALONGSIDE SHIP (FAS)
Exporter quotes a price for the goods alongside a vessel at a port. Seller handles cost of unloading and wharfage; loading, ocean transportation, and insurance are left to buyer

to the goods or additional costs after the dispatch; and finally (4) the "D"-terms, whereby the seller has to bear all costs and risks to bring the goods to the destination determined by the buyer. Figure 12.3 summarizes the most common of the Incoterms used in international marketing.

Prices quoted **ex-works (EXW)** apply only at the point of origin, and the seller agrees to place the goods at the disposal of the buyer at the specified place on the specified date or within the fixed period. All other charges are for the account of the buyer.

One of the new Incoterms is **free carrier (FCA)**, which replaces a variety of FOB terms for all modes of transportation, except vessel. FCA (a named inland point) applies only at a designated inland shipping point. The seller is responsible for loading goods into the means of transportation; the buyer is responsible for all subsequent expenses. If a port of exportation is named, the costs of transporting the goods to the named port are included in the price.

Free alongside ship (FAS) at a named U.S. port of export means that the exporter quotes a price for the goods, including charges for delivery of the goods, alongside a vessel at the port. The seller handles the cost of unloading and wharfage; loading, ocean transportation, and insurance are left to the buyer.

Free on board (FOB) applies only to vessel shipments. The seller quotes a price covering all expenses up to, and including, delivery of goods on an overseas vessel provided by or for the buyer.

Under **cost and freight (CFR)** to a named overseas port of import, the seller quotes a price for the goods, including the cost of transportation to the named port of disembarkation. The cost of insurance and the choice of insurer are left to the buyer.

With **cost, insurance, and freight (CIF)** to a named overseas port of import, the seller quotes a price that includes insurance, all transportation, and miscellaneous charges to the

FIGURE 12.3 Selected Trade Terms

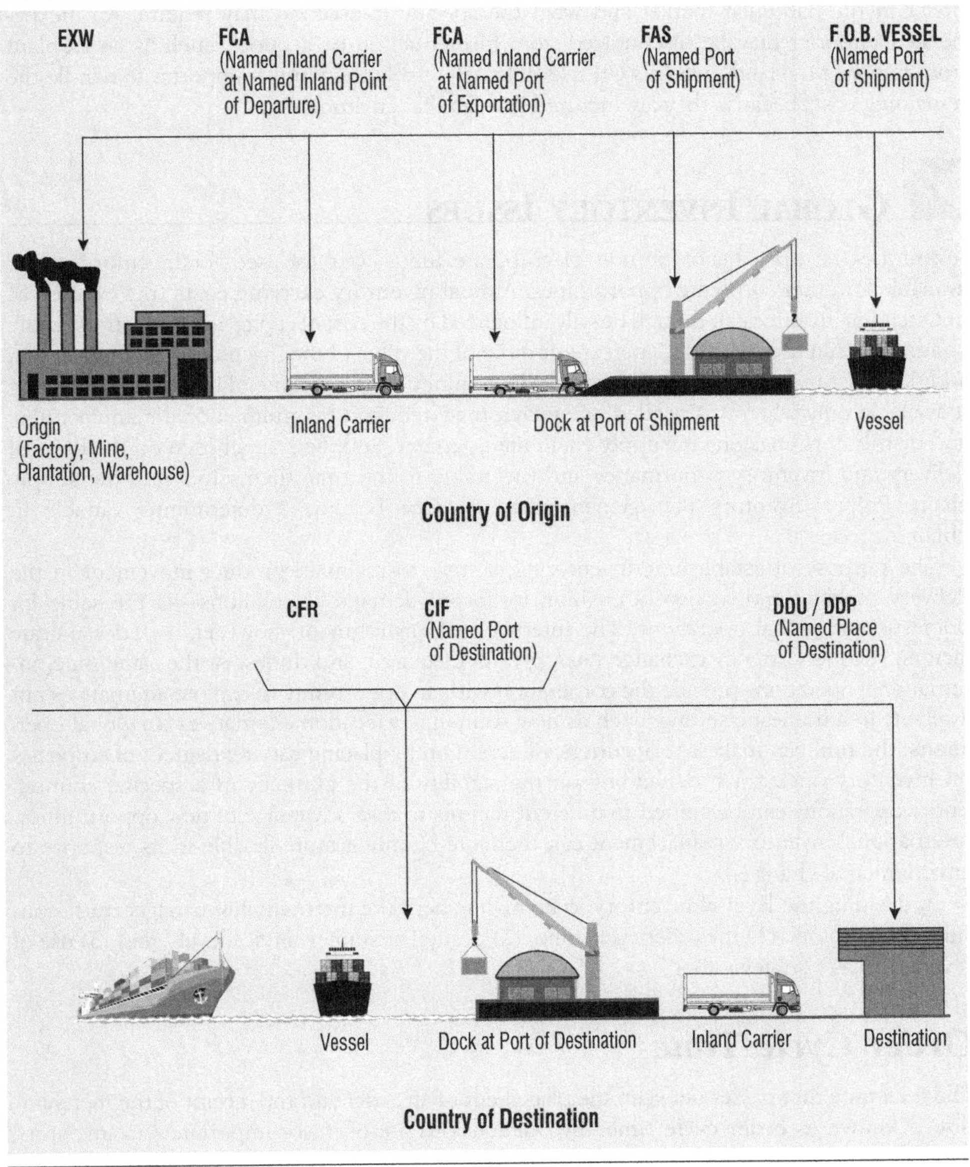

point of disembarkation from the vessel. With non-waterway transport, the terms are **carriage paid to (CPT)** or **carriage and insurance paid to (CIP)**.

With **delivery duty paid (DDP)**, the seller delivers the goods, with import duties paid, including inland transportation from import point to the buyer's premises.

With **delivery duty unpaid (DDU)**, the buyer pays only the destination customs duty and taxes. Ex-works signifies the maximum obligation for the buyer; delivery duty paid puts the maximum burden on the seller.

Careful determination and clear understanding of terms used, and their acceptance by the parties involved, are vital in order to avoid subsequent misunderstandings and disputes, not only between the parties but also within the marketer's own organization. These terms are

FREE ON BOARD (FOB)
FOB is the term used when received the ownership or liability of goods passes from the seller to the buyer at the time the goods cross the shipping point to be delivered.

COST AND FREIGHT (CFR)
Seller quotes a price for the goods, including the cost of transportation to the named port of debarkation; cost and choice of insurance left to the buyer

COST, INSURANCE, AND FREIGHT (CIF)
Seller price includs insurance, all transportation, and miscellaneous charges to the point of debarkation from the vessel or aircraft

CARRIAGE PAID TO (CPT)
The price quoted by an exporter for shipments not involving waterway transport, not including insurance

CARRIAGE AND INSURANCE PAID TO (CIP)
The price quoted by an exporter for shipments not involving waterway transport, including insurance

DELIVERY DUTY PAID (DDP)
Goods, with import duties paid, including inland transportation from import point, delivered to the buyer's premises

DELIVERY DUTY UNPAID (DDU)
Only the destination customs duty and taxes paid by the consignee

also powerful competitive tools. The exporter should therefore learn what importers usually prefer in the particular market and what the specific transaction may require. An inexperienced importer may be discouraged from further action by a quote, such as an ex-plant from Jessup, Maryland, whereas CIF Helsinki will enable the Finnish importer to handle the remaining costs because they are incurred in a familiar environment.

Global Inventory Issues

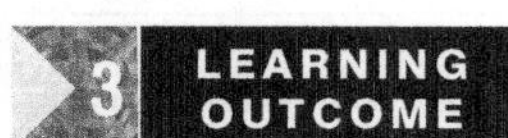

INVENTORY CARRYING COSTS
The expense of maintaining goods in storage

Inventories tie up a major portion of corporate funds. Capital used for inventory is not available for other corporate opportunities. Annual **inventory carrying costs** (the expense of maintaining inventories), though heavily influenced by the cost of capital and industry-specific conditions, can account for 25 percent or more of the value of the inventories themselves.[7] In addition, just-in-time inventory policies, which minimize the volume of inventory by making it available only when it is needed, are increasingly required by multinational manufacturers and distributors engaging in supply-chain management. Suppliers are chosen on the basis of delivery and inventory performance and the ability to integrate themselves into the supply chain. Proper inventory management may therefore become a determining variable in obtaining a sale.

The purpose of establishing inventory systems—to maintain product movement in the delivery pipeline and to have a cushion to absorb demand fluctuations—is the same for domestic and global operations. The international environment, however, includes unique factors, such as currency exchange rates, greater distances, and duties. At the same time, international operations provide the corporation with an opportunity to explore alternatives not available in a domestic setting, such as new sourcing or location alternatives. In global operations, the firm can make use of currency fluctuation by placing varying degrees of emphasis on inventory operations, depending on the stability of the currency of a specific country. Entire operations can be shifted to different nations to take advantage of new opportunities. International inventory management can therefore be much more flexible in its response to environmental changes.

In deciding the level of inventory to be maintained, the international manager must consider three factors: (1) the order cycle time, (2) desired customer service levels, and (3) use of inventories as a strategic tool.

Order Cycle Time

ORDER CYCLE TIME
The total time that passes between the placement of an order and the receipt of the merchandise

ELECTRONIC DATA INTERCHANGE
The direct transfer of information technology between computers of trading partners

The total time that passes between the placement of an order and the receipt of the merchandise is known as **order cycle time**. Two dimensions are of major importance to inventory management: the length of the total order cycle and its consistency. In international business, the order cycle is frequently longer than in domestic business. It comprises the time involved in order transmission, order filling, packing and preparation for shipment, and transportation. Order transmission time varies greatly internationally, depending on the method of communication. Supply-chain-driven firms use **electronic data interchange (EDI)** rather than facsimile, telex, telephone, or mail.

EDI is the direct transfer of information technology between computers of trading partners. The usual paperwork the partners send each other, such as purchase orders and confirmations, bills of lading, invoices, and shipment notices, are formatted into standard messages and transmitted using a direct-link network or a third-party network. EDI can save a large part of the processing and administrative costs associated with traditional ways of exchanging information.

The order-filling time may also increase because lack of familiarity with a foreign market can make anticipating new orders more difficult. Packing and shipment preparation require more detailed attention. Finally, of course, transportation time increases with the distances involved. Larger inventories may have to be maintained both domestically and internationally to bridge the time gaps.

Consistency, the second dimension of order cycle time, is also more difficult to maintain in international business. Depending on the choice of transportation mode, delivery times may vary considerably from shipment to shipment. The variation requires the maintenance of larger safety stocks to be able to fill demand in periods when delays occur.

REVERSE LOGISTICS **Reverse logistics**—the handling and disposition of returned products and use of related materials and information—is an important way for firms to improve customer service and increase revenue. With the growth of direct-to-customer Internet sales, the reverse supply chain has exploded, amounting to more than $100 billion per year—greater than the GDP of two-thirds of the world's countries! Industries facing the highest return volume are magazine and book publishing (50 percent), catalog retailers (18 to 35 percent), and greeting card companies (20 to 30 percent).[8] Just the disposal of returned merchandise can result in major headaches and costs.

REVERSE LOGISTICS
A system responding to environmental concerns that ensures a firm can retrieve a product from the market for subsequent use, recycling, or disposal

CUSTOMER SERVICE LEVELS The level of customer service denotes the responsiveness that inventory policies permit for any given situation. A customer service level of 100 percent would be defined as the ability to fill all orders within a set time—for example, three days. If, within the same three days, only 70 percent of the orders can be filled, the customer service level is 70 percent. The choice of customer service level for the firm has a major impact on the inventories needed. In highly industrialized nations, firms frequently are expected to adhere to very high levels of customer service.

Yet service levels should not be oriented primarily around cost or customary domestic standards. Rather, the level chosen for use internationally should be based on expectations encountered in each market. The expectations depend on past performance, product desirability, customer sophistication, and the competitive status of the firm.

Because high customer service levels are costly, the goal should not be the highest customer service level possible, but rather an acceptable level. Different customers have different priorities. Some will be prepared to pay a premium for speed, some may put a higher value on flexibility, and another group may see low cost as the most important issue. If, for example, foreign customers expect to receive their merchandise within thirty days, for the international corporation to promise delivery within ten or fifteen days does not make sense. Indeed, such delivery may result in storage problems and will likely reduce price competitiveness.

Inventory As a Strategic Tool

The international corporation can use inventories as a strategic tool in dealing with currency valuation changes or to hedge against inflation. By increasing inventories before an imminent devaluation of a currency, instead of holding cash, the corporation may reduce its exposure to devaluation losses. Similarly, in the case of high inflation, large inventories can provide an important inflation hedge. In such circumstances, the international inventory manager must balance the cost of maintaining high levels of inventories with the benefits that might be accrued from hedging against inflation or devaluation. Many countries, for example, charge a property tax on stored goods. If the increase in tax payments outweighs the hedging benefits to the corporation, it would be unwise to increase inventories before a devaluation.

WORLD VIEW
When There Is More to a Name

Products imported into Asia often carry brand names that are translated from their original names. The product names are either direct translations (which result in a different-sounding but same-meaning name in the local language) or phonetic (which result in the same sound but usually a different meaning). Given the globalization of markets, marketers not only need to decide whether to translate their brand names but also must consider the form, content, style, and image of such translations.

In Europe and the Americas, brand names such as Budweiser, Canon, and Coca-Cola have no meaning in themselves, and few consumers are even aware of the origins of the name. But to Chinese-speaking consumers, brand names include an additional meaning. Budweiser means "hundreds of power and influence," Canon stands for "perfect capability," and Coca-Cola means "tasty and happy."

Chinese and Western consumers share similar standards when it comes to evaluating brand names. Both appreciate a brand name that is catchy, memorable, and distinct, and also says something indicative of the product. But because of cultural and linguistic factors, Chinese consumers expect more in terms of how names are spelled, written, and styled, and whether the names are considered lucky. In a study of Fortune 500 companies in China, the vast majority of marketers were found to localize their brand names using, for the most part, transliteration. Following this insight, when Frito-Lay introduced Cheetos in the Chinese market, it did so under a phonetically similar Chinese name that translates as "Many Surprises."

SOURCES: Nader Tavassoli and Jin K.Han "Auditory and Visual Brand Identifiers in Chinese and English," *Journal of International Marketing* 10, no. 2 (2002): 13–28; F.C. Hong, Anthony Pecotich, and Clifford J. Schultz, "Brand Name Translation Language Constraints, Product Attributes and Consumer Perceptions in East and Southeast Asia," *Journal of International Marketing* 10, no. 2, (2002): 29–45; Fuming Jiang and Bruce W. Stening, *The Chinese Business Environment* (Northampton, MA: Edward Elgar Publishing, 2007).

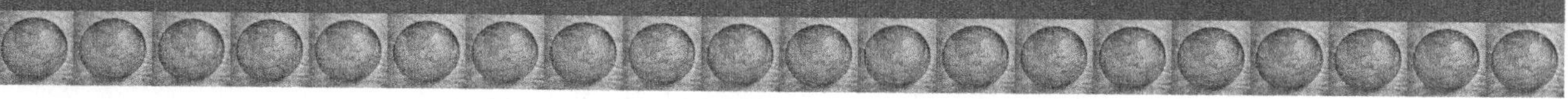

Global Packaging Issues

The responsibility for appropriate packaging rests with the goods' shipper. The shipper must therefore ensure that the goods are prepared appropriately for international shipping. Packaging is instrumental in getting the merchandise to the ultimate destination in a safe, maintainable, and presentable condition. Packaging that is adequate for domestic shipping may be inadequate for international transportation because the shipment will be subject to the motions of the vessel on which it is carried. Added stress in international shipping also arises from the transfer of goods among different modes of transportation. Figure 12.4 provides examples of some sources of stress in intermodal movement that are most frequently found in international transportation.

Packaging decisions must take into account differences in environmental conditions—for example, climate. When the ultimate destination is very humid or particularly cold, special provisions must be made to prevent damage to the product. The task becomes even more challenging when one considers that, in the course of long-distance transportation, dramatic

FIGURE 12.4 Stresses in Intermodal Movement

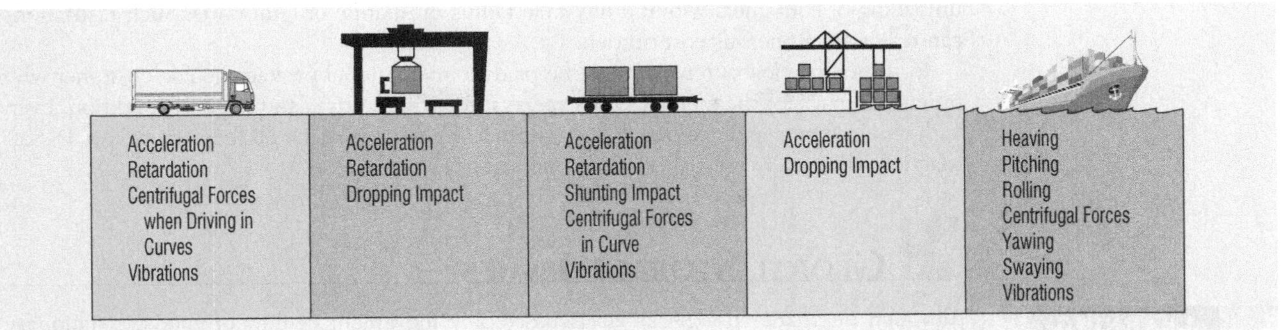

Note: Each transportation mode exerts a different set of stresses and strains on containerized cargoes. The most commonly overlooked are those associated with ocean transport.

SOURCE: David Greenfield, "Perfect Packing for Export," from *Handling and Shipping Management*, September 1980 (Cleveland, Ohio: Penton Publishing), p. 47. Reprinted by permission.

changes in climate can take place. Still famous is the case of a firm in Taiwan that shipped drinking glasses to the Middle East. The company used wooden crates and padded the glasses with hay. Most of the glasses, however, were broken by the time they reached their destination. As the crates traveled into the drier Middle East, the moisture content of the hay dropped. By the time the crates were delivered, the thin straw offered almost no protection.[9]

The weight of packaging must also be considered, particularly when airfreight is used, as the cost of shipping is often based on weight. At the same time, packaging material must be sufficiently strong to permit stacking in international transportation.

Another consideration is that, in some countries, duties are assessed according to the gross weight of shipments, which includes the weight of packaging. Obviously, the heavier the packaging, the higher the duty will be.

The shipper must pay sufficient attention to instructions provided by the customer for packaging. For example, requests by the customer that the weight of any one package should not exceed a certain limit or that specific package dimensions should be adhered to, usually are made for a reason. Often they reflect limitations in transportation or handling facilities at the point of destination.

Although a product's packaging is often used as a form of display abroad, international packaging can rarely serve the dual purpose of protection and display. Therefore, double packaging may be necessary. The display package is for future use at the point of destination; another package surrounds the product for protective purposes.

One solution to the packaging problem in international logistics has been the development of intermodal containers—large metal boxes that fit on trucks, ships, railroad cars, and airplanes and ease the frequent transfer of goods in international shipments. Developed in different forms for both sea and air transportation, containers also offer better utilization of carrier space because of standardization of size. The shipper, therefore, may benefit from lower transportation rates. In addition, containers can offer greater safety from pilferage and damage.

Container traffic is heavily dependent on the existence of appropriate handling facilities, both domestically and internationally. In addition, the quality of inland transportation must be considered. If transportation for containers is not available and the merchandise must be unloaded, the expected cost reductions may not materialize.

In some countries, rules for handling containers may be designed to maintain employment. For example, U.S. union rules obligate shippers to withhold containers from firms that

Fast Facts

What trade route connects the Atlantic and Pacific oceans?

The Panama Canal. The dream of digging a water passage across the Isthmus of Panama, uniting the Atlantic and Pacific Oceans, dates to the early sixteenth century and can be traced to the 1513 isthmus crossing of Vasco Nuñez de Balboa. He discovered that only a narrow strip of land separated the two oceans.

do not employ members of the International Longshoremen's Association for the loading or unloading of containers within a fifty-mile radius of Atlantic or Gulf ports. Such restrictions can result in an onerous cost burden.

In summary, close attention must be paid to international packaging. The customer who orders and pays for the merchandise expects it to arrive on time and in good condition. Even with replacements and insurance, the customer will not be satisfied if there are delays. Dissatisfaction will usually translate directly into lost sales.

GLOBAL STORAGE ISSUES

Although international logistics is discussed as a movement or flow of goods, a stationary period is involved when merchandise becomes inventory stored in warehouses. Heated arguments can arise within a firm over the need for and utility of warehousing merchandise internationally. On the one hand, customers expect quick responses to orders and rapid delivery. Accommodating the customer's expectations would require locating many distribution centers around the world. On the other hand, warehouse space is expensive. In addition, the larger volume of inventory increases the inventory carrying cost. Having fewer warehouses allows for consolidation of transportation and therefore lower transportation rates to the warehouse. However, if the warehouses are located far from customers, the cost of outgoing transportation increases. The international logistician must consider the trade-offs between service and cost to the supply chain in order to determine the appropriate levels of warehousing.

Storage Facilities

STORAGE LOCATION DECISION

A decision concerning the number of facilities to establish and where they should be situated

The **storage location decision** addresses how many distribution centers to have and where to locate them. The availability of facilities abroad will differ from the domestic situation. For example, although public storage is widely available in some countries, such facilities may be scarce or entirely lacking in others. Also, the standards and quality of facilities can vary widely. As a result, the need for large-scale, long-term investments often accompanies a firm's storage decision. Despite the high cost, international storage facilities should be established if they support the overall logistics effort. In many markets, adequate storage facilities are imperative to satisfy customer demands and to compete successfully. For example, because the establishment of a warehouse connotes a visible presence, a firm can convince local distributors and customers of its commitment to remain in the market for the long term.

Once the decision is made to use storage facilities abroad, the warehouse conditions must be carefully analyzed. As an example, in some countries warehouses have low ceilings. Packaging developed for the high stacking of products is therefore unnecessary or even counterproductive. In other countries, automated warehousing is available. Proper bar coding of products and the use of package dimensions acceptable to the warehousing system are basic requirements. In contrast, in warehouses that are still stocked manually, weight limitations will be of major concern. And if no forklift trucks are available, palletized delivery is of little use.

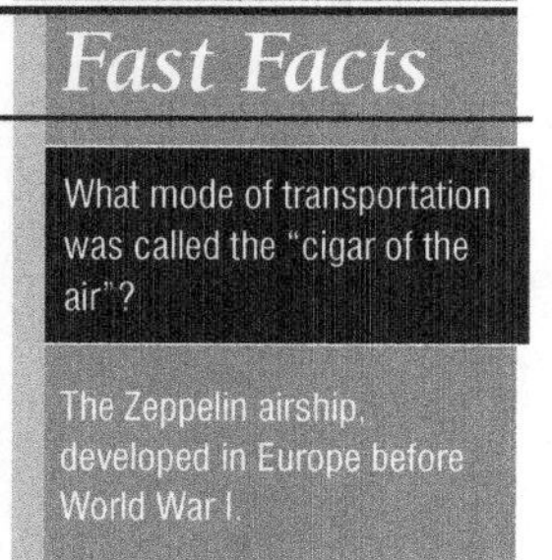

To optimize the logistics system, the logistician should analyze international product sales and then rank products according to warehousing needs. Products that are most sensitive to delivery time might be classified as "A" products. "A" products would be stocked in all distribution centers, and safety stock levels would be kept high. Alternatively, the storage of products can be more selective if quick delivery by air can be guaranteed. Products for which immediate delivery is not urgent could be classified as "B" products. They would be stored only at selected distribution centers around the world. Finally, "C" products for which there

Quick Take *Keep It Green!*

From the outside, the intermodal steel container may not appear to be a very exciting piece of transportation equipment, but inside, some of them incorporate advanced technology that maintains the condition and value of the cargo. Such is the case of Maersk Sealand's "Fresh Mist" humidity-controlled refrigerated containers, designed to prevent dehydration of fresh produce during long ocean voyages. It does this by maintaining the moisture inside a refrigerated container at optimal levels, which keeps the produce fresh longer. The fresh produce arrives heavier and better looking, with a longer shelf life that commands a higher price in overseas markets.

Inside the container, sophisticated microprocessor technology atomizes water into minute particles and injects them into the air stream—maintaining optimal humidity levels without damage to the product packaging. In addition to including advanced technology in its shipping containers, Maersk Line has also made efforts to use environmentally friendly resources when possible. For example, it has more than 10,000 containers made with bamboo flooring. According to Maersk Line, bamboo is a quick-growing grass that can be harvested every three to four years and thereby constitutes an environmental friendly alternative to the traditional wooden floorboards.

SOURCE: **http://www.maerskline.com**, accessed February 24, 2008.

is little demand would be stocked only at headquarters. Should an urgent need for delivery arise, airfreight could again assure rapid shipment. Classifying products enables the international logistician to substantially reduce total international warehousing requirements and still maintain acceptable service levels.

Special Trade Zones

Areas where foreign goods may be held or processed and then re-exported without incurring duties are called **foreign trade zones**. The zones can be found at major ports of entry and also at inland locations near major production facilities. For example, Kansas City, Missouri, has one of the largest U.S. foreign trade zones.

FOREIGN TRADE ZONES
Special areas where foreign goods may be held or processed without incurring duties and taxes

The existence of trade zones can be quite useful to the international firm. For example, in some countries, the benefits derived from lower labor costs may be offset by high duties and tariffs. As a result, location of manufacturing and storage facilities in these countries may prove uneconomical. Foreign trade zones are designed to exclude the impact of duties from the location decision. This is done by exempting merchandise in the foreign trade zone from duty payment. The international firm can therefore import merchandise, store it in the foreign trade zone, and process, alter, test, or demonstrate it—all without paying duties. If the merchandise is subsequently shipped abroad (that is, re-exported), no duty payments are ever due. Duty payments become due only if the merchandise is shipped into the country from the foreign trade zone.

Trade zones can also be useful as trans-shipment points to reduce logistics cost and redesign marketing approaches. For example, Audiovox was shipping small quantities of car alarms from a Taiwanese contract manufacturer directly to distributors in Chile. The shipments were costly, and the marketing strategy required high minimum orders, which stopped distributors from buying. The firm resolved the dilemma by using a Miami trade zone to ship the alarms from Taiwan and consolidate the goods with other shipments to Chile. The savings in freight costs allowed the Chilean distributors to order whatever quantity they wanted and allowed the company to quote lower prices. As a result, sales improved markedly.[10]

All parties to the arrangement benefit from foreign trade zones. The government maintaining the trade zone achieves increased employment and investment. The firm using the trade zone obtains a spearhead in the foreign market without incurring all of the costs customarily associated with such an activity. As a result, goods can be reassembled, and large shipments can be broken down into smaller units. Also, goods can be repackaged when packaging weight becomes part of the duty assessment. Finally, goods can be given domestic "made in" status if assembled in the foreign trade zone. Thus, duties may be payable only on the imported materials and component parts, rather than on the labor that is used to finish the product.

EXPORT PROCESSING ZONES
Special areas that provide tax- and duty-free treatment for production facilities whose output is destined abroad

SPECIAL ECONOMIC ZONES
Special tariff-free areas where there are substantial tax incentives and low prices for land and labor to which the government hopes to attract foreign direct investment

In addition to foreign trade zones, governments also have established export processing zones and special economic areas. **Export processing zones** usually provide tax- and duty-free treatment for production facilities whose output is destined abroad. The maquiladoras of Mexico, described in Chapter 5, are one example of a program that permits firms to take advantage of sharp differentials in labor costs. Firms can carry out the labor-intensive part of their operations in Mexico, while sourcing raw materials or component parts from other nations.

One country that has used trade zones very successfully for its own economic development is China. Through the creation of **special economic zones**, in which there are no tariffs, substantial tax incentives, and low prices for land and labor, the government has attracted many foreign investors, bringing in billions of dollars. The investors have brought new equipment, technology, and managerial know-how and have increased local economic prosperity.

For the logistician, the decision whether to use such zones is framed mainly by the overall benefit for the supply-chain system. Clearly, additional transport and re-transport are required, warehousing facilities need to be constructed, and material handling frequency will increase. However, the costs may well be balanced by the preferential government treatment or by lower labor costs.

SUMMARY

As competitiveness becomes increasingly dependent on efficiency, global logistics and supply-chain management gain major importance. The supply chain is concerned with the flow of materials into, through, and out of the international corporation and therefore includes supplier and customer relationships, as well as materials management and physical distribution.

The logistician must recognize the total system demands on the firm, its suppliers, and customers to develop trade-offs between various logistics components. By taking a supply-chain perspective, the manager can develop logistics systems that are supplier- and customer-focused and highly efficient. Implementation of such a system requires close collaboration between all members of the supply chain.

International logistics differs from domestic activities in that it deals with greater distances, new variables, and greater complexity because of national differences. One major factor to consider is transportation. The international manager needs to understand transportation infrastructures in other countries and the various modes of transportation. The choice among these modes will depend on the customer's demands and the firm's transit time, predictability, and cost requirements. In addition, non-economic factors, such as government regulations, weigh heavily in this decision.

Inventory management is another major consideration. Inventories abroad are expensive to maintain, yet they are often crucial for international success. The logistician must evaluate requirements for order cycle times and customer service levels to develop a global inventory policy that can also serve as a strategic management tool.

Global packaging is important because it ensures arrival of the merchandise at the ultimate destination in safe condition. In developing packaging, environmental conditions, such as climate and handling conditions, must be considered.

The logistics manager must also deal with international storage issues and determine where to locate inventories. International warehouse space will have to be leased or purchased, and decisions will have to be made about utilizing foreign trade zones.

Key Terms and Concepts

supply chain
materials management
physical distribution
systems concept
total-cost concept
trade-off concept
supply-chain management
just-in-time inventory systems
logistics platform
land bridge
sea bridge
intermodal movements
liner service
bulk service
tramp service
roll-on-roll-off (RORO)
lighter aboard ship (LASH) vessel
transit time
predictability
tracking
preferential policies
straight bill of lading
shipper's order
commercial invoice
Incoterms
ex-works (EXW)
free carrier
free alongside ship
free on board (FOB)
cost and freight (CFR)
cost, insurance, and freight (CIF)
carriage paid to (CPT)
carriage and insurance paid to (CIP)
delivery duty paid (DDP)
delivery duty unpaid (DDU)
inventory carrying costs
order cycle time
electronic data interchange
reverse logistics
storage location decision
foreign trade zones
export processing zones
special economic zones

Review Questions

1. Explain the key aspects of supply-chain management.
2. In what ways does international transportation differ from domestic transportation?
3. Contrast the use of ocean shipping and airfreight.
4. Explain the meaning and impact of transit time in international logistics.
5. How and why do governments interfere in "rational" freight-carrier selection?
6. How can an international firm reduce its order cycle time?
7. What aspects of packaging influence the transportation decision?
8. What are special trade zones, and how do they benefit global companies?

Critical Skill Builders

1. Why should customer service levels differ internationally? For example, is it ethical to offer a lower customer service level in developing countries than in industrialized countries? Discuss in a debate format.
2. Choose a small or mid-size business in your area, or research one on the Internet. Discuss ways in which the company may benefit by improving its supply chain. What recommendations would you make?
3. You work for a restaurant chain close to the Mexican border that receives requests for deliveries into Mexico. What steps can you take to fulfill those orders? What issues arise that do not also pertain to domestic sales?
4. You work for a company that makes educational toys and that sells mainly to teachers but also directly to parents. In early September, you learn that, due to a pending longshoreman's strike in Los Angeles, your shipment, due to leave Singapore next month, is likely to be delayed. What steps can you take to cut down on your losses during one of your main selling seasons, the run-up to Christmas? Create a crisis action plan for the business.

On the Web

1. What types of information are available to the exporter on the Transport Web? Go to **http://www.transportweb.com**, and give examples of transportation links that an exporter would find helpful and explain why.
2. Use an online database to select a freight forwarder. (Refer to **http://www.freightnet.com** or **http://www.forwarders.com**, directories of freight forwarders.)
3. When you first set up your web site featuring a designer line of specialty pens and stationery, you did not expect to receive orders from abroad. But from time to time, you receive orders from Europe, Australia, Canada, and Japan that you would like to fill. Create a plan for delivery of your products using airfreight. Check the web sites for UPS, FedEx, and Airborne Express to compare rates and find out more about making small, occasional shipments abroad. See **http://www.fedex.com**, **http://www.ups.com**, and **http://www.airborne.com**.

Endnotes

1. Council of Supply Chain Management Professionals, **http://www.cscmp.org/website/aboutcscmp/definitions/definitions.asp**, accessed February 14, 2008.
2. Accenture Global, **http://www.accenture.com.global/service/by_subject/supply_chain_mgmt/ client_successes/enhancedmanagement.htm**, accessed October 14, 2013.
3. David A. Ricks, *Blunders in International Business*, 4th ed. (Malden, MA: Wiley-Blackwell Publishing, Incorporated, 2006), p. 20.
4. Michael E. Porter, *The Competitive Advantage of Nations* (New York: The Free Press, 1990).
5. **www.iata.org**, accessed October 18, 2013.
6. International Chambers of Commerce, Incoterms 2010 (Paris: ICC Publishing, 2000).
7. Dennis Lord, "The Real Cost of Carrying Inventory," **http://www.imsconsulting.ca/article.php?name=highcost**, accessed October 24, 2013.
8. "Reverse Logistics: superior performance through focused resources commitments to information technology," **www.sciencedirect.com**, accessed February October 21, 2013.
9. David A. Ricks, *Blunders in International Business*, 4th ed. (Malden, MA: Wiley:-Blackwell Publishing, Incorporated, 2006), p. 29.
10. Marita von Oldenborgh, "Power Logistics," *International Business*, October 1994, pp. 32–34.

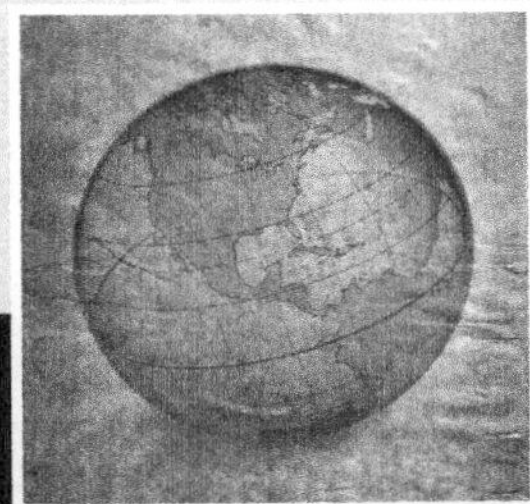

CHAPTER 13

MANAGING GLOBALLY

Strength in Structure

Globalization is at the heart of Procter & Gamble's structuring of its organization. This global structure replaced a region-driven apparatus with the goal of making employees stretch their abilities and speed up innovation as well as moving products and processes across borders. It combines the global scale benefits of an $84 billion global company with a local focus to win with consumers and retail customers in each country where P&G products are sold.

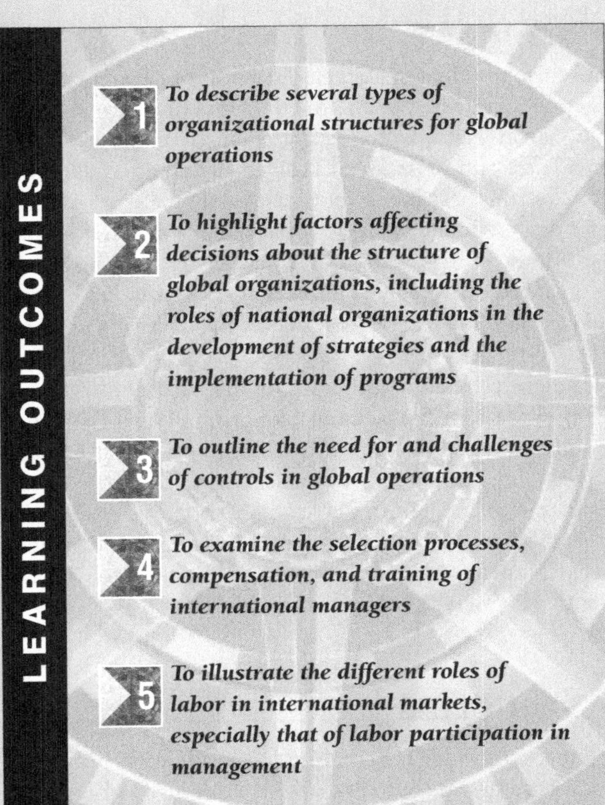

LEARNING OUTCOMES

1. ***To describe several types of organizational structures for global operations***
2. ***To highlight factors affecting decisions about the structure of global organizations, including the roles of national organizations in the development of strategies and the implementation of programs***
3. ***To outline the need for and challenges of controls in global operations***
4. ***To examine the selection processes, compensation, and training of international managers***
5. ***To illustrate the different roles of labor in international markets, especially that of labor participation in management***

P&G's structure has removed many of the traditional overlaps and inefficiencies that exist in many large companies.

Market Development Organizations

Global Business Units: **Beauty & Grooming** | **Household Care**

Global Business Services
Shared Services
Corporate Functions
Governance, Capability, Functional Innovation

Global business units (GBUs) focus solely on consumers, brands, and competitors around the world. They are responsible for the innovation pipeline, profitability, and shareholder returns from their businesses. They span a broad range of product categories that are household names around the world, including Pampers, Gillette, Tide, Ariel, Downy, Pantene, Head & Shoulders, Olay, Oral-B, Crest, Dawn, Fairy and Always.

Market development organizations (MDOs) are charged with knowing consumers and retailers in each market where P&G competes and integrating the innovations flowing from the GBUs into business plans that work in each country. P&G entered the prestige male skincare category in Korea, Hong Kong, and Taiwan with SK-II Men Facial Treatment Essence, a product designed to revitalize men's skin, making it look clearer and more vibrant in just fourteen days.

Global business services (GBS) utilizes P&G talent and expert partners to provide best-in-class business support services at the lowest possible costs to leverage P&G's scale for a winning advantage. GBS provides more than 170 employees and business services, including IT, finance, facilities, purchasing, and employee services as well as business building solutions

Corporate functions ensure ongoing functional innovation and capability improvement. P&G earned fifth place among *Fortune's* 2011 list of the World's Most Admired Companies. And as of April 2011, P&G has won twenty-two "Product of the Year" recognitions, as voted on by consumers in the United States, United Kingdom, France, Holland, Italy, Spain, and South Africa.

Changes to P&G's culture should create an environment that produces bolder, mind-stretching goals and plans bigger innovations with greater speed. For example, the reward system has been redesigned to better link executive compensation with new business goals and results. Collaborative technologies, including chat rooms on the company's intranet, are transforming the company's conservative culture to one that encourages employees to be candid, test boundaries, and take chances.[1]

As You Read This Chapter

1. How well does P&G's new structure meet the needs of a global organization?
2. Does it serve as a model for all firms that plan to go global?

GLOBAL BUSINESS UNITS (GBUS)
Focus solely on consumers, brands, and competitors around the world and responsible for the innovation pipeline, profitability, and shareholder returns.

MARKET DEVELOPMENT ORGANIZATIONS (MDOS)
Know consumers and retailers in each market and integrate the innovations flowing from the GBUs into business plans that work in each country.

GLOBAL BUSINESS SERVICES
Provide best-in-class business support services at the lowest possible costs.

CORPORATE FUNCTIONS
Ensure ongoing functional innovation and capability improvement.

As companies grow from purely domestic to multinational, their organizational structures and control systems must change to reflect new strategies. With growth comes diversity, in terms of products and services, geographic markets, and people in the company itself, creating a new set of challenges for the company. Three critical issues are basic to all of these challenges: (1) the type of organization that provides the best framework for operational effectiveness, (2) the optimal approach to implementing corporate strategy globally, regionally, and locally, and (3) the type and degree of control to be exercised from headquarters to maximize total effort.[2] Organizational structures, an organization's ability to implement strategies and control systems, have to be adjusted as market conditions change, as seen in the chapter's opening vignette.

Organizations have two general human resource objectives. The first is the recruitment and retention of a workforce made up of the best people available for the jobs to be done. The recruiter in international operations will need to keep in mind both cross-cultural and cross-national differences in productivity and expectations when selecting employees. Once they are hired, the firm's best interest lies in maintaining a stable and experienced workforce. The second objective is to increase the effectiveness of the workforce. This depends to a great extent on achieving the first objective. Competent managers or workers are likely to perform at a more effective level if proper attention is given to factors that motivate them.

Organizational Structure

The basic functions of an organization are to provide (1) a route and locus of decision-making and coordination and (2) a system for reporting and communications. Authority and communication networks are typically depicted in the organizational chart.

The basic configurations of global organizations correspond to those of purely domestic ones; the greater the degree of internalization, the more complex the structures can become. The types of structures that companies use to manage activities can be divided into four categories, as shown in Table 13.1.

TABLE 13.1 How an Organization's Structure Changes as It Becomes More Involved in Global Business Activities

Degree of Company Globalization	Unit Typically Responsible	Typical Title of Unit Manager
1. Occasional export order	Domestic sales department	Domestic sales manager
2. Increasing volume of sales	Newly formed unit-export sales department	Manager or director—export sales
3. Major corporate effort to extend reach into markets	International division (may involve some joint ventures or direct investment)	Vice president
4. Total corporate commitment to conduct operations on a global basis	Wholly owned subsidiaries, joint ventures, and/or other forms of inter-firm cooperation	Senior vice president

Little or No Formal Organization

In the early stages of global involvement, domestic operations assume responsibility for international activities. Transactions are conducted on a case-by-case basis, either by the resident expert or with the help of facilitating agents, such as freight forwarders. As demand from the international marketplace grows and interest within the firm expands, the organizational structure will reflect it. As shown in Figure 13.1, an export department appears as a separate entity. Organizationally, the department may be a subset of marketing or may have equal ranking with the various functional departments. The choice will depend on the importance the firm assigns to overseas activities. Because establishing the export department is the first real step toward internationalization, it should be a full-fledged marketing function and should not be limited to sales. VEAB are the leading manufacturer of electrical duct heaters and have significant exports to about thirty-five countries all over the world. Products that are meant for the contractor and professional markets are distributed through a network of distributors and agents.[3]

The more the firm becomes involved in foreign markets, the more quickly the export department structure will become obsolete. For example, the firm may undertake joint ventures or direct investment, which requires those involved to have functional experience. The firm therefore typically establishes an international division.

Fast Facts

Most firms also remain quite domestically rooted in other aspects of their business, such as where they do their production or research and development or where their shareholders live. BMW, for example, derived 51 percent of its sales revenue from outside of Europe in 2011, but still maintained roughly 64 percent of its production and 73 percent of its workforce in Germany.

FIGURE 13.1 Export Department Structure (VEAB)

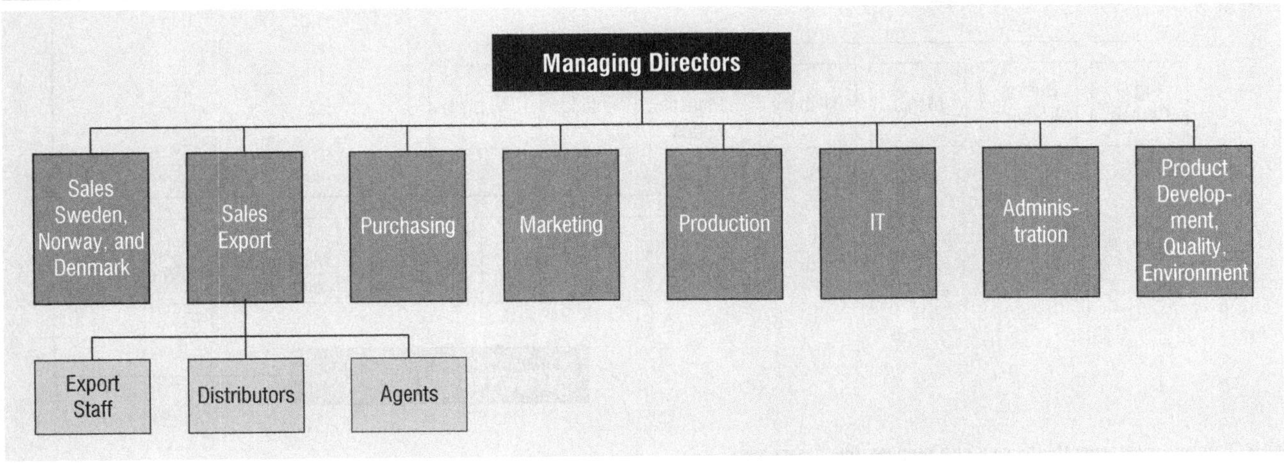

Fast Facts

- Luanda, Angola, is the world's most expensive city for expatriates.
- Moscow and Tokyo rank costliest for Europe and Asia, respectively.
- A cup of coffee in Moscow can cost $8.29 compared to $1.54 in Managua, Nicaragua.
- A fast-food hamburger meal in Caracas can cost $13.49 compared to $3.62 in Kolkata.

The International Division

The international division centralizes all of the responsibility for global activities, as illustrated in Figure 13.2. The approach aims to eliminate a possible bias against global operations that may exist if domestic divisions are allowed to serve international customers independently. The international division concentrates international expertise, information flows concerning market opportunities, and authority over international activities. However, manufacturing and other related functions remain with the domestic divisions to take advantage of economies of scale.

To avoid putting the international division at a disadvantage in competing for products, personnel, and corporate services, coordination between domestic and global operations is necessary. Coordination can be achieved through a joint staff or by requiring domestic and international divisions to interact in strategic planning.

General Mills, a notable exception among consumer goods companies, was still using the international division structure with sales from international customers at approximately 20 percent. In addition to its global brands (e.g., Pillsbury and Betty Crocker), General Mills also offers several local brands, such as La Salteña pastas and tapas in Argentina and Jus-Rol pastries in the United Kingdom. General Mills participate in two international joint ventures: Cereal Partners Worldwide (Nestlé) and Häagen-Dazs Japan.[4]

Companies may outgrow their international divisions as their sales outside of the domestic market grow in significance, diversity, and complexity. European companies have traditionally used international divisions far less than their U.S. counterparts do because of the relatively small size of their domestic markets. Philips, or Nokia, for example, would never have grown to their current prominence by relying on their home markets alone. Globalization of markets

FIGURE 13.2 International Division Structure (General Mills)

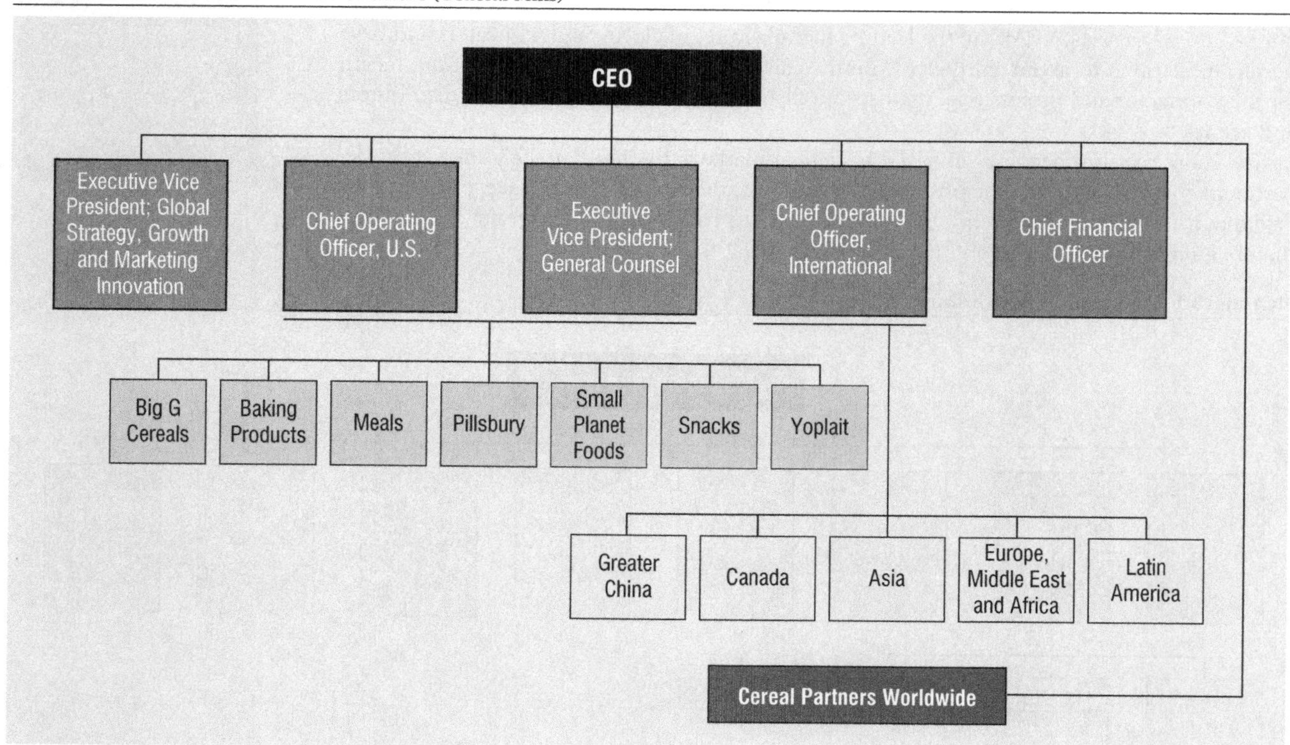

SOURCE: **http://www.generalmills.com/en/Company/Businesses.aspx**

and the narrowing ratio between domestic and international sales make international divisions increasingly less appropriate.

The Global Organization

Global structures have grown out of competitive necessity. In many industries, competition is on a global basis. As a result, companies must have a high degree of reactive capability.

Six basic types of global structures are available:

1. Global product structure, in which product divisions are responsible for all manufacture and marketing worldwide
2. Global area structure, in which geographic divisions are responsible for all manufacture and marketing in their respective areas
3. Global functional structure, in which functional areas (such as production, marketing, finance, and personnel) are responsible for the worldwide operations of their own functional area
4. Global customer structure, in which operations are structured based on distinct worldwide customer groups
5. Mixed—or hybrid—structure, which may combine the other alternatives
6. Matrix structure, in which operations have reporting responsibility to more than one group (typically, product, functions, or area)

GLOBAL PRODUCT STRUCTURE

An organizational structure in which product divisions are responsible for all global activity

GLOBAL PRODUCT STRUCTURE A **global product structure** gives worldwide responsibility to strategic business units for the marketing of their product lines. Most consumer-product firms use some form of this approach, mainly because of the diversity of their offerings. One of the major benefits is improved cost efficiency through centralization of manufacturing facilities. This is crucial in industries in which competitive position is determined by world market share, which in turn is often determined by the degree to which manufacturing is rationalized.[5] Adaptation to this approach may cause problems because it is usually accompanied by consolidation of operations and plant closings. Stanley Black & Decker rationalized many of its operations in its worldwide competitive effort against Makita, the Japanese power-tool manufacturer. In a similar move, Ford merged its large and culturally distinct European, North American, and Chinese auto operations by vehicle platform type to make more efficient use of its engineering and product development resources against rapidly globalizing rivals.[6] The Ford Fusion was designed by one team of engineers for worldwide markets. Other benefits of the product structure are the ability to balance the functional inputs needed for a product and the ability to react quickly to product-specific problems in the marketplace. Product-specific attention is important because products vary in terms of the adaptation they need for different foreign markets. A product structure means that even smaller brands receive individual attention. All in all, the product approach is ideally suited to the development of a global strategic focus in response to global competition.

At the same time, the product structure fragments global expertise within the firm because a central pool of international experience no longer exists. The structure assumes that managers will have adequate regional experience or advice to allow them to make balanced decisions. Coordination of activities among the various product groups operating in the same markets is crucial to avoid unnecessary duplication of basic tasks. For some of these tasks, such as market research, special staff functions may be created and then filled by the product divisions when needed. If they lack an appreciation for the global dimension, product managers may focus their attention only on the larger markets or only on the domestic markets and fail to take the broader, long-term view.

GLOBAL AREA STRUCTURE
An organizational structure in which geographic divisions are responsible for all global activity

GLOBAL AREA STRUCTURE Firms that adopt a **global area structure** are organized on the basis of geographical regions; for example, operations may be divided into those dealing with North America, Latin America, the Far East, and Europe. Central staffs are responsible for providing coordination and support for worldwide planning and control activities.

Integration of trade zones has increased the attractiveness of area structures. For example, with the integration of European markets, many multinational corporations relocated their European headquarters to Brussels, where the European Union is based. Cultural similarity also favors the establishment of an area structure. In some cases, historical connections between countries lead companies to choose this type of structure, combining, for example, Europe with the Middle East and Africa.

The area approach follows the marketing concept most closely because it allows for concentrated attention on individual areas and markets. If market conditions vary dramatically with respect to product acceptance and operating conditions, an area structure is appropriate. It is also a good choice for companies that have relatively narrow product lines with similar end uses and end users.

GLOBAL FUNCTIONAL STRUCTURE
An organizational structure in which departments are formed on the basis of functional areas, such as production, marketing, and finance

PROCESS STRUCTURE
A variation of the functional structure in which departments are formed on the basis of production processes

GLOBAL FUNCTIONAL STRUCTURE Of all the approaches, the **global functional structure** is the simplest from the administrative viewpoint because it emphasizes the basic tasks of the firm, such as manufacturing, sales, and research and development. The approach works best when both products and customers are relatively few and similar in nature. Coordination is typically the key problem, which is why many companies create staff functions to interact between the functional areas.

A variation of the functional approach is one that uses processes as a basis for structure. The **process structure** is common in the energy and mining industries, where one corporate

Quick Take *Rethinking Boundaries*

Global organizations have long sought to realize scale benefits by centralizing activities that are similar across locations and tailoring to local markets any tasks that need to differ from country to country. Today, as more and more companies shift their weight to emerging markets, boundaries between those activities are changing for many organizations.

At some point, they will need to adapt their structures and processes to acknowledge this boundary shift, whose nature will vary across and within companies, depending on their industry, focus, and history. International publishing company Bertelsmann created global vertical structures made up of people who work on content and delivery technology for similar publications around the world. But it was careful to leave all sales and marketing operations in the hands of local country managers because, in publishing, these activities can succeed only if they are tailored to local markets.

IBM sought out pools of competitive talent with the skills required to perform each service at different cost points. Then it built teams of specialists geographically close to the relevant pool to meet the region's needs in each service. So now, for example, IBM's growth market operations are served by human resource specialists in Manila, accounts receivable are processed in Shanghai, accounting is done in Kuala Lumpur, procurement in Shenzhen, and the customer service help desk is based in Brisbane. Globalizing functions that were previously country based has been a huge corporate-wide undertaking for IBM.

Source: Martin Dewhurst, Jonathan Harris, and Suzanne Heywood, "The Global Company's Challenge, *McKinsey Quarterly*, June 2012, 76–80; and Toby Gibbs, Suzanne Heywood, and Leigh Weiss, "Organizing for an Emerging World," *McKinsey Quarterly*, June 2012, 81–91.

entity may be in charge of exploration worldwide and another may be responsible for the actual mining operations.

GLOBAL CUSTOMER STRUCTURE Firms may also organize their operations using the **global customer structure**, especially if the customer groups they serve are dramatically different—for example, consumers, businesses, and governments. Catering to such diverse groups may require concentrating specialists in particular divisions. The product may be the same, but the buying processes of the various customer groups may differ. Governmental buying, for example, is characterized by bidding, in which price plays a larger role than when businesses are the buyers.

GLOBAL CUSTOMER STRUCTURE
An organizational structure in which divisions are formed on the basis of customer groups

MIXED STRUCTURE A **mixed structure**—or hybrid structure—combines two or more organizational dimensions simultaneously. It permits adequate attention to product, area, or functional needs, as required. A mixed structure may only be the result of a transitional period after a merger or an acquisition, or it may come about because of unique market characteristics or a unique product line. It may also provide a useful structure before the implementation of a worldwide matrix structure, which will be discussed next.

MIXED STRUCTURE
An organizational structure that combines two or more organizational dimensions, for example, products, areas, or functions

Naturally, organizational structures are never as clear-cut and simple as presented here. Whatever the basic format, product, functional, and area inputs are needed. Alternatives could include an initial product structure that would subsequently have regional groupings or an initial regional structure with subsequent product groupings. However, in the long term, coordination and control across such structures can become tedious. The Nestlé Group (in figure 13.3) is managed by geographies (Europe, Americas, and Asia/Oceania/Africa) for most

FIGURE 13.3 Global Mixed Structure (Nestlé)

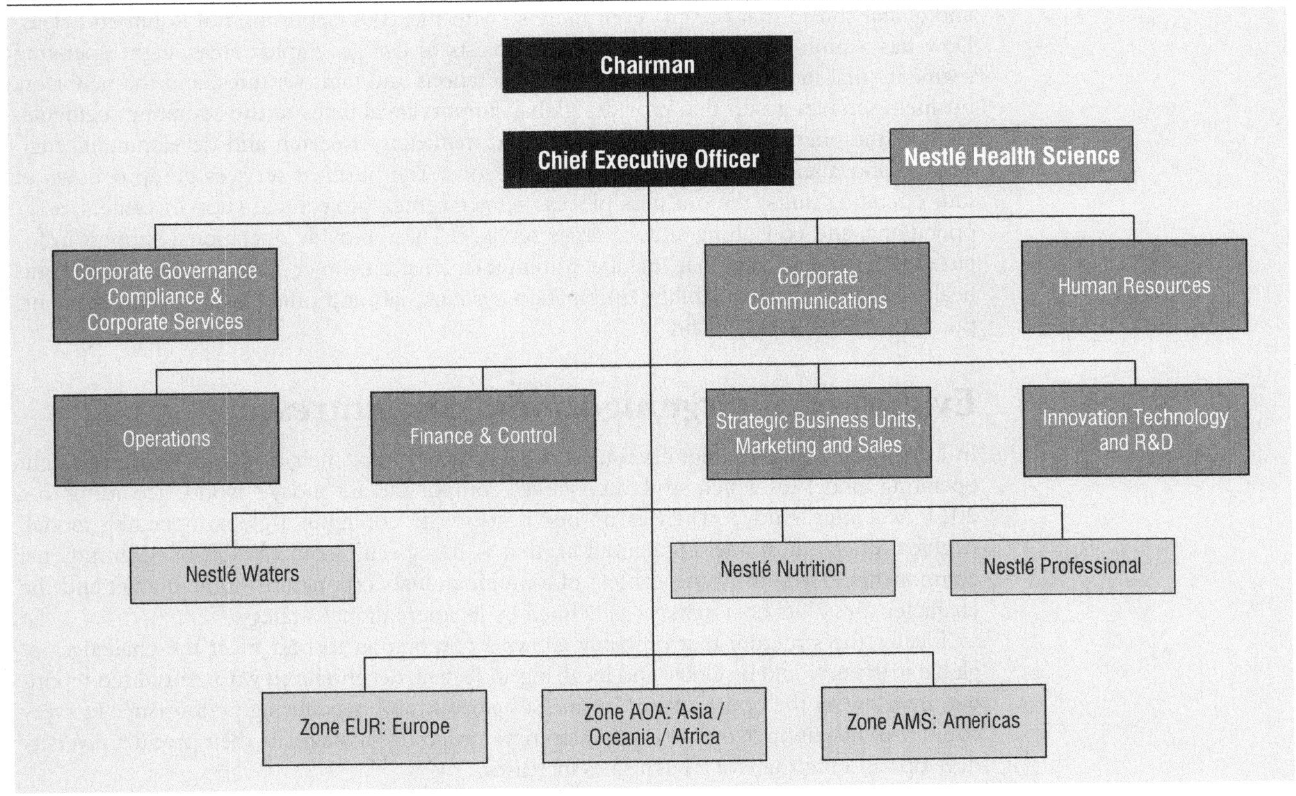

SOURCE: **http://www.nestle.com/ABOUTUS/MANAGEMENT/Pages/Management-landing.aspx**

of the food and beverage business, with the exceptions of Nestlé Waters, Nestlé Nutrition, Nestlé Purina Petcare, Nespresso, Nestlé Professional and Nestlé Health Science, which are managed on a global basis.[7]

MATRIX STRUCTURE
An organizational structure that uses functional and divisional structures simultaneously

MATRIX STRUCTURE Many multinational corporations, in an attempt to facilitate planning for, organizing, and controlling interdependent businesses, critical resources, strategies, and geographic regions, have adopted the **matrix structure.**[8] Business is driven by a worldwide business unit (for example, photographic products or commercial and information systems) and implemented through a geographic unit (for example, Europe or Latin America). The geographical units, as well as their country subsidiaries, serve as "the glue" between autonomous product operations.

A significant problem with a matrix structure arises from the fact that every management unit may have a multidimensional reporting relationship, which may cross functional, regional, or operational lines. Because of the dual, or even multiple, reporting channels, conflicts are likely to erupt. Furthermore, complex issues are forced into a two-dimensional decision framework, and even minor issues may have to be solved through committee discussion. Ideally, managers should solve the problems themselves through formal and informal communication; however, physical and cultural distances often make that impossible. The matrix structure, with its inherent complexity, may actually increase the reaction time of a company, a potentially serious problem when competitive conditions require quick responses. As a result, the authority has started to shift in many organizations, from area to product, although the matrix still may officially be used.

Organizational matrices integrate the various approaches already discussed, as the example in Figure 13.4 illustrates. Matrices vary in terms of their areas of emphasis and the number of dimensions. For example, Dow Chemical's structure reflects its diversified chemicals business and global spread that became even more so with the 2009 acquisition of Rohm and Haas. Dow has a multidimensional matrix that consists of five geographic areas, eight operating segments that include both wholly owned operations and joint ventures, and the new Dow business services group that provides global support capabilities to the operating segments. Each of the operating segments has sales and marketing, research and development, engineering and manufacturing, and finance functions. The business services group consists of four operating units: the business process service center, project and support centers, asset operations, and consulting and expertise services. These provide operational support in focused service functions that include communications, customer service, environment and health safety and sustainability, information systems, lab and office facilities management, purchasing, and supply chain.[9]

Evolution of Organizational Structures

In fact, 95 percent of senior executives say that they doubt their companies have the right operating model (of which structure is a key component) for today's world, according to a 2011 Accenture study.[10] There is no one best way to configure a global operating model. A global operating model configuration, that is the specific combination of organizational components, needs to fit the context of a multinational corporations home market and the characteristics of its host markets as defined by its international strategy.

Ideally, the structure that probably allows a corporation to best meet the challenges of global markets would be global and local, big and small, decentralized with centralized reporting, by allowing the optimizing of businesses globally and maximizing performance in every country of operation. Companies develop new structures in stages as their product diversity develops and the share of foreign sales increases.

FIGURE 13.4 Global Matrix Structure (Dow Chemical)

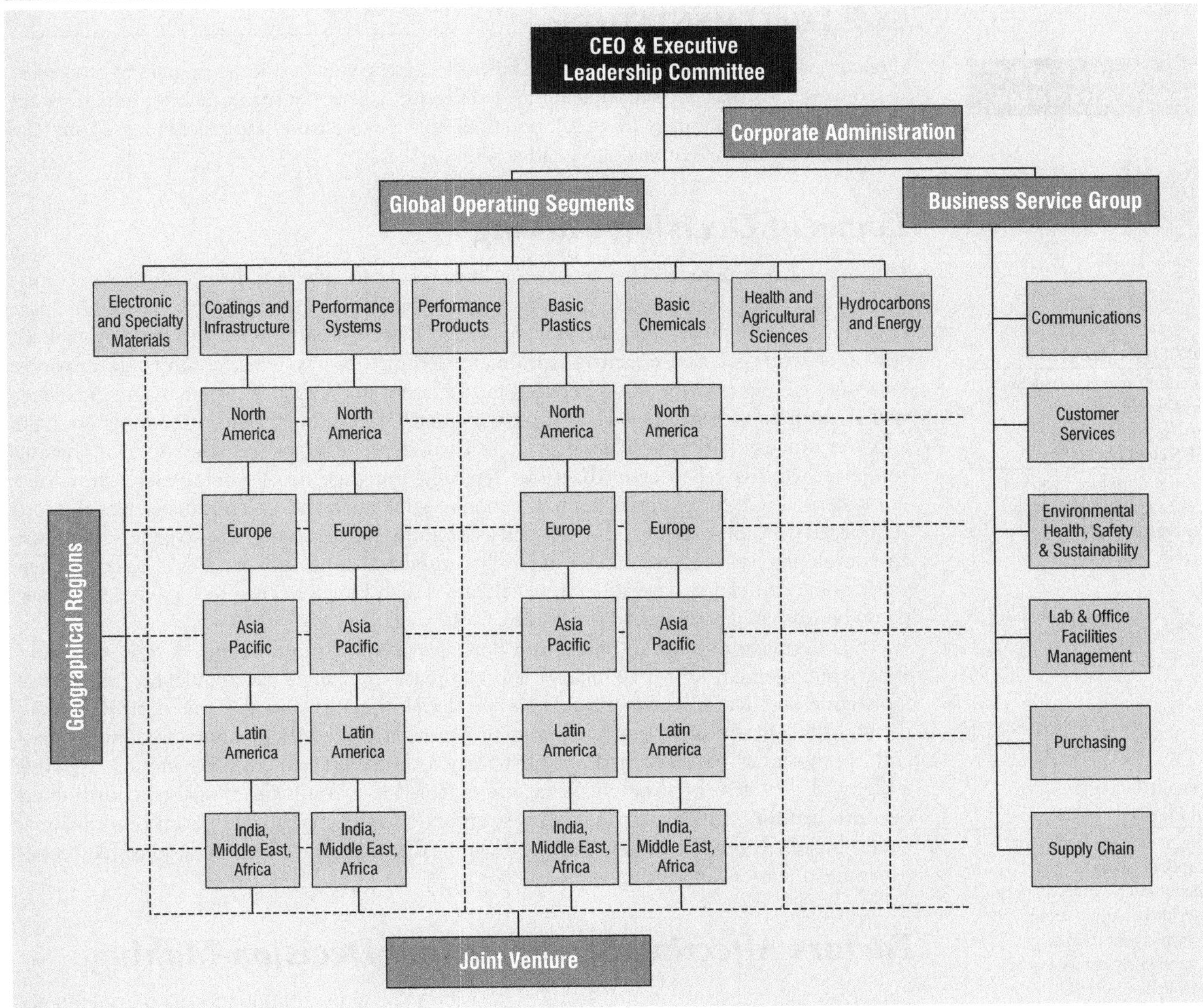

SOURCE: Derived from information from the Dow Chemical Company.

A new structure called the **T-shaped organization** is now emerging. Multinational subsidiaries in emerging markets must reorganize themselves so that they can better cope with two sets of pressures: management models that promote cross sharing and knowledge transfer at all levels of the organization, while promoting individual expertise. GE develops new jet engines, but they rely on their Chinese unit's designs to manufacture them; the India unit adds the analytical and materials aspects, while the German labs use the wind tunnel testing. GE research and development design engineers from around the world collaborate effectively speaking all the same language of Six Sigma.[11]

T-SHAPED ORGANIZATION
Cross-functional management model that promotes sharing and knowledge transfer at all levels of the organization while promoting individual expertise

Implementation

Organizational structures provide the frameworks for carrying out decision-making processes. However, for that decision-making to be effective, a series of organizational initiatives are needed to develop strategy to its full potential, that is, to ensure implementation of strategy decisions both at the national level and across markets.

Locus of Decision-Making

DECENTRALIZATION
Granting subsidiaries a high degree of autonomy

CENTRALIZATION
Concentrating control and strategic decision-making at headquarters

Organizational structures, by themselves, do not indicate where the authority for decision-making and control rests within the organization, nor do they reveal the level of coordination between units. If subsidiaries are granted a high degree of autonomy, the decision-making system at work is called **decentralization**. In decentralized systems, controls are relatively loose and simple, and the flows between headquarters and subsidiaries are mainly financial; that is, each subsidiary operates as a profit center. On the other hand, if controls are tight and the strategic decision-making is concentrated at headquarters, the decision-making system at work is called **centralization**. Typically, firms are neither completely centralized nor decentralized; for example, some functions—such as finance—lend themselves to more centralized decision-making; others—such as promotional decisions—do so far less. Research and development in organizations is typically centralized, especially in cases of basic research work. Some companies have added research and design functions on a regional or local basis, partly because of governmental pressures.

COORDINATED DECENTRALIZATION
The provision of an overall corporate strategy by headquarters, while granting subsidiaries the freedom to implement their own corporate strategies within established ranges

The advantage of allowing maximum flexibility at the country-market level is that subsidiary management knows its market and can react to changes more quickly. Problems of motivation and acceptance are avoided when decision makers are also the implementers of the strategy. On the other hand, many multinationals faced with global competitive threats and opportunities have adopted global strategy formulation, which, by definition, requires a higher degree of centralization. What has emerged as a result can be called **coordinated decentralization**. This means that overall corporate strategy is provided from headquarters, while subsidiaries are free to implement it within the range agreed upon in consultation between headquarters and the subsidiaries.

Factors Affecting Structure and Decision-Making

The organizational structure and locus of decision-making in a multinational corporation are determined by a number of factors, such as (1) its degree of involvement in international operations, (2) the products the firm markets, (3) the size and importance of the firm's markets, and (4) the human resource capability of the firm.[12]

Culture Clues A gateway model to reduce the tension between global integration and local responsiveness has been proposed. As new markets emerge, the need to manage increased complexity is necessary. For example, ten gateway countries could serve as hubs for the developed markets (United States, Japan, Germany, the United Kingdom, France, Italy, Spain, Canada, Australia, and the Netherlands) and another ten countries could perform the same role for emerging markets (China, India, Brazil, Russia, Mexico, South Korea, Indonesia, Turkey, South Africa, and Thailand). Each hub would serve the gateway market as well as other similar markets. For example, the German hub would manage Austria, Hungary, and Switzerland; Brazil would support Argentina, Bolivia, Chile, Paraguay, and Uruguay.

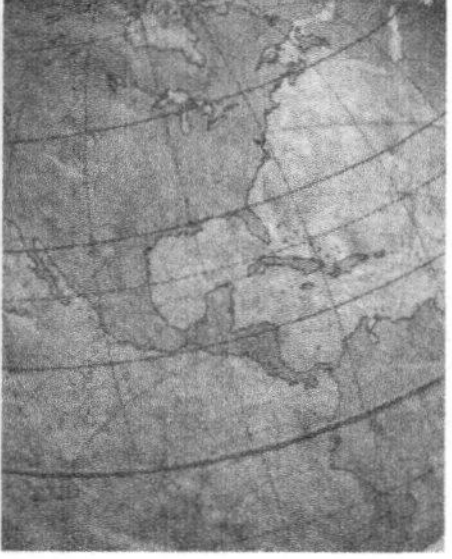

The effect of the degree of involvement on structure and decision-making was discussed previously. With low degrees of involvement, subsidiaries can enjoy high degrees of autonomy, as long as they meet their profit targets. Consider, for example, Alcatel Lucent, which generates 30 percent of its worldwide revenues from North America, mostly from the United States. The company is organized into three geographies (Americas, Europe-Middle East-Africa, and Asia-Pacific) and three corporate functions (customer care, solutions and marketing, and quality assurance). However, its U.S.-based Bell Labs, the company's "innovation engine," enjoys considerable autonomy because it is at the leading edge of communications technology development, although it is still within the parent company's planning and control system.

The type and variety of products marketed affects organizational decisions. Companies that market consumer products typically have product organizations with high degrees of decentralization, allowing for maximum local flexibility. On the other hand, companies that market technologically sophisticated products—such as GE, which markets turbines—display centralized organizations with worldwide product responsibilities.

Apart from situations that require the development of an area structure, the unique characteristics of particular markets or regions may require separate and specific considerations for the firm. For example, Yum! Brands has a structure that emphasizes its individual brands, including KFC, Pizza Hut, Taco Bell, and Long John Silver's, but also has three operational units: one for the U.S. market, an international division, and a separate China Division (covering mainland China, Thailand, and Taiwan) because of the size and strategic importance of China.[13]

The human factor in any organization is critical. Managers at both headquarters and the country organizations must bridge the physical and cultural distances separating them. If country organizations have competent managers who rarely need to consult headquarters about their challenges, they may be granted high degrees of autonomy. In the case of global organizations, local management must understand overall corporate goals, in that decisions that meet the long-term objectives may not be optimal for the individual local market.

Global Networks

No international structure is perfect, and many business leaders have challenged the wisdom of even looking for an ideal structure. Rather, attention to new processes is recommended; processes that would, within a given structure, help to develop new perspectives and attitudes that reflect and respond to the complex, opposing demands of global integration and local responsiveness. The question thus changes from which structural alternative is best to how the different perspectives of various corporate entities can better be taken into account when making decisions. In structural terms, nothing may change. Philips, for example, has not changed its basic matrix structure, yet major changes have occurred in its functional sectors and its internal relations. Philips has organized on an operating sector basis with each of its three sectors, healthcare, consumer lifestyle, and lighting, responsible for the management of its businesses globally. In addition, Philips created an Innovation and Emerging Businesses sector to invest in future-oriented projects outside of the operating sectors and the Group Management and Services sector to provide support in areas such as brand management for the operating sectors. Philips operates as a networked global organization, rather than a decentralized federation model, as depicted in Figure 13.5. The term **glocal** has been coined to describe this approach.

GLOCAL
Reflecting or characterized by both local and global considerations

Companies that have adopted the glocal approach have incorporated the following three dimensions into their organizations: (1) the development and communication of a clear corporate vision, (2) the effective management of human resource tools to broaden individual perspectives and develop identification with corporate goals, and (3) the integration of

FIGURE 13.5 The Networked Global Organization

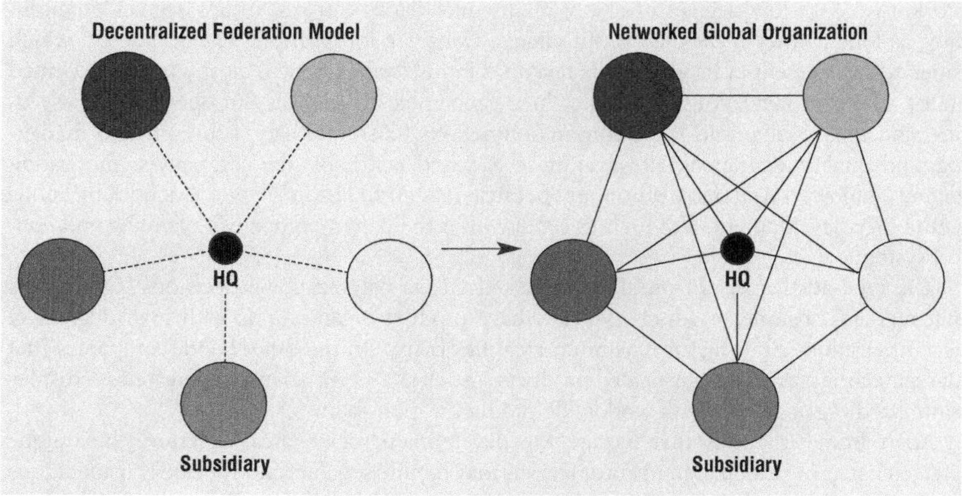

SOURCE: **http://www.accenture.com/us-en/Pages/insight-emerging-market-multinationals creating-global-operating-models-future-summary.aspx**; and Thomas Gross, Ernie Turner and Lars Cederholm, "Building Teams for Global Operations," *Management Review*, June 1987, 34; permission conveyed through Copyright Clearance Center, Inc.

individual thinking and activities into the broad corporate agenda. The first dimension relates to a clear and consistent long-term corporate mission that guides individuals wherever they work in the organization. Examples of this are Johnson & Johnson's corporate credo of customer focus, Coca Cola's mission of leveraging global beverage brand leadership "to refresh the world," and Nestlé's vision to make the company the "reference for nutrition, health, and wellness." The second dimension relates both to the development of global managers who can find opportunities in spite of environmental challenges, as well as the creation of a global perspective among country managers. The third dimension relates to the development of a cooperative mind-set among country organizations to ensure effective implementation of global strategies. Managers may believe that global strategies are intrusions on their operations if they do not have an understanding of the corporate vision, have not contributed to the global corporate agenda, or are not given direct responsibility for its implementation. Defensive, territorial attitudes can lead to the emergence of the **not-invented-here syndrome**, that is, country organizations objecting to or rejecting an otherwise sound strategy.

NOT-INVENTED-HERE SYNDROME
A defensive, territorial attitude that, if held by managers, can frustrate effective implementation of global strategies

The network avoids the problems of effort duplication, inefficiency, and resistance to ideas developed elsewhere by giving subsidiaries the latitude, encouragement, and tools to pursue local business development within the framework of the global strategy. Headquarters considers each unit a source of ideas, skills, capabilities, and knowledge that can be utilized for the benefit of the entire organization. This means that subsidiaries must be upgraded from mere implementers and adaptors to contributors and partners in the development and execution of worldwide strategies. Efficient plants may be converted into international production centers, innovative research and development units are centers of excellence (and thus role models), and leading subsidiary groups are given the leadership role in developing new strategies for the entire corporation.

Promoting Global Internal Cooperation

In today's environment, the global business entity can be successful only if it is able to move intellectual capital within the organization; i.e. transmit ideas and information in real time. If

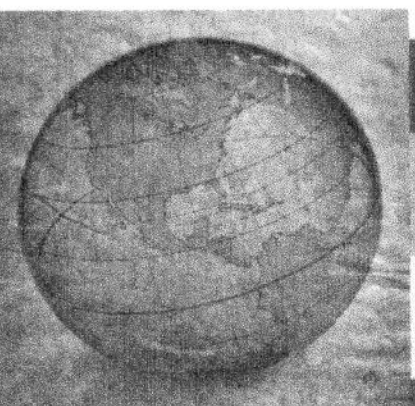

WORLD VIEW

Office-less Companies

Web company Automattic has employees worldwide: twenty-six countries, ninety-four cities, and twenty-eight U.S. states. Automattic hosts a blogging platform for companies such as WordPress.com. Work can be done anywhere with employees using Skype and Internet chat to conduct virtual meetings.

How they make it work:

- Assignments with deadlines are posted on internal blogs.
- Meetings with team members take place on blogs, Skype, or Internet chat.
- Internal "water cooler" blogs enable workers to engage in virtual chitchat.
- There is an annual meeting once a year for all employees to gather face to face.

The biggest advantage of a remote workforce is that companies can tap into a wider talent pool. Firms are also saving on real estate, but travel can offset these savings. The concept of office-less companies is slowly growing but still represents 2.5 percent of the U.S. workforce. Increasingly employees are choosing to work remotely worldwide with advances in video, social-networking, cloud storage, and mobile technology. New companies are debating whether to operate virtually or open an office. But virtual employment is not for everyone: some people need face-to-face contact, others have difficulty creating boundaries between work and home, and some people actually miss the morning commute.

Source: Rachel Emma Silverman, "Step into the Office-Less Company," *The Wall Street Journal*, September 5, 2012, B6; **http://automattic.com/about/**.

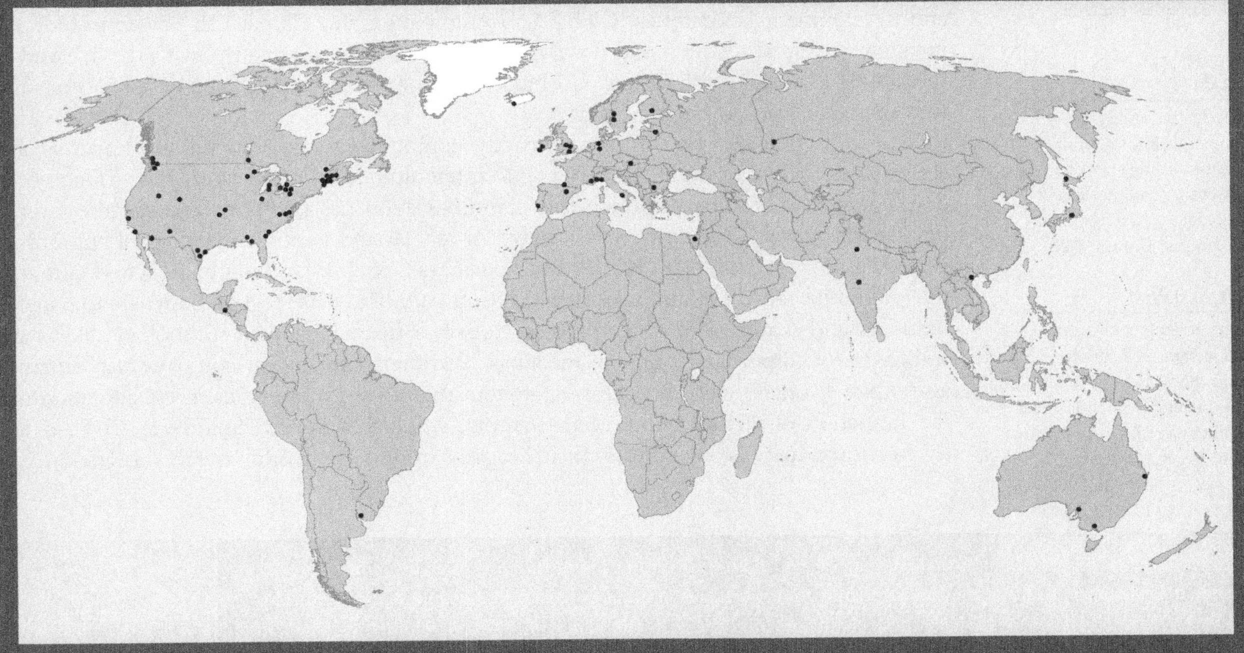

there are impediments to the free flow of information across organizational boundaries, important updates about changes in the competitive environment might not be communicated in a timely fashion to those tasked with incorporating them into strategy.[14]

One of the tools is teaching through educational programs and executive development. The focus is on teachable points of view, that is, an explanation of what a person knows and believes about what it takes to succeed in his or her business. For example, Procter and Gamble makes recruitment and teaching future leaders a priority for its top executives. All of the top officers at the company teach in the company's executive education programs and act as mentors and coaches for younger managers. P&G takes global executive development seriously and grooms its top management prospects through a series of career building assignments across business units and geographies. Of the company's top management, 85 percent has had one or more international assignments.[15]

Another method to promote internal cooperation for global strategy implementation is the use of international teams or councils. In the case of a new product or program, an international team of managers may be assembled to develop strategy. Although final direction may come from headquarters, the team has been informed of local conditions, and implementation of the strategy is enhanced because local-country managers were involved in its development. The approach has worked even in cases involving seemingly impossible market differences.

On a broader and longer term basis, companies use councils to share **best practices**, such as an idea that may have saved money or time, or a process that is more efficient than existing ones. Most professionals at the leading global companies are members of multiple councils. In some cases, it is important to bring in members of other constituencies (e.g., suppliers, intermediaries, service providers) to such meetings to share their views and experiences and make available their own best practices for benchmarking. In some major production undertakings, technology allows ongoing participation by numerous internal and external team members. The Swiss-Swedish engineering firm ABB created two group research and development laboratories, Global Lab Automation and Global Lab Power, to link and integrate its global research and development operations in Germany, Switzerland, Sweden, the United States, Poland, China, and India with universities and other external partners in a fully networked online environment.[16]

The term network also implies two-way communications between headquarters and subsidiaries themselves. This translates into intercultural communication efforts focused on developing relationships. Although this communication has traditionally taken the form of newsletters, traveling executive road shows, or regular and periodic meetings of appropriate personnel, new technologies are allowing businesses to link far-flung entities and eliminate the traditional barriers of time and distance. Companies now use regular **podcasts** to transmit seminars and conferences to employees globally. Streaming media technology allows live **webcasts** for important company meetings. **Intranets** integrate a company's information assets into a single, globally accessible system that allows more efficient collaboration and the formation of **virtual teams**. For example, employees at Levi Strauss & Co. can join an electronic discussion group with colleagues around the world, watch the latest Levi's

BEST PRACTICES

Idea that may have saved money or time, or a process that is more efficient than existing ones

PODCASTS

A podcast is a digital medium consisting of an episodic series of PDF, audio, and video

WEBCASTS

Media presentation that uses Internet streaming media technology to distribute a single content source to many simultaneous listeners or viewers

INTRANET

A process that integrates a company's information assets into a single accessible system using Internet-based technologies, such as e-mail, news groups, and the Web

VIRTUAL TEAM

A team of people who are based at various locations around the world and communicate through intranet and other electronic means to achieve a common goal

Culture Clues Virtual team members find it difficult to prevent the workplace from intruding on private life. Managers feel that they are stretching their workdays in order to have meetings in other time zones. However, managers who can navigate these challenges are rewarded with being able to work with the highest and most motivated professionals. Global Business Services introduced Video Collaboration Studios (VCS); P&G now has more than eighty studios globally. The immersive environment created by VCS allows employees to connect face to face from any part of the world—as if they were in the same room. These studios greatly reduce the need for travel—saving money and time and reducing P&G's carbon footprint.

commercials, or comment on the latest business programs or plans. The benefits of intranets are (1) increased productivity in that there is no longer a time lag between an idea and the information needed to assess and implement it; (2) enhanced knowledge capital, which is constantly updated and upgraded; (3) facilitated teamwork enabling online communication at insignificant expense; and (4) incorporation of best practice at a moment's notice by allowing managers and functional-area personnel to make to-the-minute decisions anywhere in the world.

Role of Country Organizations in Decision-Making

Rather than making them a part of the decision-making process, headquarters quite often sees country organizations as merely the coordinators or adapters of strategy in local markets. Furthermore, they often view all country organizations as the same, despite their unique characteristics, or even their levels of sales. This view severely limits utilization of the firm's resources and deprives country managers of the opportunity to exercise creativity.

The role that a particular country organization can play naturally depends on that market's overall strategic importance, as well as its organizational competence. The role of a **strategic leader** can be played by a highly competent national subsidiary located in a strategically critical market. A strategic leader serves as a partner to headquarters in developing and implementing strategy. For example, strategic leader markets may have products designed specifically to cater to their needs. Nissan's Z-cars have been traditionally designated for the U.S. market, starting with the 240Z in the 1970s to the latest 350Z and 370Z of 2010. Design work for the Z-cars takes place in La Jolla, California. A **contributor** is a country organization with a distinctive competence, such as product development. Increasingly, country organizations are the source of new products. For example, in 2009, GE created a portable ultrasound machine in China and a handheld electrocardiogram device in India. Both products cater to local conditions without sacrificing quality and are meant for price-conscious consumers: The ultrasound machine sells for as little as $15,000, whereas the ECG machine comes at a price tag of $1,000. Both these innovations have not only been successful in emerging markets, but they have also found new customers back in the United States with ambulance teams and in emergency rooms.[17]

STRATEGIC LEADER
A highly competent subsidiary located in a strategically critical market

CONTRIBUTOR
A national subsidiary with a distinctive competence, such as product development

Implementers provide the critical mass for the global effort. These country organizations may exist in smaller, less-developed countries with less corporate commitment for market development. Although most entities are given this role, it should not be slighted because the implementers provide the opportunity to capture economies of scale and scope that are the basis of a global strategy. The **black hole** is where the international marketer must work out of a bad situation. A company may be in a "black hole" situation because it has read the market incorrectly. For example, Philips focused its marketing efforts in the North American market on less-expensive items instead of the up-market products that have made the company's reputation worldwide. Or it might be a situation where the government restricts the company's activities. For example, the Indian government has been careful to limit foreign investment in single-brand retailers. Sweden's IKEA, the world's biggest furniture retailer, recently called off a $1 billion investment plan due to these restrictions.[18]

IMPLEMENTER
The typical subsidiary role, which involves implementing a strategy that originates with headquarters

BLACK HOLE
Situation that arises when an international marketer has a low-competence subsidiary or none at all in a highly strategic market or where a government may restrict a firm's activities

CONTROLS

Within an organization, controls serve as an integrating mechanism. They are designed to reduce uncertainty, increase predictability, and ensure that behaviors originating in separate parts of the organization are compatible and in support of common organizational goals despite physical, cultural, and temporal distances.

Types of Controls

OUTPUT CONTROLS
Organizational controls, such as balance sheets, sales data, production data, product-line growth, and performance reviews of personnel

BEHAVIORAL CONTROLS
Organizational controls that involve influencing how activities are conducted

Table 13.2 provides a brief overview of the types of control and their objectives. Control can be viewed in two ways: the control of output and the control of behavior. **Output controls** include balance sheets, sales data, production data, product-line growth, and performance reviews of personnel. All these make output easy to measure and compare. **Behavioral controls** require the exertion of influence over behavior after—or, ideally, before—it leads to action. Behavioral controls are qualitative rather than quantitative and can be achieved through the preparation of manuals on topics such as sales techniques and made available to subsidiary personnel or through efforts to fit new employees into the corporate culture. Corporations rarely use one pure control mechanism. Rather, most use both quantitative and qualitative measures, placing different levels of emphasis on different types of performance measures and on how they are derived.

TABLE 13.2 Comparison of Bureaucratic and Cultural Control Mechanisms

	Type of Control		
Object of Control	Pure Bureaucratic or Formalized Control	Pure Cultural Control	Characteristics of Control
Output	Formal performance reports	Shared norms of performance	Headquarters sets short-term performance target and requires frequent reports from subsidiaries
Behavior	Company policies, manuals	Shared philosophy of management	Active participation of headquarters in strategy formulation of subsidiaries

SOURCE: Peter J. Kidger, "Management Structure in Multinational Enterprises: Responding to Globalization," *Employee Relations*, August 2001, 69–85; and B. R. Baliga and Alfred M. Jaeger, "Multinational Corporations: Control Systems and Delegation Issues," *Journal of International Business Studies* 15 (Fall 1984): 28.

Bureaucratic or Formalized Control

The elements of a bureaucratic/formalized control system are (1) an international budget and planning system, (2) the functional reporting system, and (3) policy manuals used to direct functional performance.

Budgets refers to shorter-term guidelines regarding investment, cash, and personnel policies, whereas *plans* refers to formalized plans with more than a one-year horizon. The budget and planning process is the major control instrument in headquarters-subsidiary relationships. It has four main purposes: (1) allocation of funds among subsidiaries; (2) planning and coordination of global production capacity and supplies; (3) evaluation of subsidiary performance; and (4) communication and information exchange among subsidiaries, product organizations, and corporate headquarters.

Functional reports are another control instrument used by headquarters in managing subsidiary relations. These reports vary in number, complexity, and frequency. Typically, the structure and elements of the reports are highly standardized, which allows for consolidation at the headquarters level. Because the frequency of reports required from subsidiaries is likely to increase because of globalization, it is essential that subsidiaries see the rationale for the often time-consuming exercise. Two approaches, used in tandem, can facilitate the process: participation and feedback.

On the behavioral front, headquarters may want to guide the way in which subsidiaries make decisions and implement agreed-upon strategies. U.S.-based multinationals tend to be far more formalized than their Japanese and European counterparts, with a heavy reliance on policy manuals for all major functions. Manuals cover such topics as recruitment, training, motivation, and dismissal policies.

Cultural Control

An alternative to bureaucratic control is seen in the organization that emphasizes corporate values and culture, with evaluations based on the extent to which an individual or entity fits in with the norms. Cultural controls require an extensive socialization process to which informal, personal interaction is central. Substantial resources have to be spent to train the individual to share the corporate culture, or "the way things are done at the company."

In selecting home country nationals and, to some extent, third-country nationals, global companies are exercising cultural control. They assume that these managers have already internalized the norms and values of the company and that they tend to run a country operation with a more global view. In some cases, the use of headquarters personnel to ensure uniformity in decision-making may be advisable. Expatriates are used in subsidiaries not only for control purposes but also for initiating change and to develop local talent. Companies control the efforts of management specifically through compensation, promotion, and replacement policies.

Management training programs for overseas managers as well as visits to headquarters will indoctrinate individuals to the company's way of doing things. Similarly, visits to subsidiaries by headquarters teams will promote a sense of belonging. These may be on a formal basis, as for a strategy audit, or less formal—for example, to launch a new product. Some innovative global marketers assemble temporary teams of their best talent to build local skills. Multinational companies will increasingly have to move people from emerging markets, especially Chinese and Indian managers, into leadership positions. Companies in financial services, consulting, and technology, where opportunities have migrated quickly to China and India, have been among the first to do so. As a bridging mechanism, companies like P&G rotate non-U.S. executives in and out of headquarters. Many corporations, including P&G and Unilever, have asked the China and India heads to report directly to the worldwide CEO or have accorded them the status of regional heads. Samsung's China CEO, for example, is regarded as one of the company's top three executives worldwide.[19]

Corporations rarely use one pure control mechanism. Rather, emphasis is placed on both quantitative and qualitative measures. Corporations are likely, however, to place different levels of emphasis on the types of performance measures and on the way the measures are taken. To generate global buy-in, annual bonuses have shifted away from the employee's individual unit and toward the company as a whole. This sends a strong signal in favor of collaboration across all boundaries. Other similar approaches to motivate and generate changes in thinking exist. For example, in the past Kraft used incentives based on total performance of a country (China, for example) to calculate bonuses for the general managers. Optimally a corporation wants to use incentive approaches to motivate and generate collaboration across all boundaries.[20]

Culture Clues To build common vision and values, managers spend a substantial share of their first months at Panasonic in what the company calls "cultural and spiritual training." Although more prevalent in Japanese organizations, many Western entities have similar programs, such as Philips' "organization cohesion training" and Unilever's "indoctrination."

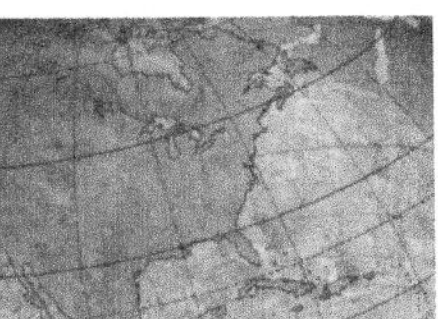

MANAGING GLOBAL MANAGERS

The importance of the quality of the workforce—from executive level down to the factory floor—cannot be overemphasized, regardless of the stage of globalization. While in the early stages, the focus is typically on understanding cultural differences; as firms become more global, they move toward integrating country-to-country differences within the overall corporate culture.

The competency that companies indicated as contributing to global success was having a global mindset (54.5 percent), signaling an understanding that the ability to work globally is different from working domestically in one's own country. The next top critical competencies for global success are risk tolerance (44 percent), cultural intelligence (44 percent), accommodation and flexibility (38 percent), and being adaptable to change (36 percent).[21]

Early Stages of Globalization

As noted earlier, in the early stages, the marketing or sales manager of the firm is usually responsible for initiating export activities. As sales increase, an export manager will be appointed and given the responsibility for handling export documentation, developing and maintaining customers, interacting with the firm's intermediaries, and planning for overall market expansion.

Typically, firms will hire an experienced export manager from outside the firm, rather than promote an inexperienced candidate from within. The reason is that knowledge of the product or industry is less important than international experience. In the early stages, a highly entrepreneurial spirit with a heavy dose of trader mentality is required.

Advanced Stages of Globalization

As the firm progresses from exporting to an international division to foreign direct involvement, human resources planning activities will initially focus on need vis-à-vis various markets and functions. Existing personnel can be assessed and plans made to recruit, select, and train employees for positions that cannot be filled internally. The four major categories of overseas assignments are (1) CEO, to oversee and direct the entire operation; (2) functional head, to establish and maintain departments and ensure their proper performance; (3) troubleshooters, who are utilized for their special expertise in analyzing, and thereby preventing or solving particular problems; and (4) white- or blue-collar workers. Many technology companies have had to respond to shortages in skilled employees by globalized recruitment using web sites or by hiring headhunters in places such as China and India. Colgate (with 75 percent of its sales outside the United States) has eight non-native Americans in its brain trust of nine top operating executives—including people from India and Colombia. More than half of the 200 people in its senior management ranks, including those in staff and support roles, are not originally from the United States.[22]

One of the major sources of competitive advantage for global corporations is their ability to attract talent from around the world. As shown in Figure 13.6, corporations need systematic management-development systems, with the objective of creating and carefully allocating management personnel. Increasingly, plans call for international experience as a prerequisite for advancement.

In global corporations, there is no such thing as a universal global manager, but rather a network of global specialists is found where four general groups of managers have to work together. Global business (product) managers have the task to further the company's global-scale efficiency and competitiveness. Country managers have to be sensitive and responsive to local market needs and demands but, at the same time, be aware of global implications. Functional managers have to make sure that the corporation's capabilities in technical, manufacturing, marketing, human resources, and financial expertise are linked and can benefit from one another. Corporate executives at headquarters have to manage interactions among the three groups of managers, as well as identify and develop the talent to fill the positions.

SEATTLE TIMES.COM

Amazon.cn, *formerly* **Joyo.com**, *is a Chinese shopping website located in Beijing. In 2004, it was acquired by* **Amazon.com**. *On October 27, 2011, Amazon Chinese name was changed to Amazon China.*

Global companies should show clear career paths for managers assigned overseas and develop the systems and the organization for promotion. This approach serves to eliminate many of the perceived problems and thus motivates managers to seek out foreign assignments. Furthermore, when jobs open up, the company can quickly determine who is able and willing to take them. Foreign assignments can occur at various stages of the manager's tenure. In the early stages, assignments may be short term, such as a membership in an international task force or six to twelve months at headquarters in a staff function. Later, an individual may serve as a business-unit manager overseas. Many companies use cross-postings to other countries or across product lines to further an individual's acculturation to the corporation. A period in a head office department or a subsidiary will not only provide an understanding of different national cultures and attitudes but also improve an individual's "know-who" and therefore establish unity and a common sense of purpose, necessary for the proper implementation of global programs.

FIGURE 13.6 Global Management Development

Selecting Managers for Overseas Assignments

The traits that have been suggested as necessary for the global manager cover a broad range, as summarized in Table 13.3. Their relative importance may vary dramatically, of course, depending on the firm's situation, as well as where the choice is being made.

COMPETENCE FACTORS An expatriate manager usually has far more responsibility than a manager in a comparable domestic position and must be far more self-sufficient in making decisions, conducting daily business, and leading others. However, regardless of management skills, a new environment still requires the ability to adapt the skills to local conditions. For this reason, cultural knowledge and language ability are important selection criteria.

ADAPTABILITY FACTORS The manager's own motivation, to a great extent, determines the viability of an overseas assignment and consequently its success. Adaptability means a positive and flexible attitude toward change. The manager assigned overseas must progress from factual knowledge of a culture to interpretive cultural knowledge, trying as much as possible to become part of the new scene, which may be quite different from the one at home. Because

TABLE 13.3 Criteria for Selecting Managers for Overseas Assignment

Competence	Adaptability	Personal Characteristics
Technical knowledge	Interest in overseas work	Age
Leadership ability	Relational abilities	Education
Experience, past performance	Cultural empathy	Sex
Area expertise	Appreciation of new management styles	Health
Language	Appreciation of environmental constraints	Marital status
	Adaptability of family	Social acceptability

such an assignment often puts strains on the manager's family, the adaptability criterion extends to the family, too. Historically, family adjustment, children's education, partner resistance, difficult location, and partner's career have been the top five criteria choices.[23]

PERSONAL CHARACTERISTICS Despite all of the efforts made by global companies to recruit the best people available, demographics still play a role in the selection process. Because of the level of experience typically needed, many foreign assignments go to managers in their mid-thirties or older. Normally, companies do not recruit candidates from graduating classes for immediate assignment overseas. They want their international people first to become experienced and familiar with the corporate culture, and this can best be done at the headquarters location. Health conditions and marital status also factor into the selection decision. Such characteristics as background, religion, race, and sex usually become critical only in extreme cases in which a host environment would clearly reject a candidate based on one or more of these variables.

Fast Facts

The percentage of female assignees increased to 23 percent in the 2013 Brookfield Global Relocation Trends Survey. A third of all new board members at Europe's biggest firms this year are women, according to Egon Zehnder International's 2012 European Board Diversity Analysis. Women now make up 15.6 percent of all board seats, up from just 8 percent in 2004—and 86 percent of companies now have at least one woman on their board, compared to 61 percent eight years ago.

Companies like Bayer have taken positive steps to propel women managers into global careers. Bayer's initiative takes the form of a program that embraces diversity awareness training, multiple mentoring programs, career development and international delegate programs, employee networks, and succession planning. As part of the company's Diversity Advisory Council, women and minority candidates are given overseas assignments of two to three years' duration.[24]

Compensating Global Managers

A firm's expatriate compensation program has to be effective in (1) providing an incentive to leave the home country on a foreign assignment; (2) maintaining a given standard of living; (3) taking career and family needs into consideration; and (4) facilitating re-entry into the home country. To achieve these objectives, firms pay a high premium, beyond base salaries, to induce managers to accept overseas assignments. The costs to the firm are 2 to 2.5 times the cost of maintaining a manager in a comparable position at home. Corporate cost cutting has been eroding some of the benefits packages of the past years.

Compensation can be divided into two general categories: base salary with salary-related allowances and non-salary-related allowances. Although incentives to leave home are justifiable in both categories, they create administrative complications for the personnel department in tying them to packages at home and elsewhere. As the number of transfers increases, firms develop general policies for compensating the manager rather than negotiate individually on every aspect of the arrangement.

Base salary, as with domestic positions, depends on qualifications and responsibilities. To ensure the manager maintains the same standard of living experienced at home, most compensation packages include **cost-of-living allowances (COLA)**, described in World View: International Cost Comparisons.

Some firms offer a **foreign-service premium**, which is, in effect, a bribe to encourage a manager to leave familiar conditions and adapt to new surroundings. Usually, it is calculated as a percentage range of 10 to 25 percent of base salary.

BASE SALARY
Salary, not including special payments, such as allowances, paid during overseas assignments

COST-OF-LIVING ALLOWANCE (COLA)
An allowance paid during an assignment overseas to enable the employee to maintain the same standard of living as at home

FOREIGN-SERVICE PREMIUM
A financial incentive to accept an assignment overseas, usually paid as a percentage of the base salary

Quick Take *Life for an Asia Expatriate*

Western companies doing business in Asia are now looking to locals to fill the most important jobs in the region. Companies now want executives who can secure deals with local businesses and governments without the aid of a translator and who understand that sitting through a three-hour dinner banquet is often a key part of the negotiating process in Asia.

In fact, three out of four senior executives hired in Asia by multinationals were Asian natives already living in the region, according to a Spencer Stuart analysis of 1,500 placements made from 2005 to 2010. Just 6 percent were noncitizens from outside of Asia.

To help companies fill Asia-based executive roles, they have begun classifying executives in four broad categories: Asia natives steeped in local culture but educated in the United States or Europe; the foreigner who has lived or worked in Asia for a long time; a person of Asian descent who was born or raised in a Western country but has had little exposure to Asia; and the local Asian executive who has no Western experience. What's more, a failed expatriate hire can be a costly mistake and slow a firm's progress in the region.

German conglomerate Siemens AG in 2010 hired Mei-Wei Cheng, a China-born Cornell University graduate, to head its Chinese operations, a role previously held by European executives. Although Siemens's European executives had made inroads with Chinese consumers—building sales in the region to nearly one-tenth of global revenue—the firm realized it needed someone who could quickly tap local business partners.

SOURCES: Leslie Kwoh, "Asia's Endangered Species: The Expat," *The Wall Street Journal,* March 28, 2012, B6; and "A Tale of Two Expats," *The Economist,* January 1, 2011, 62–64.

In addition, **hardship allowances** compensate managers for relocating to difficult environments, such as countries that are politically or economically unstable or where the living conditions are unhealthy and isolation. For example, hardship premiums vary from 15 percent (Moscow) to 30 percent (Vladivostok).

HARDSHIP ALLOWANCE
An allowance paid during an assignment to an overseas area that requires major adaptation

Because housing costs and related expenses are typically the largest expenditure in the expatriate manager's budget, firms usually provide a **housing allowance** commensurate with the manager's salary level and position.

HOUSING ALLOWANCE
An allowance paid during an assignment overseas to provide appropriate living quarters

One of the major determinants of the manager's lifestyle abroad is taxes. A U.S. manager earning $100,000 in Canada would pay nearly $40,000 in taxes—in excess of $10,000 more than in the United States. For this reason, 90 percent of U.S. multinational corporations have **tax-equalization plans**. When a manager's overseas taxes are higher than at home, the firm will make up the difference. However, in countries with a lower rate of taxation, the company simply keeps the difference. The firm's rationalization is that it does not make any sense for the manager in Hong Kong to make more money than the person who happened to land in Singapore. Tax equalization is usually handled by accounting firms that make the needed calculations and prepare the proper forms. Managers can exclude a portion of their expatriate salary from U.S. tax; for 2012, the amount was $95,100, but income above that is subject to high effective taxes.[25] The amount expatriates can exclude or deduct for housing costs has been limited in the last few years.

TAX-EQUALIZATION PLAN
Reimbursement by the company when an employee in an overseas assignment pays taxes at a higher rate than at home

Non-Salary-Related Allowances

Other types of allowances are made available to ease the transition into the period of service abroad. Typical allowances during the transition stage include (1) a relocation allowance to

WORLD VIEW

International Cost Comparisons

Living cost comparisons of Americans residing in foreign areas are developed four times a year by the U.S. Department of State Allowances. For each post, two measures are computed: (1) a government index to establish post allowances for U.S. government employees and (2) a local index for use by private organizations. The government index takes into consideration prices of goods imported to posts and price advantages available only to U.S. government employees.

The local index is used by many business firms and private organizations to determine the cost of living allowance for their American employees assigned abroad. Local index measures of eighteen key countries around the world are shown in the accompanying table. Maximum housing allowances, calculated separately, are also given. Also included are cost of living hardship and differential rate percent. (Danger pay, which includes Kabul, Afghanistan, Algiers, Algeria, and Port-au-Prince, Haiti, can also be found.)

The reports are issued four times annually under the title "U.S. Department of State Indexes of Living Cost, Abroad, Quarters Allowances, and Hardship Differentials by the U.S. Department of Labor."

How Far Will Your Salary Go?

	Cost of Living Index (Washington, D.C. = 100)		Maximum Annual Housing Allowance		
Location	Cost of Living Survey Date	Index	Family of Two	Cost of Living Hardship	Differential Rate Percent
Buenos Aires	Dec-10	135	$56,500	35	0
Canberra	Jul-10	135	30,600	50	0
Brussels	Mar-11	173	44,000	35	0
Brasilia	Jun-11	177	46,700	25	10
Shanghai	Oct-09	145	17,500	35	15
Cairo	Mar-06	96	22,900	0	15
New Delhi	Dec-10	129	17,500	15	20
Paris	Dec-09	201	77,300	60	0
Frankfurt	Mar-10	171	39,600	20	0
Hong Kong	Apr-10	151	114,300	35	0
Tokyo	May-11	213	126,300	80	0
Mexico City	Mar-09	99	47,900	0	15
The Hague	Apr-09	152	61,400	30	0
Moscow	May-11	206	90,900	50	15
Cape Town	Feb-11	130	17,500	15	10
Geneva	Nov-10	217	88,300	90	0
London	Mar-11	178	85,100	70	0
Hanoi	May-08	113	46,800	5	20

SOURCE: **http://aoprals.state.gov**

compensate for moving expenses; (2) a mobility allowance as an incentive to managers to go overseas, usually paid in a lump sum and as a substitute for the foreign service premium; (3) allowances related to housing, such as home sale or rental protection, shipment and storage of household goods, or provision of household furnishings in overseas locations; (4) automobile protection that covers possible losses on the sale of a car (or cars) at transfer and having to buy a car overseas, usually at a higher cost; (5) travel expenses, using economy class transportation, except for long flights (for example, from Washington to Taipei); and (6) temporary living expenses, which may become substantial if housing is not immediately available. Also, companies are increasingly providing support to make up for income lost by the accompanying spouse.

Education for children is one of the major concerns of expatriate families. In many cases, children may attend private schools, perhaps even in a different country. Firms will typically reimburse for such expenses in the form of an **education allowance**. In the case of college education, firms reimburse for one round-trip airfare every year, leaving tuition expenses to the family.

EDUCATION ALLOWANCE
Reimbursement by company for dependent educational expenses incurred while a parent is assigned overseas

Finally, firms provide support for medical expenses, especially for medical services at a level comparable to the expatriate's home country. Other health-related allowances are in place to allow the expatriate to periodically leave the challenging location for rest and relaxation.

Some expatriates in Mexico City get $300 to $500 per family member each month to cover a getaway from the pollution of the city.[26]

The following table provides a visual comparison between practices appropriate to developed (United States, United Kingdom, and Singapore) and developing locations. China was cited as the most challenging destination for program managers by 14 percent of respondents followed by Brazil (10 percent), India (9 percent), and Russia (8 percent).

TABLE 13.4 International Assignments

Element	Developed Location	Developing Location
Foreign service premium	Not offered	Required
Hardship premium	May not be included if company does not expect assignments to qualifying locations	Required
Rest and relaxation leave	May not be included even if company includes a hardship allowance in policy	Standard
Goods and services allowance	Cost-of-living allowances (COLA)	May be provided at expatriate level in locations with a negative index, even if some elements(e.g., meals, "shopping leave") are provided directly
Home leave	Once per year to home location	May be provided more frequently and other destinations may be covered
Host transportation	Allowance may be provided; if car and driver, typically only for employee	Car and driver may be provided for spouse as well

SOURCE: Brookfield Global Relocation Services, "To Developing Locations Spotlight Report 2012."

MANAGING THE GLOBAL WORKFORCE

The dramatic show changed in the nature of globalization during the past decade, when U.S.–based multinationals concentrated their growth opportunities abroad. The latest data show that firms cut 864,600 workers in the United States between 1999 and 2009 and added 2.9 million workers abroad. The faster growth aboard was concentrated in emerging markets, such as China, Brazil, India, and Eastern Europe.[27] A firm's objectives can not be realized without a labor force, which can become one of a firm's major assets or one of its major problems, depending on the relationship that is established. Because of local patterns and legislation, headquarter's role in shaping relations is mainly advisory, limited to setting the overall tone for the interaction. However, many of the practices adopted in one market or region may easily come under discussion in another, making it necessary for multinational corporations to set general policies concerning labor relations. Often multinational corporations have been instrumental in bringing about changes in the overall work environment in a country.

Labor strategy can be viewed from three perspectives: (1) the participation of labor in the affairs of the firm, especially as it affects performance and well-being; (2) the role and impact of unions in the relationship; and (3) specific human resource policies, in terms of recruitment, training, and compensation.

Labor Participation in Management

Over the past quarter-century, many changes have occurred in the traditional labor-management relationship as a result of dramatic changes in the economic environment and the actions of both firms and the labor force. The role of the worker is changing both at the level of the job performed and in terms of participation in the decision-making process. To enhance workers' role in decision-making, various techniques have emerged: self-management, codetermination, minority board membership, and works councils. In striving for improvements in the quality of work life, programs that have been initiated include flextime, quality circles, and work-flow reorganization. Furthermore, employee ownership has moved into the mainstream.

The degree to which workers around the world can participate in corporate decision-making varies considerably. Rights of information, consultation, and codetermination develop on three levels:

1. The shop-floor level, or direct involvement, for example, the right to be consulted in advance concerning transfers
2. The management level, or through representative bodies, for example, works council participation in setting new policies or changing existing ones
3. The board level, for example, labor membership on the board of directors

CODETERMINATION
A management approach in which employees are represented on supervisory boards to facilitate communication and collaboration between management and labor

MINORITY PARTICIPATION
Participation by a group having less than the number of votes necessary for control

In some countries, employees are represented on the supervisory boards to facilitate communication between management and labor, thereby giving labor a clearer picture of the financial limits of management and providing management with a new awareness of labor's point of view. The process is called **codetermination**. In Germany, companies have a two-tiered management system with a supervisory board and the board of managers, which actually runs the firm. The supervisory board is legally responsible for the managing board. In some countries, labor has **minority participation**. In the Netherlands, for example, works councils can nominate (not appoint) board members and can veto the appointment of new members appointed by others. In other countries, such as the United States, codetermination has been opposed by unions as an undesirable means of cooperation, especially when management-labor relations are confrontational.

A tradition in labor relations, especially in Britain, is **works councils**. They provide labor a voice in corporate decision-making through a representative body, which may consist entirely of workers or of a combination of managers and workers. The councils participate in decisions on overall working conditions, training, transfers, work allocation, and compensation. Around 10 million workers across the European Union have the right to information and consultation on company decisions at the European level through their EWCs (European works councils). The Works Council Directive applies to companies with 1,000 or more employees, including at least 150 in two or more member states.[28]

WORKS COUNCILS

Councils that provide labor a say in corporate decision-making through a representative body that may consist entirely of workers or of a combination of managers and workers

The countries described are unique in the world. In many countries and regions, workers have few, if any, of these rights. The result is long-term potential for labor strife in those countries and possible negative publicity elsewhere. The countries leading in days lost in all industries and services in 2006 are as follows: Canada (186), Spain (170), Denmark (164), Italy (88), and Finland (75).[29]

In addition to labor groups and the media, investors and shareholders also are scrutinizing multinationals' track records on labor practices. As a result, a company investing in foreign countries should hold to international standards of safety and health, not simply local standards. This can be achieved, for example, through the use of modern equipment and training. Local labor also should be paid adequately. This increases the price of labor, yet ensures the best available talent and helps avoid charges of exploitation. Companies subcontracting work to local or joint-venture factories need to evaluate industrial relations throughout the system not only to avoid lost production due to disruptions such as strikes, but to ensure that no exploitation exists at the facilities. Several large firms, such as Adidas and Nike, require subcontractors to sign agreements saying they will abide by minimum wage standards. Areas of labor compliance are captured by reference to seven core standards (dealing with forced labor, child labor, discrimination, wages and benefits, working hours, freedom of association, and disciplinary practices). Although companies have been long opposed to linking free trade to labor standards, the business community is rethinking its strategy mainly to get trade negotiations moving.[30]

The Role of Labor Unions

The role of labor unions varies from country to country, often because of local traditions in management-labor relations. The variations include the extent of union power in negotiations and the activities of unions in general. In Europe, especially in the northern European countries, collective bargaining takes place between an employers' association and an umbrella organization of unions, on either a national or a regional basis, thereby establishing the conditions for an entire industry. On the other end of the spectrum, negotiations in Japan are on the company level, and the role of larger-scale unions is usually consultative. Another striking difference emerges in terms of the objectives of unions and the means by which they attempt to attain them. In the United Kingdom, for example, union activity tends to be politically motivated and identified with political ideology. In the United States, the emphasis has always been on improving workers' overall quality of life. In China, the objective of the All-China Federation of Trade Unions, the only legal union umbrella group, is to build a harmonious society. It is the largest trade union in the world with 134 million members in 1,713,000 primary trade union organizations.[31]

Investment decisions can also be guided by union considerations. For example, of the more than 30 automobile plants in the United States owned by foreign companies, none have been organized by the United Auto Workers. Foreign automakers have located plants in Southern states where the UAW has little presence and where right-to-work laws prevent unions from forcing employees to join and pay dues. In Northern states, automakers have mostly chosen locations in rural areas away from UAW strongholds.

Fast Facts

The number of U.S. workers in unions declined sharply in recent years, the Bureau of Labor Statistics reported in 2012, with the percentage slipping to 11.9 percent, the lowest rate in more than seventy years. Levels of union density vary widely across the European Union, from more than 70 percent in Finland and Sweden to 8 percent in France.

Labor Union Membership Map

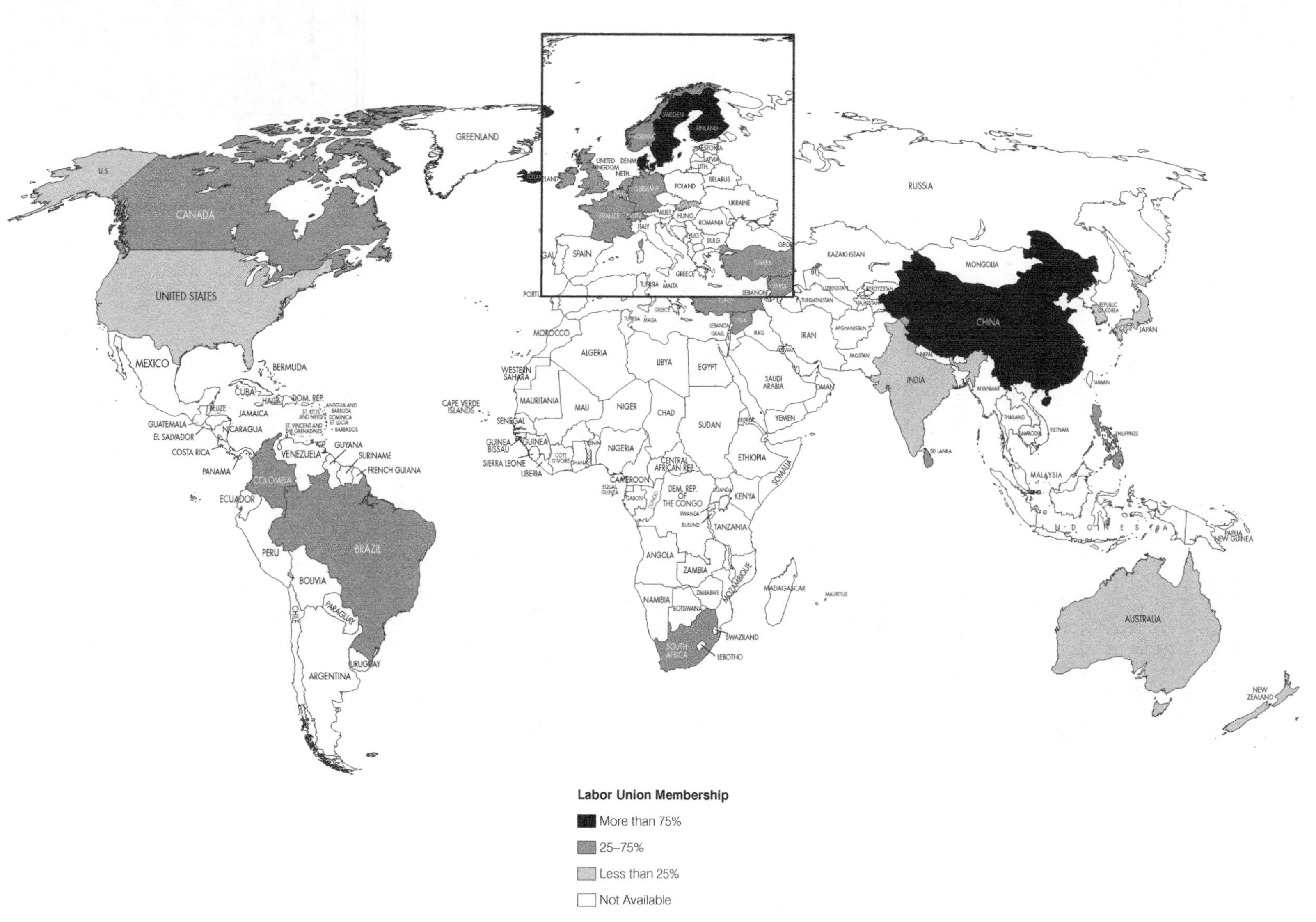

SOURCE: International Labor Organization, available at **www.stat@ilo.org**

Quick Take Labor Unions Attack IKEA

IKEA, the Swedish furniture giant, is moving to guard its reputation in Turkey. IKEA has about 2,000 employees in five stores in Turkey, including two in Istanbul (Umraniye and Bayrampasa), Bursa, Izmir, and Ankara. The dispute dates back to 2011 and stems from claims by Turkey's Koop-Is (a union already representing hundreds of IKEA workers) that alleges that IKEA Turkey has been pressuring workers not to join the union. IKEA Turkey is operated by independent franchisee Mapa Mobilya. The head of the commerce division at UniGlobal Union, which has more than 20 million service workers worldwide, said the problem is that the franchise run by Mapa Mobilya is a local Turkish company, and they can do whatever they like and don't need to comply with IKEA's global standards. UniGlobal plans to urge IKEA to ensure fair play for the Turkish union and to urge IKEA Turkey to sign a joint social dialogue agreement. UniGlobal wants IKEA to acknowledge it does not matter who owns or runs the stores; workers' rights and collective bargaining must be respected worldwide. IKEA Turkey fired back that the allegations were "unfounded and groundless" and were disrupting the calm and peace of the work environment, and they were open to discussion with Koop-Is. A spokesperson for IKEA's global operations said the company respects the rights of workers and welcomes dialogue with global unions.

SOURCE: Emre Peker and Jens Hansegard, "IKEA's Turkish Labor Issue," *The Wall Street Journal,* September 12, 2012, B9; "IKEA must tackle anti-worker culture present in its global network," May 22, 2013, **http://www.uniglobalunion.org/news/ikea-must-tackle-anti-worker-culture-present-its-global-network**, accessed April 16, 2014.

To maintain participation in corporate decision-making, unions are taking action individually and across national boundaries. Individual unions refer to contracts signed elsewhere when setting the agenda for their own negotiations. Supranational organizations such as the AFL-CIO—which is affiliated with the International Trade Union Confederation (ITUC), the worldwide union network (based in Brussels the ITUC represents 175 million workers through its 311 affiliated organizations within 155 countries) —and industry-specific organizations such as the International Metal Workers' Federation exchange information and discuss bargaining tactics. The goal is also to coordinate bargaining with multinational corporations across national boundaries. The International Labor Organization, a specialized agency of the United Nations, has an information bank on multinational corporations' policies concerning wage structures, benefits packages, and overall working conditions.

Human Resource Policies

The phrase "**quality of work life**" has come to encompass various efforts in the areas of personal and professional development. Its two clear objectives are to increase productivity and to increase the satisfaction of employees. Of course, programs leading to increased participation in corporate decision-making are part of the programs; however, this section concentrates on individual job-related programs: work redesign, team building, and work scheduling.[32]

By adding both horizontal and vertical dimensions to the work, **work redesign programs** attack undesirable features of jobs. Horizontally, task complexity is added by incorporating work stages normally done before and after the stage being redesigned. Vertically, each employee is given more responsibility for making the decisions that affect how the work is done. Toyota does not modify its automobiles to local needs; it customizes both products and operations to the level of customer sophistication in each country.

QUALITY OF WORK LIFE
Various corporate efforts in the areas of personal and professional development undertaken with the objectives of increasing employee satisfaction and increasing productivity

WORK REDESIGN PROGRAMS
Programs that alter jobs to increase both the quality of the work experience and productivity

TEAM BUILDING
A process that enhances the cohesiveness of a department or group by helping members learn how to organize their work and assume responsibility for it

QUALITY CIRCLES
Groups of workers who meet regularly to discuss issues related to productivity

WORK SCHEDULING
Preparing schedules of when and how long workers are at the workplace

Closely related to work redesign are efforts aimed at **team building**. For example, in car plants, work is organized so that groups are responsible for a particular, identifiable portion of the car, such as interiors. Each group has its own areas in which to pace itself and to organize the work. The group must take responsibility for the work, including inspections, whether it is performed individually or in groups. The group is informed about its performance through a computer system. The team-building effort includes job rotation to enable workers to understand all facets of their jobs. Another approach to team building makes use of **quality circles**, in which groups of workers regularly meet to discuss issues relating to their productivity. Team building efforts have to be adapted to cultural differences. In cultures that are more individualistic, incentive structures may have to be kept at the individual level and discussions on quality issues should be broad-based rather than precise.

Flexibility in **work scheduling** has led to changes in when and for how long workers are at the workplace. Flextime allows workers to determine their starting and ending hours in a given workday; for example, workers might arrive between 7:00 a.m. and 9:30 a.m. and leave between 3:00 p.m. and 5:30 p.m. The idea spread from Germany to the European Union and to other countries, such as Switzerland, Japan, New Zealand, and the United States. Some 40 percent of the Dutch working population holds flex- or part-time positions. In January 2009, accounting giant KPMG unveiled its new Flexible Future program for its 11,000 UK-based employees. The options include a four-day workweek and a 20 percent reduction in base pay, a four- to twelve-week sabbatical at 30 percent base pay, a combination of the two options, or sticking with the status quo.[33]

Firms around the world also have other programs for personal and professional development, such as career counseling and health counseling. All of them are dependent on various factors external and internal to the firm. Of the external factors, the most important are the overall characteristics of the economy and the labor force. Internally, either the programs must fit into existing organizational structures or management must be inclined toward change. In many cases, labor unions have been one of the major resisting forces. Their view is that firms are trying to prevent workers from organizing by allowing them to participate in decision-making and management.

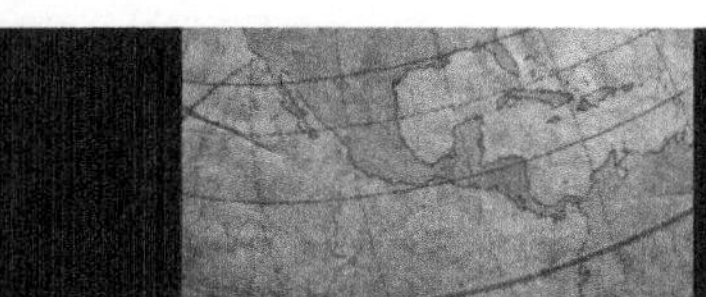

SUMMARY

This chapter discussed the structures and control mechanisms needed to operate in the international business field. Regardless of the size of the international business or the stage of internationalization, the quality of the workforce cannot be overemphasized.

International firms can choose from a variety of organizational structures, ranging from a domestic organization that handles *ad hoc* export orders to a full-fledge global organization. The choice will depend heavily on the degree of internationalization of the firm, the diversity of international activities, and the relative importance of product, area, functions, and customer variables in the process.

A determining factor of organizational structure is the degree to which headquarters wants to decide important issues concerning the whole corporation and the individual subsidiaries.

It is important to grant autonomy to country organizations so that they can help optimize corporate effectiveness. Control can be exercised through bureaucratic means, which emphasize formal reporting, or less formal ways, in which corporate culture plays a pivotal role. 3

Issues relating to the selection, screening, and compensation of global managers relate to the level of globalization. The more globalized the firm becomes, the greater the care and expense that goes into the process. 4

Increasingly, workers worldwide are taking an active role in the decision-making of a firm and in issues related to their overall welfare. International firms need to be aware and sensitive to these movements especially when the workers are away from the corporate headquarters.

Key Terms and Concepts

global business units (GBUs)
market development organizations (MDOs)
global business services
corporate functions
global product structure
global area structure
global functional structure
process structure
global customer structure
mixed structure
matrix structure
T-shaped organization
decentralization
centralization
coordinated decentralization
glocal
not-invented-here syndrome
best practices
podcasts
webcasts
Intranet
virtual team
strategic leader
contributor
black hole
output controls
behavioral controls
base salary
cost-of-living allowance (COLA)
foreign-service premium
hardship allowance
housing allowance
tax-equalization plan
education allowance
codetermination
minority participation
works councils
quality of work life
work redesign programs
team building
quality circles
work scheduling

Review Questions

1. Firms differ, often substantially, in their organizational structures, even within the same industry. What accounts for the differences in their approaches?
2. Discuss the pros and cons gained by adopting a matrix form of organizational structure.
3. A networked global model is intended to reduce the tension between global integration and local responsiveness. Is such a result possible?
4. Is there more to the "not-invented-here" syndrome than simply hurt feelings on the part of those who believe they are being dictated to by headquarters?
5. Video Collaboration Studios (VCS) now has more studios globally. The immersive environment created by VCS allows employees to connect face to face from any part of the world as if they were in the same room. These studios greatly reduce the need for travel—saving money and time and reducing carbon footprint. What factors are overlooked?
6. What are the most important criteria for selecting an expatriate manager during the selection process? How do you weight them on importance?
7. Your new manager moves from Houston, Texas, to Mumbai, India. What compensation package (salary and nonsalary) keeps the manager happy and production high?
8. What are the general policies that the multinational corporation should follow in dealing (or choosing not to deal) with a local labor union?

Critical Skill Builders

1. "Implementers are the most important country organizations in terms of buy-in for a global strategy." Comment.
2. The seven principles used by Matsushita at his company (Panasonic) today serve as principles for other Japanese companies. These guiding principles are an extension of the Japanese business culture. Will these seven principles (service to public, fairness, teamwork, united effort, courtesy, respecting nature, and gratitude for blessings) work internationally?
3. If a man wants to be a chief executive twenty-five or fifty years from now, he will have to be well rounded. There will be no more "Is he a good lawyer, is he a good marketing guy, is he a good finance guy?" His education and his experience will make him a total entrepreneur in a world that has really turned into one huge market. He better speak Chinese or German. He better understand the history of both of those countries and how they got to where they are, and he better know their economics pretty cold. Discuss the ramifications of this.
4. Expat women face a different set of challenges than men do. Safety can be a major obstacle for single women working abroad. What other issues are challenges for women, and what can they do to mediate these issues. Are there web sites to help expat women?
5. Workers at the new Volkswagen plant near Chattanooga, Tennessee, are paid about $27 an hour in wages and benefits. Volkswagen closed its last U.S. plant in 1988 after inheriting a unionized work force. Detroit labor costs under UAW are around $70 an hour. VW plans to make a new version of the Passat sedan for the U.S. market with a starting price of $20,000. They plan to sell more than one million cars by 2018. What options are available to U.S. automakers and unions (UAW)?

On the Web

1. Colgate is a good example of how to implement a successful human resources strategy. Industry analysts have determined that the company has institutionalized a "process that encourages, rewards, moves around, provides incentives, and closely manages the careers of the best performers worldwide, no matter their national origin." Why? **http://www.colgate.com/app/Colgate/US/Corp/LivingOurValues/Diversity/HomePage.cvsp**
2. Every big company has in-house experts. Search systems that apply social-computing tools such as internal blogs, wikis, and social networks can fill these critical gaps. Innovation at Dell shows how customer-driven innovation leads to solutions and services that address real-world needs. **http://content.dell.com/us/en/corp/our-story-case-studies.aspx**.
3. You want a job overseas: pick a country and even a city at jobs.goabroad.com and then calculate your salary and cost of living at **www.worldsalaries.org**. You can even calculate your salaries purchasing power at **www.xpatulator.com**.

Endnotes

1. Procter & Gamble Annual Report, 2012; "At P&G, the Innovation Well Runs Dry," *Businessweek*, September 2012, 24–26; Lafley, A. G., "What Only the CEO Can Do," *Harvard Business Review*, 87 (May 2009), 54–62. See also **http://www.pg.com**.
2. Jonathan D. Day, "The Value of Organizing," *McKinsey Quarterly*, June 2003; and Jonathan D. Day, "Organizing for Growth," *McKinsey Quarterly*, May 2001.
3. VEAB Heat Tech AB, "Complete Solutions," **http://veab.com/en/about-veab/about-veab/complete-solutions**, accessed April 14, 2014.
4. General Mills, Company: **http://www.generalmills.com/en/Company.aspx**, accessed March 19, 2014
5. Anil K. Gupta, Vijay Govindarajan, and Haiyan Wang, *The Quest for Global Dominance: Transforming Global Presence into Global Competitive Advantage*. New York: Jossey-Bass, 2008, chapters 1 and 2.
6. "Ford Tries a Global Campaign for its Global Car, *The New York Times*, February 24, 2011, B4; and **www.ford.com**.
7. Nestle, About Us, Management: **http://www.nestle.com/ABOUTUS/MANAGEMENT/Pages/Management-landing.aspx**, accessed March 19, 2014.

8. Christopher A. Bartlett and Sumantra Ghoshal, *Managing across Borders* (Cambridge, MA: Harvard Business School Press, 2002), chapter 10.
9. Dow Chemical, **www.dow.com**, accessed March 19, 2014.
10. Accenture, Consulting, Operations: **http://www.accenture.com/us-en/Pages/insight-emerging-market-multinationals-creating-global-operating-models-future-summary.aspx**, accessed March 19, 2014.
11. Nirmalya Kumar and Phanish Puranam, "Have You Restructured for Global Success?" *Harvard Business Review* 89 (October 2011): 123–8.
12. Stéphane J.G. Girod, Joshua B. Bellin, and Robert J. Thomas, "Are Emerging-Market Multinationals Creating the Global Operating Models of the Future? *Accenture, Research Report*, **http://www.scribd.com/doc/42761894/Accenture-Emerging-Markets-Create-Global-Operating-Models**, May 2009, accessed April 14, 2014.
13. Yum Brands, Defining Global Company That Feeds the World, **http://www.yum.com/brands/**, accessed March 19, 2014.
14. Gary L. Neilson, Karla L. Martin, and Elizabeth Powers, "The Secrets to Successful Strategy Execution," *Harvard Business Review*, 86, June 2008, 61–70.
15. Procter and Gamble, 2009 annual report, **http://annualreport.pg.com/annualreport2009/leadership/index.shtml**, accessed March 19, 2014.
16. The ABB Group, **http://www.abb.com/**, accessed March 19, 2014.
17. Jeffrey R. Immelt, Chris Trimble, and Vijay Govindarajan, "How GE Is Disrupting Itself," *Harvard Business Review*, 87 (October 2009), 56–63.
18. India's First Wal-Mart Draws Excitement, Not Protest Venture Comes With Limits That Protect Merchants," *Washington Post*, Monday, July 13, 2009.
19. Nirmalya Kumar and Phanish Puranam, "Have You Restructured for Global Success?" *Harvard Business Review* 89 (October 2011): 123–8.
20. Introduced by Chairman and CEO Irene Rosenfeld, "Inside the Kraft Foods Transformation," *Strategy + Business*, August 27, 2009.
21. "Preliminary Finding of Going Global Readiness Report Released," *HR.com*, July 25, 2008; Jeitosa Group International, **http://www.jeitosa.com**, accessed March 19, 2014.
22. J. Holstein, "It's Getting Diverse at the Top," *Strategy + Business*, January 6, 2009, 1–5.
23. "Global Relocation Trends," Brookefield Global Relocation Services, 2009; and Bronwyn Fryer, "The Problem with Short-Term Overseas Assignments" *Harvard Business Review*, July 20, 2009.
24. "Bayer Corp. Honored for Preparing Women for Global Leadership," April 18, 2002, **http://www.hirediversity.com/news/2002/4/18/bayer_corp_honored_for_preparing_women.htm**, accessed April 14, 2014.
25. Courtesy of Thomas B. Cooke, Esq.
26. "Expat Life Gets Less Cushy," *The Wall Street Journal*, October 26, 2007, pp. W1, W10.
27. David Wessel, "U.S. Firms Eager to Add Foreign Jobs, "*The Wall Street Journal*," November 22, 2011, B1.
28. "European Works Councils," European Trade Union Confederation (ETUC), 2008.
29. "International Comparisons of Labour Disputes in 2006," *Economic & Labour Market Review*, April 2008, Volume 2, Number 2.
30. "Sport Matters: Sustainability Performance Review 2008," **http://www.adidas-group.com/media/filer_public/2013/08/27/adidas-online-review-2008_en.pdf**, accessed April 14, 2014; and Gary Gereffi, Ronie Garcia-Johnson, Erika Sasser, "The NGO-Industrial Complex," *Foreign Policy*, July/August 2001, 56–66.
31. All-China Federation of Trade Unions, **http://www.acftu.org.cn/template/10002/index.jsp**, accessed March 19, 2014.
32. Hirotaka Takeuchi, Emi Osono, and Norihiko Shimizu, "The Contradictions that Drive Toyota's Success," *Harvard Business Review*, 86(June 2008): 96–105.
33. Hewlett, Sylvia, "FlexTime: A Recession Triple Win," *Harvard Business Review*, August 2009.

CHAPTER 14

THE FIRM AND SOCIETY

Bank Bonuses and Aristotelian Finance

Many in society find it quite difficult to understand the financial community's culture of very large annual bonuses, especially during a time when so many people in the greater public were suffering from the lack of a job or wage freezes. In the European Union and United States, there is public anger over lucrative corporate compensation structures, especially after many of the top banks were recipients of government support or perceived "bailouts." Some have called for curbs or taxes on bonuses, while others have sought government punitive action against financial industry executives and increased regulation of banks.

Mervyn King, governor of the Bank of England, addressed the British Parliament in January 2012 on the subject of excessive financial industry rewards: "We've been through a crisis where the squeeze on real living standards has been unprecedented. And that squeeze on real living standards has been on people who clearly were no way responsible for this crisis. I think the reputation of those institutions will be affected if their senior executives reward themselves, particularly in a period when the performance of the banks in terms of their share prices has hardly been stellar, if they reward themselves with very substantial compensation."

In 2013, the European Parliament voted to impose a "cap" on bankers' bonuses effective in 2015, limiting payments at one year's base salary or double that if a large majority of the company's shareholders approve. European Commission President José Manuel Barroso said of the vote: "The rules will put an end to the culture of excessive bonuses, which encouraged risk-taking for short-term gains.... This is a question of fairness. If taxpayers are being asked to pick up the bill after the financial crisis, banks must also make a contribution." The United Kingdom had opposed this cap because of worries that it would damage London's attractiveness as a financial center. In a global environment, bankers and banks will look at alternative centers such as Hong Kong, Singapore, Geneva, or New York. Given today's mobility of both industries and employees, banks that are convinced of their righteousness can fight back and move core units to more business-friendly locations.

Businesses, however, need to remember that they are only part of society. Their actions should reflect their firm's long-term best interests within an overall societal context. Business educators without an emphasis on such context and proportionality must revise such shortcomings in their teaching. Legislators and government in turn need to recognize that their actions can trigger a corporate response. Eliminating a comparative advantage and successful clusters without a productive replacement is a risky strategy.

In 2011, Martin Sandbu of the *Financial Times* wrote that businessmen and bankers in particular "would do well to read the great moral philosophers, with the courage to follow their thinking wherever it might lead. Bankers

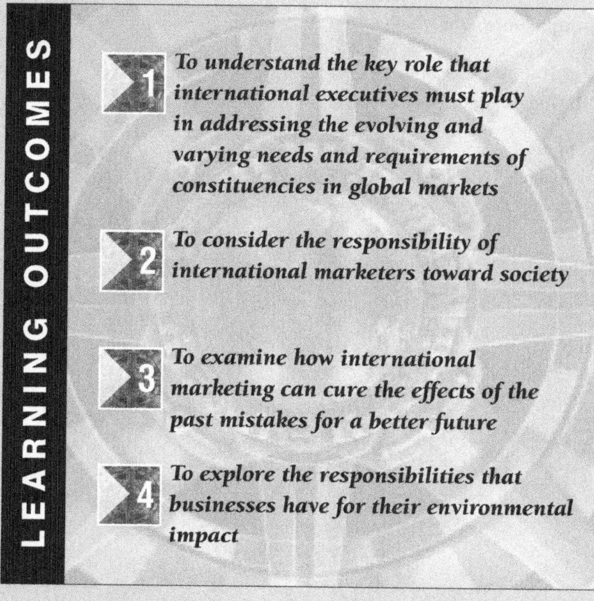

LEARNING OUTCOMES

1. ***To understand the key role that international executives must play in addressing the evolving and varying needs and requirements of constituencies in global markets***
2. ***To consider the responsibility of international marketers toward society***
3. ***To examine how international marketing can cure the effects of the past mistakes for a better future***
4. ***To explore the responsibilities that businesses have for their environmental impact***

whose inquisitiveness matches their acquisitiveness might, for instance, ponder Aristotle's view that the virtues of a profession are what fulfill its social purpose. That could prompt reflection on how to forge new ethics for investment banking along the lines of the medical or legal professions." Sandbu went on to suggest that society could benefit from more "philosopher-executives" and that reading Aristotle's works "may be one of the best investments they can make."

In a letter in response to Mr. Sandbu's article published in the *Financial Times*, Professor Charles Skuba of Georgetown University agreed with Sandbu writing "...at Georgetown, we educate many executives and bankers-to-be. We require them to study Aristotle and other philosophers before they turn to finance and other business disciplines. We seek thought about what constitutes virtue and explore the social purpose of an enterprise to endow our students with a knowledge foundation we hope will make them business and social leaders." Skuba made the point that "Aristotle distinguishes between intellectual virtue and moral virtue, ascribing the former to be the result of teaching and the latter of habit. The best banks and businesses work to develop habits that are socially responsible." As a part of the "philosophical inquiry" Mr. Sandbu advocates, bankers will benefit from ingraining a culture that values moral virtue, or corporate social responsibility, along with making money and managing risk.

SOURCES: Juergen Baetz, AP, "EU lawmakers vote for banker bonus cap," *USA Today*, April 16, 2013; Joe Rundle, "Would EU bonus cap spark banker flight?," CNN, March 1, 2013; Michael R. Czinkota and Charles J. Skuba, "Government May Put the Financial Industry at Risk, Roll Call, February 1, 2010, **http://www.rollcall.com/issues/55_84/-42798-1.html**, accessed March 19, 2014; Martin Sandbu, "Why Aristotle is the banker's best friend," *Financial Times*, January 13, 2011; Charles J. Skuba, "Best banks and businesses work at good habits," Letter to the *Financial Times*, January 18, 2011.

As You Read This Chapter

1. Why should businesses be concerned about carbon emissions?
2. What is sustainability?
3. How does the concept of shared value apply to global corporate social responsibility?

The Power and Responsibility of International Business

The rapid expansion of globalization has been driven in large part by international business. Economic liberalization has opened the door for billions of people to enter the world marketplace from countries like China, India, and the former Soviet Union, generating dramatic growth in disposable income and quality of life in these markets and others. Along with rapid economic expansion have come revolutionary improvements in communications and transportation systems. As Chapter 1 indicated, world trade has increased exponentially in the past several decades. International business has never been more important or more powerful. Yet there are also fears and challenges emanating from the field and its activities. Like the two-faced Roman god Janus, who embodies the notion of contradiction to modern thinkers, international business brings both good and bad to the global marketplace.[1] Exploitation of factory workers by global apparel and footwear companies or by electronics and computer brands, exemplifies the negative consequences of globalization.

The role of global businesses and marketers in the financial crises that began in 2008 has led to public anger and increased scrutiny by society, particularly those who experienced great hardships. As noted in "Bank Bonuses and Aristotelian Finance" at the beginning of this chapter, recent legislative efforts have worked to increase regulation of business, such as curbs on bank bonuses in the European Union. These efforts have a moral foundation in the need by societies to ensure social justice while also promoting prosperity. In his papal address of January 1, 2013, Pope Benedict XVI criticized "the predominant model of recent decades that (*sic*) called for seeking maximum profit and consumption, on the basis of an individualistic and selfish mindset, aimed at considering individuals solely in terms of their ability to meet the demands of competitiveness." He advocated that "the creation of ethical structures for currency, financial, and commercial markets is also fundamental and indispensable; these must be stabilized and better coordinated and controlled so as not to prove harmful to the very poor."[2]

Recognizing Challenges and Dilemmas

With increased power comes increased concerns and responsibility—*noblesse oblige*. International businesses are playing a leading role in societies and the lives of people around the world. Serious social implications need consideration. If firms do not respond to these, governments will impose their own rules.

Janus, the two-faced Roman god.

Janus was not only a god of contradiction, but a god whose countenance the Romans put on doors and gates as a symbol of transition. Many in times of transition have come new to the market and even new to marketing. Changes have made life more complex, both for marketers and those to whom they market. For example, some slogans offered routinely to customers in markets with some experience of marketing promotion, such as "you may have won a new car," may be interpreted quite differently by newcomers to the marketing world. Their high expectations may lead to disappointments and even hostility. Because marketers are the initiators of new practices, it is their responsibility to avoid causing harm.

As economic growth in emerging and developing markets allows millions of people to enter the middle class, it brings great new opportunities for them to experience and enjoy a better quality of life with goods and services that help them in many ways. It also exposes them to the challenge of rising aspirations with limited income. Indeed, the gap between the rich, the rising middle class, and the poor presents practical and ethical dilemmas. New international consumers must learn how to manage their aspirations as they experience emotional marketing appeals for products and services that might not be considered practical or "good for them." Philip Kotler has posed two dimensions of "the **marketing dilemma**": (1) What if the customer wants something that is not good for him or her? (2) What if the product or service, while good for the customer, is not good for society or other groups?[3] How consumers, businesses, and societies manage that dilemma in international markets will need to be resolved on a country-by-country and culture-by-culture basis.

MARKETING DILEMMA

Considering the power of marketing and its ethical impacts

All too often cultures are insufficiently studied or wrongly interpreted by newly entering outsiders. As Chapter 2 has shown, cultural differences continue to challenge international businesses and can significantly affect the success or failure of deals. Despite frequent talk about how we understand each other so much better than in the past, the reality looks different. The actual overlap between societies is typically miniscule. A number of Chinese industry leaders may have been to the United States or Europe and developed a clear understanding of Western cultures, but they represent a very small fraction of the Chinese population. The average Chinese person may knowledgeably understand as much about Columbus, Ohio, as the average Buckeye State resident knows about Tianjin. The consequence of that limitation is a danger of misunderstandings and susceptibility to hostility.

One key Western business dimension is the glory of victory in competition. Such an adherence to victory often means a lack of mercy for the vanquished. This plays out in particularly harsh dimensions when it means the loss of jobs and feelings of security about a way of life for many employees of Western firms. Not everywhere are such approaches supported, desired, or accepted. In some regions, the goal becomes for the victor to mend fences, reinvigorate a feeling of togetherness, and provide a cause for standing together. In many societies it is expected that one not take advantage of what could be done, but rather consensually do what ought to be done, particularly given the cultural importance of long-term relationships.

Such context makes it far less acceptable to practice what we have called **vampire marketing**, where the airline or hotel or communications company extracts bloodsucking prices for additional services or products from its captive audience after the major purchase decision has been made. Perhaps global businesses can learn valuable lessons from this context and consequently make themselves more valuable to their customers.[4]

VAMPIRE MARKETING
Exploiting captive customer situations

International business and societal orientation interact closely. For example, in the United States, the individual is considered the key component of society. But such a perspective is not uniformly taken around the world. Typically in socialist or tribal societies, the group receives preference over the individual, and the family is accorded top billing. In such cases, just imagine how different emphases in making financial decisions can be reinterpreted in various settings. What may be corruption and bribery to some may turn out to be filial devotion to others. With the strict administration of the U.S. Foreign Corrupt Practices Act and the new, more stringent U.K. anti-bribery law, businesses and individuals who neglect these laws may face harsh consequences.

The saying goes that "distance makes the heart grow fonder," but in international business, distance can also provide temptation for the abdication of responsibility. Businesses sometimes clearly demonstrate their desire not to know. When host country regulations have been less demanding than those in home countries, some firms sell products that may not meet home country expectations in terms of quality or benefit. As developing nations develop greater regulatory capability and more expectations of the responsibility of firms, irresponsible marketers may encounter a less tolerant face in host countries. The chairman of a multinational corporation may feel removed from local issues. Due to the evolution of a firm through mergers and acquisitions, he or she may see actions as being strictly business issues. However, the locals take all of the firm's actions very personally. When Olympic Games officials in London selected Dow Chemical as a 2012 sponsor, Indian activists protested vehemently because of outstanding claims against Dow by survivors of the Bhopal chemical disaster of 1984 caused by a leak from the factory owned by Union Carbide, which Dow bought in 1999.[5] Their injured and sick are still with them.

We can use Janus as a god of contradictions and transitions, but we cannot turn to him for guidance in morality, ethics, or even law. International businesses will confront dilemmas and challenges. How well they pursue the confluence of highly effective marketing and ethical practices and social responsibility will inevitably be reflected in the loyalty of customers and the judgment of host governments.[6]

THE INCREASED ROLE OF GOVERNMENT

Today, a substantial transformation is characterized by the response of governments to the failures and weaknesses in the global economy and financial system that triggered the economic crisis in 2008. In the developed economies, public anger and frustrations arising from the crisis led to massive government interventions to prevent systemic collapse, stabilize financial markets, and reinvigorate economic activity. Political pressures to correct currency and trade imbalances have also increased in many countries.

Policy and regulatory efforts to reform the system to correct mistakes and abuses that may have caused the crisis will have continuing major implications for the private sector in the coming years. Governments have increased regulation of complex financial instruments and require greater securitization for banks. Bank sizes and the extent of their activities have been limited. Overall, governmental control over financial markets continues to grow in the European Union and the United States. For example, the U.S. Consumer Financial Protection Agency was created by the Dodd-Frank Wall Street Reform and Consumer Protection Act and launched in 2011 to prevent and correct abuses by marketers of credit cards, mortgages, and other financial products.[7]

Ironically, although the financial and economic crisis caused a loss of confidence in "American-style capitalism," it may have also worked to demonstrate the resilience and underlying strength of market economics. It certainly revealed the importance of emerging markets and showed the extent of interconnectedness among markets worldwide. Emerging markets and developing countries have a "greater say" in the global economic system. This means that they must expect that the system is working in their interests and not just the interests of the developed economies. The gap between rich and poor nations and the potential for developing countries to close that gap will play a more important role going forward on the global economic stage.

Leaders of the G20 nations have pledged to work together to grow the global economy, avoid protectionism, and strengthen international systems and institutions. They promised to avoid the mistakes made during the Great Depression of the 1930s, when protectionist legislation in the United States led to similar actions by other countries and escalating trade sanctions. The G20 nations intend to focus on the private sector. In November 2011, at the G20 Leaders Summit in Cannes, France, the leaders specifically pledged to work together to reform the financial sector and enhance market integrity. They promised: "We will not allow a return to pre-crisis behaviors in the financial sector, and we will strictly monitor the implementation of our commitments regarding banks, OTC markets, and compensation practices."[8] A tangible sign of this being practiced is the Basel Committee on Banking Supervision, the forum based at the Bank for International Settlements in Geneva, Switzerland, for regular international cooperation on banking supervision. This committee develops guidelines and standards for implementation by individual countries. Basel III is the set of reform measures that this committee developed to strengthen the "regulation, supervision, and risk management for the banking sector" in response to the financial crisis that began in 2008. In 2013, half of the G20 countries had issued regulations to implement Basel III with the remainder committed to do within the year.[9]

Increased government involvement will also be manifested in interrelated efforts to tackle climate change, energy consumption, environmental damage, poverty, malnutrition, and food security. The G20 leaders have specifically committed to "improving energy markets and pursuing the fight against climate change."[10] Development goals are also on the G20 agenda, and the private sector will play a role in this area: "We also agree that, over time, new sources of funding need to be found to address development needs and climate change. We discussed a set of options for innovative financing highlighted by Mr. Bill Gates. Some of us have implemented or are prepared to explore some of these options. We acknowledge the initiatives in some of our countries to tax the financial sector for various purposes, including a financial transaction tax, inter alia to support development."[11]

Whenever the subject of new sources of funding comes up in government circles, it is likely to have a major impact on private sector firms because it refers to either higher taxes or greater voluntary funding expectations. Governments cannot be expected, for the sake of the theoretical ideals of "free trade" and "laissez faire economics," to sit back and watch the disadvantages and detrimental effects that capitalism and international marketing often bring alongside their benefits. In every country, many powerful interest groups have deep suspicions about market economics. The most that can be expected from leaders and legislators in the major economies is that they will permit an open-market orientation subject to the needs of domestic policy. Such open-market orientation will be maintained only if governments can provide reasonable assurances to their own citizens and firms that the openness applies to foreign markets as well. Therefore, unfair trade practices, such as governmental subsidization, dumping, and industrial targeting, will be examined more closely, and retaliation for such activities is likely to be swift and harsh. When firms violate

Quick Take Apple Apologizes to Chinese Customers

In March 2013, China Central Television, the government-owned television network in China, broadcast a criticism of Apple for its poor treatment of customers. The report highlighted the company's practice of iPhone customer service and limited warranty. In China, Apple provided a one-year warranty despite the country's law requiring two-year warranties. This television report triggered a frenzy of additional reports by other state-owned media outlets including a paper in *The People's Daily* titled "Destroy Apple's Unparalleled Arrogance, and other social media coverage." Then, China's State Administration of Industry and Commerce called for "strengthened supervision of Apple."

Responding to this criticism, Tim Cook, CEO of Apple, soon issued an apology: "We realize that a lack of communication in this process has led the outside to believe that Apple is arrogant and doesn't care or value consumers' feedback.... We sincerely apologize for any concern or misunderstanding this has brought to the customers." With China already Apple's second-largest market, the company was taking no chances.

Some observers speculated that the criticism of Apple may have been caused by U.S. government criticism of China regarding computer hacking attacks on American companies or by U.S. restriction of Chinese investment in the U.S. telecommunications market. Apple appears to have chosen in China to follow the old American adage of "you can't fight City Hall."

PHOTO SOURCE: Apple, **http://www.apple.com/pr/products/apple-retail-stores/apple-retail-stores.html**

Apple Retail Store in Bejing.

SOURCES: David Barboza and Nick Wingfield, "Pressured by China, Apple Apologizes for Warranty Policies," *New York Times*, April 1, 2013; Adam Minter, "Mao Would Have Loved Apple's China Apology," *Bloomberg*, April 2, 2013.

societal norms through their customer, labor, and environmental practices, they are likely to face stern government reaction and stiff penalties. As shown in Quick Take: Apple Apologizes to Chinese Customers, international businesses must be increasingly sensitive to issues that might trigger governmental involvement in any country. Government is now a key player in the international business environment, much more than in the past several decades, and is likely to remain that way.

Diminished Trust

The size and scope of global corporations in the twenty-first century is unprecedented. Global corporations have vast reach and enormous economic power. The Coca-Cola Company sells it branded products in more than 200 countries.[12] With operations in eighty countries, Procter & Gamble estimates that 4 billion of the world's 7 billion people buy P&G brands in 180 countries every year.[13] If one were to equate the annual revenues of the largest global corporations with the size of the world's leading economies, many firms would rank among the top economic powers. As Figure 14.1 shows, Walmart Stores, with 2010 revenues of approximately $422 billion, would rank as the twenty-third largest economy in the world, ahead of countries like Norway and Venezuela. Royal Dutch Shell would rank twenty-sixth,

FIGURE 14.1 Economic Power Of Global Companies 2010

Combined Ranking	Company/Country	Revenue (*Fortune* Magazine 2010)/ GDP (World Bank 2010) both in millions of US dollars
1	United States	14,582,400
2	China	5,878,629
3	Japan	5,497,813
4	Germany	3,309,669
5	France	2,560,002
6	United Kingdom	2,246,079
7	Brazil	2,087,890
8	Italy	2,051,412
9	India	1,729,010
10	Canada	1,574,052
23	Walmart stores	421,849
26	Royal Dutch Shell	378,152
31	Exxon Mobil	354,674
35	BP	308,928
38	Sinopec Group	273,422
39	China National Petroleum	240,192
44	State Grid	226,294
47	Toyota Motor	221,760
50	Japan Post Holdings	203,958

SOURCES: World Bank, Gross Domestic Product 2010, **http://siteresources.worldbank.org/DATASTATISTICS/Resources/GDP.pdf**, and Fortune Global 500 2011, **http://money.cnn.com/magazines/fortune/global500/2011/full_list/**, accessed January 27, 2012, Analysis by Charles J. Skuba and Joao Almeida, Georgetown University McDonough School of Business.

ahead of Austria, Saudi Arabia, Argentina, and South Africa. Exxon Mobil would rank thirty-first, ahead of Iran, Thailand, and Denmark. BP would rank thirty-fifth, ahead of Greece. This analysis also reveals that forty-five companies would be listed in the top 100 economies.[14]

With such economic power come greater expectations for corporate governance, responsibility, and ethics across many fronts from many stakeholder audiences. Businesses do not have impunity in the global economy. The capitalist system and the corporations that it creates exist at the will of the societies and nations in which and across which they operate. The tolerance of these nations for allowing market capitalism latitude is always subject to their confidence that good business brings good benefits to societies. Business does not enjoy carte blanche at any time and especially when societies evidence distrust in the truthfulness and responsibility of business to perform for the greater good. In an editorial in October 2011, the *Financial Times* advocated that "in order to preserve the capitalist model, it is vital to reform. For without public support, it will not thrive."[15]

Public trust in business may be seen as a measurement that corresponds to the willingness of societies to allow international firms greater leeway to do business. Since 2000, the public relations firm Edelman has been conducting a global survey of public trust toward government, business, and other institutions: The Edelman Trust Barometer. Observing the findings of that survey since its inception, one can conclude that trust in business is generally stronger when a greater number of people realize the benefits of business. Even in the developed economies, the economic disruptions caused by the financial crisis and recession shook severely the level of trust in businesses. Trust in business in developed economies reached a nadir in the depths of the crisis in early 2009 with less than 40 percent of respondents in the United States, Germany, and France indicating that they trusted business "to do what is right."[16] In 2013, although trust in business had rebounded from its 2009 lows, trust in government had dropped. Public frustrations resulting from the continuing euro currency crisis, the anemic economic growth rates in the developed economies, the daunting debts of governments, and the inability of political leaders to work together effectively to solve problems in the United States had damaged the credibility of governments.

The problems confronting the world are complex and intimidating. Anxiety over them increases when there is a dearth of optimism and no clear direction about how to solve them. So Edelman's findings about lack of trust in government are logical. Though overall trust in business had improved in 2013 in the developed countries, as shown in Figure 14.2, trust in business remained much stronger in emerging markets. With the promises of increased prosperity more tangible and with less exposure to economic problems, trust in business was more than twice as strong in China and India as it was in the United States, as Figure 14.3 reveals. In 2013, trust in government and business leaders was generally lowest in Japan and Europe, where economic problems were particularly challenging to citizens.

In 2013, trust in both business and government leaders regarding ethics, morality, and truthfulness was very low. Overall, Edelman cautioned in 2012 that while trust in business leaders exceeded trust in government officials, "business leaders should not be cheered by government's ineptitude, especially as trust in the two institutions tend to move in synch. There is still a yawning trust gap for business, as evidenced by one half of informed public respondents saying government does not regulate business enough. Yet what most stakeholders want from the government—consumer protection and regulation ensuring responsible corporate behavior—are actions business can take on its own."[17]

FIGURE 14.2 Credibility of CEOs vs. Government Officials/Regulators

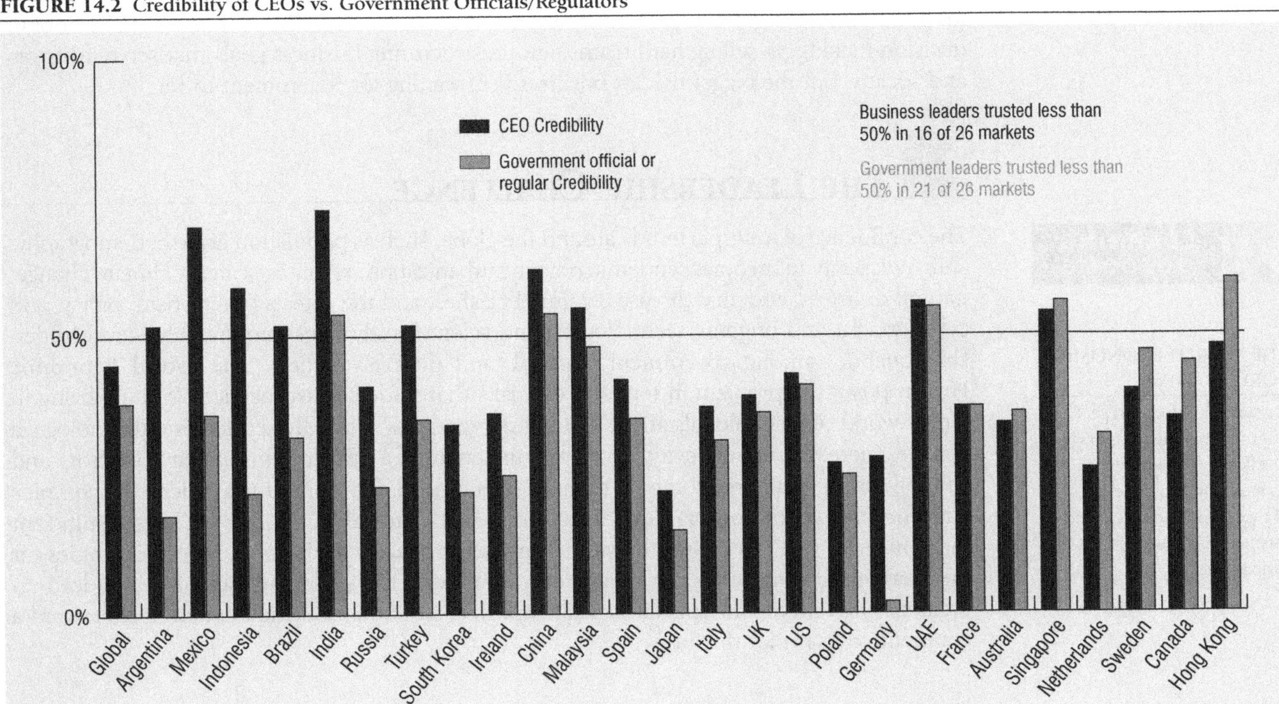

SOURCE: Edelman Trust Barometer 2013 Annual Global Study.

FIGURE 14.3 Trust in the Truthfulness of Leaders

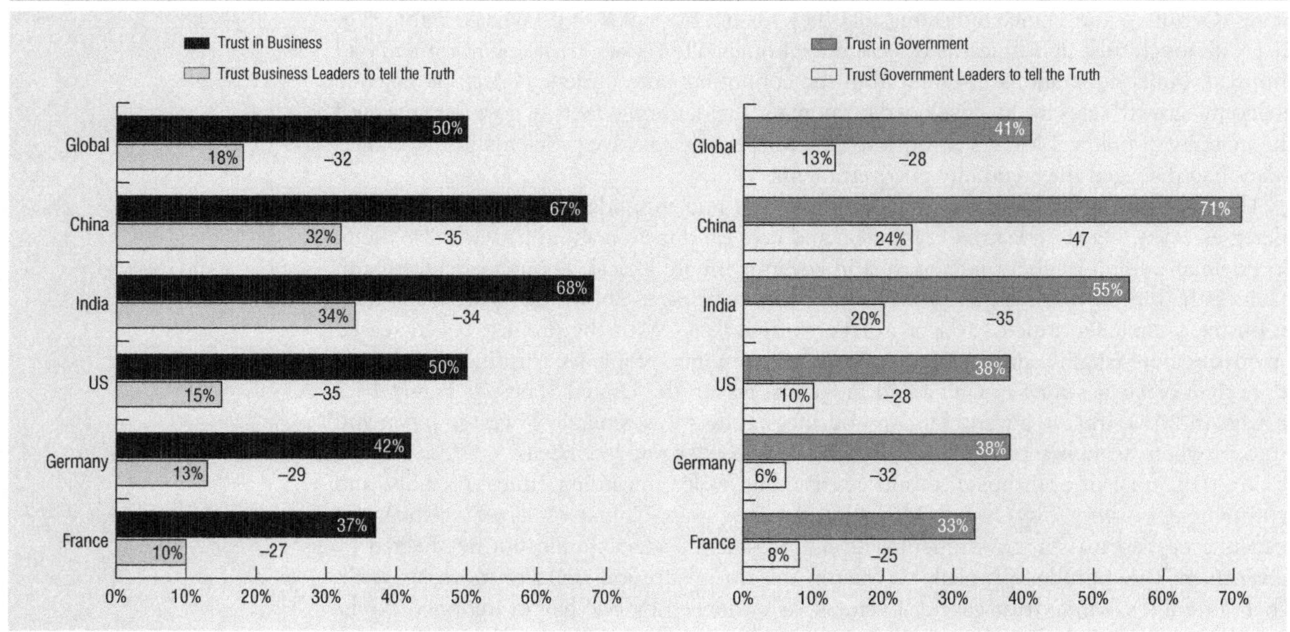

SOURCE: Edelman Trust Barometer 2013 Annual Global Study.

Edelman maintains that "business is now better placed than government to lead the way out of the trust crisis. But the balance must change so that business is seen both as a force for good and an engine for profit.... Business is a force for good. Yes, there are risks in bold decision-making, in telling hard truths, and in structuring business goals that serve investors and society. But the bigger risk for business is in waiting for government to act."[18]

The Leadership Challenge

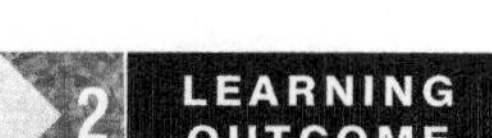

THE WORLD ECONOMIC FORUM

Organization focused on international business and its effects; best known for its annual global meeting of mostly policymakers and business executives in Davos, Switzerland

The confluence of multiple trends around the globe, such as population growth, demographic shifts, disparity in incomes, endemic poverty, urbanization, resource scarcity, climate change, natural disasters, endemic diseases, cultural clashes, and the threats of terrorism, piracy, and cyber-attacks and ongoing technological and scientific advances, requires high-level leadership qualities among government, societal, and business leaders. **The World Economic Forum** poses the problem in terms of the risks that leaders must manage: "We are living in a new world of risk. Globalization, shifting demographics, rapidly accelerating technological change, increased connectivity, economic uncertainty, a growing multiplicity of actors and shifting power structures combine to make operating in this world unprecedentedly complex and challenging for corporations, institutions and states alike."[19] It is no longer sufficient for a business CEO to "mind the store." Among the major challenges and opportunities for international businesses is the choice of leaders with the skills and capabilities to lead an organization with its multiple customer, employee, and other stakeholder audiences toward a competitive vision for the future.

Aligning Strategy, Products, and Societal Interests

Companies like IBM, GE, and Siemens are aligning their corporate strategies as well as their product offerings with societal interests and the global trends that impact societies. Many of their largest customers are national, state, and municipal governments that are confronted with complex challenges. With product and service offerings in areas like healthcare, aviation, energy, electrical distribution, railroad engines, water treatment, and lighting, GE has a large intersection with societal interests. GE's marketing positioning reflects the needs of its government customers and is centered on the notion of using imagination and innovation "to solve the world's biggest problems." The company claims that "GE works on things that matter. The best people and the best technologies taking on the toughest challenges. Finding solutions in energy, health and home, transportation and finance. Building, powering, moving and curing the world."[20] Similarly, as a major competitor to GE, Siemens provides products and services in areas like energy, healthcare, rail systems, power grids, construction, information technology, transportation and logistics management, and infrastructure logistics. Siemens is a huge global employer with more than 360,000 employees from more than 140 countries in operations in 190 regions.[21] Siemens positions itself as "a pioneer of our time" and to "reap particular benefit from the megatrends demographic change, urbanization, climate change, and globalization."[22] One of Siemens newest initiatives is its "Infrastructure and Cities sector," which is specifically designed to bring its product and service offerings to address the needs of global urban governments.

> *The megatrends urbanization, climate change, globalization and demographic change will shape the future of cities. With the need to improve the quality of life and economic competitiveness, cities have to become more resource-efficient and environmentally friendly.*[23]

Not all companies make products that directly contribute to meeting societal goals. However, all international businesses have an integral relationship with the home and host countries in which they do business. Part of that relationship is a responsibility of the company to act as a responsible citizen. We must appreciate that governments are playing a new and growing role in international businesses. In part, this has been the outgrowth of the global crises, which market forces had not anticipated or addressed. Today, there are new global regulations and restrictions. However, we have not yet established what indicators are more accurate, the siren calls of the market place with its market signals or the plans and mandates of governments. We know that governments are not always free from fault and ambition.[24] International businesses must learn the advantages and disadvantages of following one direction over the other. They must understand new paths to follow in order to operate successfully in different countries. International business in the twenty-first century requires a new kind of leader to see and navigate these unfamiliar paths.

Corporate Social Responsibility

What Is the Responsibility of Business?

In his famous 1970 *New York Times Magazine* article, Milton Friedman attacked the concept of "social responsibilities of business in a free-enterprise system" directly in his headline "The Social Responsibility of Business Is to Increase Its Profits." He described those business executives who spoke in favor of corporate social responsibilities as being "incredibly shortsighted and muddleheaded" and "preaching pure and unadulterated socialism" with their arguments being "notable for their analytical looseness and lack of rigor."[25] To understand

Friedman's point-of-view accurately, one has to understand the political circumstances that were influencing business conditions in the United States at that time and reflect on the issue of wage and price controls and Friedman's concerns about its threat to the free enterprise system that he so fiercely championed. At that time, inflationary pressures were causing criticism of the capitalist system and businesses pursuing profits with some calling for businesses to act responsibly in their pricing policies. Friedman argued that

> *the doctrine of 'social responsibility' taken seriously would extend the scope of the political mechanism to every human activity. It does not differ in philosophy from the most explicitly collectivist doctrine. It differs only by professing to believe that collectivist ends can be attained without collectivist means.... I have called it a 'fundamentally subversive doctrine' in a free society, and...in such a society, there is one and only one social responsibility of business—to use its resources and engage in activities designed to increase its profits so long as it stays within the rules of the game, which is to say, engages in open and free competition without deception or fraud.*[26]

Friedman represented one end of the spectrum of opinion on the responsibility of business in society. A prevailing argument from those who held Friedman's viewpoint was that profitable corporations would create private wealth, which could then choose to channel it toward philanthropic purposes. The United States has a long tradition of philanthropy and is the leading country for private philanthropic donations per capita in the world. The Carnegie Corporation of New York annually awards the Carnegie Medal of Philanthropy. This award is given to those who donate their private wealth to "do real and permanent good for the world."[27] Some believe that a corporation should not be distracted from the efficiency of its primary purpose and maximizing the return of the shareholders' investment. The other end of the spectrum maintains that the corporation has multiple roles and effects in society other than wealth creation. The corporation exists and operates in nations and communities, employs individuals, uses community resources, creates waste and byproducts through its manufacturing and operations, and has multiple integral relationships with society. For the sake of their own advancement, corporations are treated by governments as persons rather than merely financial entities. So it does not seem farfetched to expect them to respond to society's needs as persons rather than financial entities as well. A spectrum of opinion across the globe regarding Friedman's contention exists. As Figure 14.4 shows, when asked if they agreed with Milton Friedman that "the social responsibility of business is to increase its profits," there were broad differences among national respondents. Although 84 percent of respondents in the United Arab Emirates, 72 percent in Japan, and 70 percent in India and South Korea agreed with that viewpoint, only 30 percent of respondents in Spain, 33 percent in Italy, and 35 percent in Germany agreed.[28] Whether one agrees precisely with Friedman or not, it is common sense that an international marketer will need to be profitable if it is to practice corporate social responsibility at a high level.

Defining Corporate Social Responsibility

CORPORATE SOCIAL RESPONSIBILITY (CSR)
Corporate activities to benefit stakeholder communities

Corporate social responsibility (CSR) carries different meanings to different audiences. Research has shown that many people are confused by the term. In a 2007 study in the United States by the public relations firm Fleishman Hillard and the National Consumers League, most respondents identified either "commitment to community" or "commitment to employees" as the principal meanings of CSR. Other meanings included "responsibility to the environment" and "providing quality products." The study found that American consumers expected corporate commitment to encompass more than just charitable and philanthropic giving and that treating and paying employees well was of prime importance.[29]

CSR is a broad term that includes many specific corporate practices. The European Commission defines it as "the responsibility of enterprises for their impacts on society" and

FIGURE 14.4 What is the Social Responsibility of Business?
Milton Friedman: *The social responsibility of business it to increase its profits." —* percentage of those who agree

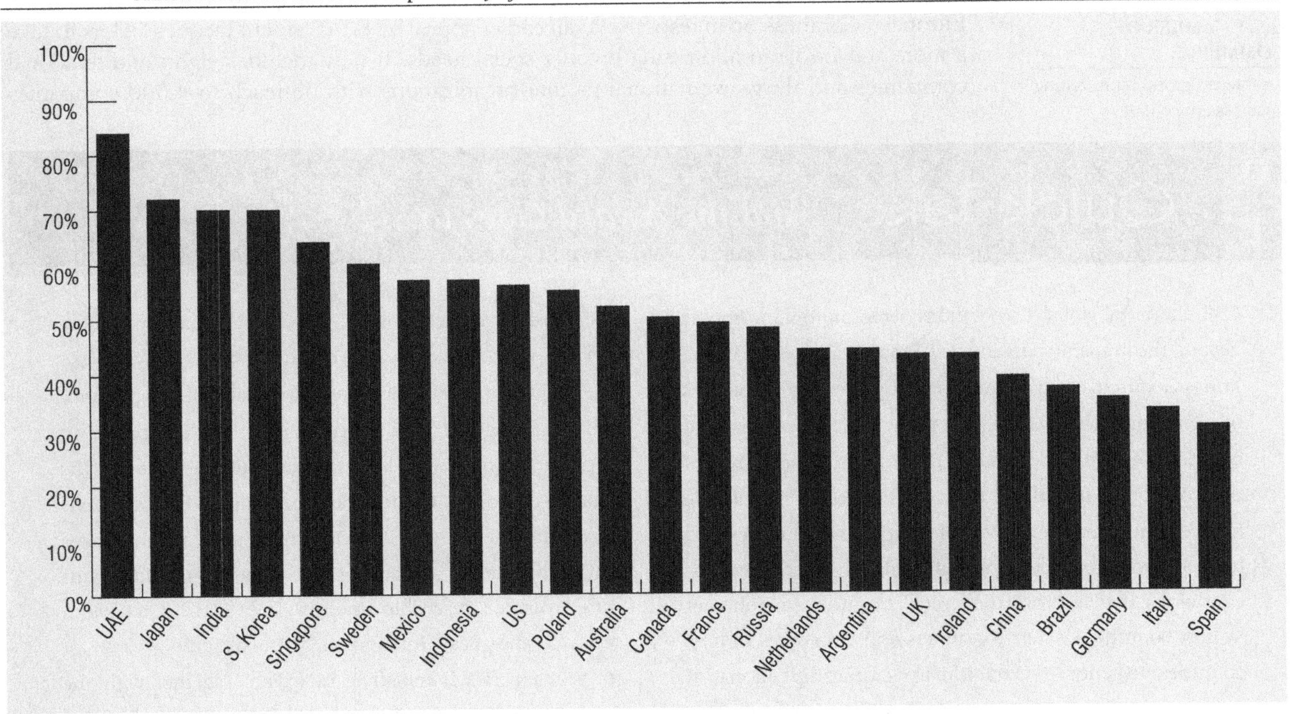

SOURCE: Edelman Trust Barometer, **http://www.edelman.com/trust/2011/**, accessed January 31, 2012.

stipulates that "enterprises should have in place a process to integrate social, environmental, ethical, human rights, and consumer concerns into their business operations and core strategy in close collaborations with their stakeholders."[30] The broader meaning of the term is also captured by other expressions used by many corporations and individuals, such as **corporate citizenship**. Historically, many companies have supported their local and national communities through a variety of roles, including support for nonprofit organizations vital to a community's social development such as board memberships, employee volunteer programs, and charitable donations. Another frequently used term is **corporate philanthropy**, which has a narrower context specific to the philanthropic or charitable contributions of a firm. As this chapter will address under the specific subject of **sustainability**, CSR also includes a range of issues related to the environmental impact of the firm's operations and products.

CORPORATE CITIZENSHIP
Corporate involvement in and support of community activities to reflect the company's role as a citizen of the community

CORPORATE PHILANTHROPY
Corporate financial donations to specific causes and activities

SUSTAINABILITY
Practices that work to harmonize organizational goals with environmental impact

Corporate citizenship practices have been around for centuries. In Augsburg, Germany, the *Fuggerei* is a Roman Catholic housing settlement for the poor that Jakob Fugger "The Rich" founded in 1520 and that still exists today through the support of the original charitable trust. The 145 residents of the Fuggerei, many of them elderly widows, pay an annual rent of less than one euro to live in the quaint community on the condition that they pray for the Fugger family. (Was he hedging his bets?) Fugger was an international marketer and financier who even financed a trade mission to India.[31] Fugger may be a good example today for international marketers to follow in combining successful business practices with social responsibility.

The International Chamber of Commerce (ICC) defines CSR as "the voluntary commitment by business to manage its activities in a responsible way."[32] The ICC encourages its membership to take initiatives on their own volition that make good sense for their company's overall strategy. CSR practices are now encouraged by governments and business associations worldwide as Quick Take: "And the Award Goes To...." describes for the United States.

European CSR efforts are also leading examples of the practice. To provide such leadership, CSR Europe was founded in 1998 by business leaders across Europe in cooperation with the European Commission in response to an earlier appeal by EC President Jacques Delors to take a more active role in addressing broader social needs. It now includes eighty multinational companies and thirty-five national partner organizations with outreach to 4,000 companies

U.S. CHAMBER OF COMMERCE
An interest group representing business concerns

Quick Take *"And the Award Goes to..."*

CSR efforts by global corporations serve multiple purposes beyond the humanitarian and developmental goals set by the firms. Good citizenship programs empower the employees of companies to channel effectively their own desire to help local communities and to be proud representatives of the companies for which they work. Socially responsible firms are also representatives of their home countries and help to promote good diplomatic relationships as well as conditions that improve the overall business environment in host countries. When consumers and employees in host countries experience extraordinary citizenship efforts, it reflects well on both the companies and the home countries.

Recognizing that good citizenship is also good business for American businesses and the United States government, the U.S. Department of State created the American Corporate Excellence (ACE) award in 1999 to honor the contributions that American businesses make around the world. According to the State Department, "The ACE helps define America as a positive force in the world. It highlights our increasing outreach to the business community, our public-private partnerships, and our public diplomacy efforts."

Among the winners of the ACE award were Sorwathe, a U.S. tea production company doing business in Rwanda, and Intel for its practices in Vietnam. The ACE award recognized Sorwathe in the small-medium-size company category particularly for its efforts to eradicate child labor in Rwanda's tea sector but also for its efforts to support adult literacy, workers' rights, and practice sustainable forestry and water management while producing high-quality tea. Intel was selected "for its leadership in environmental protection though the generation of electricity through solar power; in transformative educational programs that focus on faculty and curriculum development, including sending local educators for university training in the U.S.; and providing scholarships to disadvantaged children, youth, and women."

The U.S. business community also realizes the importance of recognizing the good work of American companies to improve the quality of life in other countries through the creation of the **U.S. Chamber of Commerce**'s Business Civic Leadership Center (BCLC). Working to improve the image of U.S. businesses abroad, the BCLC has presented awards for Corporate Citizenship since 1999. In 2012, Qualcomm received the Best International Ambassador award for its Wireless Reach initiative, in which, together with the Grameen Foundation, it developed Ruma, "an Indonesian social enterprise that brings telecommunications through micro franchises to the country's most remote regions. More than 15,000 Ruma entrepreneurs serve some 1.5 million customers." The Association of American Chambers of Commerce presented their 2012 Western Hemisphere Corporate Citizenship Award to the Coca-Cola Foundation of Ecuador (CCFE), a nonprofit organization created in 2000 by Coca-Cola of Ecuador and ARCA Continental. "CCFE has focused its actions under the platform "Live Positively," to make a positive difference in the world by ensuring sustainability as an integral part of everything they do."

Such awards serve to validate and encourage CSR practices. The U.S. Chamber maintains that the recognition of efforts will serve as a model for other companies. It may not be glamorous like the Oscars, but these awards are very important recognition of companies.

SOURCES: U.S. State Department, **http://www.state.gov/e/eb/ce/2014/index.htm**, accessed July 28, 2014; U.S. Chamber of Commerce, **http://bclc.uschamber.com/press-release/us-chamber-announces-2012-corporate-citizenship-award-winners**, accessed July 28, 2014.

across Europe.[33] CSR Europe has launched the Enterprise 2020 initiative to help companies collaborate to develop profitable, innovative businesses practices that lead "the transformation towards a smart, sustainable and inclusive society." The initiative envisions that the "enterprise of the future" will have societal issues at the heart of its strategy.[34]

The Chamber's Ireland organization presents CSR awards annually since 2004 to "recognize the work being carried out by Irish and multinational companies to improve the lives of their employees and to enhance the civic environment in which they operate."[35] The Council of British Chambers of Commerce in Europe, in the spirit of William Wilberforce who convinced the British Parliament to abolish slavery in the nineteenth century, has created a specific CSR initiative to stop Human Trafficking through educational programs and other efforts.[36]

There have been efforts by governments to codify more specifically what they expect of companies regarding CSR practices. The ICC warns against a kind of "one-size-fits-all" approach and defends the voluntary nature of CSR: "Government's role is to provide the basic national and international framework of laws and regulations for business operations and that essential role will continue to evolve. Beyond this, good corporate practice is usually spread most effectively by strong corporate principles and example, rather than by codes of conduct. A commitment to responsible business conduct requires consensus and conviction within a company. Voluntary business principles have the advantage of bridging cultural diversity within enterprises and offering the flexibility to tailor solutions to particular conditions. Voluntary approaches minimize competitive distortions, transaction costs associated with regulatory compliance, and inspire many companies to go beyond the regulatory baseline, thus often eliminating the need for further legislation."[37]

Strategic Focus

Early corporate citizenship initiatives were often directed at supporting community causes ranging from charitable organizations to cultural institutions like municipal symphonies and operas. Companies have been historically helpful in developing the cultural infrastructure of many communities. Whether these corporate philanthropy efforts were beneficial to the company or only to selected individuals is very subjective. However, many of these early efforts were not scrutinized for their contribution to the strategic objectives of the firm. Michael E. Porter and Mark R. Kramer have argued that a company needs to choose its social initiatives strategically. They have advanced the concept of **shared value**, which they define as "policies and operating practices that enhance the competitiveness of a company while simultaneously advancing the economic and social conditions in the communities in which it operates. Shared value creation focuses on identifying and expanding the connections between societal and economic programs."[38] Porter and Kramer identify three approaches that apply to international businesses: (1) delivering attractive products that are truly beneficial to society; (2) removing problems in the supply chain that are both costly and socially detrimental, such as reducing greenhouse gases; and (3) enabling local cluster development to help communities become more competitive.[39] They argue that "we need a more sophisticated form of capitalism, one imbued with a social purpose. But that purpose should arise not out of charity but out of a deeper understanding of competition and economic value creation."[40] The best international businesses are driven by the desire to create value and improve their competitive positions so shared value becomes the right and smart thing to do.

SHARED VALUE
Harmonizing corporate competitiveness goals with community goals in CSR activities

CSR Reporting

Porter and Kramer distinguish between shared value and CSR by claiming that the latter mostly focused on corporate reputation rather than on directly improving a company's profitability and competitive position.[41] This distinction can be misleading. Many companies have certainly used their CSR initiatives to build their reputations through marketing communications, but that is not inimical to a strategic approach to CSR. Crucial is the CEO's commitment to a holistic CSR program. If the CEO takes up the flag in leadership, the company is more likely to rally to the cause and integrate it deeply into the very fabric of the operation. Some deeply committed companies, like GE and IBM, reflect this by embedding CSR initiatives into their overall strategic business model.

How companies communicate their involvement and commitment to CSR is very important. Edelman advocates that companies should "practice radical transparency." Radical transparency can be accomplished by communicating effectively with various stakeholder groups, especially employees, about the company's CSR goals and its progress toward meeting those goals. Enabling employees to take that conversation further with others individually and through the increasingly important social media channels can be particularly convincing to other audiences.[42]

The most common means of formal communication is through regular dedicated reports. Most large companies issue annual or periodic reports on their CSR practices. The reporting procedure and the quality of the reports are a good lens to view the actual commitment of the company to responsibility programs. KPMG has analyzed the CSR reporting practices of companies. In its International Survey of Corporate Responsibility Reporting 2011, KPMG reported that "while CR reporting was once seen as fulfilling a moral obligation to society, many companies are now recognizing it as a business imperative. Today, companies are increasingly demonstrating that CR reporting provides financial value and drives innovation, reflecting the old adage of 'what gets measured gets managed.'"[43] The thirty-four country analysis in Figure 14.5 shows that European companies were "leading the pack" in the professionalism of the process they used and the quality of the communication. Many companies in countries like South Africa, Romania, Mexico, Nigeria, and Russia, as well as Denmark and Finland, were "starting behind" in both categories. Companies in the United States, Canada, Brazil, Japan, and Israel were just "scratching the surface," providing quality communications but a low level of process maturity. These companies "had the highest risk of failing to deliver on the promises they make in their CR report and/or targets they have set."[44] Such failures can lead to harsh responses by stakeholders. KPMG reported a dramatic rise in the number of companies reporting on CSR activities. As Figure 14.6 illustrates, almost all global companies now have some form of reporting. In 2011, 95 percent of the 250 largest global companies (G250) and 64 percent of the 100 largest companies in the thirty-four countries analyzed (N100) now report on these activities. This kind of reporting only began among global companies around 1999 and picked up dramatically after 2002.[45] A separate Georgetown University analysis of top U.S. companies found a spike in these reports in 2007 and then a rebound in 2010 after a short drop.[46] One important indicator of a company's CSR commitment is the degree of transparency and honesty in these reports, often expressed through establishing clear goals and reporting on progress toward meeting them. Another important indicator is the quality of the messaging from the CEO, often in the form of a letter. One can tell the difference between sincere conviction and the company merely covering the topic.

SUSTAINABILITY

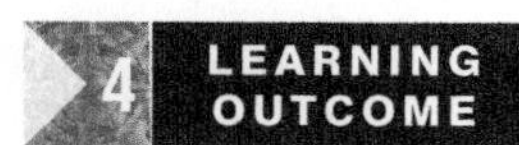

Issues related to the environment make up perhaps the most important individual element of CSR. Of the U.S. Fortune 100 corporations that issued some form of CSR report since 2010, more than one quarter specifically included some variation of "sustainability" or "environment" in their titles.[47] The focus on these issues is very logical when one considers the impact that large companies have upon the environment in relation to water usage and disposal, en-

FIGURE 14.5 Reporting On Corporate Social Responsibililty — Quality of Communications and Process Maturity

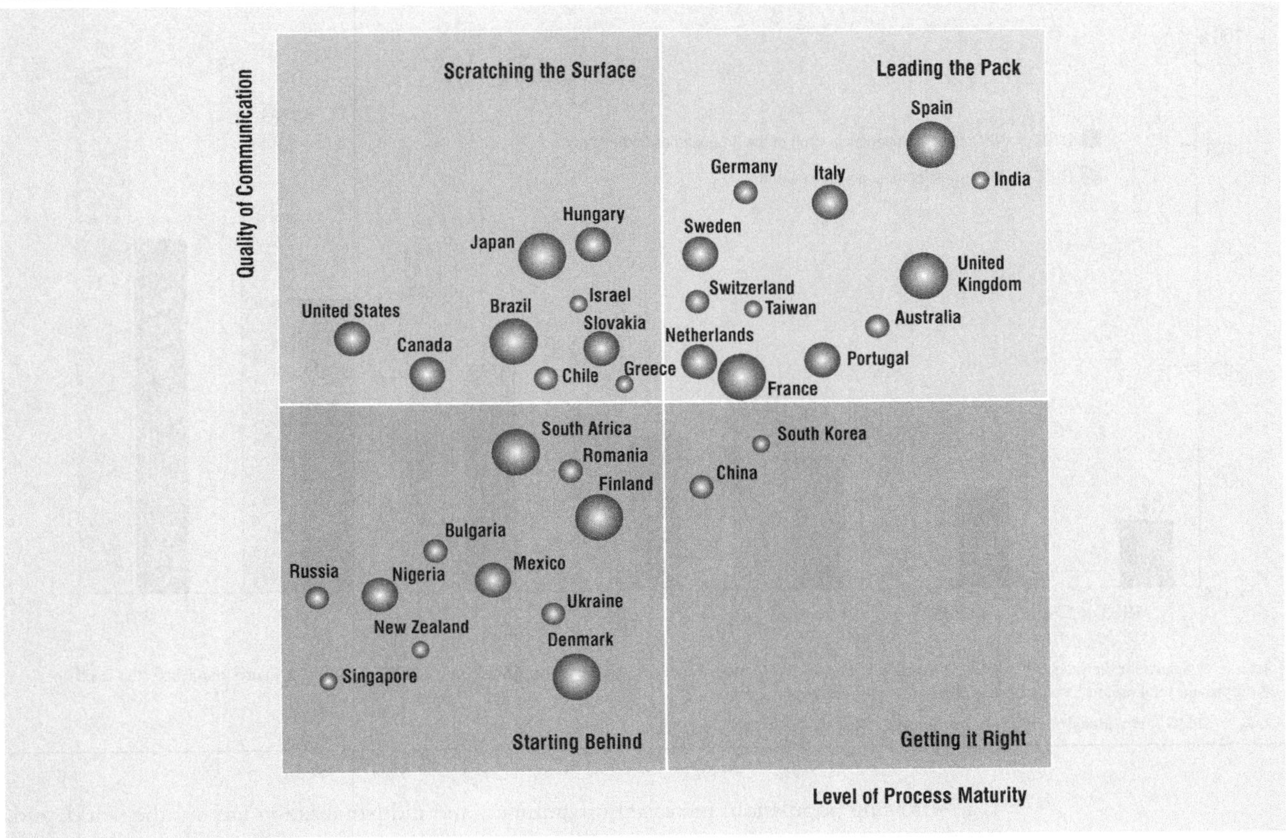

SOURCE: KPMG International Survey of Corporate Social Responsibility Reporting 2011.

ergy consumption, energy emissions, continued availability of natural ecosystems, the effects of chemical components of products and packaging, product and packaging disposal, and overall wastes from operations. More of the leading global operations have begun to embrace sustainability issues not only to improve their reputation, but as a part of their core corporate strategy to improve efficiencies and even increase revenues.

A Sustainable Future?

Just like the broader term of CSR, sustainability also carries multiple meanings to different audiences. Inevitably, groups and organizations that are interested in specific issues related to the environment tend to define the issue in narrow terms. It is helpful to understand the term in its most general sense, which often involves some sense of marrying commercial needs with preserving the natural environment for the future. Several definitions can help. The 1986 World Commission on Environment and Development (Brundtland Commission) definition of sustainable development could reasonably be applied to sustainable business practices: "development that meets the needs of the present without compromising the ability of future generations to meet their own needs."[48] A simple but powerful expression is that of Robert Gillman: "do unto future generations as you would have them do unto you."[49]

FIGURE 14.6 Percent of Companies Reporting on Corporate Social Responsibility Activities

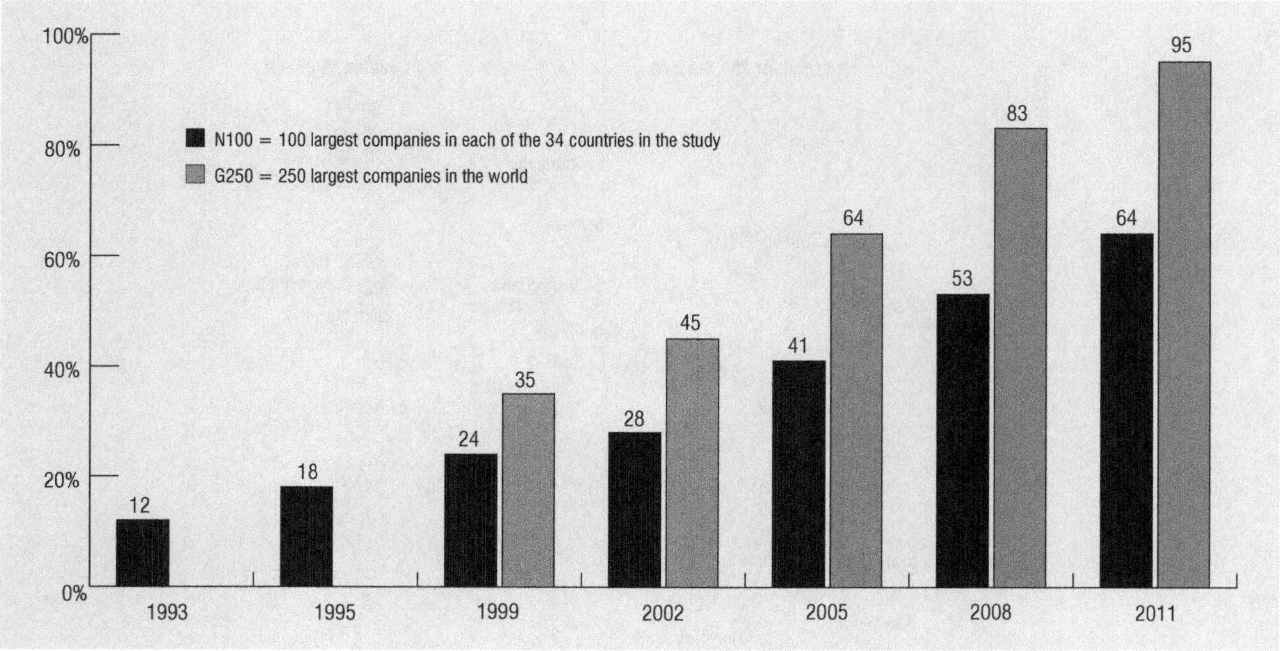

N100 = 100 largest companies in each of the 34 countries in the study
G250 = 250 largest companies in the world

	1993	1995	1999	2002	2005	2008	2011
N100	12	18	24	28	41	53	64
G250			35	45	64	83	95

Note: Survey results for the years 1993 to 2002 represent separate CR reports only. Due to the increasing trend in integrated reporting, the figures published after 2005 represent total reports, separate and published as part of annual reports.

SOURCE: KPMG International Survey of Corporate Social Responsibility Reporting 2011.

Growing population, increased urbanization and industrialization around the world, and dramatic increases in production and consumption all have a significant impact upon the environment. This has led to increased pressures from nongovernmental organizations and multilateral institutions to create greater awareness and to improve practices by governments, businesses, and individuals to lessen the detrimental impact. This sometimes raises political and philosophical disagreements as to the extent of problems and the nature of the proposed solutions. An example of this is the 1997 Kyoto Protocol, an international agreement linked to the United Nations Framework Convention on Climate Change. This agreement sets binding targets for thirty-seven industrialized countries and the European Community for reducing national levels of greenhouse gas emissions.[50] The United States declined to join this agreement because it excludes major developing economies like China, India, and Brazil, which are also major greenhouse gas emitters. Controversy continues over whether these greenhouse gases are causing "climate change" and/or "global warming." Within individual nations, political disagreements regarding the wisdom and necessity of "green" policies and practices often show varying opinions about whether "green is good." For example, the EU announced a carbon emissions tax on all airlines flying into Europe. This has raised protests from the U.S. and Chinese governments. Also, U.S. and European regulations that set new standards for the amount of light emitted per watt of power used effectively require the use of compact fluorescent bulbs and make incandescent light bulbs obsolete. Subsequently, concerns have emerged about mercury content in the new bulbs and how to dispose of them, as well as whether they are as effective in illumination. As a result, some people are hoarding old lightbulbs.[51] Similar issues and a secondary market in old toilets have resulted from regulations on low-flow toilets to save water. International marketers will need to pay attention to multiple regulations governing environmental impact of products. The EU has implemented

REACH, (Registration, Evaluation, Authorization, and Restriction of Chemical substances), a set of broad reaching regulations on the use of chemicals, to motivate businesses to exclude dangerous chemicals like cadmium in products such as personal computers and cell phones.

Where problems exist, business opportunity may exist as well. As we have outlined in this chapter, companies like IBM, GE, and Siemens are adjusting their corporate strategies and their product offerings to address some of the planet's environmental challenges and governmental plans to tackle them. In President Obama's 2011 State of the Union address, he called for the United States to generate 80 percent of its electricity from clean energy sources by 2035. Depending on the evolving definition of "clean energy," this may mean good opportunity for companies that have products and services in renewable energies, nuclear power, efficient natural gas, coal with carbon capture and sequestration, wind power, and solar energy. Some businesses objected, contending that the goal was unachievable because of existing regulatory barriers.[52] Business groups and environmental organizations in many countries often clash over various regulations that affect access to energy supplies. Even "clean energy" can pose environmental disputes as illustrated by the issues of shale gas drilling and pipelines in the United States and the movement away from nuclear power in Germany.

Sustainable Practices

Irrespective of the many disagreements that exist in relation to the "green" movement, most large international marketers have realized that sustainable practices can make good business sense. As Quick Take: Can a War on Carbon Be Good Business? illustrates, reduced emissions are often directly related to lower fuel costs and increased operational efficiency. Leading global companies are seeing strategic value in making sustainability a corporate imperative. McKinsey's 2011 Global Survey on the Business of Sustainability finds "that a handful of companies are capturing significant value by systematically pursuing the opportunities sustainability offers. We believe the trend is clear: more businesses will have to take a long-term strategic view of sustainability and build it into the key value creation levers that drive returns on capital, growth and risk management as well as the key organizational elements that support the levers. Each company's path to capturing value from sustainability will be unique, but these underlying elements can serve as a universal point from which to get started."[53]

Growing Importance To Consumers And Governments

In the long run, sustainability will be important to international businesses because it will be important to governments, to consumers, and to employees. Doug Oberhelman, the CEO of Caterpillar, captured the strategic fit of sustainability from an international marketer's customer-centric viewpoint: "It's a perfect fit. Our strategy is all about serving our customers. And our customers are asking us how we can help make them more efficient and help them meet their sustainability challenges. That pull from customers is really all we need, but our people are also pushing us. Caterpillar employees get really excited about making our products more sustainable and also making our own operations more efficient. And guess what? One of the key groups on our strategy pyramid—stockholders—like sustainability too. I've yet to meet a stockholder that doesn't believe in investing for the future and providing superior products, services and solutions that meet our customers' needs. And that's what we are doing when we deliver sustainable solutions to our customers."[54]

Quick Take *Can a War on Carbon Be Good Business?*

In 2010, at the "Creating Climate Wealth" conference at the Georgetown University McDonough School of Business, Richard Branson, CEO of Virgin Group, along with a group of global entrepreneurs, business leaders, and organizations, officially declared world war on carbon emissions. In defining the nature of the war, Branson said: "I have described the increasing levels of greenhouse gases in the atmosphere as one of the greatest threats to the ongoing prosperity and sustainability of life on the planet. The good news is that creating businesses that will power our growth, and reduce our carbon output while protecting resources, is also the greatest wealth-generating opportunity of our generation." Branson believes that good profitability opportunity exists in providing fuels and technologies while reducing the harmful effects of greenhouse gases.

One of the first theaters in the Carbon War Room's plan of battle is the shipping sector, a source of one billion tons of carbon emissions annually, about 5 percent of the world's carbon output. Toward the goal of proving that sustainable shipping and efficiency are not incompatible but rather reinforcing, the organization provides information, data analysis, and strategic resources to governments, organizations, and industry. For example, it used data from the European Union and the International Maritime Organization to create ratings standards for energy efficiency of ships. Their statistics revealed that the shipping industry could reduce emissions by a third through improved route structures, smarter types of fuel, and better maintenance. Not only would emissions be dramatically reduced but so would costs and fuel usage.

In 2013, the Carbon War Room announced partnerships with a number of key shipping stakeholders, including Pricewaterhouse Coopers and Forum for the Future. Chief Operating Officer Peter Boyd is very positive about the industry's reduced carbon future: "PwC has a very enlightened and forward-thinking sustainability team, and with them we've gathered shipowners, the charterers who actually pay for the fuel, providers of innovative technologies and the third-party funders needed to get efficiency technologies actually onto vessels in the same room to look at how we can create new financing mechanisms to drive further progress."

PHOTO SOURCE: Carbon War Room, **http://www.carbonwarroom.com/sectors/transport/shipping**

Carbon War Room.

SOURCES: Carbon War Room, "After the Storm," May 31, 2013; Richard Branson, "A letter from our Founder—If we don't act, mother nature will," **http://www.carbonwarroom.com**, accessed July 28, 2014; Keren Blankfeld, "Branson's Call to Green Entrepreneurs," Forbes.com, April 22, 2010, **http://www.forbes.com/2010/04/22/branson-green-technologies-carbon-war-virgin.html?boxes=businesschannelsections**; Fiona Harvey and Robert Wright, "Online service to track shipping emissions," *Financial Times*, December 6, 2010, **http://www.ft.com/intl/cms/s/0/1add9296-0098-11e0-aa29-00144feab49a.html#axzz17SYKPT5T**, accessed January 18, 2012.

Although we have seen that consumers may lack trust in business and are skeptical of sustainability claims, international marketers must understand the importance of sustainability to a growing number of consumers in the long run. Gallup's 2011 research found that a large majority of consumers "seem willing to reward companies for focusing on the environment" and prefer brands that are "environmentally friendly."[55] Of course, when consumer awareness of an issue is significant, customer-focused companies need to address it. An essential part of marketing is having products and claims that stand up to the test of consumer scrutiny. The involvement and potential endorsement of key stakeholders and governments can work to the advantage of smart companies. As the opening to Chapter 1 points out, environmental labels, like the **EU Ecolabel**, are an indicator that companies are addressing increasing consumer concerns about the environmental impact of numerous products through efforts facilitated by governments and nongovernmental organizations.

EU ECOLABEL
Setting of standards that encourage the use of environmentally sound processes, products, and practices

Another example of governments working together to resolve confusion is the cooperation between the United States, Japan, Korea, Australia, and the European Union to create ENERGY STAR, a voluntary appliance specific label governing energy efficiency for office equipment.[56] The EU also has voluntary labeling programs that international marketers of products such as consumer appliances, detergents, and paints need to consider. The EU Eco-Label program sets a variety of ecological criteria that helps consumers understand health and environmental impact issues for a number of products and allows them to make an informed purchase decision. Another voluntary environmental program in Germany is the **Blue Angel Program**, the oldest environment-related label in the world, which sets standards of occupational health and safety, ergonomics, economical use of raw materials, service life, and disposal. The Blue Angel "seal of approval" is awarded to products that meet the standards, allowing consumer confidence in their choices of products.[57]

BLUE ANGEL PROGRAM
German program that identifies environmentally sound products and services

McKinsey sums up the issue of sustainability: "The choice for companies today is not if, but how they should manage their sustainability activities. Companies can choose to see this agenda as a necessary evil—a matter of compliance or a risk to be managed while they get on with the business of business—or they can think of it as a novel way to open up new business opportunities while creating value for society."[58]

SUMMARY

International businesses are playing a leading role in societies and the lives of people around the world. Serious social impacts of business operations need consideration by firms. If firms do not respond to these issues, governments will impose their own rules.

Today, a substantial transformation is characterized by the response of governments to the failures and weaknesses in the global economy and financial system that triggered the economic crisis in 2008. Policy and regulatory efforts to "reform" the system to correct mistakes and abuses that may have caused the crisis will have continuing major implications for the private sector in the coming years. We must appreciate that governments are playing a new and growing role in international business.

The size, scope, and power of global corporations have increased dramatically with globalization.

With such economic power comes greater expectations for corporate governance, responsibility, and ethics across many fronts from many stakeholder audiences. Businesses do not have impunity in the global economy.

Public trust in business may be seen as a measurement that corresponds to the willingness of societies to allow international firms greater leeway to do business. Generally, public trust in business is stronger when a greater number of people realize the benefits of business. The economic disruptions caused by the financial crisis and recession shook the level of trust in businesses severely in the developed economies.

International business in the twenty-first century requires visionary and responsible leadership to see and navigate the unfamiliar paths that a rapidly changing and interconnected environment presents.

Part of that is a responsibility of the company to act as a responsible citizen to satisfy the expectations of societies and governments.

CSR efforts by global corporations serve multiple purposes beyond the humanitarian and developmental goals set by the firms. Good citizenship programs empower the employees of companies to channel effectively their own desire to help local communities and to be proud representatives of the companies for which they work. When consumers and employees in host countries experience extraordinary citizenship efforts, it reflects well on both the companies and the home countries. Smart CSR programs are structured to create value and promote the strategic advantage of the firm as well as the communities in which they operate. Issues related to the environment make up perhaps the most important individual element of CSR. More of the leading global operations have begun to embrace sustainability issues not only to improve their reputation, but as a part of their core corporate strategy to improve efficiencies and even increase revenues.

Key Terms and Concepts

marketing dilemma
vampire marketing
The World Economic Forum
corporate social responsibility (CSR)
corporate citizenship
corporate philanthropy
sustainability
U.S. Chamber of Commerce
shared value
EU Ecolabel
Blue Angel Program

Review Questions

1. Why has trust in business dropped in developed countries but remains high in countries like China and India?
2. Identify three reasons why businesses should be concerned about carbon emissions.
3. Distinguish between corporate social responsibility and corporate philanthropy.
4. Why is sustainability a "perfect fit" for Caterpillar's international business strategy?

Critical Skill Builders

1. Are environmental labeling programs by governments and nongovernmental organizations beneficial to consumers? Should international businesses participate in these programs? Why or why not?
2. In teams, debate Milton Friedman's contention that the only responsibility of business is "to use it resources and engage in activities designed to increase its profits so long as it stays within the rules of the game."
3. Do global companies, like Apple and Nike, which work with contract manufacturing suppliers in other countries, have a responsibility for the labor and environmental practices of their suppliers?
4. Is the European Union's legislation to curb bankers' bonuses good for the people of Europe? Discuss the advantages and disadvantages of this move. Should the United Kingdom be concerned about the legislation's effects on its financial community?

On the Web

1. Identify ten non-European headquartered companies belonging to CSR Europe. Go to **http://www.csreurope.org/members.php**.

2. What are the key elements of the new banking regulatory reforms that are recommended as a part of Basel III developed by the Basel Committee on Banking Supervision? Refer to **http://www.bis.org/bcbs/basel3.htm**.

3. Which U.S. companies have been recently awarded the U.S. State Department American Corporate Excellence (ACE) award and the U.S. Chamber of Commerce's Business Civic Leadership Center (BCLC Best International Ambassador award? Refer to **http://www.state.gov/e/eb/ace/ and http://bclc.uschamber.com/citizens-awards**.

4. Identify a firm that proves its leadership in sustainability in an industry of your choice. For example, go to the sustainability reports on the web sites of leading global brewing companies and compare their metrics for important performance indicators.
   http://www.sustainabilityreport.heineken.com/
   http://www.ab-inbev.com/go/social_responsibility/global_citizenship_report
   http://www.millercoors.com/Great-Beer-Great-Responsibility/Home.aspx

Endnotes

1. Michael Czinkota and Charles Skuba, "The Two Faces of International Marketing," *Marketing Management*, Winter 2011, pp. 14, 15.
2. Pope Benedict XVI, "Blessed are the Peacemakers", January 1, 2013.
3. Jagdish Sheth and Rajendra Sisodia, *Does Marketing Need Reform: Fresh Perspectives on the Future*, M.E. Sharpe, 2006.
4. Charles J. Skuba, "Consumers can shine sunlight on exploitative vampire brands," Letter to the *Financial Times*, July 11, 2011.
5. Shahzeb Jillani, "Indian anger at Dow Olympics sponsorship," *BBC News*, August 8, 2011.
6. Michael Czinkota and Charles Skuba, "The Two Faces of International Marketing," *Marketing Management*, Winter 2011, pp. 14, 15.
7. **http://www.consumerfinance.gov/the-bureau/**, accessed June 6, 2013.
8. G20 Leaders Summit— Final Communiqué, November 3–4, 2011, pp 12–17, **http://www.g20.org/documents/#p2**, accessed June 6, 2013.
9. Communiqué, Meeting of Finance Ministers and Central Bank Governors, Washington, April 2013, **http://www.g20.org/documents/**, accessed June 6, 2013.
10. G20 Leaders Summit— Final Communiqué, November 3–4, 2011, pp. 20–21, **http://www.g20.org/documents/#p2**, accessed June 6, 2013.
11. Ibid, pp. 25–27.
12. The Coca-Cola Company, **http://www.thecoca-colacompany.com/ourcompany/index.html**, accessed January 27, 2012.
13. Procter & Gamble, **http://za.pg.com/about**, accessed January 27, 2012.
14. World Bank, Gross Domestic Product 2010, **http://siteresources.worldbank.org/DATASTATISTICS/Resources/GDP.pdf**; and Fortune Global 500 2011, **http://money.cnn.com/magazines/fortune/global500/2011/full_list/**, accessed January 27, 2012.
15. *Financial Times*, "Capitalism and its global malcontents," editorial, October 24, 2011.
16. 2010 Edelman Trust Barometer Executive Summary, **http://www.scribd.com/full/26268655?access_key=key-1ovbgbpawooot3hnsz3u**, accessed January 27, 2012.
17. 2013 Edelman Trust Barometer, **http://www.edelman.com/trust-downloads/global-results-2/**, accessed June 6, 2013.
18. 2012 Edelman Trust Barometer Executive Summary, **http://trust.edelman.com/trust-download/executive-summary/**, accessed June 6, 2013.
19. World Economic Forum, "Global Risks 2012", **http://www.weforum.org/issues/global-risks**, accessed January 27, 2012.
20. GE, **http://www.genewscenter.com/**, accessed June 6, 2013.

21. Siemens, **http://www.siemens.com/about/en/worldwide.htm**, accessed June 6, 2013.
22. Ibid., **http://www.siemens.com/about/en/values-vision-strategy/strategy.htm**, accessed June 6, 2013.
23. Ibid., **http://w3.siemens.com/topics/global/en/sustainable-cities/Pages/home.aspx**, accessed June 6, 2013.
24. Michael R. Czinkota and Charles J. Skuba, "A contextual analysis of legal systems and their impact on trade and foreign direct investment," *Journal of Business Research*, 2014.
25. Milton Friedman, "The Social Responsibility of Business Is to Increase Its Profits," *The New York Times Magazine*, September 13, 1970.
26. 2011 Edelman Trust Barometer, **http://www.edelman.com/trust/2011/**, accessed January 31, 2012.
27. The Carnegie Medal of Philanthropy, **www.carnegiemedals.org/**, accessed February 2, 2012.
28. 2011 Edelman Trust Barometer, **http://www.edelman.com/trust/2011/**, accessed January 31, 2012.
29. "Rethinking Corporate Social Responsibility," Fleishman-Hillard and the National Consumer League Study, Executive Summary, May 2007.
30. European Commission, **http://ec.europa.eu/enterprise/policies/sustainable-business/corporate-social-responsibility/index_en.htm**, accessed June 6, 2013.
31. Mike Esterl, "In This Picturesque Village, the Rent Hasn't Been Raised Since 1520," *The Wall Street Journal*, December 26, 2008.
32. The International Chamber of Commerce, "Business in society: Making a positive and responsible contribution," **www.iccwbo.org/Data/.../Nine-practical-steps-to-responsible-business**, accessed June 6, 2013.
33. CSR Europe, **http://www.csreurope.org/pages/en/about_us.html**, accessed February 2, 2012.
34. Ibid.
35. Chambers Ireland, **http://www.csrawards.ie/**, accessed June 6, 2013.
36. Council of British Chambers of Commerce in Europe, **http://www.cobcoe.eu/about/corporate-social-responsibility/humtraf/**, accessed June 6, 2013.
37. The International Chamber of Commerce, "Business in society: Making a positive and responsible contribution," **http://www.iccwbo.org/products-and-services/trade-facilitation/9-steps-to-responsible-business-conduct/**, accessed June 6, 2013.
38. Michael E. Porter and Mark R. Kramer, "Creating Shared Value," *Harvard Business Review*, January–February 2011.
39. Ibid.
40. Ibid.
41. Ibid.
42. 2012 Edelman Trust Barometer Executive Summary, **http://trust.edelman.com/trust-download/executive-summary/**, accessed June 7, 2013.
43. KPMG International Survey of Corporate Responsibility Reporting 2011, Executive Summary, p. 2.
44. Ibid.
45. Ibid.
46. Joao Almeida and Charles Skuba, Georgetown University research, May 2012.
47. Ibid
48. United Nations Brundtland Report, "Our Common Future," 1986, **http://www.un.org/en/globalissues/environment/**, accessed February 4, 2012.
49. Robert Gilman, "Sustainability: The State of the Movement," *In Context*, Spring 1990, p.10; **http://www.context.org/ICLIB/IC25/Gilman.htm**, accessed February 5, 2012.
50. United Nations Framework Convention on Climate Change, **http://unfccc.int/kyoto_protocol/items/2830.php**, accessed February 5, 2012.
51. Edward Wyatt, "Give up Familiar Light Bulb? Not without Fight, Some Say," *New York Times*, March 11, 2011.
52. Anne C. Mulkern, "U.S. Chamber, Renewable Groups Clash Over Ability to Meet Obama's Clean Energy Goal," *New York Times*, February 2, 2011.
53. McKinsey & Company, "2011 Global Survey Results— The Business of Sustainability," October 2011, **http://www.mckinsey.com/insights/energy_resources_materials/the_business_of_sustainability_mckinsey_global_survey_results**, accessed July 24, 2014.
54. Caterpillar, 2010 Sustainability Report, Chairman's Message.
55. Bryant Ott, "Time to Green Your Business," *Gallup Management Journal*, April 22, 2011, **http://gmj.gallup.com/content/147221/time-green-business.aspx**.
56. EU ENERGY STAR, **http://www.eu-energystar.org/en/index.html**, accessed June 7, 2013.
57. **http://www.blauer-engel.de/en/index.php**, accessed June 7, 2013.
58. McKinsey & Company, "2011 Global Survey Results—The Business of Sustainability."

PART 6

THE FUTURE

All global businesses face constantly changing world economic conditions. This is neither a new situation nor one to be feared because change provides the opportunity for new market positions to emerge and for managerial talent to improve the competitive position of the firm. Recognizing change and adapting creatively to new situations are the most important tasks of the global executives, as Part 6 will show.

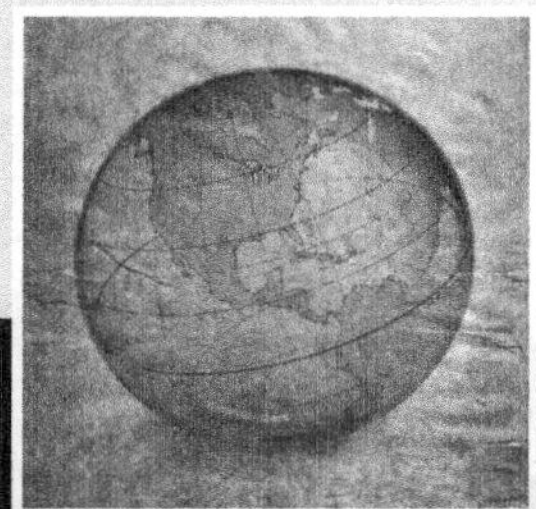

CHAPTER 15

THE FUTURE

No More Global Currency

"Euros only," blared the headlines. Supermodel Gisele Buendchen supposedly accepted payment only in euro. Robert Chu, owner of East Village Wines in New York told reporters that many people come to his store trying to pay in euro—and he was happy to accept them. European tourists increasingly come to the United States for extended shopping sprees—the low dollar value means huge discounts compared to their home markets. Some stores, like Billy's Antique & Props on East Houston Street in Manhattan, even had signs in their windows that read "Euros Only." But this was short lived.

Back in 2008, during the dark time of the U.S. economy, when a euro was worth almost $1.50, storeowners were increasingly willing to accept the euro. Then, the cost of exchanging the currency was well worth the hassle. Today, though, with the shaky European economy, the tables have turned.

Balthazar, a famous brunch locale for European tourists in SoHo did not accept the euro then nor does it today. With its large menu offerings, it would be difficult to convert each item into various currencies, especially with the fluctuating exchange rates. The same goes for the home-furnishing store Ankasa, which claims, "We accept dollars only," and if people insist on euros "we would probably send them down the street to the bank." So, instead of one global currency, both dollars and euros are desirable.

SOURCES: Angela Moore, "NYC Stores Begin Accepting Euro," *Reuters*, February 8, 2008; Robin Shulman, "New York Merchants Embrace Euro," *The Washington Post*, February 25, 2008, A3; Connor Adams Sheets, "Manhattan Small Businesses Move Away From Accepting Euro As Payment," *International Business Times*, March 27, 2013, Accessed October 23, 2013.

LEARNING OUTCOMES

To understand trends in the political environment that change the shape of global competition

To learn how changes in the global financial environment affect firms both internationally and domestically

To appreciate how the ever-accelerating pace of technology drives change

To learn how governments can trigger changes that affect trade relations

To consider how firms must prepare to shift their products, pricing, distribution, and communications strategies to keep pace with global change

To learn about different career opportunities in global business

As You Read This Chapter

1. Discuss the many concerns that CEOs face in a global marketplace.

In today's complex business environment, changes occur more frequently and more rapidly, and they have a more severe impact than ever before. Due to growing real-time access to knowledge about customers, suppliers, and competitors, the global business environment is increasingly characterized by high speed bordering on instantaneity.[1] As a consequence, the past has lost much of its value as a predictor of the future. What occurs today may not only be altered in short order but be completely overturned or reversed. For example, political stability in a country can be disrupted over the course of just a few months. A major, sudden decline in world stock markets leaves corporations, investors, and consumers with strong feelings of uncertainty. Currency declines result in an entirely new business climate for global suppliers and their customers and can have quite unexpected effects, as the opening vignette showed.

This chapter will discuss possible future developments in the global business environment, highlight the implications of the changes for international business management, and offer suggestions for a creative response to the changes. The chapter also will explore the meaning of strategic changes as they relate to career choice and career path alternatives in global business.

The Global Business Environment

This section analyzes the global business environment by looking at political, financial, societal, and technological conditions of change and providing a glimpse of possible future developments, as envisioned by an international panel of experts.[2]

The Political Environment

The global political environment is undergoing a substantial transformation characterized by the reshaping of existing political blocs, the formation of new groupings, and the breakup of old coalitions.

Planned Versus Market Economies

Political, economic, and military competition between the United States and the Soviet Union shaped the second half of the last century, which resulted in the creation of two virtually separate economic systems. This key adversarial posture has now largely disappeared, with market-based economic thinking emerging as the frontrunner. Virtually all of the former centrally planned economies are undergoing a transition with the goal of becoming market-oriented.

Global business has made important contributions to this transition process. Trade and investment have offered the populace in these nations a new perspective, new choices, new jobs, and new alternatives for marketing their products and services. At the same time, the bringing together of two separate economic and business systems has resulted in new and sometimes devastating competition, a loss of government-ordained trade relationships, and substantial dislocations and pain during the adjustment process.

Many business activities will be subject to regional economic and political instability, increasing the risk of international business partners. To encourage progress toward the institution of market-based economies, it will be important to develop institutions and processes internally, to assure domestic and foreign investors of protection from public and private corruption, and to establish respect for property rights and contractual arrangements.

The North-South Relationship

The distinction between developed and less developed countries (LDCs) is unlikely to change. The ongoing disparity between developed and developing nations is likely to be based, in part, on continuing debt burdens and problems with satisfying basic needs. As a result, political uncertainty may well result in increased polarization between the haves and have-nots, with growing potential for political and economic conflict. Demands for political solutions to economic problems are likely to increase. According to the United Nations, 2.6 billion people live on less than $2 per day.[3]

The developing countries of Africa continue as a relatively "cool" region for global business purposes. Political instability and the resulting inability of many African firms to be consistent trading partners are the key reasons for such a pessimistic view. In light of global competition for investment capital, these drawbacks are instrumental in keeping both investment and trade at a trickle. Corporations are unlikely to address this starvation for funds. Periodic surges in the social conscience of industrialized nations may result in targeted investments by governments, multilateral institutions, and nongovernmental organizations (NGOs), but these funds are likely to be insufficient for a transformation of the economic future of the region. Debt forgiveness for heavily burdened nations has helped clean the slate of past mistakes. Special provisions granting these nations easier access to developed country markets will make a marginal difference in export performance. Most important, however, is internal reform and the benchmarking of production so that competitive products and services can be offered. It would appear unlikely that government assistance alone can overcome market reluctance. An emphasis on education, training, and the development of a supportive infrastructure is crucial because that is where the investments and jobs go.[4] It is not enough to expect a rising tide to raise all boats. Significant effort must also be expended to ensure the seaworthiness of the boat, the functioning of its sails, and the capability of its crew. Market-oriented performance will be critical to success in the longer run.

ENVIRONMENTAL PROTECTION
Actions taken by governments to ensure survival of natural resources

The issue of **environmental protection** will also be a major force shaping the relationship between the developed and the developing world. In light of the need and desire for economic growth, however, industrializing nations may strongly disagree as to what approaches to take. Of key concern will be the answer to the question: Who pays? For example, nations that intend to pursue all options for further economic progress will find it difficult to accept simply placing large areas of land out of bounds for development. Corporations, in turn, are likely to be more involved in protective measures if they are aware of their constituents' expectations and the repercussions of not meeting them. Corporations recognize that by being environmentally responsible, a company can build trust and improve its image—therefore becoming more competitive. For example, it was early in the 1990s that the first annual corporate environmental report was published; now more than 2,000 companies publish such reports.[5]

In light of divergent trends, three possible scenarios emerge. One scenario is that of continued global cooperation. The developed countries could relinquish part of their economic power to less-developed ones, thus contributing actively to their economic growth through a sharing of resources and technology. Although such cross-subsidization will be useful and necessary for the development of LDCs, it may reduce the rate of growth of the standard of living in the more developed countries. It would, however, increase trade flows between developed and less-developed countries and precipitate the emergence of new international business opportunities.

A second scenario is that of confrontation. Because of an unwillingness to share resources and technology sufficiently (or excessively, depending on the point of view), the developing and the developed areas of the world may become increasingly hostile toward one another. As a result, the volume of international business, both by mandate of governments and by choice of the private sector, could be severely reduced.

A third scenario is that of **isolationism**. Although developing and developed nations may cooperate some, both groups, in order to achieve their domestic and international goals, may choose to remain economically isolated. This alternative may be particularly attractive if each region believes that it faces unique problems and therefore must seek its own solutions.

ISOLATIONISM
A policy that minimizes the economic integration between nations

Emerging Markets

Much of the growth of the global economy will be fueled by the emerging markets of the Asia-Pacific region, particularly China and India. For the industrialized nations, this development will offer a significant opportunity for exports and investment, but it will also diminish, in the longer term, the basis for their status and influence in the world economy. Although the nations in the region are likely to collaborate, they are not expected to form a bloc of the same type as the European Union or NAFTA. Rather, their relationship is likely to be defined in terms of trade and investment flows (e.g., Japan) and social contacts (e.g., the Chinese business community).

China's rapid emergence is particularly significant. Companies already present in China and those willing to make major investments there are likely to be the main beneficiaries of growth. Long-term commitment, willingness to transfer technology, and an ability to partner either with local firms through joint ventures or with overseas Chinese-run firms are considered crucial for success. The strategic impact of Chinese trade participation is also likely to change. China is likely to assume a much higher profile in its trading activities. For example, rather than be the supplier of goods that are marketed internationally by others under a Japanese or U.S. label, Chinese firms will increasingly develop their own brand names and fight for their own name recognition, customer loyalty, and market share.[6]

Among the other promising emerging markets are Korea and India. Korea could emerge as a participant in worldwide competition, whereas the size of India's potential market could make it important. Korean firms must still improve their ability to adopt a global mind-set. Some experts are also concerned about the chaebols' (a South Korean form of business conglomerate) status as Korea becomes democratized. In addition, the possible impact of the reunification of the Korean peninsula on the country's globalization efforts must be taken into account.

With the considerable liberalization that took place in India, many expect it to offer major international marketing opportunities because of its size, its significant natural wealth, and its large, highly educated middle class. Although many experts believe that political conflict (both domestic and regional), nationalism, and class structure may temper the ability of Indian companies to emerge as a worldwide competitive force, strong agreement exists that India's disproportionately large and specialized workforce in engineering and computer sciences makes the nation a power to be reckoned with.

Overall, the growth potential of these emerging economies may be threatened by uncertainty in terms of international relations and domestic policies, as well as social and political dimensions, particularly those pertaining to income distribution. Concerns also exist about infrastructural inadequacies, both physical—such as transportation—and societal— such as legal systems. The consensus of experts is, however, that growth in these countries will be significant.

The Effects of Population Shifts

The population discrepancy between the less-developed nations and the industrialized countries will continue to increase. In the industrialized world, a population increase will become a national priority, given the fact that in many countries, particularly in Western Europe, the population is shrinking. The shrinkage may lead to labor shortages, and major societal difficulties may result when fewer workers have to provide for a larger elderly population.[7]

POPULATION STABILIZATION

An attempt to control rapid increases in a nation's inhabitants

In the developing world, **population stabilization** will continue to be one of the major challenges of governmental policy. In spite of well-intentioned economic planning, continued rapid increases in population will make it more difficult to ensure that the pace of economic development exceeds population growth. If the standard of living of a nation is determined by dividing the GNP by its population, any increase in the denominator will require equal increases in the numerator to maintain the standard of living. With an annual increase in the world population of 100 million people, the task is daunting. It becomes even more complex when one considers that within countries with high population increases, large migration flows take place from rural to urban areas. As a result, by the end of this decade, most of the world's ten largest metropolitan areas will be in the developing world.[8] Within those areas, a large youth cohort may reach adulthood too quickly for the government to adapt. Problems are likely to emerge if society is unable to fulfill basic needs such as employment, housing, and education for large groups.[9]

FINANCIAL ENVIRONMENT

Debt constraints and low commodity prices create slow growth prospects for many developing countries. These countries will be forced to reduce their levels of imports and to exert more pressure on industrialized nations to open up their markets. Even if the markets are opened, however, demand for most primary products will be far lower than supply. Ensuing competition for market share will therefore continue to depress prices.

Developed nations have a strong incentive to help the debtor nations. The incentive consists of national security concerns and the market opportunities that economically healthy developing countries can offer. As a result, industrialized nations may very well find that funds transfers to debtor nations, accompanied by debt-relief measures such as debt forgiveness, are necessary to achieve economic stimulation at home.

The dollar will remain one of the major international currencies, with little probability of gold returning to its former status in the near future. However, some international transaction volume, in both trade and finance, is increasingly likely to be denominated in non-dollar terms, particularly using the euro. The system of floating currencies will likely continue, with occasional attempts by nations to manage exchange-rate relationships or at least reduce the volatility of swings in currency values. Yet, given the vast flows of financial resources across borders, it would appear that market forces, rather than government action, will be the key determinant of a currency's value. Therefore, factors such as investor trust, economic conditions, earnings perceptions, and political stability are likely to have a much greater effect on the international value of currencies than domestic monetary and fiscal experimentation.

Given the close links among financial markets, shocks in one market will quickly translate into rapid shifts in others and could easily overpower the financial resources of individual governments. Even if governments should decide to pursue closely coordinated fiscal and monetary policies, they are unlikely to be able to negate long-term market effects in response to changes in economic fundamentals.

Culture Clues In China, business appointments need to be made in advance. The more important the person, the more lead time is required. The Chinese do not like to conduct business over the telephone and generally do not take cold calls. Punctuality is considered a sign of courtesy, but arriving up to 10 or 15 minutes late is acceptable. Lateness does, however, require an apology.

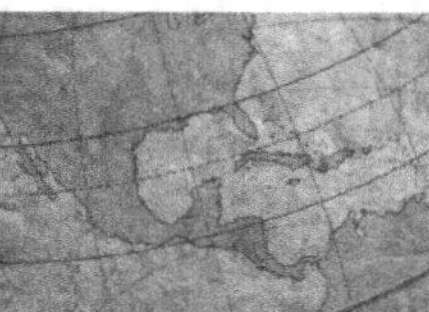

A looming concern in the international financial environment will be the **international debt load** of the United States. Both domestically and internationally, the nation is incurring debt that would have been inconceivable only a few decades ago.

INTERNATIONAL DEBT LOAD
Total accumulated, negative net investment position of a nation

In 1985, the United States became a net negative investor internationally. The nation entered the new century with an international debt burden of more than $2 trillion. This debt level makes the United States the largest debtor nation in the world, owing more to other nations than all the developing nations combined. Others argue against an unsustainable scenario, believing that special mitigating circumstances let the United States tolerate this burden, such as the fact that most of the debts are denominated in U.S. dollars and that, even at such a large debt volume, U.S. debt-service requirements are only a relatively small portion of GNP.[10] Yet this accumulation of foreign debt may very well introduce entirely new dimensions into the international business relationships of individuals and nations. Once debt has reached a certain level, the creditor, as well as the debtor, is hostage to the loans. The U.S. goods and services balance of payments deficit nearly doubled from 2000 to 2007, increasing from $377 billion in 2000 to $699 billion in 2007.[11] Since then, this deficit has been working its way back down, made evident by the 2012 deficit of $535 billion, as seen in Figure 15.1.

As of October 30, 2013, the total U.S. national debt passed $17 trillion, a near doubling from 2008's value of $10.6 trillion. However, while the public tends to fixate on this amount, it overlooks the government's long-term unfunded liabilities, which amounted to $126 trillion in late 2013. The key drivers of this large sum are the two entitlement programs the United States holds very dear, Social Security and Medicare.[12]

Yet, even with these large sums of debt, the United States government remains an attractive investment for foreigners, as seen in Figure 15.2. Concern, though, does exist about the volatility of the dollar and its status as the world's reserve currency. According to a survey by the McKinsey Global Institute, less than 20 percent of surveyed business executives expect the dollar to be the dominant global reserve currency by 2025.[13]

However, borrowing from abroad can lead to greater susceptibility to international market fluctuations and a variety of associated risks. Former Federal Reserve chairman Ben Bernanke

FIGURE 15.1 U.S. International Trade in Goods and Services
Balance of Payment Goods and Services: United States, Jan. 2000 to Dec. 2012

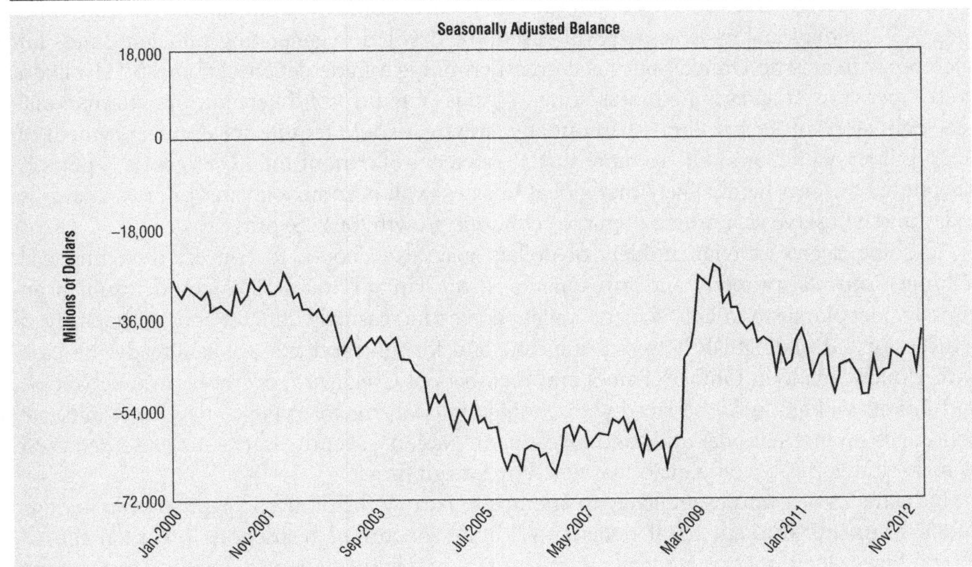

SOURCE: **www.census.gov**. Accessed October 24, 2013.

FIGURE 15.2 Foreign Ownership of U.S. Treasuries

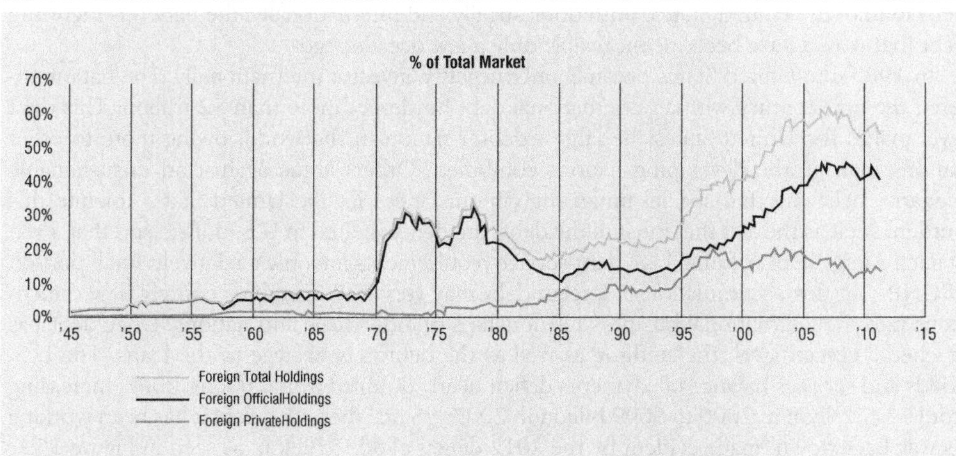

SOURCE: U.S. International Trade in Goods and Services Balance of Payment Goods and Services: United States 1945 to 2012, accessed November 5, 2013.

stated that the U.S. current account deficit is certainly not sustainable at its current level.[14] The primary reason for concern is that a rapid capital outflow from the United States, similar to a bank run on a global scale, could lead to a serious financial crisis or "hard landing" for the U.S. economy. If central banks and sovereign wealth funds in the Middle East and Asia were to dispose of their huge dollar reserves because of fear of capital losses from dollar depreciation, the results for the American currency and economy could be very difficult. The dollar has been weakening for a while, which could compromise the ability of the United States to borrow in order to finance its trade deficit. Yet, it is important to keep the value of the dollar in perspective. Though lately the euro has been stronger in relation to the U.S. dollar, the EU is very much concerned about long-term disinflation forces. These effects are already visible in Greece because smaller countries are more susceptible to deflation.[15]

Because foreign creditors expect a return on their investment, a substantial portion of future U.S. international trade activity will have to be devoted to generating sufficient funds for such repayment. The United States is currently running a trade deficit of about $741 billion dollars per year. At an assumed interest rate (or rate of return) of 5 percent, the international U.S. debt stock of $4.5 trillion—without any growth—would require the annual payment of $225 billion, which amounts to more than 14 percent of current total U.S. goods exports.[16] Therefore, it seems highly likely that global business will become a greater priority than it is today and will serve as a source of major economic growth for U.S. firms.

To some degree, foreign holders of dollars may also choose to convert their financial holdings into real property and investments in the United States. This could result in an entirely new pluralism in U.S. society. It will become increasingly difficult and, perhaps, even unnecessary to distinguish between domestic and foreign products—as is already the case with Hondas made in Ohio. Senators and members of Congress, governors, municipalities, and unions will gradually be faced with conflicting concerns in trying to develop a national consensus on international trade and investment. National security issues may also be raised as major industries become majority-owned by foreign firms.

Industrialized countries are likely to attempt to narrow the domestic gap between savings and investments through fiscal policies. Without concurrent restrictions on international capital flows, such policies are likely to meet with only limited success. Lending institutions can be expected to become more conservative in their financing, a move that may hit smaller firms and developing countries the hardest. At the same time, the entire financial sector is likely to face continuous integration, ongoing bank acquisitions, and a reduction in financial intermediaries. Large customers will be able to assert their independence by the increasing ability to present their financial needs globally and directly to financial markets and obtain better access to financial products and providers.

A Changing Growth Perspective

There may well be a reconsideration of the economic growth construct, particularly regarding growth expectations. We have come to the point where mere stability and constancy are seen as wrong and as indicative of "falling behind." Imagine an executive telling his shareholders that he wants his company's sales to remain stable—most analysts would probably run him over on their way to other firms. But is not stability in itself worthwhile and good? What ever happened to catching one's breath?

We are all familiar with the phrase "getting ready (or saving) for a rainy day." There is no implication that temporary setbacks are fatal. Rather, there is implied an acceptance, forged from experience with Mother Nature, that there are seasons and that life has its ups and downs.

Even eagles occasionally descend to lower heights so that they can catch an updraft and soar again. There is nothing to be ashamed of if resources have to be rearranged and if one accepts that not everything is linear. It may well emerge that growth, particularly on a global level, is increasingly seen in the context of the angles on a protractor: Growth does not always have to take place at all degrees, on all levels, and simultaneously because there are many different areas to grow.

Technological Environment

The Internet

The concept of the global village is commonly accepted today and indicates the importance of communication. Worldwide, the estimated number of people online in June 2012 was 2.405 billion, an almost sixfold increase since 2000. Asia has the highest number of Internet users, with 1.076 billion (45 percent of total). A persistent digital gap exists around the world, with Africa accounting for only 3.4 percent of Internet users, despite the fact that it accounts for 14.2 percent of the world's population. However, as Figure 15.3 shows, the gap is closing. The number of Internet users in Africa has grown 900 percent during the past seven years. Both the private and public sectors make heavy use of the Internet and expand into new activities. Almost all business conducted by the cabinet of the Slovenian government, for example, is on the Web. The country's fifteen cabinet members receive government business over a secure system, allowing politicians to discuss and vote on issues online.[17]

For both consumer services and business-to-business relations, the Internet is democratizing global business. It has made it easier for new global retail brands—like Amazon.com and eBay.com—to emerge. The Internet is also helping specialists like Australia's high-sensitivity hearing-aids manufacturer, Cochlear, to reach target customers around the world without having to invest in a distribution network in each country. The ability to reach a worldwide audience economically over the Internet spells success for niche marketers, who could never make money by just servicing their niches in the domestic market. The Internet also allows customers, especially those in emerging markets, to access global brands at more competitive prices than those offered by exclusive national distributors.

FIGURE 15.3 Cost of Business Travel to International Cities

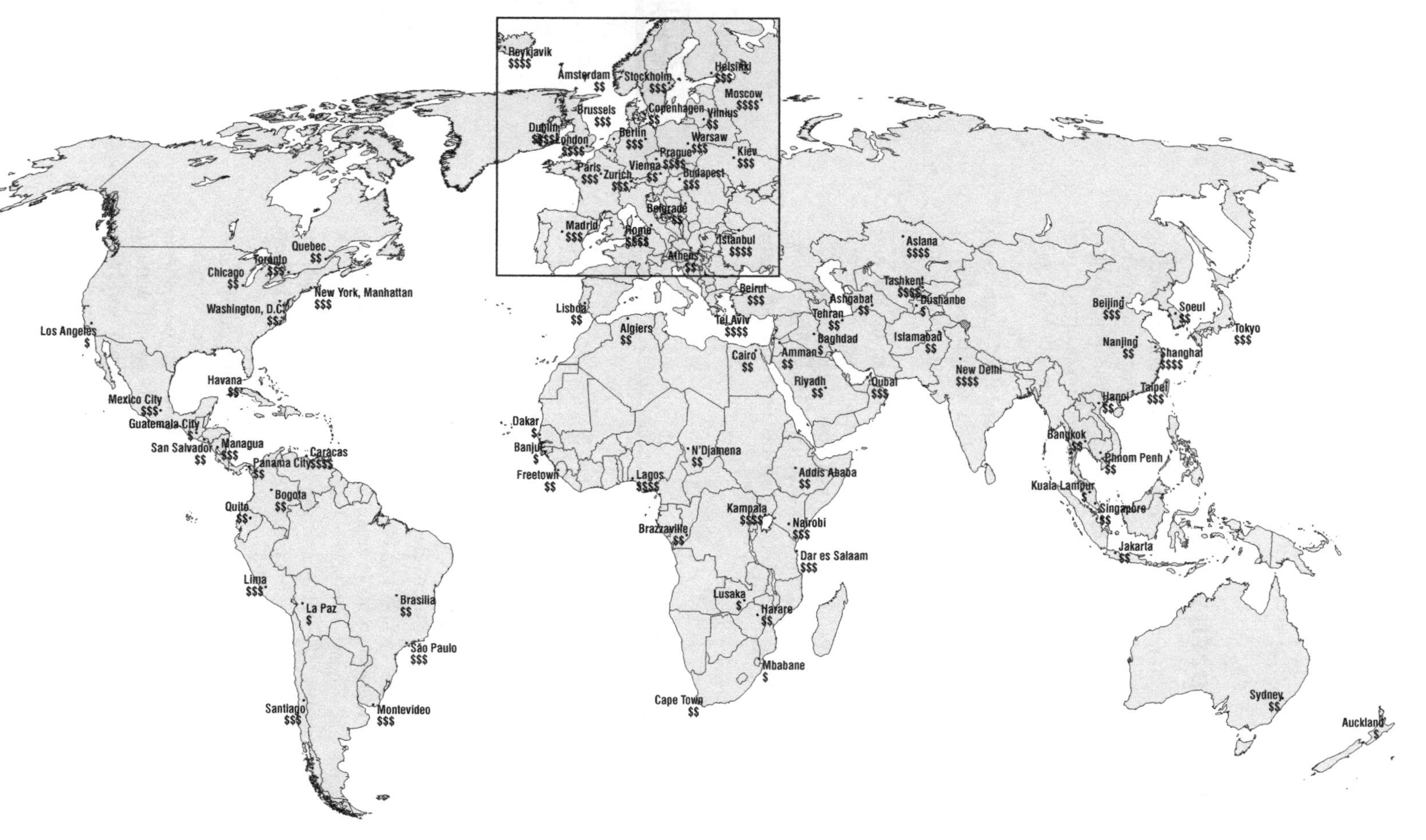

SOURCE: U.S. Department of State

Starting a new business will be much easier, allowing a far greater number of suppliers to enter a market. Small and medium-sized enterprises, as well as large multinational corporations, will now be full participants in the global marketplace. Businesses in developing countries can now overcome many of the obstacles of infrastructure and transport that limited their economic potential in the past. The global services economy will be a knowledge-based economy, and its most precious resource will be information and ideas. Unlike the classical factors of production—land, labor, and capital—information and knowledge are not bound to any region or country but are almost infinitely mobile and infinitely capable of expansion. This wide availability, of course, also brings new risks to firms. For example, one complaint can easily be developed into millions of complaints by using the Internet. Also of great impact on product marketing and customer feedback is the increasingly popular blogosphere—a new world of online journalism, where everyone with a computer is a potential critic or advertising target. The greater reach also makes firms subject to much more scrutiny and customer response on a global scale. Overall, as World View: Technology Is Not Always the Best Solution explains, technological advances offer companies, large and small, exciting new opportunities to conduct business on a global scale.

High technology will also be one of the more volatile and controversial areas of economic activity internationally. Developments in biotechnology are already transforming agriculture, medicine, and chemistry. Genetically engineered foods, patient-specific pharmaceuticals, gene therapy, and even genetically engineered organs are on the horizon. Innovations such as these will change what we eat, how we treat illness, and how we grow as a civilization.[18] However, skepticism about such technological innovations is rampant. In many instances, people are opposed to such changes for religious or cultural reasons or simply because they do not want to be exposed to such "artificial" products. Achieving agreement on what constitutes safe products and procedures, of defining the border between what is natural and what is not, will constitute one of the great areas of debate in the years to come. This is evident in the continuing debate over the relative safety of milk and meat from cloned animals.[19] Firms and their managers must remain keenly aware of popular perceptions and misperceptions and of changing government policies and politics in order to remain successful participants in markets.

Data and Information

Even though a greater diversification of information sources may typically provide for better knowledge evolution, there is an expectation of fewer data sources offering an increasingly large quantity of data, be it due to mergers, cost cutting, or a limited user willingness to pay. Such development is likely to affect accuracy and reliability—making data use heavily trust-dependent. To a growing degree, data users may demand more insights into the origin of information in order to gauge its believability. Just as butchers increasingly are expected to label the meat they sell with its precise origins (obtained from Farmer Joseph Smolensk, 5 km from here), information providers may need to offer data locale and source of origin in order to achieve trustworthiness. Under such conditions, the locality of data can be systematically used to enhance credibility—for example, through increased use of local debt-rating agencies.

Due to more transparent sourcing, firms and individuals will be less willing to offer information. Nebulous laws and restrictions increase the threat of lawsuits. Also, the gains from free information, that have greatly helped businesses and individuals in the last decade, are likely to shrink.

There may be a tendency toward "organic" data—unaltered by manipulation or interpretation. Another alternative may be "comparative" data sets, which, on an ongoing basis, provide multi-source perspectives. In addition, quantitative data are likely to be combined increasingly with qualitative information, resulting in a diagnostic perspective that permits

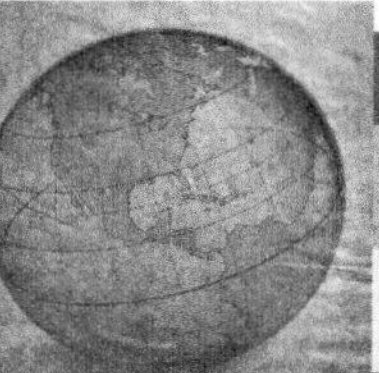

WORLD VIEW

Technology Is Not Always the Best Solution

When a renegade programmer for the National Security Agency revealed the agency's spy programs in 2013, individuals from all over the world commented on the matter. The leaked NSA documents allowed the public to know that not only are the phones and e-mail traffic of average Americans under surveillance but so are top international officials!

German Chancellor Angela Merkel has been the most vocal about this issue. Historically, the German people have often been under surveillance by their government. This makes wiretapping a very controversial issue. It brings back parallels to the Nazi and Stasi regimes and raises the importance of trust in today's society.

However, not all top government officials around the world are equally exposed to wiretapping from the United States. Indian Prime Minister Manmohan Singh takes special pride in this matter. He is arguably the one of the last remaining top officials not to have a private cell phone. He prefers to talk the "old-fashioned way," namely through landlines. This in spite of the *Financial Times* report that India is "a country with more mobile phones than toilets."

The prime minister's limited use of technology does not stop with mobile devices. He also does not have a personal e-mail address. It may seem as if he is purposely refraining from using easily hacked technology. But Singh's office runs a Twitter account for him in addition to various other job-related sites. It is only in his personal life that he has chosen not to have access to the new world of technology. He is therefore one of the few leading politicians who can claim not being affected by the NSA's surveillance programs. The issue itself certainly remains controversial as the Quick Take on chicken and the NSA shows.

SOURCES: "Singh: No email, no smartphone, no worries," *Financial Times*, Wednesday October 30, 2013; Charles Lane, "NSA's spying humiliates Germany, again," *Washington Post* Opinions, **http://www.washingtonpost.com/opinions/charles-lane-nsas-spying-humiliates-germany-again/2013/11/04/f13eba14-456d-11e3-b6f8-3782ff6cb769_story.html**, November 4, 2013, accessed April 19, 2014; Anton Trioanovski, Sioban Gorman, and Harriet Torry, "European Leaders Accuse U.S. of Violating Trust," **http://online.wsj.com/news/articles/SB10001424052702304799404579154950188871722?KEYWORDS=NSA+merkel**, October 24, 2013, accessed November 1, 2013.

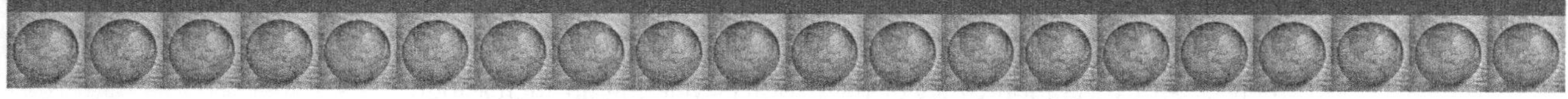

for a helicoptered perspective while holding the hand of the patient. Once data pass the trust threshold, they can then be used in a much more aggressive and insightful way, going far beyond the traditional retrospective use of statistics to look at history, toward making trends and prognoses for the future.

Advancements in information technology and convergence of new technologies will increasingly allow any new equipment to be more sophisticated and able to perform more functions with high performance at low cost. Even though companies will be willing to adopt these new technologies faster than ever before, doing so will only provide a competitive edge if it is done with ease of use and customer friendliness in mind. Whereas youth markets will be quick to use new capabilities, more mature buyers will be reluctant to invest in products that require a high degree of additional learning. Excelling in technology alone has no intrinsic value. It is the application of technology to satisfy human needs and values, at a profit, that counts.

Global Trade Relations and Government Policy

In spite of the World Trade Organization (WTO), ongoing major imbalances in trade flows will tempt nations to apply their own national trade remedies, particularly in the anti-dumping field. Even though WTO rules permit retaliation against unfair trade practices, such actions would only result in an ever-increasing spiral of adverse trade relations.

A key question will be whether nations are willing to abrogate some of their sovereignty, even during difficult economic times. An affirmative answer will strengthen the multilateral trade system and enhance the flow of trade. However, if key trading nations resort to the development of insidious nontariff barriers, unilateral actions, and bilateral negotiations, protectionism will increase on a global scale, and the volume of international trade is likely to decline. The danger is real, and it is here that international business academics are, or should be, the guardians who separate fact from fiction in international trade policy discussions. Qualified not by weight of office but by expertise, international business experts are the indirect guarantors of and guides toward free and open markets. Without their input and impact, public apathy and ignorance may well result in missteps in trade policy.[20]

The efforts of governments to achieve self-sufficiency in economic sectors, particularly in agriculture and heavy industries, have ensured the creation of long-term, worldwide oversupply of some commodities and products, many of which, historically, had been traded widely. As a result, after some period of intense market-share competition aided by subsidies and governmental support, a gradual and painful restructuring of these economic sectors will have to take place. This will be particularly true for agricultural cash crops, such as wheat, corn, and dairy products, and industrial products, such as steel, chemicals, and automobiles.

Government Policy

International trade activity now affects domestic policy more than ever. For example, trade flows can cause major structural shifts in employment. Links between industries spread these effects throughout the economy. Fewer domestically produced automobiles will affect the activities of the steel industry. Shifts in the sourcing of textiles will affect the cotton industry. Global productivity gains and competitive pressures will force many industries to restructure their activities. In such circumstances, industries are likely to ask their governments to help in their restructuring efforts. Often, such assistance includes a built-in tendency toward protectionist action.

Restructuring is not necessarily negative. For example, since 1900, U.S. farm employment has dropped from more than 40 percent of the population to less than 3 percent.[21] Yet today, the U.S. farm industry feeds more than 304 million people in the United States and still produces large surpluses.[22] A restructuring of industries can greatly increase productivity and provide the opportunity for resource reallocation to emerging sectors of an economy.

Governments cannot be expected, for the sake of the theoretical ideal of "free trade," to sit back and watch the effects of deindustrialization on their countries. The most that can be expected is that they will permit an open-market orientation subject to the needs of domestic policy. Even an open-market orientation will be maintained only if governments can provide reasonable assurances to their own firms and citizens that the openness applies to foreign markets as well. Therefore, unfair trade practices, such as governmental subsidization, dumping, and industrial targeting, will be examined more closely, and retaliation for such activities is likely to be swift and harsh.

Increasingly, governments will need to coordinate policies that affect the international business environment. The development of international indexes and **trigger mechanisms**,

TRIGGER MECHANISMS
Specific acts or stimuli that set off reactions

which precipitate government action at predetermined intervention points, will be a useful step in that direction. Yet, for them to be effective, governments will need to muster the political fortitude to implement the policies necessary for cooperation. For example, international monetary cooperation will work in the long term only if domestic fiscal policies are responsive to the achievement of the coordinated goals.

At the same time as the need for collaboration among governments grows, it will become more difficult to achieve a consensus. As the aftermath of September 11, 2001, is brought to the fore, economic security and national security are often seen as competing with each other, rather than as complementary dimensions of national welfare that can operate in parallel and, to some degree, even be traded off against one another. Unless a new, key, common sense of purpose can be found by governments, collaborative approaches and long-term alliances will become increasingly difficult.

Governmental policymakers must take into account the international repercussions of domestic legislation. For example, in imposing a special surcharge tax on the chemical industry, designed to provide for the cleanup of toxic waste products, they need to consider its repercussions on the international competitiveness of the chemical industry. Similarly, current laws, such as antitrust legislation, need to be reviewed if the laws hinder the global competitiveness of domestic firms.

Environment, Conservation, and Sustainability

China will demonstrate a lack of concern toward the environment, even though environmental problems will have a major effect on its ability to compete as a global manufacturing center. Medical, environmental, and other social costs will dramatically reduce the advantages of firms to manufacture in China—therefore leading to a move of foreign direct investment (FDI) to other locations, including the United States and Europe.

One consequence of China's and India's rapid growth will be an ongoing depletion of natural resources. Aspirations for economic progress and better lifestyles will cause shortages in natural resources. As a consequence, the sourcing and controlling of important raw materials will be a key strategic issue, often leading to preferential bilateral agreements, perhaps even in contradiction to multilateral arrangements. Governments will attempt to put more land into grain production and also use tools such as subsidies and price controls. Scarcity will also drive up the price of consumer alcohol. Protection of materials within society from theft will become a key issue (e.g., cutting electrical wires to steal copper). Recycling and recovery will grow as vital business opportunities. Farming will become highly attractive and profitable again, as fuel production from food accelerates.

The global shortage of potable water will be rediscovered as a key issue and a key constraint on global advancement and well-being. Government investments in desalination and reverse osmosis technologies will increase, as will emphasis on water conservation.

In light of public concern about climate change, there will be growing preference for energy-saving technologies and a reduction and limit to energy use. A stream of scientific and nonscientific proof will be offered for global warming, with any unusual natural phenomenon being blamed for global warming. Public impressions and perceptions will lead to changes in living patterns—for example, the population of arid and hot climate areas may well shift due

Culture Clues In India, confusion often arises because of the reluctance of people to say "no." The Indian culture has a general belief that telling someone "no" is just too unkind. People will go to great extremes to avoid saying "no," even to a simple request. For example, if you ask someone for directions, whether they know the way or not, they do not want to disappoint you and may send you off in the wrong direction entirely!

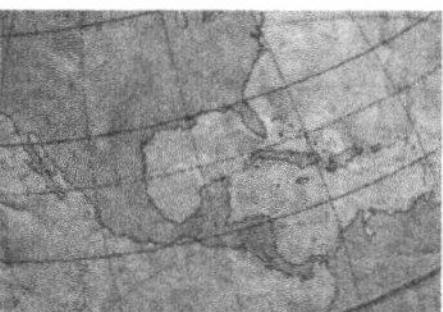

WORLD VIEW

Of Chicken Slaughter and NSA Wiretaps: Do We Really Want to Know?

On October 29, 2013, the *Washington Post* reported on the inhumane treatment of poultry on the processing line. Normally, the heads of birds are electrocuted first, and then their necks are cut, followed by scalding water and a defeathering process. However, 1 percent of the time this goes amiss, and these birds survive until they enter the boiling water. Almost a million chicken a year are alive when dunked into scalding water.

Clearly, this article appeals to the emotions of the *Post's* readers. Some believe this inappropriate chicken mortality to be a drastic case of "inhumane" animal killings. But in reality, chicken deaths are not foremost on our minds. After all, chicken are for eating and appear to us mostly in the form of nuggets or other compressed versions. How many of us have seen live chickens apart from those on the chicken retrieval trucks? They have to die somehow and, for many of us, are not marked by particular attention or friendship.

Take the example of the lobster. If you go to a top of the line seafood restaurant, typically you are given the option to pick out your personal lobster, live from the tank. Before it makes its way onto your plate, it will be dropped into boiling water, where, after some frantic clawing against the pot with its claws, it will die—or better—be prepared for you. Of course, lobsters cannot neigh or bark, and we've always had a certain fear of being attacked by their claws—so there is not too much concern.

Think about the oceans: If tuna fishermen catch some dolphins on the side and they die, we are most unhappy—we even require "dolphin safe" tuna meals, if they are to come to the United States. We mourn the wounded and grieve the injuries of dolphins because we have all seen *Flipper* (what a cute creature). At the same time, we fear and resent the great white shark, which is much more endangered than dolphins. But we all remember *Jaws* and know what that fish is after.

Back to the chicken: 50 years ago, you could pick out your chicken at the market where it was beheaded in front of you. The bird would run around headless until it eventually died from blood loss. At that time, all you were worried about was dinner on your plate.

The deeper focus of this whole matter is that sometimes too much information is not seen as helpful. Ultimately, we do not want to know nor do we sufficiently care about the process of how our poultry is slaughtered. As long as the bird is sufficiently cleaned and later cooked, we will not make a fuss. It will taste the same in the end and serve the same purpose of filling our stomachs.

This same procedure and ideal can be applied to the recent NSA accusations of the United States spying on foreign nations' top officials. We simply prefer not to know, and we think that foreign dignitaries should not know either, nor should they worry. Naturally, we all assumed that such spying occurred on some level, given the advances in technology, in addition to national security purposes. The time when gentlemen did not read other gentlemen's mail has long passed. We know what is needed, and we do what needs to be done. Therefore, the question remains, were we really that surprised?

That is what chickens have in common with the NSA. As long as they give us a good product at the end, it is probably best not to discuss the process that leads to the product. After all, we are all friends.

SOURCES: Kimberly Kindy, "USDA plan to speed up poultry-processing lines could increase risk of bird abuse," *Washington Post*, October 29, 2013, **http://www.washingtonpost.com/politics/usda-plan-to-speed-up-poultry-processing-lines-could-increase-risk-of-bird-abuse/2013/10/29/aeeffe1e-3b2e-11e3-b6a9-da62c264f40e_story.html**, accessed October 30, 2013; and "Chicken deaths, NSA wiretaps: How much do we want to know?," *The Straits Times*, Singapore, November 13, 2013.

to water shortages and possible limits to the use of air conditioning technology. Such effects will occur even if it becomes generally accepted that global warming is dependent on human activities—given the overriding argument of: What can it hurt?

Africa may well emerge in offering the most opportunities for green investments and the accumulation of carbon credits. However, as the transfer of resources resulting from carbon trading grows, such trading will become, in the eyes of governments, nonsustainable and therefore prohibitive. It is more likely that there will be an increase in international agreements (both multilateral and bilateral) that set a framework for corporations, promotion and subsidies for technologies, and products that protect the environment. Rich countries will give more importance to this concern, and most internationally operating companies will take this concern seriously. Key sectors for industry creation and expansion will focus on the protection of public health; the need for sustainability; the conservation of energy, water and natural resources; the growth of biotechnology, genomics, and nanotechnology; and the creation and promotion of "eco"-products, services, and processes. For example, sustainable water recycling technologies will spawn new industries. Governments will adopt and encourage more advanced pollution control policies, particularly for heavy metals and engineered (non-naturally occurring) substances.

Terrorism

Terrorism has precipitated many major shifts in international business practices. In many ways, it has made the world a smaller place, confronted with events that occur at greater speed. There are clear expectations that terrorism is an ongoing phenomenon that will have to be confronted. Combating terrorism is a fact of life and history, resulting in a continuous job for push back, which has to be done multilaterally, without second thoughts or trade-offs. Counter-terrorism will be dangerous, and it will be important to maintain the will of the people and of governments to oppose the terrorists. Janus-like repercussions arise from the frailty of corporate and human memories.

Over time, impressions shift. During the days following a terrorist event, for example, typically the predominate feeling is "but for some good fortune, it could have been me."

This feeling may eventually change to "this was an aberration and cannot happen to me," leading to an underestimation of danger and, often, insufficient policy measures.[23] However, the root causes of terrorism need to be kept in strong focus. Dimensions to be considered are policies toward immigrants and the sometimes-dividing role taken on by advocates of specific religions, cultures, regions, or races. Ways to address these dimensions can be education, improved nourishment, and the ability to control one's own destiny.[24]

There is major global ambivalence about which approaches to take to mitigate terrorism. Some believe very strongly that materialism and "having something to lose" are key dimensions in providing important values for those who see themselves as excluded from the benefits of globalization. Others, however, suggest a prime role for spirituality, empathy for, and understanding of cultural differences. Perhaps value combined with valuation will be the future direction.

There will also be a growing emphasis on national interests accompanied by limited readiness for multilateral solutions. It will be a key task for governments to diffuse such desires rather than accede to popular demands. Only with the collaboration of parties in conflict can one avoid local and regional protectionism, the emergence of de-globalization, and the spiraling reduction of the quality of life. The greatest imperative will be to develop and maintain the power to achieve and sustain peace.

Consumers appear willing to change their consumption habits if necessary for security needs. In response to cultural diversity and cross-border cultural conflicts, many may abrogate from earlier preferences, giving the impact of country of origin a totally new meaning.

Corporations are likely to revive ethnocentric and polycentric policies and use export activities, much more than FDI, as the dominant form of international business relations. They will either pull out from countries that lack law and order or service them only at a very high-risk premium. Other specific international business responses to terrorism can be found in four key areas: customer management, product management, logistics management, and people management.[25]

CUSTOMER MANAGEMENT Rather than just selling wherever possible, firms now focus more on where to sell, what to sell, and to whom to sell. Managers are developing a new appreciation for the type and degree of risk exposure in certain regions of the world. Leading risk factors include the policies of home and host governments, exchange-rate fluctuations, and economic turmoil.

More firms are developing trade portfolios that allocate effort and limits in different regions of the world. These portfolios are intended to achieve two goals: (1) to limit dependence on any region or customer in order to reduce a firm's exposure to conflict or unexpected interruptions; and (2) to systematically develop markets to balance existing exposure, to diversify a firm's risk, and to offer a fallback position.

FDI and exporting also present a greater scrutiny of the alternative opportunities. FDI demonstrates the long-term nature of a firm's objectives and makes use of local advantages. It also facilitates collaboration and reduces the firm's exposure to the vagaries of border-crossing transactions. At the same time, FDI renders the firm vulnerable to the effects of government policies and any divergence between home and host country. Some firms are looking beyond the strict economic dimensions of foreign direct investment. They use it to signal full confidence in an area or a partner, thus demonstrating commitment. Such a focus on relationship may well alter some of the approaches used by government agencies in charge of encouraging FDI inflow.

Exporting, in turn, permits a broader and quicker coverage of world markets with the ability to respond to changes. Risks are lower, but costs tend to be higher because of transshipment and transaction expenses. Even though an export orientation is seen to be less risky, many firms are not as aggressive as they used to be in seeking new business or new accounts. A desire to deal with old, established customers, with "people who we know and with whom we have developed a feeling of trust" has emerged, perhaps leading to a redevelopment of high-context relations around the world. An export approach appears to be the preferred method of new market entry these days. It may remain the principal tool of international expansion for firms new to the global market or those highly concerned about international risk.

Closely associated with an export strategy are increasing concerns about export controls at the corporate level. Ironically, this increase in self-examination occurs during a time when better linkages and cooperation between governments have made it possible to ease the levels of technology that can be traded internationally. Corporations have become more sensitive to the possibility of diversion or misuse of their exports and do not want to be accused of aiding and abetting an enemy. As a result, there is more intensive scrutiny of orders received, of customers who have placed these orders, and of product-use evaluation before an order is shipped.

PRODUCT MANAGEMENT Members of the supply chain now make it an imperative to identify and manage their dependence on international inputs. Industrial customers, in particular, are often seen as pushing for U.S.-based sourcing. A domestic source simply provides a greater feeling of comfort. As one executive said, "When we tell our customers their goods will be produced in West Virginia or Kentucky, they feel so much better than when we inform them about the shipments coming from Argentina, Greece, or Venezuela. They're worried about interruptions or other problems."

Some firms also report a new meaning associated with the "made-in" dimension in country-of-origin labeling. In the past, this dimension was viewed as enhancing products, such as perfumes made in France or cars made in Germany. Lately, the "made-in" dimension of some countries may create an exclusionary context by making both industrial customers and consumers reject products from specific regions. As a result, negative effects may result from geographic proximity to terrorists, as has been claimed by some for textile imports from Pakistan.

LOGISTICS MANAGEMENT The international pipeline has slowed down, but the structure of the pipeline and the scrutiny given to the materials going through the pipeline have become important.

Firms that had developed elaborate just-in-time (JIT) delivery systems for their international supplies have been exposed to increased security measures that have reduced the speed of international transactions. These firms and their service providers continue to be affected by increased security measures. Firms are also focusing more on internal security and need to demonstrate externally how much more security-oriented they have become. In many instances, government authorities require evidence of threat-reduction efforts to speed shipments along. Also, insurance companies have increased their premiums substantially for firms that are exposed to increased risk.

In the past, cargo security measures concentrated on reducing theft and pilferage from a shipment. Increasingly, additional measures concentrate on possible undesirable accompaniments to incoming shipments. With this new approach, international cargo security starts well before the shipping even begins. One result of these changes—perhaps unintended—is a better description of shipment content and a more precise assessment of duties and other shipping fees.

Carriers with sophisticated hub-and-spoke systems have discovered that trans-shipments between the different spokes may add to delays because of the time needed to re-scrutinize packages. While larger "clean areas" within ports may help reduce this problem, a redesign of distribution systems may lead to fewer hubs and more direct connections.

Firms with a JIT system are also using alternative management strategies, such as shifting international shipments from air to sea. More dramatically, some firms are replacing international shipments with domestic ones, in which truck transport would replace trans-border movement altogether and eliminate the use of vulnerable ports.

PEOPLE MANAGEMENT The heightened degree of scrutiny also extends to the employees of corporations. Without necessarily differentiating based on the country of origin of applicants for employment, firms now take a much closer look at credentials and claims of past achievements and activities. Some U.S. firms—even though globally oriented—are becoming more cautious in their practices for hiring foreign nationals. Accepting the reality that controlling an individual's access to information is much more difficult once that person is inside the organization, these firms appear to have decided not even to consider for employment nationals from highly controversial countries. The World View on the return of expatriates discusses some of the problems associated with employment and the protection of information.

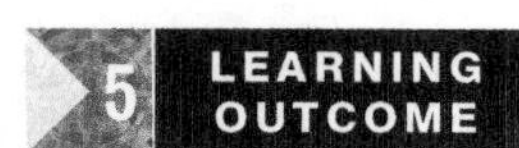

The Future of Global Business Management

Global change results in an increased risk, yet participation in the global marketplace remains the only way to achieve long-term success. International markets are a source of high profits, as a quick look at a list of multinational firms shows. International activities also help cushion

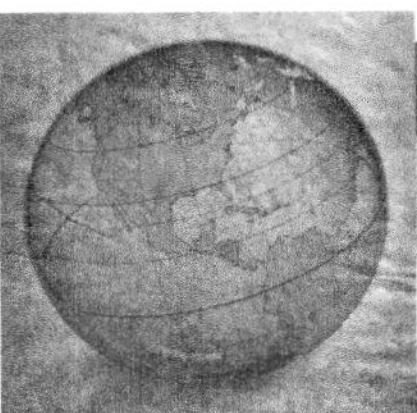

WORLD VIEW

When Expatriates Return Home

When governments change policies, when restrictions are lifted, or when new opportunities emerge, expatriates may decide to come home. For example, when Syria's president Bashar al-Assad introduced new economic liberalization policies, investment projects increased by 250 percent, mainly due to expatriates investing their money and expertise in the country.

China is planning to reverse past brain drain by luring back Chinese students who have studied abroad. It used to be that students went abroad (typically to the United States), found employment there, and stayed on. However, due to support measures introduced by the Chinese government and due to different regulations, many expatriate former students have returned to China. If the government wants to encourage somebody to return home, it provides start-up funds for a new company or money for housing and cars. Particularly in the medical research field, the availability of resources, such as embryonic stem cells and the permission to carry out exploratory research, is attractive to leading scientists.

Other nations are also thinking about implementing attractive repatriation measures. For example, the German government is increasingly searching for ways to bring back university researchers who have left the country. At one time, many researchers came to the United States to receive their Ph.Ds. Afterwards, they continued their work as university professors and were pleased to be in the United States. For instance, Professor Michael Czinkota, a co-author of this text, came from Germany to the United States in the 1970s and has worked both as a faculty member and in the political realm. Although he loves it in the United States, he, along with other expatriate faculty, do not rule out eventually spending more time in Germany. Because research is seen as very instrumental to the competitiveness of a nation, there is a large effort underway by many countries to bring researchers "back home."

One emerging policy issue concerns the security effects of such labor mobility. For example, in order to work in government laboratories, such as Los Alamos in the United States, a researcher must have U.S. citizenship. This requirement is designed to protect highly classified information and limit its dissemination to potential adversaries. But what about the researcher who became a citizen but wants to leave a few years or even decades later? How can secrets be kept?

SOURCES: Julien Barnes-Dacy, "Syrian Expatriates Return Home in Hopes of New Wealth," *The Christian Science Monitor*, December 27, 2007; "Many Expatriate Scientists Find Reasons to Return to China," *The Washington Post*, February 20, 2008, D5; and Claudia Reischauer, "Wissen kennt keine Grenzen," Absatzwirtschaft Sonderheft 2010, December 2010, **http://michaelczinkota.com/wp-content/uploads/2010/12/absatzwirtschaft-Sonderausgabe2010_Wissen-kennt-keine-Grenz1.pdf**, accessed November 1, 2013.

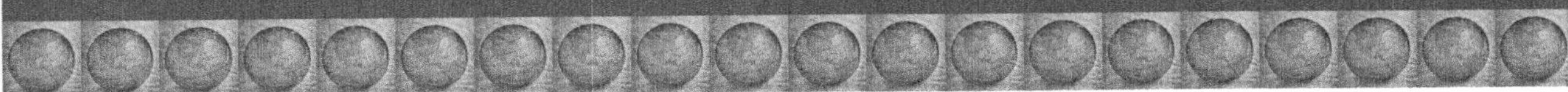

the firm from fall-offs in domestic demand that may result from adverse domestic conditions. For this reason, global participation may be crucial to the very survival of the firm. International markets also provide firms with foreign experience that helps them compete more successfully with foreign competitors in the domestic market.

Reputation Management

Firms appreciate the fact that public perceptions drive actions by consumers, governments, and competitors and thus make an effort to consider the effects of corporate actions on the public's view of the enterprise—both in the short as well as the long term.

Reforming the Global Corporation

Corporations are likely to face increasing pressures from a wide variety of stakeholders, including governments, unions, media, and the public at large. These grow increasingly more intense in light of a corporate migration from a Western-style organization to multi-polar structures, accompanied by a shift from a West-North to an East-South orientation. Accountability and transparency will be the basis for key developments.

Accounting systems will recognize and develop procedures for calculating the value of and the change of intangible corporate assets so that increasingly they can be used to drive corporate capitalization and performance. Such assets will gradually become the prime measure of corporations and will have key influence on predicted future cash flows and stock prices. Value investors will recognize that the building of intangible assets is a multiyear, multifaceted endeavor. Consequently, buy-and-hold strategies will become more dominant and quarter-to-quarter performances will become less important in the investing decision.

Corporate responsibility will be interpreted to include broad-based activity and profit sharing. Low capital manufacturing facilities will be expected around the world. Stakeholders will demand greater involvement and, for better or for worse, will play a major role in the image building of the corporation. Because lapses in ethics or social responsibility will have a major negative impact on brand equity, strong corporations will increasingly be indicated with strong corporate social responsibility (CSR) programs and strong corporate ethical conduct.

There will be a backlash against excessive executive remuneration—not only from regulators but also from shareholders and inside managers and employees. Executive compensation will again be determined in comparison to average pay levels—which may well lead to pay raises for those at lower levels.

Emerging markets will increasingly account for larger portions of corporate profits and sales, particularly in light of their representation of more than two thirds of the total consumer base. Corporations will be expected to provide improved product access and help overcome difficulties in logistics and infrastructures. For many products, the development strategies will need to shift from utmost sophistication to increased affordability.

Corruption is seen increasingly as a significant detractor from global welfare and local economic development. Its consequences are roads that are shoddily built, structures that collapse, and clinics with equipment that is either purchased too expensively or unable to do the necessary job. In all such circumstances, vast public expenditures do not achieve their envisioned use.

Typical side payments are between 10 to 15 percent of all major public expenditures, with much higher levels of misrouting in the developing world. "It is human nature to lubricate relationships with gratuity" is often said. More diversion is attributed to high-context cultures (e.g., Latin America, Latin Europe, Asia) and less to low-context ones (e.g., U.S., Nordic, Germanic). Yet the social acceptance of corruption is a big danger because it protects the elite from domestic scrutiny and control. Therefore, the ongoing impact of the U.S. Foreign Corrupt Practices Act (FCPA) and of the Organisation for Economic Co-operation and Development (OECD) discussions will be seen as instrumental in reducing or at least containing such misappropriations. However, more multilateral actions are necessary to ensure the enforcement of measures against corruptors.

Global Product Policy

Worldwide introduction of products will occur much more rapidly in the future. Already, global product life cycles have accelerated substantially. Whereas product introduction could previously be spread out over several years, firms now must prepare for product life cycles that can be measured in months or even weeks. As a result, firms must design products and plan even their domestic marketing strategies with the global product cycle in mind.

Early incorporation of the global dimension into product planning, however, does not point toward increased standardization. On the contrary, companies will have to be ready to deliver more mass customization. Customers are no longer satisfied with simply having a product: They want it to meet their needs and preferences precisely. **Mass customization** requires working with existing product technology, often in modular form, to create specific product bundles for a particular customer, resulting in tailor-made jeans or a customized car.

MASS CUSTOMIZATION
Taking mass-produced product components and combining them in a variety of ways to result in a specific product for a particular customer

As global manufacturing becomes increasingly the norm for many firms, manufacturing technologies are moving around the world at an extraordinarily fast pace. As emerging nations race to catch up, their knowledge and ability to duplicate technologies means that all global companies must be constantly innovative in order to stay ahead. The ability to develop consistent comparative advantage is particularly important because emerging country competitors are likely to have access to large and increasingly skilled labor pools at labor rates much lower than in Europe, Japan, or the United States.

An increase will occur in the trend toward strategic alliances that enable firms to take risks that they could not afford to take alone, facilitate technological advancement, and ensure continued international market access. These partners do not need to be large to make a major contribution. Depending on the type of product, even small firms can serve as coordinating subcontractors and collaborate in product and service development, production, and distribution.

Global Pricing

Global price competition will become increasingly heated. As their distribution spreads throughout the world, many products will take on commodity characteristics. Even complex products are fast becoming commodities. With commodities, small price differentials per unit may become crucial. However, because many new products and technologies will address completely new needs, forward pricing—which distributes development expenses over the planned or anticipated volume of sales—will become increasingly difficult and controversial as demand levels are impossible to predict with any kind of accuracy.

For consumer products, price competition will be substantial. Because of the increased dissemination of technology, the firm that introduces a product will no longer be able to justify higher prices for long; domestically produced products will soon be of similar quality. As a result, exchange-rate movements may play more significant roles in maintaining the competitiveness of the international firm. Firms can be expected to prevail on their government to manage the country's currency to maintain a favorable exchange rate. Technology also allows much closer interaction on pricing between producer and customer. The success of electronic commerce providers, such as eBay (**http://www.ebay.com**), demonstrates how auctioning and bidding, alone or in competition with others, offers new perspectives on the global price mechanism.

Through subsidization, targeting, government contracts, or other hidden forms of support, nations will attempt to stimulate their international competitiveness. Because of the price sensitivity of many products, the international manager will be forced to identify such unfair practices quickly, communicate them to his or her government, and to insist on either similar benefits or on rapid government action to create an internationally level playing field.

Fast Facts

Which is the best city in the world to live in?

Of course, we are all entitled to our personal opinions, but according to a survey by William M. Mercer, Zurich comes out on top. Evaluated in terms of quality of life, Geneva and Vancouver are close behind. Try to avoid assignments in Baghdad, Port-au-Prince, New Delhi, and Belgrade—all rank close to the bottom.

SOURCE: William M. Mercer Consulting. **http://mthink.mercer.com/quality-of-living-rankings-spotlight-emerging-cities/**, accessed July 17, 2014.

At the same time, many firms will work hard to reduce their customers' price sensitivity. By developing relationships with their markets, rather than just carrying out transactions, other dimensions—such as loyalty, consistency, the cost of shifting suppliers, and responsiveness to client needs—may become much more important than price.

Distribution Strategies

Innovative distribution approaches will determine new ways of serving markets. For example, television, through QVC, has already created a shopping mall used by more than 179 million customers.[26] The use of the Internet offers new distribution alternatives. Self-sustaining, consumer-distributor relationships may emerge through, say, refrigerators that report directly to grocery store computers when supplies are running low and with home delivery billed to the customer's account.

The link to distribution systems will also be crucial to global firms in the business-to-business sector. As large retailers use sophisticated inventory tracking and reordering systems, only the firms able to interact with such systems will remain eligible suppliers. Therefore, firms need to create their own distribution systems that are able to respond to JIT and direct-order entry requirements around the globe.

More sophisticated distribution systems will, at the same time, introduce new uncertainties and fragilities into corporate planning. For example, the development of JIT delivery systems makes firms more efficient yet, on an international basis, also exposes them to more risk through distribution interruptions. Therefore, a strike in a faraway country may be newly significant for a company that depends on the timely delivery of supplies.

Globally, there will be a greater emphasis on the markets offered by "second-tier cities," which are large cities not yet in the political or economic spotlight—particularly in Russia, China, and India. Firms will need to expand their distribution and market entry strategies to these large cities, thus creating new regional hubs. There must also be collaboration with the public sector to encourage infrastructural investments in these regions, which, in turn will increase their political and economic importance.

Global Communications

The advances made in international communications will also have a profound impact on international management. Entire industries are becoming more footloose in their operations; that is, they are less tied to their current location in their interaction with markets. Most affected by communications advances will be members of the services sector. International outsourcing of services makes it possible for corporations to center entire functions, like customer service, in countries where labor costs are low.

For manufacturers, intranet and Internet networks allow for instant sharing of massive amounts of data, documentation, and product images and specifications in globally dispersed locations. This opens opportunities not only for faster-paced research but for vastly improved supplier-manufacturer relationships.

Culture Clues What is the last course in an authentic Chinese meal? Soup is the last course.

Careers in Global Business

As you have learned in this book, a career in global business is more than jet-set travel between New Delhi, Tokyo, Frankfurt, and New York. It is hard work and requires knowledge and expertise. As this final section will show, there are numerous ways to prepare yourself—and the rewards are substantial.

Further Training

Further study (for example, enrolling in a graduate business school program in global business) is always a good option. You can study either at home or abroad.

According to the Institute of International Education, 283,000 U.S. students studied abroad for academic credit in 2012—an increase of 200 percent since 1995, when there were 90,000 students. At the same time, business and management are the most popular fields of study for the 820,000 international students at American universities in 2013.[27] To supplement your studies, several organizations offer programs to assist students interested in studying abroad or in gathering foreign work experience.[28]

Employment Experience

For those ready to enter or rejoin the "real world" of global business, several opportunities await. One career option is to seek employment with a large multinational corporation. These firms constantly search for personnel to help them in their international operations.

Many multinational firms, while seeking specialized knowledge such as languages, expect employees to be grounded firmly in the practice and management of business. Rarely, if ever, will a firm hire a new employee at the starting level and immediately place him or her in a position of global responsibility. As explained in Chapter 13, job placements abroad are costly, and firms usually want a new employee to become thoroughly familiar with the company's internal operations before considering transfer to a global position. Once you do get a chance to travel, data like that presented in Table 15.1 will be invaluable. The chart evaluates the top five cities of the world, ranking them in terms of quality of life, according to thirty-nine factors. They include political stability, personal freedom, air pollution, and the quality of health care, schools, restaurants, and theaters.

TABLE 15.1 Mercer Human Resource Consulting Worldwide Global Quality of Life Survey 2012, Top Five Cities

Rank 2012	Rank 2007	City	Country
1	3	Vienna	Austria
2	1	Zurich	Switzerland
3	5	Auckland	New Zealand
4	8	Munich	Germany
5	3	Vancouver	Canada

SOURCES: William M. Mercer Consulting **http:www.mercer.com** Accessed October 21, 2013.

An alternative to working for a large multinational firm is to take a job with a small or medium-sized firm. Often, such firms have only recently developed a global outlook, and the new employee will arrive on the "ground floor." Initial involvement will normally be in the export field—evaluating potential foreign customers, preparing quotes, and dealing with activities such as shipping and transportation. With a very limited budget, the export

WORLD VIEW

Global Experience Leads to the Top

International work experience has long been trumpeted as essential for middle managers in multinational corporations, but these days, even chief executives are going global. To keep up with the growing importance of foreign markets, more companies are requiring candidates for top management positions to have strong international résumés. As a board member of a Canadian oil company stated, "For a multinational firm, a culturally fluent and internationally experienced CEO and board are becoming increasingly important to remain globally competitive." When the Cochrane Corporation was hiring a new CEO in 2012, its key selection criterion was "international experience." There is a strong positive relationship between international experience and the likelihood of being selected CEO. International experience early in one's career seems to encourage professional advancement. More than 40 percent of the CEOs in the S&P 100 reported having international experience. However, international experience alone is no longer enough to remain competitive, as shown in IBM's 2010 Global CEO study. It portrays how creativity is now a crucial element to success.

In today's rough economic times, this does not come as a shock. In order to remain successful in postrecession economic times with less consumer spending, CEOs need to be globally focused on emerging markets and creative in how they market to developed nations. Creative strategies are needed for success in both types of marketplaces.

SOURCES: Russell Reynolds Associates, "Interviews and Findings – A World of Experience: A Board Perspective on CEO Succession in the Global Era 2010," **http://www.russellreynolds.com/content/world-of-experience-board-perspective-ceo-succession-aus-can**, accessed November 1, 2013; The Cochrane Collaboration, "Recruitment process for a new Chief Executive Officer (CEO) of The Cochrane Collaboration," July 4, 2012, **http://www.cochrane.org/news/news-events/current-news/recruitment-process-new-chief-executive-officer-ceo-cochrane-collabora**, accessed October 31, 2013; Peter Magnusson and David Boggs, "International Experience and CEO selection: An empirical study," *Journal of International Management*, Issue 1, March 2006, pp. 107–125; J. Warner, Route to the top, *Chief Executive 205* (2005), pp. 20–25 (Jan/Feb); IBM, "IBM 2010 Global CEO Study: Creativity Selected as Most Crucial Factor for Future Success," May 18, 2010, **http://www-03.ibm.com/press/us/en/pressrelease/31670.wss**, accessed November 1, 2013.

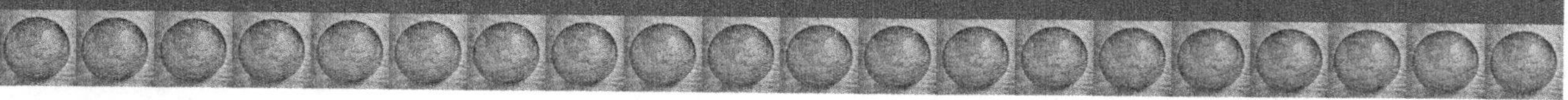

manager will only occasionally visit international markets to discuss business strategies with distributors abroad. Most of the work will be done by mail, by fax, by e-mail, or by telephone. The hours are often long because of the need, for example, to reach a contact during business hours in Hong Kong. Yet the possibilities for implementing creative business transactions are virtually limitless. It is also gratifying and often rewarding that one's successful contribution will be visible directly through the firm's growing export volume.

Alternatively, international work in a small firm may involve importing—that is, finding low-cost sources that can be substituted for domestically sourced products. Decisions often must be based on limited information, and the manager is faced with many uncertainties. Often, things do not work out as planned. Shipments are delayed, letters of credit are canceled, and products almost never arrive in exactly the form and shape anticipated. Yet the problems are always new and offer an ongoing challenge.

As a training ground for international activities, there probably is no better starting place than a small or medium-sized firm. Later on, the person with some experience may find work with a trading or export management company, resolving other people's problems and concentrating almost exclusively on the international arena.

Self-Employment

A third alternative is to hang up a consultant's shingle or to establish a trading firm. Many companies are in need of help for their international business efforts and are prepared to part with a portion of their profits in order to receive it. Yet it requires in-depth knowledge and broad experience to make a major contribution from the outside or to run a trading firm successfully.

Specialized services that might be offered by a consultant include global market research, international strategic planning, or—particularly desirable—beginning-to-end assistance for international entry or international negotiations. For an international business expert, the hourly billable rate typically is as high as $400 for principals and $150 for staff. Whenever international travel is required, overseas activities are often billed at the daily rate of $2,000 plus expenses. Even at such high rates, solid groundwork must be completed before all of the overhead is paid. The advantage of this career option is the opportunity to become a true international entrepreneur. Consultants and those who conduct their own export-import or foreign direct-investment activities work at a higher degree of risk than those who are not self-employed, but they have an opportunity for higher rewards.[29]

SUMMARY

This final chapter has provided an overview of the environmental changes facing global managers and alternative managerial responses to the changes. Global business is a complex and difficult activity, yet it affords many opportunities and challenges.

Shifts in the political environment will affect the conduct of business among and between the world's trading regions. Continued growth of emerging markets will add to already intense competition. 

Technology, including the Internet, will continue to drive change at an accelerated pace. Although technology presents opportunities for innovation, it may also allow developing nations to catch up quickly with developed world competitors. 

While global trade negotiations under the World Trade Organizations will continue, governments will balance their needs for trade with the best interests of their citizens. 

Firms must respond to change through their global strategy development, product policies, pricing policies, distribution strategies, and communications. 

There are multiple options for students desiring a career in global business, including further study. 

There are multiple options for employment in large and small business and self-employment as a global consultant. 

Key Terms and Concepts

environmental protection
isolationism
population stabilization
international debt load
trigger mechanisms
mass customization

Review Questions

1. In what ways are trends in the global political environment likely to affect global trade in coming years?
2. For many developing countries, debt repayment and trade are closely linked. What does protectionism mean to them?
3. Should one worry about the fact that the United States is a debtor nation?

Critical Skill Builders

1. What is the danger in oversimplifying the globalization approach? Would you agree with the following statement: "If you want to succeed globally, you better believe that if something is working in a big way in one market, it will work in all markets."
2. Outline the basic reasons why a company does not necessarily have to be large and have years of experience to succeed in the global marketplace. Is this likely to change in future years?
3. Because crisis situations are more likely to occur in international locations than at home, it is better to manufacture at home during periods of global recession or political unrest. Prepare your arguments and debate in class.
4. Create a résumé and cover letter presenting yourself to a multinational company of your choosing for consideration for an entry-level position. Make sure that you research the global activities of the company first and tailor your letter accordingly.
5. "You learn more, faster, and better at a multinational corporation than at a mid-sized company that is active in only one or two markets." Is this necessarily the case? Discuss your job preferences, both in the short term and in terms of career development.

On the Web

1. What are the top ten trading partners for the United States? Use the U.S. Foreign Trade Highlights tables on the Department of Commerce's International Trade Administration site, **http://www.trade.gov**. Summarize the ways in which these trade relationships are likely to change in the future.

2. Using the site Living Abroad (**http://www.livingabroad.com**), research several international schools that may interest you. What are the most interesting links to other web sites concerning international issues? Why are you particularly interested in them?

3. Use a search portal to gain a competitive advantage. Examples: Google Trends and Yahoo Buzz, which provide real-time snapshots of consumer interests; Google reader, an RSS reader that can be mined for useful data; Google Analytics and Yahoo! Site Explorer, which show consumer traffic at company web sites.

4. The site **http://www.overseasjobs.com** provides valuable information for those interested in jobs overseas. What skills do international employers seem to value most? Peruse the job listings and find several jobs that you might interest you. Also, take a look at the profiles of several international companies that you might be interested in working for. What characteristics do the international firms listed here possess?

Endnotes

1. William Lazer and Eric H. Shaw, "Global Marketing Management: At the Dawn of the New Millennium," *Journal of International Marketing*, 8, 1, 2000, pp. 65–77.
2. The information presented here is based largely on an original Delphi study by Michael Czinkota and Ilkka A. Ronkainen, using an international panel of experts, The Georgetown 2008 Delphi Study, Georgetown University, 2008.
3. Human Development Report 2007/2008: Fighting Climate Change, UN Development Program, **www.UNDP.org**, accessed March 6, 2008, p. 251.
4. "Bringing the Poor Online," *The Economist*, February 22, 2008.
5. "Corporate Disclosure Resources," Washington University, **http://faculty.washington.edu/krumme/projects/disclosure/disclosurewebs.html**, accessed February 15, 2008.
6. "Shifting the Balance: Chinese and Indian Capitalism," *The Economist*, January 24, 2008.
7. *Environmental Change and Security Program Report*, Issue 12, 2006–2007, The Woodrow Wilson International Center for Scholars, Washington D.C., 2007, p. 95.
8. "Urban Population, Development and Environment Dynamics," Committee for International Cooperation in National Research in Demography, Paris, 2007, pp. 19–23.
9. Richard P. Cincotta and Jack A. Goldstone, "The Security Demographic, Assessing the Evidence," *Environmental Change and Security Program Report*, Issue 12, 2006–2007, The Woodrow Wilson International Center for Scholars, Washington D.C., 2007, p. 77.
10. Catherine L. Mann, "Is the U.S. Trade Deficit Still Sustainable?" Institute for International Economics, Washington, D.C., March 1, 2001; "The Dollar and the World Economy," *The Economist*, December 19, 2007.
11. U.S. Census Bureau, press release of March 11, 2008, **www.census.gov**, accessed March 11, 2008.
12. Steve Forbes, "U.S. National Debt: $1.1 Million per Taxpayer," *Chicago Tribune*, October 30, 2013, **http://www.chicagotribune.com/news/politics/chi-nsc-u-s--national-debt-1-1-million-per-taxpayer-20131030,0,6187466.story**, accessed November 1, 2013.
13. Jonathan Masters, "U.S. Debt Ceiling: Costs and Consequences," Council on Foreign Affairs, October 2, 2013, **http://www.cfr.org/budget-debt-and-deficits/us-debt-ceiling-costs-consequences/p24751**, accessed November 1, 2013.
14. Chairman Ben S. Bernanke, Bundesbank Lecture, Berlin, Germany, September 11, 2007, **http://www.federalreserve.gov/newsevents/speech/bernanke20070911a.htm**, accessed February 14, 2008.
15. Robin Wigglesworth and Delphine Strauss, "Euro on the slide as traders back ECB Rate cut," *Financial Times*, November 5, 2013, **http://www.ft.com/cms/s/0/e4f8c082-457d-11e3-b98b-00144feabdc0.html#axzz2jo7Czjd0**, accessed November 5, 2013.
16. Trade in Goods and Services, 1992–present, **bea.gov**, accessed November 19, 2013.
17. **http://www.internetworldstats.com/stats7.htm**. Accessed February 2, 2008.
18. Stephen Baker and Heather Green, "Social Media Will Change Your Business," *BusinessWeek*, February 20, 2008.
19. Andrea Thompson, "Cloned Milk and Meat: What's the Beef?" *MSNBC*, January 9, 2008.
20. Michael R. Czinkota, "The Policy Gap in International Marketing," *Journal of International Marketing*, 8, 1, 2000, pp. 99–111.
21. Labour Force Statistics, 1986–2006, Paris, OECD, 2007.
22. U.S. Census Bureau Population Clock, **http://www.census.gov/population/www/popclockus.html**; accessed April 19, 2014.
23. Peter W. Liesch, John Steen, Gary A. Knight, Michael R. Czinkota, "Internationally Managing in the Face of Terrorism-Induced Uncertainty," *21st Century Management: A Reference Handbook*, Charles Wankel, Ed. Thousand Oaks, CA: Sage Publications, 2008, pp. 200–208.
24. Michael R. Czinkota and Ilkka A. Ronkainen, *The 2008 Georgetown Delphi Study*, Georgetown University, Washington D.C., 2008.
25. Michael R. Czinkota, "From Bowling Alone to Standing Together," *Marketing Management*, April 2002.
26. QVC corporate web site, **http://www.qvc.com/qic/qvcapp.aspx/app.html/params.file.|cp|mainhqfact,html/left.html.file.|nav|navhqabout,html/walk.html.|nav|navhqwel,html**, accessed March 8, 2008.
27. William M. Mercer Consulting, **http://www.mercer.com/referencecontent.jhtml?idContent=1128060**; retrieved Feb. 28, 2008; and 2013 Open Doors Report, Institute for International Education, Washington, D.C., **http://www.iie.org/Who-We-Are/News-and-Events/Press-Center/Press-releases/2013/2013-11-11-Open-Doors-Data**, accessed May 10, 2014.
28. "American Students Studying Abroad at Record Levels: Up 8.5%," Press Release by the Institute for International Education, November 12, 2007; available **http://opendoors.iienetwork.org/?p=113744**; accessed February 18, 2008.
29. The following sites are a good starting point for finding more information: **http://www.iiepassport.org**, **http://www.studyabroad.com**, **http://www.overseasjobs.com**; **http://www.egide.asso.fr**.

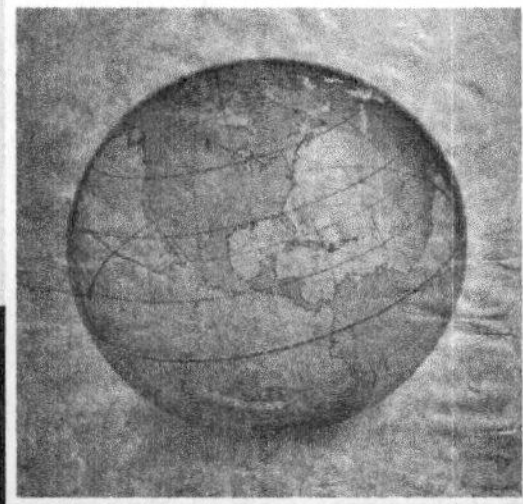

GLOSSARY

Abandoned product ranges The outcome of a firm narrowing its range of products to obtain economies of scale, which provides opportunities for other firms to enter the markets for the abandoned products

Absolute advantage A country that is capable of producing a product with fewer labor hours

Accounting diversity The range of differences in national accounting practices

Acculturation The process of adjusting and adapting to a specific culture other than one's own

American Depository Receipts (ADRs) Receipts to bank account that holds shares of a foreign firm's stock in that firm's country

Anti-dumping law Legislation that allows the imposition of tariffs on foreign imports, designed to help domestic industries injured by unfair competition from abroad in cases where imported products are sold at less than fair market value

Antitrust laws Laws that prohibit monopolies, restraint of trade, and conspiracies to inhibit competition

Arbitration The procedure for settling a dispute in which an objective third party hears both sides and makes a decision; a procedure for resolving conflict in the international business arena through the use of intermediaries such as representatives of chambers of commerce, trade associations, or third country institutions

Area briefings Training programs that provide factual preparation prior to an overseas assignment

Arm's length principle A basis for intracompany transfer pricing; the price that an unrelated party would have paid for the same transaction

Attitudes Evaluation of alternatives based on values

Autarky Self-sufficiency; a country that is not participating in international trade

Backtranslation The retranslation of text to the original language by a different person from the one who made the first translation, useful for finding translation errors

Balance of payments (BOP) A statement of all transactions between one country and the rest of the world during a given period; a record of flows of goods, services, and investments across borders

Base salary Salary, not including special payments, such as allowances, paid during overseas assignments

Bearer bond A bond owned officially by whoever is holding it

Behavioral controls Organizational controls that involve influencing how activities are conducted

Best practices Idea that may have saved money or time, or a process that is more efficient than existing ones

Bilateral agreement Agreement or treaty between two nations focusing only on their interests

Black hole Situation that arises when an international marketer has a low-competence subsidiary or none at all in a highly strategic market or where a government may restrict a firm's activities

Blue Angel Program German program that identifies environmentally sound products and services

Boycott An organized effort to refrain from conducting business with a particular seller of goods or services; used in the international arena for political or economic reasons

Bretton Woods Agreement An agreement reached in 1944 among finance ministers of forty-four Western nations to establish a system of fixed exchange rates

Buffer stock Stock of a commodity kept on hand to prevent a shortage in times of unexpectedly great demand; under international commodity and price agreements, the stock controlled by an elected or appointed manager for the purpose of managing the price of the commodity

Bulk service Ocean shipping provided on contract, either for individual voyages or for prolonged periods of time

Capital account transaction Any international transfer of a financial asset or the acquisition and disposal of a nonfinancial asset

Capital budget The financial evaluation of a proposed investment to determine whether the expected returns are sufficient to justify the investment expenses

Capital control Any government imposed restriction that limits or prevents the free movement of capital in and out of a country

Capital flight The rapid outflow of capital from a country when owners of the capital, whether they be domestic or foreign residents, fear for the preservation of the capital's value. The flow of private funds abroad because investors believe that the return on investment or the safety of capital is not sufficiently ensured in their own countries

Capital outlays Upfront costs and expenses of a proposed investment

Capital structure The proportions of owner's equity (own-capital) and debt (capital provided by external creditors) that fund the organization

Caribbean Basin Initiative (CBI) Extended trade preferences to Caribbean countries and grants of special access to the markets of the United States

Carriage and insurance paid to (CIP) The price quoted by an exporter for shipments not involving waterway transport, including insurance

Carriage paid to (CPT) The price quoted by an exporter for shipments not involving waterway transport, not including insurance

Cartel An association of producers of a particular good, consisting either of private firms or of nations, formed for the purpose of suppressing the market forces affecting prices

Cash Pooling Used by multinational firms to centralize individual units' cash flows, resulting in less spending or foregone interest on unnecessary cash balances

Centralization Concentrating control and strategic decision-making at headquarters

Change agent An institution or person who facilitates change in a firm or in a host country

Channel design The length and width of the distribution channel

Code law Law based on a comprehensive set of written statutes

Codetermination A management approach in which employees are represented on supervisory boards to facilitate communication and collaboration between management and labor

Commercial invoice A bill for transported goods that describes the merchandise and its total cost and lists the addresses of the shipper and seller and delivery and payment terms

Committee on Foreign Investments in the United States (CFIUS) A federal committee, chaired by the U.S. Treasury, with the responsibility to review major foreign investments to determine whether national security or related concerns are at stake

Commodity price agreement An agreement involving both buyers and sellers to manage the price of a particular commodity but often only when the price moves outside a predetermined range

Common agricultural policy (CAP) An integrated system of subsidies and rebates applied to agricultural interests in the European Union

Common law Law based on tradition and depending less on written statutes and codes than on precedent and custom; used in the United States

Common market A group of countries that agree to remove all barriers to trade among members, to establish a common trade policy with respect to nonmembers, and also to allow mobility for factors of production—labor, capital, and technology

Comparative advantage The ability to produce a good or service more cheaply, relative to other goods and services, than is possible in other countries

Confiscation The forceful government seizure of a company without compensation for the assets seized

Consortium/consortia A partnership among multiple companies in the same industry, usually with the aim of conducting costly research and development work and with costs and the results shared among participating companies

Contractual hedging A multinational firm's use of contracts to minimize its transaction exposure

Contributor A national subsidiary with a distinctive competence, such as product development

Coordinated decentralization The provision of an overall corporate strategy by headquarters, while granting subsidiaries the freedom to implement their own corporate strategies within established ranges

Coordinated intervention A currency-value management method whereby the central banks of the major nations simultaneously intervene in the currency markets, hoping to change a currency's value

Corporate citizenship Corporate involvement in and support of community activities to reflect the company's role as a citizen of the community

Corporate functions Ensure ongoing functional innovation and capability improvement

Corporate philanthropy Corporate financial donations to specific causes and activities

Corporate social responsibility (CSR) Corporate activities to benefit stakeholder communities

Corporation A separate legal entity organized under law which possesses legal rights and responsibilities separate from those of its owners and employees

Correspondent banks Banks located in different countries and unrelated by ownership that have a reciprocal agreement to provide services to each other's customers

Cost and freight (CFR) Seller quotes a price for the goods, including the cost of transportation to the named port of debarkation; cost and choice of insurance left to the buyer

Cost leadership strategy The ability of a firm to price its output lower than the competition due to efficiencies in production

Cost-of-living allowance (COLA) An allowance paid during an assignment overseas to enable the employee to maintain the same standard of living as at home

Cost-plus method A pricing policy in which there is a full allocation of foreign and domestic costs to the product

Cost, insurance, and freight (CIF) Seller price includs insurance, all transportation, and miscellaneous charges to the point of debarkation from the vessel or aircraft

Counterfeit goods Any goods bearing an unauthorized representation of a trademark, patented invention, or copyrighted work that is legally protected in the country where it is marketed

Country of origin (COO) The nation where a product is produced or branded

Creative strategy Development of the content of a promotional message such as an advertisement, publicity release, sales promotion activity, or Web-based promotion

Critical commodities list A U.S. Department of Commerce file containing information about products that are either particularly sensitive to national security or controlled for other purposes

Cross rate Exchange rate quotations that do not include the U.S. dollar as one of the two currencies quoted

Cross-subsidization The use of resources accumulated in one part of the world to fight a competitive battle in another

Cultural assimilator Training program in which trainees for overseas assignments must respond to scenarios of specific situations in a particular country

Cultural convergence Increasing similarity among cultures accelerated by technological advances

Cultural imperialism Promoting Western behaviors and values along with products and into other cultures, encouraging homogeneous demand across markets

Cultural universals Manifestations of the total way of life of any group of people, including concrete elements such as language, infrastructure, social institutions, education, or abstract elements such as religion, values and attitudes, manners and customs, and aesthetics

Culture shock Pronounced reactions to the psychological disorientation that most people feel when they move for an extended period of time into a markedly different culture

Culture An integrated system of learned behavior patterns that are characteristic of the members of any given society

Currency flows The flow of currency from nation to nation, which in turn determines exchange rates

Current account transaction Any international economic transaction with income or payment flows occurring within the year, the current period

Current Account An account in the BOP statement that records the results of transactions involving merchandise, services, and unilateral transfers between countries

Current transfers account A current account in the BOP statement that records gifts from the residents of one country to the residents of another

Customer relationship management The collecting, storing, and analyzing of customer data to develop and maintain two-way relations

Customs union Collaboration among trading countries in which members dismantle barriers to trade in goods and services and also establish a common trade policy with respect to nonmembers

Debt-equity structure A firm's combination of capital obtained by borrowing from others, such as banks (debts), and capital provided by owners (equity)

Debt The capital provided by a creditor, like a bank, that will be eventually repaid and that has no rights or responsibilities associated with ownership of the organization

Decentralization Granting subsidiaries a high degree of autonomy

Deemed export Addresses people rather than products where knowledge transfer could lead to a breach of export restrictions

Delivery duty paid (DDP) Goods, with import duties paid, including inland transportation from import point, delivered to the buyer's premises

Delivery duty unpaid (DDU) Only the destination customs duty and taxes paid by the consignee

Delphi studies A research tool using a group of participants with expertise in the area of concern to interact long term in order to predict and rank major future developments

Differentiation strategy Takes advantage of the company's real or perceived uniqueness on elements such as design or after-sales service

Direct exchange quotation A foreign exchange quotation that specifies the amount of home country currency needed to purchase one unit of foreign currency

Direct intervention The process governments used by governments to alter the current value of their own currency by buying or selling their own currency in the market using their reserves of other major currencies

Direct investment account An account in the BOP statement that records investments with an expected maturity of more than one year and an investor's ownership position of at least 10 percent.

Direct taxes Taxes applied directly to income

Diversification A market expansion policy characterized by simultaneous entry and expansion growth in a relatively large number of markets or market segments

Division of labor The practice of subdividing a production process into stages that can then be performed by labor repeating the process, as on a production line

Domestic policy Public policy concerned with national issues but that may have direct or indirect bearing on foreign trade and investment

Domestication Government demand for partial transfer of ownership and management responsibility from a foreign company to local entities, with or without compensation

Double-entry bookkeeping A method of accounting in which every transaction produces both a debit and a credit of the same amount

Dual pricing A price-setting strategy in which the export price differs from the domestic price

Dual-use item Good or service that is useful for both military and civilian purposes

Dumping An unfair international trade practice involving the selling of a product in an importing country at a price less than the price in an exporting country or below the cost of production

Economic and monetary union Umbrella term for the group of polices aimed at converging the economics of all EU states

Economic channel The principle that if an organization pursues corporate sustainability objectives it is still pursuing profitability and is therefore still aligned with the objectives of maximizing profit and pursuing business growth; actions, while legal, are defined by self-interest, and not morality

Economic exposure The potential for long-term effects on a firm's value as the result of changing currency values

Economic infrastructure The transportation, energy, and communication systems in a country

Economic union A union among trading countries that has the characteristics of a common market and also harmonizes monetary policies, taxation, and government spending and uses a common currency

Education allowance Reimbursement by company for dependent educational expenses incurred while a parent is assigned overseas

Electronic data interchange The direct transfer of information technology between computers of trading partners

Embargo A governmental action, usually prohibiting trade entirely, for a decidedly adversarial or political rather than economic purpose

Environmental protection Actions taken by governments to ensure survival of natural resources

Environmental scanning Obtaining ongoing data about a country, region, or condition

Equity The capital provided by the owner of a company

Ethnocentrism Regarding one's own culture as superior to other cultures

EU Ecolabel Setting of standards that encourage the use of environmentally sound processes, products, and practices

Eurobond A bond that is denominated in a currency other than the currency of the country in which the bond is sold

Eurocurrency A bank deposit in a currency other than the currency of the country where the bank is located; not confined to banks in Europe

Eurodollars U.S. dollars deposited in banks outside the United States; not confined to banks in Europe

Euromarkets Money and capital markets in which transactions are denominated in a currency other than that of the place of the transaction; not confined to Europe

Ex-works (EXW) Price quotes that apply only at the point of origin; the seller agrees to place the goods at the disposal of the buyer at the specified place on a date or within a fixed period

Exchange controls Controls on the movement of capital in and out of a country, sometimes imposed when the country faces a shortage of foreign currency

Experiential knowledge Acquisition of cultural competence through personal involvement

Experimentation A research method capable of determining the effects of a variable on a situation

Export complaint systems Efforts of the firm to encourage international customers to allow final customers to contact the original supplier of a product in order to inquire about products, make suggestions, or present complaints

Export license A license obtainable from the U.S. Department of Commerce Bureau of Industry and Security, which is responsible for administering the Export Administration Act

Export management companies (EMCS) Domestic firms that specialize in performing international business services as commission representatives or as distributors

Export processing zones Special areas that provide tax- and duty-free treatment for production facilities whose output is destined abroad

Export trading company (ETC) The result of 1982 legislation to improve the export performance of small and medium-sized firms that allow businesses to band together to export or offer export services; bank participation in trading companies and relaxes antitrust provisions permitted under law

Export-control systems A system designed to deny or at least delay the acquisition of strategically important goods to adversaries in the United States, based on the Export Administration Act and the Munitions Control Act

Expropriation The government takeover of a company with compensation frequently at a level lower than the investment value of the company's assets

External economies of scale Lower production costs resulting from the interaction of many firms

Factor intensities/factor proportions The proportion of capital input to labor input used in the production of a good

Factor mobility The ability to freely move factors of production across borders, as among common market countries

Factor proportions theory Systematic explanation of the source of comparative advantage

Factors of production All inputs into the production process, including capital, labor, land, and technology

False invoicing The illegal practice of falsifying or altering the amount of an international transaction in order to move funds in or out of a country

Field experience Experience acquired in actual rather than laboratory settings; training that exposes a corporate manager to a cultural environment

Financial Account An account in the BOP statement that records transactions involving borrowing, lending, and investing across borders

Financial incentives Monetary offers intended to motivate; special funding designed to attract foreign direct investors that may take the form of land or buildings, loans, or loan guarantees

Financial infrastructure Facilitating financial agencies in a country, such as, banks

Financing cash flows The cash flows arising from the firm's funding activities

Fiscal incentives Incentives used to attract foreign direct investment that provide specific tax measures to attract the investor

Fixed exchange rate The government of a country officially declares that its currency is convertible into a fixed amount of some other currency

Floating exchange rate Under this system, the government possesses no responsibility to declare that its currency is convertible into a fixed amount of some other currency; diminishes the role of official reserves

Focus group research A research method in which representatives of a proposed target audience contribute to market research by participating in an unstructured discussion

Focus strategy A deliberate concentration on a single industry segment

Foreign bond Bonds issued by a foreign corporation or government for sale in a country different from its home country and denominated in the currency of the country in which it is issued

Foreign currency exchange rate The price of any one country's currency in terms of another country's currency

Foreign direct investment (FDI) The establishment or expansion of operations of a firm in a foreign country; like all investments, a transfer of capital is assumed

Foreign policy The area of public policy concerned with relationships with other countries

Foreign trade zones Special areas where foreign goods may be held or processed without incurring duties and taxes

Foreign-service premium A financial incentive to accept an assignment overseas, usually paid as a percentage of the base salary

Forward exchange rates Contracts that provide for two parties to exchange currencies on a future date at an agreed-upon exchange rate

Franchising A form of licensing that allows a distributor or retailer exclusive rights to sell a product or service in a specified area

Free alongside ship (FAS) Exporter quotes a price for the goods alongside a vessel at a port. Seller handles cost of unloading and wharfage; loading, ocean transportation, and insurance are left to buyer.

Free carrier (FCA) Applies only at a designated inland shipping point; seller responsible for loading goods into the means of transportation; buyer responsible for all subsequent expenses

Free on board (FOB) FOB is the term used when the ownership or liability of goods passes from the seller to the buyer at the time the goods cross the shipping point to be delivered

Free trade area An area in which all barriers to trade among member countries are removed, although sometimes only for certain goods or services

General Agreement on Tariffs and Trade (GATT) An international code of tariffs and trade rules signed by 23 nations in 1947; headquartered in Geneva, Switzerland; 159 members currently; now part of the World Trade Organization

General Agreement on Trade in Services (GATS) A legally enforceable pact among GATT participants that covers trade and investments in the services sector

Geographical indications Place names (in some countries also words associated with a place) used to identify products that come from that place

Global area structure An organizational structure in which geographic divisions are responsible for all global activity

Global brands A brand/product that has worldwide recognition

Global business services provide best-in-class business support services at the lowest possible costs

Global business units (GBUs) Focus solely on consumers, brands, and competitors around the world and responsible for the innovation pipeline, profitability, and shareholder returns

Global customer structure An organizational structure in which divisions are formed on the basis of customer groups

Global functional structure An organizational structure in which departments are formed on the basis of functional areas, such as production, marketing, and finance

Global media Media vehicles that have target audiences on at least three continents and have a central buying office for placements

Global product structure An organizational structure in which product divisions are responsible for all global activity

Globalization approach Creation of a regionally or globally similar marketing mix strategy

Globalization Awareness, understanding, and response to global developments and linkages

Glocal Reflecting or characterized by both local and global considerations

Glocalization A term coined to describe the networked global organization approach to an organizational structure that also includes consideration of regional or local issues

Gold standard A standard for international currencies in which currency values were stated in terms of gold, for example, $20.67 per ounce of gold

Goods trade account An account of the BOP statement that records funds used for merchandise imports and funds obtained from merchandise exports

Gray marketing The marketing of authentic, legally trademarked goods through unauthorized channels

Gross domestic product (GDP) Total monetary value of goods produced and services provided by a country over a one-year period

Hardship allowance An allowance paid during an assignment to an overseas area that requires major adaptation

Hedging Taking an investment position, for example by using a financial derivative, to offset the gains or losses associated with an underlying position of the investor

High-context culture Culture in which behavioral and environmental nuances are an important means of conveying information

Housing allowance An allowance paid during an assignment overseas to provide appropriate living quarters

Implementer The typical subsidiary role, which involves implementing a strategy that originates with headquarters

Import substitution A policy for economic growth adopted by many developing countries that involves the systematic encouragement of domestic production of goods formerly imported

Import-export trade The sale and purchase of tangible goods and services to and from another country

Impossible Trinity The theoretical structure that states that no country can have all three of the following (1) maintain fixed exchange rates; (2) allow the free movement of capital; and (3) conduct independent monetary policy. The political and economic leadership of a country must pick two of the three but cannot have all three at the same time.

In-depth studies A market research tool that is used for gathering detailed data after studying consumer needs across markets

Income account An account of the BOP statement that records current income associated with investments that were made in previous periods

Incoterms International Commerce Terms; widely accepted terms used in quoting export prices

Indirect exchange quotation Foreign exchange quotation that specifies the units of foreign currency that could be purchased with one unit of the home currency

Indirect taxes Taxes applied to non-income items, such as value-added taxes, excise taxes, tariffs, and so on

Information system Can provide the decision maker with basic data for most ongoing decisions

Input–output analysis A method for estimating market activities and potential that measures the factor inflows into production and the resultant outflow of products

Intellectual property rights (IPR) Legal right resulting from industrial, scientific, literary, or artistic activity

Interbank interest rates The interest rate charged by banks to banks in the major international financial centers

Interest When a person or group is potentially affected by the actions of an organization or firm

Intermodal movements The transfer of freight from one type of transportation to another

Internal bank A multinational firm's financial management tool that actually acts as a bank to coordinate finances among its units

Internal economies of scale Lower production costs resulting from greater production within one firm for an enlarged market

Internal economies of scale When the cost per unit of the product of a single firm continues to fall as the firm's size continues to increase

International agent A representative or intermediary for the firm that works to develop business and sales strategies and that develops contacts

International bond A bond issued in domestic capital markets by foreign borrowers (foreign bonds) or issued in the eurocurrency markets in currency different from that of the home currency of the borrower (eurobonds)

International debt load Total accumulated, negative net investment position of a nation

International distributor A representative or intermediary for the firm that purchases products from the firm, takes title, and assumes the selling risk

International law The body of rules governing relationships between sovereign states; also certain treaties and agreements respected by a number of countries

International Monetary Fund (IMF) A specialized agency of the United Nations established in 1944; an international financial institution for dealing with Balance of Payment problems; the first international monetary authority with at least some degree of power over national authorities

Intra-industry trade The simultaneous export and import of the same good by a country; of interest due to the traditional theory that a country will either export or import a good but not do both at the same time

Intranet A process that integrates a company's information assets into a single accessible system using Internet-based technologies, such as e-mail, news groups, and the Web

Inventory carrying costs The expense of maintaining goods in storage

Isolationism A policy that minimizes the economic integration between nations

Joint venture Formal participation of two or more companies in an enterprise to achieve a common goal

Just-in-time inventory systems Materials scheduled to arrive precisely when they are needed on a production line; minimizes storage requirements

Lags Paying a debt late to take advantage of exchange rates

Land bridge Transfer of ocean freight among various modes of land-based transportation

Law of One Price The theory that the relative price of any single good between countries, expressed in each country's currency, is representative of the proper or appropriate exchange rate value

Leads Paying a debt early to take advantage of exchange rates.

Leontief Paradox Wassily Leontief's studies that indicated that the United States was a labor-abundant country, exporting labor-intensive products; a paradox because of the general belief that the United States was a capital-abundant country that should be exporting capital-intensive products

Letter of credit (L/C) Undertaking by a bank to make payment to a seller upon completion of a set of agreed-on conditions

Licensing A method through which one firm allows another to produce or package its product or use its intellectual property in exchange for compensation

Lighter aboard ship (LASH) vessel Barge stored on a ship and lowered at the point of destination to operate on inland waterways

Liner service Ocean shipping characterized by regularly scheduled passage on established routes

Litigation To resolve disagreements and conflicts by the use of the judicial system

Lobbyists Well-connected individuals or firms who can provide access to policymakers and legislators to communicate new and pertinent information

Local content regulation Regulation to gain control over foreign investment by ensuring that a large share of the product is locally produced or a larger share of the profit is retained in the country

Logistics platform Vital to a firm's competitive position, determined by a location's ease and convenience of market reach under favorable cost circumstances

Low-context culture Culture in which most information is conveyed explicitly rather than through behavioral and environmental nuances

m-commerce The exchange of goods and services using mobile devices that allow Web browsing

Maastricht Treaty A treaty, agreed to in Maastricht, the Netherlands, in 1991, but not signed until 1993, in which European community members agreed to a specific timetable and set of necessary conditions to create a single currency for the EU countries

Macroeconomic level Level of business concerns at which trading relationships affect individual markets

Management contract The firm sells its expertise in running a company while avoiding the risks or benefits of ownership

Managerial commitment The desire and drive on the part of management to act on an idea and to support it in the long run

Maquiladoras Mexican border plants that make goods and parts or process food for export back to the United States. They benefit from lower labor costs

Marginal cost method Method that considers the direct costs of producing and selling goods for export as the floor beneath which prices cannot be set

Market development organizations (MDOs) know consumers and retailers in each market and integrate the innovations flowing from the GBUs into business plans that work in each country

Market segment Overlapping ranges of trade targets with common ground and levels of sophistication

Market segmentation Grouping of consumers based on common characteristics such as demographics, lifestyles, and so on

Market-differentiated pricing A price-setting strategy based on market-specific demand rather than cost

Marketing dilemma Considering the power of marketing and its ethical impacts

Marketing infrastructure Facilitating marketing agencies in a country, such as market research firms, channel members

Mass customization Taking mass-produced product components and combining them in a variety of ways to result in a specific product for a particular customer

Materials management The timely movement of raw materials, parts, and supplies into and through the firm

Matrix structure An organizational structure that uses functional and divisional structures simultaneously

Media strategy Strategy applied to the selection of media vehicles and the development of a media schedule

Mercantilism Political and economic policy in the seventeenth and eighteenth centuries aimed at increasing a nation's wealth and power by encouraging the export of goods in return for gold

Microeconomic level Level of business concerns that affect an individual firm or industry

Microfinance A source of financial services for entrepreneurs and small business lacking access to banking services

Migrant A person who comes to a country and stays, or intends to stay, for a year or more

Minority participation Participation by a group having less than the number of votes necessary for control

Mixed aid credits Credits at rates composed partially of commercial interest rates and partially of highly subsidized developmental aid interest rates

Mixed structure An organizational structure that combines two or more organizational dimensions, for example, products, areas, or functions

Money laundering The process of transforming the proceeds of some criminal or illegal activities into legitimate money or other assets

Moral channel The principle that the corporation, regardless of whether it is required to by law or not, should pursue business activities which are aligned with and in support of both socially and environmentally responsible and moral outcomes

Most-Favored Nation (MFN) A term describing a GATT clause that calls for member countries to grant other member countries the same most favorable treatment they accord any country concerning imports and exports, now also known as normal trade relations

Multidomestic approach Policy of adapting the marketing mix to suit each country entered

Multilateral agreement Trade agreement or treaty among more than two parties; the intricate relationships among trading countries

Multinational corporations Companies that invest in countries around the globe

National sovereignty The supreme right of nations to determine national policies; freedom from external control

Net errors and omissions account Makes sure the BOP actually balances

Net present value (NPV) The sum of the present values of all cash inflows and outflows from an investment project discounted at the cost of capital

Netting Cash flow coordination between a corporation's global units so that only one smaller cash transfer must be made

New trade theory The new theoretical developments of Paul Krugman that emphasized imperfect competition's impacts on markets and of Michael Porter and his work on industry specific competitive forces that alter international competitiveness

Nonfinancial incentives Nonmonetary offers designed to attract foreign direct investors that may take the form of guaranteed government purchases, special protection from competition, or improved infrastructure facilities

Nontariff barriers Barriers to trade, other than tariffs; examples include buy-domestic campaigns, preferential treatment for domestic bidders, and restrictions on market entry of foreign products, such as involved inspection procedures

Not-invented-here syndrome A defensive, territorial attitude that, if held by managers, can frustrate effective implementation of global strategies

Observation research A research method in which the subject's activity and behavior are watched

Official reserves account An account in the BOP statement that shows (1) the change in the amount of funds immediately available to a country for making international payments and (2) the borrowing and lending that has taken place between the monetary authorities of different countries either directly or through the IMF

Offshore banking The use of banks or bank branches located in low-tax countries, often Caribbean islands, to raise and hold capital for multinational operations

Operating cash flows Cash flows arising from the firm's everyday business activities

Operating risk The danger of interference by governments or other groups in one's corporate operations abroad

Operational hedging When a firm arranges to have foreign currency cash flows coming in and going out at roughly the same times and same amounts and exposure is managed by matching offsetting foreign currency cash flows

Opportunity cost Cost incurred by a firm as a result of taking one action rather than another

Order cycle time The total time that passes between the placement of an order and the receipt of the merchandise

Output controls Organizational controls, such as balance sheets, sales data, production data, product-line growth, and performance reviews of personnel

Ownership risk The risk inherent in maintaining ownership of property

Ownership stake The strongest form of stake is when a person or group holds legal title to an asset such as a firm

Personal interviews Face-to-face research method, the objective of which is to obtain in-depth information from a knowledgeable individual

Personal selling Marketing efforts focusing on one-on-one efforts with customers

Physical distribution The movement of finished products from suppliers to customers

Podcasts A podcast is a digital medium consisting of an episodic series of PDF, audio, and video

Political risk The risk of loss by an international corporation of assets, earning power, or managerial control as a result of political actions by the host country

Political union A group of countries that have common foreign policy and security policy and that share judicial cooperation

Population stabilization An attempt to control rapid increases in a nation's inhabitants

Portfolio investment account An account in the BOP statement that records investments in assets with an original maturity of more than one year and where an investor's ownership position is less than 10 percent

Positioning The perception by consumers of a firm's product in relation to competitors' products

Predictability The degree of likelihood that a shipment will arrive on time and in good condition

Preferential policies Government policies that favor certain (usually domestic) firms; for example, the use of national carriers for the transport of government freight, even when more economical alternatives exist

Price control Government regulation of the prices of goods and services; control of the prices of imported goods or services as a result of domestic political pressures

Price elasticity of consumer demand Adjusting prices to current conditions; for example, a status-conscious market that insists on products with established reputations will be inelastic, allowing for more pricing freedom than a price-conscious market

Price escalation The increase in export prices due to additional marketing costs related specifically to exports

Primary research The collection and analysis of data for a specific research purpose through interviews, focus groups, surveys, observation, or experimentation

Private ownership An organization that is owned exclusively by a private party (individual, family, organization of some kind) with ownership extended only to other parties at the exclusive owner's permission

Process structure A variation of the functional structure in which departments are formed on the basis of production processes

Product cycle theory A theory that views products as passing through four stages—introduction, growth, maturity, decline—during which the location of production moves from industrialized to lower-cost developing nations

Product differentiation The effort to build unique differences or improvements into products

Production possibilities frontiers A theoretical method of representing the total productive capabilities of a nation used in the formulation of classical and modern trade theory

Public ownership An organization in which any individual or citizen has the right to purchase a share of ownership

Punitive tariff A tax on an imported goods or services intended to punish a trading partner

Purchasing power parity (PPP) A theory that the prices of tradable goods will tend to equalize across countries, and hence the exchange rate between the two currencies should be the ratio of prices in the two countries

Qualitative information Data that have been analyzed to provide a better understanding, description, or prediction of given situations, behavioral patterns, or underlying dimension— typically based on understanding of context rather than statistical data support

Quality circles Groups of workers who meet regularly to discuss issues related to productivity

Quality of life The standard of living combined with environmental and cultural factors; determines the level of well-being of individuals

Quality of work life Various corporate efforts in the areas of personal and professional development undertaken with the objectives of increasing employee satisfaction and increasing productivity

Quantitative information Data gathered in large masses to search for statistical significance or trends

Quotas Legal restrictions on the import quantity of particular goods, imposed by governments as barriers to trade

Re-invoicing The policy of buying goods from one unit, selling them to a second unit, and re-invoicing the sale to the next unit, to take advantage of favorable exchange rates

Reference group A group, such as the family, co-workers, and professional and trade associations, that provides the values and attitudes that influence and shape behavior, including consumer behavior

Remittances International transfers of funds sent by migrant workers from the country where they are working to people, typically family members, back to the country from which they originated

Representative offices An office of an international bank established in a foreign country to serve the bank's customers in the area in an advisory capacity; does not take deposits or make loans

Reverse innovation Innovations from emerging markets and then distributed to developed markets

Reverse logistics A system responding to environmental concerns that ensures a firm can retrieve a product from the market for subsequent use, recycling, or disposal

Rights When a person or group has a legal claim, a contract, or some other existing arrangement to be treated in a certain way or have a particular right protected

Roll-on-roll-off (RORO) Transportation vessels built to accommodate trucks that can drive on in one port and drive off at their destinations

Royalty The compensation paid by one firm to another under a licensing agreement

Sales promotion Short-term inducements that provide extra value and incentives to sales personnel, intermediaries, and consumers

Sanction A governmental action, usually consisting of a specific coercive trade measure, that distorts the free flow of trade for an adversarial or political purpose rather than an economic one

Scenario analyses The identification of crucial variables and the investigation of the effects of their variations on business conditions

Sea bridge The transfer of freight among various modes of ocean freight

Secondary research The collection and analysis of data originally collected to serve another purpose rather than the specific objectives of the firm

Self-reference criterion The unconscious reference to one's own cultural values

Selling forward A market transaction in which the seller promises to sell currency at a certain future date at a prespecified price

Sensitivity training Human relations training that focuses on personal and interpersonal interactions; training that focuses on enhancing an expatriate's flexibility in situations quite different from those at home

Services trade account An account of the BOP that records the international exchange of personal or professional services, such as financial and banking services, construction, and tourism

Shared value Harmonizing corporate competitiveness goals with community goals in CSR activities

Shareholder wealth maximization model (SWM) The theoretical model where the primary objective of the business organization is to create and grow value for the owners of the organization

Shipper's order A negotiable bill of lading that can be bought, sold, or traded while the subject goods are still in transit and that is used for letter of credit transactions

Single European Act The legislative basis for the European integration

Social infrastructure The housing, health, education, and other social systems in a country

Social media The use of communications technology to facilitate meaningful interaction among individuals and organizations

Social networks A communal structure consisting of individuals or organizations connected with each other through friendship, common interest, commercial transactions, information exchange, or other types of relationships

Social stratification The division of a particular population into economic classes

Special economic zones Special tariff-free areas where there are substantial tax incentives and low prices for land and labor to which the government hopes to attract foreign direct investment

Spot exchange rates Contracts that provide for two parties to exchange currencies, with delivery in two business days

Stake An interest or a share in some organization or undertaking

Stakeholder capitalism model (SCM) The theoretical model where the business organization is to maximize the wealth of all stakeholders in the business or corporation, including owners, employees, creditors, as well as community, customers, and suppliers

Stakeholders An individual or entity which has an interest, financial or nonfinancial in nature, in the prospects and activities of some organization

Standard of living The level of material affluence of a group or nation, measured as a composite of quantities and qualities of goods

Standard worldwide pricing A price-setting strategy based on average unit costs of fixed, variable, and export-related costs

Standardization approach Policy of making no or minimal changes to the marketing mix for the global marketplace

Storage location decision A decision concerning the number of facilities to establish and where they should be situated

Straight bill of lading A non-negotiable bill of lading usually used in prepaid transactions in which the transported goods involved are delivered to a specific individual or company

Strategic alliances A term for collaboration among firms, often similar to joint ventures, but not necessarily involving joint capital investment

Strategic leader A highly competent subsidiary located in a strategically critical market

Supply chain A complex global network created by a firm to connect its vendors, suppliers, other third parties, and its customers in order to achieve greater cost efficiencies and to enhance competitiveness

Supply-chain management Connecting the value-adding activities of a company's supply side with its demand side

Survey research A research method involving the use of questionnaires delivered in person, by mail, telephone, or online to obtain statistically valid, quantifiable research information

Sustainability Practices that work to harmonize organizational goals with environmental impact

Systems concept A concept of logistics based on the notion that materials-flow activities are so complex that they can be considered only in the context of their interaction

T-shaped organization Cross-functional management model that promotes sharing and knowledge transfer at all levels of the organization while promoting individual expertise

Tariffs Taxes on imported goods and services, instituted by governments as a means to raise revenue and as barriers to trade

Tax policy A fiscal means by which countries may control foreign investors

Tax-equalization plan Reimbursement by the company when an employee in an overseas assignment pays taxes at a higher rate than at home

Team building A process that enhances the cohesiveness of a department or group by helping members learn how to organize their work and assume responsibility for it

Technology transfer The transfer of systematic knowledge for the manufacture of a product, the application of a process, or the rendering of a service

Terminal cash flows Salvage value or resale value of the project at its termination

Territorial approach to taxation The principle that taxes are levied on the income earned by firms within the legal jurisdiction of the host country, and not on income earned in any other legal jurisdiction outside the host country

Total-cost concept A decision concept that identifies and links expenditures in order to evaluate and optimize logistical activities

Tracking The capability of a shipper to determine the location of goods at any point during the shipment

Trade creation A benefit of economic integration; the benefit to a particular country when a group of countries trade a product freely among themselves but maintain common barriers to trade with nonmembers

Trade diversion A cost of economic integration; the cost to a particular country when a group of countries trade a product freely among themselves but maintain common barriers to trade with nonmembers

Trade-off concept A decision concept that recognizes interactions within the decision system

Trademark licensing The licensing of instantly recognizable logos, names, or images for use on unrelated products such as gifts, toys, or clothing

Trading bloc Formed by agreements among countries to establish links through movement of goods, services, capital, and labor across borders

Trading company A company, such as the *sogoshosha* of Japan, that acts as an intermediary for multiple companies in such areas as import-export, countertrade, investing, and manufacturing

Tramp service Ocean shipping using irregular routes, scheduled only on demand

Transaction exposure The potential for losses or gains when a firm is engaged in a transaction denominated in a foreign currency

Transfer pricing The pricing of products as sold by a firm to its own subsidiaries and affiliates

Transfer risk The danger of having one's ability to transfer profits or products in and out of a country inhibited by governmental rules and regulations

Transit time The period between departure and arrival of a shipment

Translation exposure The potential effect on a firm's financial statements of a change in currency values

Treaty of Rome The original agreement that established the foundation for the formation of the European Economic Community

Triangular arbitrage The exchange of one currency for a second currency, the second for a third, and the third for the first in an effort to make a profit

Trigger mechanisms Specific acts or stimuli that set off reactions

Turnkey operation A specialized form of management contract between a customer and an organization to provide a complete operational system together with the skills needed for unassisted maintenance and operation

U.S. Chamber of Commerce An interest group representing business concerns

U.S. Commercial Service A department of the U.S. Department of Commerce that gathers information and assists business executives in business abroad

Value-added tax (VAT) A tax on the value added at each stage of the production and distribution process; a tax assessed in most European countries and also common among Latin American countries

Values Shared beliefs or group norms internalized by individuals

Vampire marketing Exploiting captive customer situations

Virtual team A team of people who are based at various locations around the world and communicate through intranet and other electronic means to achieve a common goal

Voluntary restraint agreements Trade-restraint agreements resulting in self-imposed restrictions that are used to manage or distort trade flows but do not violate existing international trade rules

Webcasts Media presentation that uses Internet streaming media technology to distribute a single content source to many simultaneous listeners or viewers

Work redesign programs Programs that alter jobs to increase both the quality of the work experience and productivity

Work scheduling Preparing schedules of when and how long workers are at the workplace

Working capital management The management of a firm's current assets (cash, accounts receivable, inventories) and current liabilities (accounts payable, short-term debt)

Works councils Councils that provide labor a say in corporate decision-making through a representative body that may consist entirely of workers or of a combination of managers and workers

World Bank An international financial institution created to facilitate trade

World Economic Forum Organization focused on international business and its effects; best known for its annual global meeting of mostly policymakers and business executives in Davos, Switzerland

World Trade Organization (WTO) The institution that supplanted GATT in 1995 to administer international trade and investment accords

Worldwide approach to taxation The principle that taxes are levied on the income earned by firms that are incorporated in a host country, worldwide, regardless of where the income was earned (e.g., in other countries)

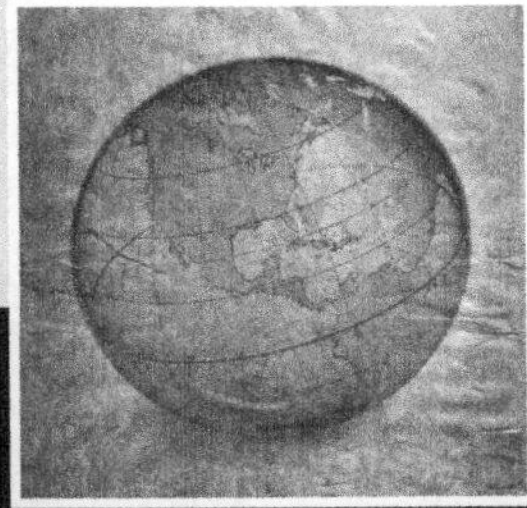

NAME INDEX

A

ABC 240
Accenture 304
ACE Group 111
Aero Engines 239
Aerospatiale Matra 242
AES 240
Airbus Industries 108, 242, 281
Air France 240
Alcatel 239, 307
Allen, Paul 200
Amazon.com 10, 260, 315, 359
AMC 44
American Airlines 240
American Express 230
Amoco 3
AOL 269
ApexBrasil 65
Apple 5, 9, 10, 61, 253, 258, 271, 333
Arvind Mills 256
Atari 8
AT&T 252
Audiovox 293
Automattic 309

B

Bank of Japan 51
Bell Labs 307
Berkshire Hathaway 10
Bertelsmann 302
Big Five 209
Big Mac 6, 7, 176, 177
Black & Decker 301
Blizzard Entertainment 270
BMW 241, 253, 299
Boeing 108, 142
BP 3, 334
British Airways 240
Brooks Brothers 4
Budweiser 4, 290
Burger King 4

C

Cadbury 251
Canon 290
CASA 242
Casual Corner 4
Caterpillar 219, 239, 345
Cereal Partners Worldwide 35
China National Petroleum Corporation (CNPC) 200
Cisco 117, 253
CNN 6, 43, 47, 329
Coca-Cola 10, 22, 121, 232, 248, 250, 253, 266, 290, 308, 333, 340
Cochlear 359
Colgate 314
Compartamos 120
Coyote 202, 203
Crown Royal Canadian whiskey 4

D

Daihatsu 252
Daimler 242
Daimler-Benz Aerospace AG 242
Dalian Wanda Group Corp. 4, 44
Danone 119, 256
Dell 259, 261
Delta 240
Desi Hits 35
Deutsche Telekom 252
DHL 260, 279, 284
Diageo 4
Diet Coke 250
Disney 5, 10, 22, 33, 43, 253, 269
Dow Chemical 91, 304, 305, 331

E

East Dawning 249
eBay 230, 258, 260, 359, 371
Economist Intelligence Unit 37, 227
Emirates Integrated Telecommunications Company 35
Endaka Construction 212
Enron 197, 198, 208, 209
Ericsson 76, 100, 239
Euro Disney 33
European Aeronautic Defense and Space Company (EADS) 242
Expedia 24
ExxonMobil 200

F

FedEx 10, 76, 260, 275, 279, 284
Fiat 96, 239, 269
First Automotive (FAW) 240
Flickr 269
Focus 190, 223, 228, 229, 298, 341
Ford 116, 241, 269, 301
Foursquare 270
Fresh Mist 293
Fujitsu 239, 275

G

General Electric (GE) 26, 65, 117
General Mills 300
General Motors (GM) 261
Gestamp 277
Gillette 297
GKN Aerospace 108
Goldman Sachs 118
Google 25, 77, 250, 253
Google+ 267
GrameenBank 120
Grey Goose Cherry Noir 270
Gruma 251
Guinness Brewery 238

H

Heinz 4
Henkel 34
Hitachi 239
Honda 58, 101, 191
Honeywell 108
Hotels.com 24
Huawei 53, 251
Hyundai 239, 264

I

IBM 10, 119, 200, 239, 253, 302, 337, 342, 345, 374
IKEA 275, 323
InBev 4
Indian Central Bank 164
ING Bank N.V. 76
Intel 34, 117, 230, 253, 340

Iron Chef 33
Itaú 264

J
Johnson & Johnson 195, 265, 308
José Cuervo 4

K
Kellogg's 35
Kentucky Fried Chicken 22
KFC 307
Komatsu 219, 239
Korres Natural Products 194
KPMG 324, 342
Kraft Foods 107

L
La Boulange 223
Lenovo 116, 119
LG 34
Louis Vuitton 33
Lufthansa 240

M
Maersk Sealand 293
Makita 301
Manchester United 240
McAfee 219
McDonald's 7, 32, 33, 61, 82, 176, 191, 252, 253
Medion AG 116
Mercedes-Benz 241, 253
Microsoft 25, 200, 253
Mitsubishi 188, 219, 237, 239
Mondeléz International 19
Monsanto 73
Motorola 239
Mountain Dew 271
MTV 6, 233

N
Nabisco 19
NBC 239, 240
Nestlé 275
New United Motor Manufacturing, Inc. (NUMMI) 241
New World Group 47
New York Yankees 240
Nike 5, 33, 269, 321
Nissan 29, 82
Nokia 100, 101, 122, 252, 253, 257, 258, 269, 300

O
Oneworld (alliance) 240
Opel 117
OREO 19

P
Pacific First Bank 212
Panasonic 313
PayPal 152, 260
PepsiCo 35, 252
PetroChina 200
Pfizer 72
Philips 300, 307, 311, 313
Pizza Hut 249
Pratt & Whitney 239
Procter & Gamble 256, 261, 297, 333

Q
QQ 268
QVC 372
Qype 270
Qzone 268

R
Ralls 52
Red Eléctrica de España 82
Renran 268
Rolls-Royce 239
Rolls-Royce, Motoren-und-Turbinen Union 239

S
Samsung 39
Saudi Aramco 200
Second Life 271
Shell 3, 333, 334
Sheraton 240
ShipGreen 283
Siemens 65, 115, 278, 317, 337, 345
Siemens AG's Medical Solutions Group 278
Sina Weibo 23
Skype 309
Smithfield Foods 44
SoftBank 51
Sony 234
Southwest Airlines 10
Sprint 51
Star (alliance) 240, 262
Starbucks 10, 33, 223, 242, 243, 251
State Bank of India 164
Sunny Hawaii 220
Symantec 219

T
Tandy Corporation 30
Target 85, 116, 232
Tesco 2, 122
Texas Instruments 239
Time 262, 282, 288
Toshiba 239
Toyota 82
Toyota Motor 334
Transportadora de Electricidad 82
Twitter 23, 25, 72, 267, 269, 270, 362

U
Unilever 2, 29, 120, 218, 256, 261, 265, 268, 313
Union Carbide 331
United Technologies 239
UPS 260, 279, 281, 284

V
Vanport 212, 213
Vivendi 4
Volkswagen 3

W
Walmart 2, 260, 333
Weibo 268
Weixin 268
World of Warcraft 270

Y
Yelp 270
Yokohama Bank 212, 213
Youku 72
YouTube 29, 72, 269, 270

Z
Zara 232
ZTE 53

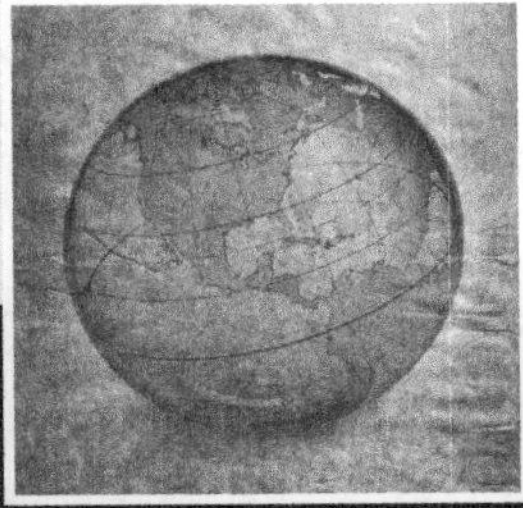

SUBJECT INDEX

A

Abandoned product ranges 142
Absolute advantage 132
  example of 133–134
Accounting
  double-entry bookkeeping 154
  global diversity 208
  international 208–209
  standards 208
  standards, worldwide 208
Accounting exposure. *See* Translation exposure
Accounting systems
  macro-uniform 209
  micro-based 209
Acculturation 21
  language and 23
Adaptability factors 315
Advertising 261–265
  Internet, and 261
  product placement 262
  regional campains 122
  social media, and 267
Aesthetics 34
Africa
  economic groupings 112
African Industrial Property Office (ARIPO) 91
African Union (AU) 112
Agricultural products 48, 57, 98, 100, 113
Agricultural subsidies 50, 52
Airfreight 281. *See also* Transportation
Alliances
  informal 240
  strategic 238–239
  successful 242
Alves, Cheryl Schaefer 220
American Depository Receipts (ADRs) 191
American Idol 239
Andean Common Market (ANCOM) 109, 110
Andean Trade Preference Act (ATPA) 110
Anti-dumping laws 84
Antitrust laws 77
Area briefings 39
Argentina
  exchange controls, and 84
Argentina currency collapse 5
Argonaut 40
Aristotle 329
Armament exports 74
Arm's length principle 258
ASEAN+1 111
ASEAN+3 111
ASEAN Free Trade Agreement (AFTA) 111
Asian financial crisis, 1997–98 164, 166
Asia Pacific Economic Cooperation (APEC) 111
Association of Southeast Asian Nations (ASEAN) 99, 111
Attitudes 33
Autarky 130

B

Backtranslation 24
Bailouts 328
Balance of payments (BOP) 151, 152, 153, 154, 155, 157, 158, 160, 161, 162, 164, 165, 166, 168
  basic economic and accounting relationships 160
  Capital account 157
  deficits in 155
  direct investment 158–160
  Direct Investment account 158
  double-entry bookkeeping 154
  Financial account 157
  financial assets 153
  forcasting economic crisis with 162
  illegal activity and 169
  net errors and omissions account 161
  portfolio investment 160
  Portfolio Investment account 158
  real assets 153
  total for the United States 162
Bangladesh 5
Bank for International Settlements (BIS) 179
Banking liquidity and management 165
Banks 189, 331
  conducting business within a foreign country 189
  correspondent banks 189
Bank secrecy 85
Base salary 316
Bearer bond 189
Behavioral controls 312
Best practices 310
Big Bang Theory, The 24
"Big data" 70
Big Mac Index 176, 177
Bill of lading 285
Blogs 269, 309
Blood diamonds 131
Blue Angel Program 347
Body language 26, 33
Bolivarian Alliance for the Peoples of Our America (ALBA) 110
Bonds
  bearer 189
  eurobonds 189
  foreign 189
  international 189
BookCrossing 269
Boycotts 75, 77, 82
BRICS (Brazil, Russia, India, China, and South Africa) 114, 115
Brain drain 61, 101, 369
Branding 2. *See also* Markets
  color and 34
Brands 33, 119, 290
  global 254
Branson, Richard 346
Brazil
  manufacturing ability 109
  population 15
Bretton Woods system 165, 166, 181
  explained 182
Bribery 77, 279, 331
"Bringing owls to Athens" 194
Buddhism 32
  Culture Clues 12
Budgets 312
Buffer stock 114
Bulk service 280
Bureaucratic/formalized control 312
"Bureaucratic overkill" 76

C

Canada
  NAFTA, and 107
Capital 99, 159
  abundance of 138

Capital *(continued)*
  mobility of 144
  movement of 101, 105
Capital account 157
Capital account transactions 165
Capital budget 201, 202
Capital controls 167, 168
Capital flight 66, 84, 164, 166, 168, 169
Capital flows 166, 169, 358
  capital account transactions 165
  current account transactions 165
  restrictions 167
Capital inflows 165
Capitalism 332
Capital mobility 165, 166
  historical patterns of 166–167
Capital outflows 168
Capital outlays 201
Capital structure 204
Captain Morgan 4
Carbon emissions 283, 329, 344, 346
Cargo 280
Caribbean Basin Initiative 98
Caribbean Common Market (CARICOM) 110
Carriage and insurance paid to (CIP) 287
Carriage paid to (CPT) 287
Cartels 113, 113–117, 114
Cash flows 201, 202, 203, 204
  cash pooling 205
  exchange rate risk, and 206
  financing 205
  internal banks, and 205
  leads and lags 205
  management of 205–206
  netting 205
  operating 204
  re-invoicing 205
Cash pooling 205
Catholicism 30
Central American Integration System (SICA) 110
Centrally planned economies 353
Change agents 21, 61, 78, 122
Chávez, Hugo 174
China
  brain drain, and 369
  brand names and 290
  Cultural Clues and 26
  culture clues 231
  current account balances 160
  current account surplus 11
  East China Sea dispute 82
  Facebook, and 268
  fiscal stimulus 118
  foreign investment by 116
  Google, and 250
  Internet advertising, and 262
  internet use 72
  investment in Africa 86
  market for movies, and 247
  "most-favored nation" 90
  monetary policy, and 54
  rapid emergence 355
  regional disputes 101
  Special Economic Areas 108
  use of prison labor 78
  WTO, and 49
Christianity 30
Church of Jesus Christ of Latter-day Saints 230
Civil unrest 80
"Clean energy" 345
Code law 88
Codetermination 320
Coffee 2, 35, 114, 131, 223, 243, 251, 300
Color 34, 278
Commerce Department Bureau of Industry and Security (BIS) 76
Commercial invoice 285
Commercial whaling 78
Committee on Foreign Investment in the United States (CFIUS) 51
Commodities 8, 114
  "sensitive" 74
Commodity price agreements 113–117, 114
Common Agricultural Policy (CAP) 52, 105
Common law 88
Common market 98
Common Market of the South. *See* Mercosur
Communication
  advances in 120
  international 6
  Intranets 310
  language and 23
  services 120
Comparative advantage 133, 136
  cost differences 137
  example of 133–134
Compensation 316
Competence factors 315
Competition 11, 100, 121
  analysis of 223
  strategies, and 223
Competitive advantage 314
  demand conditions, and 143
  factor conditions, and 143
  firm strategy, structure, and rivalry, and 143
  related and supporting industries, and 143
Competitive factors 219
Competitiveness 143. *See* Competitive advantage
Confiscation 73, 82, 86
Confucianism 32, 81
Consortia 241–242
Consortium. *See* Consortia
Consultants 375
Consumer culture 248
Consumer groups 218, 252
Consumption patterns 248
Content communities 269
Contractual agreements 240
Contractual hedging 207
Controls 311
  behavioral 312
  bureaucratic/formalized 312
  cultural 313–314
  output 312
Coordinating Committee for Multilateral Export Controls (COCOM) 12
Copper 57, 113, 120
Copyrights 83, 211, 237, 255
Corporate
  citizenship 339
  functions 298
  goodness 198
  governance 165, 334
  philanthropy 198, 339
  responsibility 198, 199, 330, 334, 337–338, 354
  social responsibility (CSR) 198
  sustainability 199
Corporate socialism 164
Corporate social responsibility (CSR) 338, 340, 341. *See also* Corporate responsibility
  initiatives 342
  reporting 342
  sustainability 342, 343
Corporation(s) 195
  economic channel 199
  financial goals 199
  moral channel, and 199
  operational goals 200
  responsibility of 197–200
  "the pursuit of the triple bottom line" 199
Correspondent banks 189
Corruption 74, 77, 79, 110, 254, 279, 331, 353, 370
Cost 286
Cost and freight (CFR) 286
Cost factors 218
Cost, insurance, and freight (CIF) 286
Cost leadership strategy 223
Cost-of-living allowances (COLA) 316
Cost-plus method 255
Counterfeit brands 81
Counterfeit goods 254
Counterfeiting 81, 83, 254
Country of origin (COO) 252
Court battles 88
Creative strategy 264
Credit risk 212
Critical commodities list 74
Cross rate 179
Cross-subsidization 234
"C"- terms 285
Cuba
  embargo, of 76
Cultural assimilator 39
Cultural competence 38
Cultural controls 313
Cultural convergence 27
Cultural imperialism 22
  France and 25

Cultural universals 22
Culture
cultural attitudes 33
cultural competence 38
defined 20
differences between 25–26
elements of 22
exposure to other 27
family relations, and 28
formal training prgrams for 38–39
gaining knowledge of 37
high-context 21
infrastructure of 26
language, and 22
low-context 21
management styles 29
manners and customs of 33
negotiation styles 34
recognizing differences 35–37
religion and 30–33
shock 39–43
U.S. Department of Commerce's Country Commercial Guides of 37
Culture Dimension Scores 36
Culture shock 39
Currencies, Market for 177
Currency
exchanged. *See also* Exchange rates
fluctuations 288
reserves 161
spot transactions of 177
symbols 177
Currency devaluing 174
Currency exchange
coordinated intervention 184
market for 179
renminbi 183
Currency flows 50, 51
Currency shortages 84
Currency war 54
Current account 154
current transfers account 155
goods trade account 154, 155
income account 154
services trade account 154
services trade and investment income 155
transactions 165
Current-rate method 208
Current transfers account 155
Customer relationship management 265
Customer service 289
Customs 33–34
Customs union 98

D

Data. *See also* Research
collection of 70
privacy 70
Debt 204
forgiveness 354
Debt-equity structure 204
"Deemed export" 76
Delivery duty paid (DDP) 287
Delivery duty unpaid (DDU) 287
Delphi studies 231
Developing nations 26, 48, 49, 52, 55, 59, 60, 65, 66, 83, 113, 139, 226, 331, 354, 357
Diaoyu 82
Differentiation strategy 223
Digital gap 359
Direct exchange quotation 178
Direct foreign investment
domestication 82
governmental scrutiny 59
Direct intervention 183
Direct investment account 158
Direct taxes 211
Distribution 118
Distribution channels 258–261
channel design 258–259
e-commerce as 260
managing channel relationship 259
problems and remedies 259
Distribution systems 372
Diversification 232
Division of labor 132, 136
Dollar, U.S.
removal from the gold standard 182
"Dolphin safe" tuna 365
Domestication 82, 83
Domestic policy 45–46, 50, 53, 56
Domestic regulations. *See* Domestic policy
Double-entry bookkeeping 154, 160
Drug trade 169
"D"-terms 286
Dual pricing 255
Dual-use items 74
Dumping 48, 53, 57, 84, 221, 332, 363
Dutch Disease 169
Duties 293

E

East African Community (EAC) 112
E-commerce 72, 228, 235, 247, 260, 261, 283
privacy issues, and 261
Economic and monetary union (EMU) 99
Economic channel 199
Economic collapse, 1930s 181
Economic Community of Central African States (CEEAC) 112
Economic Community of West African States (ECOWAS) 112
Economic crises 162, 164
banking liquidity and management 165
corporate governance, and 165
corporate socialism, and 164
Economic crisis, 2008 81, 331
responses by government 332
Economic exposure 207
Economic infrastructure
defined 26
Economic integration 98, 99
benefits 110
changing competitive landscape 121
common market 98
costs and benefits of 99
customs union 98
economic union 99
factor mobility 99
free trade area 98
in Asia 110–112
in North America 106
lobbying company concerns about 122
management, and 121
in the Middle East 112
Economic Integration 97
"pains" 108
in Africa 112
effects 100
in Latin America 109–110
in Latin America 109
nationalism, and 101
Economic stability 55
Economic systems 353
Economic union 99
Economies of scale 10, 99, 100, 101, 103, 107, 131, 142, 143, 146, 205, 218, 219, 221, 232, 233, 236, 300, 311
external 142
internal 142
Economist, The 3, 13, 23, 43, 72, 116, 164, 176, 237, 317
Edelman Trust Barometer 334
Education 28, 38
Education allowance 319
Electronic data interchange (EDI) 288
Electronic information services 227
Embargoes 73, 73–74
arms 76
Cuba, of 73, 76
Emerging markets 27, 28, 54, 57, 113, 114, 115, 117, 119, 166, 218, 219, 234, 302, 305, 306, 311, 313, 320, 332, 335, 355
Employees. *See also* Labor
posted overseas 59
Employment 66
experience 373
Endowment, of a country 137
Environmental
concerns 283, 342, 343, 344, 346, 347, 364
conditions 290
costs 2
factors 218
protection 78, 354
scanning 231
Epitafios 239
Equity 204

"E"-terms 285
Ethical standards 75, 78, 79, 330, 331, 339, 370
Ethics
  issues 330
  and trade 131
Ethnocentrism 35
EU Ecolabel 347
Eurobonds 189
Eurocurrency 184
Eurodollars 184
Euroequity markets 191
Euromarkets 185, 187
Europe
  history of trade 131
European Free Trade Area (EFTA) 98
European Parliament 106
European Patent Office 91
European sovereign debt crisis 6
European Union 97, 102–106
  development of 103–105
  Economic and Monetary Union (EMU) 103–105
  membership 103
  organization of 105–106
  Turkey, membership 104
Excess capacity 221
Excessive financial industry rewards 328
Exchange controls 84
Exchange rates 51, 161, 178, 202, 203, 206, 207, 208, 356. *See also* Global monetary system; currency exchange
  and eurocurrency interest rates 185
  Big Mac Index, and 177
  coordinated intervention 184
  cross rate 179
  direct intervention 183
  equations for determining 175, 179
  eurocurrency, and 185
  forward rates 185
  pegs 166
  pupose of 175–177
  quoting 179
Expatriate compensation 316–319
  cost comparisons across countries 318
  other types of allowances 317–319
Experiential knowledge 37
Export Administration Act and the Munitions Control Act 74
Export complaint system 231
Export-control policies 12
Export controls 74–75, 76, 83
Export-control systems. *See* Export controls
Export-Import Bank of the United States 59
Export licenses 74, 75, 76
Export management companies (EMCs) 235
Export managers 314
Export processing zones 294
Export promotion 58–59
Export restrictions 58
Exports 109, 110, 156, 166, 234–235
  documentation, and 285
  growth 10
  mercantilism, and 131
  pricing 255
Export strategies
  terrorism, and 367
Export trading companies (ETCs) 236
Export Trading Company Act of 1982 77
Expropriation 80, 82, 86, 237
External economies of scale 101
Extortion 81
Ex-works (EXW) 286

F

Facebook 25, 72, 262, 267, 268, 269, 270
  branding, and 19
"Facilitation payments" 77
Factor
  conditions 143
  intensities 137
  mobility 99, 101, 145
  prices 137
  proportions 137
Factor proportions theory 137, 138
Factors of production 65, 97, 101
  Comparison of costs 107
Fair Labor Association (FLA) 5
Fair trade products 2, 131
False invoicing 169
Field experience 39
Financial account, the 157
Financial assets 153
Financial crises 55, 169, 329
Financial crisis, 2008 55, 81, 85
Financial environment, future of 356–357
Financial incentives 66
Financing
  cash flows, of 205
  letters of credit (L/C), and 212
Firm strategy 143
Fiscal incentives 66
Fixed exchange rate 161
Floating exchange rate 161
Focus group research 228
Focus-groups 34
Focus strategy 223
Foreign bonds 189
Foreign currencies 208
Foreign-currency-denominated accounts 184
Foreign-currency-denominated deposit 184
Foreign currency exchange rate 177
Foreign direct investment (FDI) 144
  2011, total 5
  2012 flows 64
  defined 4
  factors of production, and 65
  home-country perspectives 64
  investment policies 60
  mobility of capital 144
  negative effects 61–66
  policies to attract 66
  positive effects 60–61
  restrictions 66
  sources 159
  strategic implications of 146–147
  terrorism, and 367
  theory of 144
Foreign exchange 256
Foreign exchange market. *See* Currency exchange
Foreign markets
  access to 189
Foreign policy 46, 73, 99
Foreign-service premium 316
Foreign subsidiaries 204, 205, 208
  financing 204
foreign trade zones 293, 294
Forest Stewardship Council (FSC) 2
Foriegn investment
  Chinese 44
Forward exchange rates 177
Forward rates 185
  equations for 186, 187
Forwards 177
Franchising 238
Fraud 85
Free alongside ship (FAS) 286
Free carrier (FCA) 286
Free on board (FOB) 286
Free trade 96, 100, 105, 108, 136
  customs unions, and 98
  free trade area 98
Free Trade Area of the Americas (FTAA) 109
Friedman, Milton 337, 338
"F"-terms 285
Fugger, Jakob 339
Full ownership 242
Funding, of a firm 204
Funds, transfers of 151

G

G-20 nations 49, 85, 104
Gains from trade 136
Gates, Bill 200
General Agreement on Tariffs and Trade (GATT) 48, 49, 53, 211
General Agreement on Trade in Services (GATS) 48
Generally Accepted Accounting Principles (GAAP) 208
Genetically modified organisms (GMO) 73
Gillman, Robert 343
Global area structure 302
Global brands 253–254
Global business
  anit-Western attacks 81
  benefits of 11
  careers in 373
  host-country laws 88

marketing 119
political risk 80
"satisfaction" 4
Global business environment 353–356
Global business services (GBS) 298
Global business units (GBUs) 297
Global companies. *See also* Multinational corporations
employment, and 61
Global corporations
future of 370
human resources, and 65
Global credit crisis, 2008 169
Global expansion 221–224. *See* International expansion
Global financial markets
gaining access to 191
Global firms
regulation, and 75
Global functional structure 302
Global Internet penetration 260
Globalism
marketing benefits 254
Globalization 1, 167, 169, 297, 320
approach 249
conflict between developing and industrialized nations 55–59
corporate responsibility, and 329
cutural issues and 33
dark side of 5
defined 3
domestic policy conflict 50
driving factors 218–219, 220–222
economic integration 98
effects 100
leadership challenges, and 336
Global linkages
communication 6
Global logistics 276–278
Global markets 10
Global media 262
Global monetary system 181
Bretton Woods System 182
development of 181–184
floating exchange rates 183
gold standard 181
interwar years, 1919–39 181
times of crisis, 1971–73 182
Global networks 307–308
Global organizations 301
advanced stages of globalization 314
black hole subsidiaries 311
centralization 306
contributor subsidiaries 311
controls 311–313
coordinated decentralization 306
country organizations, role of 311
decentralization 306
decision making, and 306
development of structures 304
early stages of globalization 314
global area structure 302
global customer structure 303
global product structure 301
global workforce management 320–324
Implementer subsidiaries 311
matrix structure 304
mixed structure 303
promoting internal cooperation 308–311
T-shaped organization 305
types, of 301–304
virtual teams 310
Global political environment 353
Global poverty 129
Global price competition
future of 371
Global product policy
future of 371
Global product structure 301
Global storage issues 292
Global strategies 6, 218, 219, 308
recruitment 28
Global structure
global functional structure 302
Global trade
changes in interdependence 8
Glocal 307
Gold standard 166, 181
Goods trade account 154
Governance 195
Governance structure, corporate 197
Governmental regulations 344
Government policies 73, 84, 86, 252, 331, 363, 371
e-commerce, and 261
influencing 90, 122
intellectual property rights 83
nationalist 82, 84, 86
preferential treatment 145
sources of revenue 85
Governments
preferential treatment by 105
regulation 331
as sources of reasearch 226
taxation, and 209–212
Government stability 80
"Great Firewall of China" 72
Gray marketing 257
Greece 190
"Greenfield" construction 147
"Green" policies 344
Gross domestic product (GDP)
defined 9
Guanxi 29
Gulf Cooperation Council (GCC) 112

H

Hardship allowances 317
Heckscher, Eli 136
Heckscher-Ohlin theory 136
Hedging 207
Hinduism 30, 32, 252
Holidays 30, 88
Hollywood 247
"Honorable merchant" 78, 79
House of Cards 239
Housing allowance 317, 318
Human resources 314, 323–324

I

Illiteracy 28
Immigration policy 105
Imperfect Competition 142
Import controls 100. *See* Import restrictions
Import-export trade
defined 4
Import promotion 59
Import restrictions 56, 84, 89
effects 57–58
responses to 58
Imports 156, 166, 234–235
mercantilism, and 131
restrictions of 145
standard of living 10
Import substitution 145
Impossible trinity 166
Income account 154
Incoterms 285
In-depth studies 34
India
culture clues 364
Culture Clues 9, 21
Indirect exchange quotation 178
Indirect taxes 211
Industrial espionage 83
Industrialized countries 27, 28, 55, 105, 106, 113, 278, 285, 344
Industrial Revolution 131, 132, 189
Inflation 84, 289
Informal alliances 240
Information sources 361
Information system 231
Information technology 362
Infrastructure 109, 112, 278
"Inhumane" animal killings 365
Innovation 3, 143
Innovation economies 38
Input-output analysis 138
Insurance 8, 86, 107, 111, 184, 185, 212, 256, 286, 287, 292, 368
Intellectual property rights (IPR) 11, 53, 81, 83, 90, 96, 109, 110
Interbank interest rates 184–185
Intermodal movements 280
Internal banks 205
Internal economies of scale 100, 142
International Accounting Standards Committee (IASC) 208
International agent 235
International bond market 189

International business. *See also* International trade
- acquisitions, and 44–45
- and markets 3
- antitrust legislation, and 77
- as a strategic imperative 219
- balance of payments, and 153
- begining international operations 217
- bilateral and multilateral agreements, and 90
- boycotts, and 75
- bribery, and 77
- cash flows, managing 205–206
- challenges 4
- competition 11
- competitive skills, and 10
- conflict between legal systems 91
- consultants 375
- consumer benefits 3
- corruption, and 77
- costs of regulation 71–73
- country organizations, vs headquarters 311
- cross-cultural issues 38
- culture shock, and 39–43
- diminished 333
- economic exposure 207
- economic power 334
- entry strategies 117
- ethical role of 329
- ethical standards, and 78
- expanding internationally 223, 234–238, 238
- as exploiters of imperfections 145
- financial goals 199
- financing 204
- financing operations 212–215
- global networks 307
- governance structure 197
- government policy, and 82
- host-country laws 88
- international divisions of 300, 314–315
- international law 91
- international legal environment 91
- inventories 288
- kidnapping of personel 81
- language ability and 23
- licensing, and 237–238
- local distribution 118
- local laws, and 86
- local regulations 88
- market entry by 122
- moving operations 108
- operational goals 200, 201
- organizational structure 298–305
- political and legal environment 90
- political environment and 91
- politics, and 71, 90
- poverty, and 121
- production strategies 6
- religions and 30
- research and 224–225
- service activities, and 8
- social interests, and 337
- social media, and 267–274
- societal orientation 331
- sources of profit or opportunity 145
- storage issues 292
- strategic alliances 238–239
- strategies 223–224
- tax burdens 84
- terroism, responses to 366–369
- transaction exposure, and 206
- transportation systems 278–280
- violence and conflict 81

International business transactions 152, 152–154
International capital markets 187
International communications 372
International Court of Justice 78
International debt 164
International debt load 357
International direct investment 8. *See also* Direct foreign investment
International distributor 236
International division, of an organization 300
International economic activity 153
International economic transactions. *See also* International business transactions
International Equity Markets 190
International expansion 223
- contractual agreements, and 240
- export trading companies (ETCs) 236
- full ownership 242
- joint venture 241
- market entry 234–238
- trading company 236
- turnkey operation 240

International financial markets 175, 191
International financial transactions
- defining 187–189

International freight movement. *See* Transportation
International Intermediaries 235
International investment
- theory of 144

International investments 201
- decision criteria 201–202
- foreign subsidiaries, and 204
- proposed, example 202–203
- risk, and 203–204

Internationalization 219, 222, 231, 255, 299
International law 91
International mergers and aquisitions 44, 45, 51
- national security considerations 52

International Monetary Fund (IMF) 55, 151
International money markets 184–187
International operations
- exchange rates and 206

International Payments 151
International political environment 91
International politics 90
International research. *See* Research
International search engine marketing (SEM) 24
International security markets 189–190
International service trade 105
international shipping. *See* Transportation
International Stock Exchange (ISE) 191
International trade
- absolute advantage 132
- abundance of capital and labor 138
- access to markets and buyers 144, 145
- in Africa 112
- among Canada, Mexico, and the United States 108
- in Asia 110–111, 111, 111–112
- barriers to 13, 56–59
- benefits 108, 129
- benefits of 50
- capital controls, and 168
- competition 13
- complexity of 50–51
- composition of 8
- development of 130
- disagreements 53
- division of labor 132
- domestic policies, and 45–47, 97
- factor mobility 99
- financing, and 212
- foreign policy, and 46
- free 96
- free trade area 98
- futre of 363
- gains from 135–136
- General Agreement on Tariffs and Trade 48
- global policy environment of 49–53
- import restrictions, and 56–59
- in services 59
- international export control 12
- Intra-industry trade 142
- Leontief Paradox 138
- in manufactured goods 139
- macroeconomic level 10
- in the Middle East 112
- microeconomic level 10
- motivations for 129–130
- nationalism 101
- national security 59
- national security, and 74
- performance of other nations 9
- protected geographical indications 89
- restrictions 53
- risk 86
- rules of 49
- sanctions, and 73–74
- standard of living, and 5
- subsidies 52
- terrorism, and 11
- trade barriers 99
- trade creation 100
- trade diversion 100
- volume 4

International Trade Union Confederation (ITUC) 323
International transactions
 identifying 153
Internet 359, 372
 advertising and 261
 social media, and 268
 use statistics 262
Internet restrictions 72
Intra-industry trade 142
Intranets 310
Inventory 288
 as strategic tool 289
 carrying costs 288
Inventory systems 278
Investment
 "greenfield" 147
 theory of 145
Iran
 differing government policies towards 74
 sanctions 73
Iron ore 113
Islam 30, 88, 252
 Culture Clues 12
 finance, and 32
Isolationism 355

J

Janus 4, 329, 330, 331, 366
Japan
 East China Sea dispute 82
 litigation, and 88
 regional disputes 101
 self-defense force 12
Japanese NIKKEI 6
Japan External Trade Organization (JETRO) 59
Joint Research and Development Act of 1984 241
Joint venture 117, 241
Jurisdictional clause 91
Just-in-time (JIT) systems 278, 368

K

Kinship 28
Kissaten 243
Knowledge workers 101
Kotler, Philip 330
Kramer, Mark R. 341
Krugman, Paul 142
Kyoto Protocol 283, 344

L

Latin America
 Economic Integration in 109, 109–110
Labeling
 environmental 2
 EU Ecolabel 2
Labor 99, 108, 119, 314, 320
 abundance of 138
 abuses 5, 107, 131
 exploitation of 329
 global shifts 320
 laws 82
 living wage, and 5
 Mexican 107
 movement of 101, 108
 recruitment 28
 satisfaction of 323–324
 wages 10
Labor costs 71
Labor unions 321–323
 membership 322
Land bridges 280
Language 22
 acculturation and 23
 and advertising 264
 English 24
 foreign language skills 38
 nonverbal 25
 top ten world 24
 translation 24
Latin America 55
Law 88
 basic systems of 88
 code 88
 common 88
 influencing local 90
 international 91
 international legal environment 91
 legal environment, and 90
 Roman 88
Law of One Price 176–177
Lawsuits 88
Leadership challenge 336
Leads and lags 205
"Legal personality" 195
Legal systems 88, 355
Legislation 52, 53, 58, 59, 71, 77, 83, 89, 106, 217, 236, 241, 320, 332, 341, 364
Leontief Paradox 138
Leontief, Wassily 138
Less-developed nations 55, 355
Letter of credit (L/C) 212
Licensing 237, 240
"Limited liability" 195
Linder, Staffan Burenstam 138
Liner service 280
Lisbon Treaty (2009) 99
Litigious societies 88
Liu, Lucy 252
Living standards 5
Lobbying 50, 122, 250, 252
Lobbyists 90
Local content regulations 82
Logistics 282. *See* Global logistics platform 279
Logistics management
 terrorism, and 368
London interbank offer rate (LIBOR) 185, 186

M

Maastricht Treaty 99
Malthus, Thomas 128
Management
 as change agents 78
 career paths for managers 315
 commitment to overseas expansion 219
 contracts for 240
 cultural competence, and 38
 cultural controls, and 313
 domestication 82
 expatriate compensation 316
 export managers 314
 future of communications 372
 gaining cultural knowledge 37
 global logisitcs, and 278
 global organization structures and 301–304
 government activity, and 73
 imperfections in 146
 influencing local politics and laws 89
 international considerations 4
 inventory decisions 288
 kidnapping, of 81
 labor, or 320
 logistics and 282
 managerial commitment 222
 not-invented-here syndrome 308
 of global managers 314–319
 overseas assignments 314, 315
 political and legal environment 90
 political decisions, and 89
 political risk, and 84
 recruitment by 28
 recruitment of 119
 regulation, and 71
 regulation varying between countries 75
 relgion and 30
 reorganization 122
 social organization 29
 terrorism, and hiring practices 368
 training programs 39, 313
 work experience, and 374
Management contracts 240
Managerial commitment 222
Managers. *See* Management
Manners 33–34
Manufacture. *See* Production
Manufacturing trade 156
Maquiladoras 108, 294
Marginal cost method 255
Marine Stewardship Council (MSC) 2
Market-based economies 353
Market development organizations (MDOs) 297
Market-differentiated pricing 255
Market entry 122
Market factors 218
Marketing 44
 cultural issues, and 34
 research, and 120
 strategic planning 121

Marketing dilemma 330
Marketing infrastructures
defined 26
Markets
access to 145
analysis of 223
and economic exposure 207
benefits of globality 254
developing 26–27, 119, 121, 233–234
developing global 218
developing message strategy 264
development strategies 238–246
distribution channels, and 258–261
entering new 19
entry 34
entry into 234
global brands and 253–254
global expansion, and 221–224
globalization approach 249
global organizational structures and 301–304
global pricing strategies 255–256
gray marketing 257
growth in emerging 27
imperfections in 145
improving access 120
international divisions, and growth 300
internet marketing 359
marketing dilemma, and 330
multidomestic approach 249
positioning 250
pricing 255
promotional strategies 261–267
public relations 266
research and 225
segmentation 26, 232–233
social media 269
social responsibility, and 331
standardization approach 249
standardization versus adaptation 248–249
strategic leader 311
target country selection 232
vampire marketing, and 331
Market segmentation 232
Market segments 139
Materials
flow of 276–296
management 276
Matrix structure 304
Maturing Product 140
"Maximize value" 200
M-commerce 260
Media strategy 261
Mercantilism 131–132
Merchandise trade
U.S. 8
Mercosur 109, 110
membership 109
Mergers and acquisitions 331
Merkel, Angela 362
Metallic reserves 161
Mexico
NAFTA, and 107
Middle East
economic integration 112
Microfinance 120
Micro information 226
Migrant 151
Migration 151
Millennium Development Goals (MDGs) 128
Minimum-wage legislation 71
Mininationals 220
Minority participation 320
Mixed aid credits 59
Mixed structure 303
Mobile payment services 27
Modernization 33
Monetary policy 51, 54, 166, 184
Money laundering 169
Money markets 184
Monsanto 73
Moral channel 199
Mouvement des Entreprises de France (MEDEF) 101
Multidomestic approach 249
Multilateral agreements 91
Multinational companies 61
Multinational corporations 10
defined 8
entering new markets 19
influence to hose country 64
Multinational enterprise (MNE). *See* International business

N

Nationalism 101
National security 74, 99, 358, 364
National Security Agency 70, 362
National sovereignty 45
Negotiaton 34
Net present value (NPV) 201, 202
Netting 205
New product 139
Newsletters 227
New Trade Theory 142
Nice Treaty (2001) 99
Nixon, Richard M. 182
"No license required" (NLR) conditions 75
Noblesse oblige 330
Nonfinancial incentives 66
Nontariff barriers 53, 56, 57, 363
North America
economic integration 106
North American Agreement on Labor Cooperation (NAALC) 107
North American Free Trade Agreement (NAFTA) 82, 98, 106–107
Not-invented-here syndrome 308
Nuclear proliferation 12

O

Oberhelman, Doug 345
Observation research 229
Ocean shipping 280
bulk service 280
lighter aboard ship (lash) vessel 280
liner service 280
roll-on-roll-off (roro) 280
tramp service 280
Office, The 239
Office-less Companies 309
Official reserves account 161
Offshore banking 188
Ohlin, Bertil 136
Oil production 114
On the Principles of Political Economy and Taxation (1819) 133
Operating cash flows 201, 204
Operating exposure. *See* Economic exposure
Operating risk 80
Operational hedging 207
Opportunity cost 135
Order cycle time 288
Organizational structures 298–305. *See also* Global organizations
decision making, and 306–307
global networks 307
implementation 306–311
Organization for Economic Cooperation and Development (OECD) 77, 91, 111
Organization for Economic Development (OECD) 64
Organization of Petroleum Exporting Countries (OPEC) 114
Output controls 312
Outsourcing 28, 101
Overfishing 2
Overproduction 221
Overseas assignments 314
factors for manager selection 315
Overseas Private Investment Corporation (OPIC) 86
Ownership risk 80
Ownership stakes 196

P

Packaging 290–292
adequate 290
waste 252
wieght of 291
Pakistan 13
Patent Cooperation Treaty (PCT) 91
Patents 91
Personal characteristics 316
Personal interviews 228
Personal selling 265
Personal space 25
Philanthropy 199, 266, 338, 339, 341
"Philosopher-executives" 329
Physical distribution 276

Plans 312
Podcasts 310
Political changes
in South America 109
Political decisions 73, 88, 89
regionalism, and 109
Political instability 353, 354
Political risks 80, 81, 84
Political stability 55, 86, 90, 91, 145, 165, 356
Political turmoil 112
Political union 99
Politics 90, 101
hampering economic integration 110
political union 99
stability 80
Pope Benedict XVI 329
Population shifts 355
Population stabilization 356
Porter, Michael E. 142, 143, 280, 341
Portfolio investment account 158
Positioning 250
Potable water 364
Poverty
world, statistics for 128
Price controls 84, 338, 364
Price elasticity of consumer demand 256
Price escalation 256
Price fixing. *See* Cartels
Price wars 11
Pricing 256
arm's length principle 258
coordination 257
transfer 257
Primary goods 113
Primary research 228–234
Privacy 261
Privately held firms 200
Private ownership 199
Proactive motivations 220
Product
adaptation decisions 253
adapting to local buying patterns 120
characteristics 251
counterfeit 254–255
country of origin, and 252
cycle theory 139–141
decisions 250
differentiation 142
introduction 35
labeling 2
management and terrorism 367
perishable 282
placement 262
placement in media 262
standardization, and 252
Product cycle 139–140
theory of 139
trade implications of 140–142
Product cycle theory 139
Production 132
cost of 142
cultural influences 22
cultures and product introduction 35
economies of scale, and 142
factor intensity and 136
factor mobility, and 145
factor prices 137
factors of 97, 99, 101
flow of materials, and 276
inventory, and 288
multiple countries of origin 6
order cycle time 288
packaging issues 290–292
product cycle, and 139
and quantities of the labor, capital 138
resources for 145
shifts in 8
specializing in 134–135
strategies 6
supply-chain management 277
transportation issues 278
Production possibilities frontier 134, 136
Productivity
improvements 10
Profits 201
Projects. *See* International investments
Protectionism 97, 363
Protestantism 30
Publicly held firms 200
Public ownership 199
Public relations 266
Public trust 334
in business 334–336
Purchasing power parity (PPP) 175

Q

Qualitative research 228
Quality circles 324
Quality of life 46
Quality of work life 323
Quantitative easing 51, 54
Quantitative research 228
Quotas 56, 57, 66, 88, 98, 114, 145
defined 56

R

Radical transparency 342
Rail freight 279
Rana Plaza factory collapse 5
Reactive motivations 221
Real assets 153
Recycling 252, 364
Reference groups 29
Regionalism 101, 109
Regional trade agreements 102–114
Regulations 71–73, 75, 77, 88, 89, 122, 331
Re-invoicing 205
Related and supporting industries 143
Religion 30
Religious holidays 225
Remittances 151, 152
Renminbi 54, 179, 183
Repatriation 369
Representative offices 189
Resale value 202
Research
consortia 241
Delphi studies 231
environmental scanning 231
excellence in 230
experimentation, in 231
focus groups 228
government sources 226
international online databases 227
international organizations as sources 226
interpreting 227–228
joint 241
licensing of 237
market expansion 225
observation 229
ongoing 231–232
pre-entry type 224
primary 228–234
qualitative 228
quantitative 228
reasons for 224
scenario analysis 232
secondary 226
survey 229
Research and development 237
Reserve, U.S. Federal 6
Reverse innovation 117
Reverse logistics 289
RFID technology 275
Ricardo, David 133
Rights, corporate 196
Risk 11, 13, 36, 80, 191, 203, 206, 212, 256, 367
economic 84
forms of transportation 282
managing 86
of violence and conflict 81
operating 80
ownership 80
political 80, 82, 86
reward and 86
transfer 80
Rivalry 143
Roll-on-roll-off (RORO) 280
Royalties 237, 238
Rubber 8, 114
Russia
Culture Clues 8, 83
WTO, and 49

S

SAARC 97
Sabotage 86

Safe Harbor certification 71
Safety standards 46, 78, 252
Salary 316
Sales promotion 265
Salvage value 202
Sanctions 73–74
Scenario analysis 232
Sea bridges 280
Secondary research 226
Self-determinism 101
Self-employment 375
Self-reference criterion 35
Selling forward 187
Senkaku 82
September 11, 2001 11, 81, 364
Service firms 8
Service organizations 227
Shanghai World Financial Center 34
Shared value 341
Shareholder wealth maximization model (SWM) 196
Sharia 30, 88
Shipment and sale, terms of
  carriage and insurance paid to (CIP) 287
  carriage paid to (CPT) 287
  cost and freight (CFR) 286
  cost, insurance, and freight (CIF) 286
  "C"- terms 285
  delivery duty paid (DDP) 287
  delivery duty unpaid (DDU) 287
  "D"-terms 286
  "E"-terms 285
  ex-works (EXW) 286
  Free alongside ship (FAS) 286
  free carrier (FCA) 286
  Free on board (FOB) 286
  "F"-terms 285
Shipper's order 285
Shipping industry
  emissions, and 346
Singh, Manmohan 362
Six Sigma 43, 305
Skilled workers, recruitment 119
Slideshare 269
Smith, Adam 132
Smuggling 75
Social costs 2, 57
Social infrastructure
  defined 26
Social institutions 28
Social media 267, 268, 269
  opportunities and challenges 268–274
Social networks 247, 267, 270, 309. *See also* Social media
Social responsibility of business 337
Social stratification 29
Societal orientation 331
Soft peg 166
Software
  translation 24
South America
  infrastructure 109
South Asian Association for Regional Cooperation (AARC) 97, 111
South China Sea
  tensions in 90
Southern African Development Community (SADC) 112
South Korea
  Culture Clues 81
Sovereign debt 6, 104, 169, 190, 194
Spain
  Culture Clues 225
  entry into the EU 99–100
Special economic zones 294
Spot exchange rates 177
Spot transaction 177
Stake 196
Stakeholder capitalism model (SCM) 196
Stakeholder interests 196
  interest versus a right 197
Stakeholders 195, 196–197
Standardization approach 249, 252
Standardized product 140
Standard of living 46
Standard worldwide pricing 255
State Owned Enterprises (SOEs) 199–200
Statistical Yearbook 226
Stock Exchange Automated Quotation System (SEAQ) 191
Storage
  facilities 292
  issues 292–296
  location decision 292
  location decisions 292
Straight bills of lading 285
Strategic alliance 238–239
Strategic leader 311
Strategic planning
  global expansion, and 221–224
Strategies 223, 234, 238, 249, 255
  aligning with social interests 337
  future of distribution 372
  inventory 289–292
  labor 320
  Pricing 255–258
  product 249–251
  promotional 261–267
  shared value 341
Structure 143
Subsidies 22
Sugar 35, 52, 107, 114, 248
Supplier Base 118
Supply chain 276
  electronic data interchange (EDI) 288
  managing 277, 277–278
  Reverse logistics, and 289
  selecting modes of transportation 281–285
  social issues, and 341
  storage issues 292
Survey research 229
Sustainability 283, 339, 342, 343, 345, 347, 364
  importance to consumers 345
Sweatshops 78
Systems concept 276

T

Tariffs 13, 49, 56, 98, 100, 108, 109, 111, 131, 144, 145, 256, 293, 294
  punitive 53
Taxation 209–212, 256, 317
  direct 211
  indirect 211
  jurisdictions 210–211
  territorial approach 210
  types 211–212
  value-added tax (VAT) 211
  worldwide approach 210
Tax-equalization plans 317
Taxes 84
Tax policy 84
Team building 324
Technological
  advantage 220
  changes 9
Technology 99
  advances in 3, 9, 26, 53, 120, 361
  transfer 60, 75
  transfers 12
Terminal cash flows 202
Terms of sale 285
Terms of shipment 285
Territorial approach 210
Terrorism 11, 12, 80, 81, 86, 336, 366, 366–369
  business activities, and 12
  international reaction 12
Text messaging 8
Tin 114
Tourism 47, 154, 228
Tracking 283
Trade. *See* International trade
  associations 227
  barriers 13, 99
  classical, theory of 136
  creation 100
  deficit 10
  disputes 53
  diversion 100
  motivations for 129
  negotiations 48
  theory of 129, 143
  types 4
Trade Agreements, Major Regional (Table) 102
Trade embargoes. *See* Embargoes
Trademark licensing 238
Trademarks 83, 237, 255
Trade-off concept 277
Trade secrets 83
Trade union organizations. *See* Labor unions

Trade zones 293, 294
Trading blocs 97, 100, 112
Trading company 236
Training 38
  Area briefings 39
  cultural 40
  cultural assimilators, and 39
  field experience 39
  Sensitivity 39
Tramp service 280
Transaction exposure 206
Transfer pricing 257
Transfer risk 80
Transit time 282
Translation 24
Translation exposure 207–208
Transportation 278. *See also* Ocean shipping; *See also* Shipment and sale, terms of
  adequate packagin 290
  bill of lading 285
  costs of 283
  intermodal movements 280
  land bridges 280
  modes of 280–281
  ownership of goods issues 285
  packaging weight and 291
  predictability 282
  sea bridges 280
  selecting modes 281–285
  small businesses and 284
  tracking 283
  transit time 282
Treaties 8, 71, 91, 99, 103, 209, 210, 211
Treaty of Rome 103
Triangular arbitrage 179
Trigger mechanisms 363
Truthfulness 334
T-shaped organization 305
Turkey 104
Turnkey operation 240

U

Uncertainty avoidance 36
United Auto Workers 321
United Nations Conference on Trade and Development (UNCTAD) 238
United Nations (UN) 8, 91
United Nations World Tourism Organization (UNWTO) 47
United States
  as debtor nation 8
  as the world's largest debtor nation 159
  automobile production 58
  debt load 357
  exports 9
  exports to Mexico 108
  fair trade imports 2
  foreign policy 74
  foriegn aid, and 46
  gold reserves 8
  international debt 10
  international trade position 9
  service exports 8
  trade deficit 10, 358
United Students Against Sweatshops 5
Universal Studios 4
Urbanization 344
U.S. Bureau of Economic Analysis (BEA) 151
U.S. Chamber of Commerce 340
U.S. Consumer Financial Protection Agency 331
U.S. current account deficit 358
U.S. debt-service requirements 357
U.S. Department of Commerce Commerical Service 58
U.S. Department of State 340
U.S.-EU Safe Harbor Framework 71
U.S. Foreign Corrupt Practices Act 331
U.S. national debt 357

V

Value-added tax (VAT) 211
Values 33
Vampire marketing 331
Virginia Apple Growers Association (VAGA) 217
Virtual Social Worlds 271
Virtual teams 310
Voluntary restraint agreements 56

W

Warehouses 292
War Weapons Control Law 74
Wealth of Nations, The (1776) 132
Webb-Pomerene Act of 1918 77
Webcasts 310
Westernization 33
Whaling 78
Who Wants to be a Millionaire? 239
Wikipedia 270
Wikis 268
Wireless technology 270
Wiretapping 362
Wire transfers 151
Women, role of 32
Woods, Len 275
Work experience 374
Working capital management 204
Work redesign programs 323
Work scheduling 324
World Bank 55
World Commission on Environment and Development (Brundtland Commission) 343
World Economic Forum 336
World trade 4, 329
World Trade Organization (WTO) 11, 48, 49, 50, 53, 54, 55, 83, 89, 90, 91, 96, 226, 363
World War I 166, 181
World War II 166, 181
Worldwide approach 210

Z

Zoellick, Robert 13

CPSIA information can be obtained at www.ICGtesting.com
Printed in the USA
LVOW05s1314110115

422309LV00003B/4/P